Toyota Truck & Land Cruiser

OWNER'S BIBLE™

By Moses Ludel

A Hands-on Guide to Getting the Most From Your Toyota Truck

RB

ROBERT BENTLEY
AUTOMOTIVE PUBLISHERS

Toyota Truck & Land Cruiser

OWNER'S BIBLE

Toyota history, see Chapter 1

Operator's tips, see Chapter 3

Servicing your truck, see Chapter 4

Engine tuning, see Chapter 8

TABLE OF CONTENTS

Brake and bearing servicing, see Chapter 12

Winches and accessories, see Chapter 15

Engine upgrades, see Chapter 16

Transmission upgrades, see Chapter 17

Suspension lift kits, see Chapter 18

RB ROBERT BENTLEY, INC. | AUTOMOTIVE PUBLISHERS

Information that makes
the difference.®

1033 Massachusetts Avenue
Cambridge, MA 02138 U.S.A.
800-423-4595 / 617-547-4170
Internet: sales@rb.com

The publisher encourages comments from the reader of this book. These communications have been and will be considered in the preparation of this and other manuals. Please write to Robert Bentley Inc., Publishers at the address listed on the top of this page.

This book was published by Robert Bentley, Inc., Publishers. Toyota has not reviewed and does not warrant the accuracy or completeness of the technical specifications and information described in this book.

Library of Congress Cataloging-in-Publication Data

Ludel, Moses.
    Toyota Truck & Land Cruiser owner's bible: a hands-on guide
      to getting the most from your Toyota / by Moses Ludel
         p.   cm.
    Includes index
    ISBN 0-8376-0159-2
    1. Toyota trucks--Maintenance and repair--Handbooks, manuals, etc.   I. Title
    TL230.5.T68L83   1995
    629.28'73--dc20   95–51695
                                       CIP

Bentley Stock No. GOWT

98 97 96   10 9 8 7 6 5 4 3 2 1

The paper used in this publication is acid free and meets the requirements of the National Standard for Information Sciences-Permanence of Paper for Printed Library Materials. ∞

Toyota Truck & Land Cruiser Owner's Bible™: A Hands-on Guide to Getting the Most From Your Toyota Truck, by Moses Ludel

Preface

It was 1967, late summer, and the meadowgrass stood tall around the oversized pond called Miller Lake. Our caravan, a string of early flat-fender Jeep CJs, two Land Cruisers and my 1964 CJ-5, moved West toward Cadillac Hill, the notorious trail down to Rubicon Springs.

I was the only outsider, as the rest of the crew were members of the Diablo Four Wheelers out of Concord, California. The club's president, Stan Johnson, had invited me to attend the annual run through the Rubicon. For me, the trail was unfamiliar and bore only a slight resemblance to my usual stomping grounds, the Eastern Sierras, Pinenut Range, and vast desert ranges of Northern Nevada. Equally unfamiliar were the intriguing FJ40 model Land Cruisers, which I found remarkably willing to negotiate a trail, right in step with these celebrated American 4x4s.

As we sat around our campfire at Rubicon Springs the first night, the major topic of conversation was the Sluice Box run the next morning. Several Jeep owners launched chauvinistic remarks about the "beer can" quality of the Toyota FJ40s, but the Land Cruiser owners smiled back and suggested that by dawn we'd all see what a 'Cruiser could do.

Having enough sense to set my cultural roots aside, I took the time to crawl both under and through these Japanese-built trucks and discovered that all of the engineering ingredients were in place. Having grown up in rural Nevada, where a truck's utility and stamina make the difference, I found the FJ40 more than ample with its beefy axle sizing, frame rigor and powertrain mass.

My hunch proved right. The Land Cruiser's short 90-inch wheelbase excelled at crawling through rocks and negotiating tight terrain. When it came time to pull a stranded I-H Scout off a pile of rocks in the middle of the Sluice Box, which required plying a precarious hillside and twisting between a set of thick trees, it was a Land Cruiser that passed the stuck truck and provided a winch source for freeing the heavy American 4WD.

Not only did U.S.-export versions of the FJ models prove themselves, they subsequently established a record of indomitible durability, rugged dependability, and unrelenting service. Within a brief span of years, as acceptance grew, the FJ40 won the respect of all four-wheel drive enthusiasts and the hearts of many hardcore off-highway and foul-weather users.

My turn to own a Toyota FJ40 Land Cruiser came in the mid-1980s, when these models were among the best values in the used four-wheel drive market. I began with

Preface

a 1971, a three-speed model with a dashboard-mounted transfer case shifter and the classic F engine.

Once oriented to the Land Cruiser, I turned to a 1976 model as a project vehicle for magazine stories. During the 1976–83 model years, the FJ40 reached its zenith, with vacuum assisted disc front brakes, a four-speed synchromesh transmission and options like power steering (1979) and dealer installed air conditioning.

The Project Rubicon Land Cruiser quickly became one of *Off-Road* Magazine's most popular feature trucks. Both Land Cruiser owners and knowledgeable 4WD enthusiasts joined me as I focused on one of the most successfully engineered 4WD trucks ever built. Each step of the way, from stone stock to fully modified, "Project Rubicon" remained formidably trailworthy and predictable under the widest range of driving conditions.

In 1983, due largely to emission control and fuel economy requirements, Toyota phased out the FJ40 from the U.S. market. By this time, the Toyota 4WD pickup, which had gleaned much of its chassis and geartrain layout from the Land Cruiser, was the premier small truck in America.

Through my magazine feature stories, technical question-and-answer columns, vehicle road tests, and research on two- and four-wheel drive trucks, I have become convinced that Toyota builds some of the finest truck products in the world. My exposure to Toyota trucks ranges from the rare Stout and ground breaking Hi-Lux mini-trucks to the modern compact pickup, 4Runner, T100 and Tacoma models. Each of these truck designs displays quality engineering, meticulous assembly technique and a feel for consumer needs.

My years of knuckle busting began as a truck fleet mechanic. In fleet truck service, the emphasis is on preventive maintenance, a philosophy that I promote throughout this book. Routine maintenance can reduce the demand for major repair work. Such down-time prevention can contribute to powertrain reliability, chassis integrity, and vehicle longevity. The odometers on my two Land Cruisers went well past the century mark, and within this book I explain in detail why *all* of my trucks provide long and comparatively trouble-free service.

In the performance chapters, you will discover the close relationship between proven engineering and useful performance modifications. Often, truck needs differ dramatically from those of passenger cars. These performance chapters focus solely on 2WD and 4WD Toyota truck and Land Cruiser requirements.

Ease of maintenance means that Toyota trucks offer a rewarding place to sharpen your mechanical skills. Equipped with this book and a genuine Toyota repair manual for your model truck, you can perform many repairs on your own—or even tackle the full mechanical restoration of a legendary high mileage pickup or Land Cruiser.

For the do-it-yourself owner, this book serves as a hands-on technical guide for working on your Toyota truck. Even the owner who prefers not to work on his or her vehicle will find the repair and troubleshooting sections of real value. By understanding your truck's service needs, you can effectively interact with Toyota dealership personnel or an independent shop. Increased awareness contributes to proper diagnosis and quality repairs.

When asked by my publisher, Robert Bentley, Inc., which types of vehicles I would include in my truck book series, Toyota was a top choice. It is with great pleasure and admiration that I offer this book, a tribute to a truck line that has earned worldwide respect and the appreciation of millions.

Chapter 1

History

TOYOTA'S ENTRY INTO THE U.S. MARKET was far short of spectacular. The first import models, Toyota Crown cars, arrived on the West Coast in August 1957. Intended to compete with the Volkswagen "Beetle" and other sub-compact European economy cars, the Crown's tiny engine suffered severely under the stress of America's fast-paced highways.

The slow acceptance of Toyota cars was more an issue of identifying American automotive needs than concern for product quality. Toyota was fully capable of building a good car or truck. The challenge was to design vehicles for the uniquely American driving environment.

By the mid-1960s, clear about the expectations of U.S. buyers and the meteoric sales success of Volkswagen's popular Beetle, Toyota introduced the Corona car. Here the Japanese manufacturer's capacity for quality was apparent, and the Corona quickly earned its share of popularity and brisk sales within the sub-compact car market.

By 1975, in the brief span of a decade, the highly successful Corona and Celica, the economical Hi-Lux pickup, and the rugged four-wheel drive Land Cruiser truck and station wagon helped secure Toyota's role in the U.S. automotive market. Toyota became the number one motor vehicle importer to America, a distinction that eventually contributed to Toyota's current stature as the second largest producer of motor vehicles in the world.

The stellar growth of Toyota Motor Company and Toyota Motor Sales has been the result of intensive emphasis on product quality and advanced production methods. Early on in the company's history, Toyota abandoned the traditional American and European method of single-task assembly line production. In its place, the Toyota Production System relies on the unique "Just-In-Time" parts procurement and assembly methodology, and on *jidoka*, the ability to monitor machine processes and halt the production line if a tolerance fluctuates. Jido-

0019000

Fig. 1-1. Toyota began marketing the 4WD FJ25 Land Cruiser in 1958. Supreme quality and a durable design was quickly recognized by users. The FJ25 and FJ40 Land Cruisers set a precedent for all Toyota trucks that followed. Few manufacturers can boast a "300,000 Mile Club" of satisfied owners, a distinction held by Toyota.

Fig. 1-2. Highly evolved 1994 compact 4WD Xtracab SR5 V-6 proved popular. A long history of durable truck design as- sures Toyota owners of exceptional service and lasting value.

ka means that no vehicle will "slide by" quality control checks and become a consumer's problem.

In Japan, a stable workforce (assured lifetime employment and periodic wage increases based solely upon seniority) implements these multi-task, highly skilled assembly methods. The Toyota Production System has also proven itself at Toyota's U.S. and Canadian plants, where skilled North American workers readily match the finished product quality of Japanese-built vehicles. This production process contributes to the cost-competitive, consistently durable products that Toyota buyers have come to appreciate.

The Birth Of Toyota Trucks

When Kiichiro Toyoda dreamed of building a domestic Japanese automobile and truck industry, the demand for vehicles was relatively small. By 1935, when the first "Toyota" trucks became available, the company's plant and production capacity was still in its infancy, largely subsidized by a parent company, the successful and globally respected Toyoda Automatic Loom Works.

Owing largely to the demands of Japan's militant foreign policy and expansionist advances into China, the Japanese domestic truck market grew. Kiichiro Toyoda, who harbored reservations about his nation's ambitions, was at least pleased that his appreciation for trucks and automobiles had gained wider support.

The early Toyota trucks were actually amalgams of Japanese engineering mixed with American parts and design features (primarily Chevrolet and Ford). Much of the development was trial and error, and during the fledgling days of Toyota vehicle manufacturing, it became clear that field service and feedback from service personnel would prove vital to product improvement and viability. Listening to field mechanics prevails to this day and accounts, in part, for Toyota's quick response to design or product problems.

Unlike some Japanese industrialists, Kiichiro Toyoda had a realistic sense for the political posture of his government. Although a devoted citizen of Japan and adherent to the cultural premise of cooperation and support for his country's leadership, Kiichiro Toyoda was realistic in his assessment of the Japanese capacity to wage war against nations like the United States.

Shoji Kimoto, author of the biography *Quest for the Dawn*, discovered a memo written at the entry of Japan into World War II. Here, Kiichiro Toyoda stated flatly, from the viewpoint of an automobile and truck builder, Japan's fate:

"There is no way that Japan can win a war with the United States. We must stop such a foolish war as soon as possible—even a day earlier than that. What is the truth of our situation in comparison to the United States? In 1939, for example, automobile production in the United States totaled 3.59 million; Japan's was 34,500. In 1940, production in the United States turned out 4.47 million versus Japan's 46,000. That's the real truth of our chances of victory. We're out-ranked by a factor of one hundred. Even if we were to utilize our car engines to build airplanes, and the United States were to do the same thing, they could produce one hundred planes to our one. On the European battlefields of World War I, the German Army had 120,000 vehicles, while the Allied forces consisted of France's 97,000 vehicles, and the U.S.'s and Britain's combined 100,000. That difference of almost 80,000 vehicles determined victory. With a weapons ratio of one hundred to one against us, how much of a chance does Japan have?"

Mr. Toyoda's automotive vantage point eventually proved prophetic. Japan's ultimate surrender to the Allied Forces was due to many factors, with the country's overall resource capacity, total numbers of mechanized pieces of military equipment and the logistics of the Pacific military theater each playing key roles.

During the early post-World War II period, Toyota Motor Company struggled to survive, repeatedly stating to the Allied occupation authorities that the company wished to play a role in Japan's development of a peacetime economy. More than once, Toyota Motor Company nearly failed.

In an agonizingly slow process, the Toyoda family of businesses showed signs of stabilization. Oddly, the misfortune of a war on the nearby Korean Peninsula provided the pivotal spark for both Toyota Motor Company's survival and the beginning of Japan's phenomenal, historically unprecedented postwar economic boom.

1. THE LAND CRUISER: BATTLE BORN

During the peak of conflict on the Korean Peninsula, Toyota and other Japanese vehicle manufacturers were awarded contracts to build military vehicles for the United States Government. Here, Toyota's truck engineering

prevailed, producing an extremely rugged and versatile 4WD vehicle. This military utility truck, ultimately offered in civilian form as the Land Cruiser, established Toyota as a company capable of building quality trucks.

Anyone exposed to the FJ25 or FJ40 Land Cruisers will attest to their attributes and striking similarity to the better 4WD military "general purpose" truck designs. Although quickly turned toward civilian police and emergency services use in Japan, the early FJ25 was clearly competitive with Willys' four-wheel drive M38-A1 (Jeep CJ body prototype).

Superior traction at the front axle sets the FJ25 or FJ40 Land Cruiser apart from all other 4x4s trucks in its class—with the possible exception of the Nissan Patrol, a model that Nissan stopped exporting to the U.S. over two decades ago. Incredible climbing ability, enhanced by tight approach and departure angles, gave these early Toyota FJ 4WD models a distinct edge over other utility 4x4s.

Close Look at the Early Land Cruiser 4WD

Toyota's Land Cruiser gained steady acceptance in the United States and became the notable success of Toyota's first import models. Available through dealers in 1958, the FJ25 models offered two distinct geartrain layouts.

The less conventional geartrain included a four-speed (non-synchromesh compound low gear) transmission with a single speed transfer box, much like Ford's 1965 and newer F-100 4x4 trucks. The other version was a typical three-speed transmission with two-speed transfer case. This second setup would carry forth into the early FJ40, FJ45 and FJ55 models.

Looking to some like an inflated Jeep CJ model, the FJ25 Land Cruiser was a clear departure from the Jeep 1/4-ton 4WD truck. In particular, the FJ25's in-line six cylinder engine far outclassed Willys' F-head four cylinder.

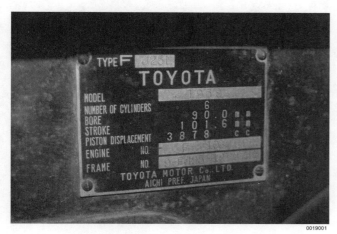

Fig. 1-3. *The Korean War played a crucial role in the survival of Toyota Motor Company. Military vehicle contracts from the U.S. Government spurred the development of a prototype Land Cruiser and other vehicles. As Japan's economy recovered, Toyota's Land Cruiser 4WD FJ25 emerged as a civilian utility model.*

Fig. 1-4. *The 236.7 cubic inch overhead valve in-line six-cylinder Toyota F engine, often described as a design knock off of an early GMC in-line six or the 235 cubic inch Chevrolet powerplant, holds a distinct advantage over Willys' M38-A1 F-head 134 cubic inch four cylinder engine. The larger Toyota engine offers substantially more torque and usable horsepower, plus the added weight of heavy iron castings that extend forward over the front driving axle.*

Land Cruiser owners marveled at the long-term durability and impressively strong performance of the FJ25 and FJ40 powertrains.

Built to metric standards and incorporating massive iron castings, the 3878cc (236.7 cubic inch) Toyota F engine borrowed many of the physical and service features of the popular Chevrolet/GMC in-line sixes. Likely the U.S. Government request for a Korean War military vehicle encouraged the use of such components. American mechanics certainly were familiar with this parts layout.

The F engine features both the assets and some liabilities of the 235 Chevrolet six. Until 1974, the F's oil system used a by-pass filtration method, which exposes the main bearings to the risk of contamination and scoring from debris. With this design, crankcase oil can leave the oil pump and travel directly to the main bearings. If the oil pressure and volume are high enough, some of the oil will "bypass" (via a pressure regulator) through the cartridge oil filter. An otherwise rugged block assembly, the F engine uses four very large main bearings and six insert-type rod bearings, heavy connecting rods, durable pistons, and a massive iron flywheel.

Another weak area in the F and early 2F sixes is exhaust valve life-span. Burning an exhaust valve(s) was not uncommon, especially on vehicles subjected to long term operation at highway speeds, a situation common to American roads. Later 2F engines gain better quality exhaust valve material and improved durability. (The earlier F or 2F cylinder head can be upgraded. See service chapters for details.)

One of the endearing features of the earliest F engine was its simple one-barrel carburetor. Although some owners replaced this unit with an American-built carburetor from an earlier Chevrolet in-line six, Toyota's origi-

Fig. 1-6. *Routine service for the F and 2F engines is much like a 235 Chevrolet, especially earlier models with breaker point ignitions. Valve adjustment, points and condenser replacement, filter and oil changes and other routine service closely resemble those steps followed with the early Chevrolet and GMC in-line sixes.*

Fig. 1-7. *Two-barrel Land Cruiser carburetors have more parts and are far more complex than the early one-barrel design. Like all other U.S. market engines, a heavy dose of emission controls makes the 1971 and later FJ models more complicated to service and troubleshoot.*

Fig. 1-5. *Toyota's original F engine, with a 90mm cylinder bore diameter and 101.6mm stroke length, survives through the 1974 Land Cruiser models. Mechanics with experience around the early Chevrolet and GMC in-line OHV sixes find the Land Cruiser's F engine familiar and easy to service.*

nal carburetor is both functional and easy to service. Later two-barrel Land Cruiser carburetors have more parts, appear complex and suffer from their close interaction with a heavy complement of emission controls.

NOTE —
Many owners use aftermarket retrofit kits to remedy OEM carburetor troubles; however, this often violates emission laws. (See engine performance chapter for details.)

The overall structure and design of the Toyota FJ25 departs from the civilian and military Willys/Jeep models in several ways. The emergency brake at the rear of the transfer case is of contracting band type, with a floor mounted rachet-type lever, much like the U.S. M38-A1. However, the four-wheel drum wheel brakes feature cleanout ports, unlike similar American-built 4WD models.

Wipers at both sides of the windshield came standard on these first FJ trucks, with a push-up type air vent in the center of the cowl at the windshield base. Considered "tall-roof" models, these trucks featured more headroom and an available hardtop with small rear side windows and no rear corner windows.

The battery mounted beneath the vehicle, at the driver's side. Sheet metal was distinctive and established the basic style that would last through the last U.S.-export Land Cruiser FJ40 model in 1983.

The Early FJ40 Series

When the FJ25 officially came to the U.S. shores in 1958, the similar 90-inch wheelbase FJ40 soft and hardtop models were close behind. The first generation of U.S. FJ40s were the 1960–69 models, which also included the rare FJ43 (95.7 inch stretched wheelbase) and the FJ45 models, originally offered with either a long pickup body (FJ45P-B on a 116.1 inch wheelbase), the four-door station wagon body (FJ45V on a 104.3 inch wheelbase), and a shorter bed pickup based on the FJ45V wheelbase.

Most three-speed trucks had column shift linkage with a front axle engagement knob at the dash. (The 4-wheel drive system engaged with a vacuum shift mechanism, while the transfer case's high-neutral-low range engagement lever fit just beneath the dash.) This arrangement was adequate and generally reliable, although the three-speed transmission had no synchromesh on first gear and required a virtual dead stop or double clutching to engage first gear without clash.

Low volume sales levels kept these early models very similar, and in the early 1960s, a one- or two-year-old frame would often sell as the current year's model.

NOTE —
Owners curious about the true year of production of an early FJ model should check the number stamped at the right front frame rail. The number that precedes the "FJ40" indicates the year of frame production, i.e., "1FJ40-" means 1961; "2FJ40-" means 1962, and so forth.

The early front axle has the unique "monkey's fist" drive joint and does not use an inboard front axle seal. Instead, the inner bushing has a thread-like groove that returns oil to the differential housing and prevents gear oil from leaking into the knuckle cavity. A worn, loose or misaligned bushing will allow gear oil to fill the knuckle cavity and find its way into the wheel bearings, brake lining and onto the wheel assembly.

Two clutch assemblies were available during these years, the heavier unit having more springs than the light duty type. Likewise, the chassis' four leaf springs were available in different rates, with color codes that identified each rating.

The early brake and hydraulic clutch master cylinders used metal caps, while 1967 and newer model brake master cylinders are of tandem design (front wheel brake sys-

Fig. 1-8. *The FJ40 and its counterpart FJ45 Station Wagon and pickup models firmly established Toyota as a 4WD truck builder. The Land Cruiser was quickly recognized for its ruggedness, structural integrity, superior engineering and stamina. Many of the early U.S.-market Land Cruisers still deliver quality service.*

Fig. 1-9. *In response to U.S. DOT requirements, 1967 and newer model brake master cylinders are of tandem design (front wheel brake system separated from the rear). Pedals are of the suspended type on all FJ models, and these trucks use a hydraulic clutch linkage system.*

tem separated from the rear). Pedals are of the suspended type on all FJ models, and a cable controlled hand throttle was standard on earlier models, ideal for Power Take-Off (PTO) use.

One of the prized features of FJ40s with side-folding rear seats was the heater at the rear floor. Although some early soft-top FJs (fold-down tailgate models) did not offer a heater, the factory front and rear heating system surely appealed to Willys/Jeep CJ owners. The earlier soft top models also offered solid plexiglass windows, an unusual and distinctly Toyota feature.

Fig. 1-11. *FJ45 short- and long-bed pickups (round and square cornered) were rare but appreciated. Today, an FJ45 pickup in top shape is a collectible value, prized by Land Cruiser aficionados. Hard and soft tops were available.*

Fig. 1-10. *A welcome feature on many FJ40 models with folding rear side-seats was the rear floor heater. This asset likely won over a lot of Willys and Jeep CJ owners who were tired of a cold neck and numb rear passengers. The factory hardtop option was equally advantageous.*

Distinctive FJ Features and One-off Models

Early FJ U.S. models afforded a surprisingly broad range of variations. An FJ45 pickup had its counterpart in the four-door custom bodied (Yamaha built) FJ45 station wagon. Military prototype parts, like a heavy windshield or a centerline "basket style" inside roof rack, were available on occasion.

FJ45 short- and long-bed pickups (round and square cornered) were also seen, along with hard and soft tops on pickup models. In 1969, popularity of the FJ45 station wagon encouraged the introduction of an FJ55 wagon with an optional electric tailgate window.

Earlier FJ40 hoods have a unique "gore cut" (curved-V) front edge that allows forming of a compound curve. This somewhat involved process was eventually replaced by fully stamped hoods that do not have the center nose trim found on early gore-cut types.

In the glovebox of all early FJ40 Land Cruisers was a set of canvas safety straps for running without the doors. Along with these parts, each truck had an owner's handbook, a trouble light and touch-up paint. (I remember pricing an FJ40 in 1970, and the price for one of these rugged trucks was little more than an accessorized Volkswagen Beetle!)

Early models boasted an internal folding (bi-fold) upper tailgate. The value of this feature was the ability to open the tailgate without moving the spare tire. Tops for these models, built through 1964, featured a factory rear roof vent.

The early FJ three-speed transmission was of side shift (top loader) design. Armor-strength skid plates, like I saw on FJ40s during my first Rubicon run in 1967, protected the exhaust pipe of these early Land Cruisers. In 1968, the demand for safety and comfort prompted the switch to a padded dash top, with the addition of a functional single windshield wiper motor and linkage between the two wipers.

Consistent with the design of durable trucks and military vehicles, the first FJs offered front and rear PTO outlets for winches and utility drives. Like the early Jeep CJs, the austere design of the Toyota FJ models did not provide for a dash-mounted radio, which led to the common practice of hanging a radio beneath the dash—where it often interfered with the driver or passenger's legs.

The early FJ 12-volt electrical systems have a generator instead of an alternator, and for electric winches, this is a liability. (See accessory chapter for upgrades to the electrical and charging system.) Fuse boxes mounted to the center of the floorboard, above the driver's right foot, were susceptible to condensation and corrosion.

These rugged trucks could easily climb a steep slope, pull a heavy load, drive a PTO accessory or cruise down the highway at speed and in relative comfort—especially when compared to the spartan Jeep CJ models or even the early International Scout.

The original Toyota FJ40 could be regarded as the first real sport utility vehicle (SUV). These 4WD trucks served a wide variety of duties without a whimper or moment's hesitation. All this progress, and the F and 2F engines still featured a provision for hand cranking!

Fig. 1-12. *Early FJ 12-volt electrical systems have a generator. For running high amperage accessories, like an electric winch, this is inadequate. Early Land Cruiser owners often convert their electrical systems to an alternator.*

Fig. 1-13. *Toyota's FJ40 was a progressive multi-purpose design, likely the world's first sport utility vehicle (SUV). Despite innovation and advanced engineering, the F and 2F engines revealed their utilitarian military origins in the hand cranking provision.*

Late 1969 through 1974 Land Cruisers

Land Cruisers continued to evolve, and in late 1969 the F engine gained two-barrel carburetion and an improved induction system for an increase in horsepower. Through 1973 and some federal (49-state) 1974 models, the FJs still offered the three-speed transmission. The last three-speed model years feature a cane-type floorboard shifter.

The four-speed and its synchromesh on all forward speeds was a major breakthrough. Timely in terms of the U.S. CAFE standards and desirable for off-pavement use, synchromesh on first gear also benefitted from a more useful first gear ratio of 3.555:1, considerably lower than the previous three-speed's 2.757:1 ratio.

Along with the four-speed, however, came a transfer case with a higher (numerically lower) gear ratio of 1.992:1 in low range, compared to the earlier 2.313:1. The earlier

Fig. 1-14. *The 1974 introduction of a four-speed synchromesh transmission was a welcome change. A more useful first gear ratio of 3.555:1 meant better acceleration and closer ratio spacing between the forward gears.*

transfer case has an off-highway advantage, although the later four-speed is desirable from a driveability standpoint and in terms of ratio spacing between gears.

> **NOTE —**
> Along with transmission changes, some owners swap earlier transfer cases into later models to gain low range gear advantages. One approach is to swap in a U.S. truck-type four-speed such as the GM Muncie 420 or 465. A common version of the SM420 features a non-synchromesh first gear ratio of 7.05:1. (See performance/upgrade chapter.)

In compliance with U.S. and California emissions standards, Toyota began using electronic breakerless ignitions in 1974. As early as 1969, smog pumps were on FJs, and the usual complement of PCV and EGR valves, evaporative emissions systems and other items have also served Land Cruiser engines.

Oiling system improvements in the 1974 F engine were significant, and like the 1975 and newer 2F engine, all oil passes through the filter before reaching engine bearings. The 1975 and newer 257.9 cubic inch (4230cc) 2F in-line sixes use a full-flow spin-on type oil filter.

Also gone, beginning with the last (1974) F-engines, is the copper tube oiler to the rocker shaft. This engine and all 2F types have oil feed holes through the engine block and cylinder head.

In an effort to survive stringent emission standards, the cylinder head and valves underwent changes. Several stopgap remedies helped, but the real fix was the use of stellite (or aftermarket stainless steel) valves. Hardened steel aftermarket exhaust seat inserts also alleviate the tendency to burn valves and seats on engines originally equipped with cast-in valve seats. (See service and engine performance chapters for details.)

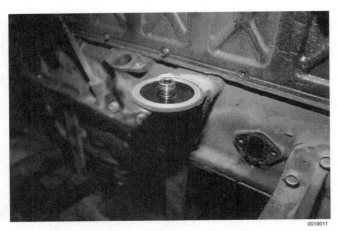

Fig. 1-15. *For 1974 F and the newer 2F engines, all oil passes through the filter before reaching the engine bearings. The 257.9 cubic inch (4230cc) 2F in-line sixes use a simple full-flow spin-on type oil filter.*

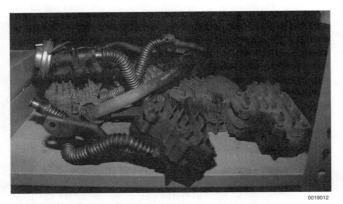

Fig. 1-16. *Helping to keep the 2F engine cool, engineers provided an ample radiator, a clutch fan, an EGR system intercooler (shown), and an engine oil cooler. An oil pan capacity of eight quarts carried forward from later F engines to the 2F.*

In 1973, a new steering column, steering wheel and steering gearbox came on line. This eliminated the leakage of steering gearbox oil into the driver's lap, a phenomenon that occurs when the pre-1973 Land Cruisers park too long on a steep tilt—angles that few (if any) other production 4x4s in the world can achieve.

Along with these steering changes, 1973 was the first FJ model with the dimmer switch on the turn signal lever. The cab was also enhanced by a pair of full front bucket seats and a dashboard location for an optional or aftermarket radio. Missing, however, was the traditional FJ40 tool box stowage beneath the driver's seat.

A fuel tank protective plate, added in 1973, reduced the fuel capacity of Land Cruiser FJ40 models by approximately two gallons. Still, these 4WD models were well suited for American off-pavement rock crawling.

The 1974 FJ40 gained the new international style taillight assemblies. Added for 1974 was the factory roll bar, and this was the last U.S. hardtop model to offer vent windows.

For added axle stamina, Toyota increased the rear axle bearing diameter. No area of the powertrain, geartrain or chassis lacked attention. The only weak link, as such, in the FJ25 through FJ55 models was the limited use of body sheetmetal galvanizing and poor anti-rust protection, factors that have prematurely retired many of these models while they were still mechanically sound.

During this era, Volvo proffered an ad that claimed exceptional service life from its cars, even when exposed to the gruelling rigors of Swedish roads. In response, Toyota's now classic advertising image was a well-used 1958 Land Cruiser from Oregon with a caption that read, "Toyota Landcruiser.... We'll know how long they last when the first one quits!"

The Last FJ40 and FJ55 Models

1975 was a milestone year for Land Cruiser engineering. The U.S. emissions control and fuel economy demands were strongly affecting trucks. The 2F engine came on line with its larger 257.9 cubic inch displacement, which helped offset the power loss of heavy emission control constraints.

More subtle changes included a fluid clutch fan on the engine and a small electric fan aimed at the carburetor. The carburetor fan was a response to the hot running engine and its tendency to percolate fuel in the carburetor bowl and fuel lines. Similarly, an auxiliary oil cooler mounted on the engine, along with an EGR valve intercooler. Toyota worked hard to maintain performance and reliability on the 2F engines, and the challenge during this period was extreme.

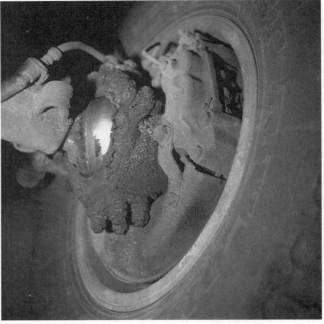

Fig. 1-17. *The addition of power assisted disc front brakes on 1976 Land Cruiser models was significant. With a four-speed sychromesh transmission, the 2F engine and disc front brakes, 1976–83 FJ40s make a supreme off-pavement machine.*

Ambulance-type rear doors, introduced in 1975 with the spare tire on the left side, eased access to the rear cargo area. A gas trap door lock is also distinctive of this model.

For 1976, the Land Cruiser gained its most significant chassis improvement: power assisted front disc brakes, utilizing powerful four-piston calipers. I can attest to the improvement, having towed a tandem axle travel trailer and a well-equipped tent trailer with my 1976 FJ40, in each case experiencing undaunted brake capacity.

> **NOTE —**
> The tandem axle trailer had electric brakes, a sway control and a load distributing hitch. (See accessories chapter for comments and details on towing.)

Cosmetically, the 1976 FJ40 gained lift-up door handles on thicker, more protective and quieter doors. No-vent windows and subtle trim changes make these models easy to spot.

The fuel requirement during this period was both unleaded or leaded, as the truck's 2F engine was emission clean without a catalytic converter (which requires use of unleaded fuel only). 1976–78 California bound models did use a thermal reactor on the exhaust manifold, but this was still not a catalytic converter.

Toyota maintained non-catalyst status until the 1979 models, which did require a catalytic converter and also the change to taller 3.70:1 axle gearing to meet CAFE standards. Previous models had 4.11:1 ratios, which

prove much more useful in off-highway environments. 1979 FJ40s also relocated the fuel tank beneath the truck, and FJ55s gained the larger international type tail lamps.

These models with a floor-mounted transfer case lever and four-speed shift cane were easy to operate, and on- or off-highway driving visibility was tops for these trucks. The FJ55 now offered factory air conditioning, and all FJs had the big front turn signals.

At the end of the 1970s, the FJ40 lost its soft-top option and canvas door straps, a sign of the safety concerns and regulatory demands of that period. Added in 1979 was a factory power steering option, a much warranted addition for any serious off-highway 4WD truck.

While Toyota adhered to OEM bias-ply M&S tires from Dunlop or Bridgestone, many owners and dealerships opted for smoother and quieter running radial tires. As with early FJ models that sometimes came with military tread tires, further Americanizing of these trucks often took place at the dealership level. Similarly, the addition of Warn or other types of free-wheeling front hubs was common.

In the last years of the U.S. model FJ40, air conditioning and power steering became popular options. This shift toward convenience and comfort was a response to SUV trends in the U.S. market. The more stylish FJ60 replaced the FJ55, adding luxury interior appointments and a refined chassis for better highway performance.

Although the transfer case became a stronger and quieter through-drive design, the PTO drive locations were no longer in place. Toyota moved the parking brake from the driveline to the rear wheel brakes, further characteriz-

Fig. 1-18. *The FJ55 Land Cruiser Station Wagon steadily gained popularity. A shift toward the Land Cruiser's current status of an upscale, more luxurious model was evident in the 1979 options of factory air conditioning and power steering.*

ing the shift to contemporary engineering. All U.S. FJ60s came with power steering and air conditioning.

1988 to Present: The Upscale Land Cruiser

Between 1988 and 1990, the FJ62 maintained the FJ60's basic body style and leaf spring suspension. However, the FJ62 gained an advanced 3F-E fuel injected engine and an upscale overdriving automatic transmission as a standard feature. The 3F-E was a smaller displacement engine (de-stroked) with a lower block deck height. The resulting higher speed engine could make more horsepower than the previous 2F engine design.

A four-headlamp system gave the FJ62 a more contemporary look, while power windows suited the class of

Fig. 1-20. The 4.0L 3F-E in-line six was a smaller displacement (shorter stroke) OHV pushrod design with a lower block deck height. A higher speed engine, the 3F-E with Electronic Fuel Injection (EFI) made more horsepower than the previous model FJ60's 4.2L engine. The 3F-E, found in FJ62 and FJ80 models, was a transition between the earlier 2F and the latest Land Cruiser DJ model's 4.5L 24-valve twin overhead camshaft engine.

Fig. 1-19. Trending toward comfort and luxury, the FJ62 Land Cruiser wagon began to distance itself from the raw utility of the original FJ45 and FJ55 station wagons.

buyers who could now afford the pricey Land Cruiser. The part-time 4x4 system, coupled with an automatic transmission, made the FJ62 a unique and highly durable multi-purpose model.

In 1991, Toyota introduced an all new chassis and body as the FJ80. Coil spring suspension provided one of the most compliant and versatile ride packages in the

Fig. 1-21. Quality and engineering superiority of the 1993–up Land Cruiser wagon is obvious. I place this vehicle over all other production 4x4s built, including the Range Rover, Hummer, Mercedes SUV models and the exotic LaForza.

Fig. 1-22. *The FJ80's coil spring suspension provided one of the most compliant and versatile ride packages in the 4WD SUV market. The use of a full-time 4x4 system, in place of the traditional part-time transfer case, placed further distance between the contemporary Land Cruiser and its utilitarian FJ45 and FJ55 roots.*

4WD SUV market. The use of a full-time 4x4 system, in place of the traditional part-time transfer case, severed the last design link to the Land Cruiser's utilitarian FJ45 and FJ55 roots.

Owners enjoy every aspect of the newer chassis, but many find that the 3F-E engine consumes too much fuel, especially under load or at higher speeds. In response, Toyota introduced the 1993 DJ model with a radical new engine design.

Maintaining the advantages of an in-line six-cylinder engine, the newest EFI powerplant features a double overhead camshaft and 24-valves with a 4.5L displacement. The bore of 3.94 inches and stroke of 3.74 inches of-

fer the first "over-square" (larger bore than stroke) design in Land Cruiser history.

The DJ engine is a highly flexible, smooth and powerful unit that produces 275 lb/ft of torque at a useful 3200 rpm, plus an impressive 212 peak horsepower at 4600 rpm. There is no engine that can provide smoother performance in its class.

For these latest models, fuel economy has jumped up dramatically. The automatic overdrive transmission and 4.10 axle ratios place the newest Land Cruiser in the 5,000 pound towing capacity range. In response to "World Class" 4WD models like the Range Rover, the new Toyota Land Cruiser is the fiercely competitive answer.

The quality and engineering superiority of the 1993–up Land Cruiser is so obvious that I place this vehicle over all other production 4x4s built, including the Range Rover, Hummer, Mercedes' SUV and the exotic LaForza. The FJ80's rugged chassis, coupled with the DJ DOHC engine and a long legacy of Land Cruiser reliability, outranks all other vehicles in this class.

Fig. 1-24. *The newest Land Cruiser is clearly a departure from the austere FJ45 Station Wagon. Stamina and product integrity remain, however, and these stylish, luxuriously appointed vehicles still rank as rugged and supremely functional sport utility trucks.*

Fig. 1-23. *The latest in-line six-cylinder engine contributes to the Land Cruiser's World Class status. 24 valves, double overhead camshafts, EFI and 9:1 compression ratio contribute to ultra-smooth performance and 212 horsepower. As vehicle weight approaches 5,000 pounds, with a matching tow capacity, this engine serves admirably.*

CHAPTER 1

2. TOYOTA TRUCKS FOR THE U.S. MARKET

While Toyota's serious bid in the U.S. truck market began with the 1969 RN11 Hi-Lux pickup, there were earlier models. Notably, Toyota brought the Stout pickup into the U.S. market, and between 1964 and 1967, this somewhat obscure model sold in small numbers.

The Stout, for that period, was really a Second- or Third-World truck. While the body and chassis were somewhat larger than a mini-truck, the engine capacity was small and aimed strictly at economy. In size, the Stout would rival today's compact class trucks, or even a Toyota T100. But with a 3RB/3RC type engine of only 1897ccs, the Stout's performance was far short of American demands, much like the original Crown car of 1957.

The Stout offered quality and durability but could not carry a substantial load at American road speeds. Sold when gasoline was 25 to 35 cents a gallon, the Stout attracted little attention with its noteworthy fuel economy. This left the Stout competing with full-size domestic trucks that, in many cases, offered 200 or more cubic inches of engine displacement than the tiny Toyota four. The

Fig. 1-26. Sluggish performance aside, the 1964–67 Stout was a sturdy, albeit homely, light truck. The four-cylinder engine was ill-suited for American highways, while the styling, something remotely like an International-Harvester or Chevrolet pickup of the period, held little appeal to U.S. buyers.

Fig. 1-25. The Stout pickup and chassis were somewhat larger than a mini-truck, but engine capacity was small and aimed strictly at economy. Timing for this product's U.S. introduction could not have been worse. With gasoline less than 30 cents per gallon for regular, Americans had very little concern for fuel economy in the mid-1960s.

U.S. of 1964–67 was simply the wrong time—or wrong geographical location—for marketing the Stout.

Toyota had no desire to compete with large displacement V-8 and six cylinder powered U.S. trucks. The Stout made a nice product for an emerging nation, where fuel is scarce and utility ranks foremost in importance.

The Toyota Hi-Lux pickup, however, would alter the American concept of a small truck forever. By the late 1960s, growing interest in small utility trucks, coupled to a steady increase in fuel costs, encouraged Toyota to press the sale of a new class of vehicles—the "mini-truck."

Like Nissan's successful Datsun pickup, the Toyota Hi-Lux made immediate inroads in various regions of the country. Consumers in the Pacific Northwest, in particular, readily accepted these tiny workhorses.

Hi-Lux size trucks were not unique to other parts of the world, and a growing first-time interest in trucks among urban, suburban and semi-rural American buyers made it possible to present such a truck concept. The 3R-C engine, a highly durable and economical progression of the 3R-B, had made an excellent reputation in the Corona passenger car. Tested thoroughly since 1965, under harsh American driving conditions, the 3R-B and advanced 3R-C designs easily satisfied the first mini-truck buyers.

A fundamental truck, with A-arm independent front suspension and torsion bars, a Hotchkiss-type rear axle with leaf springs, and a sturdy ladder frame, the Hi-Lux came as a complete package. Assembled in Japan with Toyota's policy of minimizing options, the Hi-Lux was a blessing for U.S. dealers. Initially, these trucks were much like a fleet buy—owners simply chose a color they liked. The only add-ons were dealer installed options.

This type of marketing did, however, require a re-education of American customers. Domestic trucks were available with over 100 factory options on a given model, plus the choice of many colors, trim levels and accessories.

Buyers soon realized that Toyota and Datsun mini-trucks were of exceptional value and built to last a very

Fig. 1-27. The 1969 Hi-Lux RN11 pickup began one of the most successful truck marketing ventures in automotive history. Borrowing the durable Corona passenger car powertrain plus the chassis features of popular American 2WD trucks, the early Hi-Lux offered durability and exceptional economy.

Fig. 1-28. The Toyota Hi-Lux helped rewrite the American concept of a pickup truck. By 1969, growing interest in smaller utility trucks, coupled to a steady increase in fuel costs, encouraged the sale a new class of vehicles—the "mini-truck."

Fig. 1-29. Hi-Lux pickup offered an overhead camshaft four-cylinder engine, completely foreign to traditional North American truck mechanics. Many technicians shied away from these early Toyota pickup engines, and service relied upon the skills of Toyota car and European trained mechanics.

long time. Packaged so simply, these trucks gave buyers few concerns. U.S. consumers began basing their vehicle choice on the best deal available, making a ritual of dealership-to-dealership price shopping. This habit prevails to this day, although consumers now know which import vehicles offer the best service and resale value.

Turning Point: The Oil Embargo

Early mini-truck buyers were stereotyped as econo-misers by American standards. Datsun and Toyota trucks were often the brunt of chauvinistic and demeaning remarks. Culturally, trucks symbolized American masculinity; the tiny trucks from Asia did not fit the traditional image.

Then came the worldwide Oil Crisis of 1973. U.S. vehicle manufacturers, already struggling to meet stringent emission control standards, experienced an immediate slump in the sale of gas-guzzling vehicles. Suddenly, traditional full-size truck buyers found a whole slew of reasons for looking at the mini-truck as a "second vehicle" or alternative to the popular heavy domestic hauler. Ironically, although U.S. manufacturers could not meet this sudden shift in consumer demands, there was an American precedent for economy trucks.

During the Depression years, Willys built a four-cylinder economy pickup, and even Ford Motor Company experimented with four-cylinder tractor engines in late 1930s light truck models. The relatively low cost of fuel, however, plus the strictly American marketing concept of continually increasing vehicle size to attract new buyers, dragged U.S. truck producers into the dilemma of the mid-1970s.

The "Big Three," AMC/Jeep and International-Harvester were caught off guard. The Oil Embargo, and its legacy of high fuel costs, radically disrupted the U.S. light truck market.

International-Harvester succumbed, unable to compete with its higher priced light trucks that simply could not develop decent fuel economy. Pickup truck production ceased after 1975 IH models, and Scout II production ended with the 1980 models. Jeep Corporation's J-truck and full-size Wagoneer might well have sunk AMC/Jeep had it not been for the ever successful CJ models, the introduction of the first Cherokee and the history making 1984 compact Cherokee.

Meanwhile, the Toyota, Datsun/Nissan and Mazda mini-trucks drew huge attention and sales. As a stopgap measure, GM had secured access to a stylized Isuzu-built Luv, while Ford contracted with Mazda to build the very basic (non-rotary engine) Courier.

Fig. 1-30. Even before the Oil Embargo of 1973, Toyota, Datsun and Mazda mini-trucks sales increased rapidly. The rugged 18R-C and 1975 20R (shown) four-cylinder engines cinched Toyota's huge share of the market. GM competed with a stylized Isuzu-built Luv, while Ford contracted with Mazda to build the Courier.

Dodge followed with Mitsubishi's "Ram 50" and the Montero/Raider series of trucks, which helped Chrysler overcome increasingly dismal sales of full-size Dodge trucks. Were it not for the Cummins turbo-diesel engine option, plus success with the compact Dakota truck and the newest Ram full-size models, Chrysler might easily have given up on U.S.-built Dodge truck business.

Reputation Leads the Way

Toyota mini-trucks gained a rapid following. By the mid-1970s, as the now legendary 20R engine came on line, Toyota had established its high durability standard and willingness to build a superior truck. The 1968cc 18R-C engine, an overhead camshaft design, had convinced early 1970s mini-truck buyers that Toyotas could run the distance. The 18R-C developed good torque and horsepower, and low (numerically high) axle ratios enhanced the engine's pulling power.

The 20R engine, again an overhead camshaft design, featured a cast iron block and aluminum alloy cylinder head. Simple to service, extremely sturdy by design, this engine became the final instrument of truck success for Toyota Motor Sales, U.S.A. Installed in both the mini-trucks and the Celica cars, the 20R engine provided bulletproof levels of durability plus longevity and consistently top fuel economy.

Coupled to rugged synchromesh transmissions and tough rear axles, the Hi-Lux pickup models built from

Fig. 1-31. 18R-C and 20R engines both featured rugged iron cylinder blocks and an overhead camshaft alloy cylinder head. The roller chain drive camshaft and extremely durable internal parts made these engines capable of ultra-long service. A weak link in higher mileage 18R-C engines was timing chain, sprocket and chain tensioner troubles, a problem rectified with the 1975–up 20R engine design.

1969 to 1979 established Toyota as a world leader in this market. Model year 1979 would also prove pivotal in another area of the mini-truck market, the emergence of the 4x4 version of these rugged Toyota trucks.

1979: Toyota's Legendary 4WD Pickup

The two-wheel drive mini-truck market was flourishing by the late 1970s, and an aftermarket demand for 4x4 conversion kits indicated the growing need for four-wheel drive small trucks. (Kits commonly swapped domestic light truck or CJ Jeep geartrain pieces. Some of these 1978 and earlier 4x4 mini-truck hybrids still deliver service today.) Domestic trucks had held a firm grip on the U.S. 4WD market, but Toyota also knew 4WD product and launched into this segment in 1979.

As engineering would prove pivotal here, Toyota relied upon its well-tested Land Cruiser features when building the new 4WD pickup. Toyota went with a solid front driving axle, leaf springs at all four wheels and a rugged, thoroughly tested ladder frame. Here, Toyota's conservatism in the initial design assured the truck's acceptance and immediate success.

By contrast, Datsun hastily put together a 4WD with an independent front suspension system (actually similar to the rear drive design of a Datsun Z-car). Datsun's 4WD front wheel travel and other engineering issues locked buyers into using OEM size tires at a time when oversized tires and wider wheels were a popular retrofit by American 4x4 owners.

Ride height of the Toyota and its easy accommodation of oversize tires gave American buyers what they wanted. The four-wheel drive aftermarket quickly recognized the ease with which the conventional Toyota 4WD pickup could accept accessories and suspension modifications—much like the FJ model Land Cruisers. Several vendors went into the business of personalizing the new Toyota 4WD pickup.

Fig. 1-32. *Toyota followed Land Cruiser engineering when building the 1979 4WD pickup. A solid front driving axle, leaf springs at all four wheels and a rugged ladder frame paid off in the truck's immediate acceptance and success.*

The 1979 4WD pickup, designated model RN37 (102.2 inch wheelbase with short bed) and RN47 (110.6 inch wheelbase with long bed), was available only with the four-speed transmission. This upgraded "side shift" style gearbox, dating in its original form to the 1969 RN11 Hi-Lux design, was the ideal choice for a new 4WD.

The four-speed was durable and smooth shifting, with low gearing in the first and second forward speeds of the transmission. An axle ratio of 4.30:1, plus a rugged two-speed transfer case, gave Toyota buyers the sense that they had purchased a traditional rock-crawling type of 4WD truck.

In fact, they got far more than that. The 1979 4x4 Toyota pickup is among the best four-wheel drive light trucks ever built. Although the sheet metal is typical of mini-trucks for that era, the chassis, geartrain and engine distinguish themselves as among the best designs possible. A sport package offered trim and gauge add-ons, including a tachometer. That package soon became the popular "SR5" option with a five-speed transmission. Consistent with Toyota's marketing strategy, options were minimal, although the introduction of power steering in 1979 models was a milestone. The power steering option had waited for an engineering change that placed the mechanical fuel pump at the cylinder head on the last 20R engines and the subsequent 22R carbureted engines.

1979 and 1980 4WD trucks were only available with a bench seat. With the conventional steel wheels and optional small chrome hubcaps, these trucks had a roguish, no-nonsense profile.

These looks were valid, and the Toyota RN37 and RN47 models became a marque among 4WD small trucks. Whether a buyer got the door vent window or sliding rear glass option, or simply found a base 4WD without hubcaps, these were trucks built for the long haul. Many still run fine and deliver top service to this day, much like their Land Cruiser brethren.

Assault Of The Carbureted 22R Engine

The 1981 RN38 (short bed) and RN48 (long bed) 4WD models, and all of the 2WD trucks, offered a new and larger 22R engine. Replacing the legendary 20R, the 22R maintained many of the 20R's design features. There were, however, some distinct dimension changes.

Fig. 1-33. *The 22R engine was over-square (larger bore than stroke), which typically increases mid-range and high-speed performance while sacrificing bottom end torque. The effect on bottom end torque was negligible. The 1981 carbureted 22R was a powerful and ruggedly built powerplant.*

The 2189cc 20R engine had been ample enough, but the ever increasing demands of emission controls, plus the increased weight of Toyota trucks like the 4WD models, 3/4-ton and Toyota/Chinook mini-motorhomes, demanded more power. The new 22R featured an increase in bore diameter from 88.5mm to 92.0mm. The stroke remained the same at 89mm.

As the bore increased, the 22R engine became over-square (larger bore than stroke), a measure that typically increases mid-range and high speed performance at the expense of low speed "bottom end" torque. The effect was negligible in this larger engine, though, and the 22R was simply a stronger powerplant—especially in truck models with lower (numerically higher) axle gearing.

Improvements in the staged two-barrel carburetion made the 22R perform well at all altitudes and throttle positions. The 22R is among the smoothest running four-cylinder powerplants ever built. Once again, Toyota's use of harder iron in the engine block (basically with a higher nickel content) proved virtually indestructible under normal usage.

It is not uncommon for a properly maintained 22R engine to go 200,000 miles without work on the block assembly. Even then, it is not unusual to see a block's original cylinder cross-hatch honing patterns still visible to the top of the piston ring runs.

The over-square design of the 22R was thoroughly tested in the 1981 pickup trucks. 4WD models, attempting to serve U.S. CAFE fuel standards, switched to 3.90:1 axle gearing, much like the Land Cruiser's switch from 4.11:1 to 3.70:1 ratios. This dropped the engine's rpm operating range at normal road speeds, a factor that was further compounded by the popular new five-speed manual transmission option.

In fifth-gear overdrive, at 55 to 60 mph with standard or oversized replacement tires, a 1981 4WD Toyota pickup engine runs well below its peak torque or horsepower rpm. This results in the need to downshift out of the overdrive gear or suffer the consequences of a severe load placed on both the geartrain and engine.

Further aggravating the weakness was the popularity of installing oversized aftermarket wheels and tires on these trucks. This, effectively, makes gearing even taller and further loads the engine, clutch, and transmission. This issue grew into the first major gearbox failure problem in U.S. Toyota trucks. 1981–83 overdrive (5-speed) gearboxes began knocking out the input shaft bearing on 4WD and diesel powered models.

An epidemic of failures occurred, and the first remedy was a new bearing design that offered more stamina but still fit the relatively small front bearing bore in the original transmission case. For 1984 models, anticipating an increase in OEM tire diameter, it was clear to Toyota that the interim remedy was not enough. Engineers redesigned the five-speed transmission case to accept a larger bearing, and the problem resolved.

Owners of five-speed diesel or 4x4 trucks filed numerous warranty and extended service contract claims on the 1981–83 overdrive transmissions. Toyota quickly accepted responsibility for the troubles and exacted a satisfactory and lasting repair whenever possible. This was consistent with the company's long-standing policy of maximizing customer satisfaction.

1981–85: Refinements

The wheelbases of long- and short-bed pickups worked exceptionally well for both 2WDs and 4WDs. The short-bed pickup could easily maneuver both on- and off-highway, while the longer wheelbase models offered a larger cargo area. The 1981 models introduced the popular "one touch" tailgate with a center handle.

For 1982, the Toyota gained a square headlamp system and functional 999,999 mile odometer. (Groundwork for the 300,000 Mile Club?) The stylized white spoke SR5 wheels carried over from 1981, to be replaced in 1983 by a metallic gold finished design. The 1981 4WD models gained a front axle "doubler" on the left (long) side of the axle housing to provide additional stiffness. These trucks were often put to supreme tests, as the "baby Land Cruiser" attracted hard-core 4WD users and many construction contractors.

Changes in the steering gearbox permitted easier service adjustments, and Toyota continued to increase the stamina and function of these models. For 1981, the bench seat got a center storage tray that fit flush with the seat platform. This response to consumer demands for a console had its downside, however, as three-person seating was no longer possible.

For 1984, Toyota introduced the optional Xtra Cab model, an extended cab without rear seating. Although a longer wheelbase increases the turning radius and reduces maneuverability, consumers wanted this feature.

Toyota 4x4 pickups continued to use the solid front driving axle through 1985, and this supported the marketing and user's image of a rugged design and durability. Many 4WD enthusiasts considered conventional leaf spring suspension and a solid front axle superior to the IFS designs found on other 4WD mini-trucks. Datsun 4WD sales lagged far behind Toyota, and the four-wheel drive LUV/Isuzu, Dodge Ram 50/Mitsubishi and Mazda trucks would never achieve the high sales numbers that Toyota 4WDs earned from 1979–85.

Long or short bed, standard cab or Xtra Cab, 2WD or 4WD, gasoline or diesel engine, turbocharging or non-turbo—each of these features targeted buyer niche markets. In 1985, the A340H automatic transmission secured another group of buyers. Additional power options, often found on DLX (deluxe) cab models, became more popular as pickups and the 4Runner 4x4 wagon, introduced in 1984, gained larger followings.

Restyled in 1984 with squarer body lines and no fender flares on the bed, the pickup's only sales limitation was the self-imposed quota that Toyota and other Japanese manufacturers created to prevent the implementation of a reactionary U.S. import tariff or ban. Underlying this U.S. threat was the simple fact that American vehicle manufacturers could not build cars or trucks to compete with the popular Japanese models of this period.

American buyers vied for available Japanese vehicles, and the result was a seller's market. Toyota dealers and other popular Japanese vehicle dealers exploited the scarce availability and high demand situation.

0019022

Fig. 1-34. Failure of an input shaft bearing or the fifth speed gear is not uncommon among five-speed overdrive transmissions. Fifth gear, physically smaller than the other gears, is exposed to the heaviest load of any gear in the transmission. Add oversized diameter tires, severe loads or excessive lugging in overdrive, and the punishment increases. This load flows back through the countergear to the side of the input gear, which can eventually cause input bearing failure. Toyota's early 1980s troubles are common to many other import and domestic overdrive gearboxes. (See chapter on operating your truck for tips on how to make an overdrive gearbox last.)

Fig. 1-35. *Xtra Cab models became a popular addition to the Toyota truck lineup in 1984. The added space was originally intended for stowage. Many buyers bought the first Xtra Cab* trucks because there were few vehicles available. Toyota's self-imposed quotas resulted in the rapid sale of every truck that came off the transports.

Dealers initiated the practice of tacking "additional dealer profit" to a manufacturer's suggested retail price (MSRP). In the U.S. free-market economy, this approach became so commonplace during the early- to mid-1980s that consumers often shopped for the Toyota truck with the least amount of dealer add-on profit!

Toyota trucks kept gaining popularity, due largely to their reputation for quality, a long service life and practical innovation. During the mid-1980s, Toyota offered two distinct types of bed construction. OEM bolt-on double wall protection became the standard, with Japan-built beds featuring external tie down hooks and a locking gas fill door. Beds built for on-shore U.S. installation (a procedure that classified the Toyota truck for "unassembled" import duty status) had smooth sides.

Beginning in 1985, SR5 4WD models introduced automatic front locking hubs. This was a controversial move, steered by the flood of new 4x4 buyers who demanded convenience. Like all other 4x4 truck builders, Toyota had plenty of trouble with these automatic hub systems. The permanent fix was to retrofit a set of manual hubs.

For many buyers, simply owning a Toyota was good enough. As the body style evolved and engine options increased, every new Toyota truck sold. Sales even carried over to a reasonably healthy mini-motorhome industry, which broadened the market for Toyota 3/4-ton and heftier chassis ratings. There were cab-and-chassis trucks earmarked for utility bed use. Meanwhile, the new breed of domestic compact trucks (GM S-truck and Ford Ranger class) became the only new attraction at domestic truck lots. Through the mid-1980s, these models were still not competitive with Toyota trucks.

Fig. 1-36. *1985 was the last year for a solid front axle 4WD pickup truck. Toyota enthusiasts regard this model as a marque, as many refinements were in place and its durability is legend. Rugged 1979–85 Toyota 4WD pickups fetch a premium price in today's used truck market.*

4WD 4Runner: Baby Land Cruiser Wagon

By 1984, Toyota recognized the need for an economical and more compact alternative to the bulky Land Cruiser. The advent and immediate success of AMC/Jeep's compact four-door Cherokee turned the truck industry upside down, and both Chevrolet and GMC were enjoying brisk sales of the new S-Series Blazer and Jimmy compact utility wagons.

Toyota's response was the 4Runner, built around a 4WD pickup chassis. The early 4Runner looked much like a pickup truck with a canopy, but buyers soon realized that the similarities ended at the cab's B-pillar. From just behind the doors rearward, the 4Runner was a bonafide utility wagon with a rear seat and stowage capability.

As a stop-gap model, the 1984 4Runner made an excellent crossover vehicle. A tough 4x4 chassis, proven and upgraded since 1979, provided the ideal platform for a new vehicle launch. Toyota owners and other consumers were already familiar with the cab and chassis features, and the pickup's reputation for reliability hallmarked the 1979–85 solid front axle models.

Sharing features with the pickup models has made the 4Runner a practical and rugged model. Competing within a large segment of compact SUVs, the 4Runner has established its niche: This is the proven chassis that will deliver service for a very long time.

Exceptional Four-cylinder and V-6 Engines

Between 1984 and 1987, Toyota focused on higher output engines. The general acceptance of electronic fuel injec-

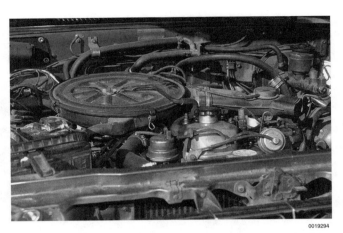

Fig. 1-38. 20R, 22R, 22R-E (EFI) and 22R-TE (turbocharged) four-cylinder engines have earned loyal followings. An iron block and sturdy alloy cylinder head form the backbone for exceptional durability. This fundamental engine design persists to the last models, a testimony to the thorough engineering that went into the original 1975 20R.

tion (EFI) prompted the introduction of 22R-E engines on some 1984 models. By 1985, SR5 models and DLXs with the durable A340H automatic offered the 22R-E EFI engine. Five-speed equipped trucks retained carburetion.

For 1985, the mildly popular 2.0L turbo-diesel was available on long-bed models only. The same option was then available on the short bed Xtra Cab chassis in 1986–

Fig. 1-37. The 4Runner continues to share many features with the 4WD pickup truck models to this day. A significant change took place with the 1990 introduction of a four-door 4Runner, which became a distinctive full-bodied wagon. Looking much like the contemporary Land Cruiser, late Toyota 4Runner styling keeps many Toyota aficionados guessing.

87. Unfortunately, the diesel continued to decline in popularity as gasoline fuel costs stabilized and buyers recognized the 22R and 22R-E for their strong performance and impressive fuel economy.

In its final form, the Toyota truck diesel featured refinements like roller rocker arms with an overhead camshaft. The turbocharged version offered more power at all altitudes, even when towing. This engine is still very popular in other parts of the world.

Competing with the domestic V-6 compact trucks, Toyota trucks needed more muscle to accommodate the heavier 4WD models with independent front suspension (IFS) and the bulky curb weight of the 4Runner. For 1986 and 1987, the solution was an efficient turbocharging system to work in conjunction with the 22R-E EFI engine.

Pilot models for this "22R-TE" gas engine option were 1986 manual transmission DLX standard cab short bed trucks and automatic transmission SR5 Xtra Cab trucks with short beds. Among Toyota truck aficionados, the 1987 gas turbo 22R-TE powered DLX short bed or SR5 Extra Cab is viewed as one of the most desirable compact truck models ever offered.

Fig. 1-40. *The 3VZ-E V-6 engine design features an overhead camshaft above each cylinder bank, a compact 60-degree cylinder bank angle and multi-point fuel injection. Capable of 150 horsepower at 4,800 rpm and 180 lb/ft torque at 3,400 rpm, this engine has powered the compact trucks, the 4Runner and even the T100 "intermediate" size trucks.*

Fig. 1-39. *Curb weight increases, especially for 4WD IFS trucks and 4Runners, demanded new engines. The turbocharged 22R-TE four-cylinder option filled the performance gap from 1986 until the introduction of the 3.0L V-6 in 1988. By 1988, Toyota trucks were clearly in the larger compact truck category and needed V-6 muscle to compete.*

The 1988 introduction of the 3VZ-E 3.0L V-6 engine ended the need for a turbocharged four-cylinder powerplant option. Gone forever was the 22R carbureted engine, as the 22R-E EFI powerplant had proven its overall superiority. The ability of a multi-point EFI engine to meet stringent emission requirements, enjoy good fuel economy and outperform the conventional carburetor system spelled the demise of carburetion.

By 1988, the overdrive four-speed automatic had gained popularity. Buyers who had formerly balked at the lackluster performance of a four-cylinder engine coupled to an automatic transmission now found the V-6 and automatic with overdrive attractive. Five-speed manual overdrive gearboxes also served well behind the four- and six-cylinder engines.

1989 to Present: Further Advancements

In 1989 the pickup and 4Runner experienced another leap forward in styling. The newly shaped truck came in a sleek standard cab version or an Xtra Cab with a new feature—rear jump seats.

For some, jump seats remain a contention. Their function has severe limitations, especially the seating position, which is awkward and of questionable safety. Toyota's creation of this option was a clear response to the huge buyer demand, and the Toyota rear jump seat option was as well engineered as any other design.

The popularity of oversize tires became overwhelming, and Toyota introduced the use of 31x10.50x15 tires as an OEM option on the new generation of "compact" 4WD trucks. Like other Toyota design changes, this was not a stopgap or cosmetic advance. The entire design of the truck came under consideration, and Toyota even altered the axle ratios to match this subtle tire change. Performance did not suffer, and the ride height and chassis alterations met the powertrain needs squarely.

This new and larger compact truck offered a double-wall bed on 4x4 models with a single inner panel. To satisfy the torque and load requirements of models like the V-6 powered 4WD pickup, Toyota installed the durable R150 series transmission in the 1989 V-6 trucks. With roots to the high performance Supra Turbo, this was the correct unit for use behind a high torque V-6 engine.

Fig. 1-41. *Independent front suspension (IFS) four-wheel drive and 31x10.50x15 tires made a formidable marketing package by the late 1980s. American buyers enjoyed the truck's rugged profile and ample power from the 3.0L V-6. 4WD mod-els held their own against competitive domestic trucks with 4-plus liter engines. Import tariffs were high, but Toyota buyers wanted quality, even at inflated prices.*

1992 was the last year for the DLX 4x4 long bed models in the U.S., and plans unfolded for shifting standard cab truck production to the NUMMI assembly plant at Fremont, California. For 1993, Toyota offered yet another change, the introduction of the T100 truck, a new class of "intermediate"-size truck.

The T100, with the 3.0L V-6 as its standard powerplant, offered chassis and load capacities up to one ton. With a bent for economy, the 1994 T100 introduced an optional 2.7L high torque four-cylinder engine that delivers as much horsepower as the 3.0L V-6.

At the introduction of the T100, many American automotive journalists bashed Toyota for failing to develop a V-8 powered truck that would compete with the domestic 4- to 8-liter engines. This was not Toyota's intent. Clearly, the T100 meets the fundamental needs of a worldwide market.

1995-1/2 signaled a significant change year for Toyota trucks. Double-overhead camshaft (DOHC) four-valve-per-cylinder technology, first introduced with the 1993 Land Cruiser 4.5L in-line six cylinder engine, became infectious.

Starting with the T100's 1994 introduction of a DOHC 2.7L four-cylinder engine, Toyota trucks have gained momentum around this design improvement. For 1995, both the T100 intermediate size truck and the new U.S.-assem-

Fig. 1-42. *Tacoma badge means a U.S.-built truck from Toyota's NUMMI (Fremont, California) plant. Truck's styling is bold and in step with the roomier cab that U.S. buyers expect. Tacoma regular cab 2WD, shown here, offers genuine truck performance with the new 3.4L V-6 engine.*

bled Tacoma compact truck offer a 3.4L V-6 DOHC 24-valve engine. Tacoma 2WD trucks offer a new (standard) 2.4L four, also with four-valves-per-cylinder.

Fig. 1-43. *3.4L V-6 DOHC features four valves per cylinder. Performance has jumped from the 3.0L SOHC V-6 engine's 150 horsepower to a powerful 190, while torque increased 40 lb/ft to 220! This is the kind of power North American buyers want in an intermediate or weightier compact truck.*

Fig. 1-45. *New 2.4L four replaces legendary 22R type engine. Four valves per cylinder offers an immediate performance jump to 142 horsepower. This engine powers 2WD models, while base engine for 4WD Tacoma trucks is DOHC 2.7L engine with 150 horsepower rating. Bigger muscle likely means a bigger market share for Toyota's pickups and 4Runners.*

Fig. 1-44. *Tacoma Xtracab meets a growing market segment. Many buyers have multi-purpose uses for their versatile Toyota pickup. Again, a forward facing rear seat provides safer and more valid seating for children. SR5 model (shown here) offers standard chrome package, stylized alloy wheels and 4WDemand four-wheel drive system, which has no freewheeling hubs and uses a front axle disconnect system for its 2WD mode.*

Fig. 1-46. *The T100's quality, not surprisingly, was so convincingly high that J.D. Power & Associates' Light Truck Initial Quality Study picked this truck as the Best Truck of 1993. Never before had a brand new model won this award.*

Looking Ahead

As new compact trucks roll from the NUMMI assembly line, Toyota celebrates an unprecedented accomplishment. Having stumbled into the U.S. truck market in 1958 with a spartan FJ25 Land Cruiser 4WD, Toyota responded in earnest to the changing demands of the American consumer. Since 1958, Toyota's original engineering goals—utility, uncompromising durability and safety—have earned that company the most dynamic growth rate of any motor vehicle builder in the post-WWII era.

Currently, Toyota design and engineering aims meet the demands of a converging global community. Responsive to environmental concerns, the issues of decreasing natural resources, the demand for motor vehicle safety and the needs of diverse consumer groups, Toyota has emerged as a leader. A worldwide enterprise, Toyota Motor Company remains devoted to the advancement of automobile and truck design, a commitment that reflects the heartfelt aspirations of the company's founder, Kiichiro Toyoda.

The Toyota Tacoma pickup trucks, T100, 4Runner and 4WD Land Cruiser serve as a tribute to Mr. Toyoda. His

Fig. 1-47. *On the eve of their introduction, I tested the T100 3.0L V-6 2WD and 4WD models. I later tested one of the first available 2.7L four-cylinder models. Both powertrains and the 3.4L DOHC V-6 deliver impressive performance. The 2.7L, with balance shaft and twin overhead camshaft design, is clearly a milestone for truck engineering. (See my evaluation of the T100 in Chapter 2.)*

firm belief that automobiles and trucks could serve humanity's needs is the inspiration behind the design and function of Toyota's modern trucks. Toyota truck owners, prospective buyers, and competitive manufacturers each hold Toyota products in the highest esteem. Toyota has become a standard by which we measure truck quality.

Chapter 2

Buying a Toyota Truck

A SUCCESSFUL TRUCK BUY begins with under-standing your needs, then finding a truck with the right chassis and options to match these goals. Even a re-stored Toyota Hi-Lux pickup, Land Cruiser FJ25, FJ40 or FJ45/FJ55 model can deliver quality service if you select the vehicle that matches your driving plans.

1. SELECTING THE RIGHT TRUCK

Aside from a vehicle flawed with mechanical defects, a prime source of dissatisfaction among new and used truck buyers is buying the wrong equipment. Whether your Toyota truck can provide multi-purpose transporta-tion or haul a massive cargo over rough roads depends upon the chassis GVWR, the right powertrain choices and useful options.

Toyota trucks and Land Cruisers can deliver value *only if you select the right chassis for your needs.* Choosing the correct chassis is easy, as each model has a distinct chassis and powertrain designed around the Gross Vehi-cle Weight Rating (GVWR).

Fig. 2-2. Toyota's original truck success was the 4WD Land Cruiser. Decades before the mini-truck boom, the Land Cruis-er captured the attention of U.S. four-wheelers. Land Cruiser FJ40 is synonymous with hardcore four-wheeling and indom-itable off-pavement prowess. As an all-weather, heavy duty utility 4x4, the FJ40 is among the best vehicles in the world.

Fig. 2-1. 1994 compact 2WD pickup offers utility, economy, and value. A truck like this one, equipped with the 22R-E or 3VZ-E engine and well maintained, could easily clock 160,000–200,000 miles without major repairs.

The earliest Land Cruiser FJ25 or FJ40 4WD chassis is distinctly different than that of the first RN11 mini-pickup. Land Cruisers, most notably the Station Wagon and rarer pickup models, were built around a bonafide full-size truck chassis that promised comparable stamina to the older (full-size) half-ton capacity domestic trucks. Some models had enough heavy duty components to support emergency equipment, construction company chores and other heavy work.

Much like the 1939–59 era GMC and 1937–62 Chevrolet in-line sixes, the Land Cruiser F and 2F engines could do a hard day's work without a whimper. These two Toyota engines easily match the GM, Ford and Dodge truck sixes of the Fifties and early 1960s.

By the mid-1960s, the advantages of newer domestic seven-main bearing slant and in-line six designs were clear. Here, due largely to the relatively small numbers of FJ Land Cruisers imported into the U.S. market, Toyota stayed with its older four-main bearing engine design.

Although the Stout pickup is best left to the aficionado of Toyota collectible models, the mini-trucks built from 1969 forward offer utility and strong character. For mini-trucks, Toyota's first big gain was the 1975 introduction of the 20R engine. This rugged four-cylinder powerplant could lug a mini-motorhome (Chinook) body with an upgraded Toyota pickup chassis and cab.

The Toyota pickup chassis has always been ample, and the geartrain stamina easily matches its load capacity. Notably, with each model year, the 2WD trucks have

improved. Used truck buyers should feel comfortable with any year model built from 1975 forward.

The 1979–85 4WD pickups rank among the best trucks ever built. My top picks would be a 1979–80 model (preferably equipped with power steering) or a 1984–85 model with power steering and the 22R engine. The 1984–85 models offer front axle and transmission upgrades for added stamina and utility, as well as better engine performance, better braking and more responsive handling.

Fig. 2-4. The 1979 4WD pickup offered front spring mount improvements (anchor end forward with the shackle at the rear of the spring) and other engineering upgrades that gave the pickup's longer wheelbase a balanced ride and excellent load carrying capacity.

Fig. 2-3. The popularity of four-wheel drive gives buyers of new and used Toyota trucks a wide variety of choices. For light hauling, the 4x4 pickup chassis is exceptionally rugged. 1979–85 models (shown) feature a solid front driving axle, much like the Land Cruiser, while 1986 and later trucks offer independent front suspension. A 1979 or 1980 4WD pickup, with its four-speed transmission and two-speed transfer case, was a rugged machine. This transmission is a better design than the 1981–83 five-speed overdrive. 1981 introduction of the larger (2366cc) and more powerful 22R engine adds performance without a loss of fuel economy.

Fig. 2-5. *Four-piston disc brake calipers and massive rotors help assure 1976 and later FJ Land Cruiser stopping power. Aftermarket oversized wheels and tires add unsprung weight and more rolling force for the brakes to overcome. Make sure that your Toyota truck operates within its braking capacity.*

I contend that there is no such thing as a Toyota pickup truck "lemon," although some year models do have design weaknesses. One such case is the 1981–83 4WDs and diesel pickups with the five-speed transmission. These models have a failure prone transmission input shaft bearing, which becomes a critical issue if the truck consistently carries a heavy load, operates with radically oversized tires or lugs excessively in the overdrive gear.

The 1986 change to torsion bar/IFS front suspension on 4x4 pickups and 4Runners is generally a good change. These models gain weight, and if oversized tires are in the plan, both axle gearing and limitations in front end geometry become an issue.

1985 and earlier solid front axle 4x4s can tolerate moderately oversize tires and wider wheel rims that require more negative offset. (These trucks have full-floating front wheel hubs that can support a small increase in wheel offset.) By contrast, 1986–up IFS 4WD models have a positive wheel offset and front end geometry that cannot tolerate the negatively offset wheel rims that accompany a change to large tires.

1989 is the first year that Toyota engineered the pickup and 4Runner front end to tolerate 31"x10.50x15 tires. This tire size is plenty big for any Toyota mini, compact or intermediate (T100) size truck. While my 1976 Land Cruiser FJ40, with disc front brakes, did tolerate 33"x12.50x15 tires on 10-inch wide rims, the lighter pickup chassis does not offer the axle, spring and chassis stamina of a Land Cruiser.

Weighing the GVWR Issue

Each of us has heard tales of trucks that carried loads way beyond their rated capacity. Rated load capacity goes beyond how much weight a set of springs can carry. If heavier springs alone made a one-ton Toyota pickup truck, the cost of heavy duty haulers would drop dramatically. While the wheelbase and body panels often match, a half-ton rated truck typically offers less chassis and geartrain stamina than a one-ton GVWR model.

Fig. 2-6. *Toyota Hi-Lux chassis features were virtually a scaled down version of U.S. truck engineering, principally patterned after 1960s General Motors light trucks. Trucks like the Hi-Lux helped North American consumers become accustomed to the concept of a mini-sized truck.*

If you can identify your hauling needs, selecting a truck becomes easier. The most significant differences in load capacity (GVWR or GCW) ratings involve the frame, spring, brake and geartrain capacities.

Among the new Toyota truck models, the T100 intermediate class chassis is the heavy hauler. Toyota offered several 3/4-ton and cab-and-chassis models during the heyday of the mini-truck era and even into the compact truck years. The new T100 was a complete departure from these earlier models. While earlier 3/4-ton Toyota trucks were essentially beefed up mini and compact models, built around the standard pickup design, the T100 began with an all-new chassis and concept.

I had the privilege of reviewing the new 1993 T100 chassis just prior to its public introduction. Rumors about this new model had stirred a great deal of anticipation. Many automotive journalists expected a large scale rival for domestic full-size trucks, possibly a 5.0L class V-8 to compete with traditional American trucks.

The T100 Intermediate-size Truck

0019047

Fig. 2-7.   The all-new Toyota T100 was a distinct departure from conventional mini and compact trucks. 4x4 version stood tall, giving a "big truck" appearance. Toyota weighed extensive survey data when designing the rugged and versatile intermediate model.

Extensive nationwide surveys within the United States indicated that buyers wanted a bigger-than-compact truck with an economical operating cost. Toyota, ever conscious of customer satisfaction, responded with the truck industry's first intermediate class truck, the stylish and work dedicated 1993 T100 pickup.

At 209.1 inches overall length, the pickup was longer than a regular cab Dodge Dakota and matched most full-size trucks for interior cab room. An eight-foot bed, engineered to carry common 4x8-foot sheets of plywood, brought Toyota buyers into the full-size truck hauling league.

Power Versus Cargo

Toyota's T100 pickup debuted with a husky 3.0L V-6 engine, aimed at fuel economy and useful pulling torque. A SOHC/EFI design, the 1993 Toyota V-6 engine produced 150 horsepower at 4,800 rpm and 180 ft/lb of torque @ 3400 rpm. With the truck's curb weight of 3350 pounds in 2WD version and 3915 pounds for 4WD models, 150 horsepower was adequate for most needs and capable of lugging up to 1550 pounds of cargo. The T100 met Toyota's goal of 5,500 pounds GVWR on 4WD models.

Toyota provided a five-speed manual overdrive transmission in 4WD T100 models, while the 2WD offered an optional ECT overdrive automatic. The manual transmission, in combination with rear wheel ABS, provided a margin of safety for both hauling and 4x4 off-pavement use.

Attention to the bed included a 97.8" length, 49.2" width between wheel wells and 61.4" overall cargo bed width. Height for the new T100 4x4 was 70.1", with a tread width of 63.1"/63.6" (front/rear). Wheelbase was a relatively lengthy 121.8" with a 75.2" overall vehicle width.

First Impressions

My first impression of the T100 cab was positive. Much roomier, the truck's interior had a distinct Toyota feel. Gauges, levers and pedals have traditional Toyota sizing, but as Chief Engineer Shigeo Asai noted, "The driver can sit comfortably with a cowboy hat in place." Cab width was ample, and 60/40 split seat claimed seating for three.

0019048

Fig. 2-8.   1993 T100 interior felt familiar and distinctly Toyota. Ergonomics allow easy access to manual controls. Smaller pedals were among the carryovers from compact truck design. Despite ample width of cab and seat, middle passenger must wriggle around the seat notch and levers, but for two occupants, cab is spacious and comfortable.

The cab did offer improved headroom, paid for in part by a noticeably lower seat platform. The cab offered ample visibility and attention to ergonomics.

The T100's V-6 performance was comparable to late Toyota compact trucks. Similar acceleration, gear change points and lugging ability give the Toyota 3.0L the same performance as comparable Japanese and U.S. trucks equipped with V-6s. But the 3.0L is modest by American big-truck standards. Serious trailer pullers find 150 horsepower restrictive. For buyers who wanted V-8-type trailering power and acceleration the earliest T100 fell short.

On a test route, I drove through hilly terrain, and these trucks, without a trailer in tow, responded much like a V-6 Toyota compact pickup or 4Runner. Axle and transmission gear ratios strike a balance between economy and good performance. Despite the increased size and weight, T100 trucks prove inexpensive to operate.

continued on next page

The T100 Intermediate-size Truck (cont'd)

The T100 4x4 featured recirculating ball power steering and an IFS chassis design proven by the 1986–up Toyota compact trucks. 2WD models offered unique rack-and-pinion steering, which provided excellent road feel and stable cornering.

Fig. 2-9. IFS is a standard now for Toyota 4x4 pickups. Proven technology of compact trucks carries over to the larger T100. T100 delivers real value, a tradition with Toyota trucks.

Fig. 2-10. Bed size and wheelbase separate T100 intermediate size truck from previous Toyota models. 4' x 8' plywood sheets will drop between wheel wells. Note six post holes atop bed sill and innovative two-tier loading.

In tests, both 4WD and 2WD models delivered a quality ride and excellent handling, much like other Toyota truck models of recent years. Importantly, driving with an empty bed did not adversely affect braking or traction.

The actual product was an entirely different concept. Toyota's manufacturing history and worldwide marketing base called for more than a gas guzzling rival to compete with American full-size trucks. Toyota compact 2WD and 4WD trucks already rivaled the best American trucks in their class, indicating that Toyota was fully capable of competing in the full-size truck realm. Philosophy of product, however, led Toyota away from that approach.

4Runner Options

IFS 4WD came on line in 1986, and all such later model pickups and 4Runners provide exceptional stamina and durability. The only drawback with the pre-Tacoma Toyota pickup or 4Runner IFS model frame is the vertical support for the lower control arms. These frame members, hanging straight down from the rugged boxed ladder side rails, permit enough flex in very rough pounding to place unusual stress on the steering linkage and front frame sections. If the driver works this design too hard in rough terrain or "jumps" the truck, it is possible to snap the idler arm loose, damage the frame and tear the steering gear loose from the frame rail.

NOTE —
An aftermarket truss support, mounted between the lower control arms, is available from Downey Off-Road. This truss helps eliminate frame and steering linkage damage caused by off-pavement pounding and the use of oversized tires. (See chassis upgrade chapter for details.)

Fig. 2-11. A pre-Tacoma era Toyota IFS 4WD model driven hard in rough off-pavement terrain can suffer frame and steering system damage. Vertical frame supports for the lower control arms can spread apart on hard and jarring impact, causing steering idler arm damage and, in the worse cases, tearing the steering gearbox loose from the frame. For off-pavement use, an aftermarket Downey Off-Road truss can help prevent lower control arms from spreading.

1989 saw a major body style change that lent the Toyota pickup and 4Runner a wider, larger appearance, and the body contours became less angular and more stylized than previous models. These later trucks hold a distinctive edge in appearance, ride quality and handling. The roomier cab is a full departure from the mini-truck image, and the Toyota became a bonafide compact truck.

The 4Runner's only limitation is power-to-weight ratio. The added weight of the back seating and canopy top places the earlier four-cylinder 4Runner at a performance disadvantage. Originally offered with the milder 22R carbureted engine, the first 4Runners drive much like a cargo-laden 4x4 pickup. This reduces trailering capacity and places a larger load on the powertrain.

Popularity of automatic transmissions, often coupled to four-cylinder 22R-type engines, further detracted from the four-cylinder 4Runner's performance. Some 4Runners feature the turbocharged 22R-TE engine, which boosts the performance level considerably. The best bet, however, for towing and other SUV hauling activities, is the later 4Runner with the 3.0L or 3.4L V-6 engine.

One of a Kind: The Land Cruiser

Although Toyota's Land Cruiser has metamorphosed into a World Class luxury 4x4, often referred to as Lexus caliber in its appointments, the basic premise remains: The Land Cruiser, for its wheelbase length and track width, is among the very best 4WD vehicles in the world.

Those looking for a used Land Cruiser 4WD will find several plateaus of refinement with these models. Today's Land Cruiser utility wagon profile is more like the early FJ45 and FJ55 Station Wagon than the 1983 and earlier FJ40 short wheelbase (90-inch) models. The FJ40 offers the most tractable and versatile type of off-pavement service in its class.

In my experience with short wheelbase SUVs, and I've tested every popular make available, the FJ40 Land Cruiser will easily outclimb any other production vehicle of its type. A lengthy and very heavy in-line six-cylinder engine places extraordinary weight on an already heavy front axle assembly. The result is a vehicle with uncanny traction at steep assault angles.

The choice between an FJ40 or the earlier FJ45/FJ55 and FJ60 depends upon your cargo demands and trailering expectations. Although an FJ40 can perform better than other short wheelbase 4x4s in a trailering situation, I find that the longer FJ55 or FJ60 wheelbase makes for a much sturdier vehicle if you plan to pull a trailer.

For anyone considering a used Land Cruiser FJ40 or FJ55 Station Wagon, the best models were built from 1976 forward. I have owned two FJ40s, a 1971 and a 1976 model. While both had exceptional off-pavement prowess, the 1976 model featured the improved 2F engine, a four-speed transmission and the first use of disc front brakes.

A 1976 or newer FJ model has disc front brakes. These models benefit from the 2F engine's improved oiling and greater power. The four-speed synchromesh transmission (1975-forward) is rugged and practical. More cab comfort adds to owner appeal, and the 1976 and newer FJ40 and FJ55 models fetch a premium price when in good, rust-free condition.

Most 1974 and earlier FJ40s and FJ55s have three-speed transmissions without synchromesh on first gear. Most have the two-speed transfer case, which in these applications features a lower low-range gear ratio than the later four-speed equipped models.

NOTE —
Rust is a problem with all Land Cruisers built before the mid-1980s. On FJ40s, It generally forms in the taillamp brows and front fender bib. For FJ55s, watch for rust in the rear quarter panels: replacement or repairs take a major amount of labor and money.

The early transfer case is desirable. It often accompanies the popular domestic V-8 swap with a truck-type four-speed conversion. (See the performance chapters for information on the popular Chevrolet V-8 with GM's four-speed SM420, SM465 or late five-speed NV4500 truck transmission swap into the earlier FJ-series trucks.)

Although later FJs offered the power steering option, many owners of earlier models have converted to power steering with the use of a GM Saginaw integral power steering system.

NOTE —
In the suspension upgrade chapter, I cover this power steering conversion in depth, along with a special changeover package, the Land Cruiser "Advanced Handling Kit." This kit reverses the front spring anchor and shackle locations and provides superior handling plus less frame stress during rugged off-pavement use.

For those seeking a later Land Cruiser Station Wagon, the FJ62 offers the 3F-E engine, a de-stroked version of the 2F engine. The 3F-E adds an EFI system for some improvement in economy. The primary complaint about FJ60, FJ62 and FJ80 models is their poor fuel economy. These otherwise rugged trucks feature air conditioning, power steering and even an automatic transmission, each of which adds to the already fuel hungry tendencies that these models inherited from earlier FJ40 and FJ55 models.

The FJ80 might have qualified as just another Land Cruiser gas guzzler, however, its four-wheel coil spring and link arm suspension chassis offers better handling and ride quality than any previous Land Cruiser model.

Those who can afford the 1993–up DJ model with the 4.5L DOHC in-line six-cylinder engine find that this is the most desirable and refined Land Cruiser model of them all. Carryover features from the FJ80 include exceptional body and interior styling, full-time 4x4 with an automatic overdriving transmission, the four-wheel coil spring suspension and a full roster of standard features that land the late DJ model in the World Class realm—right alongside the Range Rover, the high-end GM Suburban 4WD or a Mercedes Unimog.

Limited numbers of vehicles hold resale prices at a premium, yet a 1993 or newer used Land Cruiser, in good condition, still provides an exceptional value. The optional locking differentials provide a useful feature for those who plan to use their late Land Cruiser in an off-pavement environment. Like any other used vehicle buy, the goal is a well-kept model with a good history.

Testing the Late Land Cruiser

Fig. 2-12. *Four-speed automatic transmission, premium ETR sound system with nine speakers and a full-time 4x4 system with optional lockers front and rear make the new Land Cruiser anything but spartan. FJ45/55 models form a dim memory in the rear view mirrors of these new trucks.*

In 1993, I had the opportunity to test the new DJ model Land Cruiser. That 4WD SUV was quite a departure from the lumber wagon profile of the early FJ45 and FJ55 Land Cruisers. After a dozen years of intense refinement, the once cumbersome Land Cruiser had emerged as the quintessential luxury sport wagon, marked by startling comfort, utility and traditional Land Cruiser durability.

Using advanced engine developments, like electronic fuel injection and a four-valve per cylinder (double overhead camshaft) hemispherical head design, Toyota transformed the staid Land Cruiser into a sporty, high tech masterpiece. The proven in-line six-cylinder configuration of the all-new 4.5L engine delivered 275 lb./ft. of torque @ 3,200 rpm and 212 horsepower @ 4,600 rpm.

Fig. 2-13. *Core of new Land Cruiser is 24-valve, 4.5L DOHC in-line six. Engine compartment shows attention to detail, superior craftsmanship and functional layout of service items. Note ready access to dipstick, power steering reservoir, coolant fill and brake master cylinder.*

Fig. 2-14. *Optional platform tow hitch gives a solid foundation for trailer pulling. 212 horsepower and 5000 pound towing capability make the 1993–up Land Cruiser a bonafide tow vehicle. Chassis ranks among the heavyweights, more like the full-size 4WD K1500 Suburban than Jeep's Grand Cherokee or the Range Rover.*

The 37% horsepower increase, coupled with great low-end torque, blended classical Land Cruiser lugging power with spirited passing and cruising performance. The test truck had less than 200 miles on the odometer when I began the testing sequence, yet there was an immediate sense for the much stronger and *smoother* powerplant.

Matching the engine torque to the load was a new electronically controlled four-speed automatic transmission. Like other advanced transmission designs, the late Toyota automatic transmissions have an intelligent sense for road conditions, driver demands and economy. The transmission delivered power to a full-time four-wheel drive system, with optional lock-up differentials through a driver operated system that permits rear only or combined front and rear axle lock-up, a first for any production 4x4.

Chassis, Braking and Handling

Another popular and sensible option was the four-wheel anti-lock brakes (ABS), standard with the locking differential system option.

The Toyota Land Cruiser DJ chassis design is a marvel, blending traditional solid (hypoid) axles, both front and rear, with link-and-coil suspension. Stabilizer bars, a front lateral bar and carefully matched springs gave the test truck an exceptionally smooth ride.

Cornering smoothness and overall stability of the truck ranked very high. A traditional frame, solid axles and four-wheel disc brakes (included with the ABS option) lend a solid feel to this hefty 4760 pound curb weight model.

Overall, the late Land Cruiser is a formidable rival for the Range Rover. While a standard 5.7L/350 V-8 powered GM K1500 Suburban has a higher tow capacity (6500 pounds), the late Land Cruiser's 5000 pound tow limit is more conservative. I would not hesitate to pull a 24-foot travel trailer in the 4,500 pound class with a 1993–up Land Cruiser—providing, of course, that the truck had the proper factory towing/hitch package and an equalizer hitch.

CHAPTER 2

Anatomy Of A Toyota Truck

Overall, Toyota trucks have offered more product value than other import and compact truck models of comparable design. This reflects the caliber of engineering of the vehicles produced. As a result, Toyota owners enjoy the benefit of higher resale value from their trucks.

Product integrity of Land Cruiser and Toyota truck models begins with a ladder frame. (In automotive manufacturing parlance, these are "driveable chassis" designs.) All Toyota trucks feature Hotchkiss style open driveline rear axles, and with the exception of late Land Cruiser and 4Runner utility wagons, all models have semi-elliptic rear leaf springs.

Toyota 2WD trucks have always provided independent front suspension, while 4WD pickups and 4Runners use a Land Cruiser-style solid front driving axle through 1985. For 1986, Toyota switched the 4WD pickup and 4Runner to independent front suspension (IFS). Pre-Tacoma IFS models use torsion bar and double A-arm front suspension. 4WD Tacoma trucks use coil front springs.

Until the late Land Cruiser DJ model introduced a DOHC in-line six, all Land Cruiser engines have featured a pushrod type, overhead valve design with a single rocker shaft and set of rocker arms. The mini, compact and intermediate pickup trucks have each featured overhead camshaft engines.

All Toyota truck engines feature iron cylinder blocks, while only the Land Cruiser F, 2F and 3F-E engines have cast iron cylinder heads. All other engines feature durable aluminum alloy cylinder heads, and no particular Toyota engine is prone to casting cracks.

NOTE —
Land Cruiser F and earlier 2F engines are vulnerable to exhaust valve burning and exhaust seat damage. This can be remedied with use of aftermarket stellite or stainless steel valves and replacement (hard steel insert) exhaust valve seats.

For mini-trucks, even the original 8RC and 1971–74 18RC four-cylinder engines are durable. (The one weak link in the 18RC design is the timing chain tensioner and chain assembly.) Parts availability remains good for all Toyota engine designs, and for older engines, the aftermarket can supply many of the parts that the dealerships cannot—or will not—carry.

Any of the four-cylinder engines through the carbureted 22R provide relative ease of access and service. Armed with an official *Toyota Repair Manual*, a budding mechanic can successfully hone his or her mechanical skills and overhaul the 8RC, 18RC, 20R or 22R engine. Later EFI engines prove more challenging to troubleshoot and rebuild, as many additional and sensitive parts need consideration.

The Land Cruiser F, 2F and 3F-E engines each provide a reasonably easy service environment, the earliest carbureted engines being very simple by design. Challenges with these engines include tasks like carefully removing and installing the massive cylinder head assembly. A *Toyota Land Cruiser Repair Manual* for the F, 2F or 3F-E engine remains the most reliable guide for performing engine overhaul work.

0019503

Fig. 2-14. In fundamental design, the 1969 RN11 Toyota mini-pickup holds some similarities to the latest 2WD Toyota compact and T100 intermediate chassis. Load capacity of the later trucks is much greater, however, an indication of improved chassis and powertrain stamina.

Toyota trucks all have hydraulically actuated wheel brakes. All 2WD pickups have four-wheel drum brakes through 1974 models, when the Hi-Lux/Pickup models switched to disc front and drum rear brakes. The Land Cruisers offered four-wheel drum brakes through 1975, adding disc front brakes in 1976. Since 1967, all Toyota trucks and Land Cruisers feature a dual (tandem master cylinder) braking system. Anti-lock braking (ABS) is available on many late Toyota trucks.

Steering on the earlier (pre-1973) FJ25 and FJ40 Land Cruisers was worm-and-roller. Much improved and far more durable recirculating ball-and-nut steering came on line with the 1973 models. (FJ55 models gained recirculating ball-and-nut steering beginning with April 1972 production.) Hi-Lux mini-trucks and pre-Tacoma compact trucks, both 2WD and 4WD, use recirculating ball-and-nut steering.

Various Toyota truck models offer power steering, ranging from 1979 forward. With the exception of the 2WD T100 and Tacoma chassis, all Toyota power steering features an integral-type recirculating ball-and-power piston/nut design. This type of gear survives under rugged use and serves well in Land Cruisers and 2WD or 4WD pickup models. 2WD T100 and all Tacoma models feature the truck industry's first power rack-and-pinion steering.

High tech electronic fuel injection first came on line with the 22R-E four-cylinder engines, followed by the 3.0L V-6 engine and the Land Cruiser 3F-E in-line six. By the late 1980s, all Toyota engines feature EFI, although earlier carbureted models should not be considered a liability.

Equipment and Option Decisions

As noted earlier, due largely to Toyota's overseas manufacturing process, most trucks and Land Cruisers have been sold as packages. Unlike domestic trucks with their hundreds of options and computer ordering methods, new Toyota trucks generally contain a wide range of standard features, popular options and group accessories. Until recently, you could not order a Toyota pickup truck or Land Cruiser to specification. During the self-imposed quota period of the 1980s, Toyota trucks sold so fast and at such a high rate of demand, that *any* equipment package was popular.

As a result, Toyota has always offered maximum utility, durability and uniformity in each truck of a given model line. While domestic trucks require special ordering of heavy duty options, Toyota avoided this marketing approach. All Toyota trucks of a given model and engine type can haul an equal load and offer nearly identical economy figures.

As a package for work or trailer pulling, 3/4-ton and T100 one-ton models provide far greater value than a 1/2-ton in terms of component stamina and ability to move a load. Given equal chores and care, a 3/4-ton or one-ton rated Toyota truck will out-pull the half-ton model with far less strain and wear. This translates as longer component life and added resale value.

Many buyers opt for a larger truck to provide for an adequate load capacity. The only downside is fuel economy, the higher cost of tires and a shorter engine life if the axle gearing is much lower. Beyond these concerns, anyone finding a cargo need for a long-bed pickup would be wise to consider a heavy duty model.

Fig. 2-15. *A full-floating rear axle (identified on this Land Cruiser by hub design) is an important consideration if you intend to haul severe cargo loads or lug a bulky motorhome body. Most Toyota trucks do not offer such a feature. Rare Land Cruisers, later model utility cargo trucks and the recent dual rear wheel motorhome chassis offer a full-floating rear axle.*

Fig. 2-16. *Use of similar sheet metal and cab features from the B-pillar forward means that every Toyota truck and 4Runner can offer a similar level of convenience options and comfort. Driving ease and power options make the latest Toyota chassis especially popular with first-time truck buyers.*

As a rule, 4WD models have heavy duty components, although their gross payload capacity is often lessened by the additional curb weight of the truck. Most buyers choose a 4WD model for its exceptional tractability and all-season performance. Some take advantage of the added traction and put the truck to work off-pavement.

Regardless of your planned use, be clear about the truck's Gross Vehicle Weight Rating (GVWR), gross payload capacity and Gross Combination Weight (GCW). GVWR is the maximum recommended weight for the truck with its full cargo, a driver and other occupants.

The maximum payload includes the weight in the cargo area added to the weight of the vehicle's driver and occupant(s). The maximum GCW accounts for the weight of the loaded and occupied truck plus the full trailer weight. This could be a truck at maximum payload or GVWR plus a trailer weight that does not exceed the allowable GCW. Likewise, GCW could also be a truck with an empty cargo bed that pulls a heavier trailer, as long as the

Fig. 2-17. *When the load calls for maximum strength, the 2WD 3/4-ton or T100 one-ton rated trucks provide the chassis and axle stamina to get the job done. Available in a variety of wheelbases, Toyota trucks can serve a broad range of needs.*

combined weight of the two vehicles does not exceed the maximum allowable GCW.

Choosing the right Toyota truck can be both fun and rewarding. There's less confusion with the package approach, and Toyota sales literature lists load capacities and other data. Proper selection of a chassis and equipment can provide years of satisfaction and service from your truck investment.

2. INSPECTING A USED TRUCK

As a used truck buyer, there is a real fear of waking to a pile of scrap iron in your driveway. Gloomy repair expenses create anxiety about buying any used vehicle. Insight, however, can help demystify the process. Add to this the promise that no matter how much you want a

Seven Best Toyota Used Truck Buys

My seven favorite Toyota truck and Land Cruiser buys take into account reliability, utility, and versatility. Cost of operation is also a factor, so for each pick, I describe the fuel economy and parts availability/cost for the model.

In any model year, look for options that enhance the reliability of the truck. As you can tell, I prefer heavy duty options of most kinds, including engine and transmission cooling upgrades, a heavy duty charging system and battery, better springs or upgraded shock absorbers.

Shock absorbers may not be as relevant on a used vehicle, as they are a periodic replacement item. A factory shock upgrade often hints about other improvements, however, like a bigger sway bar diameter or heftier springs.

As for gearbox stamina, look for the highest GVWR weight capacity. Transmissions have torque ratings, and later model five-speed manual overdrive units have higher load capacities than the earlier designs.

The automatic overdrives offer dramatic gains in fuel economy and excellent gear ratios. First gear of an automatic overdrive is a lower ratio, and this allows use of taller axle ratios. A combination of taller axle gearing and overdriving ratio delivers exceptional highway cruising economy with performance downshifting on demand.

Four-cylinder engines, however, coupled to overdriving automatics do not offer the kind of performance that a five-speed manual transmission can. I would not recommend a four-cylinder with an automatic transmission unless the driver faces a physical challenge or there is some other sensible demand that dictates the use of an automatic. The pickup/4Runner V-6 engine and the later Land Cruiser inline sixes are far more suitable for an automatic.

Axle stamina and ratios match a given payload capacity and GVWR/GCW rating. Towing and hauling capacity, plus the curb (unladen) weight on each axle of the truck, determine which axle ratio is best. Toyota does not market optional heavy duty gearboxes or axles. Toyota builds each model with the axle ratio considered optimal for the truck's engine type, tire size, load capacity, emission output and fuel economy. You must select the model and GVWR rating that will meet your needs. Allow for unusu-

Fig. 2-18. *As a used truck buyer, look for heavy duty or longevity options like a larger output charging system and battery. Options also suggest the kind of use that the original owner had planned for the truck.*

al loads, like a front mounted winch on a 4x4 model. Before buying a truck, note its gross weight rating *per axle* and the GVWR/GCW rating. The gross load capacity per axle takes into account each axle's stamina, the brake sizing, frame strength, spring rates and tire/wheel capacity.

All Land Cruiser and truck axles, and all three- and four-speed manual transmissions, have durable service records. Five-speed manual overdrives have improved steadily since 1984.

1) 1975–up 2WD Pickups: These models feature the best engines and geartrain assemblies. The 20R, 22R, 22R-E, 22R-TE and 3.0L V-6 each offer good service and a long lifespan. Suspension, brakes, steering and other components improve steadily from 1975. Fuel economy is optimal, especially for four-cylinder models. Four-cylinder engines work best with manual transmissions, while the added performance of the 22R-TE (turbocharged) and V-6 can add the necessary power for an automatic transmission. OEM and aftermarket parts availability for any of these trucks is excellent. **continued on next page**

truck, desire won't override good judgement. This may be tough, as the search for a quality used truck sometimes leads to junk. When you finally find a presentable piece of iron, the impulse is to buy it. That's when you must be wary!

The Chassis

The condition of the frame is the most important aspect of a used truck. You can recondition cosmetic areas and mechanical assemblies, but a twisted, broken or fatigued frame means severe trouble. Several symptoms suggest that a truck's frame has sustained damage, and I always begin looking at a used truck by crawling under it and checking for obvious signs of wear and abuse.

Damage is easy to spot: bent springs, spring hangers or frame crossmembers; torn cables or hoses; a twisted skid plate on a 4x4 or damaged frame horns at the bumper attachment points. Axle misalignment shows up as worn tires. If you have suspicions about a truck's frame condition, suggest that the seller accompany you to a reputable frame and alignment shop. Have the frame checked for straightness on a four-wheel alignment rack.

Taking critical measurements between points on the frame will indicate whether the truck has sustained damage or suffers from fatigue, sag and cracks. The frame specialist can also check for wear at the steering linkage, the steering gearbox, spring hangers, bushings and steering joints.

Seven Best Toyota Used Truck Buys (cont'd)

2) 1979–80 4WD Pickup: This is a top value, offering an exceptionally reliable package if you can find a truck in top shape. Power steering is somewhat rare and very desirable, and the short bed pickup lends itself to tight off-pavement terrain, while the longer wheelbase models offer more cargo capacity and better stability when pulling a trailer. Fuel economy is good, considering the weighty chassis, and parts availability remains excellent.

3) 1984–85 4WD Pickup and 4Runner: The last two years of the solid front axle chassis. Rugged and durable, this is a tough and economical four-cylinder powered model with ample performance for light hauling. Driven respectfully, serviced regularly and treated to high grade lubricants in the engine and gearcases, this truck can often go 160,000–250,000 miles before needing major work.

4) 1986–up 4WD Pickups and 4Runner: These models feature IFS and improvements in the automatic transmission and other powertrain features. The IFS 4x4 that has not suffered off-pavement abuse is an excellent buy, and as a rule, a newer model means better engineering. I prefer the 1990 and newer 4Runner for its convenient four-door "baby Land Cruiser" profile and refinements. A V-6 is essential for 4Runners and compact pickups used for heavy hauling or towing a trailer. The T100, although fairly new as a used truck prospect, will provide exceptional 2WD and 4WD stamina plus good fuel economy—expect especially good mileage with the unique 2.7L DOHC four-cylinder.

5) 1976–83 FJ40 Land Cruiser: These are more refined versions of my favorite off-pavement 4WD utility truck. The axle gearing in 1979–up FJ40s leans toward better fuel economy while sacrificing some off-pavement prowess. Regardless, any of these trucks in top shape make an excellent buy. If the truck does not have the rare power steering option (1979–up), consider a GM Saginaw power steering conversion. Parts availability remains good through aftermarket suppliers and only fair through Toyota dealers. (Land Cruiser parts, from any source, are costly.) Fuel economy of the rugged 2F engine is marginal.

6) Land Cruiser FJ55 (1976–up), FJ60, FJ62 and FJ80 Station Wagon: Each of these models offers improvements over the previous design. The FJ55, FJ60 and FJ62 offer the last four-wheel leaf spring chassis, while the FJ62 introduc-

Fig. 2-19. 1976 and newer Land Cruiser FJ40s bring it all together: exceptional disc front brakes, a rugged four-speed iron case transmission, recirculating ball-and-nut manual steering or an integral power steering option (1979-on), plus the reliable 2F in-line six-cylinder engine.

es the redesigned (de-stroked and fuel injected) 3F-E engine. 1991 was a major shift to the newer body style, full-time four-wheel drive, and four-wheel coil spring-and-link suspension. This FJ80 chassis uses the 3F-E and an automatic transmission. Fuel economy rates poor for these models, yet each truck features a rugged chassis and powertrain. Replacement parts are expensive, while parts availability rates only fair through local Toyota dealerships. Consider one of these models only if the price is *very* right or if you find an exceptionally well kept model.

7) 1993–up Land Cruiser DJ: This is the premiere luxury SUV. The DOHC 4.5L engine ranks above all other engines in its size range, providing a broad power band, good fuel economy and traditional Toyota reliability. The appointments of this truck rank among the luxury class of automobiles. These refinements, added to a rugged frame, axles and powertrain, should keep the well-serviced 1993–up DJ model on the road or trail for decades. You'll recoil at the cost of parts, but this is the best built truck in its category.

Fig. 2-20. *Frame damage is a serious problem, sometimes impossible to repair correctly. If in doubt about the condition of a used truck prospect, take the vehicle to a reputable frame and alignment shop for closer inspection.*

CAUTION —
A braking system overhaul on an earlier Toyota truck model, especially the Land Cruisers, can be very expensive. New hydraulic cylinders, drums and rotors bear a very high price tag. Make certain that your used Toyota prospect has a sound brake system, or be prepared for a substantial repair bill or parts expenditure.

Inspecting Drivelines and Axles

Jack and support the truck safely off the ground, and depending upon the design of the front end, check the 2WD model steering knuckle ball-joints or the knuckle/kingpin bearings or ball-joints on a 4x4 model.

Grab each front wheel at six and twelve o'clock and rock the wheel in and out. Play shows inboard of the wheels at the ball-joints or kingpin bearings. Before checking for steering knuckle ball-joint play on 2WD models with coil springs or torsion bars that apply load at the lower control arms, you will need to unload the coil spring or torsion bar load by placing a floor jack safely be-

Fig. 2-21. *Front wheel driving axle trouble can mean expensive repairs. Check for wear at steering knuckle bearings, wheel bearings and axle joints. (See service chapter.) Water in an axle housing can ruin expensive gears and bearings.*

neath the lower control arm and carefully raising the arm until the upper and lower arms are free of the bump stops (bottoming stops). This will unload spring or torsion bar tension from the two ball-joints and allow an accurate check for play.

On a 4x4, note whether the knuckle seals, CV-joint boots (1986–up IFS type) or axle tubes leak grease or gear lube. With all trucks, check for wheel bearing looseness and any signs of damage at the wheel bearings, front and rear axles or universal joints. For 4x4 models, leaking seals and water are the primary destroyers of wheel assembly parts, steering knuckle pieces, gearbox assemblies and axle components.

Any indication of water in an axle housing, transfer case or transmission assembly should raise concern. These parts of the geartrain have the highest repair cost.

Check for excess play at the ring and pinion gears by rotating each driveshaft back and forth. Distinguish U-joint looseness from gear problems. While driveshafts cost plenty, axle assembly overhauls are even more expensive.

When you test drive the truck, listen for whining, clunks or growling. Axle noises telegraph during acceleration, coasting and deceleration. U-joint or driveshaft play sounds like a metallic clicking or snapping noise when you change speed or jerk the throttle open and shut, especially at a steady road speed in a higher gear.

Checking the Clutch and Transmission

The clutch can be a difficult assembly to access, especially on 4x4 models. Owners often sell their truck rather than replace a worn clutch. Official flat-rate labor to replace a clutch can run in excess of five hours on some 4x4s. Add clutch parts and flywheel machining, and the job can cost as much, or more, than a good used engine.

Check the clutch by moving the transmission shifter to high gear at 20 mph. With the clutch pedal depressed, bring the engine speed to 2000 rpm and hold the throttle steady, then quickly let the clutch pedal go. Listen carefully.

If the engine speed drops immediately to a near idle, the clutch cover (pressure plate) assembly and disc are likely okay. A gradual decrease in speed usually indicates that the clutch either slips or needs adjustment. Also make certain the clutch does not shudder during engagement.

Often the clutch needs minor adjustment, but when clutch mis-adjustment is bad enough to allow slippage, major damage is well underway. Slippage generates heat and friction, which translates as wear and fatigue.

Transmission woes telegraph unique noises. While test driving the truck, listen for crunch and gear clash. In each gear, pull gently on the shifter while accelerating lightly. If the synchronizers and shifter detents are okay, you'll feel resistance in the lever. When the transmission immediately slides out of gear, suspect a weak synchronizer assembly.

Synchronizer wear also shows up on a downgrade, as deceleration causes the transmission to jump out of gear. Bearing or gear tooth wear will also cause the transmission to slip out of gear.

Automatic Transmission

An automatic transmission may slip or chatter on take-off. Harsh shifts are another sign of trouble. A shuddering sensation, much like a bad manual clutch or weak motor mounts, also means real problems. Acrid and burnt fluid, leaks or erratic shifts each suggest that an automatic transmission is in bad shape.

For automatics, repairs generally involve a major overhaul. Again, tough access to some truck transmissions, especially on 4x4s, raises repair costs considerably. If you suspect automatic transmission troubles, get a transmission overhaul estimate before making an offer on the truck.

Engine

A common misconception about used vehicles is that the engine is most important. Especially on Land Cruisers and 4WD pickups, an axle, transmission or major brake system rebuild can exceed the cost of an engine overhaul. Installing a complete engine is often easier and quicker

Fig. 2-23. An engine oscilloscope and leakdown tester are quick means for determining engine condition. Find weakest cylinder with scope analysis, then run a leakdown test to determine source of compression loss. (See service chapter for troubleshooting details.)

than removing and overhauling the transmission or an axle assembly.

Before buying a used Toyota truck, you'll still want to make sure the engine is sound. An engine's basic requirements include: 1) normal and even compression, 2) accurate valve timing, 3) correct valve lift at each valve, and 4) normal bearing clearances and oil pressure. If you can borrow the truck or encourage the owner to comply, have the engine oscilloscope analyzed or, better yet, scoped while on a chassis dynamometer.

On a scope, a quick check of dynamic compression can compare cylinder spark loads and help determine approximate compression. Check the weakest cylinder with a compression gauge or, better yet, a cylinder leakdown tester. (You will find a complete explanation of engine troubleshooting in the service chapters.)

If you find signs of overheat, look further. Excess rust or chronic boil over can indicate aeration caused by cylinder gases leaking into the cooling system from a cracked block or head casting, a blown head gasket or a defective water pump. Run a cooling system pressure test, and also check for normal coolant circulation. (See the cooling system chapter for troubleshooting details.)

Engine Oiling System

Engine bearing and lubrication problems are tricky to diagnose. On trucks with an oil pressure gauge, it's far easier to observe oil pressure under load. Check the consistency of the engine oil to make sure that heavy additives do not disguise the true oil pressure.

Listen for knocks at cold start-up. Warm the engine completely, watching the oil pressure. Drive the truck under load, up hills and such, and constantly monitor the oil pressure. Pressure should stay within the normal operating range over the entire test drive.

An automotive stethoscope or even a long hollow tube makes an excellent diagnostic tool for finding internal engine noises. Get used to the amplified sound,

Fig. 2-22. Electronic fuel and spark management has revolutionized the automotive industry. By 1988, all Toyota truck and Land Cruiser engines feature EFI. This is the key to better fuel economy, improved performance and clean air.

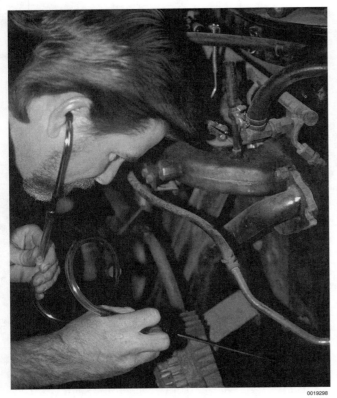

Fig. 2-24. *A stethoscope can pinpoint engine noises. If oil pressure is low or oil looks stiff, listen carefully for knocks and rattles. Thick oil or a heavy dose of additives can sometimes mask severe engine wear or damage.*

Fig. 2-25. *Body rust is the most expensive and difficult of repairs. Inspect sheet metal with a magnet if you suspect that plastic filler has concealed large areas of rust or collision damage. Routing out rust and a restoration paint job can cost more than any other repair on the truck.*

though, or the engine will resonate like a metallic thrashing machine. Learn to isolate various noises, such as the normal clicking of a mechanical fuel pump.

Isolate loose piston pin noise or a cracked piston by shorting or disconnecting each spark plug wire and seeing whether the knock is still there. Rod and main bearing noises will also decrease by eliminating spark.

If you lack the equipment or skill to do the job, consider paying a professional mechanic to check the engine, geartrain or cooling system. If you find that the truck is not in good shape, you can either negotiate a better price or consider your money well spent in that you did not buy a worn-out truck.

Body and Accessories

Sheet metal, body mounts and rubber body seals take abuse. The effects of sun, rain, snow and salted roads beat trucks mercilessly. Rubber rots, hinges twist and windows rattle in worn channels. The degree of wear can be a measurement of the overall abuse the truck has suffered.

Radio, heater and air conditioning systems are costly and time-consuming to repair. Don't accept suggestions that the air conditioner simply needs a recharge. Ask the seller to have the system charged before you agree to buy the truck.

Belts, hoses, wiring, the battery, filters and routinely serviced items speak for the truck's maintenance. Look thoroughly under the hood, and assess the kind of re-

placement parts that the owner has used. Ultra-cheap parts mean a neglected truck.

Other signs of trouble are a broken speedometer and vague records of mileage. This isn't really important on a 1958 Land Cruiser, but it sure should color your thinking about a late 1980s truck. No lube stickers, missing pedal pads, bald tires and a poor paint finish are ominous signs. You want a well kept truck, one that received regular maintenance.

Pollution Controls and Vehicle Registration

Since 1971, pollution controls on light truck engines have proliferated. The emission control era started in the early 1960s with a PCV valve and closed crankcase. Then the smog pump emerged, followed by the exhaust gas recirculation (EGR) valve and evaporative systems for fumes. The mid-1970s brought on catalytic converters and unleaded fuel, and more recently, electronic fuel injection and spark management have become part of the emission program. (See the chapter on emission controls.)

Smog laws, enforced by individual states and the federal government, mean that your used truck purchase must have a functional and complete OEM emission control system. If equipment is missing, non-operative or malfunctioning, you will have a problem registering the truck. Mandatory inspection programs have become common, with California serving as a model for a growing number of other states.

A truck engine stripped by the previous owner of its emission hardware, or an engine transplant unauthorized by your state's smog program, means real trouble. Replacing items like original equipment intake and exhaust manifolds, a smog pump, electrical and vacuum controls, the catalytic converter, an EGR valve and a host of other pieces can run beyond the cost of a good used engine.

A modified engine with non-approved aftermarket headers, intake manifold, carburetor or EFI, air cleaner, ignition and other components is a prime candidate for failing the visual portion of an emission control test.

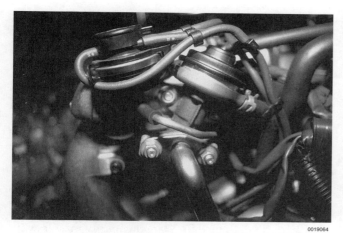

Fig. 2-26. In most states, emission control restoration is necessary for registration of a used vehicle. To pass visual inspection, all pollution control hardware must be in place, including the OEM air cleaner, correct carburetion (EFI on later engines) and approved manifolds. If you doubt the legality of a vehicle's emission system, consult an inspection facility before buying the truck.

Fig. 2-27. When continuous trailering is the plan, opt for a T100 one-ton rated chassis or heavy duty 4WD model like the Land Cruiser Station Wagon (shown). Here the frame, springs, brakes, axle stamina and powertrain will match your towing needs.

To meet legal demands, make the seller responsible for the restoration of the smog system. Otherwise, reduce the vehicle's price enough to cover the equipment necessary for compliance. If you have questions about necessary equipment or its cost, get an estimate from a licensed smog shop, an authorized Toyota dealership or your state motor vehicle pollution control agency before you buy the truck.

Engine and Transmission Choices

One of the worst fates in the aftermath of a new or used truck purchase is the discovery that the vehicle does not meet your towing or cargo load needs. This often occurs when you pick the wrong engine, transmission and axle ratio combination or when the pursuit of fuel economy overrides all other considerations.

Many of today's trailer towing gear ratios were considered economy ratios twenty years ago. These axles may work fine for breezing down the highway unloaded, but with a heavy camping trailer in tow, the strain is just too much. You snail crawl up grades, while serious engine or transmission damage develops.

> **CAUTION —**
> *A trailer of 2500-plus pounds, if towed far or often, requires a larger engine and heavy duty cooling for both the engine and automatic transmission.*

As a rule, a Toyota mini-truck or four-cylinder compact truck cannot hold up under constant trailering loads. In addition to frame or suspension shortcomings, the engine cooling capacity, braking ability, and smaller tires will compromise the truck over the long haul. For heavy hauling, economy must yield to a larger chassis. For

trailering, turn your attention toward a 3/4-ton or one-ton T100 truck with a heavy duty frame and a healthy V-6 powerplant.

Check GVWR and GCW ratings carefully, and know your cargo and trailer weights before selecting a chassis package or powertrain. Toyota offers gross load guidelines for determining the right truck and options.

Transmission Options

Automatic transmissions have become increasingly more popular. They sometimes meet special physical needs of drivers but most often satisfy those with no desire to work a manual transmission and clutch.

During the 1980s, three-speed automatics with an overdriving fourth gear came into the truck market. The demand for fuel savings and improved gear ratios have increased the popularity and availability of these late model electronically shifted overdrive automatics.

Fig. 2-28. Five-speed aluminum cased overdrive transmissions have evolved considerably. The latest Toyota units in higher GVWR trucks are rugged all-synchromesh manual gearboxes with stamina that can rival the earlier iron case four-speed transmissions found in Land Cruisers.

Fig. 2-29. *For those who prefer an automatic transmission, the Toyota aluminum cased three-speed and four-speed with overdrive units offer rugged engineering. From the late 1970s onward, various automatic transmission units find their way into pickup trucks, the 4Runner and later Land Cruisers. Later four-speed overdriving automatics with electronically controlled shifts are popular.*

NOTE —

Although automatics can offer good control in sand, a manual transmission and low (numerically high) axle ratios are usually the best approach for steep off-pavement downgrades and pulling massive loads.

For American makes of light trucks, the traditional manual transmissions of maximum durability were iron-cased, heavy duty truck four-speed units with a non-synchromesh compound low gear. The only Toyota trucks to offer such a gearbox were some rarer versions of the early Land Cruiser. (The 1975–up Land Cruiser all-synchromesh four-speed gearbox is also very tough. 2WD and 4WD pickup truck four-speeds have a good service record, too.)

Both domestic and import truck builders have struggled in their efforts to produce a reliable, heavy duty five-speed overdrive transmission. It took until the late 1980s (V-6 era) for Toyota's five-speed overdriving units to match the stamina of an FJ Land Cruiser's manual four-speed transmission.

NOTE —

To date, the most substantial five-speed overdrive transmission in the light truck industry is General Motors' NV4500-series iron-cased unit. (See the performance chapters for information on how to adapt this GM transmission to an earlier FJ-type Land Cruiser.)

Accessories for the Long Haul

Look for factory extras that will increase your truck's life expectancy. For example, air conditioning or a heavy duty trailering electrical system may include items like a heavy duty alternator, a larger battery and harnesses for trailer wiring.

Factory-installed air conditioning usually includes a heavy duty radiator and engine cooling upgrade. Again, the factory provides heavy duty options for merely the cost difference between standard pieces and these heavier components.

Some Toyota trucks have upgraded brakes. A heavy duty brake system is common to the motorhome chassis and is also available with a heavy towing package or on the heavy duty 3/4-ton or one-ton rated chassis. Heavy duty brakes might include a larger capacity master cylinder, a bigger vacuum booster and even larger brake shoes, disc pads, drums or rotors.

As a final note, factory equipment must meet high standards. When shopping for a new truck, always look for factory-installed tow hooks, tow hitch assemblies and wiring harnesses.

Fig. 2-30. *Toyota dealerships can access an extensive line of fast moving truck parts, while the aftermarket and NOS sources provide service parts or rarer restoration pieces. When older Land Cruiser parts are unavailable from the dealership, outlets like Specter Off-Road can often fill an order.*

Chapter 3

Orientation to Your Toyota Truck

MY APPRECIATION FOR LIGHT TRUCKS began in 1963, when our family moved from California to Carson Valley, Nevada. Here, surrounded by the majestic Sierras and a lesser range of desert juniper and pinion pine, sprawled fifty square miles of alfalfa fields and cattle grazing land. Crisscrossing the Valley, a host of paved and gravel roads linked the sagebrush covered foothills, broad pastures and willow-lined irrigation ditches.

During the Sixties, when harsh winters froze the ground hard and mean Sierra storms threatened livestock, pickup and stake bodied trucks lugged implements and hauled bales of cattle fodder. By early summer, when the first hay cuts came, the ranchers and their trucks labored even harder.

Fig. 3-2. *As a trailer puller, hauler or recreational vehicle, your properly equipped Toyota truck or Land Cruiser has plenty of personality. Make a place in your family photo album for this rig. Land Cruiser Station Wagon models provide the wheelbase and power for trailer pulling.*

Fig. 3-1. *Cattle country at Western Nevada's high valleys offers majestic views, bitter winters and hot, dry summers. Today, many ranchers turn to Toyota trucks and Land Cruisers for rugged reliability. Toyota 4x4 pickups and the classic FJ40 Land Cruisers serve many American farms and ranches.*

Freezing blizzards and scorching heat of August had a rancher up before dawn, often weary by mid-morning, and headed for Minden to get a friendly cup of coffee at the pharmacy next to the Post Office. Here their pickups lined up, cattle racks looped with twine ropes, the tube-type traction tires caked with mud. Two- and four-wheel drives, these iron workhorses helped raise productivity, ferried bulky goods and battled the seasonal challenges of high altitude cattle country.

Land Cruiser FJ25s and FJ40s were somewhat rare but already a topic of discussion among the local four-wheel drive enthusiasts. Hardcore wheelers suggested that the FJ40 rivalled a CJ-5 Jeep model, a remark that sparked a good deal of controversy in 1963—and still does today.

Carson Valley was surely truck country, the kind of terrain and inclement weather that sharpens wits and compels good driving skills. I soon knew trucks well and serviced plenty of them in my after school and summer service station jobs at Bud Berrum's Chevron Station in Minden.

As a light and medium duty truck fleet mechanic a few years later, I discovered that the muscle car mania of the 1960s had served as a great ground school for my craft. The intensity of interest in cars during that era heightened my appreciation for quality technology and performance tuning.

Ultimately, my experience at high performance automotive work served well in the preventive care and overhaul of trucks, and trucks have remained a part of my life since early adulthood. Around trucks, I also identify with my rural Nevada roots.

Toyota On The Scene

My appreciation for the FJ40 4WD began with a Rubicon trip in the summer of 1967. By 1969, when I worked as a fleet truck mechanic, the Land Cruiser had established a reasonable following of hardcore four-wheelers.

At the time, my flock of fleet vehicles included Chevrolet, GMC, Ford and I-H trucks. Economy versions of these models had utilitarian six-cylinder engine designs that dated from the pre-WWII period to the early 1950s— inline engines much like the Land Cruiser F powerplant.

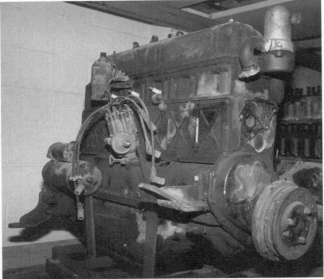

Fig. 3-3. *235 Chevy truck six (top), built from 1954–62, was a popular and rugged engine. The Land Cruiser F, 2F (bottom) and 3F-E engines share many design features with this GM powerplant. A familiar engine design made the FJ40 far easier for North American mechanics to accept.*

As a training ground, no mechanic had a better outlet than these models, as they were fundamental, simple to work on and responded readily to preventive service procedures.

In the mid-1980s, I bought my first FJ40 Land Cruiser, a 1971 model in stone stock original condition. The truck shared many design features with the mid-1950s to early-1960s Chevrolet trucks that had once been my charge as a fleet mechanic. I felt right at home with the Land Cruiser's engine, clutch, transmission, transfer case and axles.

New Powertrain Paradigm

Already familiar with Toyota's reputation for quality, I also found the new model RN11 Hi-Lux pickup of some interest. The Hi-Lux characterized an unfamiliar paradigm, and my recollection of the Hi-Lux buyer was someone interested in exceptional economy in a rugged—

albeit tiny—truck. By design, this was essentially what the Hi-Lux pickup provided.

The 1969 Hi-Lux mini-truck's 8RC engine, unlike the Land Cruiser F six, was an overhead camshaft design. For traditional American truck mechanics, and most American automotive enthusiasts, this was an exotic engine, more akin to Offenhauser's Indy powerplants or a Honda motorcycle than any U.S. built truck engine.

A period of adjustment and acceptance might well have lingered for many years, but the 1973 Oil Embargo/Crisis quickly popularized the growing class of mini-trucks. In the process, engines like Toyota's overhead camshaft 8RC, 18RC and later four-cylinder OHC powerplants became a norm for import economy trucks.

Value Like My Land Cruisers

Over the past thirty years, as a recreationalist, truck fleet mechanic, heavy equipment operator and automotive journalist, I've driven every American make of 2WD and 4WD truck, plus import trucks and SUVs built by Toyota, Land Rover, Mitsubishi, Isuzu, Nissan and Mazda. Notably, among all of the 4WD models, my two pre-owned Land Cruiser FJ40s rank as the top performers for the roughest backcountry.

My personal success with pre-owned Toyotas stems from several factors. Surely, a well built Toyota truck will deliver great service when driven wisely and maintained in accord with factory proscribed service guidelines. Here, each of my Land Cruisers benefitted from my training as a truck fleet mechanic, where constant adherence to OEM standards complements a fastidious preventive maintenance program.

Keeping your Toyota truck or Land Cruiser alive and operating well depends upon that same kind of regular service. The service chapters of this book share many of the techniques that I acquired while caring for a wide range of light and medium duty trucks.

Equally important, the ways in which you use and operate your Toyota truck will determine the degree and

Fig. 3-4. *My 1976 Land Cruiser was a pristine pre-owned truck with less than 100,000 miles on the odometer when I bought it. Two previous owners had only altered the tire size, switching to a 33x12.50x15-inch tire mounted on 10-inch rims. This required cutting out the wheel wells and installing aftermarket fender flares.*

Fig. 3-5. *Use of OEM replacement parts is one assurance that your Toyota truck will deliver maximum performance over a long service life.*

Fig. 3-6. *For any truck, long term popularity can only result from a rugged service record and consistent value. Toyota mini-, compact and intermediate size trucks and Land Cruisers offer this and more. Superior chassis and powertrain durability have been basic to Toyota design.*

quality of service possible. I believe that true "lemons" are virtually non-existent among Toyota trucks and Land Cruiser models, although any production vehicle can require warranty repairs—or even a recall for a potential safety hazard or mechanical shortcoming.

Toyota trucks, engineered for utility and even commercial service, offer a high level of performance and durability. This fact has made these trucks popular since 1957, when the first Land Cruiser FJs came into the U.S. market. Economies tighten, new vehicle prices inflate and repair costs escalate, but the buyer of a Toyota truck can take solace or, better yet, pride and satisfaction in the vehicle's inherent value.

A Toyota Truck and Your Lifestyle

Beyond their notable work skills, two- and four-wheel drive Toyota trucks complement an active lifestyle. Individually suited for family recreation, foul weather security and off-pavement chores, Toyota pickup, 4Runner and Land Cruiser models have many talents. Operated within their broad design limits, the powertrain and chassis can deliver many years of dependable service.

In our family, the children have grown up with various trucks and sport utility vehicles. 4x4s have been the family's access to hunting, fishing, hiking, firewood and some of North America's most rugged and picturesque back country. As a Search-and-Rescue volunteer, I have also made my 4x4 vehicles provide service for the community.

Trucks hold a special place in our household. As a source of recreation and cornerstone for wholesome family fun and community involvement, four-wheel-drive trucks have served us particularly well. A Toyota truck or Land Cruiser, whether new or a good used model, can provide you and your family with a rich outdoor life year round.

1. DRIVING TECHNIQUES

Although technology has changed both the appearance and comfort level of light trucks, operating techniques remain much the same. Especially for 4x4 models, irregular road surfaces pose a regular challenge. While knowing your truck's equipment and controls proves useful, understanding its handling characteristics is of even greater importance.

Lighter pickup trucks, designed to carry a cargo, generally suffer from poor weight distribution. Running empty, the back end of your pickup truck may feel loose and unpredictable on icy, wet or muddy roads. Fortunately for the Land Cruiser and 4Runner, a heftier curb weight and better weight distribution offset these liabilities to a degree.

If your truck handles strangely, first rule out any chassis-mechanical or tire related problems. (See the service chapters of the book for details.) You may find the root of your concern by running the vehicle over a set of truck scales to determine the weight on each axle. Figure the weight distribution.

Since light weight at the back of a truck can lead to trouble, many owners install a shell (cap or canopy) or permanently store useful items in the bed. A tool box is

Fig. 3-7.   A higher center-of-gravity and stiff spring rates characterize most light trucks. With the bed empty, weight bias shifts toward the front, leaving a lightened rear end susceptible to spinout on icy, off-camber highways. Under such road conditions, the rear axle can slip sideways and start the spin. Without a cargo, a "positive traction" rear differential can exaggerate these side-slip tendencies.

Fig. 3-8.   Extra weight in the bed provides better winter traction. Light trucks also need weight at the rear axle for safe braking. When the bed is empty, hard application of the brakes can start a spinout. Late model Toyota truck models have anti-lock rear brakes, which dramatically reduce the risk of spinout and dangerous loss of directional stability when braking hard with a light load.

Fig. 3-9.   If you decide that a cabover camper is a necessity, use caution when driving with a full load. Allow adequate stopping distances, take corners at reasonable speeds and observe road conditions. Avoid crisis situations that demand fast moves—such maneuvers could end in a roll over. (See suspension and accessories chapters for equipment tips that aid when trailering or hauling a heavy cargo or camper.)

another method for adding ballast to better distribute weight. During winter months, some pickup owners carry an extra load in the bed, items like snow chains or even sacks of aggregate rock laid above or rearward of the axle. A heavier step-type rear bumper also helps. Beyond this, you need to familiarize yourself with the handling characteristics of the truck.

Not A Turbocharged Supra

Driving a Toyota truck (especially the 4Runner and Land Cruiser) can be fun. However, truck and car handling differs dramatically in center-of-gravity, weight distribution and suspension responsiveness; your truck cannot respond or handle like a well tuned car suspension.

The need to carry a substantial cargo over rough roads, which requires a comparatively long wheelbase, means that truck bodies ride higher than a car. With the body mounted above a driveable chassis (separate ladder frame), the cab and bed ride considerably taller than a car. For ground clearance and wheel travel, the light truck's ladder frame rides higher than a car's frame or unibody.

Larger diameter tires, a higher frame and body height, and a powertrain that rides further above the ground mean that a Toyota truck or Land Cruiser, or any other common truck design, has a higher center-of-gravity. In simple terms, this translates as more vulnerability to roll over. Notably, the wider wheel track widths of later Toyota trucks help offset this risk to a degree.

Coupled with the higher center-of-gravity is a spring package designed for a cargo hauler. This means that the truck's springs are stiffer than a car's suspension, especially when the truck has no cargo. As a consequence, trucks respond much differently on corners. Simply put,

the cornering ability, resistance to roll over, likelihood of spinout, ability to drift, lateral force reaction or any other automotive handling yardstick will find that trucks handle differently, generally less precisely, than well engineered cars.

Moreover, your truck will handle differently when loaded or unloaded. Be aware of these factors when orienting yourself to a light truck. When you can predict the handling of your truck under a wide variety of driving circumstances, loads and tire types, you will find comfort in the fact that a late model Toyota truck or Land Cruiser can be as stable as any other light truck in its class.

Two- Versus Four-wheel Drive

Two- and four-wheel drive trucks also handle differently. 4x4 Toyota trucks ride higher than comparable 2WD models, with a higher center-of-gravity and even more awkward weight distribution. The front wheel drive system places additional weight forward of the truck's midline, while the need for ground clearance demands a taller ride height.

Toyota's pre-1986 4x4 pickups and 4Runners, and all leaf-sprung FJ Land Cruisers, have relatively high ride heights. These trucks, naturally, are more susceptible to handling quirks and roll over. 4x4 light trucks of that era draw greater attention to the high center-of-gravity issue. (See chapters on suspension modifications and tire/wheel changes.).

Fig. 3-10. *1979–85 4x4 pickups and 4Runners and all leaf-sprung Land Cruisers represent the traditional 4WD truck design. Note tall frame height and low hanging transfer case. From 1986-onward, Toyota offers IFS technology on 4WD pickups and the 4Runner. Later FJ80 and DJ Land Cruisers have four-wheel coil spring suspension. These later models have a lower center of gravity and less risk of roll over.*

Another common concern for light truck users is a tall cabover-type camper on a pickup truck. These campers raise the roll center of the vehicle substantially. Fortunately, few Toyota trucks have carried these types of campers. However, the Toyota mini-motorhome offers a similarly high roll center.

The typical chassis package for a camper, heavy cargo or trailering use will offer increased spring rates, added axle capacity and stabilizer bars for handling the extra load. Cabover campers radically alter the truck's roll center and the relationship of its center-of-gravity. Added safety equipment is a must if you plan to carry a tall camper—or even a weighty luggage rack on a 4Runner or Land Cruiser.

Whether your Toyota truck has two- or four-wheel drive, proper driving techniques for four-wheeling can help any truck operator. For this reason, I have devoted the balance of the current chapter to 4x4 and off-pavement driving concerns. Owners of two-wheel drive trucks will find much of this information both relevant and useful.

4x4 and Off-pavement Driving

The main difference between a four-wheel drive truck and a rear drive two-wheel drive truck or automobile is the 4x4's live front axle and transfer case. In addition to the customary brake, accelerator and clutch controls, a 4x4 truck's transmission and transfer case have separate shift levers.

All Toyota truck shifters for four- and five-speed manual transmissions rise through the floorboard. Some 1963 and all 1964–72 Land Cruiser three-speed transmissions use a column shift control. (Some owners retrofit a 1973–74 OEM style floor-shift control mechanism to these transmissions.)

The 4x4 transfer case also requires control levers. On part-time 4x4 models, the transfer case levers provide modes for high range, low range, neutral and two- or four-wheel drive.

Fig. 3-11. *1958–71 Land Cruiser FJs use a unique vacuum operated transfer case shift mechanism to operate the front axle engagement and disengagement. These models have manual linkage for the shifting of the transfer case from high to neutral and low range. The vacuum front axle engagement system is cable actuated.*

Fig. 3-12. *When 4WD is engaged in high or low range, a dash indicator lamp signals front axle engagement. Earlier Land Cruiser's vacuum shift mechanism and indicator lamp were years ahead of their time. A vacuum engagement system works best when the throttle is momentarily released during the shift. This reduces torque load on the axle and transfer case gears, an advantage with this kind of shift mechanism.*

The vacuum 4WD shift mechanisms of earlier Land Cruisers have either mechanical or cable operated linkage at the dashboard. Beginning with 1972 models, Land Cruisers switched to a more conventional single lever for front axle engagement and transfer case gear changes. This manual lever mounts nearby the transmission's floor shifter. The single lever type transfer case shifter is also common to all 4WD Toyota pickups and 4Runners.

The low range mode in four-wheel drive adds versatility and exceptional pulling power. Single stick transfer case control modes include 2WD high, 4WD high, neutral and 4WD low ranges. Neutral mode on pre-1981 units can operate a Power Take Off (PTO) component of the transfer case.

Fig. 3-13. *For safety sake and powertrain survival, consult your Toyota truck owner's handbook or the 4WD instruction decal or plate located in the cab for directions on operating the four-wheel drive system. This is a complex gear mechanism with very expensive components. Toyota knows what your truck's geartrain will tolerate.*

Fig. 3-14. *Land Cruisers built before 1981 offered a power take-off (PTO) drive at the transfer case. This was once a popular item for powering winches, hoisting equipment and implements. The decline in demand for mechanically driven winches influenced Toyota's decision to remove the PTO gear from U.S. models. Many earlier FJ models have mechanical winches with a PTO drive.*

Operating A 4x4 Toyota Truck

Two-wheel drive high range is much like driving a comparable two-wheel drive Toyota truck. Power flows only to the rear axle, and the transfer case operates at a 1:1 ratio. The rear driveshaft spins at the same speed as the transmission output shaft.

In 4WD high range or high-lock (late Land Cruisers with center differential lock system), both the front and rear driveshafts spin at the same speed as the transmission output shaft. High range 2WD is useful for hard surface highways and most dry and civilized driving conditions. In high range, the front or rear drive axle gear ratio, multiplied by the first gear or compound-low gear ratio, will determine the overall reduction ratio.

When in four-wheel drive high or low range, your truck offers substantially better traction, with the front axle pulling while the rear axle pushes the truck. 4x4 powertrains, however, with the exception of full-time 4x4 systems without the center differential lock engaged, cannot tolerate four-wheel drive use on hard surfaced roads. On these surfaces, front axle pull and rear axle push will not take place in full synchronization, and the result is gear bind. This condition, characterized by a frozen transfer case lever or free-wheeling hubs, can damage the powertrain.

NOTE —
To appreciate the lowest gear ratio available with a two-speed transfer case, multiply the transfer case low range ratio by the lowest gear (first or compound low) ratio in the transmission. Now multiply this number by the front or rear axle ratio. This is the overall reduction ratio in low range.

For 4WD models with a part-time 4x4 system, engaging the front axle on a hard surfaced road will adversely affect steering. (For 1991–up Land Cruisers with the lockable center differential, engaging the lock mode on a hard surfaced road will have the same effect.) As the axle shafts transmit torque, the steering assemblies will jack back and forth when the front wheels strive for traction.

On a loose surface, these symptoms are rarely noticeable. For Toyota 4WD trucks without the 1991–up Land Cruiser's full-time 4WD transfer case, you will find that dirt, snow, mud or ice can provide the necessary margin of slip for engaging the four-wheel drive system.

One exception for the use of 4WD mode on a hard surface is the short, steep pavement pull of a boat ramp. Here, I use 4x4 mode as a means for moving the trailer. Since the pull is straight, risk of gear bind is minimal. At the top of the ramp, on flat ground, you can relieve bind by rocking the truck gently forward and back as you shift the transmission from reverse to drive (forward gear) and then neutral. With the transmission in neutral (manual) or Park (automatic), move the transfer case shifter to 2WD mode, then turn hubs to FREE.

I avoid placing an automatic transmission in neutral after rocking the truck, as the transmission output shaft

Fig. 3-15. *A center differential system within the transfer case of 1991 and newer Land Cruisers provides full-time 4x4. When the center differential is not in lock mode, the high and low transfer case ranges can provide four-wheel drive on all road surfaces without the risk of gear bind. Later DJ 'Cruiser offers optional axle lock-up system (shown) for full traction at each axle.*

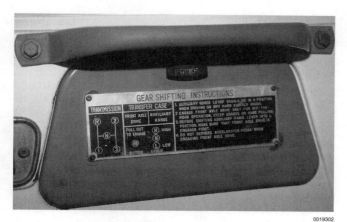

Fig. 3-16. *All Toyota 4WD trucks with part-time 4x4 have a two-wheel drive mode for running on hard surfaces. Preserving your powertrain means using four-wheel drive only when the road surface will allow some degree of slip. This limits use of 4WD low range to ice, snow, mud and off-pavement surfaces.*

Fig. 3-17. *Low range serves in rocky or dangerously steep terrain. Low range 4WD provides compression braking and far more control of the truck. Here's a typical place for 4WD low range and use of the lower transmission gears.*

Fig. 3-18. *Traditional part-time 4x4 transfer case shift positions include 2-High, 4-High, Neutral, 4-Low. Shift patterns vary, so become familiar with these modes and their locations. For safety sake, know how to shift into any position without looking at the floorboard or knob(s).*

will begin to spin when you move the transfer case shifter through its neutral range. Spinning gears can cause severe gear clash as you continue to advance the transfer case shifter into a drive range.

If your truck has an automatic transmission and you have used 4WD low range on a boat ramp, first rock the truck gently, then stop completely and place the transmission shifter in PARK mode. With the brake set firmly, you can now move the transfer case shifter from 4WD Low to 2WD High range without risk of gear clash.

Free-wheeling Front Hubs

Most 4x4 trucks spend the majority of their service life on the highway or well graded gravel roads. The front axle assembly on a part-time 4x4 system seldom sees use. Here, free-wheeling hubs can reduce wear at the front axle shafts, U-joints and the differential assembly.

The first Land Cruiser 4WDs came without free-wheeling hubs, and unless the dealer or an owner installed aftermarket hubs, the front axle shafts, differential and front driveshaft spun continuously. This creates fuel robbing drag for the life of the truck.

Now a common OEM component on 4x4s, free-wheeling hubs reduce parts wear and increase fuel economy. If your truck has manual free-wheeling hubs, use the FREE mode whenever the truck operates in two-wheel drive for a sustained period.

Fig. 3-19. During foul weather, leaving hubs in LOCK mode with the transfer case in 2WD will permit easy engagement of 4WD high range as road conditions worsen. On occasion, engaging the free-wheeling hubs for a few miles is actually valuable. This will lubricate parts, keep seals from becoming brittle and reduce the risk of condensation buildup in the axle housing.

In the early 1980s, many truck models introduced the use of automatic locking hubs that engage when you shift to 4WD mode, either high or low range. As the torque flows to each front wheel, the hub assembly has an internal clutch mechanism that automatically locks the hub.

In this mode, the hub functions much like a conventional (manual) hub in LOCK position. An exception is those automatic hub designs that fail to provide compression braking and simply free wheel on downgrades.

Although automatic locking hubs eliminate the need for manual operation, they do require backing up the truck to disengage the lock mechanisms. When road conditions once again permit use of 2WD mode, you must stop the truck, make sure the transfer case is in 2WD mode, then safely back the truck up (usually fifteen feet) to disengage the automatic hubs.

Shifting a Part-time 4WD Transfer Case

During intermittent icy highway conditions, you can leave your manual or automatic locking hubs in lock mode. During stretches of hard-surfaced road, simply shift out of front axle drive mode (4WD) with the transfer case lever. When the mountain pass or snow zone is past, stop the truck, make certain the transfer case is in 2WD mode, and either manually unlock your front hubs or, if equipped with automatic locking hubs, safely back your truck up about fifteen feet to free the hubs.

Later model transfer cases have shift-on-the-fly. These gear units allow you to move from 2WD high to 4WD high without effort. *Under no circumstance, however, can you shift any transfer case to low range without stopping the vehicle.* Although some transfer cases will tolerate engagement of low range gears at a very low vehicle speed, the best way to engage low range is at a complete stop.

For engaging the front axle drive at any speed, you will find that unloading torque from the gears helps ease the shift. If your truck has a manual transmission, you can leave the transmission in gear and momentarily depress the clutch pedal. Move the transfer case lever from 2WD high to 4WD high as if you were shifting gears in the transmission. For automatic transmission models, leave the transmission in drive range, but release the throttle as you move the transfer case lever gently from 2WD to 4WD high range.

Consult your Toyota owner's handbook or the instructional decals before engaging low range 4WD. An automatic transmission will require placing the transmission in neutral or park range before you move the transfer case lever to 4WD Low Range. Otherwise, the transmission will spin the gears at speed as the transfer case shift lever passes through its Neutral mode. Severely abusive gear clash will result if you attempt to engage the low range gears while the transfer case input shaft spins.

When To Use Four-wheel Drive

Faced with the perils of sleet and dropping temperatures, owners appreciate their 4x4 trucks. When the highway surface is wet, temperatures continue to drop, and it's still a few degrees above treacherous "black ice," the time is right to lock your manual hubs.

Early readiness is your best hedge against trouble. Lock your hubs before visibility decreases and traffic begins to stagger. Leaving the pavement when the visibility worsens could cause a wreck. The driver of the next vehicle might see your brake lamps, misinterpret your motive for leaving the road and over react by making a dangerous move.

If the weather clearly calls for ice and snow, lock your manual hubs before you leave home. You can drive for many miles with the hubs locked and the transfer case in 2WD high range without damaging the front axle system.

When I was a heavy equipment operator, I once drove my 4WD pickup from Carson City, Nevada to Jackson, California over Carson Pass in a blizzard. Reports called for a severe late winter storm, which turned into a blizzard. I engaged the truck's manual hubs at the eastern base of the Sierras and left them in LOCK until the west side, some ninety miles later. Snow was four-inches deep on the pavement at Hope Valley and over twelve inches deep across the road at the summit.

Plows were unable to keep up with the storm's pattern, and drifts continued to build. There was no parking turnout in sight. Obviously, this was one scenario where getting out of the truck to lock the hubs could have proven fatal.

With hubs locked, you can engage 4WD high range while moving. As highway conditions worsen, or if a stretch of ice lies ahead, engage 4WD and stay in this mode until you pass the hazard. At that point, simply shift the transfer case lever back to 2WD high mode. You'll likely repeat this procedure several times during long stretches of intermittent ice, snow and dry pavement.

If a dry, straight section of pavement lasts for a very short spell (1/8th mile or less), I leave the transfer case in 4WD mode, stay very light on the throttle to reduce torque application and work the steering carefully. When the road is straight, geartrain stress and risk of binding are minimal. I believe that under these conditions, shifting the transfer case in and out of 4WD places far more strain on components and creates unnecessary demands on the driver.

2. OFF PAVEMENT FOUR-WHEEL DRIVE

When the pavement ends and the dirt begins, consider your truck's traction needs. Since a softer roadway allows some slip and eliminates the risk of gear bind, it's wise to engage your hubs, whether you're using 4WD mode or not. Spinning the front axle system places a light load on the powertrain, while the benefit of locking the hubs is that four-wheel drive becomes available at the flip of the transfer case lever.

Commonly, before entering a gravel trail, four-wheelers will lock the hubs and drop tire pressures for increased traction and to lessen chassis bounce on irregular road surfaces. Lowered tire pressures can also reduce risk of tread and sidewall damage from rocks.

Unfortunately, some four-wheelers get carried away with airing down tires. Each tire design and vehicle load has a minimum safe inflation pressure. Lower pressures also increase the risk of unseating the bead. Unseating a bead or driving with severe sidewall flex can ruin your expensive tires or cause tire failure and loss of control.

My rough guideline for airing down is that a tire with a 32–35 psi maximum load pressure will tolerate no lower than 22–24 psi pressure, and this for only short distances at slow speeds. As pressure drops, so does a tire's load capacity. You trade greater traction for higher heat buildup and more risk of tire fatigue and failure. (See tire details in other chapters.).Concentrate on good driving habits and minimize your wheelspin. Wheelspin loses traction, places tires at risk and can cause environmental damage. Good driving techniques will take your truck much further than excessively low tire pressures.

Fig. 3-20. *Airing down is common vernacular for off-pavement trail runners. While ride and traction improve, airing down reduces load carrying capacity. Dropping pressures to run in sand does make sense, however, always air back up to normal when you've passed the hazards. Re-check pressures when tires are cold. (See chapter on tires.)*

WARNING —
A spinning tire is dangerous. How dangerous? General Tire suggests, "AVOID excessive tire spinning when your vehicle is stuck in snow, mud or sand. Never exceed 35 mph indicated on the speedometer. The centrifugal forces generated by a free spinning tire/wheel assembly may cause a sudden tire explosion resulting in vehicle damage and/or serious personal injury. Use a gentle backward and forward rocking motion to free your vehicle for continued driving. Never stand near or behind a tire spinning at high speed while attempting to push a vehicle that is stuck."

The number one cause of environmental damage, and the clearest sign of an inexperienced four-wheeler, is unnecessary tire spin. Your best traction is a tire tread surface that makes full contact with the road. You can minimize wheelspin by reducing throttle pressure or shifting to a higher gear in the transmission. This will apply less torque to the wheels and lessen the likelihood of tire spin.

The Terrain

Terrain dictates when to use four-wheel drive. Experience teaches that it's always better to engage 4WD before entering a hazard than once you commit your truck.

Negotiating mud and snow requires steady pulling traction, and stopping in the middle of a muddy trail courts disaster. Trying to regain traction can result in spinning tires and damage to a fragile environment. Wherever possible, keep moving while minimizing tire spin and chassis bounce.

CHAPTER 3

The Steepest Hills

If the trail gets rocky or steep and your truck begins bouncing, it's time for low range. Low range will reduce throttle effort and drastically lower the vehicle's speed. The gear reduction in low range will allow your vehicle to idle through rocky or rough stretches while tires remain in contact with the trail surface.

In 4WD high range, your truck might idle at 3–5 mph in first gear. Placing the transfer case in low range would drop speed to nearly one mile per hour. This allows far more control of the truck and reduces risk of damage. Low range stopping and starting is also simpler, especially on inclines. Use of lighter throttle pressure and less braking action reduce risk of wheelspin or dangerous skidding.

Fig. 3-21. Shift to 4WD and low range before driving up steep hills. At slow speeds, low range will provide more control and be able to reduce speed to a crawl pace on descents. Low range will drastically reduce use of brakes.

When top speed on a rough trail is 10–20 miles per hour, I place the transfer case in low range 4WD and leave it there. This allows use of all forward transmission gears to keep up with the crowd and also provides crawl speeds and excellent compression braking for moving slowly through rocky obstacles. This is the key to careful navigation and a long service life for your truck.

WARNING —
Slow down before downshifting between transmission gears in low range. The low range gear reduction will exaggerate the speed drop between gears, and the result is like slamming on the brakes.

Low range is a valuable braking mechanism. When facing a very steep decline, select the transmission gear that will control your truck's speed. Always minimize the use of wheel brakes on slick or poor traction surfaces.

If a wheel(s) locks up with application of the brakes (which they do readily on ice or sand covered granite boulders), skidding will result. Approach steep descents in sand like you would ice: if you need to slow down, apply the brakes lightly, with a gentle pumping action. Do not lock up the wheels.

The best traction is a tire that continues to rotate. At the slowest imaginable speeds, in low range first gear, your 4x4 truck's tires can still provide traction over the entire area of the tread surface. If possible, avoid skidding. Keep your tires rotating under engine compression braking to provide the highest percentage of traction.

The reduction ratio of low range also provides exceptional pulling power. Assuming that your truck can get traction, 4WD low range will permit even the most modestly powered four-cylinder 4WD pickup, which by itself weighs over 3,500 pounds in street form, to move a stalled 8,000 pound flatbed truck. Pulls like freeing a vehicle from a ditch can easily be performed if your 4x4 can get traction.

If you need to move a heavy vehicle for more than a few feet, avoid using 4WD lock mode on a hard surfaced road. Never hook the chain or strap to a trailer ball, driveshaft, spring hanger, steering components or an axle housing that has brake pipes or hoses running along its surface.

There are many situations where four-wheeling is unsafe or will cause damage to the environment. When your 4x4 truck totters on the edge of disaster, winching may be far more practical than driving. A properly angled winch cable can function as both the motive force and an anchor for your delicately balanced truck. If losing traction means poor vehicle control, use a winch. (See winching instructions in the accessories chapter.)

Uphill And Downhill

Negotiating steep hills causes more adrenaline flow than any other four-wheel drive maneuver. Angles, especially downslopes, appear distorted and ominous. This is just as well, as the real threat of losing control on a descent deserves all of your attention. When going uphill in four-wheel drive, the front wheels claw for traction and tend to pull your truck into line. Downward, these same wheels want to skid, slip sideways and search awkwardly for traction.

On ascents, minimize wheelspin. When descending, use the correct gear to minimize skidding and the need to apply your truck's brakes. Moderation has never had a better mentor than four-wheeling.

In rough and angled terrain, excess movement courts disaster. Oversteering and understeering can cross the ve-

0019082

Fig. 3-22. *When approaching an uphill section or downslope, line the truck up squarely and avoid driving sideways across the hill. Driving sideways on a slope is a roll over about to happen. Stay straight and move steadily.*

hicle up at just the wrong moment. On both ascents and descents, if your truck loses directional stability, the risk of roll over increases.

WARNING ——
• *Never drive sideways across a hill. If side tilt overcomes your truck's roll center and center-of-gravity, the vehicle is likely to turn over.*

• *If your 4x4 turns completely sideways on a steep sideslope, prepare to roll over. Always wear a seat-belt/harness and install a full roll cage if you intend to climb risky slopes. If you must get out of the vehicle, do so only on the uphill side.*

Hair-raising Hill Climb Techniques

During the Sixties, four-wheeling competitive events became popular. Organized hill climbs attracted large crowds, and the winning formula was traction, torque and solid driving skill. Typically, a 4x4 needed enough muscle to claw its way up a rocky shale slope. Exotic traction tires and axle locking devices increased the chances of a win. Here, many of us learned the finer points of high-horsepower traction.

Most hill climb courses were remarkably steep. In some of my photos from that era, course judges stand with one leg a foot and a half higher than the other, leaning into the hillside to stay upright. Walking these hills was nearly impossible. Most slopes were simply crude cuts made by a D-8 Caterpillar tractor at its maximum slope angle. Some courses were even more primitive.

Modified short wheelbase Land Cruisers, Jeeps, Scouts and early Broncos, most with modified engines or V-8 transplants, screamed at redline as they charged the

hill. The winner was, simply, the truck in each class (four-cylinder, six-cylinder or V-8) that reached the highest point on the hill.

Axles, clawing through paddle tires and spinning mercilessly, grabbed what meager traction the rocky hillside could furnish. Judges leaped out of the path of airborne 4x4s that left the ground under full power, landing forty feet off the course with their nose ends still aimed uphill. Often, with the engine throttled wide open as the tires bit, the frame jerked into line, gaining the truck an even greater height on the hill.

One of the most impressive competitors in the entire Western Nevada and Lake Tahoe Basin region was an early Land Cruiser FJ40 with a high performance 327 Chevrolet V-8 transplant. That faded green, topless Cruiser easily out-climbed, out-pulled and out-maneuvered every class of vehicle around. I learned, early on, that Toyota had the formula for maximum traction and remarkably steep gradient assaults.

The risk of getting sideways was extreme. Of all the driving techniques I gleaned from these hill climbs, the most significant was how to maintain control of a 4x4 that loses traction while climbing a steep slope. The trick is a rapid shift to reverse gear before backing down, then descending under compression braking while avoiding or minimizing the use of hydraulic wheel brakes.

This is a critical maneuver that demands quick hands and feet. As soon as the truck reaches its furthest point on the hill and traction becomes futile, you must depress the clutch pedal quickly, simultaneously shift the transmission to reverse and release the clutch pedal before the truck starts to roll backward.

Timing is all important. If you miss reverse and the transmission is in neutral, you will roll backward out of control. (The non-synchromesh reverse gear in a manual transmission will not permit a shift to reverse with the truck moving.) Stuck in neutral, the only option is to use the brakes. Applied on a steep and loose slope, the brakes want to lock the wheels, which usually throws the truck into a skid. This can swing the vehicle sideways and cause a roll over.

The important steps are: 1) shift your manual transmission to reverse just as the truck peaks its forward momentum, 2) release the clutch pedal immediately and steer straight backward with the engine idling, and 3) rely on engine compression braking with minimal, if any, application of the wheel brakes. These steps must take place in rapid succession, and if your coordination and the engine tune is right, the truck's engine should keep the tires creeping in reverse.

WARNING ——
Competitive 4x4 hill climbing is a hazardous sport. Damage to your vehicle and personal injury are real possibilities. Like other forms of competition, rules and safety regulations apply. Never attempt these competitive maneuvers without the benefit of a full roll cage, approved safety equipment, emergency medical personnel, close supervision and full acceptance of the risks involved.

CHAPTER 3

Pitfalls Of An Automatic Transmission

4x4 hill climbs place trucks with automatic transmissions at a disadvantage. Although a torque converter helps multiply torque for successful hill and sand assaults, backing down slopes with an automatic in reverse can prove hazardous. With the engine idling or stalled, the torque converter slips, acting much like neutral. This encourages use of the brakes as vehicle speed increases, and that's when trouble begins. Application of the brakes can lock the wheels, and when the tires skid, the truck may turn sideways and roll over.

An automatic transmission has many advantages, including good throttle control and torque application in sand, predictable pulling in mud and tremendous torque for going up reasonable hills that don't require backing down. If, however, your plans include negotiating serious downslopes under compression or backing down steep hills in reverse, consider the superior control of a manual transmission and clutch.

Low Environmental Impact

The popularity of four-wheeling has an effect on the environment. TREAD LIGHTLY, Inc. and other organizations encourage low impact four-wheeling and respectful use of public lands. Although the concept is new to some recreationalists, many of us have been treading lightly for decades.

In the summer of 1964, I attended Nevada Range Camp, a 4-H/USDA Extension Service project for high school students. Fifteen miles south of U.S. Highway 50 near Austin, Nevada, our base was the Reese River Valley at Big Creek. We studied erosion and other soil conservation matters, witnessed the planting of wild wheat over a vast semi-arid mountain range and learned about the fragile nature of desert environments.

If only the whole four-wheeling crowd could experience such a school. At the Reese River Reservation ranches we learned firsthand how indigenous people apply their knowledge of the land to cattle ranching. At dusk near our camp, we teased untamed fourteen-inch trout from a yardstick wide stream that feeds melted spring snow into the Reese River.

Fig. 3-23. *In a semi-arid high desert environment, we vitally protect the land from soil erosion and loss of topsoil. Three decades ago, Nevada ranchers and Native Americans dealt severely with city slick recreationalists who made tire ruts in precious soil, tore up sagebrush, meandered from designated roads, chased cattle and knocked down stream banks.*

TREAD LIGHTLY Four Wheeling

Through the efforts of Clifford G. Blake, a U.S. Forest Service manager and advocate of multiple-use policy, TREAD LIGHTLY, Inc. became the first joint public/private sector venture aimed at wise recreational use of public lands.

As National Coordinator of the U.S. Forest Service Tread Lightly program, Cliff's vision encouraged the major manufacturers of motor vehicles and outdoor recreational equipment to take a direct role in serving consumers by promoting environmentally sound use of public lands.

Charter members of TREAD LIGHTLY, Inc., now a non-profit organization, include domestic and import vehicle manufacturers, OHV and power sport equipment manufacturers, aftermarket component builders, the outdoor and four-wheel drive media, tire producers and a number of concerned groups, including the Izaak Walton League and the W.A.T.E.R. Foundation.

Toyota Motor Sales, U.S.A. has been a major contributor of funds, resources and media ad support. Toyota public relations staff have provided valuable time and corporate resources to help assure the program's success. The National TREAD LIGHTLY office works closely with the U.S. Forest Service, the BLM, U.S. Fish and Wildlife, the Army Corps of Engineers and other agencies to promote sensible use of public lands. It is the aim of TREAD LIGHTLY!'s sponsors and members to use, not abuse, the environment.

As an OHV writer and recreationalist, I joined with other concerned four-wheel drive enthusiasts in supporting TREAD LIGHTLY!, Inc. Bill Burke of 4-Wheeling America and I, each Charter Members of TREAD LIGHTLY!, were commissioned to help develop and co-instruct a national 4WD clinic pilot program. Education and low impact land use advocacy programs like TREAD LIGHTLY!, Inc., and the TREAD LIGHTLY! 4WD Clinics, will help preserve access to familiar four-wheel drive trails. For membership information, phone 1-800-966-9900.

The TREAD LIGHTLY Creed

Travel—only where motorized vehicles are permitted. Never blaze your own trail.

Respect—the rights of hikers, skiers, campers, and others to enjoy their activities undisturbed.

Educate—yourself by obtaining travel maps and regulations from public agencies, complying with signs and barriers, and asking permission to cross private property.

Avoid—streams, lakeshores, meadows, muddy roads and trails, steep hillsides, wildlife and livestock.

Drive—responsibly to protect the environment and preserve opportunities to use designated public trails.

When it comes to trail etiquette, remember hikers and horses. Your truck kicks up dust, makes noise, and raises terror in the eyes of unsuspecting people and horses. Slow down, pass with caution and be considerate. The only way we'll all maintain access to North America's grand and scenic outdoors is through sharing and cooperation. There's plenty of fun and land for everyone—and you know, sometimes it's fine to walk or hike.

For my strong belief in low impact four-wheeling, I am indebted to Nevada ranchers, the Bureau of Land Management, the USDA/U.S. Forest Service and American Indians. Neither I nor any of my four-wheeling friends have torn up sagebrush, damaged stream eco-systems, left livestock gates open or blazed our own trails across a fragile landscape.

Fig. 3-24.   Should you cross? Not if there's a bridge nearby! Aware four-wheelers always take the easiest route, one that leaves the least impact on the land. There's plenty of opportunity for high adventure along primitive trails. Save your 4x4 truck for those places.

Fig. 3-25.   A winch can take over where four-wheel traction cannot do the job. Wherever wheelspin jeopardizes the environment, use a winch. As the TREAD LIGHTLY! philosophy spreads, expect wider use of winches and protective tree saver straps. Encourage fellow four-wheelers to stay on established trails and avoid damaging fragile eco-systems.

Beyond the few bad apples, many 4x4 truck owners simply have no knowledge of how to four-wheel. Unaware of either the natural environment or the dynamics of their four-wheel drive trucks, naive recreationalists can abuse both their expensive equipment and our land.

3. SPECIAL USES FOR YOUR 4WD TRUCK

Your Toyota 4WD truck can perform a multitude of useful chores. One of the most gratifying aspects of four-wheel drive trucks is their utility value and ability to serve the community. When hazardous weather strands motorists and emergency vehicles are the only stock still rolling, 4x4 trucks lead the way.

You will undoubtedly enrich your four-wheeling experience by helping other motorists. A 4x4 truck owner is duty bound to serve, much like a Canadian Royal Mounted Police officer.

Many 4x4 owners carry this responsibility further, joining local Search-and-Rescue (SAR) organizations. Likewise, most volunteer firefighters who live at rough climate zones own 4x4 trucks. When responsibilities demand readiness, regardless of weather conditions, a 4x4 truck serves best.

SAR Volunteerism

Until recently, we lived on the west slope of Oregon's Cascade Range. I was an SAR volunteer through the local 4WD club and Lane County Sheriff's Department. In hazardous weather and during the summer when campers flow into the high country for recreation, my telephone rang at the wee hours. A number of us would roll out of sound sleep and into our gassed and ready 4x4 trucks.

For SAR, a 4x4 truck serves best. On one occasion, we pulled a 4x4 pickup, with a fifth wheel trailer in tow, from a closed roadway covered by 18-inches of snow. The paved road, plowed to a point, had suddenly turned into a snow field. The driver continued, winding up 150 yards

Fig. 3-26.   Search-and-Rescue demands a lot of people and machines, but the rewards are immeasurable. At Oregon's Cascades, I spent bitterly freezing nights with a dozen other local SAR volunteers looking for lost hikers, campers and children who strayed from camp. Here at Nevada's high desert and mountainous country, finding someone quickly is of equal necessity.

out in the slushy snow. Equipped with ham and CB radios, he called for help. We responded.

On another occasion, we searched for two 10-year-old boys who had ridden bicycles into the Waldo Wilderness and couldn't find their way out. Fall temperatures continued to drop as the evening wore on, and a drought had the local cougars and bears edgy. By two in the morning, both youngsters were safe at their families' campsites.

Typically, your local sheriff's department heads up SAR activities. If you have an interest in learning survival skills and acquiring the many tools necessary to effectively find and assist lost hikers, hunters, recreationalists and travelers, consider volunteering for SAR. The work is highly rewarding.

Fig. 3-27. 4WD trucks can be valuable emergency vehicles. Equipped with a C.B. radio, a winch, winch accessories, a Hi-Lift jack, a Pull-Pal anchor and a Max tool kit, your Toyota truck can assist stranded motorists. If you enjoy community service and own a 4WD truck, consider joining a local Search-and-Rescue unit.

Snow Plowing and Other Utility Uses

Commercial users have always appreciated Toyota 4x4 trucks and Land Cruisers. A front-mounted snowplow is a common accessory for parking lot owners, ski lodges and even private residences where steep driveways become a hazard during the winter months.

Land Cruisers and 4WD pickups are frequently seen on construction and mine sites, and their role at enhancing the productivity of American farms and ranches has increased steadily. In many of these environments, a 4x4 truck has become the standard vehicle, capable of moving heavy materials along remote and hazardous roads. For modern society, the 4x4 truck has effectively replaced mules, burros, llamas and teams of oxen as our beast of burden.

Some of the more popular accessories that have developed for industrial and agricultural uses of 4x4 trucks are PTO and electrically operated winches, posthole diggers, boom hoists, plows, harrow discs and auxiliary lighting. On-board welders can provide the field mechanic with a complete repair shop at the most remote station.

Fig. 3-28. A snow plow converts your 4x4 Toyota truck into a versatile utility machine. Make certain your chassis has necessary modifications and equipment to handle the added weight of a snow plow.

Advanced Trail Running

Faced with temptation, a hill that rises into the pastel sky or a washed out trail that accesses a favorite fishing hole, my friend Al Herndon simply shrugs his shoulders and says, "You use two-wheel drive until you get stuck... Then you lock your hubs, shift into four-wheel drive, and back out."

Fig. 3-29. Plan ahead! What was solid frozen ground in the morning may be impassable mud by the time you return in the afternoon.

Sage advice, Al. Four-wheelers, however, often scorn such practicality. Sometimes Nature provides her very own surprises. Sand that appears hard packed suddenly swallows your 4WD truck to its frame. Your frozen tracks through a bog at dawn give no hint of the underlying mud soup that will churn like homemade butter by mid-morning. Last year's solid road, now ripped by torrential

Driving Through Sand Traps

Imagine a road, not just your ordinary fire road or graded gravel road, but a trail that winds through rugged high desert country. Ahead lies a sandy wash, likely a dry riverbed of deep, loose sand. In flood season, water races through the steeply walled canyon, swirling around tall rocks that now bake under a summer sun....

Since the ancients first rotated stone wheels, the number one obstacle to travel has been sand. Granular, loose and deceptive, sand operates by its own rules. When monsoons or summer rains saturate the ground, sand can be hard, packed, and tractable. In dry weather, however, the same material defies even the best flotation tires.

For traveling loose sand, your best bet is steady forward momentum, while keeping wheelspin at a minimum. The slightest amount of traction loss—especially at both axles—and sand wins.

Traveling in sand begins with basics. Lock your front hubs before entering the wash. Engage four-wheel drive, and if the load feels heavy, use low range. High flotation tires also make a difference in sand.

Moving forward, you can feel the traction and load by listening to the engine. When I was an apprentice heavy equipment operator, the older hands taught us that the cutting depth of a dozer or grader blade translated to various levels of tension at the seat of our pants. Maintain steady progress, and concentrate on constant throttle pressure and a firm control of the steering wheel.

If your engine coughs as you bump a smooth rock and the truck momentarily bogs, watch out! As the clutch engages or you bump the throttle, the truck is highly susceptible to tire spin. Too much throttle pressure now and your 4x4 could quickly become buried to the frame at the rear wheels and down to the springs at the front.

What now? If you're alone without a winch, the tool of choice is the multi-purpose Hi-Lift-type jack. These tall, industrial strength jacks can be used for a variety of chores: pushing, pulling or lifting. In combination with a chain or cable, a multi-purpose jack can also serve as a come-along.

A hefty plywood board is usually necessary for a firm jack foot. Jack up each wheel and back fill the holes created by tirespin. Slide pieces of brush both beneath and in front of the tires. When you attempt to move the truck, avoid spinning the tires and apply power smoothly.

Plan your trip in advance. Read road and trail conditions on a map or call the local Forest Service or BLM office for road reports. Aside from getting stuck, the number one fear of all four wheelers, and justifiably so, is a roll over. Twisty, off-camber hillsides and slippery mountain trails have totalled many 4x4s. The best means for avoiding a roll over at some remote place is careful consideration of terrain.

Three conditions characterize most roll overs: 1) the vehicle faces too much side angle, which overcomes the center-of-gravity and equilibrium; 2) a shift of weight upsets equilibrium on an otherwise negotiable sideslope; or 3) exaggerated speed, in any situation, compromises stability. This last point relates to off-camber side slopes, speeding around curves, or flirting with danger on casual 4x4 terrain by adding the element of excess speed.

Unfortunately, many four-wheelers, especially newcomers to the art of off-pavement driving, confuse sport with speed. These two terms are not synonymous. Safe recreational trail driving is a far cry from desert racing. My friends Ivan "Ironman" Stewart and Rod Hall have each mastered fast desert travel on four wheels. Like other professional racers, however, they quickly discourage fast driving in sensitive and uncertain environments, especially in a production type truck.

For most recreationalists, safe and methodical trail driving proves challenging enough. This includes driving over rocky, slippery, sandy, snow-covered or mountainous terrain. The winning objective is to get your family, friends and 4x4 trucks through tough trails in one piece.

4. 4WD CLUBS

As bats darted through the treetops, silhouetted by trailing twilight, our youngest son slept soundly in his bedroll. A pair of coyotes howled as my wife stared warily across the campfire. "Moses," she asked, "why do we persist in traveling alone? Isn't there some way to have four-wheel drive fun without mimicking a Paleolithic vision quest?"

Why Go It Alone?

Runs like the Rubicon Trail tax driving skill and vehicle stamina to the maximum. If the situation gets out of hand, a solo four-wheeler could be in real danger. Group travel can provide more resources and the safety of numbers. Traveling as a group adds several other benefits: social activities, fun sporting activities and a place to build life-long friendships with those who share your appreciation for outdoor recreation. Additionally, the local, state, and national 4x4 groups serve as lobbyists for our continued access to public recreational lands.

My wife, Donna, is a prolific reader who often shoves clippings and news briefs under my nose. "Look at this copy of *IN GEAR* that you grabbed at the SCORE Show. Every off-road thing that we're interested in doing is covered here!" she exclaimed, rifling through California Association of 4WD Clubs' monthly publication. "The calendar of events lists several of the runs and family outings that we've talked about."

CA4WDC's *IN GEAR* and publications like *United's Voice*, printed by United Four-Wheel Drive Associations

flooding and muddy rock slides, lies ahead—you still need to get through safely, with your cargo intact.

Wise four-wheelers all agree, the best route through an area is the easiest one. Long before trails had fashionable difficulty classifications, experienced four-wheelers scanned hillsides, washes, streams, and rock piles, sizing up the terrain. A dozen mountaintops and desolate valleys from home, the challenge is to not get stuck. Here, a C.B. radio, winch, tree saver strap and a low impact anchoring device make essential traveling companions.

Fig. 3-30. *Some consider the wheelbase of a long-bed 4WD Toyota pickup, 4Runner or the Land Cruiser Station Wagon a bit too long for routes like the Rubicon Trail. A shortbed 4WD pickup or the FJ25 and FJ40 make the perfect rigs for that run.*

This milder 4WD trail with Mount Whitney in the background is just right for a mix of Toyota 4x4s. A caravan reduces risk in the event of equipment trouble.

(UFWDA), brim with calendar events and newsworthy reports of 4x4 club activities throughout the United States and Canada. These and other four-wheel drive publications can broaden your 4WD contacts.

Regional publications include activities suited to entire families, off road survival tips, equipment ads, vehicle classifieds, accounts of trail rides, poker runs, 4x4 breakfast runs and group barbecues. A calendar of fundraising benefits, public interest projects, social functions and future runs can help members organize their free time.

How To Find A 4WD Club

For newcomers to four-wheeling, clubs are an ideal way to learn driving skills and how to tread lightly on the land. Regional sanctioning associations promote family recreation, publish newsletters and encourage clubs to protect trails and sponsor local activities.

If four-wheeling with a group of outdoor enthusiasts sounds like your kind of good time, contact the nearest state or regional association of 4x4 clubs. The better organized local clubs usually belong to regional and national sanctioning bodies.

The umbrella over all regional, state and locally sanctioned clubs is United Four-Wheel Drive Associations (UFWDA), 4505 W. 700 South, Shelbyville, Indiana 46176, or phone 1-800-44-UFWDA. UFWDA can provide guidelines for forming your own four-wheel drive group or provide referrals to regional associations and local clubs, including the various Toyota Land Cruiser Association (TLCA) Chapters.

NOTE —
The Toyota Land Cruiser Association, Inc., can be reached at P.O. Box 607, Placerville, CA 95667-0607 or phone 916-642-2330. Toyota Trails, the official publication of the TLCA, keeps association members aware of sanctioned runs and other functions.

There are liabilities that accompany any vehicle owners' association. If you plan to form a local club or chapter, charters and by-laws should follow established guidelines. State and regional associations, the TLCA or UFWDA can furnish advice on forming a club.

Anatomy Of A Club Run

Our first outing with the TLCA was the 12th Annual Thanksgiving Run, sponsored by the Ventura Chapter. For 1987, the event centered at Lone Pine, California, where the upper end of the Mojave Desert meets the Owens Valley.

A prominent milestone and fuel stop for travelers headed for the Sierra Nevada Mountains, Lone Pine rests in the shadows of Mount Whitney. Whitney's summit lies at 14,495 feet elevation, giving the mountain its bold stature and status as the highest peak in the Lower-48 States.

I knew Ross Stuart of Land Cruiser Advanced Handling, but all of the other club members who formed the TLCA camp at Diaz Lake were new faces. My family's invitation was our Land Cruiser FJ40. Sixty-five people and close to thirty Toyota 4WD vehicles filled the northwest corner of the campground.

Fig. 3-31. *Toyota Land Cruiser Association rigs at Lone Pine, California, Annual Thanksgiving Run 1987. Sierra Nevada Mountains line the background. Lone Pine lies north. The Toyota Land Cruiser Association consists of a wonderful bunch of* Land Cruiser, Toyota 4Runner and 4WD Pickup owners' families who four wheel and travel to fun places and enjoy great camaraderie.

It was Wednesday afternoon, and we were early. A dozen Cruisers and Toyota 4x4 pickups huddled beneath the trees. Folks stood in small clusters about the camp, and a chilling breeze gusted from Mount Whitney as we found a spot to set up our self-contained travel trailer. In minutes, the group received us. Friendly handshakes and conversation made us feel welcome, a warm atmosphere despite temperatures low enough to freeze water.

A restive Thanksgiving morning allowed time to review machinery, and Bob and Jan King's FJ-40 "Red Horse" drew our attention. A bright Porsche Red finish glistened in the post dawn sunlight. Custom work on the 1971 Land Cruiser showed painstaking detail from every angle. The Kings, like other TLCA members, are very active in their club chapter. Each has held club offices, including Bob's term as president.

Thanksgiving Dinner For Sixty-five Four Wheelers

Lone Pine's Bonanza Restaurant served as the stage for the group's opening meeting, Thanksgiving dinner and all ceremonies. President Brian Schreiber pounded the official gavel, and opened the event. Once past the formality, our feasting began. The size of the group and their diverse backgrounds made the dinner all the more interesting—This was truly a meaningful Thanksgiving, a meal of plenty that commemorated the generous sharing of Nature's bounty.

The after dinner campfire at Diaz Lake Campground went well into the night. Reluctantly, the group finally went to bed, preparing for the driver's meeting that started at eight near the Visitor's Center on Highway 136.

North-south Highway 395, the route that keeps Lone Pine on the map, is a major artery. Highway 136, a California secondary route, runs quietly into the Panamint Range—the western gateway to Death Valley. Early Friday morning, this highway was empty as we drove several miles to a dirt road intersection. Turning left and facing a broad alluvial fan and sloping gravel road, the group of twenty-five Toyota 4x4s stopped in a line.

Fig. 3-32. *Bob and Jan King's show winning Cruiser looks at home against 14,495 foot Mount Whitney. "Red Horse", a 1971 FJ-40 powered by a healthy Chevrolet V-8, never misses a meet or a good run.*

The clicking of locking hubs and hissing of deflating tires echoed in the still morning air as drivers prepared for the run to Cerro Gordo. Our climb started gradually, with the Owens Valley in the rear view mirrors as the twisty canyons rose to higher plateaus. Low range and four-wheel drive was the agenda for the next six hours.

Periodically, with the group spread over a mile, the trailmaster staged a stop. 4WD pickups and Cruisers crept into the line up, their sooty tailpipes and burbling

Fig. 3-33. The Kings' Land Cruiser has horsepower that matches its stunning looks. Very warm 350 V-8 turns heads at pulls, mud bogs, and rock crawlin' trail runs through the High Sierras.

exhaust tones denoting the rarified atmosphere. None had faltered yet, but The Tram still remained miles ahead—near 9600 feet elevation.

At these elevations, 4WD pickup and 4Runner four-cylinder engines stayed wound up tightly, while the torquey F and 2F Land Cruiser inline sixes maintained their moderate pitch. Carbureted high horsepower V-8 conversions pulled strongly from an idle, loading up occasionally from the rich fuel mixtures that developed as the elevation increased.

The Tram And Cerro Gordo

For many, the highlight of the TLCA Thanksgiving Run was The Tram. In early afternoon, as the thin-aired elevation rose above timberline, we reached a high plateau. Wind ripped through the open topped FJs, and the final ascent to The Tram began.

Our stay at The Tram was shortened by the chill factor. At 9600 feet, the gusting wind carried the ominous message that winter was near. Four wheelers in open topped rigs hunched closer to their central heaters. The trail toward Cerro Gordo still lay ahead.

Downgrades, then slopes.... Trees followed by barren, brush covered hillsides.... The trail from The Tram to Cerro Gordo was a much shorter run but still rough. New mining claims dotted the roadside, explaining the fresh tire prints along the primitive trail. Ore continues to at-

Fig. 3-34. The Tram atop a 9600-foot ridge in the Inyo/White Mountains rests silently, echoing mining days long gone. The sweeping Owens Valley and the distant crags of Mount Whitney present a monumental view.

tract miners to these hills and mountains, and we followed their claims to Cerro Gordo.

Longer shadows darted across our hoods and cabs as a distant mountaintop microwave dish pinpointed our destination. Just below, against a hillside, stood the remaining Cerro Gordo minesite. Once again, the 4WD caravan wound slowly to a halt. We visited and took a tour of the Cerro Gordo Mine before continuing down an improved road to Highway 136 at Keeler. Now driving on a broad and well graded dirt super highway, our Toyota 4x4s rolled to Keeler in half an hour.

Saturday Fun And Games

On Saturday morning, following another finger warming campfire episode on Friday night, we all met again. Within a mile of Diaz Lake, the TLCA entertainment committee had sectioned off some ground for several hours of organized fun.

Everyone participated, and a number of events unfolded, including three obstacle courses. Although timed with a stopwatch, each event offered a different challenge and goal.

Fig. 3-35. Saturday's organized games included a stack-and-can obstacle run. Spirit of competition ran high, as Dan Dominy, world renowned video/film director and producer, takes two runs for his best time. Driver and navigator switch places halfway through the course.

Fig. 3-36. *Mini 4x4 pickups were not to be outdone, their 20R and 22R engines screaming to a respectable finish. Here, front tires catch air during an impressive run.*

Fig. 3-37. *I generally don't drive while wearing blackout goggles. During the blindfold obstacle run, however, my wife Donna got a rare and long awaited opportunity....She maintained total control over my driving for several minutes—and even took this flattering picture.*

The obstacle run with stick posts and tin cans was fast paced and fun. 4x4s with driver/navigator teams raced to remove cans planted on sticks along the course. At the far end, the driver and navigator changed places. On the return, the cans were remounted on the sticks. All this with no mistakes and for the fastest time.

In another event, the driver was blindfolded or given a ski mask with a blacked out lens—*zero* visibility. The navigator gave verbal signals to the driver, telling him or her how to steer the 4x4 through an obstacle course. The driver with the quickest time and least penalties won.

Once past these two challenges, participants took a crack at the Wet Lap run. Here, the navigator held a carefully measured and filled bowl in his or her hands while

Fig. 3-38. *Wet Lap game includes running through a timed obstacle course with the co-pilot holding a pre-measured bowl of water. This lady is about to wear the bowl's water.*

the driver attempted a quick run through an uphill/downhill bumpy course. Again, the stopwatch was running.

At the finish line, the judges emptied the bowl's water, if any, into a measuring glass. The winner held the fastest time with the greatest amount of water remaining.

Awards And Drawings—Better Than The Lottery!

Saturday night's banquet included the long awaited awards ceremony and raffle. Rumor of a trip to Hawaii was confirmed to be the Grand Prize. Waikiki or Maui?

Fig. 3-39. *Saturday night, the awards and raffle occupied the TLCA members for several hours. So many items were raffled that nearly everyone was a winner. Grand prize was a trip for two to Hawaii. Not bad for a fun filled, super weekend at Lone Pine and the Inyo/White Mountains.*

Not bad for a bunch of dust eating four wheelers! There were so many items raffled, from useful truck accessories to a new winch, that the event continued for hours. Nearly everyone took something home, aside from the treasured experience. The banquet night seemed a fitting way to reward each other, as the hardy bunch had clearly proven its mettle on both the trail and obstacle courses.

A number of us built one last campfire, while some folks went to Lone Pine for a night out. Eventually, all weary wheelers climbed into their tents, campers, motorhomes or trailers and went to sleep. Sunday came quickly, with home far away for most of us. My wife Donna, son Jacob and I towed the self-contained tandem axle Starcraft travel trailer nearly three-hundred and fifty miles that day—behind our 1976 FJ40 Land Cruiser.

Ross Stuart and his daughter Chelle drove back to Albany, Oregon. At that time, Ross's 1977 FJ40 still had its original 2F six-cylinder engine. Yes, Ross Stuart again won the plaque for longest distance traveled to reach the event. He and his daughter weathered 18 hours in a six-cylinder FJ-40 to be at their second outing with this group. Like other members, Ross's commitment to outdoor fun and Toyota 4x4s made the trip worthwhile.

Join The Club

If this all sounds good, guess what. It is. When four wheeling and sensible use of the environment join hands, expect sanctioned clubs to be there.

The TLCA serves popular Toyota 4x4 trucks and their owners, but that's not all. They join ranks with scores of other clubs at fun filled events throughout the U.S. and Canada. Such events and activities in no way inhibit real four wheeling. Quite the contrary—Those who enjoy competition, challenging vertical angles, and occasional

Fig. 3-40. *Road into Diaz Lake camp area has seen a lot of Toyota 4x4 trucks. At dawn on Sunday morning, our FJ40 leaves behind a memorable Thanksgiving weekend. Breathtaking High Sierras and a 20' Starcraft travel trailer filled our rear view mirrors.*

opportunities to put their pedals to the metal will go home satisfied.

Trail crawlers will feel equally welcome. So can a newcomer who wants nothing more than to learn the finer points of trail driving.

A *good, safe time* is what a sanctioned 4x4 club can offer. Our family will always remember Thanksgiving 1987, when the TLCA gave us one of the best four-day weekends we've ever had. What a great way to make friends with folks who share your outdoor interests.

Chapter 4

Working on Your Toyota Truck

E ACH TOYOTA TRUCK reflects the company's concern for serviceability. Ready access to routine maintenance components and replaceable sub-assemblies helps simplify maintenance, while a Toyota 2WD or 4WD truck's utilitarian design makes field fixes possible. Many owners learn the basics of automotive repair by working on their truck.

All Toyota trucks feature an uncomplicated chassis, a conventional powertrain layout and familiar accessory sub-assemblies. Although 1969 and newer U.S.-market vehicles have more engine emission controls and an increasingly greater number of power options, the chassis and powertrain components remain easy to identify.

Engines and geartrains for Toyota trucks are very easy to identify. Over the last decade, the introduction of automatic and manual overdrive transmissions, plus changes in the automotive industry's methods of complying with EPA and CAFE standards, have altered the engine and geartrain combinations and available options.

Light truck emission control requirements have always fit particular GVWR categories. Tiers include trucks up to 6,000 pounds GVWR (light duty emissions), 6,001–8,500 pounds GVWR, trucks between 8501–10,000 pounds GVWR (heavy duty emissions) and trucks over 10,000 pounds. Over the years, the 6,001–8,500 pound GVWR category has bounced between light and heavy duty emission control requirements.

As these categories and regulations change continually, your main concern is requirements for your particular year and model engine and chassis. When ordering replacement parts, you'll need to know the GVWR, vehicle identification number and the information on the underhood emission decal. The decal notes the engine type, family and whether 49-State (Federal) or 50-State (California) requirements apply. California engines, although typically demanding more emission controls than federal engines, must also comply with EPA/Federal emission standards. Emission equipment is also summarized on the decal.

Fig. 4-1. *A conventional ladder-type frame has assured Toyota truck stamina. Often described as a "driveable chassis" design, a rugged ladder frame supports the suspension, body and powertrain.*

1. THE TOYOTA TRUCK CHASSIS

Toyota trucks have a ladder frame chassis and similar powertrain layouts. Models covered within the service chapters of this book fit into five categories:

1. 1958–90 4WD Land Cruiser with solid-beam front and rear drive axles and four-wheel leaf springs

2. 1991–up Land Cruiser with solid-beam front and rear axles and four-wheel coil springs

3. 1969–up 2WD pickups with independent front suspension (IFS, coil spring or torsion bar) and a Hotchkiss-style (solid hypoid) rear axle with leaf springs

4. 1979–85 4WD pickups and 4Runners with solid-beam front and rear axles and leaf springs

5. 1986–up 4WD pickups and 4Runners with independent front torsion bar or coil spring suspension, rear leaf or coil springs (on 4Runners), and a solid rear hypoid axle

Fig. 4-2. *1958–90 Land Cruisers and the Toyota 4WD Pickups and 4Runners built through 1985 use leaf springs at both the front and rear. This is a conventional and highly rugged method of suspending a truck chassis. These sturdy models have solid hypoid driving axles at the front and rear.*

Fig. 4-3. *From the earliest U.S. market Land Cruiser models forward, all Toyota trucks use rubber-type bushings at the leaf spring shackles, leaf spring anchors and A-arm pivots. These types of bushings do not require grease fittings.*

Fig. 4-4. *Although springs and suspension pivots have no grease fittings, the Land Cruiser, 4WD and later torsion bar IFS 2WD trucks still require periodic lubrication at lever pivots, driveshaft joints and steering linkage. On earlier coil spring A-arm 2WD front suspension, the threaded A-arm pivot shafts do require lubrication.*

To date, the majority of Toyota trucks have featured semi-elliptic leaf rear springs. The exceptions are 1991 and newer Land Cruisers and the late model 4Runners. These two lines use coil springs and trailing link-arm suspension at the rear axle.

All 2WD trucks from 1969 forward have independent double A-arm front suspension. 1969–78 models feature coil front springs, and all later models use torsion bars. 4WD pickup trucks and 4Runners built from 1986 forward also use a double A-arm front suspension with torsion bars or coil springs (introduced on Tacoma models).

Commonly described as a driveable chassis, the Toyota light truck ladder frame has several advantages. As with full-size American trucks, these strong chassis help offset the effects of body rust and fatigue. A restorer will often replace the entire cab of an early Toyota Hi-Lux pickup, or the Land Cruiser FJ25 or FJ40-series body "tub," yet find the vintage frame intact and functional.

From a service standpoint, the ladder frame requires little maintenance. Support members, such as spring and shock absorber mounts, attach solidly to the frame. Frame rails and crossmembers are maintenance-free. Aside from periodic power washing and brushing away surface scale and debris, an undamaged frame seldom needs more than occasional paint and undercoating.

Axle and Suspension Systems

In 1958, all domestic 2WD and 4WD trucks had four-wheel leaf springs and solid-beam axles. The Toyota Land Cruiser 4WD followed this conventional design. By 1960, however, 2WD domestic trucks began their shift to independent front suspension, with GM pioneering this effort and Ford following with the Twin I-Beam front suspension in 1965.

Both the Hi-Lux and Stout featured independent double A-arm front suspension, similar in appearance to 1960s GM truck designs. All Toyota pickup trucks from the earliest Stout and RN11 Hi-Lux to the present feature leaf rear springs and a solid rear axle. Leaf springs anchor

at one end with a pivot bolt and bushings. During suspension travel, a swinging shackle at the opposite end of the main leaf permits fore and aft spring movement.

Use of pivoting double A-arms and a steering knuckle/spindle with ball-joints, the 2WD and 1986–up 4WD IFS front ends somewhat resemble passenger car engineering. The similarity ends with looks, however, as the heft of the Toyota truck's ball-joints and all other components make this a rugged suspension system. Allowing for finer adjustment, these IFS systems hold wheel alignment well and offer long service.

Fig. 4-7. In good condition, Toyota 2WD or 4WD IFS torsion bar suspension systems (shown) provide exceptional ride quality and durability. Earlier 2WD models with coil springs have an equally durable chassis layout, without the need for long torsion bars that stretch rearward from the control arms. Either suspension system is truck worthy.

Fig. 4-5. Toyota ball joints, steering linkage and A-arm shaft pivots sometimes have grease plugs instead of standard grease fittings. Straight and angled metric grease fittings can be installed as a service item and left in place if parts do not interfere during suspension or steering movement.

Fig. 4-8. Full-floating axle provides wheel support in the event of an axle shaft failure. Late motorhome and cargo vans use this type of axle with dual drive wheels. Some Land Cruisers use a full-floating rear axle (shown here) with single drive wheels. All other Toyota trucks use a semi-floating rear axle.

Fig. 4-6. Toyota's solid front driving axle, commonly called a hypoid or mono-beam type, attaches to the springs with U-bolts and offers a high degree of stamina. 4WD closed front steering knuckles of these solid axles each pivot on upper and lower kingpin bearings. Kingpin bearings, known for stability and durability, have remained a mainstay with 4WD Land Cruisers and were common to 1979–85 4WD pickups and 1984–85 4Runners. Steering linkage is simple and efficient.

Rear axles for various Toyota models are either the rarer Land Cruiser full-floating type or the more common semi-floating type. Some commercial truck models, like later motorhomes and cargo vans, feature full-floating rear axles and dual rear wheels. All Toyota axles use open driveshafts.

The last use of a solid live front axle with full-floating wheel hubs is the Land Cruiser Station Wagon. I refer to Land Cruisers and all pre-1986 4WD solid axle models as having "conventional 4x4" as opposed to the 4WD IFS front axle system with CV-joints and half shafts (found on 1986–up 4Runners and 4WD pickups). Toyota calls this IFS 4WD system "Hi-Trac."

Some argue that Toyota's IFS 4WD requires less maintenance, provides less trouble, and affords tighter turning angles than the closed knuckle solid axles. Land Cruiser and pre-IFS 4WD truck closed knuckle axles often develop seal leaks and weep grease. Also, the shimmed kingpin bearings on these axles require a precise pre-load adjustment, making service more complex.

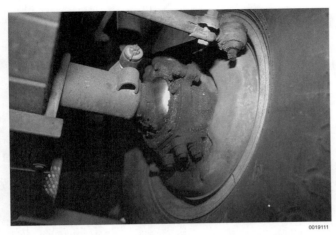

Fig. 4-9. Toyota solid axle models with closed-knuckle steering joints have sealed, ball-shaped castings that extend from the axle tubes. Inside this cavity is grease for the enclosed axle and steering knuckle joints.

Fig. 4-10. Later IFS 4WD Hi-Trac front suspension uses upper and lower ball joints that allow the steering knuckle to pivot between the two suspension A-arms. This design and its steering linkage resembles 2WD IFS. An inner driveshaft and outer stub shaft deliver power from the front differential assembly to each full-floating wheel hub. Constant velocity (CV) joints at each end of the two driveshafts allow for suspension flex and chassis movement.

Toyota engineering aims for long service life and parts integrity. By design, solid live front axles with full-floating hubs provide superior strength. The IFS 4WD chassis has CV-joints, CV-boots, half-shafts, full-floating wheel hubs and a ball-joint A-arm suspension system with lots of pivot joints. This means far more potential wear points than with a solid axle. Despite this, each of these axle designs represent durable engineering.

Torsion bars on IFS trucks are rugged and allow adjustment of the vehicle's chassis ride height. Torsion bars provide a smooth ride quality and good load capacity. The rugged double A-arm suspension can deliver the durability expected of truck components. Toyota's Hi-Trac

4WD IFS suspension complements the proven design of Toyota 2WD models.

Rear axles require little periodic maintenance beyond oil level checks and oil changes. Axle shaft bearings and full-floating front or rear wheel hub bearings offer a long service life. The overall stamina of Toyota truck axles and wheel hub assemblies is excellent.

Fig. 4-11. All Toyota trucks feature open driveshafts or "propeller" shafts. Open drivelines permit quicker service and easier removal of the transmission or rear axle and center-section assemblies.

Fig. 4-12. Toyota has preferred the drop-in carrier type design (shown) to the integral type axle assembly. Easily removed from the axle housing, a carrier type differential assembly can be serviced on the bench. Most mechanics like this feature.

2. STEERING GEAR AND LINKAGE

Toyota Land Cruisers through the 1972 models have a worm and roller type steering gear. Although very well built, this gear is not as durable nor as smooth operating as the improved recirculating ball-and-nut manual gears introduced with the 1973 Land Cruisers.

Fig. 4-13. *Recirculating ball-and-nut manual steering is superior to all other designs. Precisely machined worm shaft groove acts as an inner half of the ball bearing race, while the nut provides the matching groove. Reduced friction means easier steering and a longer service life. General Motors' recirculating ball-and-nut type manual steering gear design (shown here) set a precedent for other truck manufacturers.*

Toyota's mini and compact 2WD and 4WD models have all used recirculating ball-and-nut steering designs. (Tacoma uses rack-and-pinion.) Prior to T100 2WD and Tacoma models, Toyota truck power steering was also of recirculating ball-and-power rack/piston design.

Later (FJ60 and newer) Land Cruisers eliminate the bellcrank/center arm and have a pitman arm that moves laterally at the steering gear. The pitman arm simply moves the relay rod that attaches to the right side steering arm of left-hand drive (U.S.) models. A one piece tie-rod connects the right steering arm to the left one.

Eliminating the bellcrank helps reduce excess play, wear points, and unwarranted hardware. Many owners of Land Cruisers equipped with bellcrank steering linkage have converted to a GM/Saginaw manual or, preferably, integral power type steering gear with a laterally moving pitman arm. (See suspension upgrade chapter.)

IFS 2WD and 4WD front ends with convention recirculating ball manual or power steering share a common

Fig. 4-14. *Mimicry is a high compliment, and GM/Saginaw recirculating ball-and-nut steering has its likenesses throughout the automotive world. Toyota design (shown) is highly durable.*

Fig. 4-15. *The T100 2WD truck introduced the first use of rack-and-pinion type steering on any ladder chassis truck. This innovative gear has power assist and offers exceptionally smooth and responsive steering. Rack-and-pinion steering has been in Toyota passenger car use for many years.*

Fig. 4-16. *The demand for power steering encouraged Toyota to offer an integral power steering gear option on 1979 Land Cruisers. This is a durable but somewhat scarce item until the FJ60 offered power steering as standard equipment. The first four-cylinder 4WD pickups (shown here) immediately offered power steering as an option, and this too was a boon for driveability and off-pavement use.*

steering linkage design. These vehicles each have a laterally moving pitman arm. The linkage looks much like a passenger car system designed for double A-arm suspension. The steering pitman arm moves left to right, and a centerlink connects the pitman arm to an idler arm that mounts opposite the pitman arm at the right frame rail (on left hand drive models).

Short tie-rods attach the centerlink to the steering arm at each steering knuckle/spindle. This three-piece tie-rod assembly is similar to passenger car types, although the truck components are much sturdier. Ball-stud joints in the linkage allow the necessary movement as the IFS A-arms travel up and down with the road surface changes.

For 4x4s, power steering helps eliminate the arm wrenching of manual steering and makes rough terrain four-wheeling more enjoyable. Toyota's power gear became a popular and common option with the 1979–early '80s 4x4 pickups and became standard with FJ60 Land Cruisers and eventually all pickups and 4Runners.

> **NOTE —**
> Recirculating ball-type steering is a precise mechanism. Other than very minor sector-shaft mesh adjustment at high mileage, any excess play at the steering pitman arm or wormshaft bearings indicates internal damage. In this case, the gear needs a tear-down for inspection and overhaul. Make all adjustments in the manner described in your official OEM Toyota Repair Manual.

3. DRUM AND DISC BRAKE SYSTEMS

All U.S. market Toyota trucks have hydraulic braking systems. A hydraulic master cylinder feeds brake fluid through pipes and high strength brake hose to each wheel cylinder or disc caliper. Pedal pressure actuates the master cylinder piston (dual pistons on 1967–up tandem master cylinders), causing brake fluid to flow.

Early Toyota drum brakes have two hydraulic cylinders per wheel. Later models use more common double-piston single wheel cylinders. These later cylinders have twin, opposing pistons that move outward as fluid enters the cylinder. Depending upon the model and brake type, Toyota drum brakes apply shoe pressure to the drum via several methods, each design described generically as "self-energizing."

Overall, earlier four-wheel drum brake systems are less effective than disc front/drum rear designs. Although Toyota engineered drum brake sizes to match chassis and advertised load capacities, drum type brakes simply cannot offer the braking efficiency, resistance to fade and overall performance gains of disc brakes.

All Toyota mini trucks use drum front/rear brakes through 1974. 2WD trucks introduce disc front/drum rear brakes in 1975; Land Cruisers gain disc front brakes in 1976.

Fig. 4-18. Self-energizing brakes, with both shoes sharing a common anchor or pivot point, utilize the rotational force of the drum to force the brake shoes more firmly against the braking surface of the drum. Added force enhances braking without need for additional hydraulic pressure.

Emergency/Parking Brake

The common emergency brake system for late Toyota trucks is cable actuation of the rear brakes. Earlier Land Cruisers, however, use the classic transfer case-mounted mechanical two-shoe brake assembly. All emergency/parking brakes rely upon mechanical force to actuate the rear brake shoes—or the rear disc brake pads in the case of late four-wheel disc brake models.

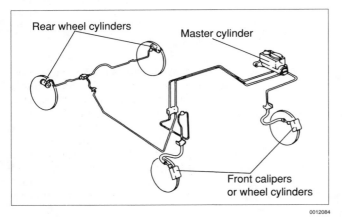

Fig. 4-17. Toyota light truck braking systems are similar to American truck designs. A pedal actuated master cylinder forces fluid into each of the hydraulic wheel cylinders or disc brake calipers. Friction brake shoes or pads act against metal drums or rotors.

Fig. 4-19. The parking brake mechanism is basic. Mechanical cable linkage activates the rear wheel brake shoes when the driver applies the emergency/parking brake lever.

Fig. 4-20. *Emergency/parking brakes are at the rear wheels of most Toyota trucks. On earlier Land Cruisers, however, the emergency brake mounts at the back of the transfer case in line with the driveshaft (shown). When brake lining is wet, muddy, oil soaked or glazed, the cable actuated emergency/parking brakes offer marginal service at best.*

Road debris and oil contamination from leaky axle or transfer case seals can lower the efficiency of the emergency/parking brakes. Also, if you have a very heavy load and need to park on a steep hill, consider using chock blocks behind the front and rear wheels as a backup.

Toyota truck braking has always been adequate, however, significant improvements began in 1967 with the dual braking systems. Disc front/drum rear brakes were a huge improvement in the mid-1970s, and by the late 1980s, Toyota trucks began offering anti-lock rear braking systems. Since 1993, four-wheel anti-lock disc braking has been an available option on the Land Cruiser.

4. Orientation to Truck Engines

> **NOTE —**
> Chapter 1 and Chapter 2 describe the design and performance of Toyota light truck engines. This section's comments apply more to general engine maintenance and serviceability. For troubleshooting, tune-up procedures and light service details, see the service chapters.

For Toyota Land Cruisers, the F and 2F OHV in-line sixes once served as a mainstay. Between 1958 and 1974, the basic 236.7 cubic inch F engine was the sole powerplant used in 'Cruisers, while the 1975–87 models benefitted from the larger 258 cubic inch (4230cc) 2F engine. The more modern 3F-E engine with EFI, introduced with the FJ62 model in 1988, featured a smaller 4.0L displacement yet higher performance output than its two predecessors.

Each of these four-main bearing engines offer easy routine service and maintain their tune for long periods of time. Like other Toyota truck engines, the F, 2F and 3F-E

powerplants have mechanical valve lifters, which require valve adjustment as part of their periodic maintenance.

For these four-main bearing in-line sixes, the earlier engines use a breaker point distributor, while all 1978 models use fully electronic distributors. The distributor and breaker points are readily accessible. Four-cylinder Hi-Lux/Pickup models use breaker points through 1977 models.

For breaker point distributors, the point sets are readily accessible. Spark plugs lie within easy reach on most Toyota truck engines, unless accessories clutter the engine bay. Ignition service, covered in the tune-up chapter, is routine and easy to perform.

The early Land Cruisers use a one-barrel carburetor. In 1968, Toyota introduced a two-barrel carburetor and intake manifold on F engines. This system carries forward with the introduction of the larger 2F engine in 1975. The 2F uses two-barrel carburetion with several intake manifold designs between 1975 and 1987. (I cover carburetor minor adjustment details in the tune-up section of the book.)

Fig. 4-21. *California, Canadian and U.S. 49-State engine equipment differs during the mid-1970s. You may find that your 1975–77 Toyota truck uses either breaker points or a fully electronic ignition, depending upon emission requirements. Some semi-electronic ignitions with breaker points were also offered during this period.*

Oil filtration on F engines through 1973 is of by-pass type. Although mid-1969 through 1973 models use a spin-on filter, this is still a by-pass design. You can distinguish these by-pass lubrication systems by their use of a pressure regulator and two external oil lines.

These earlier F engines definitely require periodic service of the by-pass filter assembly to provide adequate oil cleansing. Make absolutely certain that the air filter and oil filler seals are tight, and keep all contaminants (sand, debris, grease, etc.) out of the crankcase when checking and changing oil.

Engine overhaul of the Toyota in-line sixes involves handling very heavy castings. Iron cylinder heads weigh more than big block domestic V-8 heads. Aside from damaging the head, block or new head gasket, you can seri-

Fig. 4-22. *F, 2F and 3F-E engines have overhead valves and a rocker shaft assembly with twelve valve rocker arms and mechanical lifters. These engines require period valve adjust. This can be an oily job, but once mastered, provides satisfying results and a sense of accomplishment.*

Fig. 4-23. *All 1974–up Land Cruiser sixes, 1969–up four-cylinder engines, all V-6s and the latest Land Cruiser DOHC 4.5L engine use full-flow oil filtration. Serviced regularly, this system keeps Toyota truck engines alive for decades. Filter sets to right of distributor on this high mileage six.*

Fig. 4-24. *The next best thing to a simple breaker point ignition distributor was Toyota's switch to higher energy electronic ignitions in the late 1970s. An electronic breakerless distributor requires only an occasional rotor and distributor cap change (or module replacement when defective) and a periodic check of the base spark timing.*

Fig. 4-25. *The Toyota F, 2F and 3F-E in-line sixes are rugged and very heavy iron casting designs. In-frame engine overhaul is possible, although the sensible approach, considering the sheer mass of these engines, is to carefully remove the powerplant assembly. Use extreme caution when handling the heavy cylinder head, flywheel and other pieces.*

ously hurt yourself by mishandling a Land Cruiser cylinder head. Use a chain and hydraulic hoist if available.

Much of the tuning and routine service of Toyota truck engines is similar. Although EFI has more electronic components, these systems pose no threat to minor tune-up. EFI troubleshooting entails more details, however, with the proper testing devices and an OEM Toyota guidebook, you can even become proficient at troubleshooting much of your truck's EFI system, if so equipped. The combination of electronic fuel and spark management (EFI) have made the later Toyota truck engines even easier to maintain. Reliability of these components will keep your truck's needs to a minimum, and this translates to lower overall maintenance costs.

One area of concern worth noting, though, is the use of valve timing belts, beginning with the 3VZ-E V-6 3.0L engine. This method of rotating the overhead camshafts of that engine was unprecedented in Toyota's OHC en-

gines. Frankly, I am far more impressed with the proven chain and sprocket designs found in all previous Toyota OHC engines, and must emphasize that periodic replacement of this belt is mandatory. Follow Toyota's recommended change interval if your engine has a replaceable timing belt.

5. TRANSMISSIONS AND TRANSFER CASE

A wide range of manual and automatic transmissions have been coupled to Toyota truck engines. For four-wheel drive, the geartrain requires an additional member, the transfer case or power divider, which delivers power to each driving axle.

Diaphragm spring-type clutch covers have been used in most Toyota trucks, although pre-1975 Land Cruisers employ a three-finger design. Each clutch design is so similar to a domestic truck counterpart that anyone familiar with popular U.S.-built truck clutches will find the Toyota units simple to service. All Toyota clutches are of metric dimensions, just like hardware and machining throughout the truck's powertrain.

The clutch provides the clamping force necessary to press the clutch disc between an engine-driven steel fly-wheel and the clutch cover's face or pressure plate. This method of operation is proven and reliable.

A pilot bearing at the rear of the engine crankshaft supports the nose end of the manual transmission input shaft/gear, while the clutch release or throwout bearing rides on the front bearing retainer of the transmission.

Fig. 4-28. *Toyota trucks have used a conventional clutch and release arm mechanism. The throwout bearing rides on the transmission front bearing retainer and presses against the clutch release fingers during disengagement. A crankshaft pilot bearing centers and supports the transmission input shaft.*

Hydraulic Clutch Linkage

Toyota trucks are noted for their smooth clutch operation. This is largely due to the use of hydraulic clutch linkage. From the earliest U.S. Land Cruisers forward, Toyota truck clutch linkage has consisted of a hydraulic clutch master cylinder, hydraulic lines, a slave cylinder and a common release arm system.

Fig. 4-26. *Failure to periodically replace the timing belt on 3VZ-E V-6s and similar OHC engine types can result in major engine damage if the belt should break. I find the industry-wide trend toward replaceable timing belts most unfortunate. Toyota has a three decade track record of proven reliability from timing chains and sprockets that generally last between major engine overhauls. A timing belt failure can result in major valve and piston damage. Change this belt on time, at least every 60,000 miles.*

Fig. 4-27. *2.0L four-cylinder diesel engines have worked very well in Toyota small trucks. A diesel requires very little maintenance, however, regular filter and oil changes are crucial to diesel engine survival. Crankcase contaminants build up more rapidly in these high compression engines.*

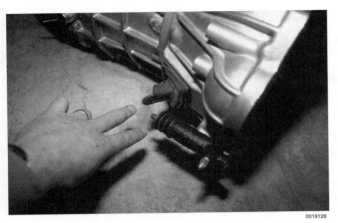

Fig. 4-29. The Toyota slave cylinder attaches directly to the engine/transmission assembly, typically at the clutch housing. This is a smart arrangement, as it prevents lost motion and clutch shake, common to mechanical linkage systems that pivot between the truck's frame and the clutch housing.

Positive and smooth clutch engagement is possible with this design, and the easy pedal pressure is refreshing. Off-pavement frame and engine flex has no effect on clutch operation. Hydraulic systems seldom fail, and when they do, you can rebuild or replace the leaking or defective parts.

Adding further to the powertrain smoothness of Toyota Land Cruiser FJ models is the four-point engine and transmission mounting system. Two mounts toward the front of the six-cylinder engine and two side mounts at the clutch housing provide a firm and stable cradle for the engine. The brute torque of the in-line six is well controlled.

Toyota trucks and 4Runners, by contrast, commonly use a three-point engine/transmission mounting system. This involves side mounts on the engine and a single rear transmission mount. This design has worked well for Toyota and, currently, all domestic light truck builders.

Hydraulic clutch linkage requires periodic inspection for leaks and air in the system. Worn parts usually fail when your truck is under load or off-pavement. For this reason, clutch linkage is a vital part of preventive care.

Durable, Sophisticated Automatic Transmissions

Toyota and other mini-truck builders were late to offer automatic transmissions. The FJ60 was the first Land Cruiser to offer an automatic, a feature that came on line somewhat later than the 2WD Toyota mini-truck models began offering an automatic transmission option.

Reluctance to offer an automatic in trucks was warranted. Four-cylinder Toyota engines through the 20R were not up to the task of driving a torque converter and working with a three-speed automatic transmission. Later overdriving four-speed automatics, with their lower first gear ratios and lock-up torque converters, provided a better opportunity for offering four-cylinder engines with automatic transmissions.

The Land Cruiser FJ40, to its last U.S. offering in 1983, never used an automatic. This was likely due to the rug-

ged truck's design and Toyota's unwillingness to reduce the fuel economy of a vehicle already considered a gas guzzler. Poorer fuel economy was also a reason for Toyota to limit the production and importation of FJ60, FJ62 and FJ80 Land Cruisers.

Remember, Toyota's market is much larger than just North America. With status as the second largest producer of motor vehicles in the world, Toyota's product planning takes on a much more global view. Until recent engineering developments, fuel economy with small powerplants and automatic transmissions has been less than with manual transmissions—and fuel economy remains a foremost consideration for Toyota marketing.

Manual Transmission Overview

The various manual transmissions used in Toyota trucks have offered good to excellent service. All Land Cruiser transmissions are durable and sufficient for a stock powertrain. 1975 and newer 'Cruiser four-speeds have superior stamina and much improved synchromesh on all forward gears.

Some special off-pavement demands and Land Cruiser V-8 or early 4WD pickup/domestic V-6 conversions might warrant the use of a heavy duty domestic truck four-speed or five-speed. (See the geartrain upgrade chapter later in the book.)

Also, the first 4WD pickup five-speed overdrives built from 1981 through 1983 have a somewhat weak input gear bearing design. These transmissions fare poorly if a heavy load is placed on the overdrive (fifth) gear. Oversized tires will create a problem here.

Transfer Cases

All Toyota transfer cases attach directly to the transmission. This reduces driveshaft needs and provides a positive coupling of the transmission and transfer case. For service and removal, this design requires no more effort than a "divorced" transfer case, which has a short driveshaft that separates a free standing transfer case from the transmission.

All part-time Land Cruiser and earlier Toyota 4WD truck transfer cases have gear drive mechanisms. Gear drive units have the most rugged service record around. I knew an early Land Cruiser owner from San Diego, California whose vintage 'Cruiser had 600,000 miles on it. The engine had been replaced twice with 283 small-block Chevrolet V-8s, yet the transfer case was original and had never been apart.

This is especially impressive, as the earlier Land Cruiser transfer cases were of side-drive design. This means that neither 2WD or 4WD mode offers a direct flow of power from the transmission output through the transfer case. In either position, power must flow sideways through an intermediate gear to the output shaft. Generally, this at least leads to bearing wear. The Land Cruiser transfer case bearings have exceptional size and longevity. Likewise, gear stamina is also great.

The first through-drive transfer cases in Toyota 4WD models were the 1979 pickup types. This change was as likely due to the centrally positioned differential of 2WD truck rear axles as an effort to match the competitive models' through-drive designs. The Land Cruiser

Fig. 4-30. *I can attest to the reliability of Land Cruiser part-time gear-drive transfer cases. My two Land Cruisers had transfer cases in excellent condition at nearly 100,000 miles. After subjecting the 1976 'Cruiser to a 280 horsepower small-block Chevrolet V-8 (including untold numbers of zero-to-sixty mph tests), I pulled a Starcraft tandem axle travel trailer with the truck. I then made a casual trip through the Rubicon. The transfer case never broke down.*

changed to a rugged split transfer case in 1981 models, although this was still a side-drive design.

1958–74 three-speed Land Cruisers have a transfer case with a lower gear ratio in low range. The four-speed models introduced in 1975 with the 2F engine have higher low range gearing.

For this reason, builders of custom off-pavement rock crawling 'Cruisers will sometimes elect to use the early transfer case mated to a domestic truck type four-speed or heavy duty five-speed transmission. Such transmissions have compound low gear ratios ranging to 7.05:1. (See geartrain upgrade chapter.) This combination provides a remarkably low "crawl ratio" for environments like the Rubicon Trail.

Some early Land Cruisers came equipped with a four-speed truck-type (compound low gear without synchromesh) transmission and a single-speed power divider instead of the customary two-speed transfer case. Fortunately, these single-speed power divider models are rare. Some early owners of three-speed Land Cruisers took advantage of the four-speed transmission, however, installing the unit and its iron bellhousing in front of their truck's two-speed transfer case.

Gear- and chain-driven part-time 4x4 systems offer a distinct two-wheel drive mode. In two-wheel drive mode, power flows from the engine through the transmission to the transfer case, then rearward to the rear axle. Here, the front propeller shaft receives no power from the transfer unit.

In 4-Wheel High or 4-Wheel Low, power flows through the front and rear driveshafts to both axles. Low

range provides a reduction gearset, with a ratio factor between 2:1 and nearly 3:1 (depending upon the year and transfer case model application). The transfer case is a crucial part of the truck's four-wheel drive system.

Toyota 4WD truck transfer units all have aluminum alloy cases. These materials are lighter yet very durable. Toyota has used both gear-drive and modern chain-drive systems with these alloy cases, proving that an aluminum case can be both reliable and lightweight.

Overall, Toyota transfer cases offer exceptional stamina and longevity. Part-time designs tend to decrease wear on the front drive system, while full-time 4x4 offers convenience and continuous 4WD advantages.

Propeller Shafts and CV-Joints

Power flow between the transfer case and drive axles on a Toyota 4WD truck is through conventional propeller shafts. Two-wheel drive trucks use a similar rear driveline between the transmission and axle.

Driveshaft U-joints are of common cross-type design, while Hi-Trac IFS 4WD front drive systems use open half-shafts with CV-joints and grease boots at each end of the half-shafts. The outer CV-joints serve as front axle knuckle joints, acting much like the enclosed Rzeppa or Birfield type joints found in solid front drive axle 4x4 models.

Fig. 4-31. *Frequently, Toyota pickups use a mid-shaft bearing (shown) and two piece rear propeller shaft (driveshaft). A single tube and slide coupler make up the typical early FJ40 Land Cruiser driveshaft.*

The longer wheelbase models employ the mid-shaft or carrier support bearing, which requires a two-piece propeller shaft. Slide couplers and splined sections compensate for axle movement by lengthening or shortening the overall driveshaft length as the axle moves with suspension travel.

Driveline service usually consists of required routine lubrication and inspection of the U-joints and spline sections. At high mileage and when damage occurs, the driveline will need repairs or overhaul. (For details on driveshaft overhaul, see service chapters.)

6. REPAIRS ON YOUR TOYOTA TRUCK

Your truck's serviceable components fit into several sub-groups. The common chassis and powertrain layout provides an easy orientation. Once familiar with your truck's design, you can readily make repairs.

Unless you must remove the crankshaft, major engine work is often possible in the chassis. The engine bays of Toyota trucks are reasonably accessible and designed to facilitate most service work. An exception to this rule are the later Toyota trucks with EFI and a full complement of power accessories.

Powertrain Orientation

You can quickly become familiar with your truck's features. Servicing propeller shafts, cables, the brakes, shock absorbers (airplane-type removable units) and wheels is fast and straightforward. On 4x4 models, the transfer case detaches from the transmission, making it easier to remove each of these units and reduce risk of damage.

Axle service, generally performed with the axle housing still in the truck, follows standard guidelines for a carrier type design. Carrier type axles have been widely used on American trucks. For Toyota, these axles have an excellent reputation for reliability.

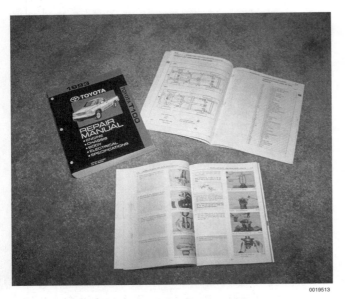

Fig. 4-32. *Official Toyota Repair Manual is your assurance of a job that meets OEM standards. If you plan to keep your truck and do your own service work, invest in a service book(s) for your particular truck model and year. (See appendix for sources of older factory guidebooks.)*

Like trained Toyota dealership mechanics, you'll find the factory service manual very valuable. By following factory recommended procedures for disassembly and installation of parts, you can perform professional level work or know when a repair is beyond the scope of your skills or tools. Your Toyota truck deserves the highest work standards and competency.

The Workplace

When servicing your truck, a clean and safe workspace is essential. Toyota truck geartrain and chassis parts are expensive. Losing parts can create lengthy delays, as many components have special order status.

By establishing neat work habits at the beginning of a repair or restoration project, you will speed up the work process and assure success. Each part has its place. Before starting a repair, lay out labelled coffee cans or similar non-breakable containers to hold the nuts and bolts.

Parts illustrations, either from this book or the detailed unit repair section of your factory Toyota shop manual, should accompany the job. Especially on an older pre-owned Toyota truck, which could have suffered years of mediocre repairs, you should account for each part illustrated in the guidebook.

Use Correct Tools

Before starting any repair, review the tools required. Toyota trucks sometimes need specialty wrenches or other devices to complete a diagnosis or repair. You will find references to such tools in this book or your factory repair manual. Avoid the loss of time and knuckle tissue by using proper tools.

Some safety basics apply when working on your truck. Repairs to the undercarriage and wheel service frequently require chassis hoisting. The use of safe floor jacks and jackstands is a must. The ideal jackstands for light truck work have four-cornered platforms and a minimum of five-ton rating per stand. Stay away from light duty tube type stands. They provide far less stability when you wrestle with a transmission or transfer case.

Jacks and Lifting

Quality hydraulic floor jacks are another safety requirement. Minimally, your floor jack must be of 1-1/2 ton or greater capacity. Whenever possible, avoid lifting the entire front or rear of the truck with a single jack. Never rely upon a hydraulic jack to support the truck while you work beneath the body or chassis. Insert jack stands immediately to avoid overloading your jack. When lifting the truck for wheel and tire removal, take extra time and use jackstands. Safety is primary.

To position your jackstands, note the design of the chassis. Your Toyota owner's handbook or a factory shop manual outlines the recommended points for lifting and positioning stands. Common support points on Toyota trucks are the frame rails and beneath the axle housing tube sections. Space jacks evenly, as near to the spring mounting points as possible. These are locations engineered to support the truck.

Avoid placing a jackstand in any area of the chassis where rocking might result. Never place a floor jack or jackstand under steering linkage, brake pipes/hoses, exhaust system parts or body sheet metal. Note the reinforced chassis sections and axle points recommended for positioning a jack. If you are uncertain about the lift points for your chassis, consult your local Toyota dealership service representative or refer to a factory repair manual covering your model.

Fig. 4-33. *Assure a margin of safety when working on your truck. These 1-1/2 ton rated floor jacks and 5-ton (per stand) rated jackstands offer features found in professional equipment. Invest in quality. Your safety is at stake.*

Fig. 4-34. *As a rule, you can position floor jacks beneath the front or rear axle housing on a solid axle 4x4 truck. Allow room to place jackstands at the frame rails or other recommended locations. Leave work room and space to remove stands.*

WARNING —
Never work under a lifted vehicle unless it is solidly supported on stands designed for the purpose. Keep the jackstands well spaced and secure. Allow an ample and unobstructed space to work. Do not work under a vehicle supported solely by a jack or other makeshift supports.

Hoisting Equipment

Powertrain and axle unit repairs involve very heavy sub-assemblies. If your service goals involve the removal and replacement of the axles, engine, transmission or transfer case, be prepared to handle these heavy units.

Consider renting the correct hoisting tool(s) or a portable engine hoist from your local rental yard. Rental firms often have transmission/transfer case jacks as well. When performing heavy work, always ask a robust friend or relative for assistance.

Hoists and specialty tools help prevent damage to your truck. Personal injuries are also less likely when hydraulic force takes the place of brute strength. The manhandling of parts, such as attempts to install a transmission by hand, can lead to broken components and severe bodily injury. This is unnecessary and avoidable.

Failure to detach all of the hardware before hoisting can result in major damage. Take time to envision the sub-assembly standing alone. Check the step-by-step service procedures and parts diagrams to make sure that you have disconnected all necessary hardware and linkages. Ask an assistant to watch progress from a different vantage point.

Fig. 4-35. *In-line sixes are long and require care during removal. A "cherry picker" hoist provides the angle and control to safely lift an engine. Use a tilt cable for added safety, and avoid swinging the engine or damaging parts. 'Cruiser engine with flywheel, clutch, and iron bellhousing nearly flattens front tires of my tractor.*

In the case of engine removal, always secure the engine with suitable chain or cables. Find balance points to assure the stability of the engine as you raise it, and also pay attention to the angle of pull. Use strong, high grade attachment hardware and, if available, an engine tilt cable that allows angle adjustments as you hoist.

Special Safety Considerations

For work around coil suspension springs, like those found on pre-1979 Hi-Lux/Pickup models (front springs), the 1991–up Land Cruisers (all four springs) and 1990–up 4Runners (rear springs), be extra careful. Also use extreme care when servicing models with front torsion bars, like the 1979–up Toyota IFS models.

Before changing springs, either allow the spring to extend and fully unload its force or constrain the spring with a special coil spring compressor. Consult your factory-level repair manual for the safest and recommended method for your model.

WARNING —
Compressed coil force exceeds a ton, and an unrestrained spring can come loose and cause severe bodily injury or damage to the truck.

Always account for the size of the transmission or transfer case assembly when placing the chassis on stands. If you intend to slide the transmission from beneath the truck, be certain that there is sufficient room. A disconnected transmission or axle, laying trapped beneath the truck, is like the story of the man who built a boat in his basement.

7. Toyota Truck Owner's Toolbox

On- and off-pavement driving environments are full of hazards and mechanical threats. The prepared truck owner carries an on-board complement of hand tools and simple diagnostic equipment.

At home, for the Toyota truck owner who performs maintenance and repairs on his or her vehicle, a variety of tools support the workshop. If you plan to work on your own truck, your tool selection must meet a wide range of service needs, including periodic maintenance and light repair work, troubleshooting, and diagnosis.

Reference Books: The Literary Tools

This book serves as an orientation to your truck and reference guide for preventive care, tune-up and diagnosis of mechanical troubles. If your skill level and ambitions include sub-assembly repairs and overhaul, I highly recommend an OEM Toyota *Repair Manual,* available through your local Toyota dealership's parts department or from a new/used book source in the case of older models.

Stick with a bonafide Toyota supported publication for a specific model and repair assemblies. These publications provide the most accurate and detailed information, greatest detail and best illustrations.

In your factory level shop manual and the owner's glovebox handbook, you will find concise information on tune-up specifications, fitup tolerances and fluid capacities. For overhaul of the engine, chassis, geartrain and electrical sub-assemblies, a factory level repair manual provides the necessary details and those specifications considered essential by Toyota truck engineers.

For over twenty-five years, my truck repair work has benefitted from the use of OEM/factory level shop manuals and professional trade manuals like MOTOR'S *Truck* and the Mitchell *Service Manual.* These books are available to the mechanical trade and other consumers.

Filling Your Toolbox

Your light truck garage requires a full assortment of metric size wrenches and tools, as Toyota has built all models to metric standards. Thread sizes and wrench sizes are all of metric proportions.

Hand tools should include metric open and box ended wrenches plus metric sockets in 1/4", 3/8" and 1/2" square drive sets. You will also need specialty sockets for spark plugs, wheel lugs and the front wheel bearing adjuster and lock nuts on 4x4s.

The wheel bearing nut wrench is a necessity. Many pre-owned 4x4 domestic trucks show signs of severely abused front wheel bearing nuts. Instead of using the correct socket, unequipped mechanics apply a hammer and chisel to the corners of the hex locking nuts. This not only

0019311

Fig. 4-36. *Front wheel bearing spindle nut wrenches are a must. This specialty socket, available through NAPA and other auto supply retailers, fits Toyota 4x4s. Such sockets are available for earlier and later hex nuts. Never use a hammer and punch to remove or tighten spindle nuts.*

ruins the nuts but also eliminates any chance of accurately measuring the torque setting on either the bearing adjusting nut or the lock nut.

4x4 front axle spindle nut wrenches are available from better retail auto parts stores. OTC, Snap-On and others produce flat-walled, 1/2" square drive hex sockets for precisely this purpose. The large nut size and small space between the nut and inner face of the hub makes use of a conventional socket or wrench impossible.

Four-wheel drive truck service also requires other specialty tools. Consult your OEM Toyota *Repair Manual* before tackling a major repair job. Make certain that you have the right tools—or resources to buy the tools. Only with the correct tools can you perform accurate and professional-level work.

Additional Chassis and Powertrain Tools

Your other chassis service tools should include tie-rod and pitman/steering arm pullers, a pickle fork and those tools commonly used for working on any other truck. For adjustments like the Toyota 4x4 kingpin bearings and the steering gear, you will need an accurate pull-type spring scale, torque wrenches and other measurement devices.

Cross-type U-joint service, a frequent truck repair procedure, may be performed successfully with a bench vise and some sockets, although more elaborate specialty tools are available. Some types of driveshaft work and other service operations may demand access to a hydraulic press, bearing/gear pullers and fixtures.

You can have such tasks done by an automotive machine shop or rent equipment at a local rental yard. The cost of equipment and frequency of use will dictate whether you should buy a hydraulic press.

For transmission and clutch alignment work, a dummy input shaft is always practical, as transmissions and attached transfer cases are very heavy—especially with a four-speed iron case Land Cruiser transmission.

Fig. 4-37. *Specialty pullers will ease steering linkage disassembly. Use of the right tool prevents damage to expensive components.*

Although axle overhaul is often a send-out repair, you can do this kind of work with the right tools and proper service data. Removing brake parts, axle shafts, wheel hubs or carrier bearings may require use of special pullers and handtools. (See your OEM Toyota shop manual.)

Precise Measurements

Competent truck repairs require precise adjustments and measurements. Shimming bearings, checking shaft end float, adjusting backlash of gears, setting wheel bearing endplay and other chores require a dial indicator. A magnetic stand or a gooseneck holding fixture will help with awkward measurements. You will also need a precision micrometer(s) for measuring shaft diameters and checking the thickness of shims, rotors and bearings.

Toyota truck service and overhaul work demand a wide range of torque wrenches: 1/4" drive inch-pound, 3/8" drive inch/foot-pound, 1/2" square drive foot-

Fig. 4-38. *Many jobs require use of a hydraulic press. If a press is beyond your budget, send your heavy bearing, gear or bushing work to an automotive machine shop. Attempts to improvise with a hammer are wasteful and dangerous.*

Fig. 4-39. *A dial indicator and magnetic stand are very useful. For adjusting wheel bearing end play and runout on shafts, you can use a dial indicator. You can also detect camshaft lobe wear with a dial indicator.*

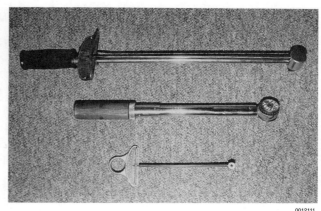

Fig. 4-40. *Torque wrenches come in a variety of sizes. This assortment serves every need from companion flange nuts to ultra-sensitive automatic transmission band adjustments.*

You can fabricate transmission locating dowels by removing the heads from long metric bolts of the correct thread pitch. Thread the bolts into the bellhousing's upper transmission mounting holes. These simple guide pins can prevent clutch disc damage during transmission installation.

pound and even a 3/4" square drive heavy duty type. If cost is prohibitive, rent or borrow a quality torque wrench. Make sure the calibration is correct.

> **NOTE —**
> Although Toyota trucks have metric dimensions and machining standards, Toyota manuals provide both metric and U.S. measurements. If you have U.S. micrometers, calipers and dial indicators, these will likely work for your Toyota repair work.

Nitty Gritty Tools

Your basic hand tools should include a hacksaw, a variety of chisels, punches, and drifts (both hard steel and malleable brass), Allen hex wrenches, and in later model trucks, Torx-type drivers. Toyota trucks have also used various Phillips head and other cross head screws.

Seal and bearing cup driver sets are optional, as careful improvisation often works satisfactorily. Wear safety goggles whenever you work with air impact tools, sharp cutting tools, hammers, chisels or punches.

Fuel Line and Brake Work Tools

For brake tubing nuts and fuel pipe fittings, a metric flare nut wrench set is mandatory. (Open end wrenches will damage compression and flare nuts.) Other brake work tools include adjuster spoon wrenches, spring pliers, retainer/hold down tools, wheel cylinder piston clamps and bleeder hose.

Disc brake work requires a pad/caliper piston spreader and a micrometer for checking disc thickness/variance. There are special hones for wheel cylinder, master cylinder and disc caliper rebuilding.

Fig. 4-41. *The right tools help assure a quality job. Both disc and drum brake systems require specialty tools. If you intend to perform brake work, invest in quality brake tools.*

Air Tools: Speed and Efficiency

Air wrenches are a major timesaver. A wide range of pneumatic tools quickly tame difficult repair jobs. In addition to time savings, air impact wrenches can add muscle to high torque, heavy duty repairs.

Fig. 4-42. *Air wrenches and other pneumatic tools save time and ease truck repair work, especially the removal and installation of shaft nuts on the transmission, transfer case or axles.*

This is especially true with older sub-assemblies suffering from semi-seized hardware and rust accumulation. (Specially hardened impact sockets should always be used with air wrenches.) Also, hardware like transmission output yoke nuts and U-joint/pinion flange nuts require high torque settings. Air tools for the removal and installation of these large nuts can eliminate the awkward use of a breaker bar and special holding fixtures.

When using air tools, avoid over tightening. Always check final torque with a torque wrench. Avoid using a pneumatic impact gun to fully torque precision fasteners.

Engine Overhaul: Tools For Hardcore Repairs

In-the-chassis engine overhaul requires common tools like a valve spring compressor, cylinder ridge reamer, hone, and ring compressor. For a major out-of-chassis rebuild, you will sublet re-boring the block, grinding the crankshaft and valves, fitting piston pins, installing cam bearings and other machine shop procedures.

Before taking on a major engine overhaul, consider the cost of tools and how often you will perform this kind of task. Professional mechanics invest constantly in specialty tools necessary to properly perform automotive work. If you want to perform professional level work, the tools needed could prove costly.

Tune-up and Engine Diagnostic Equipment

The tune-up needs of your Toyota truck engine depend upon the model and engine type. Various fuel, spark and ignition systems have different tool requirements.

Early trucks provide the arguable simplicity of a breaker point primary ignition, supported by a remote ignition coil and high tension spark cables. A common misunderstanding is that breaker points are easier to service. The more contemporary breakerless electronic distributor or distributorless ignition is equally easy to troubleshoot and repair. (See tune-up, repair and troubleshooting procedures in service chapters.)

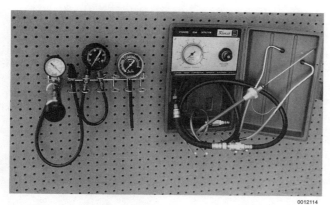

Fig. 4-43. *A vacuum pump or gauge tests ignition, carburetor and emission devices. A compression gauge and cylinder leakdown tester can diagnose internal engine troubles.*

Fig. 4-44. *Ignition tune-up tools should match your requirements. Some of my automotive tools date back thirty years. Ignition wrenches, point files, breaker cam lubricant and feeler gauges were common to the breaker point ignition era.*

Servicing your earlier Toyota truck's breaker point distributor requires traditional tune-up tools. A point feeler gauge set helps adjust the point gap. (Tappet feeler gauges are for engine valve stem clearance adjustments.) For accurate, parallel spark plug gaps, use a gapping pliers. Simpler wire-type feeler gauges work fine on used plugs and fit easily in your on-board tool kit.

A dwell-meter provides precise breaker point adjustment, while a timing light verifies timing after you have set the point dwell angle. The volt/ohm meter is an ideal companion for your electrical troubleshooting and tune-up work, offering quick, concise diagnosis of everything from shorts and open circuits to testing alternator or generator current and battery voltage.

For precise performance, setting the breaker point spring tension assures accurate spark at all engine speeds while extending point life. (Today, this is rarely necessary. Most modern replacement points have pre-set tension.)

Fig. 4-45. *A dwell meter, timing light and volt-ohmmeter help with tuning and troubleshooting. Volt-ohmmeter has become an important electronic/electrical troubleshooting tool. Some tasks require a digital volt-ohmmeter.*

Carburetor tuning requires a float height gauge and needle/seat removal tool. A complete assortment of quality screwdrivers (clutch head, straight slot, Phillips and Torx) is necessary for repairs and tuning chores.

Ignition wrenches are versatile for breaker point replacement and other electrical system repairs. A continuity tester is helpful, although the volt/ohmmeter surpasses the effectiveness of any test lamp. Although pinpoint tester probes allow testing through wire insulation, I avoid use of these testers. They can damage insulation, weaken your wiring and make the circuit susceptible to shorts.

Fig. 4-46. *Round out your tune-up tools with a fuel pump tester, vacuum gauge, float height gauge, needle/seat driver, assorted screw drivers, metric allen wrenches, Torx sockets and a distributor terminal brush. During the heyday of Land Cruiser F and early 2F in-line OHV sixes, the breaker point spring gauge served as a precision tuning tool.*

Electrical System Tools

When working alone, I find a remote starter switch handy. This permits cranking the engine from beneath the

Fig. 4-47. *Traditional Toyota starter solenoids allow reasonably easy use of remote starter switch. With this you can quickly align timing marks or check compression.*

Fig. 4-48. *Induction meters provide a quick view of starter current draw or generator/alternator output. Held over the starter cable or charge wire, meter reads magnetic field and displays this as a quantity of current.*

hood. A remote starter is helpful for compression testing. With all spark plugs removed and the high tension spark current safely isolated or eliminated (check your factory repair manual for recommended procedure), you can hold the throttle open, crank the engine and watch the compression gauge—all from beneath the hood.

Regular battery maintenance, a critical need for all trucks, requires tools for cleaning the cable terminals and posts. A battery hydrometer test is useful when you suspect a dead cell, while simpler voltmeter tests answer most battery questions.

Another quick diagnostic tool for starter and charging systems is the induction meter. These sense magnetic current flow through the starter or charge circuit cable, showing the approximate output in amperes. In seconds, you can roughly determine current flow rate or draw.

Engine Compression Versus Cylinder Leakdown

Although the compression gauge registers cranking compression (a quick reference to overall engine condition), a more reliable test is cylinder leakdown percentages. The leakdown tester pressurizes a cylinder through the spark plug hole, with the piston at top-dead-center (TDC) of its compression stroke. If the valves, rings, head gasket or castings fail to seal normally, the tester indicates the volume or percentage of the leak.

Fig. 4-49. *A leakdown tester exceeds all other methods of evaluating engine seal. Gauge can pinpointing worn valves, defective piston rings, a blown head gasket or casting cracks.*

The advantage of the leakdown test is two-fold. First, the piston rests at the point of greatest cylinder wear (maximum taper). With parts immobile, leakage and piston ring blowby show up readily. It is not uncommon for an engine to display normal cranking compression yet have 30% or higher leakdown due to poor ring seal. Eight to ten percent leakage means an engine is in top shape.

Second, the leakdown tester immediately indicates the area of the leak. If an intake valve leaks, air will blow back through the carburetor or EFI throttle body. A leaking exhaust valve sends an audible signal out the tailpipe. Piston ring wear telegraphs through the dipstick tube, oil filler hole or crankcase vent.

If a professional leakdown tester is unavailable or more costly than your budget allows, the traditional substitute is an air-hold fitting designed for changing valve springs. Screw the fitting into a spark plug hole. With the piston at TDC on its compression cycle, adjust air line pressure to a point between 60 and 80 psi. Attach the air hose coupler to the fitting. Listen for high volume leaks and pinpoint where leakage occurs.

Electronic Ignition and Emission Control Service Tools

From the mid- to late-1970s, various Toyota engines began offering high energy ignitions with an electronic module that eliminates the need for breaker points. Some earlier semi-electronic ignitions still use breaker points. Toyota's first fully electronic ignition systems still rely on vacuum and centrifugal spark advance mechanisms.

Later Toyota truck models have computer driven electronic spark and fuel management. EFI and electronic spark controls have reached their highest level of sophistication with the latest distributorless ignitions.

Fig. 4-50. Electronic ignitions have reduced service requirements. This Toyota high energy electronic distributor is accessible and serviceable. For these ignitions, the primary troubleshooting tool is a digital volt-ohmmeter.

The electronic distributor has actually reduced truck maintenance. Electronic ignitions eliminate the need to gap points and set dwell. Instead, troubleshooting now consists of ohmmeter and voltage tests. Here, a precision digital-type volt/ohmmeter proves invaluable.

Timing Light

The timing light has remained an important element of ignition tuning, as normal wear to the camshaft timing chain (or belt) and distributor drive mechanism still requires periodic tests of spark timing. The ideal timing light has a built-in advance, which allows testing the vacuum advance function and the mechanical (centrifugal) advance if so equipped.

Better timing lights are inductive variety. This means that you may hook the connector to the insulation of number-one cylinder's spark cable without disconnecting the cable from the spark plug.

Distributor machines, once popular for testing a distributor unit off the engine, have nearly become obsolete. I still prefer this method for programming distributor spark advance mechanisms. Unfortunately, few shops can provide such services any more.

Timing lights with built-in advance now use the engine as a test stand for spinning the distributor to 1000–1250 rpm (2000–2500 crankshaft rpm). The timing light's advance mechanism allows zeroing the timing to the factory TDC mark or any other degree setting within the timing light's range. This allows an accurate readout of the distributor's total spark advance.

Many Toyota truck engines have distributor vacuum and centrifugal advance mechanisms. (The late engines with EFI use the computer to adjust all timing functions.) The use of a hand held vacuum pump aids in testing the vacuum type ignition spark advance mechanism.

Stay clear of the fan when using the engine to increase distributor rpm. Fan separation or water pump shaft failure could cause severe bodily injury, even death. Limit test speeds as much as possible. (See specifications in your factory repair manual.) If you can perform tests with a cool engine, consider temporarily removing the fan belt(s) while testing the distributor on the engine. Carefully watch engine temperature, and only perform these tests while the engine remains cool.

Tools For Checking Emission Controls

A vacuum pump/pressure tester also serves as a tune-up tool for emission control devices. You can test the exhaust gas recirculation valve (EGR), found on Toyota truck engines beginning in the 1970s, with a vacuum pump. Additionally, applying vacuum to various emission control parts, like the thermal vacuum switch and bi-metallic air cleaner switch, helps locate leaks and troubles.

As many emission switches rely on coolant temperature, an accurate temperature gauge is necessary. To test the opening point for a thermal vacuum switch, for example, requires both a thermometer and vacuum test tool. Emission control troubleshooting proves far more productive when these tools are available.

On a pre-owned Toyota truck, emission control devices and hoses may be missing. Some sources you can use for restoring the system are Mitchell's *Emission Control Manual* or, again, your OEM *Toyota Repair Manual*. Either will provide diagrams and illustrations of the original equipment components. Your Toyota dealership's parts department or a good local parts store make the best sources for emission legal replacement parts.

Fig. 4-51. Fuel pump pressure affects carburetor needle and seat action. Fuel injection requires higher, precisely regulated fuel pressure. These gauges pinpoint trouble.

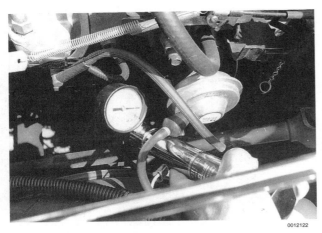

Fig. 4-52. *A hand vacuum pump/pressure gauge is valuable. Emission control devices like this Land Cruiser's EGR valve can be tested easily with a vacuum pump.*

Cooling System Tools

Toyota truck engines depend on their cooling systems for survival. Radiator cleanliness, the correct thermostat, the right coolant mixtures and a properly working fan provide the backbone of engine cooling efficiency.

For both radiator cap and cooling system tests, a hand pump tester provides quick results. Locating head gasket seepage or a cracked engine casting is also within the scope of a cooling system pressure tester.

Fig. 4-53. *STANT pressure tester can verify cooling system pressure, find leaks and determine overall condition of the cooling system. This gauge has served for fifteen years, saving a considerable amount of diagnostic time and effort.*

For anti-freeze and coolant protection tests, inexpensive radiator hydrometers are available. The reliability of your truck's radiator cap and the concentration of coolant/anti-freeze play a vital role in boil-over protection. Radiator cap pressure also raises the boiling point of the coolant mix.

It is therefore essential to maintain correct pressure in your truck's cooling system. STANT and other companies provide pressure testers for both radiator cap and radiator/cooling system diagnosis. (See the service chapter.)

Soft Tools

Conventional composition gaskets leak from the effects of heat (embrittlement), shrinkage, or their inability to fill minute gaps. The gap need not be very large—a valve cover gap of a few thousandths of an inch could easily spill an entire crankcase of oil along a remote back country trail. Aging, fatigue and oxidation can affect neoprene, rubber, cork, and even steel gaskets.

Chemical products and sealants, known in the automotive trade as "soft tools," make the ideal companion for your truck's traveling toolbox.

Fig. 4-54. *Toyota and aftermarket suppliers offer sealants and chemical soft tools that meet OEM guidelines for your truck. Specialized items, such as rubber bonder, mirror adhesive, thread locking liquids and gasket forming materials, meet rigid standards and assure a quality repair.*

RTV silicone sealants are unlike conventional gaskets. Rather than deteriorate when exposed to oils, products like Permatex/Loctite's Ultra Blue actually become more flexible, pliant and oil resistant. During engine assembly, you should use silicone products at the oil pan gasket corners, especially between cork and neoprene junctions, such as those found with intake manifold gaskets.

Along the trail or in an emergency, Ultra Blue can create a thermostat housing gasket, valve cover gasket, oil pan gasket or timing cover gasket. Ultra Blue and Ultra Copper make smart companions for off-pavement travel.

When selecting an RTV high temperature silicone for exhaust system joints and flanges, make sure the volatility level of the sealant is correct. For applications involving emission control oxygen sensors, use low-volatility sealant. Higher volatility sealants can seriously damage the sensor. Most factory warranties on emission hardware will not cover the replacement of an oxygen sensor damaged by the use of high-volatility RTV sealant.

Never use a non-automotive silicone sealant, like bathtub caulk, on your engine or geartrain parts. On manual gearboxes and axle housings, the correct RTV silicone sealant provides a sturdy, permanent fit up of parts. For some parts assemblies, Toyota now uses anaerobic sealers that cure in the absence of air. Mechanisms like gasketless transfer cases and alloy transmission housings often require anaerobic type sealants.

For axle differential covers and all oil exposed seals, automotive RTV silicone can help eliminate seepage. Toyota trucks, especially older Land Cruiser 4x4s, can flex and distort paper gaskets, and older transmission and transfer case cut gaskets are notorious for leaking. Many late powertrain components no longer use cut gaskets, substituting the more flexible silicone products.

RTV sealant allows a more direct fitup of parts, which reduces flexing, keeps hardware from loosening and helps prevent parts misalignment. Although neoprene-lipped seals still serve on many shaft surfaces, the outer jacket of these seals should also be lightly coated with automotive RTV silicone before driving the seal into place. This includes timing cover seals, transmission front shaft and output shaft seals and axle shaft seals. Although coating the jacket of a seal will not prevent the lip portion from failing, you can reduce the likelihood of housing bore-to-seal seepage.

Once you become familiar with the properties and proper uses of these sealants and adhesives, they prove as handy as your screwdrivers and wrenches. Often, soft tools provide faster, more permanent repairs than conventional gaskets—especially when your makeshift garage is in remote back country.

Miscellaneous Chores

There are other tasks that you may want to perform on your Toyota truck. In particular, front end alignment is a relatively easy job on a 4WD solid hypoid front driving axle. Adjusting toe-in may be within the scope of your service work. The setting of caster and camber, however, involves more skill, special tools and sometimes special parts. A solid front driving axle with springs in good

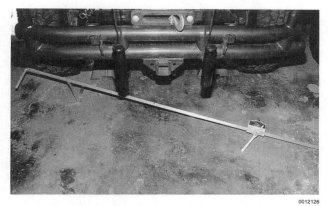

Fig. 4-55. *For front wheel alignment at home, consider an inexpensive toe-set bar. Toe-in is easy to calculate and adjust on a solid front axle truck like the Land Cruiser or pre-IFS 4WD pickup trucks.*

shape and no signs of damage seldom requires caster or camber adjustment.

Toe-in changes caused by normal wear of steering linkage takes place over time. Inexpensive toe-set alignment bars, available through Eastwood Company and other outlets, serve the home mechanic. These toe bars can easily be used on solid driving axle 4x4 trucks. Performing your truck's toe-set provides savings in both service costs and longer tire life.

A variety of miscellaneous tools serve your truck's needs. Body work and paint, detailing chores and repair of upholstery are often part of a complete restoration. With proper maintenance or restoration, your Toyota truck will deliver years of rugged service.

8. SOURCING TOYOTA TRUCK PARTS

For many models, your local Toyota truck dealer remains the most reliable parts source. Older Toyota trucks, especially Land Cruisers, have specialty suppliers.

Genuine Toyota parts provide a high standard and your assurance of proper fit-up. When restoring your truck to OEM standards, your local Toyota dealership can often assist.

The indomitable nature of Toyota trucks, the massive numbers of older Toyotas still on the road and the collectible value of particular models has encouraged aftermarket suppliers to provide replacement parts. Popularity of 1958–83 FJ40 Land Cruisers alone assures a brisk niche market for replacement Toyota parts, plus replica or rebuilt parts for models built nearly four decades ago.

Despite availability of parts, replacement Land Cruiser components can be very expensive. A brake job requiring replacement of the vacuum power booster, master cylinder and all other hydraulic cylinders, the hoses plus the brake drums and rotors can easily exceed the cost of a rebuilt/exchange long-block engine assembly.

Chassis components are available through lines like MOOG and TRW, even for many of the early pickups. For small truck engines, many with passenger car counterparts, repair pieces remain readily accessible. The sheer numbers of Toyota engines built assures the likelihood of parts availability for many years. Even the F and 2F in-line OHV Land Cruiser sixes remain popular enough for vendors to market new, reproduction or rebuilt parts.

Automotive parts outlets and machine shops throughout the entire world are very familiar with all Toyota truck engines. Perishable and fast moving items like ignition parts, filters, shock absorbers, belts and hoses are usually available through local parts outlets. Whether a new or vintage model, your Toyota truck will always be among the most popular and roadworthy vehicles in its class.

Aftermarket Geartrain Sources

Axle, transmission, driveshaft and transfer case pieces are available from a number of sources. In some instances, interchangeability of parts between Toyota models is possible. Often, though, the truck version of a gear or powertrain component is unique, which will make parts sourcing more complicated.

For older models, aftermarket parts sources often have easier access to certain parts than the modern Toyota dealership. Specialty outlets can service powertrain, chassis and body restorers. Owners of older Toyota trucks have access to engine rebuilding, re-wiring sources, fuel system repair parts, chassis/suspension and steering components, brake parts and even some new or replica body panels.

Mail-order Aftermarket

The brisk aftermarket for 4WD and off-highway vehicle parts also serves Toyota 2WD and 4WD trucks. Businesses like Specter Off-Road, BTB Products, Con-Ferr, California Mini-Truck (CMT), Downey Off-Road, Northwest Off-Road Specialties, Advance Adapters, Precision Gear, Dick Cepek and Four-Wheel Parts (Wholesalers) do a large mail-order and retail business. Product lines range from tires and off-road accessory items to winches and utility products for 4x4 trucks. Engine performance, engine conversion, geartrain, chassis lift and axle traction devices are also available.

Mail order retailers keep suburban and rural Toyota truck owners in parts. J.C. Whitney and Eastwood Company serve restorers of vintage trucks, and J.C. Whitney now caters to the burgeoning recreational truck market.

Local Parts Outlets

The local auto parts store can help with tune-up and routine service parts. Choose the best available tune-up components for your truck. Trucks demand flawless ignition performance. Bargain hunting for replacement parts is unwise.

Water crossings and foul-weather driving conditions require a much higher standard of performance from your Toyota truck. Especially with 4x4 models, water-proofing is a practical goal for your ignition distributor, coil and secondary spark cables. (See tune-up and performance chapters for ignition service and upgrades.)

Filtration

For consistent performance, use genuine Toyota replacement air, oil and fuel filters. High performance filtration systems are available from aftermarket sources like K&N Engineering.

Any Toyota truck exposed to poor quality fuels or water contamination, especially diesel engines, needs an add-on fuel filtration system. This includes diesel water trap filters and similar devices for gasoline engines that operate in regions where fuel has a high water content.

9. ASSIGNING WORK TO A SHOP

For many consumers, nurturing a second career as an automotive/truck mechanic is impractical. You may find that performing hands-on mechanical work has no appeal. Perhaps your life-style or work space is too busy for servicing your own vehicle. Sometimes, the cost of special tools or the sheer scope of a repair job ranges beyond your capacity. Chasing parts and tying up your vehicle for unreasonable periods could be costly and stressful.

Fig. 4-56. An automatic transmission or axle assembly overhaul requires special tools and skills. Unless you would enjoy a career at light truck mechanics, consider sending these types of jobs to a specialist.

Assigning such jobs to a specialist can save considerable time and assure quality workmanship. You'll save in the long run by setting your ego or the "challenge" aside and simply recognizing that you would be better off assigning the work elsewhere.

Assess the Job

Whether you enjoy servicing your vehicle or saving the cost of labor on repairs, each task has its challenges. My approach to mechanics has always taken an academic twist (which you have likely noticed by this stage of the book!). I begin all work with a thorough review of the job, starting with the factory repair manual for the vehicle. The factory manuals assist at troubleshooting problems and give step-by-step instructions for performing mechanical tasks. Each repair includes descriptions of specialty tools required.

The factory repair manual can even serve truck owners who plan to assign repairs. If you can pinpoint the actual problem, or at least narrow the field of possibilities, you have a distinct advantage when approaching a shop or dealership service facility.

The Well-Informed Customer

If you assign work to an independent shop or Toyota dealership's service department, your sense for the repairs needed can help the staff. When your diagnosis is accurate, the mechanic can focus on the actual trouble and save time—and your money—by not having to troubleshoot the job. If you suspect that extra service is being sold, your own Toyota repair manual can verify whether such service is warranted for the kind of troubles and repairs in question.

Having worked from repair orders in a truck dealership, I suggest that you approach the service department with diplomacy. Surveys often reveal that American consumers mistrust auto repair facilities. Surely, this happens with unscrupulous shops or those service operations that set profit above all other considerations, but the current trend has been toward improved customer relations.

Fig. 4-57. *Since the mid-1980s, vehicle manufacturers have placed far more importance on customer satisfaction. Ethical transactions at the service department are encouraged, often through incentives for achieving a high Customer Satisfaction Index (CSI rating). Customers are poled about service quality and ethics. As a manufacturer, Toyota ranks exceptionally high in customer satisfaction.*

Your best safeguard is information, becoming a well-informed consumer who has a sense for the task at hand and reasonable costs. In fairness, remember that the shop staff has more experience at troubleshooting and repairs. If you insist that a certain repair be done, you will pay whether that was the problem or not. When there is a gray area, you are wiser to pay for further diagnostic work and an opinion from the professional mechanic.

Flat Rate Cost Estimating

In some cases, you will find that shopping around (phoning different shops, asking friends where they do business, etc.) is an effective way to determine a fair cost for repairs. When you know the exact work needed and are certain that the truck will perform properly once a competent shop does these tasks, then you can do your own cost estimation work.

The standard practice for billing automotive service in the United States and Canada is by flat rate. This provides a basis for estimating repair costs and paying the mechanic. Flat-rate work differs substantially from actual clock time labor billing, which could vary greatly on a given job due to different mechanics' skill levels, obstacles in a given job, or tools available in the shop.

As a former fleet and dealership truck mechanic, my personal library includes flat-rate labor and parts estimating guidebooks. These books are the "trade" variety found in independent repair shops and dealerships. Automotive/truck dealerships also use the manufacturer's new vehicle warranty labor time schedules.

The flat-rate guidebook lists specific labor operations and the recognized "fair" time to perform tasks. As a consumer, you can acquire such books, new or used, and actually do your own labor estimating before shopping for repairs. It is also reasonable to ask the service writer/salesperson to provide a labor time guidebook.

Become familiar with the guide's format and how to read an estimate. For example, many procedures overlap. The overhaul of an engine will say whether the overhaul includes R&R (removal and replacement/reinstallation) of the engine from its chassis. If so indicated in the guidebook, the shop should not charge for R&R of the engine *plus* the overhaul. Tune-up procedures may include diagnosis. If so indicated, you should not pay for diagnosis as a separate procedure.

I also find the parts estimating section of these books valuable, although in fairness, parts pricing changes frequently, making guidebook prices obsolete. Here, you need current and reliable information.

Ethics and the Flat-rate System

Flat-rate pays minimal (if any) time for diagnostic work. Most vehicles brought into the shop for repair focus only on a current trouble symptom. If you want thorough service and inspection of your entire truck, that is a separate labor procedure, which bears an additional cost.

The flat-rate mechanic must make quick and accurate assessment of a problem and propose a repair procedure. When the paid repair fails to make a difference, a credibility gap develops. The shop likely contends that you should pay for the first repairs, especially if an observable improvement occurred. You, on the other hand, may feel that the shop failed to completely cure the symptoms yet took your hard earned money.

If no change in the original symptom took place, the flat rate system (when ethically applied) says that your mechanic has earned a come back. This means the mechanic absorbs the labor cost of the first repair, and sometimes the shop absorbs the parts cost. This punishment for the mechanic supposedly serves as an incentive to prevent hasty or inaccurate diagnosis.

The largest complaint that consumers have about the flat rate system is its emphasis on parts replacement. Unfortunately, since a hard hourly flat-rate program can only apply to repairs entailing R&R of parts, the system does encourage outright parts replacement.

The flat-rate system implies that automotive troubleshooting and repair estimating are an exact science. In fact, jobs like troubleshooting a late model electronic fuel and spark management system can become ensnared in the mysteries of systems overlap—or mired in the complexities and idiosyncratic nature of computer programming. Such engineering issues often reach beyond the control of a service technician.

In my view, many automotive labor procedures can fall within consistent time frames. I believe that unit repair jobs and R&R operations (like a transmission overhaul, differential rebuild, engine overhaul, alternator replacement or brake system overhaul) can be held to flat-rate criteria. However, I also believe that mechanics deserve more time for diagnostic work. This would encourage more thorough repairs and increase the likelihood of long term, preventive remedies.

Knowledge Is Your Best Friend

In the automotive flat-rate system, the R&R incentive works like this: You approach the service shop with a complaint that your truck's engine has a misfire. The eth-

Fig. 4-58.   Most repair personnel commonly replace, rather than overhaul, a sub-assembly. The argument is often cost effectiveness, even with the extreme of replacing entire commodities. Cheaper goods and cost competitive "rebuilt parts" have denigrated the role of field service technicians and mechanics who once took responsibility for actually fixing a worn or defective product or sub-assembly.

the factory recommended service guidelines. Your factory level repair manual and owner's handbook describe the normal intervals between tune-ups and other routine maintenance. Keeping a trail of maintenance work orders helps prevent an overly zealous service writer from re-selling work already done.

Ask, nicely, how the mechanic arrived at the conclusion that all of these parts need replacement. Since the diagnosis involves ignition or fuel problems, ask what diagnostic equipment aided the conclusions. Did the equipment suggest that all of these parts needed replacement to end the symptoms and restore reliable and economical operation of the engine?

Unless a problem is obvious, request thorough diagnostic procedures. Toyota's latest interactive computer diagnostic equipment and other highly advanced tools can interrogate a late fuel and spark management system or an electronically controlled transmission. If a service facility like your local Toyota dealership has such equipment, you can radically reduce the risk of engine or powertrain mis-diagnosis and unnecessary repair work. Money spent here is spent wisely.

Remember the adage "too much knowledge is dangerous." Don't flaunt your wisdom and insight. You will find that an ethical mechanic or service writer will happily share information and engage in dialog. Such an exchange is valuable, as there are many diagnostic gaps that only a professional mechanic's experience can overcome.

ical mechanic in a well-equipped shop will put the engine on an oscilloscope/infrared machine and analyze the exhaust content and ignition performance.

Let's say your six-cylinder engine shows that the #2 cylinder spark firing line is weak. (As a non-flat rate mechanic, I would check resistance of the plug wire at #2 cylinder and compare this reading with other wires.) The air filter and other parts would deserve a quick look, but once the ignition system was isolated as a problem, I'd focus on restoring the plug firing line for #2 cylinder. If I found that other wires, the distributor components or spark plugs looked marginal, some of those parts would also be replaced.

A flat rate mechanic, wanting to avoid a costly comeback and recognizing that the parts department likes additional sales, might decide to cover all possibilities. The parts list soon includes a fuel filter, air cleaner, six new platinum spark plugs, a distributor cap and rotor, a full set of spark plug wires and the PCV valve.

The service estimator/writer/salesperson usually calls the customer and gains approval for installation of these parts. Here is how the dialog might go: "Ms. Jones, your engine's misfire is ignition related, but the mechanic feels that the engine shows other wear points, and he would like to perform a complete tune-up. When was the engine tuned last?"

To the salesperson, this question is critical. If you had such work done recently, there would be no basis for buying all these parts and service. (When you use the same shop all the time, you can eliminate such game playing.) The mechanic would simply replace the one spark plug wire and bill accordingly.

As a consumer, you need to make decisions based upon your knowledge of the vehicle's service history and

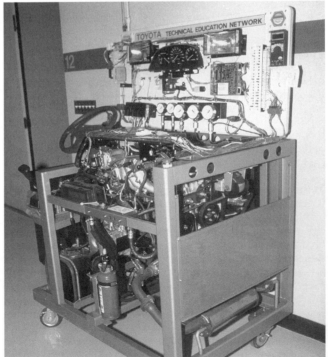

Fig. 4-59.   Toyota offers leading-edge diagnostic equipment and factory training for dealership technicians. If your truck has EFI or an electronically controlled automatic transmission, troubleshooting with advanced diagnostic equipment can offer substantial savings.

Chapter 5

Lubrication and Maintenance

REGULAR MAINTENANCE is the most important way to attain maximum service from your Toyota. Preventive care proves cost effective and assures safety and reliable performance when your truck needs it.

Preventive maintenance can reduce the risk of hazardous and costly breakdowns. As a truck fleet mechanic and heavy equipment operator, I trained at visualizing potential weaknesses in a chassis, engine and geartrain. The best place for making these observations was during routine lubrication and service.

Although much of a truck's maintenance is routine, such care has a direct effect on your safety. For 4x4 trucks that travel to remote and nearly inaccessible places, regular maintenance could prevent a serious breakdown or equipment related accident. Even simple fluid or filter changes will help ensure good engine performance and fuel efficiency when the going gets tough. A preventive maintenance schedule will keep your truck running at peak performance and extend its service life.

1. DO YOUR OWN "FULL-SERVICE" MAINTENANCE!

Most modern gasoline stations fail to meet motorists' needs. Drivers at many "Full Service" pumps pay up to two-fifths more per gallon for fuel, expecting genuine ve-

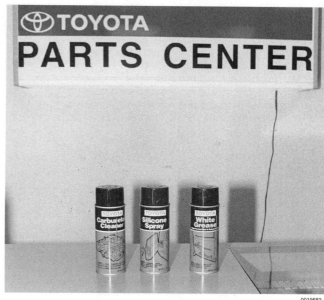

Fig. 5-2. Toyota trucks have specific lubrication and maintenance requirements. Toyota offers and recommends special gear oils, power steering fluid, wheel bearing grease, and service products. Your best assurance of long service life is quality lubrication at proscribed intervals.

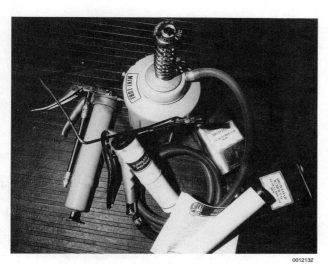

Fig. 5-1. Mini-Lube unit from C.D.U. Services in Visalia, California is a professional quality portable greasing system, ideal for the home workshop. High pressure gun makes quick chore of lubrication.

hicle care. Perhaps their windshield receives attention or the attendant will ask if the oil needs checking. After several minutes beneath the hood, some attendants return to inquire, "Where's the oil dipstick?"

When I was a high school student in the mid-Sixties, there was Bud Berrum's Chevron, at Minden, Nevada. I worked after school and summers for Bud, and he ran a real service station. We catered to customers' needs, and that meant thorough service.

If you drove into Bud's Chevron while I was on shift, your cares were over. I'd pump 94–110 octane gas into your tank, check your oil, drive belts, hoses, automatic transmission fluid, brake fluid, battery and windshield washer fluid.

Without leaving a streak, I'd whisk away the summer bugs or January ice from your windshield, wipe your sideview mirror and even clean the back window glass. If your truck's tires were cool enough, I'd check pressures at all four corners plus the spare if accessible.

What did this cost? Nothing more than your gasoline business and, if you felt like it, you could say, "Thanks!"

The lube room was always busy, with a grease job for $2.50, and a lube, oil and filter running near five dollars, depending upon the filter's cost. A thorough wheel bearing repack, even on a 4x4 truck, would be less than six dollars, including the price of new seals.

For these services, I'd take out Standard Oil's lubrication chart and look up your truck model. The guide listed each grease fitting, gear case check point and fluid type. It also noted how frequently each service procedure should be performed, and at the truck's last service, I put a dated mileage sticker on the door jamb as a reminder.

All fittings greased, the engine oil drained, gearbox and axle oil levels checked, rubber bushings dressed with rubber lube, I would inspect the clutch free-play, exhaust system and chassis. After installing a new oil pan drain plug gasket, I'd lower your truck carefully and head for the hood latch.

Armed with special data for your Toyota, I'd remove and service the oil bath air cleaner (early Land Cruisers), check the radiator coolant with a hydrometer, inspect the steering gearbox fluid level, and carefully check brake fluid—only after vacuuming or brushing away any dirt that had accumulated around the master cylinder cap(s).

Next, I'd clean the battery case, check its water and wire brush the terminals. Since early trucks had generators and wick-oiled distributors, a squirt can of motor oil was always handy. Careful not to overfill the wicks, I'd apply oil with a light squeeze of the trigger. Then, as the engine crankcase filled from the station's five-quart copper down spout can (adding two and a half more quarts to a Land Cruiser's in-line F six crankcase, plus enough oil to fill the new by-pass oil filter cartridge!), I would test all lights and the turn signals.

Finally, I'd spray lube each hood, door and tailgate hinge, the parking brake handle mechanism and even the ball bearing in your ash tray! Before the truck rolled out the door, I would vacuum the cab, clean all of the windows (inside and out), and check tire air pressures for all four tires and your Land Cruiser's rear-mounted spare.

Was this all that our customers came to expect? Oh, no! A free wash job went with each lube and oil change! Winter or summer, searing heat or low teens temperatures (complete with a frozen water bucket and wash mitten), I'd wash your truck thoroughly and be thankful for the $1.50 per hour that Bud paid me!

Well, times have changed. Few service stations offer the kind of service that was common in the 1950s and 1960s. I'm recommending that you do your own routine maintenance. You'll be better off for it. Not only will you learn more about your favorite truck, you'll also be better equipped to handle problems afield.

Bud Berrum's training gave me a darn good foundation. My first stint as a truck fleet mechanic yielded a zero breakdown record for the organization's twenty-two vehicles. I had entered the job with a thorough grasp of preventive maintenance. If you take this whole thing half as seriously as Bud and those of us who worked at the Minden Chevron station, your Toyota truck will give its all.

Defining Chassis Maintenance

Your truck's chassis, though durable and designed for longevity, requires regular maintenance. Earlier Toyota trucks demand more chassis service than later models, and Land Cruiser models, in particular, have more grease fittings and service points than the pickup trucks.

Toyota trucks use zero-maintenance synthetic and rubber bushings at most suspension wear points. Even so, such pieces still require periodic inspection and need replacement when they wear out.

According to most maintenance standards, greaseable joints on hard working models like Land Cruisers and 4WD pickups require lubrication at 1000-mile intervals, even sooner under severe service conditions. Greaseable joints also wear out over time, which means that periodic safety inspection is necessary.

Minimizing wear at friction points is the overall goal of chassis maintenance. In your Toyota truck OEM repair manual or the owner's handbook that came with the truck, you will find a chassis lubrication chart for your model. Pay close attention to the greases specified.

As a home mechanic, you will likely use a hand grease gun, which minimizes risk of grease seal damage. U-joints, in particular, require hand gun lubrication. High pressure equipment can destroy delicate seals, leaving a U-joint exposed to debris and abrasive contaminants.

Selecting Lubricants and Fluids

Various lubricants, oils, greases and fluids serve your Toyota truck. Proper oils and fluids are crucial to the safety and reliability of your vehicle. Compatibility of oils, correct quantities and proper viscosities are each essential to proper maintenance.

Earlier Toyota trucks require conventional lubricants. Typically, 90-weight gear oil fills the differential(s), manual steering gearbox, manual transmission and transfer case. With the advent of chain-drive and full-time 4x4 systems, lighter viscosity fluids have become common for the transfer case. Many late model manual gear cases also call for lighter or multi-viscosity lubricants. Always refer to your Toyota owner's handbook or repair manual when selecting proper lubricants.

Mixing oil brands and types is a mistake. Even when viscosity and type (GL or API rating) are the same, oil producers use different chemical additives with their base stocks. Strange chassis/wheel bearing greases, engine oils or gear oils may react adversely with your truck's existing lubricants. For this reason, the Toyota truck owner who maintains his or her own vehicle has a distinct advantage: the ability to assure consistent use of compatible fluids, greases and oils.

When changing engine oil, select a brand and stay with it. Carry a spare can or bottle of this type oil to assure availability in the field. Likewise, when draining and refilling the gearboxes or differential(s), adhere to a specific type and brand of lubricant.

Synthetic oils have generated much controversy. Synthetic lubricants will outperform conventional crude oil base stocks under heavy duty/severe service use. Regardless of your choice, beware of compatibility. Avoid mixing stocks of synthetic oil with either conventional oils or other synthetic brands.

Note your vehicle's warranty requirements as they relate to lubricants, oil types and ratings. When uncertain about the correct lubricant for a given area of your truck, refer to the owner's handbook or Toyota repair manual.

Fig. 5-3. Conventional chassis greases are lithium based with molybdenum disulfide additives. Many greases have all-purpose ratings, although temperature and reaction to water (washout resistance) improve with more specialized products. Many high-grade synthetic greases meet or exceed OEM specifications.

Proper Greases

Lubrication greases have become simpler in recent years. Many manufacturers use a common, multi-purpose grease for all chassis, steering linkage and wheel bearing needs. I still prefer precise greases for each application: a specified chassis/steering linkage and U-joint grease or a specific wheel bearing lubricant. Use the highest grade grease when servicing wheel bearings (usually designated as a wheel bearing grease for disc brake models).

> **WARNING —**
> *Wheel bearing adjustment is critical to vehicle safety and normal bearing life. Specifications and methods for adjusting the various Toyota wheel bearing applications differ dramatically. Consult your Toyota repair manual for the wheel bearing adjustment technique that applies to your year and model.*

Wheel bearing greases and chassis lubes have various base stocks. A major concern is compatibility of greases. Do not mix brands or types of grease. If you have just begun servicing your wheel bearings, thoroughly remove all old grease before repacking with fresh grease. (See other chapters for wheel bearing service details.)

On steering linkage and chassis joint grease fittings, simply pump fresh grease through the assembly until only new grease squeezes out. Wipe away excess with a rag. This will prevent abrasive dirt from accumulating around the joint.

> **CAUTION —**
> *Some Toyota suspension joints have full seals or a bellows-type seal that does not provide for excess grease to escape or bleed off. On these seals, you must use extreme caution not to rupture the seal by over-greasing the joint. Apply only a small amount of grease at a time.*

Gear Oil

For gear case lubricants and oils, use a slightly different strategy. Ideally, especially if your truck has higher mileage, the gear units should be drained and refilled with a high grade gear oil. As with engine oil, gear oil viscosity and type must correspond to the climate and load on your vehicle.

Once you've selected an oil brand/type, periodic inspection and topping off will be simple. If you drive your truck extensively off-pavement or to remote reaches, squeeze bottle containers are practical, easy dispensers. Major oil companies distribute gear lube in pint or quart size plastic bottles, ideal for stowage on board.

Service Intervals

The tight OEM service recommendations for early Toyota trucks, such as chassis lubrication each 1,000 miles, assume that users will give their vehicles a real workout. When subjected to severe environments or heavy work, older trucks, especially Land Cruiser 4x4s, demand closer care than later models.

Longer oil change intervals allow oil to deteriorate. The contemporary 7,500-mile oil change recommendations of many vehicle manufacturers mean that combustion contaminants will find their way into the crankcase oil for even longer periods. At such a recommended oil change point, with crude stock (conventional) oils, crankcase contamination can reach *ten percent*. On the Land Cruiser F, 2F or 3F-E engine, sludge buildup and subsequent poor oil circulation can damage the valvetrain, especially the rocker arms. On overhead camshaft engines, poor oil flow due to sludge can cause camshaft seizure and damage to the pistons.

Your truck demands the best. For maximum service life and performance, adjust oil and filter change intervals to 2,000–3,000 miles with premium grade conventional oil. Even with synthetic oil, light truck driving demands call for oil change intervals at 7,500–10,000 miles, with oil filter changes each 3,000–3,500 miles and oil top-off.

Land Cruisers and 4x4 pickup models have special requirements. Few other vehicles submerge wheel hubs and axle housings in swift running streams! If your 4x4 sees this kind of use, regular wheel bearing service and axle housing inspection is mandatory. If you stall in a fast moving stream or suspect water seepage into the wheel hubs, repack the wheel bearings immediately.

Recognizing the superior quality of modern chassis and wheel bearing greases, you can usually extend the intervals between routine wheel bearing and axle shaft service. Be certain, however, that wheel hub seals, gaskets, axle and gear unit vent hoses and the one-way vent check valves each work properly.

Synthetic Versus Mineral Oil Products

When the first Land Cruisers with F in-line OHV sixes landed on the U.S. shores, few oil choices existed. Viscosity and detergent levels were the major considerations when picking an oil. Until the 1960s, multi-viscosity oil was virtually non-existent for light truck service.

Until the advent of synthetic oils, the fundamental difference between one brand of oil and another was the additive package. Generally, we accept that a modern, multi-viscosity, high-detergent/dispersant oil will offer broader engine protection under the widest variety of engine operating conditions.

Over the last two decades, a newer debate has surfaced around mineral versus synthetic based oils and greases. This controversy will likely reign through the 1990s, but on the basis of currently available information, a higher quality synthetic oil or grease is superior to a conventional mineral or crude stock product.

A major engine killer is sludge. Plugged or restricted oil screens mean scored bearings and engine failure. Poor oil circulation always accompanies sludge. Although changing oil is the best way to resist sludge buildup, other factors also play a role. The composition of an oil, regardless of the oil drain intervals, can contribute to sludge buildup.

High temperatures also encourage sludge buildup. Teardown of a worn truck engine generally reveals sludge in the valve cover(s), timing cover, and lower block or oil pan. It is easy to spot the engine's highest temperature areas; they show the greatest sludge deposits.

The typical gasoline automotive engine, for each 100 gallons of fuel burned, produces a horrifying 1/4 to 4 pounds of nitrogen and sulfuric acid, 1 to 2 ounces of hydrochloric acid, 90 to 120 gallons of water, and 3 to 10 gallons of unburned gasoline! For the once popular lead-additive gasolines, add 6 to 10 ounces of lead salts to this medley of pollutants. At the typical 3,000-mile drain interval, petroleum oils in the crankcase have reached a contamination level of at least four percent.

How, then, do synthetic oil manufacturers extend oil change intervals up to 25,000 miles? Mobil and others claim that longer term viscosity stability (due to superior control of hydrocarbon volatility), plus greater resistance to sludge formation, contribute to these longer service cycles. Superior ingredients reduce engine heat, friction and oxidation. Higher film strength and lower volatility allow many synthetic oils to last longer and protect an engine far better than any mineral base oil currently available.

The lubrication quality, engine cooling and the cleansing action of synthetics is exceptional. Even at –40° F Mobil Delvac 1 still pours. Typical mineral based oils have already solidified. More importantly, the piston ring sealing properties of an oil largely determine the amount of contaminants that will find their way into the crankcase. Here, high grade synthetics can often provide the best protection.

Test results show Mobil 1 can operate an engine 50-degrees Fahrenheit cooler than a premium mineral based oil. As oil is responsible for cooling pistons, rings, the valvetrain, the crankshaft assembly and other critical running parts, oil temperature reduction represents a significant gain.

Under laboratory tests, high grade synthetic oils drastically reduce sludge, piston varnish, wear of metal parts and oil consumption. Prominent race engine builders confirm the merits of synthetic oils.

Notably, Smokey Yunick, quoted from a *Popular Science* interview, comments about his Indianapolis 500 engine and polyol synthetic. Upon teardown after the race, Yunick observed, "When you disassemble an engine that's been run on petroleum oil, if you examine the rings and cylinder bores with a glass, you'll see ridges and scratches—that's wear going on. With polyol [a variety of synthetic], when you take the engine apart, everything has the appearance of being chrome plated. In the engine we ran at Indianapolis, we used a polyol synthetic. When we tore the engine down, you could still see the original honing marks on the bearings...no wear at all. We put the same bearings back in because the crankshaft never touched the bearings. I've never seen that before."

Is such protection necessary for your truck? Recognizing the stresses of heavy hauling, off-road driving and harsh climates, any oil product would face hard work in a Toyota truck engine.

On the downside, many owners switching to synthetic oil on high mileage engines have trouble. Worn, varnish-coated seals and gaskets, suddenly faced with the high cleansing action and superior lubricity of synthetic oil, sometimes begin to leak. The synthetic oil has washed away the false sealing surfaces of built-up varnish and deposits.

Seals and gaskets may require upgrading before your truck's gear units or engine will adequately hold synthetic oil. Once seals meet normal standards, however, a synthetic oil could actually increase seal and gasket life.

Weigh the information available. If your Toyota truck powertrain is in top shape, relatively new or recently restored, consider use of high grade synthetic lubricants. The added protection, probability of longer component life and extension of service intervals will usually offset the higher cost of these products.

Fig. 5-4. For the 4x4 truck that makes stream crossings, consider extending the axle housing or transmission and transfer case vents upward onto the body. Using pipe thread nipples, oil resistant hose and insulated clamps, mount these vents well above the frame height. This reduces the risk of water entering important geartrain parts.

Building A Maintenance Schedule for Severe Service

Common sense should dictate your truck's service intervals. Years ago, service intervals were more frequent. Industrial and agricultural truck users changed gear lube each 300 hours, flushed the cooling system twice a year and fussed constantly over the amazing number of chassis lubrication points.

In industrial or farm work, oil bath air cleaner service takes place every 100-150 hours. (As always, dust conditions affect these figures.) If your truck has gone through twenty miles of alkaline gravel road, or at a snail's pace in high dust conditions, immediately service the oil bath air cleaner (found on early Land Cruisers) or change your later truck's felt or dry paper element.

Likewise, for 4x4 trucks, stalling the vehicle for several minutes in a thirty-inch deep, fast flowing stream raises several concerns. You will immediately need to inspect the hubs, wheel bearings, each gear unit and the engine oil for water contamination. Grease all fittings to flush out water.

Similarly, a day's play in dusty sand dunes begs a complete chassis lube and careful air cleaner service. (Keep sand from the intake area when you remove the filter.) Before performing this service, wash the chassis with a high pressure approach, like the local car wash. Toyota trucks work and play hard. Whether an older or new model, they need regular attention.

2. YOU CAN LUBE YOUR OWN TRUCK!

Many truck owners have developed a better knowledge of their vehicles by performing routine service. Aside from saving sublet labor costs, you can learn about how your truck works and contribute to its reliability.

The greatest benefit of routine service is that you can find a problem before it becomes costly to repair or causes an inopportune breakdown. You can inspect safety areas and assure that the truck's vital components are intact and properly lubricated. This, basically, is what quality preventive maintenance is all about.

You should keep an accurate account of the service you perform on the truck. Over time, various patterns emerge, and the routine begins to pay off. By keeping these records and holding onto receipts for parts purchases, you may even enhance the value of your truck at resale—especially if the sale is to an interested private party, a common method of re-selling a popular Toyota truck.

Since the best way to learn routine service is by watching close-up, I have constructed a pictorial guide for basic lubrication work. (See troubleshooting and service chapters for specific details on mechanical/safety inspection.) Compare these steps with recommended procedures found in your Toyota owner's handbook or the Toyota repair manual for your truck model.

If you follow Toyota's service interval guidelines, your truck will have a long and reliable life. Use the right tools to protect your hands and eyes, and always recycle or dispose of your drained fluids and other hazardous materials properly.

Engine Oil and Filter Change

Begin service by placing a drain pan beneath the engine's oil pan. Whether oil is warm or hot, wear an industrial rubber glove for protection. Drain oil is caustic and can contain carcinogenic agents.

Oil filters differ depending on the year of your Toyota truck. Early Toyota Land Cruiser engines have cartridge type by-pass oil filters. A replacement cartridge fits securely within the canister.

Fig. 5-5. It is better to drain the engine oil when warm. Let the oil pan drain while you perform other lube chores.

Fig. 5-6. *If your filter mounts separately from the engine, with oil lines connected to the engine block, you have a by-pass oil filter. The permanently mounted steel canister has a removable top.*

Fig. 5-8. *If your Toyota truck engine has a spin-on oil filter, replace the unit with each oil change. Remove the oil filter carefully, using a special filter wrench.*

Fig. 5-7. *While oil drains from the pan, remove the canister's top and disassemble the filter. Note parts layout. Discard the cartridge and wipe sludge and debris from the interior of the housing.*

Fig. 5-9. *It's wise to stock some new drain plug gaskets if you plan to perform your own lube and oil change service. Be careful not to cross-thread the drain plug when you install it.*

Install a new cartridge, making certain that the oil seal(s) are in place and seat squarely. Replace all pieces carefully, in the reverse order of disassembly. Re-install the mounting bolt. Install a new gasket under the mounting bolt head if wear is evident.

The first trucks to use spin-on oil filters were the Hi-Lux four-cylinder pickups and mid-1969 Land Cruisers with by-pass filtration. Use a clean shop rag to wipe the area around the filter base. Keep debris away from oil passages. Apply a small film of clean engine oil to the filter gasket before installing. Follow directions on the filter, and tighten the unit securely. Avoid overtightening, however, or you will have a very difficult time removing the filter next time.

Clean and inspect the drain plug gasket. If the gasket is damaged or worn, replace with a new gasket of the same type and size. Stock some new drain plug gaskets if you plan to perform your own lube and oil change servic-es. Be cautious when threading the drain plug, and tighten to specification.

Topside in the engine bay, wipe the oil fill cap/hole before removing the cap. Make sure that dirt cannot enter the engine during service. Pour oil carefully and avoid spilling by using a clean spout can or funnel if necessary. After filling crankcase with specified amount of oil, replace the cap and start the engine at an idle. Check for oil leaks around filter and drain plug. Shut off engine, let it set for several minutes, then re-check oil level on dipstick. Make sure oil reaches the FULL mark. Add oil as needed.

Fig. 5-10. *It's important to make sure that no dirt enters the engine through the oil filler hole. Clean the area before removing the filler cap.*

Air Filter

Toyota trucks have used two types of air filters. Older trucks use an oil-bath air cleaner, where the intake air is filtered through oil-soaked metal mesh. (See Fig. 5-11.) The second type of air cleaner is the more familiar pleated paper element.

Fig. 5-11. *If your earlier Land Cruiser engine has an oil bath air cleaner, you should service the unit every few thousand miles or at the same time that you change engine oil. An older engine with by-pass type oil filtration, like the Land Cruiser's F in-line OHV sixes through 1973 models, will benefit from frequent oil and oil filter changes.*

Whichever type, it is important to service the air cleaner regularly. A very dirty oil-bath air cleaner, unlike a paper element, will still allow reasonable engine performance. This can create the impression that the filter is okay. For maximum performance and economy, you must service the oil-bath unit more frequently when driving in dusty conditions.

To service an oil-bath air cleaner, remove the oil bath air cleaner assembly completely from the engine, then separate the filtering element from the oil cup. Clean both of these components thoroughly in a suitable solvent and allow them to air dry. Avoid the use of compressed air, as it may damage the element. Note the oil fill level, which is indicated on the inside of oil cup section. Use clean engine oil of the recommended viscosity (usually straight 30-wt., or a 20-wt. for cold temperature operation), and take care not to spill oil when re-installing the bulky oil bath assembly.

Fig. 5-12. *Oil-bath air cleaner has two components: filter element and oil cup.*

Fig. 5-13. *Oil fill level is indicated on the inside of the oil cup section.*

If your engine uses a dry paper element, you must also check it regularly. Once clogged with dirt, the dry paper element starves the engine for air. The result is similar to operating your engine with the choke on. Replace the filter element.

It is virtually impossible to thoroughly clean a dry paper element. Most manufacturers caution against reverse blowing (inside to outside) with compressed air, as this damages the paper matrix.

Fig. 5-14. *Although dry paper elements offer exceptionally good air filtration, they quickly clog when exposed to high dust levels. Check this type of filter frequently if your truck operates in a high dust environment. Disregard normal change intervals, and change the filter if you cannot see light through paper layers. It's cheap insurance for your engine.*

If you are uncertain whether the air cleaner will flow enough air, perform a simple field test. Remove the filter and gently tap its base on a clean, flat surface until loose debris has fallen free. Then, test the filter's condition by aiming it toward bright sunlight or a flashlight. (Keep away from heat or flame—the element contains flammable gasoline fumes.) Look from the center toward the light source. Rotate the cleaner slowly. A new or functional dry paper filter will show light through its wafered layers. (Compare light flow of a new filter.) If no light is visible, or light seems scarce and intermittent, assume that the filter needs replacement.

Make certain that your truck's air cleaner seals properly. Abrasive dust, seeping into the engine through an air cleaner mounting gasket leak, can quickly destroy piston rings. If the air cleaner seals look weak or seat poorly, re-

Fig. 5-15. *It is virtually impossible to thoroughly clean a dry paper element. Reverse blowing (inside to outside) with compressed air does not extend paper element life. Most manufacturers caution against such cleaning methods.*

Fig. 5-16. *For paper elements, also check the canister lid sealing gasket and where the canister seats against the carburetor. The seals must prevent dust from entering the engine.*

Fig. 5-17. *During stream fording, water drawn through the air intake snorkel can quickly pass through a paper element and into engine cylinders. If sufficient in volume, this water can act like a hydraulic ram, bending connecting rods or breaking other vital engine parts. Protect your intake system from exposure to water, and avoid use of an open faced paper filter air cleaner.*

place them immediately. Clean and ample air supply is vital to an engine's survival.

Fuel, Spark and Emission Controls

Engine service includes the fuel, spark and emission control systems. (For details on tune-up, troubleshooting and emission controls, refer to service chapters.) Closed crankcase ventilation eliminated archaic open road draft tubes. Check the positive crankcase ventilation (PCV) valve during routine service. Periodically clean or replace the valve. All Toyota trucks have closed crankcase systems.

Steering Gear

While beneath the hood, check the steering gear fluid. With the engine turned off and cool, begin by clearing away debris from the inspection plug on a manual steering gear or the power steering pump dipstick. Remove

Fig. 5-18. *The positive crankcase ventilation (PCV) valve is just one part of emission control maintenance. For more information, see Chapter 8.*

Fig. 5-19. *When checking steering fluid, clear away debris from the inspection plug (manual steering) or the power steering pump dipstick. Remove plug or dipstick, check fluid level and top off fluid, if necessary, with recommended lubricant. If you find fluid level very low, look for leaks and make repairs.*

the plug or dipstick, check fluid level and top off fluid, if necessary, with recommended lubricant. If you find fluid level very low, look for leaks and make repairs.

Manual steering gears usually use conventional gear lubricant. SAE 80-wt. or equivalent was standard on many older trucks. (In a temperate or hotter climate, 90-wt. gear lube works fine in a manual steering gear.) Power steering systems require the ATF fluid type marked on the power steering reservoir or in your truck owner's manual.

Other Lubrication Points

Early ignition distributors, generators and starters may require periodic oiling. Several drops of motor oil, applied regularly to oil wicks, assure long service. Look for spring-loaded oil caps at these locations and add clean engine oil with a squirt can. The typical manufacturer's recommendation is oiling every 1,000 miles. Avoid excess use of oil. Simply saturate the oil wicks.

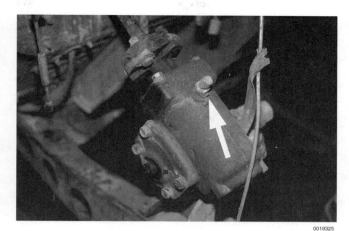

Fig. 5-20. *Manual steering gear check and fill hole (arrow).*

Chassis and Driveline Lubrication

Move to the underside of your truck. You may need to raise the vehicle. If so, always use jackstands for support.

> **WARNING —**
> *Always use jackstands to support the vehicle when raised. Never use just a jack, cinder blocks, wooden blocks, or other makeshift supports.*

Chassis and driveline lubrication includes spring shackle pivots (early models), ball joints, U-joints, steering knuckles, transmission, and differential(s). Depending on your truck model, grease the steering linkage, tie-rod ends, the drag link, the center arm or centerlink (if so equipped) and control arm bushings on earlier IFS 2WD models. *Always wipe each grease fitting before inserting clean grease, and wipe off excess after lubing.*

Fig. 5-21. *On steering linkage and suspension pivots, wipe each grease fitting with a clean rag or shop towel, then apply fresh lubricant through the grease fitting. Watch for grease to exit at open-lip type dust seals (shown). Wipe away excess grease. If the joint has a bellows type seal, apply only a small amount of grease, just enough to expand the bellows slightly.*

Fig. 5-22. *On leaf spring models, spray each bushing with rubber or silicone lubricant. Avoid use of lubricant that contains petroleum distillates or mineral/petroleum based solvents and oils. They harm rubber and cause premature wear. If your truck has a stabilizer bar, use a specified rubber lube on the bushings.*

Fig. 5-23. *Some Toyota models have grease plugs instead of fittings. You can install permanent fittings, angled or straight, if they do not interfere with moving parts.*

Fig. 5-24. *Once you have greased the front suspension and steering, lube driveshaft components, including slip collars and U-joints. Avoid overgreasing joints, especially the slip collars. If the slip collar is extended, add grease modestly. Otherwise, compression of the driveshaft will displace grease.*

Move toward the rear springs and driveshaft. On some Toyota trucks, you will find additional grease fittings that need attention, including the transfer case lever pivot (on 4WDs) and column shift linkage on some Land Cruisers.

On a 4x4 truck with closed-knuckle steering joints, the grease fill hole is much like a gearcase check point. The steering knuckle contains an axle shaft joint and upper and lower kingpin bearings. This calls for molybdenum disulfide lithium base grease (quality chassis grease) as a

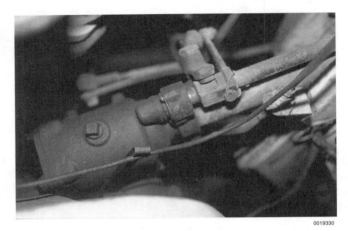

Fig. 5-25. *On earlier Toyota trucks, you will find additional grease fittings that need attention, including the transfer case lever pivot (on 4WDs) and column shift linkage on some Land Cruisers.*

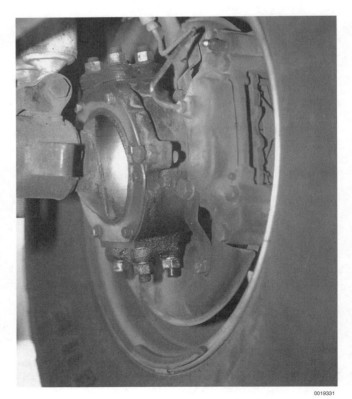

Fig. 5-26. *Closed-knuckle steering joints have a fill/inspection hole. Check grease at routine intervals*

lubricant. Use of gear lube in a steering knuckle cavity can lead to knuckle seal leaks.

When lubing closed steering knuckles, add enough grease to lightly fill the cavity. Avoid pressurizing the knuckle with grease, which could stress seals. Closed steering knuckles are notorious for seal leaks, anyway, especially at the large inner grease seal. This seal, exposed to road debris and ice, will fatigue over time.

After running on slush or ice in freezing weather, swing the front wheels to each extreme before parking your closed-knuckle equipped 4x4 truck. Knuckle wipers will sweep away debris that could otherwise freeze and damage components.

Periodic engagement of free-wheeling hubs is helpful for supplying adequate lube to upper kingpin bearings. If your truck's closed knuckle solid drive axle or later IFS 4WD front end has manual hubs, engage LOCK mode for a few miles each month. This will circulate grease at the axle shaft joints and steering kingpin bearings (on closed knuckle solid drive axles), plus reduce the effects of condensation. This is not a concern with 1991-up Land Cruiser full-time 4x4 systems or the late "A.D.D." IFS front end, which has a disconnect system and no need for free-wheeling hubs.

4x4 front axles with closed knuckles call for periodic steering knuckle/axle shaft grease changes. Front wheel bearings often call for a repack at 6,000 miles, more frequently if you run through water. If your Toyota truck is a newer model with IFS 4WD, you will find that wheel bearing re-pack intervals have been extended. For both

Fig. 5-28. Front bearing repack intervals for IFS 4WD have been extended. This older Land Cruiser full-floating front wheel hub requires more frequent attention.

Fig. 5-27. Periodically engage hubs (top) to circulate lubricant. Late A.D.D. IFS front end (bottom) has a disconnect system and no need for free-wheeling hubs.

Fig. 5-29. Since disassembly of a closed-knuckle unit is a major job, any means for extending service intervals is practical. Intact seals and superior lubricants can serve beyond the OEM clean and re-pack recommendation of 12,000 miles—if you avoid stream crossings or running in deep water. Severe service demands immediate attention.

new and older 4x4s, modern greases can lengthen periods between bearing and joint service.

On 4x4 models, the axle differentials, transfer case and manual transmission each have oil fill plugs. The fill hole also indicates the oil full mark with the vehicle stationary and level. The recommended interval for changing hard working 4x4 gear and differential lubricant is 10,000 to 15,000 miles. You should check fluid levels with each oil change or at 2,500 to 3,000 miles, and more often if seepage is apparent.

Fig. 5-30. Custom Toyota gearcase inspection/fill plug by BTB Products allows quicker access.

Your kind of driving and periods that the truck remains idle, contributes to condensation and corrosion, and governs fluid change intervals. Before multi-viscosity gear oils, SAE 80-wt. (cold weather) or 90-wt. was commonly recommended for front and rear differentials (except positive traction differentials, which require special lubricant). SAE 90-wt. accommodates the typical manual transmission and transfer case top-off. Contemporary multi-viscosity gear lubricants, including high quality synthetics, are much more resilient. These prod-

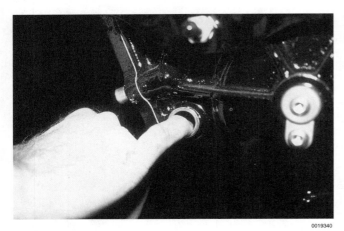

Fig. 5-31. Check fluid on level ground, using your clean finger as a dipstick. Correct level is to edge of fill hole.

Fig. 5-32. Overfilled gear cases can raise havoc, especially on 4x4 vehicles that operate on steep angles. Excess oil can cause a leak or even drive a seal loose from the gear case! If this occurs, expensive parts can starve for oil or gear lube can find its way into the clutch or emergency brake lining, ruining friction material.

ucts enable your truck to go way beyond 10,000 miles between gear lube changes.

Before removing any fill/inspection plug, clean the surrounding area. Likewise, take special care when checking an automatic transmission dipstick. Keep debris and abrasive contaminants away from openings. These are expensive gear units, responsible for taking your truck into remote back country. Cleanliness assures reliability.

With your truck on level ground, fluid should not be above the lower edge of the inspection/fill hole. If the gear unit is over full, drain it down to the lower edge of the fill hole. (Make sure your truck's chassis is level and that fluid has settled before making this determination.)

Fig. 5-33. Toyota has offered some limited slip or positive traction axles. (Many hardcore off-pavement users turn to aftermarket locking differentials like the ARB Air Locker shown here. See geartrain performance chapter for details.) Often, clutch units in OEM-type positive traction differentials require special lubricants and/or additives. A periodic flush-and-clean can slow clutch deterioration. Use only specified cleaners and lubricants when servicing your limited slip differential.

Final Lubrication Details

Several other service points require attention. Clean the battery case and cable ends, then check cells and add distilled water to the battery as necessary (do not overfill). The manifold heat riser valve, found on many engines, requires penetrating oil. With engine cold, apply a solvent/penetrant oil, like WD-40, to the riser shaft, then test to see that it moves freely and opens smoothly as the engine warms.

Fig. 5-34. *Where applicable, periodically lube the manifold heat riser valve. Make sure engine is cold when performing this service.*

Remove the speedometer cable occasionally, wipe it down and dress with speedometer cable lubricant. On early Toyota trucks, treat all control cables (steel conduit sleeve type) with a penetrating oil such as WD-40. Some lithium sprays work equally well. Always wipe off excess lube to avoid attracting dirt. If cables still balk, remove and clean them thoroughly, then lubricate with a suitable graphite or lithium based grease.

Fig. 5-35. *White lithium and silicone sprays work well on hood and tailgate hinges, latches, strikers and locks. Lithium acts more like a grease, while silicone penetrates and frees up sticky mechanisms.*

Fig. 5-36. *For rubber parts and seals, use silicone based products that are free of solvents or petroleum distillates. (303 Protectant is an exceptional anti-oxidant for trim, dashpads, tires, chassis rubber and door edge seals.) Read labels carefully to understand a product's intended use. Choose a protectant that will dry completely. Wipe off excess and keep these products away from painted surfaces.*

3. STORING YOUR TRUCK FOR LONG PERIODS

Many trucks, especially recreational models that serve seasonally, park for long periods of time. Some 4x4 models are strictly for snowplowing, idle for the other three seasons of the year. Arctic trucks often hibernate through deep freeze periods, immobile from early fall to the beginning of summer. A collectible FJ25 or early FJ40-series Land Cruiser might undergo long storage to protect its value.

When storing your Toyota truck for long periods, consider the temperature, air quality and humidity. Major areas of concern are the engine, geartrain, cooling and electrical systems, the body and interior, fuel system, tires and brakes.

Body and Upholstery

Preserving your truck's body and upholstery involves many of the chemicals used for detailing work. For exterior painted surfaces, a heavy coat of wax will help protect the finish. For long storage, apply two coats of a carnauba-base wax, buffing lightly. (A coat of cosmoline has been the long-term approach for severe climate storage or salty air.)

Vinyl upholstery, along with the dash pad, tire sidewalls and all other plastic and rubber areas, requires a liberal coating of a protectant/anti-oxidant treatment. Professional rustproofing treatment, hot wax, and spray undercoatings can help protect the underside of the body and chassis.

You can apply some products at home, like rubberized spray undercoating. Whenever your truck faces exposure to corrosive environments, especially salted roads or sea air, take every precaution to eliminate oxidation of bare metal.

Once the body, frame/chassis, wheels and tires have been thoroughly protected, you should blanket the truck with a fitted cover. An enclosed garage, barn or storage shed will further protect your truck from elemental damage. Prevent exposure to bird droppings, tree sap and other corrosive hazards that might impair wax protection and destroy paint.

Engine Protection During Dormancy

Before storing your truck, change the engine oil and install a new oil filter. Run the engine to warm up and assure clean oil flow throughout the system. Install a new air filter element (paper-type), and make sure that it fits securely. If your older Toyota Land Cruiser has an oil bath air cleaner, thoroughly clean the unit and change the oil. Be sure belts and hoses are in top condition and apply a quality belt dressing or protectant to each drive belt.

If the engine will set for a very long period, or if high humidity and varied temperatures are a factor, protect the engine's cylinder walls, valve guides, valve seats, valves and piston rings. Remove the spark plugs and squirt approximately two tablespoons of Marvel Mystery Oil or a similar fine lubricant into each cylinder.

Reinstall the spark plugs, and with the coil wire disconnected or ignition rotor removed, crank the engine just a few revolutions. This will coat the cylinder walls and other metal in the upper cylinders with a film of oil. Leave the rotor out or ignition coil wire disconnected as a safety and anti-theft measure during storage.
After the storage period, before attempting a start up, crank the engine over with the rotor or coil wire removed.

Fig. 5-37. *Removal of coil wire and rotor during storage discourages theft. After long storage period, you can crank the engine without start-up to circulate oil.*

This will pump the fine oil from the cylinders. Remove and clean the spark plugs in solvent or install a fresh set of spark plugs.

Reinstall the ignition rotor or coil wire. Start the engine, maintaining the lowest practical rpm during start-up and initial warm-up. Oil pressure should appear immediately upon start-up, quickly registering normal on the gauge.

Protect the Fuel System

If water contamination in the fuel is a concern, run a can of fuel system de-icer through the fuel tank before storing your truck. Carburetor cleaners with alcohol or other water bonding dispersants may be sprayed directly into the float bowl through the carburetor bowl's vent opening. A teaspoonful is plenty. After setting for a few minutes, run the engine to purge the float bowl of contaminants.

Fig. 5-38. *Oil bath air cleaner and sediment bowl fuel filters are common to earlier Toyota Land Cruiser models. Drain and clean bowl screen before long storage. This will remove trapped water that could corrode parts.*

Cooling System and Storage

The cooling system requires fresh anti-freeze/coolant (ethylene glycol type) with a 50/50 mixture that tests, minimally, to −34° F or lower on a hydrometer. Coolant must be thoroughly mixed, with a quality water pump lubricant/anti-rust agent added. An alternative to water pump lubricant is a small amount of traditional "soluble oil," a vegetable based, non-mineral (non-petroleum) oil that can also help preserve rubber parts.

Unless the storage area will be subject to temperatures below —34°, avoid heavier concentrations of anti-freeze. Pure anti-freeze has an insufficient expansion rate and can actually cause engine castings to crack at temperature extremes. Poor expansion capability will also cause an overly concentrated coolant mixture to boil over. Follow the mixture chart and manufacturer's recommendations described on the anti-freeze container.

Tighten all hose clamps, inspect hoses for cracking or weather checking and consider installing a new thermostat if the system requires flushing or draining. When

Fig. 5-39. Radiator hydrometer tests specific gravity of coolant/ anti-freeze. Weak concentrations allow freeze-up and also lower the boiling point. Excessive concentration adversely impacts the expansion rate of coolant mix.

Fig. 5-40. When greasing steering linkage, suspension or driveline parts, grease fittings sometimes fail. These fittings are replaceable. Take care not to overfill joints, as seals like these may rupture. Ruptured seals allow contamination of the joint or bushing.

running the engine and circulating new coolant, be certain to turn on and operate the heater. Coolant/anti-freeze of proper mix must fill the heater core , coolant recovery tank, and all hoses, or damage from freezing could result.

Chassis and Geartrain Preservation

Several powertrain items require attention. Lubricate the U-joints and all other grease fittings on your truck. With open lip-type (non-bellows) seals, force out old chassis lube and make certain fresh grease squeezes from each joint. Wipe excess grease from the area. Dress rubber shock absorber, spring and sway bar bushings with rubber lubricant to prevent surface oxidation and dehydration.

If your truck is anywhere near due for a wheel bearing repack, buy new front wheel hub seals and fresh grease. Remove the wheels and hubs, and inspect for any signs of moisture damage. Thoroughly clean, closely inspect and repack the bearings. Fit new seals during installation. (For details on front wheel bearing repack, see the service chapter.)

Check fluid levels in each gear case and the axle/differential units. Note the smell and appearance of gear oil. (A burnt, acrid odor indicates older and likely worn gear lube.) Signs of damaging moisture are a milky, greyish appearance in the fluid or around the housing cavity.

If signs of moisture appear in a manual transmission, axle housing or transfer case, drain and flush the unit with a specified flushing oil, an appropriate solvent or clean kerosene. (During the flushing operation, drive the truck at minimal load for a very short distance to thoroughly wash the gear housing walls. Do not pull a load or allow gearcase to get hot.) Drain unit immediately and

completely. Refill with fresh, proper grade gear oil, and drive the truck to circulate the new oil.

Major damage to expensive bearings, gears and shafts will result from unchecked water or condensation in the gear cases. Check all vents from the axle housings, transfer case and transmission. One-way check valves must be clean and seat properly to prevent moisture from entering gearcases during storage period.

Fig. 5-41. One-way type check valves (arrow) allow transfer case, transmission and axle housings to vent pressure. Make sure these valves are clean and seating properly to prevent moisture from entering the gear unit.

If you are storing an automatic transmission equipped truck for a lengthy period, change the transmission fluid and filter. Operate the truck long enough to fully circulate new fluid. ATF is a high detergent oil, and fresh fluid purges older, acidic lubricant that might otherwise act on seals. Fresh fluid also helps flush varnish forming agents from the sensitive valve body and friction lining.

Fig. 5-42. *Many Toyota trucks benefit from power steering. With the engine stopped, check ATF fluid at the power steering reservoir fill cap. Keep debris from entering the reservoir. Remove dipstick and wipe with a clean (lint-free) rag. Note "Hot" and "Cold" levels indicated on dipstick. Top off with ATF or power steering fluid specified for your truck.*

Prepping the Electrical System for Storage

Before you place your truck on furlough, the electrical system requires attention. Disconnect the battery cables to eliminate voltage drains from the clock or elsewhere. Clean the outer battery case thoroughly with a solution of warm water and baking soda. Use an inexpensive nylon paint brush.

> *CAUTION —*
> *Make certain that the cleaning solution does not enter any of the battery cells. Rinse away all cleaning solution with clean water. Avoid splashing cleaning solution onto painted surfaces. Wear protective goggles.*

If you remove the battery, make sure it rests on a nonconductive surface and in a state of full charge at the time of storage. Remember that a fully discharged battery, at low specific gravity, can freeze and crack.

Battery specialists recommend storage of batteries in a temperate setting. If at all possible, avoid exposing the battery to extremes of heat or cold, and always store away from spark or flame sources. After storage, bring the battery slowly up to full charge with a low amperage trickle charger. (Make certain that the charger has a built-in voltage regulator to prevent overcharging.)

Brake System and Storage

Hydraulic brake fluid is hygroscopic and readily bonds with water. On Toyota trucks, the master cylinder vents to atmosphere. Such brake systems are especially vulnerable to moisture contamination. Eventually, especially if you store the vehicle for long periods, moisture can seep into the system, lower the boiling point of the brake fluid, cause oxidation damage and pit or corrode the hydraulic brake cylinders.

As a minimal precaution, especially with an atmospherically vented hydraulic master cylinder, you should routinely flush fresh brake fluid through the hydraulic system. (A power bleeder speeds up this procedure.) The aim is to force old fluid, and any contaminants suspended in that fluid, out of the system.

The traditional, more involved method is to flush the system with denatured alcohol or a specially formulated hydraulic brake system flushing compound, then disassemble each wheel cylinder, caliper and the master cylinder. Air dry the lines and cylinders. Coat cylinder bores with special brake/rubber parts assembly lube or brake fluid, then install new rubber cups and seals. Fill/bleed the system with clean DOT 3 or higher grade brake fluid. (See service chapters for details on brake work.)

Along with a thorough flushing and installation of new rubber parts, you might consider switching to silicone brake fluid. Although expensive, silicone brake fluid nearly eliminates the water absorption problem. If you store your truck regularly, for long periods, silicone brake fluid could be practical.

When converting from conventional brake fluid to silicone, the system must be entirely purged of conventional brake fluid. (Use the silicone brake fluid during assembly of cylinder rubber parts.) Follow instructions carefully to avoid mixing incompatible chemistry. Make sure silicone brake fluid meets your vehicle's DOT brake fluid requirements.

> *WARNING —*
> *Silicone fluid and conventional brake fluid are incompatible. Do not mix or blend these substances.*

Unfortunately, even though Toyota switched to a safer dual braking system in 1967, the master cylinders remained vented to atmosphere. By contrast, most 1967-up domestic trucks are less prone to absorbing moisture. They have master cylinder covers with sealed bellows-type gaskets that offer far more protection from atmospheric contamination.

Even with a bellows seal master cylinder, I recommend periodic purging of old brake fluid using the pressure bleeding method. This reduces moisture content in the brake fluid and helps maintain a normal boiling point for safe braking.

Tires and Climate

If your truck will be dormant for more than a few months, raise the chassis and place the frame safely on jack stands. (See your Toyota truck owner's handbook or repair manual for jacking locations and where to place stands.) Tires suffer from long storage periods, which can cause sidewall distortion and damage plies or radial belts—especially if your Toyota truck happens to be a mini- or compact motorhome model! Raise the truck enough to take the weight off the tires.

Climate plays a role in the precautions you take. In desert environments, the concern is ultraviolet damage and dehydration of rubber seals and bushings. Arctic regions require protection from freezing. Moist and salt air regions call for anti-rust measures. Consider the environmental stresses that your truck will face, and prepare accordingly.

Chapter 6

Troubleshooting and Minor Adjustments

TYPICALLY, A TRUCK WILL TAKE a lot of abuse, especially when equipped with four-wheel drive and forced to carry severe loads on bad roads. While routine maintenance and inspection will enhance any truck's reliability, your talent at making emergency field repairs could mean the difference between walking or driving back to civilization.

After three decades of exposure to two- and four-wheel drive trucks, I cannot overstate the need for preventive care, those service steps that turn up *potential* problems. A truck will provide signs and symptoms before most parts fail, so the best tactic for preventing a breakdown is periodic inspection of the chassis and powertrain. Your lubrication and tune-up service should include a thorough look at the chassis, axle and driveline components.

Aftermath of a Hard Day's Work

The off-pavement work truck stretches over rocks and logs, stressing its chassis to the limit. Springs and shackles twist in every direction while bushings and joints battle awkward angles. As the dust settles from a day of tough work, your truck needs a thorough inspection.

Look beneath the front bumper at the drive axle, steering linkage, steering shock/damper, stabilizer bar, leaf springs, front leaf spring shackles, or the leading

links and coil springs (1991-up Land Cruisers). On IFS trucks, the vulnerable items on off-pavement 4WD models include the steering linkage, steering stabilizer shock, A-arms and vertical frame members that support the lower control arms.

Fig. 6-2. Spring flexing loosens U-bolts and clamps. Look for misaligned leafs, broken plates and spring sag. Toyota Land Cruisers through 1990 and 4WD pickups through 1985 have leaf-type front and rear springs. Rear leaf springs have served on all Toyota trucks until the 1990-up 4Runner and 1991-up Land Cruiser. Late 4Runners and Land Cruisers have coil springs at the rear.

Fig. 6-1. Until 1986, all Toyota 4x4s have solid front driving axles. 1986-up Land Cruiser models retain the solid axle design. Pickups and 4Runners changed to an IFS 4WD chassis design in 1986. Solid front axles, like that found on this luxurious 1995 DJ model Land Cruiser, can handle a good amount of off-pavement pounding. Solid front and rear driving axles have served on the most rugged 4x4 trucks in the world. IFS 4WD has also proven itself.

Fig. 6-3. Steering linkage, stabilizer shock/damper and tie-rod require close inspection. On solid front axle 4x4s, the single tie-rod and relay rod operate in front of the axle housing, vulnerable to rocks, stumps and debris.

Look for oil seepage or cracks along the axle housing unit, especially gear lube leaking where the axle housing sections mate up. Extreme jarring, twisting and rock banging can dislodge, distort or crack an axle housing.

Note the condition of the springs. Look for broken or out-of-line leafs and bent U-bolts. If a leaf spring appears offset from its perch on the axle, suspect a broken center bolt. Leafs out of alignment mean loose U-bolts or distorted spring clamps. Extreme flexing and twisting is the usual cause.

The tie-rod, relay rod and steering shock/damper are vulnerable on 4x4 trucks. Due to available space and the necessary position of the front driveshaft, the steering linkage mounts forward of the axle housing. Especially on 4x4s with a solid axle housing, the long tie-rod and hydraulic steering shock/damper face obstacles like rocks, tree stumps and debris.

Veteran four-wheelers know where this tie-rod rides. Aware driving involves a sense for low hanging and vulnerable chassis parts. When knocking around on boulder-strewn trails, protect your truck's axle housing(s), suspension, steering, driveshafts, brakes, fuel system and other chassis/powertrain components. Become familiar with exposed, expensive pieces.

Check the stabilizer bar (if so equipped), its support links and bushings. These parts really flex, especially off-pavement. Look closely at the brake hoses and other brake hardware. Brush, tree limbs and loose rock can damage sensitive safety items. Learn to scan along brake and fuel lines; watch for kinks or rock damage. In the worst cases, it is possible to rip whole sections of brake pipe loose from the frame or rear axle housing. Accidently backing into a rock or tree stump can crush the rear axle housing brake piping and impair brake action.

Before finishing your front end inspection, pay close attention to the steering knuckle joints. All 2WD and 4WD IFS front ends use ball-joint pivots at the upper and lower ends of each steering knuckle. Solid axle 4WD models use kingpin bearings at the upper and lower steering knuckle pivots. Vulnerable pieces in IFS steering linkage systems include the left and right tie-rods, the center link (relay rod), the idler arm and the pitman arm.

A broken or loose knuckle joint will impair steering and place your safety at extreme risk. Severe off-pavement impact can break a kingpin bearing race, crack a knuckle casting or damage a steering knuckle ball joint. On closed-knuckle 4WD front ends, watch for spindle separation from the knuckle casting and for cracks at the spindle, especially if your truck has aftermarket wide wheels and big tires.

Inspect the rear axle housing for leaks, cracks or broken welds. Springs and spring supports demand a close look for cracks, bushing wear, fatigue and damage. Look for emergency brake cable damage, signs of water in the axle housing and evidence of mud or sand in brake components.

Inspect the exhaust system for leaks, dents, kinks or any other damage that might impair flow or create unsafe and noxious fumes. Tap gently on the muffler(s) with a plastic or rubber head hammer while listening for loose and rattling internal baffles.

Driveshafts, flexing and moving constantly, are also susceptible to wear and damage. If your Toyota truck wallows constantly along rocky trails and through creek beds, keep U-joint flanges and driveshaft tubes away from rocks and stumps. It is relatively easy to spring (bend) a driveshaft tube.

Memorize the original appearance of your truck's undercarriage. When inspecting the chassis, use that image as your standard. Especially when subject to off-pavement hazards, Toyota truck reliability depends on good driving habits, the willingness to pick sensible travel routes and unrelenting chassis inspection. Skid plates are not enough.

0019159

Fig. 6-4.   Brake hoses and brake/fuel pipes require close inspection. In rough terrain, these items face many obstacles.

0019160

Fig. 6-5.   Steering knuckles, spindles, kingpin/steering knuckle bearings or A-arm ball-joint pivotal supports are vulnerable to impact damage. Inspect these safety components regularly.

1. GUIDE TO TROUBLESHOOTING

Engine failure is intimidating, especially if you use your truck in remote country or pull a conventional or light fifth wheel trailer. Your engine can quit for many reasons, and if unprepared while in the back country, you can burn as much shoe leather over a shorted ignition module as a seized connecting rod bearing.

Maintaining your Toyota truck includes troubleshooting savvy and the means to remedy common problems. Whether you perform repairs or send the work to a qualified shop, troubleshooting skill increases self-sufficiency and heightens your understanding. (For additional details on service work, see service chapters.)

NOTE —
Overhaul of specific powertrain, geartrain and chassis components is beyond the goals of this book. For overhaul and unit repair guidelines, refer to the OEM Toyota Repair Manual(s) for your model.

Lack Of Power

Low Compression can result from a pressure leak at one or more cylinders. Loss of compression suggests several possibilities: leaking or misadjusted intake or exhaust valves, worn or defective piston rings, a blown head gasket, casting cracks, or a severely worn camshaft and timing chain or gear set. Coolant loss into the engine oil (turning it milky) indicates a cracked cylinder head or engine block—or a leaking head gasket.

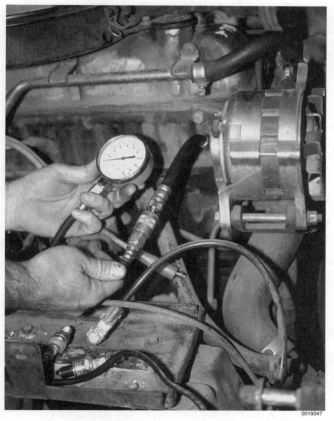

Fig. 6-6. A compression test reveals loss of cylinder pressure. When two adjacent cylinders show low pressure, suspect a warped cylinder head or a head gasket failure. Especially with an alloy cylinder head(s), severe engine overheat can warp or crack castings.

Diagnosing low compression requires a compression gauge or cylinder leakdown tester. (See other chapters for details on these test procedures.) A field testing method involves shorting cylinder spark leads, one at a time, and comparing the engine rpm drop per cylinder. A high rpm drop indicates a strong cylinder, while a low rpm drop reveals a cylinder that has either low compression or an ignition, fuel or vacuum related problem.

Internal Friction indicates major engine trouble. If the engine will not crank easily, first rule out obvious battery/starter/electrical problems. Place the transmission in neutral or Park (on an automatic), and block the wheels. Remove all spark plugs and rotate the crankshaft with a socket and ratchet. The engine should turn freely, with only the moderate resistance of the valvetrain.

Fig. 6-7. Block the vehicle's wheels, remove the spark plugs, and rotate the crankshaft with the transmission in neutral or Park (on an automatic). High resistance indicates internal damage.

To rule out manual transmission damage as a possible cause, have a helper disengage the clutch (depress the pedal) while you rotate the crankshaft. If the engine will not turn freely, suspect bearing, piston, connecting rod or valve damage.

When water (either drawn through the intake system or originating as an internal leak) prevents engine rotation, removing the spark plugs allows liquid to escape. Coolant or water exiting the cylinders suggests the possibility of severe damage, even bent connecting rods or damaged rod bearings. On some Toyota 4WD pickups, the air cleaner intake snorkel originates near the grille opening. A fast plunge into a moderately deep stream, with the engine spinning at a brisk rpm, can suck enough water through the snorkel and air filter to "hydraulic" the engine. The pistons and connecting rods will try to compress this incoming water. Rods either bend or break if the volume of water and crankshaft rotational force are great enough.

Overheat/Seizure means serious trouble. If the engine will not crank or rotate after a severe overheat or running without oil, major damage has occurred. Pistons can distort from heat, gall the cylinder walls and destroy crankshaft bearings. Lubrication generally fails during a severe overheat, causing glazing and scoring as the piston rings drag on cylinder walls. Valve stems can seize in their guides, and the camshaft may seize in its bearings. Casting cracks from severe overheat are common, especially near exhaust valve seats and along cylinder walls.

CAUTION —
If the camshaft seizes on OHC and DOHC engines, the spinning engine can drive pistons into the valves that stand open.

Fig. 6-8. *Radiator damage, overheat and loss of coolant are more than an inconvenience. Piston/cylinder wall galling and engine bearing damage result from extreme heat. The amount of heat involved will determine the extent of damage.*

The least gloomy prospect is that a cylinder head (possibly both heads on a V-6) has warped, resulting in a head gasket failure. Coolant fills the cylinders, locking up the engine. Even here, the risk of bent connecting rods and other crankshaft assembly damage remains.

Fuel Starvation results from low fuel supply pressure or volume. In addition to fuel pump malfunctions and restrictions in the supply or return lines, EFI/MPI-equipped engines can suffer from pressure regulator defects or fouled/defective injectors. A sticking carburetor float needle, although rare, is another source of trouble for carbureted engines.

Testing fuel pump pressure requires a special gauge. Pump flow volume is easier to determine. Before suspecting the fuel pump volume, flow rate or carburetion/injection troubles, consider the fuel filter(s) or the fuel line inlet filter ("sock") in the gas tank. Especially with a paper element fuel filter, a single fill-up with watery gasoline is enough to stop fuel flow.

Weak Ignition creates hard-starting problems and a lack of power. On older engines with breaker points, rubbing block wear retards ignition timing, and the points resistance increases with pitting and arcing. Condenser, rotor, distributor cap and spark cable defects can also weaken spark output.

Fig. 6-9. *A fuel pump pressure gauge quickly determines pressure output. Before condemning the pump or other expensive items, look to the simpler causes, like a plugged fuel filter.*

Fig. 6-10. *Wiring shorts, fraying and bad grounds cause the majority of field failures. Look closely at routed wires and connections.*

Check the distributor shaft for excess runout (sideplay), a common cause of erratic spark output and errant ignition timing. Dwell angle variance of more than two degrees is a sign of distributor defects. Mechanics often condemn the coil, although a coil is far less likely to fail than the breaker points, condenser, primary and secondary wiring or the distributor shaft bushings on a high mileage ignition.

Breaker point and electronic ignitions are vulnerable to wiring failures and poor connections (due to corrosion or dirt). Consider this a major cause of poor ignition performance. Check carefully for insulation breakdown and shorts to ground. Especially on an older Toyota truck with embrittled wire insulation, wiring failures and shorts can be a prime source of trouble.

Test wires between junctions. (You will find engine and chassis wiring diagrams for your Toyota truck in the OEM repair manual. Toyota manuals have a separate section for electrical and wiring needs.) If an electrical or ignition problem is not readily apparent, test circuits with your volt-ohmmeter or have the work done at a local service garage or Toyota dealership that has special testing equipment.

Vacuum Leaks, if severe, will prevent the engine from running. A sufficient leak creates low manifold pressure, stalling, lean air/fuel mixtures and backfire. Even small vacuum leaks can lean the air/fuel mixture, cause idle speed to drop and prevent smooth performance.

Fig. 6-11. A non-volatile spray solvent or penetrating oil helps detect engine vacuum leaks. With the engine idling, spray toward the intake manifold sealing edges and the carburetor base. If rpm changes, there is a leak.

The engine's sudden inability to idle indicates a vacuum leak. Check the PCV valve, all vacuum hoses, the distributor advance diaphragm and the transmission vacuum modulator and hoses, if so equipped. (On earlier Land Cruisers equipped with the vacuum front axle drive shift mechanism, add this item to the list of potential vacuum leaks.) Intake manifold bolts can loosen over time, resulting in poor gasket sealing and another possible vacuum loss. Periodically check torque at the manifold bolts and the carburetor mounting nuts or bolts. As the engine idles, spray a mist of fine penetrating oil (non-volatile) along the gasket sealing edges. Listen for a change in engine speed. This indicates a leak.

WARNING —
Always keep volatile solvents away from hot engine parts. Use a spray substance that will not ignite if it contacts a hot surface or spark.

Engine Timing is crucial. Three essentials for optimal engine performance are 1) normal compression, 2) correct valve lift and 3) proper valve timing. When troubleshoot-

ing reaches beyond spark timing adjustment, changing a fuel filter or basic tuning, make certain your engine meets these requirements.

Measure compression with a compression gauge or cylinder leakdown tester. (See tune-up chapter for more details.) Verify valve lift by removing the valve cover(s) and/or pushrod and lifter cover (Toyota F, 2F and 3F-E engines). Depending upon the test requirements found in your Toyota repair manual, measure either the height of each valve stem tip from its closed position to fully open or the amount of lift at the valve lifters (OHV in-line sixes). Respectively, this is the total valve or lifter/tappet lift produced by each camshaft lobe.

Fig. 6-12. A worn camshaft lobe or improper valve adjustment will affect valve lift. Always check valve adjustment or tappet clearance before testing valve lift.

In addition to valve lift, make note of valve timing variances that result from a severely worn timing chain, worn timing belt or defective timing gearset. If ignition timing has suddenly become retarded, yet the distributor housing remains securely clamped to the engine block, suspect excess slack in the timing chain, worn sprockets, a bad timing belt or defective timing gears. (A severely worn valve timing mechanism can allow valve timing to jump one or more teeth. When the camshaft drives the ignition distributor, this type of problem appears as suddenly retarded ignition timing.)

Clutch Slippage and related troubles are relatively easy to detect. Before testing, check and adjust the clutch at the release arm. (See service chapters for clutch adjustment tips.) Make certain that the clutch disengages and engages properly. Through the release arm opening in the bellhousing, observe whether the throwout bearing actually moves the clutch release fingers or levers.

WARNING —
Keep your fingers away from moving linkage while an assistant depresses the clutch pedal. Force of clutch linkage could easily crush a finger. Also, the clutch housing's release arm opening has sharp edges.

Fig. 6-13. *Always check clutch adjustment at the release arm. Pedal play alone is misleading, as linkage wear can masquerade as clutch free play.*

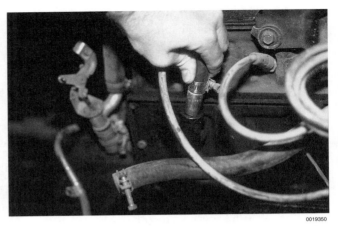

Fig. 6-14. *Tune troubles include spark timing, fuel supply and emission control components. Your truck's engine cannot idle or run properly with a defective EGR valve or even a plugged PCV valve (shown here).*

If the clutch release arm has insufficient movement, check the clutch pedal height and pushrod-to-master cylinder piston clearance. Note excessive play and correct the cause. As Toyota trucks use a hydraulic clutch linkage, first inspect the fluid level. Check for leaks at the cylinders, pipes and hoses, then bleed any air from the system. Repair or replace defective hydraulic parts.

I like to periodically flush fresh brake fluid through the hydraulic clutch linkage system. This purges the system of suspended contaminants, accumulated moisture and corrosive agents. A brake fluid flush, air bleeding, and periodic clutch adjustment helps assure smooth action and a longer life for seals and hoses.

Now drive down a deserted road at 15–20 mph. Depress the clutch pedal, and place the transmission in high gear. Raise engine speed to 2500 rpm and rapidly release the clutch pedal. Engine rpm should drop immediately. If rpm decreases gradually, the clutch unit is probably weak. Sources of trouble could include worn clutch cover springs; a worn or glazed clutch plate; a glazed or worn flywheel face; or oil on the friction disc.

Engine Will Not Run

Tune-up Problems include faulty ignition, inadequate fuel supply, flooding or vacuum leaks. On breaker point ignitions, verify point dwell angle and resistance. Both breaker point and electronic distributors require spark timing adjustment. Fuel system troubles involve dirty filters, plugged carburetor passages, a sticky needle/seat assembly in the carburetor, a defective float or a defective fuel pump. (See tune-up chapter for details on ignition timing procedures and other tune-related tasks.)

Isolate problems. Verify the strength of the ignition spark, check timing and ensure that the engine has an adequate fuel supply. Check vacuum circuits. Make certain that the emission control system is functional, especially the PCV and EGR valves. If indicated, remove and overhaul the carburetor with a quality rebuild kit. You will find instructions for the carburetor overhaul within the kit or your OEM Toyota repair manual.

Exhaust System Restriction has vexed plenty of troubleshooters. Check the exhaust system! Off-pavement or construction site pounding can flatten the tailpipe or muffler. Restricted exhaust can prevent the engine from starting or developing full power. A muffler or catalytic converter may show no external damage yet have broken baffles or internal restrictions. Include the exhaust system on your engine inspection and performance checklist.

Fig. 6-15. *Exhaust restriction is a possible cause of power loss. Off-pavement use leaves tailpipes, mufflers and catalytic converters vulnerable to damage. Tap muffler gently with a rubber or sand filled plastic hammer to test for loose baffles.*

Engine Will Not Crank

Poor Battery Maintenance/Charge Circuit Troubles remain the primary sources of starting problems. The simplest cause is dirty or corroded battery posts. Regular cleaning of the posts and battery case prevent hard starts and a stranded truck. Make certain that cables are clean and connections tight, especially on an older Land Cruiser electrical system that may have high amperage demands and a lower output 12-volt generator.

Generator or alternator troubles are easy to identify using a charge current induction meter or a simple volt-ohmmeter. Begin with the voltmeter OFF. Take care not to generate a spark near the battery. Securely attach the negative (black) probe to a good chassis or engine ground point. Attach the positive (red) probe to a battery current source some distance from the battery, such as the solenoid switch. Switch the voltmeter to D.C.

Measure the voltage level before cranking, during cranking and after starting the engine. Make certain that the maximum charge voltage reads within the regulator's normal charging range as listed in your Toyota repair manual or a similar professional-level guide.

Dead Battery Cell(s) present a difficult diagnostic problem. A high capacity battery can limp along with a dying cell for months. It takes a deep overnight freeze to bring out the worst in a battery. To avoid walking home from a chilly mountaintop, test each of your battery's cells with a hydrometer. Specific gravity should be normal and uniform at each cell.

Fig. 6-17. *A safety precaution, even for a battery that shows no sign of weakness, is the hydrometer test. Specific gravity of a fully charged battery should read uniformly at each cell. Perform this test before cold weather begins.*

Fig. 6-16. *Battery maintenance is the best preventive care for the starting circuit. Don't buy a new starter, generator or alternator before thoroughly cleaning the battery and cables and testing specific gravity.*

Fig. 6-18. *Starter defects often give warning. A clicking solenoid or erratic, dragging motor indicates trouble. An amperage draw or voltage drop test helps determine the condition of the starter. Here is a simple induction meter test for quick troubleshooting. With the tester laid across the high amperage cable to the starter, you crank the engine over. Meter reads approximate amperage draw through cable.*

Starter Motor Problems generally give warning. A solenoid switch or starter drive unit often shows signs of weakness before it fails. Run-on, clicking and erratic cranking are signs of starter and solenoid troubles.

Toyota truck engines use a variety of starters and solenoid designs, but starter principles remain universal: The solenoid acts as a relay to handle heavy amperage flow. In many Toyota starters, the solenoid actually moves the starter drive to the engagement point, much like the popular domestic Delco-Remy type starters.

Despite changes in drive styles, Toyota has adhered to brush-type motors with series-wound armatures. If the starter is high in mileage or the truck has been through repeated water fordings, you should inspect the starter for water damage, clutch drive fatigue and brush wear.

Poor cranking when hot is often due to worn brushes or armature bushing wear that allows the armature to drag on the field coils. Aftermarket exhaust headers passing too close to the starter may also cause hard starting when hot. While cranking the engine, test the draw with an induction meter directly over the starter cable. Another method is to measure the voltage drop, with a voltmeter, at the starter solenoid switch while cranking the engine. This can also be measured with a voltmeter at any other battery current junction block a safe distance from the battery.

> **WARNING** —
> *When checking voltage drop during starter tests, be sure to choose a test point well away from the battery to avoid accidently creating a dangerous spark. A spark generated by voltmeter probes near a hot or defective battery could ignite explosive battery gases.*

Geartrain Friction or Drag can prevent cranking. (Also see section on Lack of Power.) Among geartrain items that can prevent engine cranking are seizures of a transmission input shaft bearing, a gear set or the crankshaft pilot bearing. A seized pilot bearing will not allow power to disengage between the engine and transmission. However, the engine will crank in neutral.

Seized transmission components also allow the engine to crank with the clutch disengaged, but the engine will stall when you engage the clutch. (Before suspecting a damaged transmission, check clutch adjustment and operation.) A seized transmission can result from poor lubrication, severe parts stress or excessive wear.

Cooling System Troubles

Engine cooling presents a challenge, especially with high horsepower conversion engines or trips through hot desert environments. Rock crawling through the desert at high noon in August is the ultimate test for any truck's cooling system.

Before troubleshooting common cooling system problems, clarify your truck's needs. For years, the two most popular buzzwords around cooling system upgrades have been "four-row" and "cross-flow" radiators. These terms are meaningless without an understanding that horsepower equals BTUs (heat). The more horsepower, the more heat your radiator and fan system must handle.

Fig. 6-20. Pressure tester can check hoses, water pump, engine castings, gaskets and heater core. Radiator pressure cap must also seal properly, or boiling point will drop.

I once installed a 270-horsepower domestic V-8 into a truck that originally had a 110-horsepower engine. The stock down flow radiator had good size tanks and a very adequate looking core. However, the high gallon-per-minute (gpm) coolant flow rate of the transplant engine, plus its horsepower figure of more than twice the original engine's output, thoroughly overtaxed the radiator.

A radiator specialist educated me on the gpm flow needed for the new engine. He found a larger radiator core that easily fit with the original down flow radiator's top and bottom tanks. The engine ran cool ever after.

Sometimes the issue is fan air flow through the radiator core. A radiator may have plenty of flow capacity, tube size and fin surface area, but the fan draws too little air through the core. The cure in this case is a heavy duty mechanical (engine driven) fan. Well-pitched blades and a shroud may solve the cooling problem completely. Make certain that the radiator's tube size and surface area, plus the mechanical fan size, are adequate for your engine and the usage you anticipate.

Heavy-pitched truck type or high performance aftermarket mechanical fans draw far more CFM air flow than an automobile type or light duty fan. Check your truck's fan blade count and pitch. Upgrade if necessary.

Make certain a shroud captures the fan's full draft without creating an air block. (See the cooling system chapter for further details.) Fortunately, most Toyota truck models have relatively large grill openings, which makes the fan's job easier.

An air conditioning-application radiator provides a good design for the basically stock Toyota truck engine. For higher horsepower transplant engines, evaluate the heaviest duty replacement radiator available for your chassis. Order that radiator or have an adequately sized radiator built. Install a hefty mechanical (engine driven)

Fig. 6-19. A high performance engine and heavy duty radiator benefit from aftermarket stainless steel flex fan. This particular setup keeps engine within 5-degrees F of thermostat setting, even under load in the hottest climates.

fan. A fan clutch unit, which lessens engine load at speed, is often advisable.

Engine Overheat at Low Speeds suggests an under-capacity or restricted fan or radiator. Overheat can also result from insufficient water pump volume, cavitation or aeration problems. Air, either trapped within the cooling system or siphoned through a pinhole leak or defective water pump seal, can cause cavitation (air gaps and blocks). Cavitation drastically lowers cooling efficiency.

Another source of air in the cooling system is a slight head gasket leak that allows pressurized combustion gases to seep from a cylinder into an adjacent cooling port. This rapidly creates rust or oxidation, visible in the upper radiator and coolant recovery tank. As preventive care, you should check torque of the cylinder head bolts at each valve adjustment interval, periodically tighten all hose clamps, watch the water pump bleed hole for seepage and pressure check the cooling system and antifreeze each fall.

NOTE —
Restrictions in air flow through the radiator core, like from a tall winch, will cause overheating.

Engine Overheat At High Speeds involves incorrect coolant flow (either too fast or too slow) through the radiator, restrictions in the radiator core or an undercapacity water pump. Many of the symptoms for low speed overheat apply, so first follow those troubleshooting guidelines. Always check the thermostat, which regulates the coolant flow rate and temperature.

If coolant actually pushes from the radiator overflow at higher speeds, the water pump circulates more coolant than the gallon-per-minute (gpm) capacity of the radiator core. (The core is either too small or plugged with scale.) Freeze plug failure and hose leaks are not uncommon under such conditions, as excess pressure backs through the entire cooling system.

Coolant Boil-over requires careful diagnosis. Is the coolant erupting from extreme engine heat? This means the radiator and fan cannot cool the liquid sufficiently—or that the engine/powertrain produces very high temperatures due to abnormal friction, spark timing error, improper air/fuel mixtures, automatic transmission overheat or other cooling system overloads.

NOTE —
An under-capacity radiator flow rate will cause coolant overflow from the radiator—even at normal engine temperatures.

Observe when the overflow occurs. Monitor the temperature gauge closely. If the engine runs consistently hot, suspect a sticky thermostat, plugged radiator core, obstructive block mud (accumulated rust and scale in an older engine), a defective water pump or other factors that raise coolant temperature.

Fig. 6-21. *A relatively inexpensive item like the thermostat can cause major heating problems. Replace the thermostat during your periodic flush and refill of the cooling system.*

Clutch and Manual Transmission

Clutch Noises tell of bad things to come. Fatal clutch noises include the abrasive whirring of the throwout bearing during disengagement, the grinding of clutch plate rivets as the clutch engages, or the rattle of broken clutch disc torsion springs. Expect that any new, persistent and metallic sound from the clutch means trouble.

A defective pilot bearing makes noise with the transmission in gear and the clutch disengaged. Clutch disc or cover assembly noises occur during engagement and dis-

Fig. 6-22. *Clutch plate (disc) torsion springs and rivets make distinct noises. Rivets grind against the flywheel or clutch cover face while torsion springs rattle in the hub.*

engagement. (Broken clutch cover springs cause uneven engagement and severe chatter.) Throwout or release bearing noise becomes apparent with light pressure against the clutch pedal, just enough pressure to start the bearing spinning.

CAUTION —
Continued vehicle operation with a defective clutch can damage motor mounts, the flywheel and components of the transmission.

Gearbox noises grate and amplify according to load on the gear teeth. Coast and acceleration noises differ. Transmission bearing troubles give distinct cues, with countergear or counter bearing noises evident in the lower gears and overdrive, if so equipped. Input or output bearing noises correspond to shaft or road speeds. Any clutch or transmission noise requires immediate repairs.

Gear Clash in a manual transmission or transfer case has several possible causes. Before condemning the transmission, check the clutch adjustment at the release arm and note any sluggishness in the hydraulic linkage, which could be caused by a leak, air in the system or fatigued cylinders. Full range of release arm travel is necessary for disengagement of the clutch. A partially disengaged clutch causes difficult shifting and rapid wear of parts.

0019165

Fig. 6-23. Shift linkage binding or failure can prevent gear engagement or power flow. In an emergency, it may be necessary to free a 4x4's transfer case linkage by manually moving the shift rails beneath the floorboard. Shown is earlier (three-speed) Land Cruiser.

Another source of clash is hasty shifting to a non-synchromesh first or reverse gear. You must allow gears to quit spinning (or double-clutch on a first gear downshift) before engaging gear teeth. A defective synchromesh assembly will also produce this metallic clashing noise during gear shifts.

Use of the wrong gear lube can cause synchronizer balkiness and also make shifting difficult under various climate conditions. As such, gear clash and hard shifting will occur when using an overly stiff gear lube viscosity in winter months. Heavier gear and engine oils become

rigid in extremely cold environments. Multi-viscosity and synthetic gear lubricant is another cure for cold weather problems. Synchronizers are a braking mechanism, however, and if the lubricity of a gear lube is too high (too good!), there may be insufficient braking action at the synchronizer. I often advise a blend of synthetic and high grade conventional gear lube.

Synchronizers wear over time. A patterned gear clash or jumping out of any gear usually indicates bearing, shift housing, shift fork or synchronizer damage. These troubles require a transmission overhaul.

Vehicle Will Not Move means several possibilities. A failed clutch is the first consideration. A clutch permanently disengaged (linkage extended and binding, disc worn completely or clutch cover springs broken) may still allow shifting of gears.

The opposite situation is damaged clutch linkage or bad contact between the throwout bearing and clutch cover fingers, which prevents clutch disengagement. With the truck in an open area and the engine shut off, place the transmission in low gear (low range if a 4x4). Click or crank the starter. This should move the truck.

WARNING —
The engine may start. Make sure nothing is in the truck's way. Be ready to shut the ignition switch off immediately.

If the clutch works, check the transmission. On a 4x4 equipped model, also check the transfer case. On a 4x4, begin by locking the front hubs and engaging four-wheel drive. Now shift gears and try to move the truck. If your truck still will not move, power flow has stopped at the transmission or transfer case input. If the truck moves in four-wheel drive mode, suspect a broken rear transfer case output, a failed rear driveline or rear axle troubles.

When power fails to reach the axles of 4x4 trucks, defective transfer case shift linkage is a common cause. The linkage may bind or catch between gear ranges, creating a neutral effect and preventing power flow. As an emergen-

0019166

Fig. 6-24. On a 4x4, power flow includes front hubs that work properly. While the engine, clutch, transmission, transfer case, driveshafts, differentials and axles may work fine, a defective free-wheeling hub can prevent front axle traction.

cy repair, block the wheels carefully, crawl beneath the vehicle and shift the transfer case manually at its shift rails.

WARNING —
Stop the engine and place safety blocks at each wheel before attempting to engage the transfer case. The vehicle can roll with the transfer case in neutral.

Poor Traction/Erratic Wheel Spin is usually an axle or differential gearset problem. On 1991-up Land Cruisers with full-time transfer cases and a transfer case differential lock system, the transfer case's differential mechanism is much like an axle differential. Make certain this unit shifts properly and provides normal differential action. For part-time 4x4 transfer case and axle systems, rule out the much simpler possibility of a defective front axle free-wheeling hub(s).

To check the free-wheeling hubs, first engage/Lock the hubs and the 4x4 drive system. (Roll forward in four-wheel drive to engage automatic free-wheeling hubs.) Jack each front wheel, one at a time, safely off the ground. By hand, rotate the raised wheel assembly (only in a forward direction if your truck has automatic locking hubs) while the opposite wheel is still on the ground. The axle shaft should spin the front differential and cause the front driveshaft to rotate. (Note: If your 4x4 truck has a front axle positive-traction device, the wheel assembly should rotate only slightly in each direction.)

If your Toyota truck has a limited slip differential at the rear, erratic handling and odd traction are often caused by wear in the differential's clutch unit. Lurching, clicking and snapping noises indicate trouble here. A failing limited slip unit shows obvious signs: poor traction with audible symptoms of trouble, most notably as the vehicle negotiates turns.

Gear bind is a common phenomena with any 4x4 truck. If you attempt to operate your 4x4 truck on a dry, hard road surface with the front hubs locked and the transfer case in either 4WD high or low range (or diff-lock mode on full-time 4x4 systems), the rotational speed differences between the front and rear axles will act as a counterforce within the geartrain.

Gear bind prevents disengagement of the transfer case. To overcome the binding force, gently rock your truck forward and in reverse while maintaining gentle, steady pressure on the transfer case lever. There is a point of free load, somewhere between forward and reverse, where the bind loosens. At that moment, the transfer case lever will slide into the two-wheel drive position. Never apply excess force to the transfer case lever.

Driveshaft and Axle Woes

A more common driveline problem on Toyota 2WD trucks and 4x4s is U-joint and constant velocity joint failure. Especially, in rough and rocky terrain, the radical change angles place major loads on driveshaft U-joints and live front axle steering joints. Massive torque applied under high stress driving conditions can destroy a U-joint or constant velocity (CV) joint.

Fig. 6-25. *U-joints fail at inopportune times. Off-pavement, radical driveshaft angles and high torque loads place maximum stress on these components.*

The loud, metallic snap of a breaking U-joint or CV-joint is hard to forget. Back country veterans of hard-core trails carry spare U-joints for such occasions. Although proper off-pavement driving habits prevent the majority of mishaps, U-joint failure is always a concern.

Another source of driveshaft trouble is torque twisting the tubes. A properly built driveshaft, operating at normal angles and in correct phase, will withstand tremendous abuse. If, however, a shaft sustains impact damage or operates at an abnormal posture, the tube and welds may fail. Inspect your truck's driveshafts regularly, and note any shake or vibration at road speeds. A bent or sprung driveshaft will create havoc, most apparent as vehicle speed increases.

If your truck has a conventional, non-positive traction differential(s), an axle shaft or joint failure means an immediate loss of power flow. Although a truck equipped with four-wheel drive may still move when the front or rear differential fails, if a semi-floating rear axle shaft breaks, do not drive the truck.

With the exception of late model Land Cruisers, nearly all Toyota U.S. market trucks have semi-floating rear axles; the rare exceptions are dual rear wheel specialty models—motorhomes and cargo vans—with full-floating axles. On a semi-floating rear axle, a broken axle shaft offers no stability to the wheel, tire and brake drum. If the axle shaft breaks outboard of the outer bearing, or if the bearing and its pressed-on lock collar or the inner C-lock dislodges, the wheel and brake drum assembly can separate from the axle housing!

With a full-floating rear axle, it is possible to move the truck with a broken rear axle shaft. If the full-floating axle has a positive traction device, you can remove the inner section of broken axle shaft, reinstall the outer flange section, and carefully drive the truck. Some FJ Land Cruiser owners have retrofitted full-floating axles available from non-U.S. market and late model Land Cruisers. (See geartrain performance section for more details.)

On 4x4s, front axle shaft or steering CV-joint failure is another safety risk. A broken shaft, cross-type joint or constant velocity joint may wedge in the housing or steer-

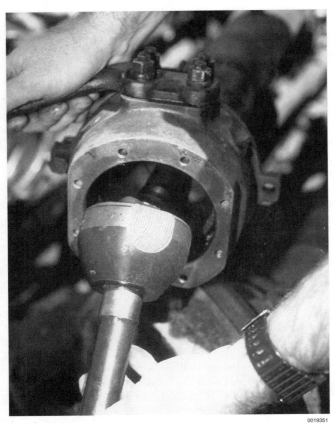

Fig. 6-26. *Front axle joint failure is dangerous. A broken shaft or joint can wedge in the steering knuckle and prevent the wheels from turning. Before driving the truck, check closely for such damage. If necessary, remove the axle shaft.*

ing knuckle cavity. This could prevent rotation of the steering knuckle and wheel spindle, causing loss of vehicle control.

On solid front axle 4x4s, if the axle shafts are still safely in line and supported, you may place the transfer case in two-wheel drive mode and turn the hubs to FREE. (Disengage automatic locking hubs by placing the transfer case in 2WD mode and backing up the truck for fifteen feet.) Drive cautiously to the nearest repair outlet and make certain that the steering knuckles continue to pivot freely.

CAUTION —
If you believe the defective axle shaft/joint could cause a lock-up of steering, remove the axle shaft assembly. Leave the transfer case in 2WD mode and the front hubs on FREE. This is a temporary fix to get home. Once back, immediately make a thorough repair.

In any instance where your truck must operate with failed axle components, understand the extent of damage. If necessary, remove the inspection cover from the differential to locate the source of trouble. (In the field, catch drain oil in a clean container and save for refilling the differential if necessary.)

Raise each wheel/tire from the ground and rotate the wheel (with both front hubs engaged) to determine whether the axle shafts and joints are intact. On an IFS open steering knuckle axle, watch joint and driveshaft rotation.

If your Toyota truck has a full-time 4x4 system like the late Land Cruiser or an IFS 4WD's A.D.D. system without free-wheeling hubs, axle shaft damage poses several driving threats, including steering impairment, risk of losing a wheel assembly, loss of braking or the possibility of increased damage to the truck.

WARNING —
If an inner component in the axle breaks, exercise extreme caution if you must move the truck at all. Do not attempt to drive the truck if the steering knuckle, outer axle shaft, steering knuckle U-joint or wheel bearings have become severely damaged.

On such a truck, the full-floating front wheel hubs permit removal of a broken front axle shaft in an emergency. If you must move a full-time 4x4 model or A.D.D.-equipped 4WD truck that has an unsafe, broken front axle shaft or joint, first remove the broken shaft, then the front driveshaft assembly. Set the transfer case in differential lock mode on the Land Cruiser full-time system or 2WD mode on an A.D.D. system. (See axle service chapter or your Toyota repair manual for details on front axle shaft removal.)

During axle oil changes, with the differential cover removed, clean and inspect all parts. Look closely for abnormal tooth contact patterns on the ring and pinion gears. Check the pinion shaft for any end play or radial movement. Inspect the seals, observe side gear/pinion backlash (play) and note the condition of the carrier bearings that support the ring gear and differential carrier housing. Preventive maintenance and careful inspection remain your best safeguards against axle troubles.

Fig. 6-27. *Ring and pinion gears, side gears and differential pinions can each fail. On models equipped with an inspection cover, remove the cover to check these parts. Excess play at the pinion shaft or axle shafts can mean trouble.*

Differential Troubles include clutch failure on positive traction units, broken differential side gears or small pinions and the stripping of teeth from the ring and pinion gears. Bearing failures, seal leaks and thrust washer wear are other trouble areas.

Fig. 6-28. Most OEM limited slip axles feature multi-plate clutches. Wear occurs over time, and traction diminishes. Toyota has offered very few factory differential traction devices, however, many truck owners opt for aftermarket traction differentials, including limited slips and "lockers." (See performance geartrain upgrade chapter.)

Steering and Tire Troubles

Wander, the tendency for steering to either drift or follow road irregularities, is a common complaint with both two- and four-wheel drive models. The usual causes are front end misalignment, cupped tire wear, a loose steering gear, defective steering linkage or suspension wear. Steering linkage, ball-joint, or kingpin bearing wear are trouble spots.

When aligning the front wheels, service should include a caster check. Insufficient positive caster angle can cause shimmy and loss of steering control. If your Toyota truck needs coaxing to steer straight after a turn, check caster and toe-in. Sagging suspension or aftermarket lift kits can also affect caster angle.

For Toyota trucks with a solid 4x4 front axle, if slight caster and camber correction is necessary and no safety problem exists, adjustment is possible. An alignment shop can install tapered steel shims between the axle and leaf springs for caster correction or install special aftermarket offset kingpin bearing caps (currently available from NAPA) to correct small camber error. (Caution: Be certain that no hazardous damage is causing the error!)

1986-up IFS 4x4 models and all 2WD IFS Toyota trucks have factory adjustment provisions for caster, camber and toe-in. (See your Toyota repair manual for details on your truck's front end design and adjustment/alignment concerns.)

Loose steering gear and linkage result from high mileage and wear, severe loads and the rigors of off-pavement pounding. Excess play translates as wander. Depending

Fig. 6-29. On Toyota trucks with a 4WD solid front axle, camber is only a concern when springs sag or an axle housing/beam fatigues or becomes bent. Worn kingpin bearings can affect both caster and camber angles—and also cause "kingpin shimmy."

upon your truck's front end design, inspect for wear at tie-rod ends, the steering gear, spring bushings and shackles, the centerlink/relay rod assembly, the center arm/bellcrank, idler arm, draglink, steering arms, kingpin bearings, ball-joints and spindles.

Front End Shimmy usually results from looseness in the steering knuckle (kingpin) bearings or ball-joints. A contributing factor is looseness in the steering linkage, front wheel spindles or wheel bearings. Sagging springs and improper wheel alignment (especially caster angle) can also cause front end shimmy.

Oversize tires exaggerate shimmy and so does severe tire imbalance. Any vibration or road shock can set off this potentially violent shaking of the front wheels. With manual steering, kingpin shimmy is a wrist-wrenching experience.

Perform a quick check of spindles, wheel bearings, kingpin bearings or ball-joints by raising front wheels safely from the ground and installing jack stands beneath the axle housing on a solid axle 4WD model or the lower A-arms of 2WD trucks. (On 2WD and 4WD IFS models with torsion bar or spring load at the upper A-arms, allow the suspension to drop by supporting the frame instead of the lower A-arms.) Grab each front wheel and tire firmly at 6- and 12-o'clock. Rock the tire in and out with a lifting motion. Note the amount of movement.

If play exists, have a helper watch the backside of the wheel and steering knuckle. Determine whether the play is at the wheel hub (loose wheel bearings or spindle) or the knuckle support (kingpin bearings or ball-joints). When wheel bearing play is excessive, adjust the wheel bearings to specification, then repeat the inspection. (See service chapters for further details.)

Wheel Run-out and Tire Imbalance is another area of concern. Especially with oversize mud-and-snow tires, the weight mass at each wheel becomes excessive. Cleated truck tires, unlike conventional passenger car types, fall out of balance with normal wear. Periodic re-balancing and rotation are essential. (Note: Switch in cross with bias ply, non-radial tires; ask your tire dealer for manu-

Fig. 6-30. *Use of a quality tire gauge is essential. Your truck requires specific pressures for on- or off-highway use. Off-highway pressures below 20 psi will reduce load capacity drastically and possibly damage the tires. Always check tire pressures cold, and follow the manufacturer's recommended inflation rates for your Toyota.*

Fig. 6-31. *Spin balancing helps guard against vibration and abnormal tire wear. In some cases, tires require truing, matching or balancing on the truck. Rotate tires every 5,000-7,500 miles, and check balance as needed.*

facturer's recommendations when rotating newer radial type tires.)

Hard-core 4x4 rock crawling can dislodge wheel weights or cause them to rotate on the rim. Tire damage, including internal belt separation of radial tires, causes vibration and shake. Bent wheel rims (runout) creates a wide range of handling and tire wear problems. The best preventive measure is periodic spin balancing of each tire and wheel. Have the technician pay close attention to rim run-out and distortion. Replace rims that show excess run-out.

Traditionally, heavy duty bias-ply tires have benefitted from truing, a procedure that trims out-of-round ma-

terial from the new tread surface. Radial tires sometimes require tread and sidewall matching, a procedure that contributes to uniform tread pressure over the full circumference of the tire.

Tire imbalance usually becomes noticeable between 45 and 55 mph. Sometimes a set of tires and wheels may balance perfectly, yet the symptoms of imbalance remain. This situation may call for balancing the tires on the vehicle, with the brake drum or rotor and hub included in the rotating mass. Balancing on the truck requires re-balancing the tires each time you rotate them.

Brake Problems

Brake Pull and Grab occur when you apply the brakes. Defects in hydraulic or mechanical parts of the brake system cause these problems. A pitted or corroded wheel cylinder or disc caliper piston bore can cause erratic piston action, while a sticking piston prevents normal movement of the brake shoes or disc pads.

An incorrectly adjusted master cylinder pushrod or dirty and corroded fluid reservoir can affect brake performance. If brake fluid cannot return to the master cylinder reservoir through the compensation port, fluid trapped in the system will keep pressure on the brakes. This can cause drag, fade and erratic braking action.

Several mechanical factors contribute to brake pull and grab. Oil on the brake lining, binding linkage, a broken shoe return spring, warped brake shoes and drums (bell mouthed or out-of-round), distorted rotors and pads, hard spots on drums or rotors and excessive lining wear each contribute to erratic braking. Poor lining quality, which leads to fade and undercapacity braking, is another source of trouble.

Slipshod brake jobs, without turning drums and rotors or rebuilding (sometimes replacing) hydraulic cylinders, can lead to problems. With exposure to water, mud and drastic climate changes, your brakes deserve quality care. Restore your brakes properly, then protect the brake system by periodically cleaning debris from shoes, backing plates, brake drums or rotors. Inspect the wheel cylinder and caliper dust seals regularly.

> *WARNING —*
> *All older brake lining contains harmful asbestos. Brake vacuum equipment and special parts washers are available to prevent exposure to harmful asbestos brake dust. If you cannot safeguard yourself from asbestos, leave brake work to a professional shop. When performing brake work, inquire whether a non-asbestos lining is available for your truck.*

Failure To Stop has two symptoms: no pedal pressure or an extremely hard pedal. No pedal pressure generally means a hydraulic system failure, especially on pre-1967 trucks with single master cylinder systems. Also, if you use your truck off-pavement, it faces environmental hazards that can damage brake pipes or hoses. If fluid loss has occurred, carefully repair the hydraulic system, bleed air out, and check for leaks before driving the vehicle.

Mechanical problems like a broken brake shoe, drum, actuating linkage, defective self-adjuster mechanism or brake shoes not adjusted properly can cause the master cylinder piston to fully exhaust its stroke before the brakes apply. (Actually, this too is a hydraulic failure, although a mechanical cause underlies the problem.)

Under extreme circumstances, misadjusted brake shoes, combined with major lining wear, will create the same effect. The brake pedal reaches the floor before lining reaches the drums. If your truck's brakes have no self-adjusters, you must periodically adjust the shoe-to-drum clearance and monitor the lining wear.

Normal lining wear lowers the level of fluid in the master cylinder reservoir. Check brake fluid at regular intervals to assure an adequate reserve. The master cylinder must displace a full stroke of fluid to actuate the wheel brakes. (See chapters on maintenance and brake service.)

An extremely hard pedal is usually the result of contaminated lining (oil, dirt or water), glazed brake lining or warped drums and/or rotors. Poor brake shoe seating, often a consequence of improper shoe arc, can prevent lining from making full contact with the drums. Binding of the linkage, actuating hardware or hydraulic cylinder pistons will also increase brake pedal pressure.

Make sure that your Toyota truck's brake pedal linkage is free of debris and moves freely. Periodically inspect the master cylinder dust boot where the pedal rod enters the cylinder. Replace the boot if loose or torn.

CAUTION —

Be aware that when stored in a damp climate or exposed to icy and wet road debris and corrosives, the pistons in the master cylinder, wheel cylinders and disc calipers sometimes rust and corrode in their bores.

In freezing weather, always check your brakes before driving the truck. Wet hardware may ice up—another cause of hard pedal. Additionally, hard pedal can result from overheated lining or fade.

There are several causes of brake fade: improper fitup of brake parts; hydraulic fluid trapped in the lines (due to a misadjusted master cylinder pushrod, bent pipe or kinked brake hose); extensive use or abuse of the brakes; excess load on the brake system; a misadjusted wheel-type emergency brake system; incorrect brake shoe-to-drum clearance (too tight); and glazed or contaminated brake lining.

Fig. 6-33. Toyota master cylinders with caps that vent to atmosphere can draw moisture and fine dust. The master cylinder's cap and pedal-side dust boot must seal properly. Otherwise, corrosive rust, abrasive dirt and other harmful contaminants will attack the walls and seals of the cylinder.

Fig. 6-34. Glazed or contaminated brake lining, rotors and drums will increase pedal pressure. A defective outer axle shaft seal permits gear lube to saturate and ruin the brake lining.

Fig. 6-32. Master cylinder pushrod clearance is crucial to safe braking. Insufficient clearance at the tip of the pushrod will prevent the piston from retracting completely.

Chapter 7

Cooling System Service

W HEN WORKING HARD, your Toyota truck places a high demand on its cooling system. The engine must maintain normal operating temperatures, whether the air outside is minus-60 degrees Fahrenheit or 130 degrees above. Dusty roads pack dirt and abrasive material into a radiator core, and rocks and debris from the tires of other vehicles can damage the radiator core just as easily as they break a windshield.

For 4x4 models, a twisting back country trail, where tires hang suspended in air, can loosen a weak radiator core support. Hose flex fatigues the radiator inlet and outlet tubes. Hard impact force can drive the fan into the radiator or fan shroud.

Add to this the burden of air conditioning and an automatic transmission. Many truck owners consider creature comfort a valid part of driving. Why suffer with 120-degree heat inside your vehicle? The installation of a factory or aftermarket air conditioner places another obstacle in front of the cooling system, as the air conditioning condenser restricts air flow through the radiator core. Many later Toyota trucks have an automatic transmission. All of the Toyota automatic transmissions cool ATF at the engine's radiator. This places an even greater load on the radiator, coolant and fan system. Likewise, an auxiliary engine or transmission oil cooler might mount within the fan's air flow. This adds extra heat that the cooling system must handle.

Another factor that increases the risk of overheat is a forward mounted winch. Often, 4x4s have such an as-

Fig. 7-2. On Land Cruisers from the mid-1970s onward, the high heat created by the use of more exotic emission controls, leaner fuel mixtures and lower fuel octane grades demanded use of auxiliary electric fans. Special fans cool items like the manifolds, EGR system and the overall engine bay.

sembly or other accessories mounted just forward of the grille. Today's better winch mounts place the winch behind or in line with the bumper, below the grille opening. This allows vital air to flow through the radiator.

Since many light trucks pull trailers, Toyota V-6s and the Land Cruiser in-line sixes offer higher horsepower engines. The ultimate cooling challenge for any truck is a high horsepower engine and a severe load. Another challenge is Toyota's 2.0L turbocharged diesel or the 22R-TE four-cylinder gas engine. Each of these smaller engines place a tremendous load on the radiator and fan system, especially when they operate under load or at full boost.

The simplest way to explain this equation is that each horsepower equals a certain number of British Thermal Units (BTUs). More horsepower means a higher BTU output or engine heat. The cooling system must adequately dissipate this thermal load.

Sufficient cooling requires maximum transfer of heat from the engine to the air. The radiator, comprised of coolant tubes and fins, handles the majority of this task. For those who like engineering formulas, here's the actual equation for engine cooling: Draw off at least 42.5 BTUs of heat per minute for each horsepower.

Since BTU heat dissipation relates directly to the area of radiator tube and fin exposure, core size is very important. Air flow and radiator core size (reflected by the number and size of the coolant tubes plus the area of the fins) will determine cooling capacity.)

Fig. 7-1. An automatic transmission and air conditioning place an added load on the engine's cooling system. The air conditioning condenser and an auxiliary transmission cooler may each block air flow through the radiator core.

system. Your truck's engine loses approximately one-third of its thermal energy as heat dissipating from the radiator, the heater core and surfaces of the engine. Another one-third of the thermal energy goes out the tailpipe as hot exhaust! (This valuable energy, when harnessed to power an exhaust turbocharger, produces considerable extra horsepower.)

The actual ignition process and combustion of fuel consume the other third of this thermal energy, as the hot gases expand and drive the pistons downward in the cylinders. Moving pistons rotate the crankshaft, which in turn propels the vehicle.

Matching Cooling System Components

Whether you are restoring an earlier model truck, retrofitting a higher horsepower engine into your truck's chassis or increasing an engine's performance, you must accurately determine the horsepower level. It's better to guess high than low, as a thermostat can regulate coolant temperatures if you install a slightly oversize radiator that cools too well. With an undersize radiator core, the engine will never run cool enough.

Fig. 7-3. *If a hot engine has a good amount of coolant still in the system, run the engine while pouring a light stream of water over the radiator core and tanks. (Avoid hitting a hot engine with cold water, as this could crack a block, cylinder head or other castings.) The temperature will drop quickly. Allow the engine and radiator to cool completely before removing the radiator cap.*

Fig. 7-4. *Here is the difference between a custom-built cross-flow truck radiator (top) and an early model Land Cruiser's down-flow unit (bottom). A high horsepower engine or air conditioning, power robbing accessories and an automatic transmission require far more overall radiator size—more tubes or a larger core surface area—than an earlier, lower output carbureted F or 2F engine.*

1. COOLING SYSTEM BASICS

Chronic cooling system problems usually originate at the radiator and sometimes at the water pump. Often, especially with larger engines, an undercapacity or clogged radiator creates trouble. Several factors apply when choosing the correct radiator, but the main issue is horsepower. Higher horsepower equates to a greater need for heat transfer, the principal job for your truck's radiator.

Engineers see horsepower output as the main variable when determining the capacity of a radiator or fan

Fig. 7-5. *A four-row core is not always bigger than a three row. Tube size and surface area also contribute to flow rate. Pay attention to gpm flow ratings and engine/chassis applications when selecting a high output radiator. Recyclers and radiator shops offer information on flow rates and applications.*

Also consider the engine's water pump volume and coolant flow rate. If the engine pumps more water into the radiator than the tubes can flow, the coolant will overflow the filler neck as engine speed increases. This is a common symptom of an inadequate radiator flow rate.

Lastly, the radiator's ability to rapidly transfer or dissipate heat must be sufficient. The engine fan plays a large role here. As an absolute minimum, you need a fan that creates an air flow rate of 725 to 1150 feet per minute through the radiator core.

Excess loads, high ambient temperatures, air restriction or unusually slow road speeds require additional fan flow and coolant flow.

Flow rate is the amount of coolant that can move through the radiator in a given interval of time. The industry standard of measurement is gallons-per-minute flow or gpm. If your truck's original radiator won't cool a transplanted bigger engine, the cause is either a deficiency in gpm flow or too little surface area.

The usual cure for low flow rate is a larger radiator or radiator core. Popular four- or even five-row radiators offer a thicker core with more rows of tubes. If you must adhere to the original radiator's height and width dimensions, and that radiator has two or three rows of tubes, the addition of a four-row core may provide the necessary gpm flow level.

The size of each tube is actually more important than the number of rows. Many three row cores, with larger tubes, offer higher BTU dissipation ratings than a four-row core with small tubes. When in doubt, consult flow and BTU charts at a local radiator shop.

Fan Air Flow

If, despite adequate coolant flow and proper thermostat action, your truck's engine overheats, air flow or fan shrouding could be at fault. With a narrow grille opening, fan draw becomes a major part of cooling. Poor fan location, a defective fan clutch, or an improperly shaped shroud can prevent air flow through the radiator core.

Some owners make the mistake of eliminating the clutch fan unit and trying to run a non-flexing metal fan. This can actually create a blockage of air flow at high road speeds. Here, air moving through the grille and radiator can travel much faster than the draw speed of the fan. For this reason, and to reduce horsepower drain, either a fan clutch assembly or an aftermarket flexible-blade fan are frequently found on high performance engines.

The shroud must capture the entire core area of the radiator. Ideal fan location will have half the thickness of the blades inside the shroud, the other half just rearward. (Aftermarket flex fans alter this formula slightly, so read instructions that come with any conversion fan.) This al-

Fig. 7-6. *The location of the fan and shroud are important to cooling. Factory fan blade lies approximately halfway into the shroud opening. Shroud captures air from the entire radiator core. Toyota truck engines use V-type or serpentine drive belts.*

Fig. 7-7. Flex-A-Lite aftermarket flex fan (right) and spacers replace a factory fan clutch and fan. Stainless steel blades will flatten at higher engine speeds to prevent air blockage. Note reverse fan rotation, required on many late engines with serpentine drive belts.

Fig. 7-8. A cooling system pressure tester is quickest check for leaks. Pump tester to normal cooling system pressure, then watch gauge. Sealing properly, no drop should occur.

lows the fan to draw under all circumstances and prevents turbulence or an air blockage within the shroud.

The last area of concern is coolant or air blockage within the cooling system. Beware of improperly installed engine gaskets, especially the head gasket(s), or an upside down thermostat. When performing a valve grind or complete engine overhaul, follow engine assembly instructions carefully. Make sure all gaskets seal properly and that coolant ports align correctly with the gaskets.

Finding Leaks

Coolant leaks can ruin your drive or vacation. As a safeguard, check your cooling system regularly with a pressure tester. External leaks are easiest to find. With the engine shut off and cool, simply pump the tester to the cooling system's normal pressure, and watch the gauge. It should not drop. If it does, look for leaks at hoses, the intake manifold, the thermostat housing, freeze plugs, or the radiator and heater cores.

If no external leaks are present, suspect an internal engine leak, including a seeping or blown head gasket, casting cracks, or an interior intake manifold/cooling passage leak. A blown head gasket or cracked casting will either leak coolant into a cylinder or create low compression in two adjacent cylinders. When coolant can enter a cylinder, compression gases also leak into the engine's cooling ports. Rapid overflow at the radiator filler neck or coolant recovery tank results when high pressure cylinder gases enter the cooling system.

Intake manifold gasket leaks at coolant passages will drain coolant into the crankcase. So will a leaking timing cover casting or gaskets that cover coolant ports. Block or cylinder head cracks cause coolant leaks into the upper cylinders and/or crankcase, depending upon the crack's location in the casting.

There are several tests for an internal coolant leak. Securely attach a pressure tester to the radiator fill neck. Have someone start the engine while you watch the gauge. If pressure rises rapidly and pegs at the high side

Fig. 7-9. Strange place for an exhaust gas analyzer probe! With the engine idling at normal temperature, an exhaust infrared tester can sniff cylinder gases just above the radiator filler neck. Combustion gases will enter the cooling system through a blown head gasket(s), a cracked cylinder head or a crack in the block. Carbon monoxide (CO) is detectable here.

of the gauge, *shut the engine off immediately*. This indicates that cylinder pressure has entered the cooling system and pressurized the radiator. A casting crack or blown head gasket is the cause.

The appearance of bubbles in the radiator often indicates the presence of cylinder gases and a head gasket or casting leak. This can be deceptive, though, since other causes of aeration, including water pump malfunctions, can also introduce air bubbles into the cooling system.

An infra-red exhaust analyzer can quickly confirm whether bubbles in the radiator are from leaking combustion gases. By holding the analyzer probe just above an open radiator fill neck or coolant recovery tank, a reading of carbon monoxide and hydrocarbons is possible. If you find these gases present in the cooling system, suspect a "blown" head gasket, warped cylinder head, cylinder block crack or head casting crack.

CAUTION —

Cylinder gases in the cooling system will create an abrupt and dangerous rise in pressure. (Imagine 100-plus psi of pressure within a cooling system designed for 17 psi.) Protect your cooling system tester by shutting the engine off immediately if pressure starts to rise rapidly with the engine running. Use extreme care when working around a cooling system. Do not remove the cap if the engine has warmed or if the tester gauge reads high. Allow time for the system to cool and pressure to drop.

Automatic Transmission Load On Cooling

An automatic transmission can overtax your engine's cooling system. Automatic transmissions operate hot, well in excess of normal engine coolant temperatures, and the truck's radiator is often the only source of cooling for the transmission. As a result, a heavily worked transmission can actually cause an engine overheat.

Toyota truck automatics have fluid lines that run to the radiator for cooling. On downflow radiators, popular on Land Cruisers and Toyota trucks, the lower tank harbors a separate cell for circulating automatic transmission fluid (ATF). (Cross-flow type radiators incorporate a transmission cooler in one of the side tanks.) Engine coolant, circulating around the outside of this cell, draws off heat from the scorching ATF.

One of the best solutions for better engine and transmission cooling is an auxiliary transmission cooler. Some trucks feature an auxiliary OEM transmission cooler, which is usually part of a heavy duty/air conditioning or trailer pulling package. Aftermarket manufacturers build units that work either in-line with the radiator or independently.

The auxiliary transmission cooler resembles an air conditioning or refrigeration condenser. Air, either from vehicle movement or from the engine's fan, moves past the fins on the transmission cooler, drawing heat away from the transmission fluid.

If you install an aftermarket transmission cooler, position it carefully. Since so much heat passes from its surface, placing the unit in front of the radiator core is not always wise. Pre-heated air can raise the temperature of the radiator fins and tubes. Often, a better approach is to place the transmission cooler safely behind the radiator, or somewhere in the vehicle's air stream, without restricting the flow of radiator air.

Keeping Late Model Engines Alive

Late model truck engines operate hot. More thorough combustion, better fuel economy plus lower CO and HC emissions result from leaner fuel mixtures and higher thermostat settings; the side effect is more heat. Years ago, a truck engine came from the factory with a 180° winter thermostat. It was common practice to install a 160° thermostat in the summer months.

Today, due largely to cooling system controls and emission restrictions, the various Toyota truck engines use 180° F, 190° F and even higher thermostat openings. "Normal" engine operating temperature can range to 230° F—well past the boiling point of water!

One way to compensate for high operating temperatures is by using the correct radiator cap and coolant mixture. A radiator pressure cap of 15 psi can raise the boiling point of a 50/50 anti-freeze and water mixture to 265° F, while a 60/40 ethylene glycol coolant mix is good for 270°. Each pound increase in radiator cap pressure raises the boil over point by three degrees. Make sure the cap pressure rating is right for your engine.

Also, while anti-freeze/coolant seems the cure-all for raising the boiling point, remember that there's a limit to its use. The expansion rates differ between water and

Fig. 7-10.   An add-on auxiliary transmission cooler takes a large load off the engine's cooling system. Install an auxiliary transmission cooler if your plans include trailer pulling or rock crawling in off-pavement environments.

Fig. 7-11.   For those who wish to swap a domestic V-8 engine into the Land Cruiser, or a domestic V-6 into the 4WD mini-pickup (see engine performance chapter for details), a stock to fully modified V-8 can range from 180 to 500 horsepower. For cooling purposes, keep in mind that horsepower equals BTUs. More horsepower requires far more radiator capacity.

anti-freeze/coolant. An excessive amount of ethylene glycol limits the solution's ability to expand within itself. Running pure anti-freeze can cause boil over——expansion right out of the system!

Too much anti-freeze/coolant also affects the freezing point. At –8° F, pure ethylene glycol anti-freeze will actually freeze, resulting in broken engine castings and/or a cracked radiator core! Never mix ethylene glycol solutions richer than the 68% maximum ratio recommended by most vehicle manufacturers. (The minimum recommended mix is usually 44%.) With quality anti-freeze, a 68% anti-freeze/32% water solution should provide engine protection to –90° F. (Read the anti-freeze manufacturer's specifications to confirm protection.)

A mix of at least 40% water is considered practical in an ethylene glycol anti-freeze/coolant solution. This can be confirmed by either mixing the solution from scratch or testing the cooling system with an anti-freeze hydrometer. Make sure that the coolant has circulated (through the heater system, too) before you attempt to check its specific gravity with a hydrometer.

When To Use An Aftermarket Electric Fan

It takes far less to cool a lower compression, low horsepower four-cylinder or in-line six-cylinder engine than a high compression, high horsepower DOHC six or V-6. The original Toyota Land Cruiser F engine produced 138 (SAE net) horsepower from 236.7 cubic inches (3878cc) with 7.8:1 compression. The late DOHC 4.5L DJ Land Cruiser engine produces 212 SAE net horsepower with 9:1 compression ratio and 4477cc displacement. Now add an automatic transmission, A/C and power options to the late engine's cooling system equation.

Auxiliary electric fans have found their way into some OEM truck applications. They typically serve as factory add-on devices for heavy duty cooling. Toyota has used OEM electric fans and auxiliary coolers for cooling manifolds, oiling systems and EGR valve systems. The engine driven fan assembly still provides primary radiator cooling, however.

For the conversion engine in a tight chassis bay, there's a temptation to use an electric fan in place of an engine driven fan. On many large V-8 conversions, the engine's mechanical fan is difficult to fit within the confines of a smaller engine bay or will not line up easily with the center of the radiator core.

The Land Cruisers accept a domestic V-8 transplant without much trouble. 4WD pickups easily accept a GM V-6 powerplant. In either of these applications, the engine bays provide room for an engine driven mechanical fan. My experience has taught that a mechanical fan is the only sensible method for cooling an off-highway engine. (See performance engine chapter for details.)

Some custom truck builders believe that the mechanical (engine driven) fan is unnecessary and that a heavy duty electric fan system, alone, can cool the engine. As a former truck fleet mechanic and long standing four-wheel drive user, I am not a supporter of aftermarket electric fans and am especially disappointed with electric fans that rely on the radiator fins for support. (These kinds of assemblies are held in place by plastic ties

Fig. 7-12.   Factory electric fans are an auxiliary source of air flow for cooling. A cooling system's principal source of air flow is still the heavy duty engine driven mechanical fan. An OEM auxiliary electric fan meets a special cooling need and works in conjunction with (not in place of) a heavy duty radiator and high output engine driven fan. Here is an OEM electric fan for cooling the carburetor on a 2F Land Cruiser.

Fig. 7-13.   If the radiator is heavy duty and the load light, most engines require little fan support by 30 or so miles per hour road speed. This is why clutch-type mechanical fans make sense, as the fan does not operate at higher road speeds. In fact, an older style non-clutch type OEM fan can actually obstruct radiator air flow at higher road speeds. Aftermarket flex fans will not obstruct flow.

through the radiator core.) With enough vibration, a fin mounted electric fan can severely damage the radiator.

A mechanical fan, if centered and shrouded properly, proves superior in all cases. A heavy-duty truck fan or any of the better aftermarket flexible (engine driven) cooling fans provide far more pitch and air draw than the typical electric fan.

An electric fan may provide adequate cooling for light load highway use where cruise speed air flow meets the majority of cooling needs. I once tested a "high output" aftermarket electric fan on my 1976 Land Cruiser with the 383 Chevrolet V-8 conversion. (See performance chapters.) The electric fan was the sole source of cooling. At crawl speeds or traffic light stops, the engine would heat up as if the cooling system was under capacity. When the vehicle reached 25–30 mph, the engine would cool rapidly, even with the electric fan turned off.

The real test of truck cooling is a high noon rock crawling episode on a mid-summer trip through the desert—or pulling a 20-foot travel trailer up a six-percent, twelve mile long grade out of El Centro, California in August—or getting stuck in the Los Angeles freeway interchange with a sailboat in tow and the ambient temperature around 100° F. Here, when used as the sole source of air flow, a heavy duty engine driven fan serves far better than any currently available aftermarket automotive electric fan.

I would consider using an aftermarket electric fan to cool an auxiliary engine oil cooler or a transmission cooler. These devices often rely on the engine driven fan for air flow, which places an added burden on the engine's cooling system.

Tenacious Overheat Problems

Cooling problems can go beyond the radiator and fan. A dirty or corroded engine block, obstructions in the block, the wrong cylinder head(s), an improperly installed head gasket or excessive internal friction can each cause overheating. Faulty ignition timing or spark advance, excess carbon, valves ground too thin, a defective thermostat, the wrong intake manifold, cross-firing spark plug wires and an overly lean or rich carburetor mix can also cause an overheat.

Water pump defects are a common cause of trouble. The most obvious pump problem is a leaking seal. Worn pump bearings allow pulley and fan blade runout, usually visible when looking sideways at the idling engine. Improper gaskets, corroded impeller vanes or a missing water pump backing plate can also cause coolant circulation problems.

A plugged exhaust system or a stuck heat riser valve will quickly overheat an engine. Pinched or air-blocked cooling hoses, excessively hot spark plugs or a loose fan belt(s) can also cause trouble. Avoid using flex type radiator hoses, as they can collapse or place excess stress on radiator inlet and outlet sleeves. Wherever possible, use OEM type molded hoses with wire reinforcement.

An older radiator may need boiling and rodding. This process involves removing the top and bottom tanks, boiling the radiator in caustic, then running rods through the scaly tubes. Reassembly and pressure testing complete the job. Late model truck cooling systems operate at higher pressures, which, in conjunction with antifreeze/coolant, raises the boiling point.

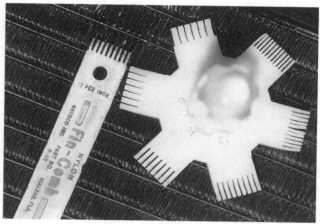

Fig. 7-15. Fin design makes a difference, with serpentine-type fins generally better for the off-highway environment. Overall, whether an oversize radiator is a downflow or cross-flow design, quality construction and adequate air flow are more important than whether coolant moves horizontally or vertically

Fig. 7-14. Even a defective spark advance mechanism or vacuum unit can cause engine overheating. The State of California once advocated a retrofit smog control that eliminated vacuum spark advance under most driving conditions. Engine overheat damage was so prevalent that California abandoned the measure.

Fig. 7-6. Check radiator solder seams and joints for coolant seepage. Have weak or loose brackets repaired by a radiator shop.

A clean, pressure tested radiator, with adequate flow rate and the proper fan cooling, should keep your truck's engine running at normal temperatures. Most radiators that test leak free at 20 psi in the shop will offer long service. A 17 psi cap affords a 260-plus degree boiling point with a 50/50 mixture of high grade ethylene glycol anti-freeze/coolant and water.

A heavily modified engine, however, may require a special radiator. Especially challenging are the domestic V-8 and large V-6 engine conversions. Here, a custom down-flow or cross-flow type radiator must have a large flow capacity. Also consider a heavy duty OE replacement radiator. Often, a radiator specialist can mount your original radiator tanks and brackets to a much larger new radiator core.

As for specialty radiators, don't rush to buy a NASCAR or SCCA aluminum road racing radiator. Such a unit may rely on high speed air flow for cooling, a non-existent commodity when your 4x4 shares a desert floor with the lizards or your fully loaded Toyota motorhome climbs the Grapevine.

2. WATER PUMP SERVICE

Eventually, every engine's water pump will fail or wear out. Although water pumps often last between engine overhauls, the load and stress placed on a hard working truck can cause earlier failure. If you periodically pressure check the cooling system, maintain an adequate amount of coolant/anti-freeze and keep proper tension on the drive belts, you will decrease the likelihood that a failed water pump will leave you stranded.

On that note, like an extra fan belt, a bottle of radiator stop leak solution is a smart accessory for your truck's

toolbox. Often, if the leak has just developed, stop leak can get your truck home or to a service garage. For the water pump in good condition, a water pump lubricant additive is of some value.

As a precaution, pressure check your cooling system regularly. Often, a water pump will only leak when under pressure. Also, with the engine shut off, rock the fan blade to test the water pump shaft bearings.

WARNING —
Be extremely careful when handling an after-market stainless steel fan. The edges are often as sharp as a knife.

At the first sign of water pump seepage, replace the pump. Don't take chances or attempt a permanent fix with a liquid or powder stop leak. A weak pump will likely fail at a critical time, such as when the engine is under load and pulling hard.

Fig. 7-18. *In an emergency, you can change the water pump yourself. Make sure the engine is completely cool before attempting to drain coolant, and use a drain pan. Avoid prolonged skin exposure to anti-freeze, sealants or parts cleaning agents. Use adequate ventilation as indicated.*

Guidelines For Water Pump Service

Prior to the advent of engine driven power options, water pump replacement was relatively easy. For later models, depending upon equipment and how many engine accessories stand in the way, this task can vary. In general, older Toyota pickups and Land Cruisers have open engine bays and ready access to the water pump.

The presence of engine driven accessories can make the water pump more difficult to access. If your engine has power steering, air conditioning, or an air injection pump(s), allow plenty of time to complete the water pump replacement.

Toyota trucks use different engines and a variety of accessories. Although the steps discussed should help guide your water pump removal-and-replacement (R&R), the job may require additional measures for your particular year, model or accessory package. If you find

Fig. 7-17. *Fortunately, water pump failure seldom occurs instantly. Signs of weakness, like coolant seepage or a wobbling shaft bearing, give forewarning. Watch the bleed hole at the pump's base. When the seal begins to fail, coolant will seep from bleed hole.*

Fig. 7-19. Later model 4Runner and pickup V-6s (top) and Land Cruiser in-line DOHC sixes (bottom) require considerable steps for removal and replacement of the water pump. I would not attempt such a repair without a thorough review of the Toyota Repair Manual's steps for the specific model involved. Make sure that you have such information and any described tools before tackling this kind of job.

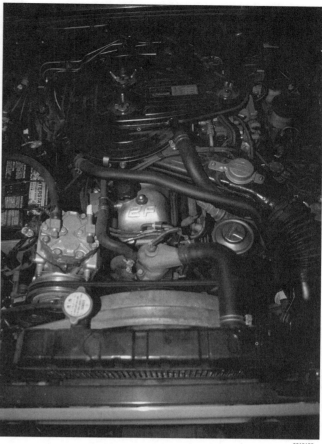

Fig. 7-20. If the air conditioner interferes with pump removal, you must follow necessary steps to move the compressor and access the water pump. A power steering pump, an alternator, an air injection pump and even vacuum fittings and electronic sensor components may interfere with a water pump's removal.

areas not discussed and have doubts about what steps to take, consult the OEM Toyota Repair Manual that covers your truck's specific engine application.

Before attempting a water pump replacement on a well-equipped late Toyota truck engine, consider the scope of the project. If you decide to proceed, outline on paper the steps and the position of each removed part. This sequence is crucial for correct reassembly. To avoid a "sour" job or the ultimate frustration of re-doing the project, take time to observe how the pieces come apart.

Begin any water pump replacement by placing a large pan beneath the radiator drain cock. With the engine cool, loosen the petcock and allow coolant to drain into the pan. (You may find that removing the radiator cap allows faster draining.) Unless this coolant is relatively new and very clean, discard it at your local recycling outlet.

Disconnect the negative battery cable if your engine requires removal of the generator or alternator and its mounting bracket. With the negative battery cable disconnected, loosen the generator/alternator belt, whether

serpentine or V-groove type. For serpentine belts, make careful note of belt routing.

Unbolt and lay the generator or alternator aside, with its wires still attached if possible. Do not stretch these wires. Support the alternator or generator properly.

On all engines, remove the radiator fan shroud, fan and fan clutch where applicable. If you have not already done so, you will need to loosen and remove the generator or alternator belt or serpentine belt to perform these steps. When the engine drives power accessories, other belts may also need removal. Note their location and routing so that you can reinstall them in the proper sequence.

If you are not removing the radiator but need to remove the shroud, reinstall one screw at each side, if necessary, to support the radiator as the shroud is detached. On some trucks, the space between the radiator and engine is enough to replace the water pump by just removing the shroud. (Consult your repair manual.) Take care not to damage radiator fins when removing the fan, pulley or water pump.

Fig. 7-21. *Serpentine belts have unique routings. Note the engine equipment and match to your Toyota truck repair manual chart or the decal beneath the hood of your truck.*

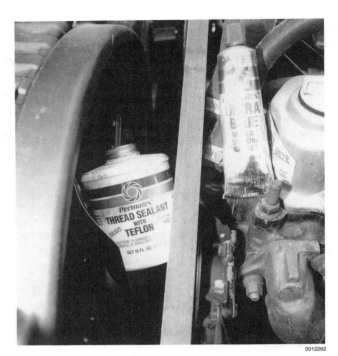

Fig. 7-22. *Use the specified gasket sealant when installing a water pump. Proper sealant is both oil and coolant resistant. Place a thin coat on each side of the gasket. Thoroughly clean bolt threads and pipe fittings, and apply thread or pipe sealant before assembly.*

Fig. 7-23. *These bolt markings represent different grades of Metric hardware. No mark is equal to U.S. Grade 2. Metric 8.8 is equivalent to U.S. Grade 5 (three marks), while 10.9 is equivalent to U.S. Grade 8 (six marks), a much higher tensile strength than the general purpose U.S. Grade 5 or Metric 8.8. In addition to these classifications, Toyota lists special grade marking charts in the back of the OEM Repair Manual for your model truck.*

When the lower radiator hose attaches to the water pump, you need to disconnect this hose at the water pump. On some engines, you may want to remove the upper hose to allow more room to work. Now loosen all other hoses attached to the water pump.

All water pump installations require wire brush cleaning of bolts and fasteners and close inspection of hardware and fittings for corrosion damage. Carefully scrape old gasket material from the water pump mounting surface. If surfaces are aluminum, use extreme caution when scraping to avoid nicking soft alloy.

Years ago, water pump rebuilding kits were available. Today, your local Toyota dealer or parts outlet can supply complete new or rebuilt replacement pumps. Make certain that the new or rebuilt pump is identical to the pump you have removed, and inspect the new gasket(s).

As required, transfer any reusable fittings or pipes from old pump to new pump. If fittings show excessive wear, replace with new parts of like kind and coat threads with a film of liquid Teflon sealant. Evenly coat both sides of new gasket(s) with a suitable gasket sealant. Apply sealant or liquid Teflon to bolt threads before installing water pump.

Find an appropriate coolant-resistant sealant approved for water pump installations. Avoid use of too much sealant on gaskets, as excess sealant finds its way into the radiator tubes. On very late model engines, anaerobic sealers sometimes take the place of a conventional gasket. Consult your Toyota repair manual on what kind of seal your engine parts require.

With the odd routing of serpentine drive belts, some late model engines have either forward or reverse rotation water pumps. Make note of which way your engine's water pump and fan rotate. Be certain that the new pump's impeller vanes match the original pump's direction of rotation.

If electrolysis or erosion has weakened your water pump bolts, discard them and replace with new, properly graded hardware. Always be certain that bolts are of the same thread pitch, thread length and overall length as original hardware. Use hardware gradings equal to or better than those indicated on the heads of OEM bolts. In-

stall new lock washers of the same kind as the original hardware, and apply coolant-resistant sealant to the bolt threads as described in your Toyota repair manual.

When a specific torque setting is not available, torque bolts according to their thread size and grade standards. These specifications are usually in the back of the Toyota Repair Manual for your truck. Many non-factory service manuals neglect the torque settings for water pump and engine accessories hardware. If you are tightening bolts into threads in an aluminum alloy casting, use caution. Tighten all bolts gradually and in cross sequence.

WARNING —

The running fan and water pump contain a lot of energy. One of the worst possible accidents is a fan coming loose and either driving through the radiator core or flying in lethal fashion from the engine bay.

Reinstall and torque power driven accessory hardware to the settings found in your OEM Toyota repair manual. Much of the hardware that you remove during a water pump installation supports components that are under stress when the engine is running. Setting proper torque is essential. Torque bolts in sequence and stages, from a light and uniform tension to the final torque setting described for your engine.

Unless otherwise specified, after tightening the water pump bolts, other parts go back in place by simply reversing the step sequence used for removing the old pump. Once you've safely secured the water pump, pulley and fan, install a new fan belt or serpentine drive belt (if wear exists) and tighten securely. Follow the factory belt tightening procedure. In some cases, a special belt tensioner or a torque wrench is necessary to meet OE requirements.

If no data or special tools are available, a V-groove belt should deflect about 1/2" when you apply heavy thumb force midway between the pulleys. (The alternator or generator pulley should rotate very slightly as you press firmly on the belt.) Serpentine belts require a large amount of tightening force. Adjust to factory specification.

Fig. 7-24. Follow factory belt tightening procedure whenever possible. If data is unavailable, adjust a V-type belt to 1/2" deflection midway between the generator/alternator pulley and fan pulley. Measure this deflection while applying firm thumb pressure to the belt. Correct tension will rotate generator/alternator pulley slightly as you apply pressure.

With coolant drained, this is also a good time to replace the thermostat. During replacement, carefully scrape old gasket material from the mounting area, taking care not to scrape gasket material into the cooling ports. (If old gasket material circulates to the radiator tubes, it can restrict coolant flow and inhibit cooling.)

Examine the radiator for rust and scale, seepage at solder seams and signs of corrosion. Consider sending the radiator unit for a boil out and pressure testing, even if no leaks are apparent. You only want to do this job once, so consider any parts that could fail in service.

Put a light coat of suitable sealant on the inner ends of hoses or outside the hose fitting threads. Install hoses with new clamps centered carefully. (Where applicable, make sure the coil of wire is in place within each radiator hose, if so equipped. This prevents the hose from collapsing.) Tighten clamps securely.

Make certain the radiator draincock is shut snugly. Pour anti-freeze/coolant and correct water mix into the radiator. Allow the coolant to settle, and keep filling until liquid reaches full level. Top off as necessary. On closed coolant systems with an overflow tank, fill radiator to the top of the filler neck, then seal with the radiator cap. Add coolant to the overflow tank's COLD line.

Install the radiator cap, turn the heater controls to HOT, and start the engine. Let the engine reach operating temperature, then turn it off and allow to cool completely. Once cool, slowly open the radiator cap.

Since the coolant has circulated thoroughly with the heater on, you can check the coolant mixture with a hydrometer. This will help you decide whether to top off with straight coolant, water or a mixture of both. Unless your climate has arctic temperatures, strive for a 50/50 coolant/water ratio, which will read around −34° F protection with an ethylene glycol anti-freeze solution.

Now, with the engine cool and shut off, you should recheck torque on all hardware and the hose clamps. Also check closely for leaks. If you suspect a leak, pressure check the system.

Water Pump Details For Earlier Engines

Earlier Land Cruiser engines and carburetor era four-cylinder models have relatively simple water pump replacement procedures. For this reason, I will offer a basic description of a water pump replacement on these models. This may assist if you cannot find more model-specific information or you have become stuck with water pump troubles at some remote location. Look closely at your engine and its accessories. If you see distinct differences, refer to a Toyota OEM repair manual for your year and model truck.

Make sure that the engine is cool enough to prevent injury, drain coolant carefully by opening the lower radiator draincock. Loosening the radiator cap will allow faster drainage. Catch all coolant in a pan for either reuse or environmentally safe disposal. Disconnect any hoses that attach directly to the water pump.

Loosen the fan shroud, making sure that the radiator remains supported once you loosen the shroud's hardware. Loosen the alternator/generator adjusting arm bracket, then remove the fan belt(s) completely. Some models have power steering or air conditioning, so you may need to loosen additional belts. Note their placement and routing.

Now you can decide whether you have safe room for removing the fan. If you cannot remove the fan without risking damage to the radiator, consider removing the radiator. With coolant drained and hoses disconnected, this will only take a few extra minutes. Handle the radiator carefully.

For trucks with an automatic transmission, you would need to carefully disconnect and drain the transmission cooler lines at the radiator and cap off the lines with clean plugs to prevent contamination of the transmission fluid. Do not reuse drained ATF. Top off with fresh ATF when the job is finished.

Plan on replacing the water pump with a rebuilt or new assembly. Do not force parts. If they do not separate readily, they may be a component in a press-fitted assembly. Do not remove a water pump pulley unless it slides readily on and off the hub and shaft. Some water pump pulleys press firmly onto the pump shaft. In such cases, the pump and pulley come off as an assembly.

You may find that the thermostat housing and additional hose fittings make removal of the pump awkward. Since you should replace the thermostat along with this job, consider removing the thermostat housing before taking the water pump loose.

Now you can remove the bolts that secure the water pump to the front end of the engine block. Carefully support the pump until you have removed all bolts. Make sure that you can easily pull the pump unit straight forward to avoid damaging the impellers. Be extremely careful to protect the radiator if it is still in place.

When piecing the project back together, reverse the steps used during the removal of the water pump. Tighten belts to specification; for V-belts, you can use the procedure I've outlined earlier in this chapter if you do not have access to Toyota Repair Manual guidelines.

Chapter 8

Engine Tune-up and Emission Controls

TUNED CORRECTLY, a properly equipped Toyota pickup, 4Runner or Land Cruiser can easily tow a sizeable trailer over Colorado's Loveland Pass or California's infamous Grapevine. At construction sites and timberlands, Toyota 4x4 work trucks spend the bulk of their service life hauling maximum payloads over bad roads and up severe grades. For top performance, dependable service and decent fuel economy, your Toyota truck's engine requires routine tune-ups and preventive maintenance.

Tuning demands have changed dramatically since 1958. Until 1978, Toyota truck engines had breaker point ignitions. Beginning in 1975, semi-electronic ignitions (still using points) gained prominence, with enhanced spark voltages, more complete ignition plus lower maintenance requirements. By 1978, all Toyota truck engines featured breakerless electronic ignition distributors.

In 1984, some pickup models (SR5 manual transmission models and DLXs with automatics) began using electronic fuel injection (22R-E engine). Other models and engine types gradually switched from carburetors to EFI, and by 1988, all Toyota gas truck engines feature EFI.

The 22R-TE (turbocharged) first came on line in 1986; the 2.0L diesel engine added a turbocharger in 1985. This 2.0L turbo diesel was an advanced design with an overhead camshaft (OHC) and roller rocker arms. The 22R-TE gas turbo served well as a stopgap performance measure until the introduction of the 3VZ-E 3.0L V-6 in 1988.

EFI boasts the use of an oxygen sensor and other sensor feedback to precisely control air/fuel ratios and the electronic spark management. Instantaneous computer controlled spark timing enhances performance without harmful detonation (ping). This type of engine requires far less routine maintenance.

0019180

Fig. 8-1. *This late Land Cruiser has a DOHC in-line six-cylinder engine, a fully electronic ignition with computer controlled spark advance, and a comprehensive emissions package that adds to the tuning requirements.*

Fig. 8-2. I find the Denco Step a handy item for tuning a taller 4x4 truck. Use of such a step and a fender cover will allow you to work on the distributor or deep in the engine bay without marring the truck's paint.

Earlier mechanical and vacuum advance ignition distributors and carburetor fuel systems often require tuning or adjustments for altitude changes and lower grade fuels. Later Toyota engines with electronic fuel and spark management automatically adjust and compensate for altitude changes, poor fuel grades and a wide range of loads and driver demands.

As an avid outdoorsperson, I have always owned or had access to a 4WD truck. Whether living at sea level or near 5,000 feet elevation, as I now do, I try to stay in condition for hiking, hunting, cross-country skiing and fishing at much higher elevations. Likewise, I tune my trucks for hard work and expect them to perform reliably from sea level to at least 10,000 feet elevation.

If your truck's engine has carburetion and a breaker point or conventional (mechanical/centrifugal and vacuum) spark advance electronic ignition, precise tuning can make a difference. Understanding your truck's tune-up needs, including the fuel, spark and emission control systems, will also improve your skills at troubleshooting and field repairs.

Moreover, tune-up skills provide a cornerstone for off-highway survival. Back country travel, effectively carrying a heavy cargo, and your truck's trailer pulling ability each rely upon proper ignition and fuel system tune.

Emission Controls and Tune-up

Emission control service, which has become an increasingly larger part of engine maintenance, also affects your truck's performance. For basic tuning, the exhaust gas recirculation (EGR) circuit and closed crankcase ventilation (PCV) system are primary concerns. Other emission devices can also affect engine tune.

The closed crankcase ventilation system requires routine care. (Toyota Land Cruisers offered closed crankcase devices early on, and California mandated such devices for all engines by the early 1960s.) Always service or replace the positive crankcase ventilation (PCV) valve when tuning your truck's engine. The idle, manifold vacuum and general performance depend upon a clean and functional PCV system.

California still demands a closed crankcase retrofit on 1955-up vehicles plus biennial smog inspection on many model years of cars and trucks. Other states and local areas, designated as "non-compliant," "non-attainment areas" or, generally, regions poor in air quality, now have similar annual or biennial inspection requirements.

To pass a visual inspection in California and the many other states and local areas that require emission compliance and testing, all OEM (factory) emission controls must be in place and operative. Your truck can fail a smog test for simply not having the flexible aluminum heat tube between the exhaust manifold and air cleaner intake. Assuming that your engine is in good condition, a tune-up will assure compliance and help pass the smog test.

Carbureted Land Cruiser sixes, especially late 1960s to 1987 models, gave up increasingly larger doses of horsepower to comply with Federal and California emission standards. Reclaiming such latent horsepower is possible, in some cases, through the use of aftermarket performance parts that have California E.O. (exemption) numbers. (See the engine performance chapter.) As a rule, however, if you want your truck to comply with emission laws and contribute to clean air, you need to preserve OEM emission controls. Emission control maintenance helps assure a successful tune-up.

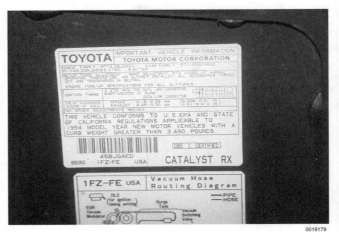

Fig. 8-3. The underhood tune-up decal offers valuable details about emission features and tune-up specifications. On this Land Cruiser, the decal offers enough information to perform a complete tune-up.

Later in this chapter, you will find details on emission controls and service. If you intend to service a 1965 or newer engine, familiarize yourself with the emission control section before attempting a major tune-up.

Fundamental Engine Requirements

The best tune-up cannot compensate for internal engine defects, wear or damage. As an adult education automotive and diesel mechanics instructor, I fielded many questions about engine needs and tuning.

In response, I devised a simple formula called "The Four Basics." An engine must meet these requirements before tuning can be a success. The Four Basics are:

1. Normal compression
2. Correct valve lift and valve opening duration
3. Correct valve timing
4. Normal oil pressure

Additionally, the engine must operate at its normal coolant temperature.

Normal compression depends on proper piston ring, valve and gasket sealing. The valvetrain and camshaft condition determine proper valve lift, valve opening duration and valve timing. Valvetrain troubles include wear at camshaft lobes, the timing chain, the timing sprockets or gears and the valve springs. Oil pressure relies on good engine bearings, polished and true bearing journal surfaces, a sound oil pump and unobstructed oil passages.

For tuning purposes, you can add steady vacuum to the checklist. If your engine meets the four basic requirements and has no vacuum leaks, your tuning efforts will be successful.

1. ENGINE ORIENTATION

As a truck fleet mechanic, when I brought an older vehicle into the shop for periodic (routine) engine service, lubrication and tuning, the first steps were a complete chassis lube, checking all gearbox fluid levels and setting the valves with the engine still thoroughly warm. With the engine speed adjusted to a very slow idle, I could set the running valves with a minimal amount of oil spillage.

Next I drained the oil and changed the oil filter, then filled the crankcase. Installation of new ignition points, a condenser and rotor followed, and I set the points with a dwell meter before disconnecting and plugging the distributor vacuum advance line to check the base timing.

Many early engines had manual chokes, and I serviced the air cleaner and made sure that the choke was operating freely. After reinstalling the air cleaner, the final step was to set the carburetor idle mixture and idle speed with the engine warmed completely.

Aside from the time spent adjusting valves, changing the valve cover gasket and setting the points with a dwell meter, the accessibility of engine parts was so good on early engines that a tune-up went quickly and always proved satisfying. Later engines have different needs. The following section outlines some of the basics of tuning each engine family.

Land Cruiser In-line OHV Six

The Land Cruiser's in-line OHV sixes built from 1958–92 provide an ideal place to learn tune-up work. All distributors mount at the side of the engine block, easily accessible and simple to service. F and 2F carburetors vary in

Fig. 8-4. *Often overlooked during tune-up is the battery. Ignition and electronic fuel systems require precise battery and charge voltages. Checking overall battery condition is easy with modern dash voltmeter gauge. Simply turn on key without starting engine and read voltage on dash gauge. Check drive belt tensions and clean battery posts regularly.*

Fig. 8-5. *The basic design of the Toyota F and 2F in-line OHV six changed little between 1958 and 1987. In 1975, the 2F six came on line and was available through 1987. 1958–87 in-line OHV sixes, like this 1983 2F type in an FJ40, look very similar. On all of these engines, the ignition distributor location provides easy maintenance.*

Fig. 8-6. F, 2F and 3F-E Land Cruiser OHV in-line sixes were four-main bearing designs. Well suited for truck service, the basic F, 2F and de-stroked 3F-E engines are easy to recognize and share common overhaul and tune-up requirements. 1978–up sixes have fully electronic ignitions; all F and 2F engines use carburetors; the 3F-E uses electronic fuel injection (EFI).

Fig. 8-7. 2F engine in mid-1970s and later FJ Land Cruisers is an anomaly. Crankshaft features an archaic hand crank provision (top), while the engine has an overwhelming load of modern emission control equipment (bottom). Heat generated by lean fuel mixtures and emission devices requires an electric fan to cool the carburetor and an EGR system intercooler.

design, earlier F engines using a one-barrel type, while all later F and 2F engines use a two-barrel design. Reaching air and fuel filters is easy, and earlier versions of these trucks were especially simple to fix alongside the road—as many have been. The emission control era takes its toll on these engines, and the simple F and 2F OHV in-line six becomes a service and troubleshooting handful in its final form. Use a Toyota repair manual when servicing emission devices, the more complex carburetors and the 3F-E EFI engines. All in-line OHV sixes have solid tappets/lifters that require periodic valve adjustment.

8RC, 18RC, 20R, 22R In-line OHC Four

These engines have similar tuning requirements. Like the simpler in-line sixes, the OHC engine's distributor is readily accessible. Installing points and adjusting point dwell angle is comparatively easy on these engines. Servicing a breakerless distributor is, fortunately, an infrequent chore. A principal concern when tuning these engines is periodic valve adjustment.

Fig. 8-8. Highly regarded 22R four-cylinder engine (shown) had its predecessors in the 8RC, 18RC and 20R. The 20R first introduced in 1975, is still regarded as among the best fours ever built. 22Rs share the basic 20R design. Tuning these engines is relatively easy and straightforward. 8RC, 18RC and early 20R engines use breaker point distributors; all 22R engines (1981–up) feature breakerless electronic distributors.

3VZ-E V-6, 2.7L Fours, 3.4L V-6

These and other late Toyota engines with timing belt or chain drives have few tune-up needs. EFI, electronic spark management and long-lasting spark plugs extend the service intervals of these engines. Valve adjustment is still essential at proscribed intervals. Again, I cannot overstress the importance of servicing the timing belt at Toyota's recommended intervals. Failure to do so can result in severe and costly damage to the engine.

Fig. 8-9. *The distributor cap of 8RC, 18RC, 20R and 22R OHC fours is easy to reach. You can make fine adjustments of the breaker points without struggling to find the point set mounting screws. This enables quick and easy dwell angle setting. Often, the easiest method of setting dwell is with the distributor cap removed and engine cranking, a procedure that may require several trial adjustments.*

Fig. 8-10. *3VZ-E 3.0L V-6 was an innovative and high tech addition to the compact truck and 4Runner engine lineup. Introduced in 1988, this engine's obvious design differences include a timing belt drive, a narrow 60-degree V configuration and a higher performance level than Toyota's four-cylinder engines of that era. The timing belt of this and subsequent timing drive belt engines requires careful and periodic attention.*

2.0L Diesel (Naturally aspirated and Turbocharged)

The designs that span 1981–87 are rugged and have few service demands. Like other diesel engines, the periodic changing of oil and filters is essential to engine performance and longevity. If your Toyota truck has a diesel engine, concentrate on high quality lubricants and frequent oil, air and fuel filter changes. "Tune-up," as such, has more to do with changing the fuel filter(s), repairing O-ring seal leaks, air cleaner service, injector cleaning and

Fig. 8-11. *Latest engines for Tacoma compact models, 4Runner and T100 trucks include the 3.4L V-6 and 2.7L in-line four. Each has four valves per cylinder, a DOHC system, advanced EFI and other refinements that allow maximum performance without an increase in fuel consumption. 3.4L V-6 produces an impressive 190 horsepower, while the 2.7L four provides 150 highly usable horses. Maintenance is low, although the valve timing mechanisms become more complex on these engines. Like the 3VZ-E 3.0L V-6, valve adjustment is an intricate process.*

glow plug repairs. Despite rising diesel fuel costs, the fuel savings, overall reliability and notable longevity of these 1981–87 Toyota diesel engines keep them attractive. At present, parts availability is not a problem.

Filter changes are very important with your diesel engine, especially fuel filters. Diesel fuel has a very high water content, and this contributes to everything from corrosive damage to the actual emergence of living bacteria cultures in your truck's fuel system.

Frequent fuel filter changes and use of a quality water trap filter will help preserve your diesel engine and ensure good performance. Become familiar with servicing a water trap filter. Fuel system anti-fungal agents are available if you suspect that a culture is alive and growing within the truck's system. (See your local diesel/truck stop.)

NOTE —

At this time, the reduction of diesel fuel sulphur content as a measure to lower tailpipe pollution is a topical issue. The lack of lubricity after the fuel hydrogenation process (one method of eliminating sulphur) can lead to injector O-ring damage and mechanical fuel pump diaphragm failure, most frequently in engines with higher mileage.

An area that sometimes requires attention is the glow plug system. Failure of the glow plug controller or relay can cause excessive glow plug operation and failure of the expensive glow plugs. Whether you service your Toyota diesel or sublet work, make certain that the glow plug relays and controls function properly.

Fig. 8-12. *Glow plug failure is not uncommon to higher mileage diesel engines. When left on too long, glow plugs can burn out.*

Fig. 8-13. *Troubleshooting your electronic fuel and spark management system requires a precise digital volt-ohmmeter. For feedback/closed-loop carburetors and EFI systems, tenths and hundredths of a volt make a difference.*

Beyond these concerns and occasional replacement of leaky injector O-ring seals, the 2.0L diesel is content with regular oil changes and filter service. If you intend to perform major work on your injector system or in-depth repairs on the engine unit, invest in the Toyota repair manual that covers these service operations.

A Closer Look At EFI Engines

Toyota trucks began using electronic fuel injection (EFI) in some 1984 22R four-cylinder engines. By 1987, the last carbureted engines were a few applications of the four-cylinder 22R (most were 22R-E and 22R-TE with EFI), plus all of the Land Cruisers. Here, Toyota's use of carburetors ended and multi-point EFI became the mainstay fuel induction system.

Although the special skills and tools for servicing EFI have kept many consumers from servicing their own engines, you can work on various aspects of the EFI system. An OEM Toyota repair manual covers repairs and troubleshooting thoroughly.

Professional mechanics often lament new technology. When the electronic (transistor) ignitions came into vogue in the 1960s and 1970s, a trip to the parts house would invariably turn up a seasoned mechanic who complained about the "lack of reliability" and huge expenses involved with electronic ignition parts—not to mention that these mysterious solid state devices would surely fail when we least expected and leave us stranded!

Today, few argue that archaic breaker points make more sense than a high voltage, precisely timed and fully electronic ignition system. I recall working with exotic dual point high performance distributors that required constant tinkering with dwell angle, followed by the mandatory re-timing of the engine on every occasion that the breaker points needed "minor" adjusting.

Toyota breaker point distributors, although simpler devices, have wearable and less precise spark advance mechanisms, a set of breaker points that need replacement periodically, and very rigid limits for spark timing

advance. Adjusting the points and setting the initial or base spark timing are the only tuning provisions.

Yes, there was a time when some electronic ignitions had marginal components, and the repair and maintenance of electronic fuel injection once meant the equivalent of an extra monthly vehicle payment for owners of high mileage cars. That has changed. Electronic fuel and spark management has revolutionized the automotive industry. Toyota's multi-point EFI systems provide exceptional fuel economy, low tailpipe emissions and improved performance.

> **NOTE —**
> Failure of an EFI/spark management system is covered under the manufacturer's warranty and also under federally mandated pollution control laws. If your truck has received proper routine maintenance (replacement of serviceable parts like spark plugs, filters, etc.) and is within the time frame/mileage for either coverage, see your Toyota truck dealership. You may have warranty against some or all of the repair expenses.

Fuel injection relies on a series of interrelated sub-systems. Engine sensors take the climate, altitude, coolant temperature, cargo loads and driver's throttle input into account. In the exhaust stream, an oxygen sensor performs much like an infrared scope analyzer, noting oxygen content in the burned fuel and instantly telling the engine's computer the air/fuel ratio. The computer, in turn, instantaneously adjusts fuel flow to maintain air/fuel ratio constants. These various ratios complement both the engine needs and driver demands under all driving conditions.

By precisely monitoring load, engine speed and manifold pressure, the fuel injection system and electronic spark timing mechanisms can adjust to changes in milli-

Fig. 8-14. *A full complement of sensors feed data to the EFI and spark management computer. Air/fuel mixtures depend on the oxygen sensor signal. The oxygen sensor and manifold pressure signals help adjust for altitude changes, a significant gain of EFI. Feedback carburetors, although electronically controlled, compensate to a far lesser degree than EFI.*

seconds. The result is precisely metered fuel and optimally timed spark for better power output, fuel economy and a clean tailpipe.

EFI and electronic spark management have meant huge savings in fuel, precise startups in the coldest weather conditions and the ability to pull a load without stressing the engine. Smooth travel at any altitude, plus successful use of the current rash of low octane fuels, are major accomplishments of EFI and electronic spark timing management.

Moreover, EFI has enabled the internal combustion piston engine to meet the challenge of increasingly higher air quality standards. Various Toyota truck four- and six-cylinder engines with EFI emit as little as 1/20th the tailpipe pollution of their counterpart late 1960s engines. And these newer EFI engines require no periodic adjustments or tinkering. Routine tuning is nearly obsolete.

EFI Tuning Needs

Although all ignition and fuel adjustments are pre-set at the factory, EFI does have needs. Air cleaner changes and periodic fuel filter changes are crucial to performance and quality service from these engine designs. The most common fuel injection troubles involve the fuel filter(s).

Aside from the more accessible in-line fuel filters, some Toyota trucks also use a pickup filter in the fuel tank. If you know the tank has corrosives and debris that could plug a pickup screen, refer to your Toyota truck repair manual for safe procedures and service steps to remove the fuel tank and/or the pickup screen.

Despite the high level of reliability of modern computer and electronic components, parts failures and some adjustment needs do occur. The idle speed controls, secondary ignition pieces (distributor cap, rotor, spark plugs and spark cables), even the injectors and their O-ring seals, can require attention. Beyond this, EFI components either work properly or they don't.

When bad tune or poor engine operation occurs, you can perform necessary troubleshooting, replace faulty sensors or repair those parts that test as defective. You may want to understand, diagnose and repair your truck's EFI and spark management system. The best way to increase your diagnostic skills is through carefully reading the OEM Toyota truck repair manual sections that cover your model. Equipped with such a guide and the necessary testing tools for EFI service (outlined thoroughly in the Toyota truck repair manual and other professional level manuals), you can competently service the EFI system.

Before condemning expensive EFI parts, check the simpler possibilities. Wiring, ground leads and vacuum hose leaks cause a variety of problems. Make a systematic check of the wire leads. An electric fuel pump mounts in the fuel tank, and during start-up, you should hear the pump operate. If the pump is not active, check the fuel pump relay, fuses and wiring.

Most components on your EFI engine are very reliable. Contrary to the views of sceptics, one of the least likely items to fail is the computer. Connectors, however, often become faulty or create too much resistance, which can radically distort the computer's sensory signals.

If you suspect sensor, fuel injector or other problems and want to perform your own service, invest first in the Toyota truck repair manual for your model or a professional service manual that covers electronic fuel injection troubleshooting and repairs in detail. OEM Toyota repair manuals offer easy-to-follow flow charts, diagrams, and steps that quickly assist with troubleshooting procedures

Although the term tune-up would today apply mostly to routine parts replacement, EFI engine performance issues require concise, sequential tests and measures. Toyota OEM and other professional repair manuals explain these steps in detail.

For me, the only limiting factors would be availability of specialty tools and whether I care to invest in some of the expensive diagnostic equipment required for troubleshooting and testing some circuits and devices. Professional service guides describe the tools needed for each procedure, so you can make an informed decision about whether or not to sublet the work to a Toyota dealership or qualified shop. Such insight will pay for your OEM Toyota truck repair manual(s) many times over.

2. IGNITION TUNE-UP

Spark plugs, the distributor cap, rotor, coil and plug cables make up the ignition's secondary circuit. The rotor and spark plugs require periodic service; less frequently, the distributor cap and spark cables.

On earlier models the primary spark circuit consists of the breaker point set and condenser. On models with electronic ignition, the module replaces the points and condenser. During routine tune-up service, the breaker points, condenser and rotor require replacement. Inspect the distributor cap for corrosion at the contacts. If you believe the wires have wear, an ohmmeter can test individual plug wires for end-to-end resistance.

If an oscilloscope is not available, and the distributor is in good condition, a simple ohm meter can confirm the

Fig. 8-15. *Ignition and other service parts are available through your Toyota dealership. Use high quality OEM or aftermarket parts. Simply put, if you pay more, you get more.*

Fig. 8-17. *This commercial tester plug is a necessity with high energy electronic ignitions. Never create a spark arc to ground. Ignition system damage could result.*

Fig. 8-16. *Difficulty reaching some ignition parts encourages replacement with high quality OEM pieces. When performing a routine tune-up at higher mileage, consider replacing the distributor cap, rotor and plug wires. Using a volt-ohmmeter, check critical items like the electronic igniter or the coil. You will find test sequences and ohm specifications in your Toyota repair manual.*

Spark Plug Service

Begin an engine tune-up by cleaning debris from the area around the spark plugs, then remove the wires. Use a clean socket to avoid dropping grit into the cylinders. A flex handle spark plug ratchet serves well with awkward spark plug locations.

On engines with carbon-core spark plug wires, use a spark cable pliers to prevent damage when removing the wires. Grip the plug insulator, not the wire section.

Use compressed air and a nozzle to blow debris away from the base of the spark plugs. Remove spark plugs carefully.

> **WARNING —**
> *Wear protective goggles when blowing debris from the spark plug area.*

condition of the spark plug cables. Read ohms resistance between the ends of each wire, a measurement of the wire's capacity to move current under load.

When testing the output of an electronic ignition, use a commercial tester plug or fabricate a similar device. You want to keep the plug's metal shell grounded to the engine block and not allow any spark wire to arc directly to ground. This tool is also handy for back country troubleshooting, enabling a fast and graphic look at spark output.

If you test spark with a plug wire removed, the misfire of one cylinder creates a rich mixture in the exhaust stream. On late engines, this can send a confusing signal to the oxygen sensor and load up the catalytic converter with raw fuel. Do not test ignition spark output for long.

Fig. 8-18. *Use of a spark cable pliers is always wise. Grip the plug insulator firmly. Avoid tugging on the wires, as carbon-core will separate easily.*

"Read" the spark plugs. Fouled spark plugs provide a valuable insight. Oily plugs generally mean worn valve guides or piston rings. A sooty black or wet plug surface indicates gasoline fouling, unless ash from burnt oil is also present. Oily plugs can denote either valve guide, guide seal or piston ring wear.

Fig. 8-19. *Spark plug cleaning machines were once very popular. However, you need a spark plug tester or engine oscilloscope analyzer to verify a used spark plug's ability to fire. Avoid trouble. Replace your spark plugs with each tune-up or at Toyota's recommended intervals.*

If caught quickly, gasoline fouling is less ominous than oil fouling. Gas fouling of only one or a few cylinders usually indicates a worn spark cable(s) or an ignition system problem such as a defective rotor, distributor cap, breaker points, condenser, coil, electronic ignition module or faulty wiring.

If all spark plugs appear gas fouled, yet the ignition tests okay, suspect a carburetion or fuel injection problem. The plugs may also show other kinds of damage, including broken porcelain. When this occurs, check for detonation or pre-ignition. On gasoline engines, overly advanced spark timing or the use of very low octane (highly volatile) fuel can also cause plug damage.

As spark plugs are relatively inexpensive, replacement of worn plugs is the best protection against mis-fire and

Fig. 8-20. *Detonation (ping) is always a symptom of engine stress. Worse yet is pre-ignition, which burns up pistons, shatters rings and even breaks connecting rods!*

Fig. 8-21. *My son, Jacob, also started young. Here he sets spark plug torque using a torque wrench. His smaller hands work really well on tight access spark plugs.*

poor starting. Before installing new plugs, verify that each plug has the correct part number and heat range for your engine. Especially on pre-electronic breaker point ignitions, a slightly hotter (stick within one heat range) spark plug may work better during extremely cold weather, when long warm-up periods tend to carbon foul plugs.

On engines with high-energy electronic ignition systems and stringent emission standards, the correct spark plug heat range and gap are crucial to engine survival. For many engines, the underhood emission control decal provides tune-up data and spark plug information.

Check each plug gap carefully. I prefer a plug gapping tool that provides a flat and parallel gap surface. Many home mechanics, however, achieve good results with a round wire gauge set. Bend the side electrode strap carefully. Never attempt to move the center electrode.

In the heyday of the Land Cruiser F-type OHV in-line sixes, it was popular to clean and reuse spark plugs. Most mechanics have abandoned this practice. Clean plugs may look good, but they may also have lost their full firing capability. The only way to test a used plug is with an oscilloscope or plug tester. New plugs eliminate costly troubleshooting problems.

If you have limited experience at tightening spark plugs, use a torque wrench. Too loose and the plug could unscrew and blow out. Over-tightening may distort the spark gap or damage the plug. I place a small amount of anti-seize compound on plugs that fit into aluminum alloy threads. Keep compound above the first spark plug thread to prevent it from entering cylinders. Anti-seize reduces the risk of thread seizure that might pull out cylinder head thread material with the next plug change.

Fig. 8-22. *Spark plug gapper is ideal tool for setting new plugs. Tool (top) adjusts strap and sets parallel gap surfaces. I would not use this kind of tool on a platinum spark plug with its delicate core wire. Gap platinum plugs with a conventional gapping tool (bottom).*

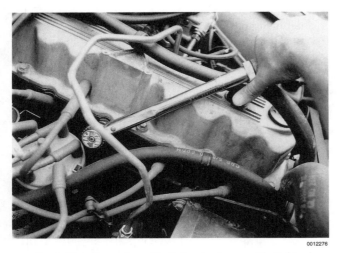

Fig. 8-23. *If you have limited experience with tightening spark plugs, use a torque wrench. Overtightening can distort the spark gap or damage the plug or cylinder head.*

Fig. 8-24. *Traditionally, Japanese-built spark plugs (NGK or Nippondenso) have been OEM Toyota plugs. Platinum plugs have become popular in late model engines with longer service intervals. Toyota has used a variety of plug thread types and wrench sizes.*

Prior to the introduction of higher output electronic ignitions in mid-1970s Toyota trucks, spark plug gaps and torque settings were very consistent. A Toyota owner's manual or repair manual offers torque specifications for these engines. For 1976-up Toyota trucks, the emission and tune decals (found in the engine bay) will describe the spark plug type and gap setting, along with point gap and timing specifications.

The 1975-up high voltage electronic spark systems sometimes require wider spark plug gaps. Your underhood decal furnishes information on tuning the engine, including the type of spark plug recommended and its proper gap.

Wires and Distributor Cap

Because modern spark cables have a carbon core to suppress radio interference, your truck's ignition wires require periodic testing for ohms resistance and shorts. The simplest volt-ohmmeter comes in handy here, providing a quick means for checking resistance between the ends of each lead. As a yardstick, longer leads typically require a minimum resistance of 4,000 ohms and maximum of 15,000 ohms.

As you check the spark cables, twist and coil each wire gently. This will reveal opens or defective segments of wire. Also look at the insulation. Carefully route wires to prevent nicks and melted insulation.

> **CAUTION —**
> *Never puncture or use a pinpoint probe on carbon core wire insulation.*

A quick preliminary test of plug wire condition is possible with a strobe timing light—preferably the induction type. Hook up the timing light lead to one spark cable at a time. With the engine idling, observe the consistency of the spark while also listening to the smoothness of the engine. Ideally, the spark should appear steady, without misfire, pause or interruption.

Fig. 8-25. *Tools for conventional ignition work include blade feeler gauge for breaker points. Use brass feeler gauges for checking electronic distributor air gap settings. Distributor tower brush cleans corrosion from cap and coil towers. Grease is for breaker cam and point rubbing block.*

Fig. 8-27. *Contacts on the distributor cap can oxidize and corrode. Replace distributor cap and rotor when corrosion or arcing has caused damage. If available, a high quality replacement cap with brass contacts makes a good investment.*

Fig. 8-26. *Check plug wires with a volt-ohmmeter. Attach leads to each end of the wire and read resistance. While testing resistance, coil the wire very gently and loosely to turn up shorts without damaging the sensitive carbon core.*

Fig. 8-28. *Often, the distributor is awkward to reach. When installing the distributor cap, center the cap carefully and make sure each clip or screw seats completely. If there is a locating notch between the cap and housing, make sure the cap seats correctly.*

There are other causes of misfire, too, including lean or rich fuel mixtures, a fouled spark plug, a defective distributor or a worn ignition coil. Remove the suspected wire and test it with your ohmmeter before investing in an expensive set of spark cables.

The spark plugs and cables are part of the secondary ignition circuit. In addition to these components, the distributor cap and rotor require attention. Replace the distributor cap when you see wear, cracks, carbon tracking (a cause of cross-firing between cylinders) or corroded electrical contacts. During routine service, I inspect the cap for cracks, examine the rotor contacts and clean the cable sockets with a distributor brush.

On high energy electronic ignitions, high voltage will eventually erode the rotor. If not corrected, electricity can short to ground through the distributor shaft. Inspect the rotor carefully. Replace the rotor if arcing, heat damage or wear is evident.

Primary Ignition System

On earlier non-electronic ignition systems, the points and condenser require periodic replacement. As for when you should replace the breaker points, consider several symptoms: point misalignment, severe rubbing block wear, pitting, arcing, blue discoloration or contact surfaces showing a peaked buildup of metal on one side (which can also mean condenser trouble).

When I entered the field of automotive mechanics, ignition point service was still popular. Light contact filing, performing spring tension tests and re-adjusting the breaker gap were routine procedures when points showed minimal wear.

Fig. 8-29. *High voltage output of electronic (breakerless) ignitions can burn a hole from the center contact or rotor to top of distributor shaft. Spark arcs to ground, shorting out ignition. Check the rotor and cap periodically.*

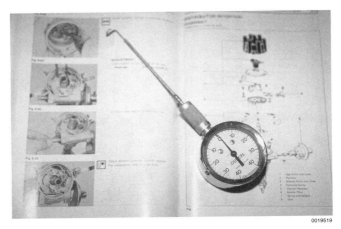

Fig. 8-30. *This spring tension gauge, still a part of my breaker point tuning tools, helps set correct tension to reduce point bounce at high rpm and also assure normal rubbing block and contact wear. When wear is minimal, filing and re-gapping ignition points extends parts life and service. Use a special points file, and clean all filings away with an electrical contact cleaner. When I began performance tuning engines in the Muscle Car Era, tools like this provided a fine edge.*

Today, we regard breaker points as a disposable item. At routine intervals, usually 8,000 to 12,000 miles, most mechanics simply install a new set of points and a condenser. Years ago, if the condenser tested okay and the points showed even wear, condenser reuse was acceptable. In fact, if the condenser tested within specification, it was often better than a new one out of the box.

Better engineered breaker point sets have eliminated the need to adjust point spring tension. However, setting the breaker point cam angle or dwell remains crucial to peak performance. Proper dwell allows full coil saturation for a hot, crisp spark and also assures good engine starts, smooth performance and long point set life. (Dwell is the number of distributor cam degrees between the spot where the breaker points close and just where they begin to open again.)

A prominent source of ignition trouble is defective primary circuit wiring. Especially on an older truck, wire can fray and short to ground against the engine block or distributor housing. Insulators on the distributor wire terminal block also wear, allowing the stud or wires to short.

Take care when installing the points and condenser. Failure to fully isolate the point spring from the distributor housing can cause hard starts, misfire or total shorting out of the ignition.

Route and attach primary wires and spark plug cables securely. Imagine your truck jostling in rough terrain. Will the breaker plate move with the vacuum advance and cause a wire short to ground? Will wires stay in place, come loose or short to ground? Before condemning your coil or other parts, look for wiring problems.

Remove the distributor cap to service the primary ignition parts (points and condenser) and the rotor. For Toyota ignition distributors equipped with a centrifugal (mechanical) advance mechanism, the centrifugal weights and springs mount beneath the breaker point plate or beneath the advance plate assembly of a fully electronic (breakerless) distributor.

Fig. 8-31. *Loose, frayed or broken primary wires will cause ignition trouble. On earlier electrical systems, embrittled wire insulation can flake off, causing shorts to ground as the wires age. Wire leads through the distributor housing wear and deteriorate. Shorts cause engine misfiring and ignition failure. Check leads whenever you service the distributor.*

All 1958–77 Toyota trucks with breaker point distributors use either centrifugal and/or vacuum spark advance mechanisms. These highly effective advance systems can accurately meet both the low and high speed load requirements of the engine. Vacuum works well at low rpm, while centrifugal advance responds to increasing engine speed.

Electronic ignitions used until the late EFI/electronic spark management era also rely on centrifugal and vacuum advance mechanisms. For emissions purposes, some vacuum spark timing systems use dual spark advance and retard diaphragms that play roles during engine acceleration and deceleration modes.

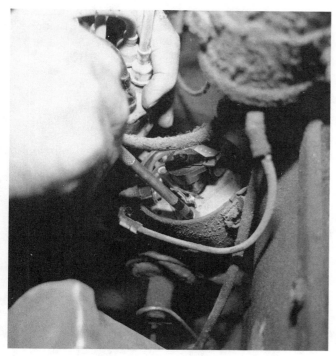

0014193

Fig. 8-32. Place points and condenser carefully on the breaker plate. (Don't drop screws, or you will be fishing for hardware or removing the distributor assembly to turn it upside down.) A spring loaded screw holder (shown here) helps.

0019356

Fig. 8-33. Place cam lubricant in this recess. As the distributor cam rotates, grease will press against the rubbing block. Grease applied to the opposite side of the rubbing block will pull away, possibly fouling the points.

If spark timing tests reveal a sluggish or erratic mechanical/centrifugal spark advance, you may need to remove the distributor for disassembly and overhaul. While some distributor vacuum advance units are adjustable or replaceable with the distributor still mounted in the engine, you will find that centrifugal advance mechanism repairs are more easily done on your work bench.

When you suspect spark advance troubles with this type of distributor, consult your OEM Toyota truck repair manual for repair and rebuilding procedures. You may decide to overhaul your distributor. Perhaps wear is so severe that installing a rebuilt or new distributor assembly makes better sense or will prove cost effective.

During breaker point installation, wipe old grease from the cam and apply a thin film of fresh lubricant. Use a special point rubbing block lubricant, applied to the thrust side (toward the direction of the distributor cam rotation) of the rubbing block.

> **NOTE —**
> When you apply the grease correctly, the rotation of the breaker cam will push the grease into the rubbing block, rather than pull grease away and scatter it.

Always reset the ignition timing after you install new points or make a dwell adjustment. Any change in the point gap or the point set's location on the breaker plate will alter the spark timing.

Dwell Meter and Setting Points

When installing or adjusting breaker points, a feeler gauge is far less accurate than a dwell meter. Using a dwell meter to adjust the breaker points will assure adequate coil saturation for high speed operation plus enough spark for easy starting. Use of a dwell meter will also extend breaker point life.

Use the ignition feeler gauge to set the points for initial start-up. Once the engine starts, you can take a dwell reading and readjust the points as needed. Since Toyota truck distributors require removal of the distributor cap to readjust points, you will want to make adjustments based on your dwell meter reading.

0019177

Fig. 8-34. Breaker point ignitions use a closed (no points adjusting window) distributor cap. This makes dwell setting more difficult, and the quickest method is with distributor cap removed and engine cranking. Adjust the points, secure screws, install the distributor cap and verify dwell once you start the engine. If necessary, shut off the engine and readjust points. Again verify cam angle (dwell) with engine running.

Breaker Point Basics

Breaker points act as an electrical switch and they require periodic attention. The gap set between the contacts determines the coil's spark output at various engine speeds.

Although you initially set the point gap with a feeler gauge, the real concern is dwell or cam-angle, which translates as the *number of distributor degrees between the time the points close and when they open.*

Dwell is critical, since a coil needs saturation of its windings to yield a snappy spark each time the points open. Wide point gaps *decrease* cam angle or dwell; narrow gaps *increase* dwell. Although it would seem that the long dwell associated with narrow gaps is desirable, narrow gaps cause unwanted arcing of spark while the points are open and excessive heat buildup in the contacts. Arcing can also cause firing of spark plugs at the wrong time.

A traditional means for increasing dwell, without risk of re-arc or short contact point life, is the use of *two* sets of breaker points. Dual-point distributors overlap the opening and closing times of the two sets, using one set to open the circuit, the other to close it. These points, gapped wider, provide high dwell degrees, allow for better coil saturation at high rpm and permit good starting.

Fig. 8-35. *A dwell meter measures the cam angle from breaker point closure to reopening. Check the dwell angle specs for your engine, and use a dwell meter for best results.*

When the engine starts, you can read dwell angle with the engine running. Once dwell is correct, consider taking the time to note the actual breaker point gap (with new points) that achieves this dwell reading. You might be able to use this setting as a more accurate starting gap for your future point set changes. Remember, you always set or read the gap at the peak of a cam lobe.

If the engine will not start with a feeler gauge setting, check all wires and connections. (Check insulators where wires attach to the points and be sure you installed these insulators in correct order.) If necessary, have an assistant crank the engine with the distributor cap removed and your dwell meter turned on. Observe spark across the points and read dwell during cranking. No spark across the points and no dwell meter reading mean either a bad electrical connection or a defective condenser. Correct this problem before setting or changing the point dwell.

> *WARNING —*
> *Do not open the points with a non-insulated screwdriver, or you may get a severe electrical shock from the condenser.*

By tightening the mounting screws just enough to still allow movement of the breaker set, you can adjust the points as the engine cranks. Move the point set (change gap) by rotating a screwdriver either clockwise or counter-clockwise at the adjusting slot. Once you adjust the dwell to within specification, tighten the mounting screws securely and confirm that dwell is still correct.

Years ago, mechanics removed the distributor from the engine and used a stroboscopic distributor machine as a testbed for routine service and repairs. You may want to sublet your distributor to a shop that has such a machine. They can test and restore the advance mechanism(s), install new points and set dwell. You would then re-install the distributor unit and set the base timing. (See timing section for instructions.)

Watch carefully for distributor shaft bushing wear. If your distributor shows a dwell variance of more than two degrees cam angle, check the shaft bushings. With the rotor removed and points open on a cam lobe, press gently against the shaft. Note the point gap. Now pull on the shaft lightly. Again measure the point gap.

The difference between these figures helps indicate distributor shaft bushing wear. When your distributor shows wear, you need to overhaul the unit or install a new or rebuilt distributor. (See performance chapter for aftermarket replacement/upgrade distributor units.)

Fig. 8-36. *Service Tip: Adjusting new points slightly wide will allow for fiber rubbing block wear. If an engine calls for a dwell angle of 37–41 degrees, set the gap toward 37. As rubbing block wear proceeds, dwell will gradually shift toward the 41-degree side. Spark timing retards slightly as the gap closes.*

Breaker gap and dwell angle settings vary on the Toyota truck engines built from 1958–77. Consult your OEM truck repair manual for details. You may need to verify the distributor part number on the distributor to confirm which unit your truck uses.

Remember, while gap settings will start the engine and provide adequate service, accurately setting the dwell angle will gain even better performance and longer service from your tune-up.

Electronic Primary Ignition System

On breakerless distributors, removing the distributor cap provides access to electronic ignition parts. The pre-EFI engines incorporate a vacuum advance unit and a centrifugal advance like breaker point distributors, but in place of the traditional breaker points and condenser, the breakerless electronic distributor uses a timer core (the "cam") and a pickup coil (the "point set"). These parts work with a replaceable external module or igniter and a conventional external coil.

Electronic ignitions offer tremendous reliability, performance tuning potential, plus they make good mechanical sense. Like earlier breaker point distributors, the centrifugal flyweights and springs lie beneath the point or pickup plate—serviceable and even ready for performance modifications. Likewise, the vacuum advance canister can be replaced with an OEM replacement or a unit with improved spark advance characteristics.

You can build performance modifications into any conventional breaker point or breakerless distributor, and this is why the design enjoys a loyal following with high performance buffs. Aftermarket or modified parts can upgrade this type of distributor to offer the same type of spark advance curves as a distributor found on high performance engines. Tuning for maximum horsepower or economy—or a reasonable point somewhere in between—is possible.

The high voltages of breakerless distributors, often well in excess of 50,000 volts in stock form, make these designs better suited to the emission control era. Long duration spark and more complete fuel burn is possible,

Fig. 8-38. These parts functioned reasonably well before the tune-up. Keep them for your off-pavement excursions to the back country. A good coil, spare igniter, breaker point set, condenser, usable distributor cap and rotor provide valuable backup parts for an outback emergency.

and the electronic ignition can easily fire across wider spark plug gaps like 0.045-inch to 0.060-inch—but only if the spark plug tips will clear the pistons and valves!

The igniter is a primary trouble spot when an electronic ignition fails. Testing electronic ignition components requires use of a sensitive digital volt-ohmmeter and other equipment, including an oscilloscope in some instances. For service and repairs beyond basic tuning, refer to your OEM Toyota truck repair manual.

Before condemning an igniter or any other electronic ignition component, check all wiring circuits and connections. Wires can fray, short and develop loose connections. Primary pickup leads can wear out, especially on vacuum advance equipped distributors. Check your engine's wiring carefully, and replace defective wires or plug connectors as needed.

> **NOTE —**
> Ignition igniters and other parts often mount near hot engine components or on the ignition coil. This may require use of a special silicone heat insulating gel, supplied with the new component(s). A coating of insulating gel, applied per instructions, helps isolate sensitive components from damaging heat.

Spark Timing

If the right quantity of current reaches fresh spark plugs, the other concern is *timing*. For older engines, the mechanical (centrifugal) advance mechanism and a vacuum advance unit require routine inspection and service.

The vacuum advance unit has a diaphragm inside and a balance spring to move at a specific vacuum pull. Vacuum can be tested with a vacuum hand pump. Look up the correct vacuum setting in your Toyota truck repair manual or a professional service guidebook that covers your engine. Then test the vacuum advance by watching

Fig. 8-37. Always read the instructions with a new coil, igniter or electronic pickup and timing core. Upgraded or superceded parts sometimes require special installation procedures.

Fig. 8-39. *Most settings call for the engine at an idle with the distributor vacuum line disconnected and plugged. Your timing light attaches to the #1 cylinder's spark plug wire. Disconnect and plug or tape off vacuum advance line before verifying base or initial timing.*

Fig. 8-40. *A distributor wrench allows easier access to the adjuster clamp nut. Loosen the bolt slightly, just enough to move the housing. The moveable distributor permits timing corrections. On many current engines, the distributor clamps in a fixed location for emission compliance; timing changes come from the engine management computer.*

the electronic advance plate or breaker point plate move as you apply vacuum. If you perform this test with the distributor cap removed, note the vacuum level where the plate *just begins to move.*

NOTE —
On later engines with electronic fuel and spark management (EFI), spark timing is electronically controlled. The engine computer receives timing signals from the ignition distributor and several other engine sensing devices. Once you verify the correct initial (idle) timing setting, there's no other timing consideration.

After inspecting the vacuum advance, check the mechanical advance mechanism. If accessible, lube the pivots for each flyweight with high temp grease and check for wear.

Be certain that the centrifugal advance unit moves easily and that the springs have tension. Once the engine is running, you can use a timing light with built-in advance to determine whether the distributor's mechanical and vacuum advance mechanisms perform properly.

NOTE —
When timing the engine, check the centrifugal advance and vacuum advance systems separately. Disconnect and tape off the distributor vacuum line before testing the centrifugal advance.

If spark advance works correctly, set the ignition *initial* spark timing to specification. This is generally done with the vacuum advance *disconnected*, unless otherwise specified in your repair manual or on the underhood tune-up decals. Initial timing is set with the engine at a specific idle speed.

Before you start the engine to verify spark timing, check the tightening torque on fan and water pump mounting hardware. Make sure the water pump shaft and bearings do not have play or wobble. When timing your engine, stay away from moving parts.

WARNING —
Do not race the engine, as the fan is more likely to come loose on a stationary vehicle than when air is moving through the radiator at road speeds. Make sure your hands, clothing and tools are well away from moving parts. Never operate the engine beyond 2,500 rpm during service work.

Always perform initial or base spark timing with the engine at its curb (fully warmed) idle speed. This means the choke is fully open, and the engine is running slowly enough to prevent the centrifugal/mechanical advance from altering the reading. Even a slight opening of the throttle will cause the vacuum advance to operate.

Initial advance settings are generally with the vacuum advance hose(s) disconnected and taped. On emission controlled engines, read the underhood decal carefully, as you may need to use special procedures or keep certain vacuum lines connected as you adjust base timing.

Use a stroboscopic timing light for best results. I like the latest induction type lights for their ease of hookup and brightness. The timing lights for my shop include a model with built-in timing advance capability.

NOTE —
Emissions law requires that an engine operate at the vehicle manufacturer's recommended setting. When you tune your engine for an emissions test, be aware that many states and local areas require a check of spark timing. Set the timing correctly to avoid failing a smog test.

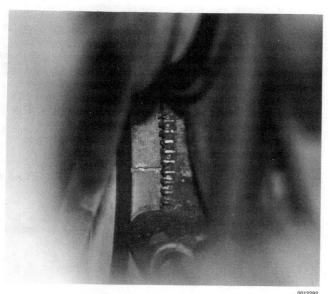

Fig. 8-41.   You will find timing marks at the engine's front timing cover. The tab is likely dirty from road debris and engine grease. With the engine safely shut off, carefully wipe the tab clean. You will index the correct marker point with the correct crankshaft line.

Fig. 8-42.   A unique and important item in earlier Toyota ignitions was the "Octane Selector." This adjustable mechanism allows quick changes in timing to compensate for fuel octane levels and altitude. When setting base timing, make certain the octane adjuster is in the "standard position." Later, you can quickly adjust several degrees of spark retard (to stop detonation from low octane fuel) or advance (to raise manifold vacuum at higher altitudes).

Your OEM Toyota truck repair manual or a professional series service guidebook lists the timing mark location, firing order, distributor direction of rotation, and initial (base or idle speed) timing specifications for your engine. With the ignition switch OFF, verify the timing mark on your engine and whether the setting is with the vacuum line disconnected and taped. Timing marks vary from a ball or timing marks on the flywheel (early in-line

sixes) to a notch or lines on the crankshaft pulley. Some timing tabs mount on the engine's front cover, just above the crankshaft pulley. Become familiar with how your engine's indexing marks or pointer align, and also know how many crankshaft degrees of timing each mark on the timing tab or crankshaft pulley represents. When you need to set the engine timing, you will be carefully observing the tab, pointer or indexing marks.

Your strobe timing light will attach to number one spark plug wire. Know which wire in the distributor cap is for number one cylinder. With a knowledge of the firing order and the cylinder numbering order (plus the direction that the distributor shaft rotates), you can also verify whether each spark plug wire is attached to the correct cylinder.

Static Timing

If you need to service your engine in the wilds, I have a static timing technique that can prove very useful on breaker point type distributors. (Electronic ignitions cannot be static timed, due to the need to generate electrical signals with a rotating distributor armature.)

Begin by locating the distributor wire lead to #1 cylinder. Remove the distributor cap and spark plugs. Manually turn the engine over in its normal direction of rotation. Watch the rotor as it approaches the #1 cylinder firing position.

Rotate the crankshaft slowly, and stop exactly where the timing marker indexes with the correct initial advance mark. On most Toyota truck engines, the marks and pointer will be visible at the crankshaft damper/pulley and timing cover. An exception is the Land Cruiser inline six cylinder with a pointer and timing mark at the clutch/converter housing and flywheel or flexplate. With the engine shut off, you may need to wipe grease off the pointer or pulley to clarify the marks.

Turn the ignition switch to the ON position. With the distributor clamped loosely, move the housing in the direction that the distributor shaft normally rotates during cranking.

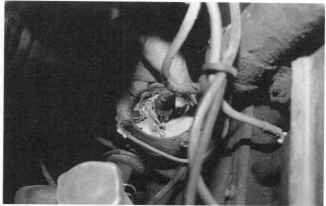

Fig. 8-43.   For static timing, rotate the distributor housing with the ignition ON, making sure your hand is away from the primary wire or stud terminal. First rotate in direction of shaft rotation, then reverse toward #1 cylinder firing position.

NOTE —
Verify the engine's firing order and direction of distributor rotation before static timing. If in doubt, remove the distributor cap and have someone "bump" the starter as you observe the direction that the rotor turns. Return the crankshaft to the timing mark you want to use for initial timing. Verify that the rotor points to #1 cylinder's firing position. If not, rotate the crankshaft 360-degrees and align the mark again.

Move the housing well past the #1 cylinder distributor lobe. Now, very slowly rotate the housing in the opposite direction of distributor shaft rotation, toward #1 cylinder firing position. Watch the point contacts carefully.

WARNING —
Avoid electrical shock by keeping your hand away from the primary coil wire. When the condenser unloads, the primary wire receives a good voltage spike. Make sure your hand isn't the ground source.

At the exact moment the points arc, you will have set timing at the number of advance degrees indicated on the pulley and timing marker. When you start the engine and verify the timing with a timing light, you may find a slight difference. This is due to camshaft and distributor drive gear lash. For start-up purposes, however, this method serves well. (When I rebuild an engine, static timing assures an immediate start-up.)

A variation on static timing also works well. With spark plugs removed from the engine, rotate the crankshaft to locate the timing marks as before. Now, reinstall the distributor cap. Place an old spark plug on #1 plug wire and ground the plug's metal shell carefully. Loosen the distributor housing clamp.

Turn the ignition switch to ON. Rotate the distributor housing in the same direction as the shaft rotates, well past the #1 cylinder firing point. Then, slowly rotate the housing in the opposite direction of shaft rotation until a spark fires across the test plug. If you tighten the distributor at this exact point, accurate static timing will result. If you pass the firing point, repeat the procedure.

By rotating the distributor first in the same direction as rotor rotation, and then in the opposite direction, you will prevent the advance mechanism from distorting your static timing results. If you overshoot the firing point, repeat the whole process to assure an accurate setting.

When you need to remove the distributor, carefully note the rotor position and scribe the distributor housing base location on the engine before pulling the distributor unit. Upon reinstalling the distributor (with the rotor and scribed marks aligned correctly), start the engine and immediately verify timing with your induction timing light.

Using a Timing Light With Built-in Advance

An easier approach to spark timing is possible with a timing light that has adjustable advance. Simply dial the advance until you index the timing cover marker with the 0,

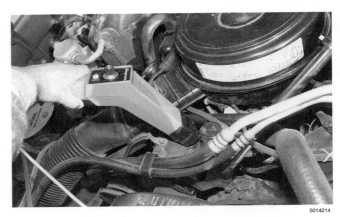

Fig. 8-44. *Timing lights with built-in advance will check performance of the spark advance mechanism. If you add initial timing degrees to the specified distributor advance degrees for a given engine rpm, the adjusted strobe light should index with the 0 (TDC) mark. This set-up proves handy for checking vacuum and centrifugal advance mechanisms.*

TDC or dot/groove on the crankshaft pulley (or the clutch/converter housing pointer and flywheel/flexplate marks on Land Cruiser in-line sixes). Read the timing light's scale. If the reading equals the correct timing specification, the engine's spark is in time.

The built-in advance light is ideal for verifying the performance of the spark advance mechanism. For engines with a vacuum and/or centrifugal advance system (without electronic computer management override), you can use an advance timing light much like a stroboscopic distributor test machine.

NOTE —
Some distributors, especially on emission controlled Land Cruisers, have a vacuum spark retard mechanism. This retard mechanism can be confusing as it looks much like a vacuum advance assembly. In this section, I refer to "vacuum advance" testing, however, you can perform similar tests on a vacuum retard system.

You can quickly test the vacuum advance unit with a vacuum pump. (In your Toyota truck repair manual or a professional service book, you will find specifications for the vacuum and centrifugal advance units.) With the engine idling, disconnect and plug the vacuum line and read the degrees of spark timing advance.

Hook the vacuum pump to the advance unit and apply the number of vacuum inches (in/hg) described in the service guidelines. Note the degrees of timing advance (or retard in the case of distributors that have a vacuum retard system) that now appear at the crankshaft pulley/damper and timing marker. (The centrifugal advance may add advance when rpm increases.) When assessing the results, note whether the service book describes "distributor degrees" or "crankshaft degrees" of advance or retard.

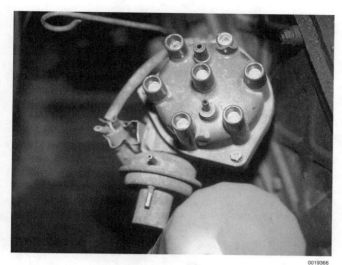

Fig. 8-45. On models with a vacuum spark <u>retard</u> mechanism, be cautious when testing spark timing. The unit looks much like a vacuum advance assembly, but is not the same. A vacuum retard distributor relies strictly on centrifugal advance for added spark timing. These vacuum retard distributors make for very poor rock-crawling performance, as low engine speeds cannot produce enough spark advance to develop needed torque and horsepower. Some distributors use a combination advance/retard vacuum device, usually in addition to centrifugal advance.

Distributor Degrees vs. Crankshaft Degrees

Your Toyota repair manual has specifications on where the vacuum or centrifugal advance unit should just begin to move and how many total degrees it should advance at full apply vacuum or a given rpm. Be aware that most service guidebook distributor specifications read in distributor rpm and distributor degrees.

These figures are exactly one-half the number of engine crankshaft degrees and one-half the crankshaft/engine rpm. When you read degrees of timing advance at the crankshaft, what you see is *twice* the distributor degrees, *plus* the number of degrees of initial spark advance. Likewise, engine speed is *twice* that of distributor rpm.

Example 1: Initial timing calls for 0 or TDC. Centrifugal advance specifications call for 5 distributor degrees of spark advance at 1250 distributor rpm. With vacuum advance hose disconnected and taped off, timing will read 10 crankshaft degrees of spark advance at 2500 crankshaft/engine rpm.

Example 2: Vacuum advance specifications call for 8 degrees of distributor advance at 13 in/hg vacuum. With the engine at an idle, you apply 13 in/hg vacuum to the vacuum diaphragm. Timing should increase 16 crankshaft degrees, (more if the engine rpm rises enough for the centrifugal advance to swing).

Consider sending out the distributor for testing if you suspect an inoperative centrifugal advance mechanism. Mark the distributor housing and rotor location. Remove the distributor. Have a shop test the advance mechanism(s) in a distributor test machine. Although these machines have become somewhat rare in this era of rebuilt/exchange parts, they were popular during the breaker point distributor era.

Vacuum vs. Mechanical/Centrifugal Advance

Many Toyota light truck distributors use a very slow or mild centrifugal advance curve and rely on vacuum advance for extra spark timing and power at low engine speeds. The reason vacuum advance works well for truck engines is that under severe loads, the engine needs spark advance quickly. By contrast, a centrifugal advance requires engine speed in order to work, and that's not often easy when the truck lugs a heavy load.

Vacuum provides the necessary spark advance for low speed power. As speed increases, a centrifugal (weight and spring) advance unit can offer engine speed related advance. At this stage, as the throttle opening widens and neither engine (manifold) vacuum nor ported carburetor vacuum can assist, engine speed alone can regulate the degrees of centrifugal spark timing advance.

Ported vs. Manifold Vacuum

When a distributor uses ported vacuum, the vacuum source is a channel just above the carburetor's throttle plate. As the throttle valve begins to open, this port becomes exposed and receives a high rate of engine vacuum, causing the spark timing to advance substantially. Ported vacuum declines gradually as the throttle valve opens further.

Manifold vacuum, which is sometimes used in a single or dual diaphragm vacuum advance system, is the vacuum from within the engine's intake plenum. Manifold vacuum is highest at an idle, remains relatively high at light loads and throttle settings, and drops as the throttle opening and engine load increase. At wide open throttle under load, manifold vacuum reaches its lowest point.

Fuel economy is best at higher manifold vacuum readings. Sluggish spark timing advance reduces manifold vacuum. Adequate spark timing advance, whether vacuum or centrifugal, maintains the best manifold vacuum. This contributes to better performance and optimal fuel economy.

3. CARBURETOR TUNE-UP

Carburetor adjustment is another aspect of your tune-up. Vacuum leaks, normal wear and dirt can inhibit a carburetor's performance. Tuning may include setting idle mixture, idle speed and adjusting choke operation.

> **WARNING —**
> *During many fuel system procedures fuel will be discharged or exposed. Do not smoke or work near heaters or other fire hazards. Have a fire extinguisher handy.*

Before setting the idle mixture, make certain that the fuel pump provides an adequate supply of gasoline. Change the disposable filter(s) on engines so equipped and clean or replace the sediment bowl filter on early Land Cruiser engines.

A plugged fuel filter will restrict fuel flow and affect engine idle. If flooding, starvation or other problems exist, consult your Toyota truck repair manual or a profes-

CHAPTER 8

Fig. 8-46. *Gummy carburetor looks threatening, though performance does not indicate need for overhaul. A can of spray carburetor cleaner and some patience will provide an impressive clean-up. Read directions, spray down primary and secondary throats, and concentrate on the venturi and exposed jet areas.*

sional level service guidebook for carburetor overhaul procedures. By far, Toyota OEM repair manuals offer the best details. You can also find detailed carburetor overhaul procedures in the instructions that come with a quality carburetor rebuild kit.

Correct idle mixture and float settings contribute to a smooth idle, stable engine performance and optimal fuel economy. Altitude changes will alter the idle mixture. If you plan to operate a carbureted truck at a higher or lower altitude than your home, for an extended period of time, expect to re-adjust the idle mix (if adjustable).

CAUTION —
Overhauling and repairing some of the later Toyota truck carburetors require expertise and special gauges, an accurate vacuum pump and exacting service data. Only with professional service guidelines will an experienced technician overhaul such a carburetor. Unless you have a good background in carburetor overhaul, either take your carburetor to a specialist for overhaul or purchase a rebuilt or new unit.

If your truck's engine runs roughly or responds poorly under acceleration (has a flat spot), suspect dirty carburetor jets, a defective accelerator pump or an ignition mis-fire. Once you rule out ignition problems, vacuum leaks, low compression or a worn timing chain or gear mechanism, consider a carburetor overhaul.

Before seeking specifications to reset the float or adjust any linkages, solenoids or the idle mixture, verify your carburetor's type and its identification or tag number. For later vehicles from the emissions era, you will find the underhood emissions/tuning decal a reliable tuning aid.

You cannot correct some types of carburetor wear. Consider the age of the carburetor and its general condition. Check for throttle plate wear at the throttle shaft, corrosion in the float bowl area, and warpage of main body parts. Also look for missing linkage pieces or loose

Fig. 8-47. *Change fuel filter as a part of routine service. The flare nut on fuel line inlet requires care. Always use a special metric flare nut wrench when working with brake pipe, fuel pipe or other flare nuts. Hold the fitting steady with an open end wrench and loosen flare nut carefully. When flare nut is too tight for flare nut wrench, this small version of plumber's chain wrench (bottom) can save the day. Chain grips nut around flats and allows good leverage.*

Carburetor Tuning Tips

Minor carburetor tune-up consists of nothing more than setting the choke linkage to specification (with the engine very cold and ignition switched off), then adjusting the choke-on fast idle. If the carburetor has idle mixture screws, warm the engine thoroughly and adjust curb idle. This is the hot engine idle speed with the choke fully open.

Carburetor specifications often vary between models. See your Toyota truck repair manual or a professional service guide for precise adjustment specifications that apply to your engine and carburetor.

Check for vacuum leaks before adjusting the carburetor. Scan all hose connections and make sure the PCV valve works. This inexpensive, replaceable valve can cause serious idle problems when stuck open—or excessive crankcase pressure when stuck closed or plugged. If in doubt, replace it.

Always set ignition timing before adjusting the idle speed or mixture screws. Also check the torque of manifold and carburetor mounting bolts.

To adjust fast idle, attach a tachometer, open the throttle and release it completely, then start the engine. Without opening the throttle, immediately adjust the fast idle speed to specification. Do not allow the choke to move the fast idle linkage and cam until you have made your speed setting.

Watch the choke open. If the vacuum pull-off is working correctly (periodically check it with a vacuum hand pump), a "blip" of the throttle should immediately tug the choke valve open slightly. As the engine warms, the choke valve should gradually open to the straight-up position. Should your choke be old or its components sticky, you can usually clean or overhaul the choke unit without removing the carburetor.

CAUTION —
Avoid burning your fingers when working around an exhaust or heated choke.

After servicing the choke, thoroughly warm the engine. You can now set the hot (curb) idle speed. Note that the emission requirements will dictate which adjustment procedure is correct for engines built since the late 1960s. You will find instructions on the underhood decal or in a Toyota truck repair manual.

Performance wise, the best idle mixtures produce the highest vacuum reading. Unless another method is specified (lean drop, propane enrichment, etc.), I always use a vacuum gauge for setting hot idle mixtures. High and steady manifold vacuum at an idle indicates an engine with proper compression seal, a quality ignition system and complete combustion. In the tune-up realm, an overly lean or rich carburetor setting—or retarded spark timing—will create a low manifold vacuum reading.

Finally, test the stroke and "squirt" of the carburetor's accelerator pump. Too little pump discharge causes engine stumbling and starvation on acceleration. Some accelerator pumps have a leaner high altitude setting for operating the engine at higher elevations. If you plan to run your truck for a long period at higher elevations, consider using the high altitude pump arm setting.

Refer to the emission control section for insight into the many emission control defects that cause rough idle and other troubles. For example, an EGR valve that cannot seat properly creates symptoms just like carburetor trouble—so can the simple PCV valve, an inexpensive and routinely replaced item. Even a plugged exhaust system can be at fault.

Fig. 8-48. *Teflon pipe sealant acts as both a sealing agent and anti-seize compound for the sensitive filter fitting. Compound or Teflon tape helps prevent thread seizure and damage to expensive carburetors and other parts. A Heli-Coil repair kit can salvage an otherwise stripped and ruined carburetor fuel inlet thread.*

and worn components. A new or rebuilt replacement carburetor can often prove practical.

On some later emission control engines, the carburetor has no provision for idle mixture adjustment. Idle screw limiter caps or, more recently, the elimination of idle screws, make emission control carburetors more difficult to tune. Federal and state laws will not allow tampering with these design features, and "by the book" tuning is crucial to proper engine operation. (See performance chapter for information on legal replacement carburetors that can enhance or restore performance.)

NOTE —
Generally, when these carburetors function correctly and idle is still poor, other problems exist, such as a vacuum leak, low compression, late valve timing (bad timing gears, chain/chain tensioners), an ignition system defect, or exhaust restriction.

Consult a Toyota or professional service book before adjusting or servicing a closed loop/feedback or "emissions calibrated" carburetor. The system may include a vacuum actuator and idle solenoid that interact with your truck's electrical accessory circuits, such as air conditioning. The curb idle speed and fast idle may be adjustable. Use your emissions and tune-up underhood decal as a guide for these rpm settings.

The mechanical fuel pumps on Toyota truck engines are single diaphragm types. Single diaphragm pumps serve only as a fuel supply for the carburetor, while dual-diaphragm fuel pumps offer both the fuel supply and an additional source of vacuum for windshield wipers. Fortunately, all U.S.-bound Toyota trucks have featured electric windshield wipers.

Before condemning either the carburetor or fuel pump, check the bolts that secure these parts to the manifold and engine block. Also check the manifold mounting hardware and for possible vacuum leaks. Look for kinks in the fuel pipes and hoses. On early fuel pumps with a glass sediment bowl, tighten the bail nut carefully to avoid breaking the glass bowl.

Fig. 8-50. *This fuel pump test gauge verifies pressure. During tests, route fuel away from the engine's spark and heat sources to avoid a fire.*

Fig. 8-49. *Early Land Cruiser engines feature an in-line sediment bowl filter. The serviceable filter or screen traps debris and functions much like a disposable modern fuel filter (shown). During service, avoid exposure to gasoline.*

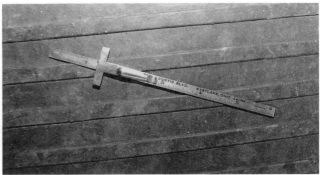

Fig. 8-51. *T-gauge rule is a common carburetor overhaul tool. Better quality overhaul kits come with detailed instructions for your carburetor model and a plastic gauge for setting the float.*

Float Settings and Fuel Pressure

When your truck's engine floods with gasoline or bucks during high speed runs, check the carburetor float setting. You can find float specifications in your Toyota truck repair manual or a professional service manual. Also use the manual for checking the float drop setting. A handy spot check for the float level is the sight glass on many Toyota carburetors.

To set the float, consult your repair manual. On carburetors with a removable air horn (top section), you may need to loosen the fuel pipe for access to the carburetor air horn and float(s). Loosen the air horn screws, then carefully remove and invert the air horn. Hold it level as you measure the float height.

NOTE —
Toyota trucks use Japanese Aisin carburetors, beginning with the one-barrel designs for F Land Cruiser engines. Mid-1968 and later F, 2F and all four-cylinder engines use Aisin two-barrel carburetors.

Fig. 8-52. *Land Cruisers first featured one-barrel carburetors. 1968 models had a newer two-barrel carburetor, a design that changed somewhat in 1975. Early one-barrel carburetors were far less complicated, as emissions demands were nil. Note fuel level sight glass, a unique and handy feature on Toyota four- and six-cylinder carburetors.*

Fig. 8-53. Aisin carburetors require removal of air horn for adjusting float. Invert the air horn and check height. Turn air horn upright to check float drop. Compare measurement against specifications found in your truck repair manual. New replacement carburetors are available for most Toyota applications.

On some of the earlier one-barrel and two-barrel Toyota carburetors, you can also check the float height without removing hardware. A sight glass on the carburetor main body allows a view of the actual level of fuel in the float bowl. A mark across the middle of the sight glass indicates the proper level for fuel. Note this level with the engine running and shut off.

> *CAUTION —*
> *Do not press the float needle into its seat when adjusting float height. Damage could result, causing erratic performance.*

Fuel Pump Pressure/Output

If the float level is correct and fuel starvation persists, check the fuel pump output. Correct pump pressure varies between models and pump designs. Verify your engine's requirements in the Toyota repair manual. Before suspecting fuel pump pressure or volume troubles, check all fuel lines from the tank forward. Look for leaks, loose connections or kinks.

The fuel pump is a common trouble spot. Early Toyota truck fuel pumps are rebuildable, and repair kits were once a common item at the local retail auto supply. Today, however, rebuilt or new replacement pumps are readily available. It is wise to carry an extra fuel pump and needle/seat kit on extended trips into back country.

An older, fatigued fuel pump diaphragm will stretch or rupture. Look closely for fuel dilution in the engine's crankcase or leaks around the pump. If the cause of low

pressure/volume is unclear, remove the pump and check the condition of the camshaft lobe or eccentric disc that operates the pump arm.

> *CAUTION —*
> *When testing fuel pump volume, make certain that your container is safe and able to catch all of the gasoline. Route gas away from spark sources or hot engine parts. Spark from the ignition or engine heat could ignite fuel and cause a serious fire.*

Idle Mixture Setting

Before adjusting the carburetor, look down its throat for carbon and debris. A spray type carburetor and choke cleaner can remove accessible varnish and carbon. Short of an overhaul, these solvents work well for periodic cleaning. If dust or grime is present, suspect an inadequate air cleaner seal. Correct the problem.

Fig. 8-54. A quality spray carburetor cleaner will remove accessible debris. Try to wash exposed bleed holes and spray cleaner into the air horn vent. This will allow cleaner to work inside the float bowl.

You can also shoot spray cleaner directly into the float chamber vent. The alcohol present in most cleaners will absorb water sediment and carry it from the float bowl to the engine's combustion chambers. Run the engine at a fast idle to clear washed down debris; then allow the engine to cool before installing new spark plugs.

> *CAUTION —*
> *Make sure your spray carburetor cleaner will not damage the sensitive oxygen sensor, if so equipped. Read labels and use these products sparingly.*

An OEM Toyota repair manual will describe overhaul procedures and give preliminary idle mixture settings. If your engine has run reasonably well, turn the engine off and carefully screw the mixture adjusters clockwise while counting each turn carefully. Do not overtighten these screws!

CAUTION —
Turn the mixture screw/needle gently. Over-
tightening the mixture screw can seriously
damage the needle end of the screw.

See how close the current adjustments come to the preliminary settings recommended in your Toyota truck repair manual or a professional level service guidebook. If there is a large difference between these two settings, suspect a vacuum leak or other problems. Return the needles to the current settings, then correct any obvious

Fig. 8-55. Idle mixture screws are easy to access. For the lat-er emission control era, many carburetors have limiter caps on their adjuster screws or depend upon electronic controls for adjustment. For emission carburetors, cleanliness and frequent filter changes enable the engine to offer continued good performance.

Fig. 8-56. On Toyota carburetors, clockwise leans mixture; counterclockwise enrichens. Adjust the screw slowly. Shown here is a popular Toyota/Aisin two-barrel carburetor's idle mixture screw.

problems. (Look for a vacuum leak, loose carburetor mounting or air horn screws, a defective EGR valve, etc.)

Before adjusting the idle mixture, run the engine until completely warm, watching the choke through its whole opening cycle. On engines so equipped, make sure the exhaust heat riser valve also opens properly, along with the coolant thermostat. Bring coolant to normal operating temperature—and make certain that the choke valve is fully open before adjusting the idle mix.

Always be certain the choke remains fully open while adjusting a carburetor's idle mixture. Do not allow the engine to idle for long periods during adjustment, or the spark plugs may foul and distort engine performance.

If you have difficulty judging the engine's smoothness, use a tachometer and vacuum gauge while you set the carburetor mixture screws. Strive for smooth running and the highest vacuum reading at a normal curb idle speed.

Try to adjust the engine to a "lean best" setting to help meet clean air standards. This is the leanest point for each adjuster screw that still allows the engine to run without mis-firing or stumbling.

On a fully warmed engine, begin the idle adjustment by turning the idle mixture screw slowly clockwise. A noticeable lean misfire should occur. Stop here. (If no lean mis-fire occurs, suspect dirty carburetor air bleeds or other troubles.)

Slowly back the idle mixture screw out (counterclockwise). Just when a smooth idle occurs, the setting is correct unless your emission decal calls for a "lean drop setting." (*Lean drop* means to turn the screws inward, toward a leaner mix, dropping the rpm a specific amount.) If the idle speed is incorrect at this point, reset the throttle or curb idle stop screw. Repeat the idle mixture adjustment if necessary.

Toyota trucks used a variety of carburetors between 1958 and 1987. The list and description of specific carburetors would make a full length service guidebook in itself. Rather than attempt to describe these carburetors, let me suggest that such information is readily available. Consult the Toyota repair manual for your model truck.

Fig. 8-57. Toyota trucks, with their lighter GVWR packages, require emission equipment like the closed-loop computer carburetor. Designed for strict emission compliance, these fuel systems provide little room for adjustment.

Mechanical Fuel Pump Installation

Fuel pump installation begins with cleaning the area around the fuel pump. Carefully detach the fuel lines at the pump. Safely cap the fuel inlet line to prevent fuel leakage during service.

WARNING —
Fuel will be exposed during this procedure. Do not smoke or create sparks. Have an approved fire extinguisher handy.

Fig. 8-58. *The mechanical fuel pump can wear over time. More often, a defective or clogged filter will cause trouble, mimicking symptoms of a worn pump. Change filters before condemning the pump, especially on applications where the fuel pump is difficult to reach. Note unique manual primer on this earlier FJ25 F-type engine.*

Fig. 8-59. *To prevent damage to the pump or misalignment with the lobe/eccentric, loosen and tighten fuel pump bolts evenly to prevent cocking or binding of the fuel pump arm.*

Loosen the fuel pump mounting bolts evenly and remove the pump and gasket. Look closely at the camshaft lobe, eccentric cam or pushrod that operates the pump arm. Make certain a worn camshaft lobe, loose eccentric or worn pushrod is not your problem.

Clean the gasket surface on the engine block thoroughly. Do not allow debris to fall into the engine. Rotate

the engine to place the pump's camshaft lobe or eccentric on the lowest (heel) side to reduce pressure.

Use a suitable gasket sealant, applied to both sides of the new gasket. Put sealant on the mounting bolt threads. Insert the bolts into the pump. Set the gasket, pump and bolts in place.

Carefully place the rubbing surface of the pump arm against the lobe or pushrod. Start the bolt threads with caution, holding the pump squarely toward the block surface. Tighten the bolts evenly until the pump is secure.

CAUTION —
Make certain the fuel pump arm remains in place and straight during installation. Wedging the pump to one side can damage the lever or housing.

4. BEYOND TUNING: MAJOR ENGINE DIAGNOSIS

If you suspect major engine trouble or your fuel and spark tune-up has little effect on performance, you need to perform further testing.

On emission era truck engines (approximately 1968 forward for Toyotas), the emission controls can cause trouble. A defective EGR valve, for example, often creates the same symptoms as carburetor and fuel supply problems. Defective electronic closed-loop carburetion or EFI sensors and fuel/spark management components can also mimic these kinds of symptoms.

Although PCV and air injection came on some of the early emission era engines, the emission control packages were simple and not likely to cause much trouble. From the late 1970s onward, emission controls play an increasingly larger role in engine performance and tune. (For details on the role of emission controls, see the emission section of this chapter.)

After years of exposure to tune-up and engine overhaul diagnostics, I now use a compression gauge only for quick referencing. A low reading usually requires squirting motor oil into the cylinder to distinguish piston ring wear from valve troubles. I go further than this and use a leakdown tester for pinpoint diagnosis.

A leak of more than 12% in any cylinder raises questions of wear, although many engines will offer reasonable service up to 20% leakage. High performance demands, such as turbocharging, require 10% or less leak in any cylinder.

Compression Seal and Testing

For quick diagnosis, a compression gauge is very handy. I prefer a threaded hose gauge, which allows one-person operation. Clean the spark plug areas, then remove all of the plugs. Screw the gauge end into #1 cylinder's spark plug threads. With the gauge secure, visible and lying away from rotating engine parts, open the throttle wide.

Consult your Toyota truck repair manual or a professional level service guide for normal cranking compression readings. Crank the engine several revolutions, until the highest stable reading occurs. Record the reading. Repeat these steps for each cylinder.

Fig. 8-60. *A cylinder leakdown test of this freshly rebuilt engine reveals normal seal. A compression gauge reading is nowhere near as accurate. Leakdown tests foretell trouble long before a compression gauge.*

If you get a low reading and want to pinpoint the problem with a compression gauge, squirt a tablespoon of clean oil in the spark plug hole for that cylinder and crank the engine again. If compression comes up to normal, you likely have an engine with defective piston rings. If no change occurs, valve or head gasket leakage is likely.

Assessing Compression Readings

According to some manufacturers' current guidelines, engine balance depends upon a maximum variance of 25% between the highest and lowest cylinder. I believe this is too great for satisfactory performance and fuel economy. Smooth operation, especially off-highway or when pulling a heavy trailer or load, demands better cylinder balance than this. A more traditional factor, 10% difference between the highest and lowest cylinder, still serves as my standard.

Higher compression readings mean carbon buildup. Excess carbon is very hard on the piston rings and valves. At its worst, carbon buildup contributes to deadly pre-ignition, the premature ignition of fuel by glowing material in the cylinders. Pre-ignition can break pistons and bend connecting rods.

Low compression readings indicate either worn rings, valve wear, a blown head gasket or cracked castings. Improper valve clearance also causes low readings. Although most service guidebooks list valve adjustment as a possible cure for low compression, this is very seldom the case.

After more than twenty-five years of exposure to engine repair and machine shop work, I find that running an engine with valves that do not seat completely will cause permanent damage to valve faces and seats. If valve clearances are so far out of adjustment that compression is low, damage has likely occurred already.

A valve adjustment cannot remove hard carbon buildup, pitting and burnout from valve faces and seats.

For these problems, only a valve grind or cylinder head rebuild can restore performance. If adjusting valves does not restore compression, assume the valves need repair.

Tight valve adjustment is a product of normal wear on engines without hydraulic valve lifters. As the valve faces wear into their seats, a process called *valve seat recession* occurs.

Cure for Unleaded Fuel

Unleaded fuel aggravates valve seat wear, especially in engines designed during the leaded gas era. Older, more heavily leaded fuels would lubricate the valve seats, faces and stems. For older leaded fuel era truck engines, the problems of unleaded gasoline and valve seat recession have a remedy. An automotive machine shop can retrofit hardened steel (replacement) exhaust valve seats into the head(s) of most OHV engines. Hardened exhaust valve seats will offset the effects of heat and reduce valve wear caused by the use of unleaded fuels. The Toyota Land Cruiser F and early 2F engines make prime candidates for this procedure.

The octane requirements for an engine are also crucial to the prevention of detonation (ping). Your Toyota truck owner's handbook describes octane requirements for your engine. Under current fuel standards, your older engine may need high test fuel to deliver top performance. If you must run your truck on 87-88 octane fuel, retard the timing a few degrees if harmful detonation occurs. Power may suffer some, but the engine will survive longer.

Re-torque Cylinder Head(s)

When you find a low compression reading, re-torquing cylinder head bolts may help remedy slight gasket seal or head warpage problems. (You will find the torque settings and sequence for tightening bolts in your Toyota truck repair manual.) Re-check cranking compression when you finish. If compression is still low, suspect head or gasket damage—or other low compression related problems.

Since you are re-torquing a head that has already been in service, one pull at the full torque setting should be enough. I like to go through the sequence a second time, as bolts will often yield slightly.

If you remove a cylinder head for service and install a new gasket with proper sealant on both the gasket and freshly cleaned bolt threads, follow the three-step torque method: In sequence, 1) bring all bolts up to a snug setting, 2) advance to a firm setting just below final torque, and 3) finish with your final setting. Some gaskets require re-torquing after the engine warms.

You may find the two- or three-stage torque figures in your Toyota truck repair manual. If unavailable, they usually run as first stage: 2/3rds of final torque; second stage: 5/6ths of the final torque figure; third stage: final torque. Let the engine set for a while after final torque, then re-tighten again at the final torque setting. Always tighten bolts in the recommended sequence.

5. VALVE ADJUSTMENT

Valve clearance should be periodically checked and adjusted if necessary. Toyota engines tolerate normal variances between adjustments—if you check and/or adjust the valves on their proper schedules.

Engines with rocker arm type adjusters require regular valve adjustments. My suggestion for a preventive care routine includes checking and, if necessary, re-adjusting valves each 12,000 miles—or certainly along with each periodic tune-up.

Single OHC fours like the 18RC, 20R or 22R, have no pushrods and tend to go longer between valve adjustments than a pushrod type engine.

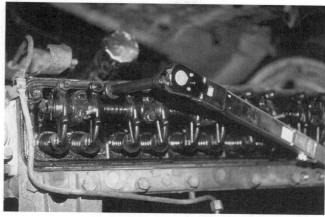

Fig. 8-62. *Periodic valve adjustment decreases the chance of burning valves. Always re-torque the cylinder head and rocker shaft assembly support bolts/nuts, if so equipped, before adjusting valves.*

Fig. 8-61. *All Toyota truck engines are of overhead camshaft (OHC and DOHC) or overhead valve (OHV) valve-in-head designs. Simpler rocker arm/valve adjustment (shown here on 22R OHC four) is possible on all engines except the V-6s and late DOHC in-line fours and sixes. These V-6 and DOHC engines use selective fit shims that require some special tools and a micrometer for service.*

Check your owner's manual or repair manual for valve adjustment schedules. You will find valve clearance settings in your repair manual. Be certain of your engine's age and application, then find the valve lash settings that apply.

Normally, mechanical lifters and rocker arms should not get badly out of adjustment or extremely noisy. If your engine has very noisy lifters, suspect poor oiling, a defective lifter(s) on OHV type engines, improper valve clearances due to bad valve seat recession or wear, or a camshaft with worn lobes. If the camshaft lobe profiles are normal, a valve adjustment of just a few thousandths of an inch will restore valve lift and valve opening points, reducing noise and improving engine performance.

In-line OHV Sixes

Before you adjust the valves on the Toyota Land Cruiser F, 2F or 3F-E OHV in-line sixes or any of the single OHC fours, warm the engine completely—I would recommend running the engine for at least thirty minutes.

V-6 and DOHC engines with shim-type valve adjustment use valve lash checks and settings on a *cold* engine.

Since Land Cruiser F, 2F and 3F-E mechanical lifter engines each call for a hot valve adjustment, I prefer running the engine to check valves on these engines. By using a low idle speed setting, just enough to keep the engine ticking over, oil spillage can be minimized. Optional methods will also work.

The static method requires that you warm the engine, shut it off and remove the spark plugs, then rotate the engine very slowly while following the cylinder firing order. (Watch the position of the ignition distributor's rotor as you bring each piston to top-dead-center or TDC.) Make sure each piston is at its firing point (TDC on the compression stroke) before setting the valve clearances on that cylinder's intake and exhaust valves.

The process of hand cranking is slow, and by the time you approach the last cylinders, the engine has likely cooled down considerably.

Fig. 8-63. *On in-line six cylinder engines, #1 and #6 cylinders align with TDC mark when these pistons reach top dead center. Likewise, on 18RC, 20R and 22R fours, #1 and #4 index together. For this reason, you must look at the rotor and distributor cap alignment to see which cylinder is up to fire.*

Fig. 8-64. *A special valve adjusting tool simplifies running valve adjustment on OHV engines like the Toyota F, 2F and 3F-E. Snap-On offers this top quality tool for general applications. A metric socket enables use on Toyota engines.*

Fig. 8-65. *For static valve adjustment, follow the distributor rotor and firing order sequence. Watch rocker arm movement. If a piston is at or near TDC on its firing cycle, both valves will be completely closed. Here, valve clearance is at its widest point. The easiest way to identify intake and exhaust valves is by looking at the manifolds.*

I prefer a hot *running* set, despite the oily mess. On Toyota F, 2F and 3F-E engines that call for hot valve lash settings, checking the running clearances is the most accurate method possible. Although hard on tappet gauge blades, the results reflect your engine in its running mode, which is far more reliable than a static adjustment. The main advantages of hot adjustments are: 1) a better feel for valve action and lift under real operating conditions, and 2) an end to tedious hand rotation of the engine while you set the valves. This method is faster, however, you must guard your knuckles from bruising on moving parts. (Wearing work gloves makes sense here.)

With the engine warmed completely, my method involves slowing the idle speed to the minimum point that the engine will continue to run. This reduces oil spray and difficulty when handling the moving parts. If possible, shield the engine bay from oil spray.

Fig. 8-66. *Flat blade tappet gauges have various thicknesses. Check your service guide for correct gap thickness, and identify the intake and exhaust valve. Make certain the blade lays flat and squarely between the rocker arm end and valve stem tip. Although rougher on gauges, adjusting valves on a running F, 2F or 3F-E engine produces highly accurate results.*

WARNING —
Keep cloth and covers away from the hot exhaust manifolds, or a fire could erupt. Remove the valve cover carefully, without burning your fingers and hands.)

Shut off the engine, and check the cylinder head bolt and rocker shaft support bolt torque. Then, with your valve adjusting tools ready, start the engine.

Identify the intake valves by looking at the intake manifold ports. Check the intake tappet clearances by inserting the feeler gauge between each intake valve stem and its rocker arm.

Start the engine. While the engine ticks over slowly, lay the clean gauge flat and squarely between the valve stem tip and the rocker arm end. Correct settings will allow a very slight drag as you gently pull and push the feeler gauge. (You are actually feeling for the moment of widest tappet clearance.)

There is a point at which the gauge blade can slide freely. If you are uncertain what this feels like, loosen the lock nut and adjuster on in-line OHV sixes or single OHC fours—very slightly. Slide the gauge in and out again.

Once you can feel where the gauge measures *clearance*, unaffected by the opening and closing movement of the valve, you can easily determine whether the setting is tight, loose or just right.

When right, the screw-and-lock nut adjusters require that you tighten the lock nut while holding the screw. You will find that by tightening the nut, the adjuster screw may move or pull up slightly in its threads.

This could be enough to distort the setting and require re-adjustment of the valve. If so, re-adjust the clearance, compensating for the distortion, and tighten the lock nut. Again check the clearance. When intake valves are all adjusted, move to the exhaust valves with your other tappet gauge.

For screw-and-lock nut adjusters, a valve adjusting tool is available that both secures the lock nut and provides a screw driver to turn the adjuster.

Such tools were popular during the era of adjustable tappets and come in different nut sizes for various engine applications. K-D Tools, Snap-On or your local NAPA dealer are good sources for these kinds of specialty tools. Blade tappet gauges are also available from these sources.

Two-position Valve Adjustment On 18R, 20R and 22R

On 18RC, 20R and 22R in-line OHC fours, valve adjustment without the engine running is simple. You can adjust the valves by indexing the crankshaft's TDC timing mark, first with #1 cylinder's piston at TDC of the compression stroke and in its firing position, then with #4 cylinder's piston at TDC of its compression stroke and in firing position. Make sure the engine is thoroughly warmed up before adjusting valves.

Confirm which piston is at its TDC firing location by first aligning the crankshaft mark with TDC. Then look at the distributor rotor location or note whether #1 or #4 cylinder's intake and exhaust valves each have stem-to-rocker clearance. When the mark is indexed for TDC, and you know which piston is in its firing position, you can adjust four valves.

When #1 piston is at TDC on its firing stroke (top of compression stroke), you can adjust the #1 cylinder intake and exhaust valves, the #2 cylinder intake valve, and the #3 cylinder exhaust valve. After adjusting these valves to spec, rotate the crankshaft 360 degrees, until #4 piston is at TDC of its compression stroke (in firing position).

Now adjust the remaining four valves (#2 cylinder exhaust, #3 cylinder intake, and #4 cylinder intake and exhaust).

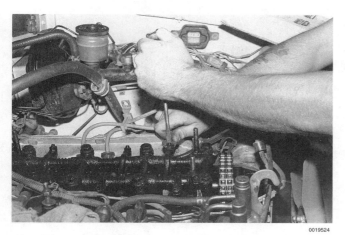

Fig. 8-67. Fig. 9-86. For single OHC fours like the 18RC, 20R and 22R, adjust the valves with the engine hot and shut off. All eight valves can be adjusted by aligning the crankshaft in just two positions. You can quickly and accurately set the valves on these engines.

In using these two crankshaft positions, you are able to accurately adjust all eight valves—not a difficult task when approached this way! Install a new valve cover gasket and check for leaks.

Fig. 8-68. Cork valve cover gaskets often shrink and distort in storage. To restore a side cover or valve cover gasket, soak in water until completely pliant.

TUNE-UP SPECIFICATIONS FOR MY TOYOTA TRUCK ENGINE

IDLE SPEED: _____

INITIAL (LOW SPEED OR IDLE) SPARK TIMING @ _____RPM:_____-DEGREES

HIGHER SPEED (2500 CRANKSHAFT RPM) SPARK TIMING_____-DEGREES

CARBURETOR IDLE MIXTURE ADJUSTMENT PROCEDURE (IF ADJUSTABLE):

_____

AIR FILTER PART NUMBER_____

FUEL FILTER(S) PART NUMBER_____

SPARK PLUG TYPE AND NUMBER_____

BREAKER POINT OR MODULE PART NUMBER _____

BREAKER POINT GAP OR MODULE AIR GAP SETTING _____

BREAKER POINT DWELL ANGLE _____

DISTRIBUTOR CAP PART NUMBER _____

Fig. 8-69. Sample of a quick reference chart for tuning your truck engine. Keep a copy of these specifications with your on-board tool kit or in your glovebox.

CHAPTER 8

6. EMISSION CONTROLS

All manufactured motor vehicles must comply with federal and state tailpipe emission standards. Since the 1960s, Toyota truck engines have required factory installed emission control devices, designed to combat air pollution. Some emission control devices help the engine achieve more complete combustion, while others work directly at reducing tailpipe pollutants.

Emission control components vary, depending upon the model year and requirements. Your truck's emission control package may include the ignition spark timing, the carburetor or EFI and a series of devices to reduce three major exhaust pollutants: 1) the poisonous gas, carbon monoxide (CO), 2) raw, unburned hydrocarbons (HC), and 3) oxides of nitrogen (NOx), the building block of visible smog.

Many engine emission controls focus on peak performance, fuel efficiency and longer engine life. The care and maintenance of these devices remains an important part of servicing your truck. Even tuning your engine requires a working knowledge of emission control components, as the idle, acceleration, gas mileage and overall performance depend upon a fully operational emission control system.

Emission Control Basics

In the early 1960s, U.S. vehicle manufacturers began installing Positive Crankcase Ventilation (PCV) systems on engines to comply with California emissions requirements. (Toyota Land Cruisers offered PCV systems even earlier.) The simple concept aimed at purging the engine crankcase of combustion blow-by and fumes.

Prior to 1961, most engines vented blow-by to the atmosphere through a road draft tube. These devices were simply open pipes with their tips cut on an angle toward the rear of the vehicle.

The road draft tube relies on low pressure vacuum, created as the vehicle moves forward, to purge the crankcase. Primitive and inefficient, an engine with a road draft

Fig. 8-71. *The more modern carburetor is plumbed for emission devices. Several vacuum sources (manifold or ported) may be built into an OEM carburetor.*

Fig. 8-72. *A very popular tool with emission control specialists is the hand vacuum pump and pressure tester. Use the tester to check EGR valves, vacuum diaphragms, vacuum hose circuits and thermal vacuum switches.*

tube pollutes the environment and permits condensation and corrosive agents to build sludge in the crankcase.

The modern PCV system allows manifold vacuum, regulated by a spring-balanced valve, to draw crankcase blow-by back through the intake manifold. This closed crankcase system continuously removes and recycles harmful combustion by-products. A PCV valve and closed crankcase contribute to better performance and longer engine life.

Fig. 8-70. *Inspect the vacuum hoses. A principle energy source for emission control switches is vacuum. Hose routing and quality are critical to peak performance. Leaks reduce performance and create tune-up problems.*

Fig. 8-73. The simple PCV valve on your truck's engine contributes to engine longevity by fighting sludge and the formation of crankcase condensation. Additionally, a closed crankcase prevents water from entering the engine during stream fording. Change the PCV valve with each spark plug replacement (30,000 miles maximum for late engines). On some engines, spark plug and PCV change interval is 12,000 miles. Also make sure that hoses and grommets seal properly.

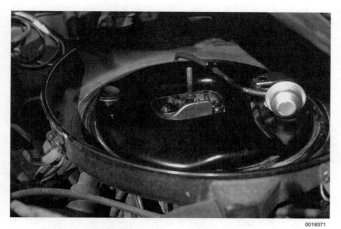

Fig. 8-74. This clean-air filter lies just inside the air cleaner canister on most closed crankcase engines. Manifold vacuum through the PCV valve creates low pressure in the crankcase. Clean air enters the engine from the filter. Without an adequate source of fresh air through the breather filter, PCV vacuum could damage engine seals and gaskets.

Air Injection System

The most visible emission control device is the air injection pump system. Found as original equipment on many truck engines built from the mid-1960s onward, the smog pump's ungainly physical features and maze of plumbing have attracted unwarranted criticism.

Air injection is an external emission control. It has no effect on either the fuel/induction or ignition system and creates a negligible amount of exhaust back pressure. Although the engine drives this pump, power loss is less than one-half horsepower—hardly noticed by a torquey Land Cruiser six or even a smaller Toyota truck engine.

Fig. 8-75. Distribution tubes direct clean air into the exhaust manifold(s) or the cylinder head exhaust ports. Toyota truck emission control systems are very typical and resemble domestic truck and passenger car designs.

Fig. 8-76. One-way or anti-backfire check valves prevent hot exhaust from reaching the air injection pump and hoses. Dangerously charred hoses and a burned pump can result from a defective check valve.

Since the air injection system is relatively passive, removal of the pump system does not improve performance.

The principle of air injection is simple: Inject oxygen into the exhaust stream near the engine exhaust ports and/or directly into a catalytic converter. Given this fresh source of oxygen, the combustion of unburned hot hydrocarbons and carbon monoxide can continue.

Your truck engine's air injection system requires little maintenance. Pump bearings are permanently lubricated, and the drive belt seldom requires adjustment. The rest of the air injection system consists of a diverter/bypass valve, anti-backfire check valves, and manifold or cylinder head distribution tubes.

Air Bypass Systems

The diverter or bypass valve receives a high manifold vacuum signal during engine deceleration, as carburetor venturi effect causes an over-rich fuel mixture. The valve

Fig. 8-77. *The air pump drive belt requires periodic adjustment and replacement. Relatively light load of this device assures long belt life. Tampering with the air injection pump system can prevent cool air from reaching the exhaust valves, manifolds and air injection tubes. Heat damage to your truck's engine will result. Maintain your air injection system.*

Fig. 8-78. *The diverter/bypass valve directs injection pump air away from the exhaust stream during deceleration. This pollution control device prevents an over-rich mixture of unburned fuel from igniting and damaging the exhaust system.*

opens, allowing pump air to vent into the atmosphere. Without a diverter valve, air pumped into rich, unburned exhaust stream gases would cause spontaneous combustion. The exhaust system could be severely damaged.

Additionally, the engine's exhaust valves, manifold(s) and even the air injection tubes rely on pump air for cooling. When an air injection system is defective, or a mechanic disables the engine's emission devices, melted injection tubes, damage to exhaust valves or a cracked manifold often result.

Examine the rubber air injection hoses for signs of charring. Check the vacuum line to the diverter. On a fully warmed engine, snap the throttle open and shut and observe whether air exits the by-pass/diverter valve under deceleration. If the valve functions properly, air should by-pass.

Exhaust Gas Recirculation

Lean fuel mixtures reduce CO and HC emissions. These lean fuel mixtures, however, also increase combustion temperatures and raise NOx emissions. In the early 1970s, engineers applied a simple, effective means for lowering combustion temperatures: recycle the exhaust gases.

Recirculating a small amount of exhaust through the intake stream dilutes fresh fuel mixtures and cools the combustion chambers, yet has little effect on the air/fuel ratio. These cooler combustion temperatures also enhance performance.

The exhaust gas recirculation (EGR) system permits the use of leaner air/fuel ratios without compromising cylinder temperatures. EGR valves serve a useful function on any engine that runs low octane fuel, requires a mild spark advance curve or operates with lean air/fuel mixtures.

Unfortunately, ill-informed mechanics see the EGR as a source of trouble or a horsepower thief. This false reasoning overlooks the EGR system's ability to lower

Fig. 8-79. *An EGR valve can lower upper cylinder temperatures by as much as 2000 degrees Fahrenheit! Lower temperatures reduce oxides of nitrogen (NOx) emissions, the key component in visible smog. The EGR valve, effective from off-idle through cruise rpm, typically operates via a ported vacuum source.*

Fig. 8-80. *EGR valve inspection is simple. Attach a vacuum pump to the valve. With the engine idling, unseat the valve by applying vacuum. Idle should get rough, often enough to stall the engine. Watch the gauge to be certain the EGR valve diaphragm holds vacuum.*

scorching combustion temperatures (which run as high as 4800° F without an EGR system) to below 2500°. Operating properly, the EGR system eliminates most detonation or ping. If, after tossing the EGR valve in the dumpster, your truck's engine now suffers severe ping, look here for the problem.

Catalytic Converter

Another anti-pollution device, found on many light truck engines since 1975, is the catalytic converter. Simply a

Fig. 8-81. *Catalytic converters resemble a muffler. These small chemical processing plants reduce carbon monoxide, hydrocarbon and oxides of nitrogen. Consider the very high temperatures generated by a catalytic converter. Avoid touching the converter during service work, and never park your truck in tall, dry brush!*

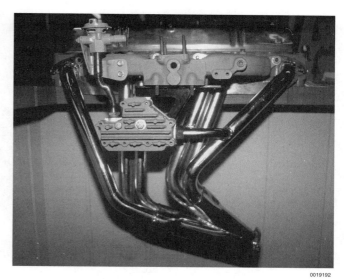

Fig. 8-82. *An emission-legal aftermarket high performance exhaust system, like this Downey Off-Road header, can reduce back pressure. Do your share for clean air, even if high performance is your goal. Be sure your exhaust system complies with federal and state regulations.*

muffler-like device, the converter operates a small chemical processing plant in your exhaust system.

Oxidizing catalysts (usually platinum and palladium) in the converter react with carbon monoxide and hydrocarbons. The by-products of this catalyzing process are harmless carbon dioxide and water. Reducing catalysts also take the oxygen out of NOx, leaving harmless free nitrogen to pass out the tailpipe.

Although the catalytic converter emits sulfuric acid and an annoying rotten egg smell during rich fuel conditions, the only cost in performance is exhaust system back pressure. Aftermarket high performance catalytic converters are now available to reduce this back pressure.

Cold-start and Warm-up Devices

All gasoline engines require cold start systems. A carburetor's choke or an EFI engine's cold start enrichment cycle must meet both cold start-up and emission control needs.

For low tailpipe emissions, the choke should open as quickly as the engine can accept leaner air/fuel mixtures. To accomplish this, a number of devices come into play. The air cleaner assembly doubles as the thermal air system to direct heated air from the outside surface of the exhaust manifold into the intake inlet of the air cleaner.

Light truck engine chokes come in a variety of shapes and sizes. Early Toyota truck models rely on manual, cable controlled choke valves. Later carbureted engines feature either a hot water (engine heated), bi-metallic or electric type automatic choke.

Observe choke operation and timing. Spray all carburetor linkages with a quality cleaner. Clean the choke valve, choke housing and vacuum piston if there is any evidence of choke stickiness. The choke should move freely when unloaded.

Fig. 8-83. *The conventional choke, either manual or automatic, must open quickly to maintain low tailpipe emissions. Adjust your truck engine's choke for safe driveability and lower pollution levels. (For proper settings, see your truck's underhood emission decal, the Toyota repair manual or a professional service guide.)*

Fig. 8-84. *Some automatic chokes operate as manifold heat reaches a bi-metallic coil spring. Others open via a heated electrical coil (shown here), activated as the ignition circuit opens. Hot, circulating engine coolant opens some Toyota chokes.*

Fig. 8-85. *Toyota automatic chokes open by engine heat (often hot coolant) or electrically. Chokes quickly become too hot to touch. Take care not to burn your fingers when handling or inspecting a choke! This electric unit is preset and riveted at the factory.*

Fig. 8-86. *Inspect the warm air vacuum motor on the thermal air cleaner. Make certain this device works properly. If the inexpensive flexible heat tube shows evidence of leakage or poor fitup, replace tube.*

Fuel injected (EFI) engines benefit from a computer controlled cold start enrichment system that maintains precise air/fuel ratios and driveability during the entire engine warm-up cycle.

Additionally, many carburetors rely on a vacuum signaled choke pull-off to allow quicker vehicle operation during warm-up. The choke pull-off unit consists of a vacuum diaphragm and choke release linkage operated by either manifold vacuum or ported vacuum.

On many emission engines, a thermal air cleaner (TAC) provides a vacuum-actuated warm air valve. The vacuum motor receives signals from a thermal vacuum switch and/or bi-metallic valve. The motor opens and closes the warm air door at the air cleaner intake.

When the engine warms sufficiently, the vacuum motor closes the warm air door, permitting cooler, fresh air to enter the air cleaner. Your engine's thermal air cleaner allows quicker choke opening and better driveability.

Exhaust Heat Riser

The heat riser, usually eliminated with the installation of aftermarket exhaust headers, also serves a vital function. During cold start-up, the riser valve stays closed, redirecting hot exhaust toward the base of the intake manifold on in-line four- and six-cylinder engines. (Some engines rely on hot coolant circulation to warm the manifold.) The heated section of the manifold sometimes houses a stove well for a bimetallic spring operated choke.

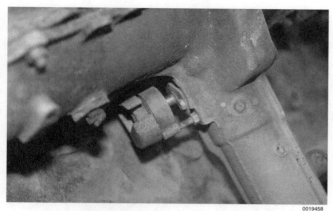

Fig. 8-87. *The heat riser valve plays an important role during engine warm-up and choke operation. A heat riser stuck shut creates severe back pressure and reduces engine power. A heat riser stuck open may cause the choke to stay on too long, affecting performance and fuel economy. Heat risers open by various energy sources. For earlier Toyota truck engines, a bimetallic spring expands and opens with engine exhaust heat.*

This heat warms the area beneath the carburetor, permitting better atomization of fuel and more thorough combustion. It is important that the manifold heat passage remain clear. Often, the passage clogs as carbon builds up.

Some riser valves open with a vacuum diaphragm/motor, while others rely on a heated bi-metallic spring.

To service the heat riser, let the engine cool completely. Spray the heat riser valve with a suitable penetrant and oil. Make certain that the valve moves freely and the bimetallic spring or vacuum diaphragm is intact and functional.

Switches, Valves and Vacuum Controls

Your truck engine's emission control devices must know when to work and usually require energy to work. A variety of electrical and vacuum switches help meet those requirements.

The ignition switch often serves as the trigger for a fuel shut-off solenoid. Other switches, such as the thermal vacuum switch (TVS), control vacuum to the distributor spark advance or an EGR valve. Most TVS switches rely on engine coolant temperature to expand an enclosed wax pellet, which opens one or more vacuum ports.

On your truck's engine, vacuum serves as a very powerful and economical source of energy. Vacuum switches, valves, and motors, like those that open and close the thermal air cleaner intake flap, can serve quickly and efficiently.

Vacuum- or electrically operated throttle positioners serve a variety of roles. Some raise the idle speed to compensate for extra loads like the air conditioner. Others serve as a dashpot, relying on a spring and resistance diaphragm to slow the throttle return. On carbureted engines, a dashpot helps reduce over-rich fuel flow (venturi effect) during deceleration.

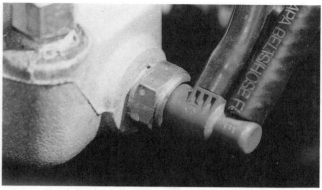

Fig. 8-88. *Thermal vacuum switches (TVS) on many truck engines activate the thermal air cleaner, EGR valve and other devices. At a preset temperature, the valve opens ports, directing vacuum to devices. Check your engine's vacuum circuit diagram to determine the role of the TV switches.*

Fig. 8-89. *Vacuum powers a number of engine devices. Some emission carburetor designs rely on a vacuum-actuated throttle positioner. Vacuum provides ignition spark advance on all pre-emission era Toyota engines and many emissions era engines as well. Emission service always includes inspection of vacuum hose circuits.*

Fig. 8-90. *Check electrical connections at switches and solenoids. Watch the solenoid as someone activates the ignition switch and air conditioning. An idle control solenoid has been popular on engines since the 1970s. Fuel cut-off solenoid (shown) has been used on many Toyota truck engines.*

Fuel Tank and Carburetor Fumes

The raw fumes from gasoline are another source of air pollution. To contain these vapors, light trucks have used evaporative emission control devices since the early 1970s. Although storage methods vary, vacuum helps capture float bowl, crankcase and fuel tank fumes, eventually recycling them through the engine's intake system.

When servicing or repairing your truck's fuel system, you must route vacuum and ventilation hoses very carefully. Follow the OEM Toyota repair manual diagrams or a professional level guide that covers your model.

Fig. 8-91. Evaporative emission controls include a vapor canister. Typically, the replaceable canister is plastic or metal with a granulated carbon element inside. The fuel tank, carburetor vent and other vapor sources each feed the evaporative emission system. Correct hose routing is critical to both performance and vehicle safety.

Inspect the evaporative canister and hoses. If the canister smells heavily like gasoline or feels weighted with liquid, safely drain the gas and replace the canister with a new unit. Evaporative canisters have check valves and require careful routing of hoses to the carburetor or EFI unit, the vacuum source and fuel tank.

> **WARNING —**
> *Gasoline fumes are highly volatile. Use extreme caution when working with the evaporative emission control system. All parts must fit according to design, including the gasoline cap.*

Conversion Engines and Emissions

Many Land Cruisers and some Toyota pickups have conversion engines. The low horsepower output of four- and six-cylinder engines has encouraged swapping to larger, more powerful powerplants. For many years, manufacturers like Advance Adapters and Downey Off-Road have produced parts for domestic engine/transmission swaps into Land Cruisers and Toyota pickup chassis.

Fig. 8-92. A domestic V-8 transplant into a Land Cruiser chassis became popular practice by the late 1960s. An entire industry developed around improving the performance level of 4WD trucks like the rugged FJ40, FJ43, FJ45 and FJ55. (See performance chapter for further details.)

Engine conversions come under Federal emission control compliance laws and the statutes of many states. Whether your truck has a conversion engine or you plan a change, be certain of emission control laws. (You will find further information on engine conversions and emission control compliance in the performance chapters.)

Passing an Emission Test

Although California has the strictest motor vehicle pollution laws in the United States, many vehicles that fail California's smog tests have sufficiently low tailpipe emissions. They fail the visual inspection part of the test.

During the visual inspection, before the engine has a chance to show how cleanly it burns, the inspector looks at the emission control system and vehicle chassis. Any missing or modified parts are cause for failure.

This is a tough test. All vacuum hoses, flexible heat tubes, the smog pump drive belt, vacuum switches, the EGR valve (if required) and closed crankcase devices must be intact and function properly. The inspector, using a detailed manual and the emission decal found under your truck's hood, checks your engine and chassis equipment against the OEM requirements.

The vehicle can fail visual inspection for something as simple as a missing two-dollar section of aluminum flex hose at the thermal air cleaner. Although many aftermar-

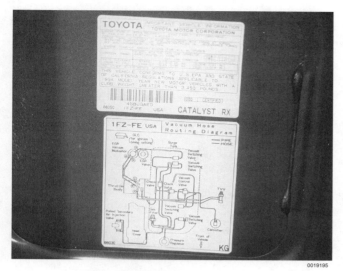

Fig. 8-93. *The underhood emission and tune-up decal is important. It describes the standards for tuning your truck's engine and also the emission control package assigned to the vehicle. The decal often describes smog devices and vacuum hose circuits.*

Fig. 8-94. *Many 1975 and newer U.S.-sold light trucks require unleaded gasoline. Note that this truck's fuel filler neck has a restrictor. In California and other states, smog inspection includes a look at fuel filler.*

NOTE —

Aftermarket components described as "not legal for use on California highways," hold a good chance of getting your engine failed on the smog inspection test. California has essentially become a model for Federal and 49-State emission control policy.

The cold start circuit is among the many items considered during the visual inspection. Although this system operates for only minutes during the warm-up cycle, every component is essential.

A hand choke retrofit kit to replace an automatic choke, a missing vacuum hose or a discarded thermal air cleaner are each cause for failure. Even raising the air cleaner bonnet with a thicker filter element results in an "F," as the open canister compromises both the cold start and closed crankcase systems.

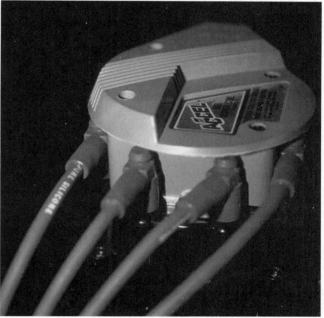

Fig. 8-95. *This Accel HEI Super Coil for a G.M. V-8 has a California E.O. number. Decal installed above distributor allows smog inspection at any Smog Chek station. If you upgrade your ignition (including legal domestic V-6 or V-8 engine conversions), stick with emission legal parts!*

ket performance parts immediately fail the visual test, some pieces comply with California Air Resources Board standards.

Approved aftermarket parts bear a special number (E.O. number) allowing your truck to be inspected at a regular California smog station. Such products even include some designs of retrofit superchargers. Increasing numbers of aftermarket high performance engine components, including intake manifolds and a number of ignition devices and exhaust pieces, also meet ARB standards. (Lists of these devices are available from the California Department of Consumer Affairs, Bureau of Automotive Repairs.)

Well tuned and running properly, your engine will meet hydrocarbon, carbon monoxide and NOx standards at both an idle and the currently required 2500 rpm. Bonafide defects, such as vacuum leaks, carburetor flooding, bad ignition cables, fouled spark plugs or a defective EGR valve, will result in a tailpipe test failure. Ignition timing must match OEM specifications for the engine.

When a California Smog Chek inspector suspects that the wrong engine is in a chassis, he or she may examine the block and/or cylinder head casting numbers. If your engine is not original for the truck, you'll receive a noncompliance certificate and referral to a referee.

Fig. 8-96. By California and U.S. EPA standards, this engine, despite a closed crankcase, EGR valve, enhanced ignition and precise tuning, is not legal. Handsome aftermarket chrome air cleaner, without a closed thermal air system, would immediately fail visual smog inspection.

The referee station identifies the engine by casting or serial numbers, determining the age and OEM emission requirements for both the engine and the chassis. (You may need sales documentation for the engine.) The referee compiles a list of necessary emission control devices for both your truck's chassis and the conversion engine. A visual inspection confirms whether the needed devices are in place. If not, the referee recommends which devices will bring your truck into compliance.

After meeting compliance, the vehicle receives a certification tag noting the required emission control devices. Currently, this enables the owner to take the truck to any Smog Chek station for either a biennial or change of ownership inspection. If the truck complies, you only need to see the referee once.

For emission compliance by California legal criteria, your engine must fit a given range of years (be the same year or newer than your truck's chassis), and meet either OEM or state-approved aftermarket parts requirements. The chassis requires such original equipment as the catalytic converter(s) and the gas tank unleaded fuel restrictor if so equipped.

Lastly, your engine must meet specific tailpipe emission standards—equal to or better than the truck's original engine in good operating condition.

Exhaust System

A truck's exhaust system is subject to severe abuse. Off-highway debris, harsh climates, corrosion, freezing, scorching temperature extremes and a variety of other hazards impact your truck's exhaust system. Aside from emission related components, like the catalytic converter, the system has several other replaceable components.

The exhaust system begins at the exhaust manifold flange and heat riser (if so equipped). The exhaust pipe leads from the manifold to either the catalytic converter or a muffler. If your truck requires a catalytic converter, a pipe exits the converter and connects to the muffler. After the muffler, a tailpipe continues to the rear of the truck.

> **NOTE —**
> Pre-1975 trucks have no catalytic converter. Some Toyota trucks through the late-1970s have no required cat system, either. (These cat exempted trucks have plenty of other devices to handle emission requirements.) You can determine emission device requirements for your truck by looking at the underhood decal for the terms CAT, catalyst, or catalytic converter.

Toyota trucks use a single exhaust system. V-type engines use a Y-shaped exhaust pipe that leads to the catalytic converter or muffler. Single exhaust systems can restrict the flow of gases on V-type engines. High performance and V-6 or V-8 conversion engines generally have dual exhausts.

The obstacle to a dual exhaust conversion is legality. Interpretation of the 1990 Federal Clean Air Act has varied. One view states that if your cat-controlled truck has a single exhaust system, you cannot convert to dual exhaust—period. Under this judgement, no muffler shop can install a two-cat, dual exhaust system on a single exhaust equipped truck. If the truck were converted before the 1990 revision of the act (and receipts are available to prove this fact), a shop can service and repair such a two-cat, dual exhaust system.

If your state requires visual inspection of the emission control system, discuss the dual exhaust option with an emission control inspector or contact the state bureau. When periodic inspection is necessary, make sure your new system is smog legal as well as functional.

Always replace any worn or damaged exhaust parts. Your exhaust system inspection should take place with each lube job. Especially on short wheelbase models, like the FJ40 Land Cruiser, or trucks equipped with a bed cap or camper unit, a safe and leakproof system is a must. Backflow of exhaust and seeping fumes present a health hazard to vehicle occupants.

By design, light truck tailpipes have always exited to the rear of the truck. This is important for health and safety, as it allows fumes to flow away from the truck's body. Some owners, however, choose to shorten their exhaust systems, thinking that less length will improve performance. Such pipes usually exit just forward of the rear wheels. This is a significant health hazard, as exhaust fumes roll upward from the sides of the truck and into the cab, especially on shorter wheelbase models.

If a muffler shop suggests short dual exhaust pipes that exit out the truck's sides, insist that the tailpipes continue to the rear of the truck. An experienced muffler technician can bend and twist pipes to fit the contours of your truck's chassis. Dual tailpipes can always exit the rear of the truck—even if both pipes must fit along the same side of the chassis.

Chapter 9

Clutch and Transmission Service

CLUTCH AND TRANSMISSION PROBLEMS are sometimes difficult to separate. The high cost of a clutch replacement or transmission overhaul makes diagnosis very important. Transmission wear is often mistaken for a bad clutch and vice versa. As troubleshooting skill is the best mechanical resource you can muster, I'd like to help you understand various clutch and transmission problems.

Troubles first appear as driving quirks. As an accurate troubleshooter, you must first isolate each symptom, then determine its cause.

1. CLUTCH AND TRANSMISSION TROUBLESHOOTING

WARNING —
The clutch disc may contain asbestos fibers. Asbestos materials can cause asbestosis. Always wear an approved respirator and protective clothing when handling components containing asbestos. Do not use compressed air, do not grind, heat, weld or sand on or near any asbestos materials. Only approved cleaning methods should be used to service the clutch disc or areas containing asbestos dust or asbestos fibers.

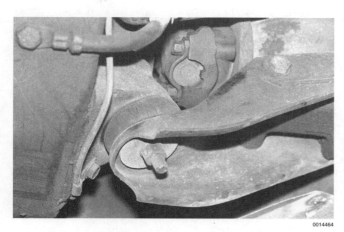

Fig. 9-1. *Defective motor mounts, differential mounts, and transmission mounts can mimic clutch chatter symptoms. Fortunately, Toyota trucks use hydraulic clutch linkage, which eliminates the shake often inherent to mechanical clutch linkage systems. Inspect all mounts before condemning your clutch assembly.*

Clutch Chatter

You release the clutch pedal, and the powertrain shudders, sometimes violently, as clutch engagement begins. If the problem has developed suddenly, especially after an unusually hard day of trailer pulling or pounding a rocky trail, examine the engine mounts and, on 4x4 models, the transmission/transfer case mount. (On some models, a torque arm helps limit transfer case or differential torque twist. Check this bracket along with the mounts.)

If none of these points appear troubled, look to the clutch unit. Disc wear, clutch damage or oil on the disc are common causes of chatter. Especially with 4x4 trucks operated at odd angles, an engine oil leak from the rear main seal or pan gasket can find its way into the clutch assembly and saturate the disc.

An attempt to burn off the oil by riding the clutch to generate friction is a waste of time and could prove dangerous. Clutches can explode under extreme stress or from over revving. There's no sure way to clean the disc

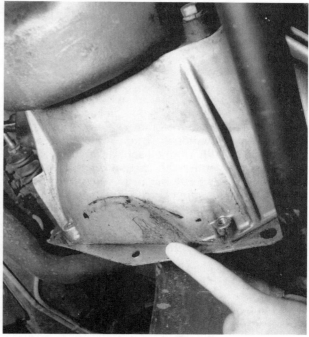

Fig. 9-2. *An engine oil leak at the rear main seal or pan gaskets can cause clutch damage. Oil saturates the clutch disc and causes chatter, slippage and failure. The only cure is clutch replacement.*

in the truck, either. If oil has entered the clutch housing and soaked the disc thoroughly, the disc is ruined.

Another source of oil on the clutch is from the transmission. The front bearing retainer seal is responsible for keeping oil within the gearcase. These seals wear, and on rare occasions, the retainer may crack or leak around its sealing gasket(s). Gear oil, acidic and tenacious, has a devastating effect on a clutch disc.

A common cause of clutch chatter is a distorted clutch cover or broken springs. Excess heat and overworking the clutch can warp a clutch cover. Springs break from fatigue or abuse. Heat also weakens springs, making them exert uneven force. Simply put, clutch chatter results from uneven application of pressure. Loose clutch cover bolts, broken torsional springs in the disc hub or a warped disc will cause chatter.

Fig. 9-3. As the clutch disc wears thin, clamping force decreases. (The clutch cover springs compress less, which reduces their apply pressure.) This is why a high mileage clutch cannot deliver the same performance as a new assembly.

Clutch slippage symptoms are obvious. In gear, the engine revs up, yet the truck does not accelerate. Slippage and chatter often have common causes. In either case, clutch cover apply pressure cannot hold the disc firmly.

Slippage results from oil saturation of the disc or extreme wear of either the friction disc or clutch cover springs. The faintest sound of rivets grating on the flywheel face or pressure plate is a sure sign of major wear. Replace the clutch assembly immediately before irreparable flywheel damage results.

Unwanted Clutch Noises

Truck owners become accustomed to particular powertrain and geartrain noises, those rhythms and pitches of whirring machinery that accompany us on long interstate pulls and dusty trails. An abnormal sound from the clutch area immediately draws attention.

A defective clutch sends a clear message. A warped or severely worn disc will grate or transmit a metallic sound as the disc engages. Broken torsional springs around the disc hub also transmit noise. The more common clutch region noises, however, are bearing defects.

The pilot bearing supports the forward end of the transmission input shaft. Pressed into the center bore of the crankshaft flange, the pilot bearing allows the clutch or input gear to rotate independently of the crankshaft during clutch disengagement. For a pilot bearing, trucks use needle and caged ball-type bearings or a fitted bronze bushing. While some pilot bearings have permanently sealed cases, others require lubrication during installation.

Fig. 9-4. There are three types of pilot bearings and bushings for various truck applications: the solid bronze bushing, a needle bearing assembly and a caged, permanently lubricated ball bearing. In some cases, you will have a choice of designs. Needle and ball bearings offer less friction, while bronze bushings have a reputation for long, trouble-free ser-

CAUTION —
A needle or ball bearing should never be used with an input gear designed for a bronze bushing. Heat treatment of gears differ, and needle bearings will damage a shaft end designed for use with a bronze bushing. Always use Toyota recommended replacement parts.

The pilot bearing or bushing should only need service during clutch replacement. A dry pilot bearing, however, is common to trucks that perform "submarine duty." Running in surf or stream crossings and other water traps can wash grease from the pilot bearing. Once dry, the bearing wears quickly and sets up a howling noise distinct from any other. With the clutch disengaged and the transmission in a gear, pilot noise is obvious.

Loss of lubricant can cause the pilot bearing to seize on the clutch/input gear nose end. This mimics symptoms of a clutch disc and pressure plate that won't disengage properly.

On rare occasions, debris from a backwoods trail enters the clutch housing. Protective plates, tinware and a rubber clutch fork boot should prevent this from happening, but in extreme cases, gravel or other abrasive material seeps through and becomes embedded or trapped in the clutch disc. The symptoms are chatter, clutch slippage and metallic grating. (Twigs or rocks make a raking or rattling sound against the spinning faces of the flywheel or clutch pressure plate.)

A time-honored clutch noise is the worn release or throwout bearing. These bearings often fail before the

Fig. 9-5. The dust boot at the clutch fork is a vital part. Water and debris entering your truck's clutch housing can damage parts. Water can wash vital grease from the pilot bearing or transmission front bearing retainer surface. Keep seals, plates and tinware in good condition.

disc and clutch cover, and the noise is easy to distinguish. First, make certain that the clutch is adjusted properly, as described later in this chapter, and that free-play exists between the clutch release fingers and the throwout bearing. At this point, with the engine running and the pedal fully released, the throwout bearing cannot make noise.

Now apply very light pedal pressure, just enough to bring the bearing against the fingers. The bearing will begin spinning and allow noise to develop. It may require firmer pressure before the bearing transmits sound. Also, to avoid confusing throwout bearing noise with pilot bearing noise, leave the transmission in neutral (with the clutch engaged) so the clutch/input gear can turn in unison with the pilot bearing.

With your transmission in neutral, the clutch fully engaged and the throwout bearing clear of the release fingers, clutch pilot and throwout bearing noise should disappear. If you hear bearing sounds now, look to the transmission for trouble.

Difficulty Shifting Gears

The simpler causes of hard shifting are a misadjusted clutch or insufficient clutch linkage travel. Begin troubleshooting by adjusting the clutch properly and examining linkage from the release fork all the way to the pedal. You need full pedal travel and proper fitup at the various links. Beginning with the truck's clutch pedal, replace any worn bushings to eliminate excess play. Adjust the pedal height and clutch master cylinder pushrod length to specifications found in your OEM Toyota truck repair manual. Each link must provide full movement when you depress the clutch pedal.

Any obstacle to complete clutch disengagement will cause hard shifting. This includes a warped disc or pressure plate, a clutch disc bound on the input gear splines, a

seizing pilot bearing or debris wedged between the clutch disc and pressure plate or flywheel.

> **NOTE —**
> For smooth shifts and complete clutch disengagement, the clutch pressure plate must move away from the disc and allow the disc to rotate freely and independently of the flywheel.

For Toyota trucks, with their hydraulic clutch linkage, look first to hydraulic system troubles. Aside from proper pushrod and pedal height adjustments, the hydraulic system requires a full stroke of fluid to release the clutch completely. This means that the master cylinder piston must retract completely, and the clutch slave cylinder piston must also have ample travel within its bore.

The clutch master cylinder piston must return to its stop when you release the pedal. Adjust the pushrod and/or pedal height to achieve correct piston-to-pushrod clearance and travel. Assuming that the master cylinder has a full fluid reservoir (check fluid first!), check the pushrod and pedal height adjustments. (See adjustment section of this chapter.)

If the fluid has run low, the system may require bleeding. Like a hydraulic brake system, the hydraulic lines can trap air, causing a loss of piston movement at the slave cylinder. Flush and bleed the system periodically with clean brake fluid to purge sludge, accumulated moisture and any air. If the system draws air regularly or loses fluid, overhaul the master cylinder and slave cylinder. (See the brake section of the book for tips on hydraulic cylinder overhaul.)

In good operating condition, bled properly and full of fresh brake fluid, the hydraulic clutch system will move the clutch release arm enough distance to disengage the clutch. If your clutch still drags, consider other causes.

Manual Transmission Troubleshooting

Toyota trucks have used a variety of manual transmission types. If you have the skill and tools necessary to overhaul your transmission, the OEM Toyota truck repair manual provides an excellent, in-depth guide for rebuilding the unit.

> *CAUTION —*
> *Never work on your truck's transmission without first reviewing a professional level repair manual. Subtle differences between synchronizer assemblies and other parts make transmission designs unique. A professional manual will provide correct step-by-step instruction, outline critical clearances and suggest the tools you need. You'll find the job rewarding and a great confidence builder.*

As hard shifting is a symptom shared with clutch troubles, take the time to distinguish causes. Begin by adjusting the clutch and transmission linkage, if possible. Although many Toyota truck transmission shifters are within the control housing and inaccessible to adjustment, some Land Cruiser three-speed transmissions have column shift linkage.

On three-speed models with column shift, the neutral gate and shift linkage alignment are crucial to shifting ease. (Refer to the shift linkage adjustment section of this chapter.) Periodically clean away all debris and lubricate the linkage.

Hard Shifts, Jumping Out Of Gear and Other Woes

Binding shift linkage is always a concern. Your truck is subject to twisting and off-highway stress, and the effects are often felt at linkages and pivotal supports. Eliminate any binding in the shifter or clutch linkage.

Before disassembling the transmission in pursuit of a shift problem, consider the gear lubricant. In late model trucks, lighter oils, including ATF and 75W-90-weight multi-viscosity gear lube, often replace traditional straight 80- or 90-weight gear lube. High grade synthetic oils claim easier shifts and a multi-viscosity lube that will work to –50° F—allowing one oil to serve year 'round.

> **NOTE —**
> Some Toyota synchronizers require either conventional or a conventional/synthetic gear lube blend. Straight synthetic lube may result in gear clash on shifting.

If your manual transmission has the wrong gear lubricant and the weather gets cold, expect trouble. The braking action and movement of synchronizers becomes difficult, and in some cases, the effect is so severe that gear clash makes cold shifting impossible.

Perfectly good clutches come under suspicion because a transmission won't shift into the lower gears when cold. The cause is often an improper viscosity lubricant which prevents normal synchronizer action.

Refer to your Toyota truck lubrication specifications when selecting correct lube—summer and winter. In extreme climates, it may be necessary to change oil in the fall and spring. If the clutch linkage, lubricant and clutch check okay, look to possible transmission problems.

Hard shifting is rarely a transmission shift fork problem, although you cannot rule out this defect. Broken shift rail detents and other shift mechanism troubles are possibilities, although that likelihood is again slim. The most common hard shift problem is a defective synchronizer assembly.

Synchronizers wear over time. The balky shift common to high mileage transmissions is usually a synchronizer problem. The tendency for a transmission to slip out of any synchronized gear is often caused by a synchronizer assembly defect. Synchronizer interlock springs, detent keys and shift rail poppet springs each help keep the transmission in gear. Wear or defects here require a transmission teardown.

Loose transmission bearings, worn synchronizer parts and excessive clearances can cause a transmission to slip out of gear. (Before condemning the transmission on column shift models, check shift linkage for full travel and smooth operation.) Worn or chipped gear teeth, excessive shaft end play, and drive gear pilot bearing wear are also causes of hard shifting and jumping out of gear. Other possibilities include a loose or misaligned clutch housing, worn motor or transmission mounts, a broken torque brace, or a defective crankshaft pilot bearing.

If you have isolated your trouble to the transmission, prepare for considerable expense. An overhaul must be thorough, replacing all worn pieces. If severe growling or gear whine noises have developed, you may wish to compare the cost of a major overhaul to that of a recycled or new transmission.

Burnt gear oil is a sign of major trouble. If fried oil and various metals come from the drain hole, expect to find heat-discolored shafts, damaged gears and failed (expensive) bearings.

Transmissions contain hard steel gear and shaft parts, bronze thrust washers and in some later units, nylon shift fork slippers. When you service your transmission, examine the lubricant carefully for the presence of these materials. Powdery bronze thrust washer material, in small quantities, is normal. These washers wear very slowly over time. However, a high degree of bronze, or the presence of harder metal pieces, means trouble.

2. CLUTCH WEAR AND SERVICE

A truck clutch will eventually fail or wear out. Fortunately, a clutch rarely breaks without warning. The key to getting the most from your clutch is to exercise reasonable driving habits, avoiding severe powertrain shock loads or continuous clutch overheating.

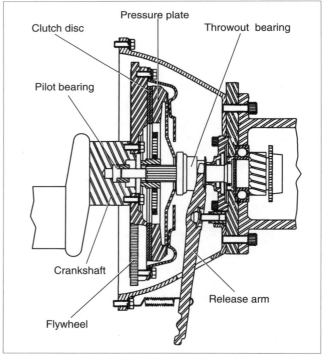

Fig. 9-6. *The spring loaded clutch pressure plate sandwiches the clutch disc face against the flywheel. As the disc's friction material wears, spring apply pressure weakens. This accounts for the slippage common with higher mileage clutch units.*

Although many accessories speed up clutch wear, oversize tires have the heaviest impact. Big wheels and tires have the same effect as installing a taller (numerically lower) set of axle gears. Unless you change axle gearing to match the new tire diameter, the new gearing will take its toll on the clutch.

A variety of causes lead to clutch slippage. Misadjusted clearance between the throwout bearing and pressure plate, overloading, slipping the clutch and other bad driving techniques usually speed up the process. Even under ideal circumstances, the clutch disc wears, becoming progressively thinner and seriously weakening the clutch cover apply pressure.

The best way to reduce clutch wear is to reduce the amount of time that the clutch plate slips during engagement. Beyond this, proper use of your gears can help. (See chapter on operating techniques.)

Clutch wear is obvious. Slippage will occur as you release the pedal, when the truck climbs steep inclines and during low speed lugging of the engine. If the clutch isn't noticeably weak, you can push the test further: Place the shifter in high gear at 15–20 mph. Disengage the clutch, and, as you hold the clutch pedal to the floor, bring the engine speed to about 2500 rpm and quickly release the clutch pedal.

Assuming that clutch free play is adjusted correctly, one of two things will happen. When the clutch is in good condition, releasing the pedal will cause an immediate and noticeable drop in engine rpm, sometimes enough to nearly stall the engine. If the clutch has excessive wear, such as glazed friction lining or weak pressure plate springs, the engine speed will either remain high for several seconds or drop slowly.

Sooner or later your truck's clutch will fail this test. When it does, a variety of rebuilt and new clutch assembly options exist to restore or improve your truck.

An aftermarket clutch can work with no modifications to your truck's existing flywheel, clutch linkage, or other clutch-related parts. A clutch replacement offers an excellent opportunity to upgrade your truck.

Identifying Your Clutch

There are three clutch types used in Toyota trucks: the common diaphragm spring design and two kinds of three-finger multiple coil spring types. Three-finger types are either centrifugally weighted (like domestic Long types) or full-spring pressure designs (like the domestic Borg&Beck units). All clutch discs have torsional springs and composition friction material.

Years ago, clutch covers with coil springs and adjustable release fingers could be rebuilt by a well equipped shop. It was common for a general repair shop to rebuild a cover or adjust the release finger height. Today, neither the three-finger types nor multi-finger diaphragm clutches require field service. Auto parts retailers and your local Toyota dealership sell fully adjusted (rebuilt or new) clutch cover/pressure plate assemblies.

When your truck needs a clutch replacement, consider installing a heavy duty replacement unit. When seeking such a clutch, you will find that diameter sometimes increases with larger displacement engines or higher GVWRs. If your Toyota truck engine shares a flywheel design and bellhousing with a heavier duty model, there could be a larger clutch assembly for your engine.

Fig. 9-7. Many Toyota trucks use the common diaphragm type clutch cover/pressure plate with its full radius of non-adjustable release fingers. Clutch disc diameter is an indication of stamina and strength. Your Toyota truck flywheel and clutch housing size will determine whether a larger diameter clutch disc and cover can upgrade the system.

Fig. 9-8. Borg&Beck clutches serve many domestic trucks. Toyota trucks have used a Japanese version of this three-finger design. Multiple coil springs offer strong clamping force and smooth operation. These clutches deliver quality service.

If the flywheel size restricts the diameter of the clutch disc and cover, consider a Centerforce II or Dual-Friction clutch. I have seen these OEM replacement size units perform heroically in Toyota trucks with grossly oversized tires, heavy loads and driver abuse. There is absolutely no clutch that shifts easier than a Centerforce, yet its superior clamping force can turn your truck's clutch into a high performance workhorse.

If you increase engine performance or the load placed on the clutch, a heavier duty unit is likely necessary. When buying a new clutch assembly, you will need to match your clutch disc diameter (unless a larger unit will fit properly), the hub spline configuration and the clutch cover design.

Toyota trucks have used a variety of manual transmissions. The clutch splines and input shaft diameter can vary between designs. Carefully identify your transmission whenever ordering parts.

Fig. 9-10. *All Toyota trucks bound for U.S. market have used hydraulic clutch linkage. Shown here is an early Land Cruiser FJ40 with its clutch and brake master cylinders. Land Cruisers and earlier pickups require periodic adjustment of the clutch release rod at the slave cylinder.*

Fig. 9-9. *Aside from the clutch diameter, the spline configuration must match the transmission input gear. It's good practice to take your complete clutch to the parts house. Always avoid inhalation of asbestos fibers from the disc.*

Clutch Adjustment

A manual transmission truck may require periodic clutch adjustment. On later models, the hydraulic clutch linkage adjusts by itself to compensate for wear. Earlier Toyota truck hydraulic clutch linkage *does* require periodic clutch adjustment. (These models are easy to distinguish, as the clutch release rod at the slave cylinder has a threaded and adjustable section.) See your OEM Toyota truck repair manual for pedal height, master cylinder pushrod clearance and slave cylinder/release pushrod adjustment.

You will need to work beneath the truck to adjust linkage at the clutch release arm and rod. Set the parking brake securely and block the wheels to prevent the vehicle from rolling, then crawl beneath the truck with a set of wrenches. Remember to loosen locknuts before attempting adjustments. Tighten lock nuts when done.

WARNING —
Always set the parking brake and block the wheels before crawling beneath your truck.

Since the hydraulic linkage slave cylinder mounts firmly to the engine/clutch housing, smooth clutch engagement is possible under all operating conditions, a distinct advantage over mechanical linkage. With mechanical linkage, engine torque can twist and shake the release rods, and this translates as jerky clutch engagement. Especially for trucks that operate with heavy loads or off-pavement, hydraulic clutch linkage is superior.

Always begin your clutch adjustment by checking freeplay at the release arm. Although proper clutch operation demands sufficient pedal travel and free play, release arm movement provides the only true measurement of the throwout bearing-to-clutch clearance. Maintaining the required gap between the clutch release fingers and the throwout bearing face assures full engagement of the clutch and a long life for the throwout bearing.

On models with adjustable clutch linkage, normal clutch wear will decrease the clearance between the clutch release fingers and the throwout bearing. If wear becomes

Fig. 9-11. *Always check clutch free-play at the release arm (arrow). Note relationship of throwout bearing and clutch release fingers. Linkage wear can make free-play measurement at the pedal inaccurate.*

Fig. 9-12. Later Toyota truck models use hydraulic clutch linkage that requires no adjustment. However, you should still check the clutch master cylinder's fluid level regularly and change the fluid at appropriate intervals. Maintenance checks still include proper pedal height and master cylinder pushrod clearance.

Fig. 9-13. The earlier model hydraulic clutch release rod (shown with adjustable threaded section) is much like mechanical linkage. You need to periodically adjust the clutch on this type of system.

excessive, the throwout bearing will actually ride on the fingers. This can cause premature failure of the clutch release bearing or damage to the release fingers.

If wear continues beyond the point of contact, the throwout bearing will not allow the clutch to engage completely. Slippage occurs, resulting in heat buildup and friction. The clutch will wear rapidly when adjusted too tightly and ruin the clutch or release bearing.

When following adjustment steps in your OEM Toyota truck repair manual, note that all release rod adjustments take place after the pedal height and master cylinder pushrod clearance have been confirmed and/or corrected. Specifications also assume that linkage is in good condition and that return springs pull the pedal and release arm to their proper stop positions. Linkage wear or weak return springs will create false readings.

> **NOTE —**
> Your truck's clutch can be costly and difficult to access (especially 4WD models), taking considerable labor to replace. Avoid trouble. Inspect and adjust clutch linkage periodically.

Clutch Adjustments: Early Models

Clutch adjustment takes place at the release arm linkage near the clutch housing. First make sure the master cylinder is full, and bleed any air from the slave cylinder. Next, verify the clutch pedal rod-to-master cylinder piston clearance. The rod must allow the piston to retract completely when the pedal rests against its bumper stop. Match the pedal height to figures found in your Toyota repair manual. Typical pushrod to master cylinder piston clearance is 1mm-5mm (1/32" to 3/16") with the pedal fully retracted against its bumper stop. I like a clearance of 1/16-inch (approximately 1.5mm) to assure full retraction of the master cylinder piston when the pedal releases.

If clearance is incorrect, the pushrod attaches to the pedal with a threaded clevis and pin. The pushrod length is adjustable, as the pushrod threads into the clevis yoke. Loosen the pushrod's lock nut and rotate the rod to attain the correct pedal rod-to-master cylinder piston clearance. Tighten the lock nut when adjustment is correct.

On models with an adjustable pushrod, slide the dust boot back, taking care not to allow debris to enter the backside of the master cylinder or the boot. Loosen the lock nut and adjust the length of the pushrod to establish proper clearance, then reinstall the boot carefully.

> **NOTE —**
> Pedal and pushrod adjustment is rare and generally addresses long term chassis wear. Your next clutch adjustment(s) will likely require nothing more than an adjustment at the clutch release arm.

Now you can go beneath the truck and check or adjust the clutch release arm clearance. Check for throwout bearing movement by moving the release arm and observing the bearing-to-finger relationship within the bellhousing. On adjustable release rods, you should find a clutch linkage/pedal return spring at the release arm or rod. Make sure all springs work properly so that pedal weight does not cause the throwout bearing to ride on the clutch cover fingers when the pedal is released.

With the clutch return spring detached, push the release arm pushrod into the slave cylinder until the pushrod stops (piston bottomed). Hold the pushrod here, and move the clutch release arm fork away from the pushrod until the throwout bearing stops against the clutch cover fingers.

You can set clearance by turning the adjuster nut after backing off the lock nut. Hold the pushrod steady as you rotate the adjuster. (Some Toyotas have lock and adjuster nuts and a release rod with a slotted end that accepts a screwdriver. With this kind of adjustment, loosen the lock nut and hold the adjuster nut while turning the rod with a screwdriver.) When adjusted properly, hold the adjuster nut and tighten the locknut. Re-check clearance.

Fig. 9-14. On models like this Land Cruiser, the clutch release rod requires periodic adjustment for proper pedal free play. When adjustment is correct, there is a distinct amount of clearance between the release/throwout bearing and the fingers of the clutch cover. You can feel this at the release arm. Check this movement whenever you perform routine service.

Follow clearance specifications in your repair manual. Generally, you will strive for 1/8" to 5/32" release arm play on Toyota models with the diaphragm type clutch and 3/32" to 5/32" spacing on models equipped with a three-finger clutch. Measure between the release rod nut or fulcrum and the release rod seat in the arm or fork.

Strive for the greater amount of release rod-to-release arm/fork clearance listed in your manual. This will protect the throwout bearing and clutch fingers from unnecessary chafing and wear. You will find that as the clutch wears normally, release rod clearance will decrease.

Reattach the return spring, which must be in good condition. Work the clutch pedal several times, then check the pedal free travel again. Measure free travel from the center of the pedal foot pad. There should be approximately 1/8-inch of pedal movement before the pushrod begins to push the master cylinder piston. (You may need to either slide the dust boot back to see this or grip the pushrod through the boot and feel for play. Keep dirt and debris from entering the backside of the master cylinder or the boot.)

Now move the pedal further with your fingertips (taking up free play), and note the pedal height where you begin to feel more resistance. This resistance is the throwout bearing starting to press against the release fingers. If you press further, you are actually releasing the clutch. Make sure pedal free play comes within the specifications in your Toyota repair manual.

Secure each locknut after adjustment, and always recheck the release bearing-to-clutch finger clearance after driving the truck.

Always keep in mind that worn or improperly adjusted linkage can create a false pedal free-play reading. Air in the hydraulic lines or a worn piston seal will also create a false reading. Check the linkage, bushings and adjustments from the pedal to the clutch release arm. Correct for any wear before measuring pedal free play.

Non-adjustable Clutch Linkage

Later hydraulic clutch linkage designs omit the use of a release arm spring. This design relies on the rotational force of the clutch to thrust the release bearing slightly away from the clutch fingers when the driver releases the pedal. These systems self-adjust, requiring no type of adjustment between clutch replacements. (Check clutch reservoir fluid with regular maintenance.)

Assuming that pedal height is correct and the clutch cylinders work properly, this type of hydraulic clutch linkage provides enough piston travel to compensate for normal wear. The system simply compensates for wear, providing correct release bearing clearance for the normal service life of the clutch.

Hydraulic systems occasionally need bleeding, and a periodic bleed/flush will provide fresh fluid and remove moisture or other contaminants. (Bleeding procedure is much the same as for hydraulic brakes.) Always use fresh DOT 3 or higher grade brake fluid and maintain cleanliness. Keep all contaminants out of the system. Clean fluid will help protect the release mechanism from premature failure.

CAUTION —
As with a brake system, clean debris from around the fluid reservoir before removing the cap. Prevent contaminants and dirt from entering the hydraulic clutch system. Always use clean brake fluid.

Clutch Replacement Tips

Replacing your truck's clutch is a major job. Before condemning your clutch, try a simple adjustment first and make sure that the mechanical linkage or hydraulic cylinder operation is correct. A hydraulic seal leak can limit the clutch release arm travel, prevent full release of the clutch and cause symptoms of a defective clutch.

Also, clutch wear or failure symptoms are often mimicked by troubles like loose or broken motor mounts, a worn limited slip axle/differential or binding clutch linkage. When clutch failure or a diagnosis like "worn out" is premature, consider other possibilities.

WARNING —
The clutch disc may contain asbestos fibers. Asbestos materials can cause asbestosis. Always wear an approved respirator and protective clothing when handling components containing asbestos. Do not use compressed air, do not grind, heat, weld or sand on or near any asbestos materials. Only approved cleaning methods should be used to service the clutch disc or areas containing asbestos dust or asbestos fibers.

When your truck requires a clutch replacement, the OEM Toyota repair manual for your model will clearly outline the steps. Rather than provide step-by-step instructions for the clutch replacement, this section provides the footnotes that OEM and professional workshop manuals, written primarily for journey-level mechanics, often omit.

Fig. 9-15. *Examine motor mounts and other areas before condemning the clutch. Mounts sag, break, loosen and become oil saturated. A 4x4 Land Cruiser, 4WD pickup or 4Runner clutch job is a major task, done only when necessary.*

The clutch in your truck mounts on the flywheel, at the back of the engine and in front of the transmission. On 4WD equipped trucks, the removal of the transmission involves far more work than on a 2WD truck.

2WD trucks require driveshaft and transmission removal for a clutch replacement. On a 4x4, the front and rear driveshafts attach to the transfer case. Clutch replacement on a 4WD model means removing the transfer case, plus numerous components that connect to the transfer case, before removing the transmission.

Obviously, if you have any good reason to remove the engine, consider performing a clutch replacement at the same time, especially on 4WD trucks. This is simply good insurance.

Clutch replacement can be done in concert with other repairs. For example, if your 4WD's radiator needs repair when the clutch also begs attention, consider doing both jobs simultaneously. Once the radiator is out, you have added engine bay space. You could then separate the engine from the bellhousing and, with a safe engine hoist, *partially* remove the engine to access the clutch.

If changing the clutch in this manner makes sense, securely support the transmission before moving the engine forward. This method is an alternative to the customary routine of removing the two drivelines, the transfer case and the transmission assembly.

The choice is yours. First read Toyota's OEM procedure for removing the engine, then the steps for replacing the clutch. Assess your truck, the available tools and your working conditions. Some later model engines have a mass of accessories and confusing A/C plumbing, special wiring considerations and a maze of vacuum hoses that could make engine removal less practical.

When removing and installing powertrain components, understand that they are very hefty and cumbersome. Use appropriate jacks and any other safety equipment to protect yourself from injury. If you cannot afford a transmission jack, rent one. This will save time, make the job easier and prevent damage to vital parts. Aligning the transmission and transfer case with the clutch is an awkward job, even with a special jack.

A truck transmission coupled to a transfer case can weigh over 200 pounds—enough to pin you to the garage floor for good! Use extreme caution with this type of bulk, as no clutch job is worth permanent injury. Use a hoist, hydraulic transmission jack or special lifting devices.

For saving time and protecting vital parts, always use clutch and transmission aligning tools. More trouble occurs during attempts to align the transmission with the clutch disc hub than any other operation. To avoid clutch disc damage, never hang weight off the clutch hub.

Take care to tighten clutch cover bolts gradually, evenly and in cross sequence, following factory guidelines. Warping a brand new clutch cover can ruin the whole job, plus require a teardown to correct the clutch shudder.

Fig. 9-17. *A Land Cruiser iron four-speed, or NV4500 conversion five-speed (shown) coupled to a transfer case, can weigh as much as 300 pounds. Separate these components and use a special transmission jack to remove and install the sub-assemblies. Floor jack and jackstands can support engine and transmission during service work.*

Fig. 9-16. *A 4x4 Toyota truck clutch replacement calls for transmission and even transfer case removal. In some cases, it may be easier to remove the radiator, detach and move the engine forward, and leave the rest of the powertrain in place. Support the transmission/ transfer case carefully.*

Inspect the flywheel surface for heat cracks, glazing and possible warpage. Again, with the magnitude of this task, don't try to cut corners. Mark the flywheel's location on the crankshaft and remove the flywheel. Send it to a quality automotive machine shop. Let them inspect the flywheel and resurface its face. If the flywheel's starter ring gear shows any damage, replace either the ring gear or the entire flywheel.

Fig. 9-18. *Check the flywheel for heat cracks, blue discoloration and glazing. If you find any of these symptoms, sublet the flywheel to an automotive machine shop for service. Note that many Toyota truck flywheels have a step to mount the clutch cover. Machine shop must surface the flywheel's step and clutch mating face to maintain proper spacing. If not, clutch apply pressure will be inadequate.*

Flywheel thickness is important for normal clutch operation, engine balance and correct positioning of the release bearing. Make sure flywheel thickness is within factory specifications. On Toyota's step-type flywheels, be certain the machine shop considers the clutch cover height when machining the flywheel. This requires surfacing both the flywheel's face and the step where the cover mounts.

The Parts List

The job is tough, and you don't want to do it over. When you make your list of necessary parts, begin with the clutch cover (pressure plate), clutch disc and throwout or release bearing. Closely inspect the crankshaft pilot bearing and clutch release arm for wear. If in doubt, replace these parts. (I generally replace the pilot bearing as a preventive measure.)

For most trucks, weather and age take their toll. The release arm sealing boot can deteriorate or be in rough shape. If worn at all, replace it. Any saggy return springs need replacement. Look closely at the clutch linkage; inspect for wear, fatigue and life expectancy. Inspect the transmission's front bearing retainer that supports the throwout bearing. If you find galling or wear, replace or repair (if the wear is very slight) the retainer.

Replace all seals that are leaking or could soon leak. This includes the front bearing retainer seal and gasket. (On some transmissions the retainer gasket is a selective fit to control bearing end play. Read your service guidebook for clearances before replacing this gasket.) Visual-

Fig. 9-19. *The transmission front bearing retainer also supports the throwout bearing. Galling or a rough surface can cause erratic clutch operation, including chatter during engagement. If you find substantial wear here, replace the retainer. If wear is limited to very slight burrs light sanding with crocus cloth may restore the surface.*

ize where a leak could develop and which parts would be especially hard to access. Restore any trouble spots now.

Toss out any worn fastening hardware and replace with equivalent grade bolts, nuts and locking devices. Know your grading (see appendix charts) and upgrade if necessary. If you remove the flywheel, install new original equipment (OE) type replacement flywheel bolts. The same with the clutch cover. Replace all locking hardware and/or washers, and clean or chase threads to assure proper torque settings.

> **WARNING —**
> *Use properly graded hardware, identical to OE design. Engineers often design bolts to serve a particular function. Match hardware perfectly, and do not install generic hardware in place of specially configured bolts. Always replace hardware with identical parts. Match bolt shoulder length, thread pitch, grading, lock washer design and other details. Do not replace specialized hardware with generic fasteners.*

Tools

For a quality job, you'll need several specialty tools. Removal of the pilot bearing generally requires a special puller. For solid bushing or sealed ball bearing pilots, you might try this alternative, which I learned years ago from a veteran mechanic: Pack the pilot cavity with grease. Find a steel shaft or an old transmission input gear with the same diameter nose as the pilot bushing bore. Tap the shaft into the pilot bore.

> **WARNING —**
> *Cushion your blows with a block of wood or a plastic hammer, and wear eye protection.*

The shaft acts like a hydraulic ram. As you tap, grease will create impact force at the back side of the pilot bushing and drive the bushing out. This only works with

Fig. 9-20. A clutch disc aligning tool is a must when fitting a new disc. Always install a new pilot bearing/bushing and clutch throwout bearing when replacing the clutch disc and pressure plate. Use OEM design bearings.

bronze bushings or sealed/caged bearings, as the driver shaft must maintain a snug seal within the bore in order to create this effect.

A clutch aligning tool is a must. An old transmission input gear with the same splines will serve to align the clutch disc as you secure the clutch cover to the flywheel.

Over the years, I have accumulated a drawer full of alignment dowels for the two upper bolt holes of various clutch housings. To make your own alignment dowels, simply cut the heads off long bolts of the proper thread size. For simpler removal, make a screwdriver slot at the end of each dowel and keep threads clean.

By installing dowel pins, you can keep the transmission aligned and on center as you slide the assembly into position. Once you've installed the lower transmission bolts, unscrew one pin at a time and replace each dowel with a transmission mounting bolt. Tighten all bolts in sequence, and establish final settings with a torque wrench.

Prevent damage to the transmission case, bearing retainer, clutch hub and pilot bearing. Carefully maintain transmission alignment during installation. Always support the transmission with a jack until all upper and lower mounting bolts are secure.

You will want some high melting point grease for the inside collar of the throwout bearing. Some manufacturers package the bearing with grease. Never clean a new throwout bearing in solvent, as this will remove grease.

Make sure you have proper sealant if you intend to remove the front bearing retainer and install a new gasket. As I commented earlier, some transmissions have selective fit bearing retainer gaskets (shims) for precisely adjusting the end play of the input gear and bearing.

Be sure you have plenty of parts cleaner and shop towels. This is a very messy job, especially on a 4x4 or truck that runs off-pavement. (Before you start work, thoroughly pressure wash the chassis and powertrain.) You will also need the best hand cleaner available. You'll be very oily when this job is done!

CAUTION —
Do not alter the thickness of selective fit shim/gaskets. Use a micrometer to confirm original thickness and match this with the new gasket stack. Some gearboxes call for a dial indicator check of end play and use of gaskets of proper thickness to restore or correct end play.

Hydraulic Clutch Linkage Service

Many domestic trucks have used mechanical clutch linkage. These systems require periodic service, as bushing wear leads to unwanted play. The rods and levers that actuate the clutch will wear and fatigue at the pivot points. Nylon bushings wear out, along with the pedal stops and return springs. If a truck uses mechanical linkage, it is necessary to replace these parts when wear develops.

Toyota trucks have all used hydraulic clutch linkage. These linkage systems consist of a master cylinder, hydraulic hose and pipe, and a clutch slave (release) cylinder. The slave cylinder actuates a release fork/arm, much like a mechanical clutch linkage system. Similar to your truck's braking system, cleanliness and fresh hydraulic brake fluid assure longer service.

When performing work on the hydraulic clutch system, you need clean hands, free of any grease, oils or abrasive contaminants. Repair kits are sometimes available for the master and slave cylinders, or you can replace these parts if they show excess wear.

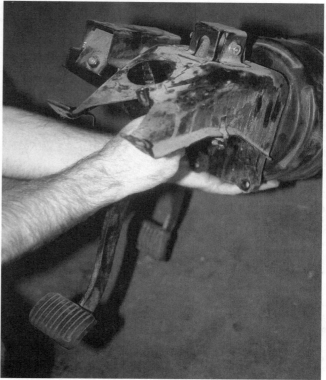

Fig. 9-21. Because Toyota trucks use hydraulic linkage the only friction points to check for wear are pedal bushings, springs and release arm pivots. Hydraulic cylinders may require rebuilding or replacement at higher mileage.

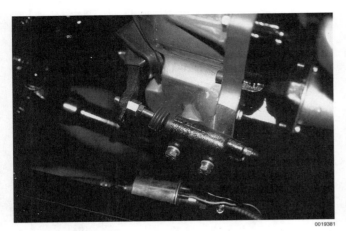

Fig. 9-22. *Hydraulic clutch linkage eliminates many problems. Twisting and body/frame flex off-highway can raise havoc with mechanical clutch linkage, especially models with suspended pedals. By contrast, a hydraulic cylinder mounts solidly to the bellhousing, maintaining constant alignment with the release arm.*

Judge cylinder wear as you would a brake cylinder. Consult your Toyota truck repair manual for safe tolerances and rebuilding details. Do not take chances here, as a clutch linkage failure could strand your truck or cause clutch and transmission damage.

Look closely at the hydraulic hose and piping. Again, like brake lines or hose, these items can wear or deteriorate. If embrittlement or dehydration has occurred, replace the hose and/or brake-type piping. Use DOT 3 or higher grade brake fluid. (See the brake section of this book for further details on hydraulic system repairs.)

3. TRANSMISSION LINKAGE ADJUSTMENTS

For Toyota truck manual transmissions, the need for linkage adjustments primarily applies to Land Cruiser three-speed column shift models. Other gearboxes feature control housing assemblies, generally considered part of the transmission assembly. Rarely does a control housing require overhaul, although in many models, you can perform such service without removing the complete transmission.

Land Cruiser three-speeds built before 1973 use column shift linkage. In 1973 and 1974, the last two years of Land Cruiser three-speed transmissions, FJ models had a floor shifter. This type of mechanism can be retrofitted to late 1963 through 1972 Land Cruisers. (Some aftermarket suppliers offer a floor shifter conversion kit. See performance chapters for more details.)

Some owners find the floor shift conversion practical, eliminating a worn column shift linkage system in one step. For other trucks, however, the OEM column shift linkage may be intact and fully functional—or perhaps an FJ model is undergoing OEM-type restoration and requires the original shift linkage.

Fig. 9-23. *Column shift linkage will wear, stretch and fatigue, requiring periodic adjustment. Worn parts require replacement. On Land Cruisers with column shift, periodically clean linkage and thoroughly lubricate lever mechanism at base of column.*

Although a Toyota truck repair manual or professional service guide provides details for adjusting the column shift linkage on a Land Cruiser, I will detail some aims.

A rod extends from one of the transmission control levers to a control lever at the steering column (just forward of the engine cowl). Another arm runs from the other transmission lever to a pivoting bellcrank. A rod extends from this bellcrank to the steering column linkage.

The driver controlled shifter lever moves fore and aft through a neutral gate. This aligns the shifter lever with one or the other column shifter arms.

One shifter arm works the first and reverse gears, while the other attaches to the second and high gear control lever at the transmission. Adjustment consists of aligning these two column shifter arms so that the shift lever can move smoothly from the first/reverse gear path, then through the neutral gate and into the second/high gear shift path.

You will find specific adjustment procedures in your Toyota truck repair manual or a professional level service manual. Three objectives apply: 1) the rod adjustments should place the steering column shifter arms in perfect alignment through the neutral gate; 2) for driver convenience, the column shifter should swing through a comfortable range; and 3) rods must move freely and permit complete engagement of all gears.

This last point is crucial. The only place to verify proper gear engagement is to block the wheels, set the parking brake and crawl beneath the truck (with the engine turned off and cold so the exhaust system won't scorch your hands) and have an assistant move the shift linkage through each gear.

Make sure that the transmission control lever moves completely into each gear position indicated. If you are uncertain, remove the shift rod at the transmission control lever and note whether the lever is completely in gear.

Automatic Transmission Adjustments

Your automatic transmission requires periodic service. Look for fluid leaks and the condition of vacuum hoses to the modulator (if so equipped). Perform periodic fluid and filter changes. Cleanliness in the service of your transmission cannot be overstated—guidelines call for lint-free shop towels when working around an automatic transmission's valve body.

Fig. 9-24. When servicing your automatic transmission, cleanliness is crucial. Dirt, even lint, in the valve body can cause shifting irregularities and other problems that lead to an overhaul. When changing the filter, use extreme care to keep contaminants out.

There are some basic adjustments for your automatic transmission. Later trucks have sophisticated electrical and electronic controls, yet the rules remain similar. First, the manual (shift) valve requires proper adjustment. This measure cannot be overstated.

A manual valve out of adjustment may direct an inadequate flow of hydraulic fluid within the transmission. Incorrect manual valve adjustment can cause weak shifts, insufficient apply pressure, slipping clutch packs and weak band application. Damage or complete transmission failure can result from incorrectly adjusted shift linkage.

The second adjustment is the kickdown or downshift linkage. The kickdown feature makes the transmission responsive to engine throttle position, causing a downshift from Overdrive (fourth gear) and Drive (third gear) to sec-

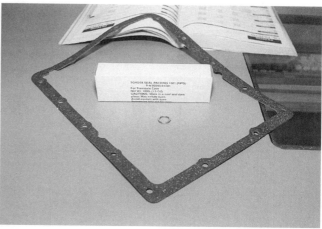

Fig. 9-25. A full service on your automatic transmission includes a fluid and filter change, adjustment of the shift and kickdown linkage or electric switches, and adjustment of the ignition neutral/park safety switch.

ond gear at full throttle if the vehicle speed is less than the limit set for the truck's axle gearing and OEM tire size.

A mechanical linkage for kickdown was common with Toyota's earlier Toyoglide transmissions. Late electronically controlled transmissions (ECT) designs use electrical kickdown switches. This process involves a variety of sensory data and electronic modules, including the engine management computer.

If your transmission has a vacuum modulator, this can also affect shifts. The modulator helps dictate upshift and downshift points. An automatic transmission that shifts erratically can suffer from either a defective governor or a bad vacuum modulator. The modulator is much easier, and less costly, to replace!

Before condemning your whole transmission, perform a full service. Change the fluid and filter. Adjust the manual linkage, centering the shift indicator for neutral and park. Readjust the neutral safety switch, if necessary, to assure that the engine will start only in neutral or park. On adjustable band-type transmissions, adjust the bands.

On older Toyoglide band-type automatics (built prior to 1978), you must periodically adjust the front and rear bands. This procedure is outlined in the OEM Toyota Hi-Lux Pickup repair manual for that era or a professional level service manual. Later Toyota transmissions do not require periodic band adjustment.

Adjust carburetor linkage on models with manual detent/kickdown controls. Check the adjustment of electrical kickdown switches on later transmissions. Check vacuum lines to any transmission controls. Make sure that they provide leak-free vacuum signals.

If none of these measures improve your automatic's performance, accept the likelihood that the unit needs in-depth repairs or a major overhaul. Like a manual clutch, automatic transmission parts wear over time.

Chapter 10

Transfer Case, Driveshaft, Axles, and Hubs

TOYOTA TRUCKS HAVE A REPUTATION for durability and hard work. Whether moving a loaded travel trailer or hauling supplies to a minesite or logging camp, a Toyota truck can more than earn its keep. In Africa, Asia, South America and Australia, 4WD Toyota trucks run wheel-to-wheel with the legendary British Land Rovers and U.S.-designed Jeep models. In North America, rural, suburban and urban owners use their Toyota Land Cruisers, pickups and 4Runners for both hard work and an active outdoor recreational life-style.

Toyota 4WDs grapple with desert sand, churning mud, deep snow, the steepest rocky grades and swampy bogs. Such a wide variety of chores requires auxiliary gearsets, and the two-speed transfer case has provided the solution. Except for the rare (very early) Land Cruisers equipped with a heavy duty four-speed transmission and single speed power divider/transfer unit, Toyota 4x4s offer a two-speed transfer case with a provision for 4WD high and low range.

1. TRANSFER CASES

The Toyota transfer case adapts to the rear of the transmission and divides power between the front and rear axles. A two-speed transfer case offers low range,

essentially an extra gearset available for four-wheel drive mode and heavy off-pavement pulling chores.

On Toyota 4WD truck geartrains, the transmission output shaft drives the transfer case input, and the transmission attaches to the transfer case. For Land Cruisers with rear engine mounts at each side of the clutch housing, the transmission and transfer case actually hang as a unit from the back of the heavy iron clutch housing.

For 4WD trucks with three-point engine/transmission mounting systems (two side engine mounts, one transmission mount), a cast adapter attaches the transmission directly to the transfer case. This adapter doubles as the rear engine/transmission and transfer case mount.

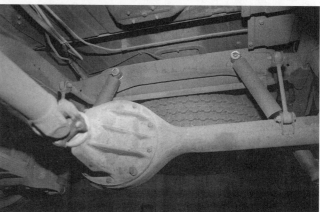

Fig. 10-2. *Land Cruisers have used side-drive type transfer cases. This means that power flows into the transfer case, then moves laterally through an intermediate gearset to the front and rear output shafts. These shafts line up with each other, and due to their offset from the transmission output centerline, they must drive to offset axle differentials.*

Fig. 10-1. *All Toyota Land Cruiser, 4WD pickup and 4Runner transmissions mate directly to the transfer case. The common term for this arrangement is a married transfer case. Some very early FJ25 and FJ40 models had a heavy duty four-speed transmission without synchromesh on first (compound low) gear and a single speed transfer/power divider. All other Toyota transfer cases feature two speeds: high and low range.*

179

Fig. 10-3. *This later Toyota pickup transfer case has a chain drive mechanism. Alloy cases on all Toyota transfer cases provide a lightweight and durable package. Toyota stayed with proven gear drive transfer cases longer than domestic light truck manufacturers and made the switch to chain drive only after extensive testing.*

Fig. 10-4. *4WD pickups have used a through-drive transfer case. This drives power directly from the transmission through the transfer case to the rear axle in 2WD and 4WD modes. The front axle drive lies offset from the rear drive. Power to the front axle is side-driven, much like the Land Cruiser's power flow.*

Traditional Land Cruiser transfer cases offered a power take-off (PTO) drive gear, which provided an auxiliary power source for a winch or other accessories. Declining interest in PTO-type winches, replaced by easier to install and less complex electric types, eventually led Toyota to remove the PTO drive gear from transfer cases.

For rock crawling or heavy off-pavement pulling in low range, the gear drive transfer case accomplishes speed reduction through engagement of a gear on the intermediate shaft. When you move the lever toward low range, a sliding gear or clutch releases the high-range gear, then moves further to engage low-range. Low range power flows through the intermediate (idler) gear.

Chain-drive transfer cases use a planetary gearset to create the low range gear ratio, a proven method com-

mon to automatic transmission engineering. Shifting still involves disengaging the 2WD power throughput, although in this case, the planetary assembly takes the place of an intermediate gearset.

> **CAUTION —**
> *No Toyota transfer unit has synchromesh between high range and low range. While Most transfer cases can shift readily from 2WD High to 4WD High modes without stopping the truck, I recommend stopping your truck completely before engaging low range. (For details, see chapter on operating your truck.)*

Both gear drive transfer cases and late chain drive types can easily meet the requirements of Toyota truck users. In terms of 2WD mode energy efficiency, a through-drive transfer case proves superior to side-drive types. However, all Toyota transfer cases have a tremendous record for durability and long service.

Although Toyota's late chain drive transfer cases reduce friction, with planetary gear systems acting in place of hefty gearsets, some buyers regret the passage of traditional gear drive units. For stamina and a remarkably long service life, there is no substitute for a gear drive transfer case. The industrial strength of Land Cruiser FJ and early 4WD pickup transfer units is legend.

Full- Vs. Part-time Four Wheeling

Until the advent of the Land Cruiser's Full-Time 4WD system in 1991, all Toyota 4WD trucks featured part-time four-wheel drive systems. Whether the original gear-drive or later chain-drive types, part-time transfer cases connect and disconnect power flow to the front axle when the driver selects 2WD high range or either of the two 4WD modes (high and low range).

On later Full-Time 4WD systems, power flows at all times to both front and rear axles. You can select 4WD high or 4WD low range for various driving conditions.

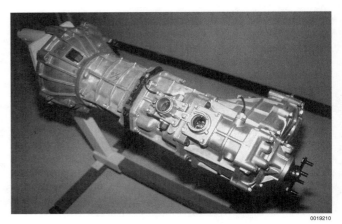

Fig. 10-5. *Toyota 4WD trucks evolved from spartan FJ-series utility vehicles into multi-purpose SUVs, spending more time on the highway than off. To meet stiffer tailpipe emission and fuel economy standards, Toyota and other manufacturers have reduced two-wheel drive mode wear and frictional losses by changing to chain drive part-time 4x4 transfer cases.*

A manual locking differential within the Full-Time 4WD transfer case allows more driver control of the system. When shifted into lock mode, the transfer case delivers power to both axles without any "differentiation"—this means that both axles receive equal torque at all times, a useful device for severely loose off-highway traction surfaces.

The differential system in All-Time 4WD systems serves in similar fashion to a drive axle's differential mechanism. The design continuously delivers power to both the front and rear axles, however, the differential "senses" speed variances between the axles and compensates by permitting one driveline to rotate slower or faster than the other, much like an axle's differential. This prevents gear bind between the front and rear axles.

On very late part-time 4WD systems, Toyota has eliminated the need for front wheel locking hubs. A front axle disconnect system, called A.D.D., disconnects the power flow through the left axle shaft. This effectively stops the flow of power through the front axle to the front wheels. (Dana pioneered this concept on domestic trucks.)

Although A.D.D. allows for a part-time transfer case and adds the convenience of no locking hubs, it increases wear at front CV-joints and their dust boots. Some axle/differential parts now turn for the entire life of the truck, even though they have no torque load when the transfer case is in 2WD mode.

Transfer Case Troubleshooting

Overhauling your truck's transfer case is a job much like a manual transmission overhaul. If you need to do such work, you will find step-by-step overhaul procedures in a OEM Toyota truck repair manual or a professional level service manual. Within the scope and aims of this book, I am outlining some general troubleshooting guidelines for common transfer case problems. This should help you determine what measures to take. Your shop manual can help with step-by-step removal/installation (R&R) and overhaul procedures.

The most frequent transfer case trouble is hard shifting. Often, the remedy is really simple, requiring nothing more than cleaning the linkage and properly lubricating these parts. Sometimes the problem is bent or damaged linkage, the result of off-pavement abuse.

If external linkage is not the problem and your transfer case slips out of gear or front wheel drive, anticipate more serious trouble. Before condemning the transfer case, I would suggest that you check the transfer case-to-transmission attaching hardware. A loose transfer case housing can cause gear binding and internal side loads or pressure on the gears.

Deeper Troubles

Most repair manuals list the shift mechanism among the possible causes of transfer case problems. Poppet balls and springs are of concern in earlier transfer case shift mechanisms, but noises, jumping out of gear and difficult shifting usually indicate more serious troubles.

Before removing the transfer case from your truck for overhaul, it's always prudent to check the condition of the shift rail springs and poppet balls. There are instances when a worn or broken spring does cause trouble, but

more likely the culprit is transmission or transfer case bearing damage, a bent shift fork or other internal defects.

If your high-mileage transfer case has never been through an overhaul, suspect bearing fatigue at the very least. Although gear-drive transfer cases have a solid record for longevity, you should always replace worn bearings, as excessive gear clearance and poor tooth contact can quickly cause gear failure and expensive damage.

Chain Drive Transfer Case Troubles

Failure of a fork or shift mechanism can leave your 4x4 stranded. Trouble symptoms include jumping out of gear, failure to engage the low, high or neutral range, or noisy operation. Before tearing into the unit, however, check the easy possibilities.

Fluid deserves a look. (Various applications use lighter viscosity oils, so check your truck's requirements.) Leaks develop at seals, case halves, and castings. Pay close attention. Shift linkage sometimes needs adjustment or alignment. Make certain the linkage does not bind or interfere with the truck's body parts. When simpler fixes fail, plan to remove the transfer case unit for overhaul.

Removal of the Transfer Case for Overhaul

A Toyota truck transfer case is relatively easy to remove. For earlier Land Cruisers with three- and four-speed manual transmissions, the transfer case actually hangs from the back of the transmission. This enables detachment and removal of the transfer case without a need to support the engine and transmission assemblies. You do, however, need to safely support the transfer case during its removal and installation.

On later Land Cruisers, 4WD pickups and 4Runners, the transfer case is supported by a rear motor mount. For these models, you will need to safely support the transmission when removing the transfer case. The general procedure begins with placing the shifter in neutral and draining fluid. You will need to disconnect all cables, transfer case shift linkages and both driveshafts.

Drain fluid, then separate drivelines from the input and output shaft companion flanges. Scribe driveshaft-to-flange fitups before disassembly. Keep splined driveshafts together and in phase for proper reassembly.

See whether the exhaust pipe or brake cable interferes, and check the top of the transfer case and transmission for any switch wires and vent hose(s) that need detaching. Remove the propeller shaft upper dust cover and dynamic damper on models so equipped.

With all external parts disconnected, place a transmission jack beneath the transfer case. With the assembly supported and weight off the rear motor mount, carefully remove the mount. Place a stable jackstand beneath the transmission to support the engine/transmission.

Now unbolt the transfer case or adapter from the transmission while carefully supporting both the engine/transmission assembly and transfer unit. The transfer case will come out as an assembly. With the use of a floor jack or the help of a friend, you can free the transfer case or transfer case and adapter from the transmission.

Protect seals and castings by keeping all parts level until the input shaft completely clears the transmission or transfer case. Place the complete transfer case assembly on your workbench. Follow the step-by-step overhaul procedures outlined in the OEM Toyota repair manual or a professional level service guidebook.

Remember to replace all seals. Always refer to an OEM Toyota repair manual or a professional level service manual for detailed procedures on the removal, overhaul and reinstallation of your particular transfer case.

> **CAUTION —**
> *When towing a 4x4 truck, consult the owner's handbook for special towing instructions that apply to the model and transfer case design. Severe geartrain damage can result from failure to observe Toyota's requirements.*

2. DRIVESHAFTS

A light truck's driveshaft(s) take tremendous punishment. On 4WD models, excessive suspension travel, weighty loads, radically changing driveshaft angles and modifications like an overly zealous suspension lift kit can tear your U-joints and driveshafts to pieces.

Fig. 10-7. *Trent Alford at M.I.T. in El Cajon, California aligns hefty replacement parts for a heavy duty rear driveshaft that will increase a truck's stamina.*

Fig. 10-6. *A variety of U-joint failures directly relate to poor maintenance or bad driveshaft angularity.*

Fig. 10-8. *Many 2WD Toyota pickup trucks use a mid-shaft bearing. Wear here will cause severe driveline vibration.*

Often, the cause of a U-joint failure is misconstrued. Sure, wear takes a rapid toll on trucks that ford streams, flex their springs to the maximum and crawl through tortuous rocks with massive torque applied through low range gears. On 2WD models that pull trailers or lug a camper, the loads on drivelines also become excessive.

Poorly fitted driveshafts also provide a major cause of failure. Shafts pieced together out-of-phase or badly angled are the worst culprits. Wear in the rear driveshaft slip yoke, stub spline or mid-shaft bearing can produce an unusual vibrating sound during a float condition (period between acceleration load and deceleration). This is especially noticeable on trucks with driveline-mounted parking brakes (like the earlier Land Cruiser), as the brake drum amplifies noise.

Driveshaft U-joints must also be "in phase" with each other. (Cross-joints match at each end of the shaft.) As a simple maintenance concern, proper grease intervals and grease gun pressures contribute to driveshaft longevity.

Fig. 10-9. *Although they look similar, replacement U-joint at left fits a one-ton domestic truck. Middle joint is found in most half- and 3/4-ton domestic models or a Toyota 4WD truck. At right, small size joint fits driveshaft of a light duty domestic compact 2WD and some 4WDs. When it comes to driveline stamina, bigger is better.*

Driveshaft Angularity

Angles and rotational arcs make or break U-joints and driveshafts. While torque load determines the proper size U-joint, engineers design driveshafts for an 85% efficiency factor. To understand the highest load placed upon your driveshafts, the formula is: Lowest Gear Torque = Net Engine Torque X Transmission Low Gear Ratio X Transfer Case Low Range Ratio (if a 4x4 with low range) X 0.85.

Two angles affect a driveshaft: side-view drop and plane-view shift. Side view is simply the angle that the driveshaft slopes downward from the transfer case to each axle's differential. Plane view is the lateral angle of the driveshaft, viewed from directly above the frame.

For your truck's driveshafts to live, the angles on each end of the driveshaft (the side-view drop combined with the plane-view shift) must create as little non-uniform motion as possible. U-joint angles, in simple terms, must rotate on nearly identical arcs, with the vertical faces of the U-joint flanges nearly parallel. (Spicer/Dana recommends that the limit of inequality must not exceed that of a single U-joint operating at a 3-degree angle.)

The included U-joint angles should remain identical on each end of the driveshaft. When the shaft rotates, joints should move in similar arcs, with bearing cross shafts each running at the same tilt.

Speed dictates maximum allowable driveshaft angles. A driveshaft rotating 5000 rpm (somewhat obscure for a truck, unless flat out in a desert race) tolerates no more than 3 deg., 15 sec. of operating angle, while the same shaft spinning 1500 rpm will work at an 11 deg., 30-sec. angle. Driveshaft length affects this formula, too, with longer driveshafts tolerating more operating angle.

Owners who lift their trucks with shackle kits or springs must also consider that a 3/4-degree change in the differential pinion angle will change the U-joint operating angle about 1/4 of a degree.

Shimming the axle housing at the spring perches is a common method for restoring the pinion angle and U-joint operating angles. Driveline specialists insist that appropriate steel shims be used or, if the angle is radically off, cut the spring perches from the axle housing, reposition to the correct angle, and re-weld the perches. Brass and aluminum shims tend to pound flat during off-road bashing.

Before hybridizing your engine, transmission or transfer case angles, take accurate measurements of the shaft angles. When lifting a 4x4, the side angles of the driveshafts also change. Small changes are acceptable, as long as the axle swings up and down on its original arc of movement. Problems begin when the side angle becomes excessive.

An excellent source of information, including formulas and professional driveshaft service tips, is Spicer/Dana's *Trouble Shooting Guideline*, available through Spicer distributors or Dana Corporation, Drivetrain Service Division, P.O. Box 321, Toledo, Ohio 43691. This quick reference guide and the *Spicer Universal Joints and Driveshafts Service Manual* are the last word on professional driveshaft service, maintenance and construction.

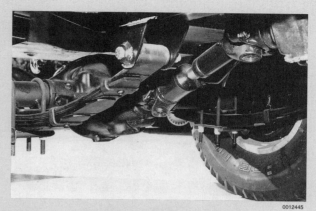

Fig. 10-10. *Looking upward from below the rear driveshaft, the line between the U-joint flanges is evident. A short driveshaft, like that found at the rear of an FJ40 Land Cruiser, demands precise side and plane angles.*

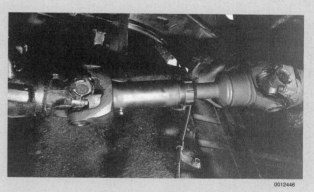

Fig. 10-11. *Side view angle shows the relationship between the sloping driveshaft and the U-joint flanges. Note that flange centerlines are parallel.*

Fig. 10-12. *Short wheelbase 4x4s (like the FJ40 Land Cruiser) sometimes boast a long front driveshaft with very slight slope (side view angularity). As length reduces torque load, a heavy duty replacement shaft will easily handle the chores.*

CHAPTER 10

Beyond these factors, driveshaft survival depends mostly on torque loads. These include the weight placed on the vehicle, the amount of engine torque applied to the

Fig. 10-13. *Use of a custom built driveshaft(s) assures resistance to torque loads. Land Cruisers with a domestic V-8 conversion, compound low gear truck four-speed and sets of low (numerically high) ratio axle gears can produce a reduction/crawl ratio in excess of 70:1! (See performance chapters for details.) Such torque is tremendous.*

Fig. 10-14. *Dramatic difference between an OEM front driveshaft tube section and a replacement heavier wall thickness tube is obvious.*

joints and also the departure and receiving angles between the driving and driven yokes of the driveshaft.

A common problem with trucks that have a suspension/spring lift kit is too much angle on the joints. This results from the radical difference in height between the axle pinion shafts and the transfer case output shafts.

Rotating the axle pinion shaft upward is a shoddy method that some lift kit installers use to reduce U-joint angles. This approach can lead to another crop of problems, those caused by unmatched U-joint angles. U-joints rotating on widely dissimilar arcs can create enough rotational vibration and stress to break a gear case housing!

Driveshaft survival depends upon joint size, tubing diameter and wall thickness, plus the ability of the assembly to compensate for speed, length and angle changes. Often, a driveshaft that would work perfectly well in its original mode cannot handle a chassis lift or increased horsepower. Here, a custom heavy duty driveshaft is necessary.

Fig. 10-15. *This step is critical during driveshaft construction. Proper driveshaft phasing requires that U-joint cross yokes are absolutely in line. Before welding, a spirit level or protractor and a perfectly flat benchtop assure alignment.*

Fig. 10-16. *Before MIG wire-feed welding, the shaft is carefully tapped into alignment. The builder will work this section until total runout is less than 0.005-inch. Such tolerances are necessary for vibration-free results and illustrate the importance of protecting your driveshafts from bashing.*

Proper Lubrication

U-joint survival depends upon correct lubrication. Stream crossings, wintry highways and sandy deserts take their toll. Assuming that U-joint dust seals are in top shape, follow either your Toyota owner's handbook or Spicer's on/off highway lubrication guidelines: 5000–8000 miles or every three months (far more often if your truck is subject to either severe service or exposure to water). A high-quality lube gun is a prerequisite to preserving U-joints and their delicate seals.

When selecting U-joint and driveshaft greases, follow the OEM Toyota or Spicer's guidelines. Use National Lubricating Grease Institute (NLGI) Extreme Pressure Grade 1 or 2 greases. Avoid heavier greases. Severe service requires lithium soap base or EP grease with a temperature range of +325 to -10° F.

Fig. 10-17. U-joint failure usually follows loss of grease. Worn seals allowed moisture into these joints. Brindling resulted from lack of grease.

U-joint Service and Repair Tips

U-joint replacement always begins with driveshaft removal. Before loosening a driveshaft, mark the shaft's order of assembly. Drivelines must be in-phase, with couplers kept in line with their original splines.

> **NOTE —**
> If your driveshaft has two pieces, scribe an indexing line on each section. Reassembly in the original position will assure satisfactory service, alignment, and balance.

Cleanliness is essential, regardless of the locale in which you make the repairs. (I and others have replaced U-joints on the tailgate of a pickup and even atop granite boulders!) If the work area is particularly gritty, beware. New U-joints, freshly coated with grease, attract dirt like a horseshoe magnet draws pig iron from beach sand. As-

suming that the shaft isn't damaged, you can make a permanent U-joint installation in the field if you approach the job with professional expectations.

The tools needed to remove and replace a U-joint are minimal. In the field, a good mechanic's hammer, solid punch, blade screwdriver, a variety of sockets and a set of pliers can handle the job. Specialty or homemade tools can help, although the principles remain the same.

If your technique is correct, even the most trying environment will not prevent a quality job. Find a solid surface to work on, preferably steel plate like a platform hitch bumper, a front winch mounting plate, or a hefty wooden board placed across the floor of a pickup bed). Get out of the weather if gale winds prevail, and plan on several minutes of painstaking work.

U-joint Installation

Although an arbor press or specialized U-joint tools are helpful, don't be misled. Some of the best craftsmen in the automotive repair industry still replace U-joints with hand tools. The reason? U-joint bearing caps fit precisely

Fig. 10-18. Coupler types and U-joints vary. Double Cardan (constant velocity) joints have become common on many 4x4 driveshafts. Joint to yoke attaching methods also vary.

Fig. 10-19. Disassembling a joint requires few tools. On cross-type (original Spicer design) U-joints, you must remove two external snap rings. Some Toyota cross-type U-joint bearing caps use an internal snap ring, a design like domestic Detroit style U-joints.

Fig. 10-20. *Clean the driveshaft for close inspection and reassembly. This will assure proper fitup of parts.*

Fig. 10-21. *Once both bearing caps are free of the driveshaft, you can separate the U-joint.*

Fig. 10-22. *Protect these snap ring grooves during service. Striking a groove with a hammer or punch could cause permanent driveshaft damage.*

into their saddles and bores, and the slightest cocking of a cap during installation can ruin a driveshaft. Presses and hefty tools eliminate the *feel* of the cap moving into its bore. Hand tools maintain your awareness of fit.

Once you have completed the U-joint replacement and reinstalled the driveshaft in the truck, grease the U-joints. Do not grease a U-joint before bolting it into the yoke, as you will force the bearing caps out of position.

Fig. 10-23. *Install the first bearing cap. Use the hammer carefully and support the bearing needles (spiders) with the cross section of the U-joint. If you doubt your hammer skills, use a socket to drive the bearing cap into its recess. Install the cap far enough to insert the snap ring.... Install the second cap. Again, carefully keep the cross section centered to hold needle bearings in place. If all needles remain intact, the second bearing cap will just clear its snap ring groove. Install the snap ring. Make sure snap rings seat completely.*

Fig. 10-24. *New U-joints come with snap rings and a grease fitting. Make sure needle bearings stay in place during assembly. Always align the grease fitting to permit easy access and service. Field lubrication of double Cardan joints requires special grease gun tip.*

(See your OEM Toyota repair manual for hardware torque specifications.)

If you left the grease gun home, new joints usually contain enough grease for the drive back. Permanently sealed joints, in fact, have very high quality grease and seals, and they require no further greasing. Other joints, equipped with grease fittings, require periodic lubrication.

Fig. 10-25. *A constant velocity, double Cardan U-joint has a precise assembly sequence. On some applications of the double Cardan joint, be aware of the spring, which must be in place when installing the new joints. Reassemble in exactly the reverse sequence of disassembly.*

Fig. 10-26. *Some Toyota U-joints resemble the domestic Detroit style. Note use of internal snap rings at bearing caps. Typically, Toyota uses a full circumference flange casting or yoke to support each of the four bearing caps. This approach is superior to the detachable straps used on many domestic trucks.*

3. AXLE ASSEMBLIES

The mysteries within the axle housing, the maze of gears and bearings, are responsible for turning horsepower and torque into motion. How that happens is as significant as any other aspect of your truck's powertrain. Although axle overhaul is beyond the scope of this book, your knowledge of tell-tale wear signs could prevent serious trouble, reduce damage and contain the repair costs. Let's begin with some axle basics.

Engine power flows through the clutch or torque converter, transmission, transfer case (4WD models) and driveline(s). The driveshaft rotates the axle's pinion shaft/gear (attached to the U-joint companion flange) to carry power into the axle. Supported by bearings in the axle housing, the pinion shaft's bevel gearhead transfers

Fig. 10-27. *Ring and pinion gear size and method of bearing support indicate stamina. Land Cruiser axle (shown) boasts a larger ring and pinion gearset than mini- and compact-pickups or the 4Runner. All Toyota axle assemblies have notable strength and durability.*

Fig. 10-28. *Land Cruisers and pre-IFS 4WD pickups feature removable front and rear axle center section assemblies. Shown is a Land Cruiser front axle with closed steering knuckles and a removable center section. One piece axle housing offers rigid strength. 1979–85 4WD pickups boast a similar design. Differential service takes place on workbench.*

Fig. 10-29. *Another tip-off to axle stamina is differential side gear size, axle shaft diameter and splines that mate to side gear. Land Cruiser was built like a heavy duty domestic 1/2-ton full-size truck, able to handle the torque of an in-line OHV six cylinder engine. These Land Cruiser shafts offer more heft than lighter design found in Toyota pickup and 4Runner.*

power to a matching ring gear, which changes the direction of the power flow by 90°.

Together, the ring and pinion gears serve two functions: 1) changing the power flow direction, and 2) increasing torque, proportionally, by reducing the rotational speed of the axle shafts. A 4.10 gear ratio (41 teeth on the ring gear and 10 on the pinion) rotates axle shafts with nearly four-and-one-tenth times the torque of the driveshaft—and at slightly less than one-fourth of the driveshaft's speed.

The ring gear bolts to a case, generally called the differential carrier. Bearings support the differential carrier in either the hypoid axle housing or a removable third member housing. Toyota trucks have used both the integral-type hypoid axle housing and the removable center section/carrier design. The removable carrier (also called the third-member or center-section) has been a popular approach for Toyota rear axles and non-IFS front driving axles.

If the axle shafts connected directly to the ring gear's case, both wheels would spin continuously at the speed of the ring gear. Such a locked assembly or spool, although maximizing traction, is incapable of adjusting for the vehicle's left or right turns.

All four-wheeled vehicles require unequal wheel speed to negotiate a turn. The inside wheels rotate slower than the outside wheels. If all four wheels turned at equal speed, serious trouble would result. Tires would skid and axle shafts would work against each other.

Here the differential becomes important. The right side wheel speed must be able to vary from wheel speed at the left side of the vehicle. In a straight ahead mode, the ring gear turns both shafts at equal speed, that speed determined by the axle ratio, transmission gearing and engine rpm. For turns, however, the individual axle shaft speeds adjust for smooth traction at each wheel.

Imagine your truck's driveshaft(s) rotating at 2000 rpm. With ten teeth on the pinion gear and forty teeth on

the ring gear, the axle shafts will spin at 500 rpm. Note: Although useful for illustration purposes, an axle ratio of exactly 4-to-1 would cause the pinion gear teeth to continuously find the same ring gear teeth, an undesirable tendency. Instead, engineers devise ratios like 4.10, with a 41/10 tooth arrangement that constantly renews tooth contact.

Differential Action

As your truck enters a corner, the inside wheel turns slower than the outside wheel. The speed at each wheel must differ. To allow for the speed change, the differential contains a series of gears inside the rotating carrier case. While ring and pinion speeds are constant, the differential gears allow axle shaft speeds to vary.

The differential carrier housing is hollow, and the axles slide through the space in the housing, entering from each side. Splines on the inner ends of the axle shafts engage the differential side gears. These side gears, in non-locking differentials, also have bevel teeth, meshing with two smaller gears, called pinions or spider gears.

The spider gear teeth, facing inward toward the center of the carrier case, engage with the side gear teeth. The spiders float on a pinion shaft, which mounts rigidly through the center of the carrier case. Effectively, the four gears can move independently of the carrier.

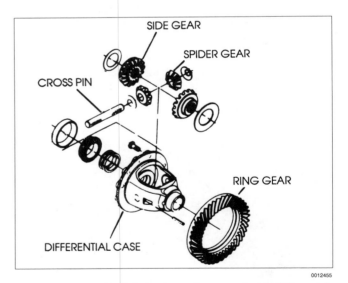

Fig. 10-30. *Exploded view of conventional differential shows gear locations.*

The result: 1) If road speed at both wheels remains the same, the gears all rotate like a solid unit in unison with the differential carrier case; 2) when turning a corner, the four gears can rotate at the speed necessary to apply more rpm at the outside wheel and proportionally less at the inside wheel; and 3) at times, the conventional differential mechanism directs power to the wheel with the least resistance. This last point remains the primary shortcoming of conventional, non-locking differentials.

When watching a 2WD truck negotiate rocks, sand and loose terrain, it's easy to distinguish the conventional rear axle. One wheel will often spin furiously, while the opposite wheel, with solid traction, stands still. Four-wheel drive models, even with conventional axles, fare much better than a 2WD truck.

Controlling Wheelspin

Traction loss is a serious problem. The other extreme is damage caused when no differential action takes place. A truck's handling with a permanently locked rear axle would be very dangerous, too. For this reason, we depend upon systems that provide more positive traction but still allow differential action.

Factory/OEM limited slip differentials enjoy a variety of trade names. Several aftermarket performance systems have also been developed, many suited for street, drag strip and off-pavement use. (See the performance section for detailed information on aftermarket traction devices.)

Typically, a limited slip unit is built around a clutching mechanism within the differential. Simply put, the clutching device enables torque delivery to the axle and wheel with traction. The basic difference between factory limited slip and aftermarket locker differentials is the design of the clutching or lock-up mechanism.

By design, the clutch type limited slip unit can still allow variance of wheel speed on corners. The differential behaves in much the same manner as a conventional unit, permitting the inner wheel to rotate slower.

WARNING —

Use caution with any limited slip or positive traction differential. Your truck will tend to go sideways when both wheels of an axle lose traction at the same time. On ice or slick pavement, locked traction at both wheels of an axle can cause sideward motion of the vehicle, most often toward the low side of the road. (See chapter on driving techniques for details.)

Axle Types

Although integral housing hypoid axles require more tools for disassembly, they also provide substantial ring and pinion carrier support. Toyota introduced this kind of axle at the front of IFS 4WD trucks in 1986. (The concept was popularized by Spicer's domestic truck axles, used from the 1940s to the present.)

Integral housings take up less space, a necessity with the IFS 4WD pickups and 4Runner. For major repairs, the axle housing and gear assembly typically comes out as a unit. Once on the workbench, the differential case, ring-and-pinion gearset and all other service or repairs can take place.

Semi- Versus Full-floating Rear Axles

Semi-floating axles offer less safety margin than full-floating axles. On the semi-floater, a single outer wheel bearing supports the axle shaft, while the splined inner end of the axle shaft relies on the differential side gear for support. A broken axle shaft can cause real trouble.

Most semi-floating axles rely upon bearing retainer plates at the outer bearing to hold the axle in place. If the

axle shaft should break in the wrong place, the broken axle shaft, hub and wheel can slide out the side of the vehicle.

Semi-floating Toyota truck axles also use a C-lock at the inner end of each axle shaft, but the risk of losing an axle remains. C-locks and the inner axle shaft end can wear out, or the axle shaft could break and come loose, much like an axle shaft without a C-lock.

Full-floating axle shafts, by contrast, act simply as a drive bar. The wheel and hub ride on bearings much like on the front end of a Toyota 4x4 truck. A retaining nut(s) provide for hub bearing adjustment and also hold the wheel hub on the spindle.

The spindle is a component part of the axle housing, and the axle shaft fits through the spindle's bore. Engaging a differential side gear at its inner end, the axle shaft's outer flange bolts to the wheel hub. If an axle shaft breaks, the hub and wheel continue to rotate safely on the spindle.

To remove the broken shaft, you unbolt its flange from the wheel hub and fish out the broken section. The wheel and tire remain on the ground, supported by the wheel hub bearings, so there is no need to even jack up the truck.

With the exception of special use cargo van and motorhome models that have dual rear wheels, all U.S.-market Toyota trucks have used semi-floating rear axles. Outside the U.S. market, Land Cruisers have offered full-floating rear axles. These non-U.S. axle assemblies will retrofit to other Land Cruisers, and some performance enthusiasts make this investment. For truck use, especially hauling cargos, carrying a fifth-wheel trailer or working hard off-pavement, the added stamina and safety of a full-floating type axle is significant.

Toyota 4x4 Front Axle Styles

NOTE —
Since a broken front axle shaft or steering knuckle joint could impair steering and cause further axle damage, it's best to remove the axle shaft assembly before moving the vehicle.

Much to Toyota's credit, 4x4 trucks to date have featured full-floating type front wheel hub systems. Whether equipped with manual locking hubs, automatic locking hubs or solid drive plates, each wheel hub assembly has an inner and outer bearing set that rides on the spindle. The axle shaft fits through the hollow spindle and drives either the free-wheeling hub or a steel drive flange that attaches to the outer face of each wheel hub.

Only one major change has occurred in Toyota 4x4 front axles. The shift to independent front suspension (IFS) on the 1986-up 4WD pickup and 4Runner chassis has been the major engineering change in 4WD technology.

Free-wheeling manual and automatic front locking hubs have served with both the solid housing and IFS driving axles. Part-time 4WD/A.D.D. equipped models do not require free-wheeling hubs, and the Land Cruiser Full-Time 4WD system (1991-up) also has no need for free-wheeling front hubs. (Both A.D.D. and Land Cruiser models offer full-floating wheel hubs with solid drive plates.)

NOTE —
Full-floating front hubs plus manual or automatic locking hubs provide the only means for eliminating excess front axle and driveline wear. I always choose rugged and reliable manual locking hubs.

Toyota's closed-knuckle solid front axles use tapered roller type upper and lower kingpin bearings. IFS front ends feature double A-arm suspension with an open steering knuckle assembly that pivots on upper and lower ball-joints.

Closed-knuckle solid axles feature fully enclosed front axle shaft joints (either Rzeppa or Birfield constant velocity types) that receive grease from within the sealed knuckle cavity. (See lubrication chapter for details.) IFS drives use open axle half-shafts, CV-joints and permanently sealed boots.

NOTE —
Permanently sealed joints are easy to distinguish. They have no provision for a grease fitting. IFS drive systems have permanently sealed CV-joints that do not require lubrication unless the boot tears or the joint becomes defective and requires replacement.

Drive Axle Troubleshooting

Before suspecting trouble with your truck's axle(s), check the fluid levels and also the type of gear lubricant required. On limited slip units, special lubes prevent multiple-plate clutches and other components from sticking together. If you introduce a non-specified oil to these axles, symptoms of differential trouble can result.

Try to isolate any abnormal noise. Tire sounds, front or rear wheel bearing noises, engine and transmission troubles and even the type of road surface can confuse the situation. Especially with oversize tires, light trucks often develop noises that have nothing to do with the differential or any other axle component, yet the sound comes from that area. Check each of these other possibilities before condemning your axle(s).

A clicking or patterned ratcheting noise at the rear wheels is a possible wheel bearing problem. By supporting the rear axle safely on jack stands, you can rotate each wheel by hand and feel for bearing roughness. (See other chapters of the book for front wheel bearing inspection and service.)

If you detect an actual wheel bearing problem, consult your Toyota truck repair manual or a professional level service manual for details on axle shaft removal and wheel bearing service.

Differential side gear and small pinion (spider) gear noises are most often heard when the vehicle turns. If your truck has a conventional or limited slip rear axle that makes noises as the vehicle negotiates a corner, suspect differential trouble. Similar front axle noises, especially with the hubs engaged and the transfer case in 4WD, also suggest differential trouble, although a defective axle shaft joint can mimic these sounds.

Fig. 10-31. *Watch the closed-knuckle spindle's eight attaching bolts closely. If they work loose, these bolts can shear or rip cleanly from the threaded holes in the steering knuckle. Note that on earlier Toyota applications, a tie wire helps keep bolts from loosening. Consult your OEM Toyota repair manual for safe methods of securing these fasteners and use of tie-wire (where required).*

A continuous grating noise that varies with vehicle speed suggests pinion bearing failure. Trucks that run in deep water without frequent changes of gear lubricant are vulnerable to ring gear, pinion gear or bearing failure.

Ring and pinion noise is distinguishable under various driving conditions: coast, drive or float. Deceleration creates coast noises. Drive noises are detectable as you accelerate the truck. Float noise occurs under light throttle situations and easy loads that keep the ring and pinion gears spinning with the least amount of pressure.

When your truck's axle gear lubricant smells badly burned, remove the inspection cover and examine the gear teeth and bearings. Blue discoloration usually indicates extreme heat, fatigue and poor lubrication.

CAUTION —
If lubricant is very low for any length of time, the axle is subject to major damage. Always watch for seal leaks or symptoms of fluid loss.

Seal Leaks

Seal failure is a primary cause of fluid loss on truck axles. Look closely for fluid loss at the axles whenever you service your truck, and watch for oil drips when you park the vehicle. The locations for axle seal leaks are easy to monitor, beginning with the pinion shaft seal, the ventilation valve (if so equipped) and the axle shaft seals.

The pinion shaft seal is very easy to locate. Follow the driveshaft to the U-joint flange, then note the point at which the pinion shaft enters the axle housing. The seal that surrounds the shaft at the entrance to the axle housing is the pinion shaft seal.

Axle shaft seal leaks appear as oil dripping from the bottom of the rear brake backing plates or at the steering knuckle inner seal and free-wheeling hub of a closed-knuckle 4WD front end. An axle seal leak on a closed-knuckle front end can lead to dangerously diluted wheel bearing lubricant. Often the closed knuckle system's large diameter inner steering knuckle seal will leak visibly. (See brake section for details on parts damage from leaking axle seals.)

When a seal leak occurs, first check the lubricant levels. Overfilled steering knuckles or differentials will cause leaks and can even dislodge a seal by hydraulic pressure. Again, a common leak on all closed-knuckle front ends is the large inner oil seal. This seal at the inner side of the steering knuckle will leak grease from the knuckle cavity. You can replace this seal without removing the entire steering knuckle.

Fig. 10-33. *This tool, fabricated twenty years ago with simple materials, holds the U-joint flange. The pinion shaft nut torque is very high, and heavy leverage is necessary. Today, the option for most mechanics is an air impact gun. Always set and check final torque with a torque wrench.*

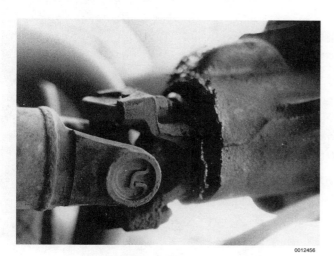

Fig. 10-32. *A pinion seal leak is easy to spot. Loss of lubrication can lead to expensive parts damage.*

Axle Seal Installation Tips

Front drive axle seals are difficult to replace. Rear axle seals are also a handful. You'll want to do the job right the first time. Axle pinion seal replacement requires a holding tool to keep the U-joint flange from rotating while you loosen its nut. As an option, mechanics usually use an air impact gun when performing this work.

Before installing a pinion seal, clean the housing bore thoroughly. Be certain to apply a thin film of gasket sealant to the outer edge of the seal. Coat the inner lip of the

seal with light grease. (Older trucks sometimes use leather seals that require soaking the seal in oil before installation. Neoprene replacement seals are now available.)

Tap the seal gently and evenly in cross. I like to use a rubber or plastic sand head hammer to avoid damaging or distorting the steel portion of the seal. Although I've always had access to special seal drivers, I feel that carefully placed hammer taps can produce the same results—and often better. Without a solid driver, you can maintain the *feel* for what you're doing by using a soft headed hammer and a light touch.

Coat the backside of the pinion flange washer with a thin film of gasket sealant, and install a new self-locking nut if required. Torque the nut to OEM specifications found in your OEM Toyota truck repair manual or a professional level guidebook.

Other seals, including the front and rear axle shaft seals, are more difficult to access. Consult your OEM Toyota repair manual before attempting to replace seals on a Toyota drop-in center section (semi-floating type) rear axle or full-floating solid live front axle. The job is messy and involved. Make certain you have the time, tools and a sense for the scope of the task before attempting an axle shaft seal replacement or accessing C-locks on the inner ends of the axle shafts.

NOTE—
When servicing a closed knuckle front end, be aware that spindle bolts can loosen on the steering knuckle and shred the spindle gasket (if so equipped). Once loose, a very unsafe condition exists, with the risk of shearing the spindle attaching bolts or stripping the threads that attach the spindle to the knuckle casting.

Two remedies for this kind of spindle bolt problem include: 1) drilling and wire tying the bolt heads to aircraft standards (an OEM Toyota approach), 2) replacing the bolts with Aircraft Grade Metric studs secured with

Fig. 10-34. *Conical washers, popular on domestic Dana/Spicer axles, have a full locking surface and offer long service life. They do not spread or break apart like common split-ring washers. Used in conjunction with Loctite 242 on cleaned threads, bolts with conical washers provide a safer attaching method.*

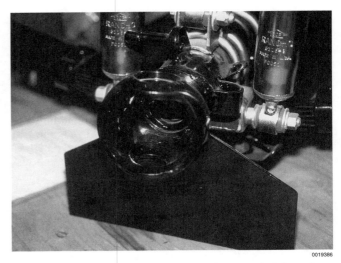

Fig. 10-35. *Closed knuckle steering has served U.S. market Land Cruisers from 1958 to the present. Pre-IFS 4WD pickups also feature closed-knuckle solid front driving axles. Wear on these systems occurs at pivot pin/kingpin bearings, seals and steering linkage.*

thread locking compound, then use appropriate washers as needed and Aircraft Grade Metric self locking nuts to secure the spindle.

> **NOTE —**
> While some Toyota spindles attach with bolts and split lockwashers, others use bolts with a locking shoulder built into the head. If your earlier Land Cruiser has a tendency to loosen spindle attaching bolts and split-ring lockwashers, consider the later style bolts or use of conical washers.

Closed-knuckle Axle Repairs

At one time, all 4x4 solid live front axles had closed-knuckle steering mechanisms. Toyota's Land Cruiser and pre-IFS 4WD pickup trucks use a front axle design common to other early 4x4 trucks built in the U.S., Great Britain and elsewhere. This closed-knuckle style solid housing axle, a durable and stable design, prevails in the latest and most luxurious Land Cruisers and British Range/Land Rovers.

Full-floating front axle designs, many of these closed-knuckle Toyota Land Cruisers and pre-IFS 4WD pickups now have several *hundred thousand* miles on their chassis. Eventually, even with a superior solid front axle design, fatigue and wear occur.

Before tackling a 4WD steering knuckle or axle system repair, consult your OEM Toyota repair manual. The section detailing axle overhaul offers numerous illustrations, tips and step-by-step repair procedures. You will find that a competent rebuild requires special tools and gauges, a spring scale and torque wrenches. Some press and puller work is also involved.

Individual model years require different specifications. See an official Toyota truck repair manual for your model. The drive axle, suspension and steering sections list specifications and repair procedures for your truck's live front axle.

Fig. 10-36. *Toyota closed-knuckle solid front driving axles are easy to spot. Axle shaft joint is within the spherical housing end, enclosed by the steering knuckle casting. Knuckles pivot on pins and tapered roller bearings.*

Fig. 10-37. *Protect yourself from overexposure to harsh solvents, petroleum distillate products, caustic cleaners and dirty, acidic lubricants. Taking a cue from contemporary automotive technicians, I use these disposable latex gloves as a barrier to chemicals and means of preventing minor nicks, cuts and abrasions. It took less than an hour to become accustomed to working with these gloves.*

Fig. 10-38. *Most solid front axle repairs begin with removing tie-rod assembly and relay rod. I use a puller available from Eastwood Company to safely remove tie-rod ends. Inspect for wear and replace any worn pieces.*

Fig. 10-39. *First part of steering knuckle work resembles wheel bearing repack: remove free-wheeling hub or drive flange (shown) and brake drum or rotor. Where parts are frozen together, it may be easier to remove drum and wheel hub as an assembly. (Closed-knuckle live front axles have either drum or disc brakes.)*

Fig. 10-40. *Toyota 4WD truck wheel bearing applications have used double hex nuts and a lock plate. Consult your Toyota repair manual for specifications on wheel bearing service and adjustment. (See wheel bearing chapter for tips on wheel bearing service and how to interpret bearing wear.)*

Fig. 10-41. *During a steering knuckle rebuild, upper and lower bearing cap fasteners are torqued to specification before checking steering knuckle drag (bearing preload). Rotate knuckle at steering arm/tie-rod socket and read pull with a spring scale. The large inner knuckle seal and steering linkage are not attached during this check. Your Toyota truck repair manual will give required spring scale and bolt tightening specifications.*

4. FREE-WHEEL LOCKING HUBS

Free wheeling hubs stretch drivetrain component life by many thousands of miles. Manual or automatic locking hubs eliminate front axle shaft rotation during two-wheel drive operation. Hubs save wear on front axle joints, seals, the differential assembly, and front driveshaft components. Drag, especially in cold weather, translates to added engine load, increased clutch effort, and a loss of fuel economy.

On most 4x4 full-floating front wheel spindles and hub castings, you can install retrofit manual or automatic locking hubs. By design, a full-floating system affords safe operation and rotation of the wheels, with or without

Fig. 10-42. *Aftermarket free-wheeling hubs have existed since the 1940s. Hubs come in many shapes and sizes to fit various axle splines and wheel hub flanges.*

Fig. 10-43. *This very early Warn system was clearly manual. The hub cap bolted in place of an OEM drive flange and permitted wheel hubs to rotate without turning the axle shafts. By 1958, when Toyota exported its first U.S. market Land Cruiser, Warn hubs were far past this pioneer design and had become a 4WD industry standard.*

an intact axle shaft. This type of spindle and hub flange also allows use of free-wheeling hubs.

Full-floating wheel hubs, supported by inner and outer wheel bearings, ride on the spindle. The axle shaft fits through the hollow recess of this spindle, and the spindle attaches to the steering knuckle.

At the splined outer end of the axle shaft, a drive flange attaches to the wheel hub casting, much like the systems found on many domestic 3/4-ton and larger truck rear axles. Here, the axle delivers its rotational force to the wheel hub, wheel and tire.

All early 4x4 locking hubs were manual. Highly dependable, manual hubs survive to this day. Although locking mechanisms differ between manufacturers, each design disconnects power flow from the axle shafts to the front wheel hub flanges. Providing a means to disconnect

rotational force, free-wheel/locking hubs allow the wheel hub, wheel and tire to free-wheel on the spindle.

Automatic locking hubs came in the 1980s as an alternative to full-time 4WD. The 1970s domestic full-time 4x4 systems, although costly to maintain and taxing to fuel economy, had eliminated free-wheeling hubs. Consumers expected ease of operation, and automatic hubs were the solution.

Many owners appreciate the convenience of not having to operate hubs. Automatic hubs provide for easier operation of a part-time four-wheel drive system. I still prefer manual hubs, despite their inconvenience. (See chapter on vehicle operation for tips on making manual hub use easier.)

Maintaining Your Locking Hubs

Many four-wheelers wrestle with their front wheel locking hubs. Some go to extremes, fabricating special tools for muscling the manual hub knob. Whenever more than light hand force is necessary, there's something wrong with the hub mechanism or its installation.

Laid out, the hub pieces can include a clutch mechanism, springs, locking clips or drive plates. Manual hubs utilize sleeve bushings, needle bearings, ball or roller bearings. Periodic bench stripping and service of the front hubs will assure free movement and proper lubrication of all parts.

Free-wheeling hub bearings and bushings cannot tolerate the rotational loads of parts running at speed. If pressed into such service, as when one hub is accidently left in LOCK while the other is on FREE, a free-wheeling hub assembly will quickly fail. Periodic disassembly and cleaning help reduce the risk of dragging hubs.

Servicing hubs is relatively simple and should accompany every front wheel bearing repack. Repeated or prolonged submersion of your 4x4 truck in deep, fast-running water requires immediate hub disassembly and inspection for water damage. The sealing areas of hubs deteriorate over time, another reason for periodic inspection and service.

Service Work

Servicing front wheel locking hubs is well within a competent mechanic's ability. Hub disassembly requires basic hand tools, including a torque wrench and snap ring pliers. As always, seek out an OEM-level service guidebook. A detailed schematic of the hubs will eliminate guesswork as you inventory parts.

Servicing hubs requires cleanliness and order. Remove parts carefully, noting their relationship to each other. Lay pieces on clean newspaper or shop towels. Clean pieces carefully in solvent. (Avoid cleaners that affect plastic parts.) Clean grease will not adhere properly to solvent coated parts. Rinse away solvent with a dish detergent solution and a clean water rinse, then air dry (preferably with compressed air) before regreasing parts.

CAUTION —
Never spin a bearing with compressed air. High speed, excess friction and stress could score the bearings or cause the assembly to explode. This could result in risk of serious bodily injury.

Use a grease recommended for your hubs. If wheel bearing type is acceptable, use the same grease that you use for your front wheel bearings. This often falls into the category of high temp wheel bearing grease, recommended for disc brake equipped applications. Such greases have excellent heat resistance yet afford the viscosity needed for free hub movement on those -40 degree F mornings in North Dakota.

CAUTION —
Avoid mixing unknown grease types. If necessary, perform a major wheel bearing repack at the same time.

Service kits are inexpensive, providing cheap insurance against hub sealing problems. The O-ring or paper gasket that looks marginal is a risk. For a few dollars, new seals and other hardware will keep water out of your hubs and wheel bearings. Properly and sparingly applied, a silicone compound like Permatex Ultra-Blue can provide additional protection in areas that require gasket sealant.

Fig. 10-44. *For ease of maintenance, Toyota and most after-market hub manufacturers offer service kits for their hubs. Warn's kits consist of paper gaskets, snap rings, O-rings, new attaching screws, and bolt lock tabs as required.*

Fig. 10-45. *First step in overhaul of Warn hub is removal of free-wheeling hub unit from the wheel hub flange.*

As with any mechanism, inspect parts carefully. Look for bushing wear, galling, scoring and binding of parts. Include emery cloth in your service tools for light touch-up of rough or scratched pieces. Clean thoroughly after sanding. Dry the parts before repacking with grease.

Fig. 10-46. *Disassembly begins with clutch mechanism flange screws.*

Fig. 10-47. *Drive hub rides in needle bearings on this early Warn hub design. Watch out for falling needle bearings!*

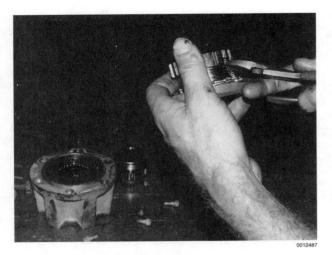

Fig. 10-48. *Spring roll pin locks clutch unit to flange.*

Fig. 10-49. *Mark or scribe location of plate to flange.*

Fig. 10-50. *Now remove the spring clutch mechanism.*

Fig. 10-51. *Snap ring holds hub knob to flange.*

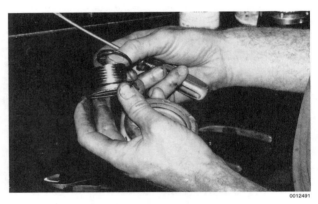

Fig. 10-52. *With knob removed, important O-ring is accessible. Here's where water often seeps into hub units.*

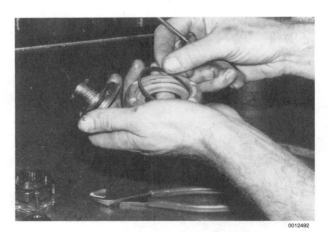

Fig. 10-53. *Another critical O-ring is found here.*

Fig. 10-54. *Scrape gasket material from surfaces before thoroughly cleaning parts.*

Fig. 10-55. *After a hot tank dip, thorough rinse and air blow drying, these clean pieces can go back together.*

Fig. 10-56. *Pack the cavity of the needle bearing bore with a compatible wheel bearing grease. Needles are carefully replaced. Last bearing holds set together by keystone effect.*

Fig. 10-57. *Drive hub, with proper spacer/thrust washers in place, goes easily into bearing bore.*

Fig. 10-58. *Fig. Snap ring secures drive hub.*

Fig. 10-59. *Install new O-rings, greased lightly, to base of brass knob assembly and to cover.*

Fig. 10-60. *Install the hub knob and place in FREE position.*

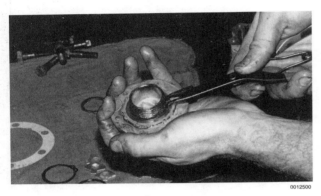

Fig. 10-61. *New snap ring, provided in Warn service kit, fits at base of knob.*

Fig. 10-62. *With clutch spring mechanism screwed into place, reinstall spring roll pin.*

Once clean, the hubs reassemble easily on the workbench. After putting each unit back together, make certain that the finger control works freely and smoothly. Hubs that test friction-free on the bench should provide easy operation on the vehicle.

Before reinstalling the hubs, carefully inspect the wheel hub mounting flange. Internal splines must be free of debris, rough edges or galling. High-grade hardware, specified for this installation, is necessary.

Fig. 10-63. *Check clutch movement by rotating hub knob to LOCK, then slide clutch mechanism into the clean, lightly greased hub body bore. Careful fitup, torquing bolts, and bending lock tabs (where required) will assure proper operation.*

Mounting bolts are subject to tremendous stress, so tighten them in sequence. Recheck final torque before securing new lock tabs. Some bolt applications require wire tying, Loctite (thread locking compound) or special lock washers.

Free-wheeling hub or drive plate mounting bolts on some U.S./domestic truck applications loosen or even shear. This is not very common on Toyota models, especially since most Land Cruisers, 4WD pickups and 4Runners use tapered cone washers to safely center and more tightly secure the free-wheeling hub flanges to the wheel hubs. Toyota engineering continually strives for safety and quality.

On models without cone washers, consider use of Metric Aircraft Grade studs with self-locking Aircraft nuts. Set the studs into clean threads with Loctite 242 or equivalent, then install the free-wheeling hub flanges with necessary washers and self-locking aircraft style nuts.

Lastly, especially if your 4x4 truck was purchased used, be certain that all locking hub parts are present. Often, after several services, small pieces get "lost." Find a blow-up schematic in a service guide, parts catalog or manufacturer's literature. Compare your pieces with those required, and restore the hubs accordingly.

Retrofitting New Hubs

Eventually, your truck's free-wheeling hubs will wear out. The effects of weather, age and abuse take their toll. (Late model automatic locking hubs may simply fail to meet your requirements.) Fortunately, you can retrofit a set of quality manual hubs.

A variety of new hubs are available through aftermarket suppliers. When selecting new hubs, consider your driving habits and intended use of the truck. Although price often influences your decision, weigh the cost against the inconvenience of walking home from a remote mountain range or the desert.

Since free-wheeling hubs require the same stamina as the differential, transfer case or transmission, consider upgrading your equipment. The controversy around automatic locking hubs continues. I maintain a singular view on the subject: Unless you need automatic hubs to offset a physical disability/challenge or health problem, forget them!

Whenever possible, I request new test vehicles with manual hubs or a delete-automatic-hubs option. I always retrofit manual hubs if I buy a used 4x4 equipped with automatic hubs. To me, stepping from the truck to twist manual hubs into LOCK mode is worth it. At least I'm certain the hubs have engaged. Uphill or down, I know that positive engine power and compression braking will assure safe four-wheeling.

0019211

Fig. 10-64. *Most four-wheelers can pull a lever, twist a manual hub or read an instruction decal. I would prefer that four-wheel drive systems remain available in true part-time form—with manual free wheeling hubs. For consumers who want or need full-time 4WD or an A.D.D. part-time system, such components could be offered as an option.*

Chapter 11

Suspension and Steering

SEVERAL YEARS AGO, my journalist's duties had me interviewing Jim Sickles at Downey Off-Road. When my questions shifted to worn suspension parts, Jim commented, "Springs are a perishable commodity." No vehicle proves this point better than a light truck, whether 2WD or a 4x4.

Fatigue, owner upgrades and modifications limit the life-span of springs, shock absorbers, shackles, bushings and steering linkage. Changes in tire diameter or the need to carry an extra load call for more body clearance. For these reasons, suspension modifications and improvements have become popular.

Fig. 11-1. *Rear leaf springs are common on all Toyota trucks except 1991–up Land Cruisers and the 1990–up 4Runners that feature link arm and coil rear springs. (Late Land Cruisers also feature coil springs and leading link suspension at the solid front driving axle.) This FJ40 chassis features a ladder frame with leaf springs at all four wheels.*

1. SPRINGS

Three criteria govern your truck's spring height and rates: 1) the necessary eye-to-eye length of leaf springs, 2) arch of leaf springs, and 3) plate thickness for each spring leaf. Coil springs, like those found on front ends of 1969–78 Toyota mini-pickup 2WD models and the late Land Cruiser and 4Runner models, have specific wire diameters and free length/standing height.

Leaf spring arch or coil spring length also determines your truck's ride height, while leaf plate thickness and taper control the spring rate, as does coil spring wire diameter. For serious off pavement use, special spring rates can offer an advantage.

Fig. 11-2. *All Toyota 2WD trucks have independent front suspension (double A-arm type IFS) with either torsion bars or coil springs. 1986–up IFS 4WD trucks feature torsion bars that, uniquely, apply force to the upper A-arms. (Late Tacoma trucks have IFS with coil springs.) These torsion bars mount high and out of the way, and steering linkage is also well up and protected within the chassis. IFS improved ride quality without compromising durability.*

For light trailer pulling, heavy cargos or off-pavement four-wheel drive use, custom springs and shock absorbers can remedy a multitude of quirks. In some cases, you can buy a Toyota truck equipped with "sport" or "heavy duty" components. In other cases your truck may need special suspension products, available through aftermarket vendors or a custom spring shop.

Although inexpensive modifications meet some tire clearance and ride height needs, the right springs offer a much better solution. For oversized tire clearance, a properly engineered lift spring kit can raise chassis/body height without compromising axle caster or pinion/driveshaft angles.

A reputable aftermarket spring/suspension installation kit can meet most OE engineering requirements for your truck and still provide a safe and moderate amount of lift. When age and fatigue become a problem, a traditional spring/blacksmith shop can also fabricate stock-type replacement springs that will improve both the suspension longevity and ride quality.

> **WARNING —**
> *Front axle spacer blocks and homemade lift kits are not only unsafe but also illegal in most states. Toyota 2WD and 4WD IFS models are especially vulnerable to handling quirks when lifted incorrectly. See the suspension upgrade chapter for details on safe kits and what to seek when modifying your truck chassis.*

Installing New Leaf Springs

Leaf spring replacement is relatively simple. Unlike torsion bar and coil spring installations, there is no threat of a loaded spring flailing out of its socket like a missile. If you keep the axles safely away from the springs until all spring mounting hardware is attached, there's very little risk of injury. Although awkward, truck leaf spring replacement is reasonably easy.

When aligning the parts, mount the spring in the frame anchor first, and secure the hardware. Then attach the shackle assembly at the opposite end of the spring, tightening all hardware to specifications found in your OEM Toyota truck repair manual.

You may find it easier to bend out a slight amount of arch from the spring before clamping the axle U-bolts into place. On a chassis with the springs riding over the axles, compress the spring slightly with a safe garage-type floor jack placed beneath the axle, just enough for the axle's spring pad to align squarely with the spring's center-bolt.

On models with the spring beneath the axle(s) place the garage floor jack at the spring, just outboard of the axle mounting location. Carefully compress the spring enough for the center-bolt to align squarely with the axle's spring perch pad.

Especially with new lift springs, spring compression may be necessary to achieve spring conformation at the original axle center point. Use a garage-type floor jack, which will place you safely away from the axle and the loaded spring.

Attach the U-bolts carefully, tightening U-bolt nuts uniformly. Watch the exposed thread lengths to determine equal tightening. Torque nuts in sequence. (See your Toyo-

ta truck repair manual for tightening specifications.) Gradually tighten each nut until you have reached full torque value and the bolt threads extend evenly past the nuts. Properly installed springs often live well past 100,000 miles, depending on how and where you drive your truck.

> **NOTE —**
> After driving a few miles, re-torque these spring U-bolt nuts. It's also a smart policy to re-check U-bolt torque periodically, especially on 4x4 models.

Shackles and Bushings

The leaf springs on your truck move in a shackle. All Toyota truck models use low-maintenance rubber-type bushings. Although very durable, these shackle bushings will eventually wear out. Always replace the shackle bushings when noticeable wear develops.

> **CAUTION —**
> *Spring bushings and frame hanger designs vary. Each type requires specific torque settings for both the pivot bolts and shackle nuts. Refer to your Toyota truck repair manual for further details on safe and correct spring assembly methods and torque settings.*

Torsion Bar and Coil Spring Front Suspension

Double A-arm (wishbone) independent front suspension (IFS) has been a Toyota mainstay since the first 2WD mini-trucks. IFS 2WD and 4WD front end systems use double A-arms at each front wheel. This is a popular suspension method that allows excellent wheel and tire alignment in all steering and wheel travel positions. Toyota's IFS provides superior ride quality, improved handling characteristics and an excellent reliability record.

By basic design, Toyota coil spring and torsion bar IFS systems have changed only slightly since the 1960s. Key

Fig. 11-3. *Toyota 2WD IFS suspensions incorporated coil springs through 1978, then torsion bars from 1979–up. 4WD IFS models use torsion bars until the introduction of the Tacoma with coil springs. This basic engineering has proven reliable and easy to service and tune. Shown is Downey Off-Road's popular "lifted" suspension package.*

IFS components include 1) double A-arms of unequal length, 2) knuckle/spindles attached to the A-arms by pivoting ball-joints, 3) a hefty front frame crossmember to support the A-arm suspension (plus the coil springs on pre-1979 2WDs) and 4) steering linkage that accommodates the movement of paired independent A-arms at each front wheel. A-arms pivot on bushings mounted at the control arm shafts on all IFS trucks.

Conventional (solid front axle) 4x4s include the 4WD Land Cruiser, 1979–85 4WD pickups and the 4Runners through 1985. These well built models carry the earlier technology to the modern era. Today, the only remaining solid front axle Toyota 4x4 is the 4WD Land Cruiser with advanced link arm and coil spring suspension.

IFS Wear Points

Toyota trucks with independent front suspension (IFS) have several wear points. Control arm (shaft) bushings, spindle/knuckle ball-joints and steering linkage components deteriorate over time, a factor that affects wheel alignment, handling and even safety.

Fig. 11-4. Spindle/knuckle ball-joint and steering linkage wear can cause looseness in the steering. This affects wheel alignment and safe handling. Always consider these wear points when your Toyota truck with IFS wants to wander or track poorly.

Most IFS front ends have greaseable ball-joints and steering linkage components. Knuckle/spindle ball-joints, whether permanently sealed or greaseable, require routine inspection for wear. When greasing the ball-joints and other steering components, I prefer a hand grease gun, as the dust boots are vulnerable to rupture when too much grease is applied too quickly. (See lubrication chapter for details.)

CAUTION —
Do not overfill joints. On non-sealed boots (those boots with an open flap edge), apply just enough grease to force old lube out. On joints with a grease plug and a fully sealed boot, do not add more grease than enough to slightly swell the boot. Any more grease than this will cause the boot to rupture and create a need for parts replacement.

2WD and 4WD IFS ball-joints wear over time and require replacement at high mileage. The Toyota truck repair manual describes the procedure for replacing ball-joints, which can require special pullers and a press in some cases.

CAUTION —
Older or high mileage truck's ball-joints may be difficult to remove from the A-arms. Use protective safety eyewear when replacing steering knuckle ball-joints and A-arm cross-shaft bushings. Some materials are exceptionally hard, and you must not damage the A-arms. Most owners prefer to send this job to a well equipped front end alignment and frame shop.

The procedure for changing ball-joints on 2WD and 4WD IFS models, plus information about alignment corrections, is within the Toyota truck repair manual for your model or a professional level service guidebook. Review this task before proceeding. You may decide that subletting such work is appropriate.

Frame Damage

Off-pavement pounding and heavy hauling can damage your truck's frame. All Toyota trucks feature a driveable chassis or ladder frame. Subject to severe twisting and overload, frame damage is possible.

During routine service, inspect your truck's frame. Look closely for tears, cracks, wrinkles, loose rivets or damaged fasteners. Inspect axle housing mounts and spring hangers, all pivot bolts and other friction points. Make certain crossmembers are intact. On 4x4 models, consider the skid plates and transmission crossmember an integral part of the frame. Structural support and frame stiffness depend on intact crossmembers.

Those leaf spring Land Cruisers with front spring anchors at the rear of the springs (shackles at the front) may experience frame damage near the spring anchor if the truck is severely abused off-pavement. The anchor (rear) end of the springs receives a great deal of punishment, as road and trail obstacles want to drive the front axle from beneath the truck. The frame receives the brunt of the punishment and can crack under extreme conditions.

Under the most severe service, spring shackles on a leaf spring 4x4 can break, along with the spring shackle upper frame supports. Extreme off-pavement pounding with harsh push and pull on the upper shackle supports can break the bracket or frame rail. (See suspension upgrade chapter for more details.)

WARNING —
Fatigued or stress damaged spring shackles, frame brackets or spring hangers pose a safety hazard. Broken leaf springs can cause complete loss of vehicle control. Inspect your truck's springs, frame and spring supports regularly.

Another area of concern are the vertical frame members that support the lower control arms (A-arms) on torsion bar IFS 4WD trucks. Without an aftermarket truss support, the control arms will bend these frame members and spread apart under severe off-pavement punishment.

As the control arms spread apart, the steering idler arm and even the power steering gear can rip loose from the frame! Watch this area, and if you plan oversized tires or hard off-road use of the truck, consider a Downey Off-Road lower control arm (A-arm) truss. (See the performance suspension chapter for details.)

2. SHOCK ABSORBERS

Single, dual and gas shocks... The market seems glutted with shock absorbers! What do you need? Which shock design works best? Is there a formula for choosing the right shock absorbers? You bet!

Shock absorbers make a major contribution to your truck's handling, ride, braking and safety. As shocks wear and fatigue, they lose their effectiveness. On most off-highway vehicles, the original shock absorber set fails before any other chassis item. Shocks deteriorate rapidly under excessive heat, friction and overwork. Due to wear over time, shock absorbers are a perishable item.

Anatomy Of A Shock Absorber

All shock absorbers have the same aims: 1) damp the oscillating motion of the vehicle frame and body, 2) limit the rebound effects as uneven loads affect each wheel, and 3) keep the wheels safely on the ground when suspension moves violently, like over rough washboard roads.

Your safety depends upon adequate shock absorbers. Off-pavement, your truck's suspension travels constantly, from full extension to pounding compression. The shock absorbers pay the price, often succumbing to leakage or faulty performance. A bone jarring ride, squeaks and rattles develop when shock absorbers fail.

Of the two common shock absorber designs, single tube and twin tube, most truck manufacturers install the lighter duty single tube types, avoiding the more expensive and dependable twin tube or gas filled designs. Original equipment shocks concentrate on highway ride and driver comfort.

A single tube shock absorber has a machined steel cylinder and a rod/piston assembly. The shock body holds

Fig. 11-6. Piston head and cylinder have valves and precisely metered orifices. Doetsch Tech's Pre-Runner shocks boast progressive valving.

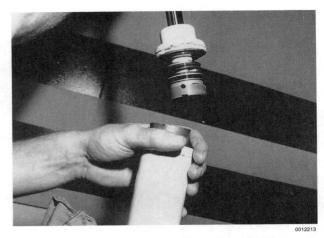

Fig. 11-7. O-ring sealing on these valves is sign of better quality.

Fig. 11-5. Laid out, twin tube shock absorber components consist of an outer tube, inner tube and cylinder, plus the rod and valve assembly. Fluid fills the reservoir of this sealed Doetsch Tech unit.

an oil (plus nitrogen on gas filled types) that resists the force of the moving piston. Valving in the piston controls oil flow, which helps regulate the movement of the rod.

Twin-tube shock absorbers provide the added benefit of a second valving and reservoir system. Beyond the valves on the piston head, these shocks provide a bottom check valve, permanently affixed to an inner, machined cylinder. Valving in the piston head allows fluid to bypass during shock absorber compression and rebound. The second, fixed valve enhances damping sensitivity. Located between the inside cylinder tube and outer shell reservoir of the shock absorber body, this valve enables fluid or gas pressure to act as an additional damping force.

When resistance against the piston is too great, the suspension cannot move. Too little damping will cause serious handling and ride problems. Therefore, the most important job for your truck's shock absorbers is to sense road forces and continually work to control them. The heat generated during rapid movement of the piston compounds that task by weakening the damping ability. Fluid fade directly corresponds to the velocity of the piston.

Shock absorber valving faces its greatest challenge when your truck tackles a washboard road. The better shock designs, which boast as many as ten stages of valving, compensate for the varying fluid velocities and heat demands found in severe off-pavement conditions.

Gas Shocks

Foaming (aeration) of fluid inhibits shock absorber action by creating gaps that cause erratic shock behavior or fade. The best counter measures employ gases such as freon (now outlawed as an environmental hazard) and nitrogen. These substances offset many of the troubles associated with hydraulic oils, including heat buildup.

When high performance and constant pounding demand real shock action, gas shocks do the job. Non-gas shocks suffer from oil thinning. They operate best under moderate piston velocities. By contrast, nitrogen gas keeps shocks cooler and foam-free, allowing valves and fluid to continue working, even at extreme piston velocities.

Popular nitrogen gas shocks come in two varieties: low and high pressure. As gas filled shocks place high loads on the rod and piston, many recreational and off-pavement users prefer low pressure cellular gas shocks. (By contrast, desert racing demands high pressure, 200 psi-plus nitrogen gas damping.) Due largely to their off-pavement superiority, reliability and predictable behavior, cellular gas or pressurized gas shocks have become a popular aftermarket item.

Selecting A Quality Shock Absorber

Most OEM shocks feature one- to 1-1/8-inch piston diameters. I feel that the minimum piston size for overall good performance should be 1-5/16". Popular for many years, the even larger 1-3/8" piston head satisfies all but the most brutal off-pavement maulers and heavyweight haulers.

> **NOTE —**
> Some Toyota trucks come with gas-filled or heavy duty shock absorbers. If your truck is so equipped, be certain to replace these shocks with a similar type.

A typical high performance shock is Rancho's RS-7000 series, a gas cell design with 1-5/8" piston diameters. The operating pressures of these shocks hover around 200 psi with chrome-hardened 17.3 millimeter rods. Sealing ability contributes to the life expectancy of such shock absorbers. (See suspension upgrade chapter for additional details on performance shock absorbers.)

Pistons should be O-ring sealed, and the cylinder requires a tough double wall. Oversize fluid reservoirs provide better cooling and more resistance to fading. Refinement of the valve mechanism, that ability to sense terrain and load demands, will determine a shock absorber's worth. Proper shock damping serves as a primary element in a truck's suspension system.

Lastly, shock mounting grommets and eyes must hold up to road and load demands. A shock absorber is useless when detached or loose. A weak set of grommets allows wasted movement and undamped travel.

3. 4x4 STEERING KNUCKLE AND LINKAGE

Off-highway driving can punish your truck's steering and suspension components. On 4x4 equipped trucks, the live front axle design, especially with Full-Time 4WD or Toyota's IFS/A.D.D. system, places an extra load on steering linkage and knuckle pivots (kingpin bearings or ball-joints).

On a solid front axle 4x4, replacing a steering knuckle kingpin bearing set is a major job, requiring removal of the wheel hub assembly, spindle, axle shaft and steering knuckle. For repairs on your live front axle unit, including axle shaft removal, refer to the OEM Toyota truck repair manual or a professional service manual.

> **NOTE —**
> On some 4x4 systems, the steering arms, free-wheel hub flanges and bearing caps have split cone washers. Do not attempt to force these components apart without loosening and removing the cone washers first. The washers have a taper, and you can try gently prying them out. If gentle doesn't work, use a plastic hammer (sand-filled head preferred) to provide the necessary jarring. Tap the plastic hammer at the side of the flange (working sideways against the cone washers) to loosen the washers and flange.

The 4x4 closed knuckle axle's kingpin bearing caps are critical safety parts, responsible for aligning the knuckle and setting an exact pre-load on the bearings for normal steering control and reasonable parts life. When steering knuckle service takes place, proper pre-load adjustment is very important. Follow guidelines and methods described in the OEM Toyota truck repair manual for your model.

Fig. 11-8. *Use of proper tools is crucial to safe, dependable work. Steering knuckle replacement requires each if these tools. For many applications, a spring scale is also necessary.*

CHAPTER 11

4WD steering knuckle repairs, 2WD or 4WD IFS ball-joint replacement or front brake service each provide a good time for front wheel bearing re-packing. (See chapter on wheel bearing service.) Assemble wheel bearings carefully and adjust to spec. Include new inner wheel grease seals with the bearing pack. Follow procedures and adjustment specs outlined in your OEM Toyota truck repair manual or a professional service guide.

Always use new self-locking nuts, new lock tabs or retainers and new cotter pins. Clean assembly methods during fit-up of parts, proper use of tools, and correct procedures for cleaning, re-packing and adjusting bearings will assure a safe job.

> **CAUTION —**
> *Never bang directly on ball joints, tie-rod ends or their studs. Keep hammer blows away from joints and dust boots. Never use a pickle fork when you intend to reuse ball-joints, steering linkage joints or their dust boots.*

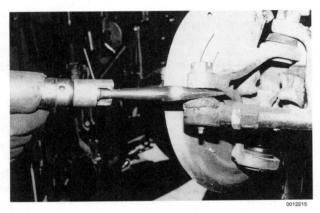

Fig. 11-9. *Loosen tie-rod nut, leaving a few threads in place to prevent tie-rod from falling. Only if joint will not be reused, insert a pickle fork between tie-rod joint and steering arm to separate the ball stud from its tapered seat in the arm. (Never use pickle fork if you plan to reuse the ball-joint.)*

Fig. 11-10. *Alternate method for loosening tie-rods is a pair of hefty hammers. Place one at the back of the steering arm's tie-rod seat and rap the other hammer on the front of the arm. A sharp rap will dislodge the tapered ball stud from its seat. Take care not to damage the steering arm or tie-rod threads.*

> **CAUTION —**
> *Do not re-use any fasteners that are worn or deformed in normal use. Many fasteners are designed to be used only once and become unreliable and may fail when used a second time. This includes, but is not limited to, nuts, bolts, washers, self-locking nuts or bolts, circlips and cotter pins. For replacement always use new part(s) of OEM grade and quality.*

Fig. 11-11. *Another method for loosening a ball stud is to simply strike the flange near ball stud. With a few solid blows directed at flange, ball joint should drop. If this does not work, do not use excessive force. Find an appropriate puller or spreader, as described in the repair manual for your truck.*

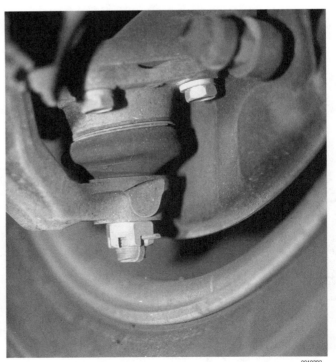

Fig. 11-12. *Castellated nuts always require a new cotter pin during service. Note how Toyota fastens the cotter pin, and duplicate that method. Replace worn self-locking nuts or locking hardware with new and identical OEM Toyota pieces.*

Fig. 11-13. *Install new lip-type seals in the same manner as originals. Seal lips must face in proper direction. (If in doubt, consult the OEM Toyota repair manual.) Some seals have a sealant/coating at the outer edge. If not, consult your OEM Toyota repair manual about whether or not you should apply sealant to the outer edge of seal.*

Fig. 11-15. *Once steering knuckle/spindle and dust shield are securely in place, you can proceed with wheel bearing service and assembly. (See wheel bearing service chapter or your OEM Toyota truck repair manual for details.) After carefully adjusting wheel bearings, install brake calipers (if so equipped) and torque all bolts and steering linkage nuts to specification. Always install new cotter pins.*

4X4 Closed-knuckle Axle with Kingpin Pivots

Toyota 4x4s with closed-knuckle axles use kingpin bearings rather than ball joints. At the bearing caps, shims control steering knuckle bearing preload. When your closed knuckle 4x4 truck has high mileage, the kingpin bearing clearance may increase enough to cause looseness at the knuckles or a "kingpin shimmy." If inspection reveals excessive play, consider replacing the bearings and their races.

> **WARNING —**
> *When a large amount of kingpin play appears suddenly, suspect kingpin bearing race, knuckle or axle housing damage. Immediately replace defective parts—safety is at stake.*

Fig. 11-14. *When adjusting wheel alignment or installing new steering linkage pieces, always center tie-rod ends in their sleeves. The ball studs and their sockets should line up evenly before you tighten the sleeve clamps. Make sure each tie-rod end has full range of motion.*

Fig. 11-16. *Shims beneath the bearing caps on closed knuckles control steering knuckle preload. Proper placement of shims is crucial. If these bearings need adjustment, use a spring scale and follow OEM guidelines in your repair manual.*

I have found that when kingpin bearings feel loose and re-torquing the bearing cap bolts to specification does not correct the problem, bearings have excessive wear. Usually, new OEM bearings and races (or equivalent), installed with the original shims at their original locations, will restore proper preload and safe steering.

After installing the new bearings and races with shims in their original locations, torque bearing cap bolts and check pre-load with a spring scale. (You will find pull specifications in the OEM Toyota repair manual for your truck.) Replacement bearings meet exact sizing standards, so try this procedure before performing the elaborate bearing adjustment method described in the Toyota repair manual.

If the knuckle has sustained damage or original shims were removed during previous repair work or service, you may find that the pre-load measurement with new bearings and races is not correct. Look closely for any steering knuckle or axle housing damage. If pre-load is not correct and their is no damage, you will need to perform the shim adjustment procedure described in the OEM Toyota repair manual.

When you disassemble a closed steering knuckle, always note bearing cap shim placement. Keep shims together and tagged for re-installation in their exact, original locations. Shims must be clean and flat during installation. If a shim is badly damaged, measure it carefully with a micrometer. Replace the shim with one of the same thickness. Make sure bearings and races are clean and greased properly. Races must seat firmly in clean bores. Use a torque wrench to tighten bearing cap bolts in even steps and cross sequence.

4. THE STEERING SYSTEM

Whether your truck serves utility needs, lugs a travel trailer or plies recreational back country, safe vehicle control depends on a reliable steering system. Toyota truck steering system layouts differ, both in design and function.

Your truck's suspension and steering linkage design dictate the location of the steering gear, while driving requirements and engineering intent determine the speed or ratio of the steering gear. Responsive handling results from correctly matching the suspension, steering linkage and steering gear, while a chassis lift and other suspension modifications often compromise the steering geometry.

NOTE —
"Bump steer" and other handling anomalies result from the misalignment of suspension and steering linkage. See chapter on suspension upgrades for details.

Production trucks, especially older models with manual steering systems, have slower steering response and less suspension feedback than passenger cars. Concerned about safety and liability, truck manufacturers "de-tune" suspension to meet a wider audience of drivers. Later models feature quicker power steering ratios, which gives the light truck a sportier feel, nimbler parking habits and easier trailer backing ability.

Types Of Steering Gears

Toyota's choice of recirculating ball-and-nut manual steering gears on all pickups and 1973–up Land Cruisers was a wise decision. (Land Cruisers prior to 1973 use the higher friction worm-and-roller type steering gears.) Recirculating ball-and-nut steering gears offer much smoother, safer operation and a higher degree of durability.

The popularity and superior quality of recirculating ball-and-nut gears—both manual and integral power piston types—has made these units a standard among quality truck manufacturers.

Fig. 11-17. *In 1940, GM pioneered recirculating ball-and-nut steering gears. This engineering breakthrough revolutionized the safety and driving ease of trucks, and GM's patented design was decades ahead of all competition. Toyota recognized the quality of this design, and pickups and the 1973–up Land Cruisers feature recirculating ball-and-nut steering gears. For early Land Cruisers, a GM-style Saginaw power steering gear conversion kit is available from the aftermarket. (See suspension upgrade chapter for details.)*

NOTE —
A common cause of steering gear damage comes from towing an early Land Cruiser that has a worm-and-roller steering gear. The gear design does poorly with reverse flow of energy, like when the road causes the primitive roller/sector shaft teeth to rotate the worm shaft. If you must transport a truck that does not have recirculating ball-and-nut steering, consider using a low-bed car hauling trailer.

On all Toyota steering gears except rack-and-pinion types, the pitman arm attaches at the outer end of the sector or cross-shaft. Clockwise and counterclockwise rotation of the sector- or cross-shaft translates as the fore and aft swing of the pitman arm on pre-IFS solid axle 4x4 pickups and earlier Land Cruisers with bellcrank (center arm) steering linkage. By contrast, all later Land Cruisers and IFS models without rack-and-pinion steering rely on lateral movement of the pitman arm.

The manual recirculating ball-and-nut gears drastically reduce friction. A ball nut, machined internally to form the top half of a ball race, rides on ball bearings. These ball bearings run in the worm shaft's precisely machined groove. The machined groove serves as the inner half of the ball bearing race.

Machined teeth on the outer surface of the ball nut engage teeth on the pitman (cross/sector) shaft. Steering wheel and worm shaft rotation translate as up and down movement of the ball nut. This movement of the sector teeth rotates the sector shaft and pitman arm.

The major gain of recirculating ball-and-nut steering gear designs is the reduction of stress and friction. Gliding motion of the ball nut, up and down the worm shaft, takes place with ball bearing smoothness. Wrist wrenching steering kickback is drastically reduced with a ball-and-nut design, especially the integral power assist type. Moreover, even with severe four-wheel drive use, these gears survive.

Fig. 11-18. *On Toyota IFS models, the pitman arm and steering linkage move laterally. On solid front axle 4WD pickup models and Land Cruisers with center arm/bellcrank steering linkage, the draglink and pitman arm move fore-and-aft, as shown here.*

CAUTION —

A steering gear that needs a significant amount of adjustment always suggest internal damage and time for a complete gear overhaul. Service adjustment, although rare with ball-and-nut gears, focuses solely on the mesh between the ball nut's teeth and the pitman/sector shaft teeth. Worm shaft bearing pre-load is also adjustable, although this procedure is rare between steering gear overhauls. Never attempt a steering gear adjustment without instructions from an OEM-level repair manual.

The antiquated worm-and-roller gears suffer from sector teeth and worm gear chipping and, in the worst cases, seizure from jammed tooth debris. Friction and shock loads translate to wear that requires periodic adjustment. Hard use often leads to unseen damage. My experience with both domestic and import worm-and-roller and worm-and-sector steering gears has taught me that any steering gearbox with an excessive amount of play deserves a teardown for inspection and replacement of defective parts.

Power Steering

Power steering, once considered a horsepower-robbing accessory for lazy drivers, is now a light truck standard feature. Major design breakthroughs, especially the switch to integral power steering gears, popularized domestic light truck power steering by the late 1960s. Toyota's first truck use of power steering came as options with the 1979 Toyota Land Cruiser and early 4WD pickups. These were durable and integral/recirculating ball-and-rack type gears.

The reliability of General Motors' recirculating ball-type Saginaw manual and power steering gears is legend. For early manual steering Land Cruisers, a conversion to power/integral steering has become popular among 4x4 off-pavement enthusiasts. A conversion kit, available from Advance Adapters (see suspension upgrade chapter), makes this conversion easier. This is the premier steering gear for a hard-core off-pavement 4WD truck.

A Saginaw-type integral power gear provides the best features and attributes found in light truck power steering. (As noted, Saginaw integral power steering also makes popular swap material for an older FJ-series Land Cruiser.) For this reason, and since OEM Toyota gears are of similar design, I am offering a description of the Saginaw integral power gear.

The Saginaw integral power gear employs a rotary valve that opens ports and directs high pressure fluid to help during turns. The degree of assist corresponds directly to the driver's steering wheel effort.

Some Saginaw integral units offer a unique variable ratio, produced by using unequal length teeth on the pitman/sector shaft and rack piston. As you steer full left or right, the pitman shaft speed increases, quickening the steering. Straight ahead, steering is very stable, with a slower ratio that provides more road feel.

Saginaw integral power steering gears are sensitive, precise mechanisms operating under close tolerances and very high fluid pressures. Service on a power gear is rare, but when necessary, requires intricate preload adjustments and special assembly tools. Your safety depends upon proper fit-up of parts.

> **NOTE —**
> Despite basic similarities between recirculating ball-and-nut manual gears and the Saginaw integral power units, you need much greater skill to service a power gear.

When Toyota truck owners retrofit Saginaw integral power gears to an early truck chassis (typically a vintage 4WD Land Cruiser), such a conversion project requires skill, plus a thorough knowledge of steering safety and chassis fabrication requirements.

> *CAUTION —*
> *Do not attempt a conversion without the requisite skill level. The most common mistakes that inexperienced installers make are 1) misalignment of steering linkage (causing bump steer or limiting travel), 2) failure to make sure that the steering gear is in its center position when the vehicle's wheels aim straight ahead, and 3) not setting the steering knuckle/wheel stops properly, which could allow the steering gear's ball nut to hyper-extend at the extremes of its travel and severely damage the gear assembly.*

Advance Adapters and others make conversion kits for retrofitting a Saginaw recirculating ball type integral power steering gear to an earlier truck chassis. (See the suspension upgrade chapter.) The few horsepower lost in running a power steering pump is worth the trade-off: smooth and durable modern steering.

Steering Linkage and Control

Although lock-to-lock steering ratios affect turning quickness, the true blueprint for off- and on-highway handling is the precise delivery of steering signals. The wheels must respond readily to linkage movement.

Later 4x4 model steering linkage often includes a stabilizer shock designed to eliminate severe road kickback. Although an OE or aftermarket stabilizer is a major asset, it's not a substitute for replacing worn steering components. Before tackling steering wander, you must eliminate worn or dangerously loose linkage.

If your truck wanders, check for excess play at the wheel bearings, steering knuckle ball-joints, kingpin bearings or the steering linkage. The pitman arm, drag-link, tie-rod ends, idler arm, steering knuckle ball joints and kingpin bearings are acute wear areas.

The best procedure for checking steering linkage, ball-joint, kingpin bearing or wheel bearing play is to shake the tire and wheel assembly. Jack and secure the front end safely off the floor. On 2WD IFS suspension, place jacks safely beneath lower control arms to unload the spring or torsion bar pressure from the A-arms and ball-joints.

On IFS 4WD torsion bar models, place the jacks at frame members and allow the control arms to extend downward, unrestricted, to their travel limits. On solid axle models, you can place a pair of jackstands beneath the axle housing, spaced far enough apart to safely support the vehicle.

Grip each front tire at 6 and 12 o'clock to check ball joints, kingpin bearings or wheel bearings. Shake each raised tire from a 3 and 9 o'clock position to note steering linkage wear. Have a partner watch for play at each tie-rod end and the other joints while applying a shaking, back-and-forth force.

Begin your inspection with the wheel bearings and knuckle joints or kingpin bearings. Next, check the steering linkage. Worn tie-rod ends and other joints cause steering looseness, road wander, and the risk of losing steering control.

Suspension frame mounts, control or link arm bushings and spring shackles are also wear points that can cause poor vehicle handling and loss of control. Especially on a 4x4 model or a truck used extensively off-pavement, off-road pounding can stress the suspension and steering system to its limits.

Fig. 11-19. Excess play in ball-joint steering knuckles (shown) causes "kingpin shimmy," characterized by a violent shake of the steering wheel and the entire front end. Kingpin bearing shims on solid axle 4x4s allow for very minor adjustment. Any more than very slight adjustment calls for bearing and parts replacement or a knuckle assembly rebuild. Ball-joint play cannot be adjusted. Any sign of wear calls for replacement.

Fig. 11-20. *Excess spring movement contributes to wander. Always inspect spring bushings for wear. OE-type hard rubber bushings can wear over time and leave your truck's front end wobbly and unstable.*

Rear spring position also affects steering control. Check for misaligned springs, loose U-bolts, broken spring center bolts and defective spring or link arm bushings. Wander and "rear wheel steer" can result from rear suspension defects.

Worn steering linkage and suspension parts are not serviceable. When defective, you must replace them. (One exception is the rebuildable spring-and-cup drag-link assembly on an earlier Toyota 4x4 solid axle model.) Parts removal requires care and should follow professional service guidelines found in an OEM level repair manual.

> **NOTE —**
> You may need special tools, including pullers. Cleanliness is essential. Debris must not interfere with the tight fitup of tapered ball studs on tie-rod ends and ball joints. You must torque self-locking and castellated nuts to factory specs. (Always install a correctly sized new cotter pin on the castellated nut.)

Periodic steering linkage maintenance is simple, consisting of wiping dirt from fittings, then greasing joints with clean chassis lube through a hand grease gun. Safety inspection should include dust boots, joint wear, and straightness of rods. Always replace bent steering linkage components with new parts. Straightening a bent tie-rod compromises safety. Stretched one way, then the other, tie-rod tubes and steel rods can weaken and break. Do not compromise with safety.

Inspecting the Steering System

Restoration of steering linkage, knuckle joints, kingpin bearings and wheel bearings usually eliminates steering play. If looseness remains, make certain that the frame, spring bolts, control arm cross-shafts, all pivot bushings, link arms and spring attachments are intact and that hardware is secure.

Tires and front end alignment are also a concern, as wander often occurs when tires have abnormal wear pat-

Fig. 11-21. *Sway/stabilizer bar bushings are also perishable. On later trucks, inspect these pieces for wear, looseness and deterioration. Too loose, the bar serves no purpose. Control in corners benefits greatly from the sway bar. Also look for bushing wear at sway bar links and torque arms (shown).*

terns. On Toyota 4WD trucks with solid front driving axles and kingpin knuckle pivot bearings, wheel alignment is simple. Unless you've bent the axle beam/housing or the truck's frame, alignment consists only of setting the toe-in.

> **NOTE —**
> As mentioned later in this chapter, on a solid axle 4x4 with closed knuckles and kingpin bearings, you can make slight camber adjustments with aftermarket offset bearing caps. On leaf spring front suspension 4x4s, you can also set caster with steel wedge shims placed between the axle and leaf stack.

If steering play still exists, suspect the steering gearbox. For a quick check, center the steering and carefully rotate the worm or steering shaft. (This may require a helper on the early trucks with an enclosed steering shaft/column.) Note the amount of rotational movement necessary to just move the pitman arm.

On a later truck with an exposed steering shaft, this operation is very easy. Park your truck with the wheels straight ahead. Turn the shaft at the input end of the steering gear while holding the pitman arm with your other hand. It's easy to detect pitman movement by gently rotating the steering shaft.

CHAPTER 11

Fig. 11-22. *The coupler above the steering gear (arrow) is also a wear point. An open column and coupler like this enables a quick check for steering gear damage and excess gear backlash.*

Be sensitive to the exact point at which the pitman arm responds to the steering shaft movement. Rotate the shaft in the opposite direction to determine the degree of play. If wear or play is evident, either steering gear adjustment or overhaul is necessary.

Note that the steering gear must be in its center position when checking for play. Steering gears have a high point in the exact center position that creates a very slight pre-load in the straight ahead driving position. Turned left or right of this point, sector play or backlash will increase. If you suspect a mis-centered steering gear, disconnect the steering linkage at the Pitman arm and very gently rotate the steering to one extreme.

Now count the exact turns back to the opposite extreme, then divide that number by two. Turn the wheel back this amount, and your steering gearbox will be on center. Check for play and over-center (high point) pre-load at this position. (Never turn the shaft hard against its extremes, as damage to ball races could occur.)

Signs of Steering Gearbox Trouble

Sudden development of steering gear play or symptoms of wander, clicking noises or binding imply internal damage to the gear. Although later steering gears have great resiliency, hard-core abuse or four-wheeling can damage even the best steering unit.

Unless high mileage dictates a minor readjustment to compensate for acceptable limits of wear, any more than a slight amount of steering gear play suggests internal gear damage. Since the gear's inner workings are invisible without a teardown, you must make a judgement call here.

Before considering a steering gear teardown, review the OEM Toyota truck repair manual for your model. Understand the tools, close tolerances, and sequence of disassembly and reassembly.

Power steering gears, in particular, require special care, cleanliness and safe work habits. Consider a new, factory rebuilt or low mileage recycled gear. Sometimes a rebuilt/exchange unit proves cost effective. Individual power steering gear pieces get very expensive.

Unless you find a recycled truck with well under 100,000 original and easy miles on the odometer, the manual or power steering gear likely has substantial wear. If you have a manual unit and decide to rebuild it, always install new parts in a sound housing. Always use new seals, bushings, bearings, a new worm shaft, a new ball-nut and a new pitman/sector shaft assembly. Never mix or fit up old and new parts, especially gear pieces. If you cannot find parts at your local Toyota dealership, try for NOS (new original stock) pieces through a restoration source that specializes in parts for even the earliest Land Cruisers.

Steering Linkage and Suspension Damage

Normal wear over time and the off-pavement use of light trucks can affect wheel alignment. Rough terrain and obstacles like rocks, stumps, slick mud, and streambeds each threaten the chassis and front end system. Damaged steering linkage and badly mis-aligned front wheels can ruin a brand new set of tires in just a few miles.

Off-pavement pounding can cause serious suspension trouble. Especially sensitive are the leaf spring centering bolts and the spring U-bolts (which shear or break and allow the axle to shift out of alignment). Toyota coil springs ride above the control arms or axle, and unless stressed to the limit, these coils seldom break, even under tight off-pavement twisting. Coil springs can dislodge, however, from serious suspension bashing.

Steering linkage is a major area of concern. Steering linkage must move with the axle to maintain wheel alignment. Generally, a solid axle tie rod lies just above the axle centerline, making this linkage the most vulnerable steering component. On 4x4 solid axle models, the drivetrain layout has the front driveshaft angling from the transfer case to the backside of the front axle. Due to this design, the steering linkage must ride in front of the axle.

Tree stumps can easily damage the relay or tie rod(s) or a steering stabilizer. If the stabilizer shock damper (found on most 4x4 models) becomes bent, steering bind is possible. If obvious damage exists, remove the stabilizer shock damper. Other than some wander and possible shakiness, the truck can get home without this unit. Replace with a new stabilizer shock damper immediately.

5. WHEEL ALIGNMENT

Subjected to normal wear-and-tear or off-pavement pounding, your truck demands regular steering system inspection and front wheel alignment. The longevity of expensive tires and your safety both depend upon proper front wheel tracking.

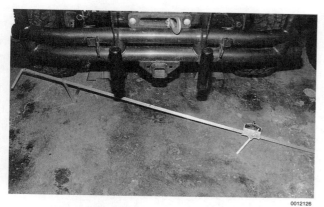

Fig. 11-23.   Toe-set is a regular part of chassis service. Especially on vehicles subjected to off-pavement pounding, tire life depends on periodic checks of front wheel toe-set. Radial tires have different toe-set requirements than bias-ply types. Adjust toe-in when installing new tires. On solid front axles like an FJ40 Land Cruiser, toe-in is normally the only adjustment required. Caster or camber changes result from axle, chassis or suspension damage and wear.

Fig. 11-24.   Note use of a special tie-rod sleeve wrench. After rain, slush, mud, and water crossings, joints require fresh chassis grease to displace water and foreign matter.

Front end alignment also reveals defective steering and suspension components. Consider wheel alignment an important part of your truck's preventive maintenance program.

Steering Geometry

For the Toyota truck, periodic front end alignment always includes toe-in. Toe-in is the measurement between the centerlines of the tire tread at the tire's horizontal midline.

Imagine lines scribed at the center of your front tire treads, running the full circumference of the tire. Each line references 360° of tire tread surface and offers an easy measurement at the front and rear of the tire. The object when setting toe-in is to properly distance these two reference points.

Vehicle manufacturers establish toe settings with consideration for rolling resistance and chassis geometry. Generally, older bias ply tires require a slight (1/32" to 1/8") toe-in. Modern radial tires have less rolling resistance and need only minimal inward toe. They often call for a zero-degree/inch toe set, or tires that run perfectly parallel in the straight ahead mode.

Normal steering and reasonable tire wear also depend upon correct caster and camber geometry. Camber is simply the upright angle or tilt of the tire. The camber angle can change when an axle housing, steering spindle, or steering knuckle becomes bent or when excess wear develops at the knuckle pivots (kingpin bearings, pivots or ball-joints).

Caster is trickier to define. The caster angle is the tilt of an imaginary line drawn through the centerline of the steering kingpins. On ball-joint front ends like Toyota 2WD and 4WD IFS designs, we draw this line through the orbital centerline of the upper and lower ball joints.

This line's angle tilts rearward (positive caster) or forward (negative caster). Its purpose is to encourage straight ahead orientation of the wheels—the feature that causes the steering wheel to center naturally as we leave a

Fig. 11-25.   Caster and camber gauges clamp to the wheel. Once on a center line with the wheel spindle, levels indicate steering and wheel tilt angles.

Fig. 11-26. All 2WD and IFS 4WD Toyota trucks have provisions for caster and camber adjustment. On torsion bar models, ride height is also adjustable. Solid front axle 4x4 models are restricted here. All models allow for toe-in setting.

turn. Caster also helps prevent kingpin shimmy, the violent back and forth shaking of the front wheels.

The last front end geometry issue is steering axis inclination. Effectively, steering axis inclination is two angles (caster and camber) in one, with the steering knuckle/spindle angled to maintain a specified arc during turns. Steering axis inclination depends upon the condition and integrity of the steering knuckle and spindle. If axis of inclination differs from the OEM specification while caster, camber and toe-in measurements are correct, suspect a bent or defective steering knuckle or spindle.

Many manufacturers and specialists assert that caster and camber should never be adjusted by bending a solid axle beam (hot, cold or otherwise). If these measurements are beyond specification, look for bent, worn or damaged parts. Don't overlook sagging springs and ride height. You will find chassis, alignment and ride height measurements in your OEM Toyota truck repair manual.

Wheel Alignment Features

IFS double A-arm front suspension systems allow both caster and camber adjustments by tilting the top of the wheel inboard (negative camber) or outboard (positive camber) from its vertical axis. Such systems also provide fore and aft adjustment of the kingpin centerline for setting proper caster.

Solid live front axle 4x4s have no provision for camber or caster adjustment. You can, however, set caster by placing shims (tapered steel wedges) between the axle spring perches and leaf springs. Accurately degreed, these wedge-shaped shims can restore proper tilt angle of the kingpin centerline. Make sure that sagging springs are not at fault when caster reads out of specification.

Modest camber corrections on solid closed-knuckle 4x4 front axles are possible with replacement offset steering knuckle bearing caps (available currently through aftermarket sources). Before installing such parts, be absolutely certain that none of your truck's suspension or steering components have become damaged. Never compensate for collision or wear damage with the use of

shims or offset bearing caps. Replace defective parts before adjusting caster or camber. It is not advisable to bend the axle housing to make a caster or camber correction.

IFS models with torsion bars have the added benefit of adjustable ride height, i.e., a means for adjusting the A-arm position to restore proper frame height. This adjustment also contributes to correct caster and camber settings.

Field Fix To Get Home

A front end alignment is a good safeguard after any serious off-pavement pounding or hard bout with washboard. In an emergency, you can restore toe-in in the field—at least close enough to keep your precious tire rubber from peeling away like an apple's skin.

Back woods straightening of the tie rod could save a walk home and allow your truck to track reasonably straight. As for the permanence of such a fix, realize that any straightened steering linkage part should be replaced as soon as possible.

> **CAUTION —**
> *Many frame and axle specialists can skillfully straighten a slightly bent solid axle (and even pull out several degrees of frame kink). No professional, however, will reuse a bent piece of steering linkage.*

For just getting back to civilization, be very cautious not to break the parts as you straighten them. Use care to distribute force over a broad area, while centering the pull at the bent section. If the kink is at the threaded portion of a tie rod, leave it alone. Threads respond badly to stretching, and breakage is very likely.

Attach a tow strap to an immoveable object—like the tree stump that caused all this trouble! Use the truck's power to gently pull the tie rod straight.

If your truck has a winch, a tree and a snatch block provide an ideal alternative. Park the truck in low range and low gear (manual transmission) or Park (automatic) and low range. Shut off the engine, set the parking brake and block the wheels securely.

> **CAUTION —**
> *On models with automatic transmission, never use only Park range when you winch another vehicle from a stationary location. Severe loading of the chassis could break the tiny parking pawl within the transmission. Always set the parking brake firmly.*

Anchor the snatch block securely, with a tree-saver strap if required. Run the cable forward, and loop it 180° through the snatch block. Attach the hook to the tie-rod. Use your winch remote control to operate the winch while watching the tie-rod from a safe distance.

Straighten the tie rod only enough to provide safe clearance for moving parts and approximate wheel alignment. Once you straighten the tube or sleeve, adjust toe-in if possible.

When adjusting wheel alignment or installing new steering linkage pieces, always center the tie-rod ends.

The ball studs and their sockets should align correctly before you tighten the sleeve clamps. Make sure each tie-rod end has its full range of motion. Also be sure that each tie-rod end is safely threaded into the sleeve.

A Wooded Backdrop For Your Alignment Shop

Temporary toe-in can be set with a few hand tools, a tie-rod sleeve wrench, a tape measure, and a portable frame jack. Center the steering (pitman arm) before beginning. Set the steering wheel for normal, straight ahead driving, then jack one front wheel slightly off the ground. Without a toe adjusting bar and scribe for drawing lines around the tire centerlines, the next best tool for a primitive "get home only" alignment is a piece of chalk.

Fig. 11-28. *Loosen the tie rod clamps and stabilizer mount, then turn the tie rod tube or sleeve to adjust its length. The adjusting tube, often stubborn from rust and scale at the tie rod threads, may require a pipe wrench(s) or sleeve adjuster tool to rotate.*

Fig. 11-27. *After straightening the tie-rod with a tow strap, the Lantern Alignment Shop opens. Raise the driver's side wheel slightly from the ground and reference mark the front tire tread. Keeping the steering wheel straight ahead, measure between the front treads of the tires and the rear reference marks. This will indicate the degree of misalignment.*

Fig. 11-29. *Safely position the sleeve clamps after confirming the final measurement. Clamps must not interfere with steering linkage movement or other components.*

Carefully note the tread pattern of your front tires. Find reference niches that are easy to identify. Hold the tape measure level, close to the mid-point of each tire's diameter. Make sure that the tape does not interfere with suspension parts, and pull it snugly from the opposite tire's mark.

If you encounter an obstacle while pulling the tape straight, drop the level of the tape, rematch the tread pattern, and try again. Once the tape is level, make an accurate note of the length between your two niche marks.

Perform the same procedure at the rear of the front tires. Again, attempt to draw a level line, close to the tire's horizontal mid-line without parts interference. Note the length between these tread pattern niches. (Make sure your chosen tread patterns match those used at the front.)

These two measurements form the basis for your toe-in alignment. For simplicity, use an emergency toe-in spec of zero. Both front and rear measurements should read the same. (Were our goal 1/8" toe-in, the rear measurement would be 1/8" longer than the front. Simple? Well, with practice it gets easier.)

A bent tie rod shortens the distance between the steering arms. On a solid axle 4x4 truck with its steering linkage forward of the axle housing, this toes the front wheels inward. Under such conditions, the bend will cause a long measurement at the backside tread.

To shorten or lengthen the tie rod, loosen the tie rod end clamps to allow rotation of the adjusting tube/sleeve. Note the left-hand or right-hand threads at each end of the tube, and also the amount of thread screwed into each sleeve end. If you must lengthen the tie rod, be careful not to unthread the tube so far that the tie-rod thread fitup becomes too shallow and unsafe.

The tube may not rotate easily. Moisture, rust, and scale cause seizure of tie-rod end threads. A rust penetrant will sometimes help. Rotate the tube, checking the

Fig. 11-30. Make sure plenty of tie rod thread remains within the sleeve/tube ends. Tighten clamps and make certain that parts move freely as you turn the steering wheel. Envision suspension movement, and make sure of adequate clearance when the chassis, control arms or axle beam moves.

Fig. 11-31. A new spring centerbolt replaces sheared item at the axle's spring perch. These bolts can break during heavy off-pavement pounding. The result is axle shift and misalignment. Odd steering can result.

fore and aft tire measurements often. When the measurement is correct, tighten the clamps securely.

Many of us have been fortunate enough not to hit tree stumps or rocks. It's wise, however, to travel prepared. Whether we experience trouble or find ourselves able to help others, survival skills help. A slow drive to pavement with a temporary field fix sure beats walking! Success can sometimes be a twelve-mph trip to civilization—with your truck's heater humming, windshield wipers swishing and headlights leading the way.

Chapter 12

Brakes and Wheel Bearings

P ROPERLY FUNCTIONING WHEEL BEARINGS and brakes are essential to safe driving. Inspect your truck's wheel bearings and brakes regularly. Perform all brake work with careful attention to cleanliness, correct specifications and proper working procedures.

> *WARNING —*
> *• Brake friction materials such as brake linings or brake pads may contain asbestos fibers. Do not create dust by grinding, sanding, or cleaning the pads with compressed air. Avoid breathing any asbestos fibers or dust. Breathing asbestos can cause serious diseases such as asbestosis or cancer, and may result in death. Use only approved methods to clean brake components containing asbestos.*
>
> *• Brake fluid is poisonous. Wear safety glasses when working with brake fluid, and wear rubber gloves to prevent brake fluid from entering your bloodstream through cuts and scratches. Do not siphon brake fluid with your mouth.*

1. FRONT WHEEL BEARINGS

All U.S. market Toyota trucks have used tapered roller type front wheel bearings. Tapered roller bearings provide for slight float. While maintaining the vehicle load, properly adjusted rollers can still move laterally (axially) within the clearances of the inner and outer bearing races. Ball bearings, by contrast, cannot tolerate any axial play and require a pre-load rather than end play adjustment.

Any type of rolling bearing will micro-slip (slide or scuff) slightly, and all bearings suffer chronic wear at their rollers, balls, and races. The most common bearing race, roller or ball steel is a chromium-alloy, usually SAE 52100 bearing race steel.

This is tough stuff (ranging between 60 and 68 on the Rockwell C scale tests for hardness). These materials furnish high rolling mileage, but the hardness makes races vulnerable to impact damage and pitting from abrasive contaminants. For this reason, thorough cleaning, inspection, and periodic bearing repacking with a suitable grease is necessary.

Bearing Fundamentals

Although wheel bearing service procedures and exact adjusting specifications differ among models, some general points apply to all Toyota trucks. (Adjustment standards and methods for your truck are available in the OEM Toyota repair manual or a professional level service guide.)

Fig. 12-1. *Tapered roller front wheel bearings require an end play adjustment. On trucks with inner and outer tapered roller front wheel bearings, a specified in and out movement of the bearing assembly provides proper running tolerance. Toyota measures this tolerance in spring scale pull at the wheel lug studs and/or axial (end) play at the hub.*

Fig. 12-2. *Inspect the spindle surface where the wheel bearings ride. On both 2WD and 4x4 front spindles, any wear, galling or play will affect the adjustment of the bearings. Check closely for cracks, especially if your truck has overly wide aftermarket wheels and oversize tires. Always replace worn parts.*

For tapered roller wheel bearings, precise wheel bearing adjustment takes end play into account. End play is measurable with a dial indicator attached to the wheel hub, outer brake drum face or rotor. Push the brake drum

Fig. 12-3. *The disc rotor and wheel hub rotate as an integral unit. Correct disc brake rotor lateral runout is critical. Trueness of rotor and proper adjustment of the wheel bearings provide acceptable runout.*

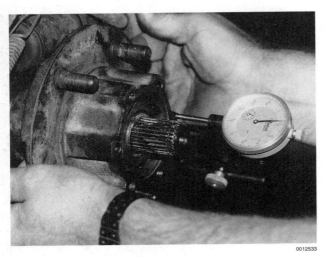

Fig. 12-4. *Dial indicator on magnetic stand measures wheel bearing end play on models with tapered roller wheel bearings. This measurement addresses the acceptable range of bearing roller movement (axially) on the races. Hold the hub flange at 9 and 3 o'clock, push the hub straight in and pull straight out while measuring end play. Check your OEM repair manual for end play specifications.*

or rotor straight inward with both hands. (Push evenly to avoid cocking the hub to one side). Take a dial indicator reading, aiming straight toward the spindle.

The dial indicator measures end play when you pull the hub outward. Do not rock the drum or rotor, or a false reading will result. End play is the straight inward and outward (lateral) movement of the hub along the spindle's axis.

Bearing Survival

The two most common causes of bearing failure are poor maintenance and abuse. Poor maintenance includes neglecting periodic cleaning or failure to repack and properly adjust the bearings.

For 4x4 trucks, abuse takes on several additional forms. Such a truck may sport oversized custom wheels and tires, or perhaps a change in weight on the front end, the result of a V-8 transplant or a front mounted winch. Operating the truck with either too much load on the bearings or excessive lateral stress can cause damage.

Often, bearing failure results from using radically offset (reversed) custom wheels. Shifting the tire centerline outboard from the stock location causes vehicle weight to act as leverage against the wheel hub and bearings. With a front mounted winch or a weighty V-8 engine transplant, even more weight bears directly on each wheel hub! If that same weight applies with the tire centerlines located further outboard, the bearings must now resist an added amount of leveraged force.

Wheel Bearing Service

Always service wheel bearings with the correct grease. All wheel bearing greases are not the same. Mixing grease types can severely damage parts and compromise your safety.

When repacking your truck's front wheel bearings, begin with a thorough solvent cleaning. Make certain that no solvent residue remains on the bearings before repacking them. Also clean the spindle, inner wheel hub and races. Wash, wipe and dry parts thoroughly to remove any traces of solvent before repacking the bearings with fresh, clean grease.

> *WARNING —*
> *Never spin the bearings with compressed air. Severe bodily harm could result from a bearing assembly flying apart at speed.*

> *CAUTION —*
> *Use the recommended wheel bearing grease for your model and type of wheel bearings. Disc brake equipped vehicles demand exacting wheel bearing adjustments and highly heat resistant lubricant.*

Always replace grease seals. Do not attempt to reuse them. Installing new front or rear wheel seals lowers the risk of parts failure. At the front wheel hubs, they prevent moisture and dirt from entering the hub assembly. Rear axle seals prevent grease or gear lubricant from ruining brake lining and causing failure of the rear brakes.

Use proper tools, refer to your OEM- or professional-level repair guidebook, and take your time when servicing your wheel bearings. On Toyota 4x4 models with a bendable locking washer between the two spindle nuts, install a new washer whenever fatigue is obvious. On 2WD models, always install a new cotter pin after adjusting the castellated or adjuster nut and aligning the retainer (if so equipped) with the cotter pin hole. Done properly, a wheel bearing re-pack and seal replacement will last for many miles.

CAUTION —

Wheel bearing service and adjustment is a critical part of vehicle maintenance. Your safety and the truck's reliability depend upon proper bearing adjustment. Always follow the adjusting procedure and specifications described in your OEM Toyota truck repair manual or a professional-level service guidebook. On models so equipped, use the correct size and type of cotter pin, and secure the cotter pin properly.

Fig. 12-6. *Clean and dry hub and rotor assembly. Swab clean grease on the hub's inner cavity, filling the grease recess and providing a dam to prevent hot grease from leaving the bearings. Install the freshly packed inner wheel bearing and a new grease seal. The hub is ready for installation. Keep grease away from brake linings. (Shown here is a 4x4 front hub)*

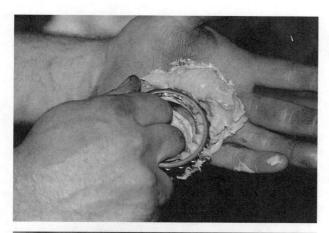

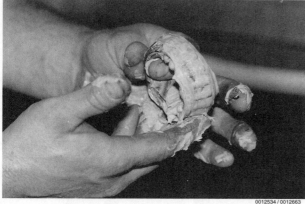

Fig. 12-5. *When hand packing a bearing, squeeze the grease between the wider end of the bearing cage and the inner race. Make sure grease flows out the opposite end of the rollers. Go around the entire bearing assembly at least two full times to assure thorough saturation. Once grease fills all spaces between the rollers, spread a generous film of grease around the outside of the bearing and cage. Special wheel bearing packers make this job easier and assure complete grease penetration of the rollers.*

Fig. 12-7. *Install the repacked outer wheel bearing. I build a dam of additional grease between outer side of bearing and face of thrust washer.*

Fig. 12-8. *Thread the adjuster nut carefully onto the spindle. 4x4 front wheel hubs require a special spindle nut wrench. Consult the OEM Toyota truck repair manual for adjustment procedures and torque figures.*

Fig. 12-9. *Confirm layout and order of parts assembly in your repair manual. 4x4 models use this type of lock washer between two hex nuts. Once end play is correct with outer lock nut torqued to specification, bend lockwasher tabs (shown here) to secure the nuts. This is a safety procedure. To ensure that nuts will not loosen, secure tabs properly by bending one tab inward and one outward against hex nut flats. When finished, check hub end play with a dial indicator.*

2. THE BRAKING SYSTEM

All Toyota truck models covered in this book have brakes that actuate by hydraulic pressure. The basic hydraulic apply system begins with a brake pedal and master cylinder. 1958–66 Land Cruiser brake systems have a single reservoir master cylinder mounted against the firewall and actuated by a suspended brake pedal.

In 1967, the U.S. Department of Transportation invoked safety standards requiring dual hydraulic circuits on the master cylinder. All U.S. market Toyota trucks from that year forward have separate hydraulic supply lines for the rear and front brakes. If either end of the system should fail, brakes still operate at the opposite axle.

For light trucks, the dual brake system was a major advancement, eliminating the risk of total brake loss in the event of a fluid leak. For the many truck chassis exposed to fallen trees, jagged rocks and raw terrain, the pre-1967 single braking system offers little protection. If a brake hose snaps or a steel pipe tears, the system loses pressure and the brakes fail completely.

> *WARNING* —
> *Brake friction materials such as brake linings or brake pads may contain asbestos fibers. Do not create dust by grinding, sanding, or cleaning the pads with compressed air. Avoid breathing any asbestos fibers or dust. Breathing asbestos can cause serious diseases such as asbestosis or cancer, and may result in death. Use only approved methods to clean brake components containing asbestos.*

Pedal Warning Signals

A spongy brake pedal is caused by air in the hydraulic system or low brake fluid level. This leads to poor braking action and rust within the system. Check for leaks and bleed any air from the system.

Low fluid can be due to normal lining wear. Periodically verify the thickness of lining, check for proper lining-to-drum clearance, and top off fluid after adjusting the brakes. On models with rear wheel emergency/parking brakes, be certain that the emergency/parking brake is released before adjusting the wheel brakes.

Another sign of trouble is the pulsating brake pedal, characterized by a rhythmical pumping action during braking. Causes could include warped drums or rotors, defective brake hardware, a bent front spindle or rear axle shaft, and loose wheel bearings. These symptoms can occur suddenly, often following an off-road pounding or submersion in water.

> *CAUTION* —
> *Old brake fluid has likely drawn moisture, especially in a truck with an atmospherically vented master cylinder. (Conventional brake fluid is "hygroscopic.") This lowers the boiling point of brake fluid, increasing the risk of brake fluid failure under hard braking.*

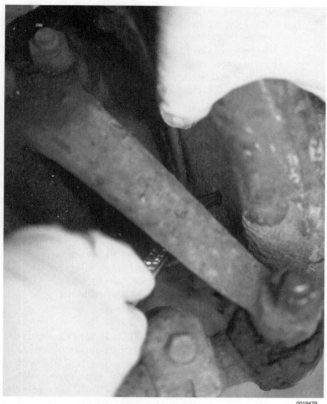

Fig. 12-10. *On earlier truck models without self-adjusting brake mechanisms, you must periodically adjust the drum brake lining to avoid a low pedal. With the exception of earlier Land Cruisers, Toyota truck rear brakes double as the parking/emergency brake. Watch for oil, grit and contaminants that will make your wheel brakes—and parking brake—ineffective. Also check the parking brake cable frequently, and lube it periodically.*

Trailer pullers and those who use their Toyota truck for hauling heavy cargos should change brake fluid periodically and avoid overheating the brakes whenever possible. (Recreational or tow vehicles that set for long off-season periods are especially vulnerable to brake fluid moisture contamination.) Always use lower gears on a steep downgrade to relieve the load on your truck's brakes. Let the brakes cool down thoroughly when severe heat-up has occurred. Any pedal fade is a sure sign of trouble.

High pedal pressure accompanied by increased stopping distance is brake fade. Fade suggests poor lining quality, drum or rotor warpage, contaminated brake fluid, excessive rotor runout or materials that have fatigued severely.

Brake pull, another common trouble symptom, results from contaminated brake lining, misadjusted shoes or sticky hydraulic cylinders. If brake pads or shoes require replacement, always change lining at both wheels of that axle to avoid uneven braking. Ideally, you should change lining and renew the brake cylinders at all four wheels (both axles) for optimal braking efficiency.

Other Brake Woes

Metallic brake noise signals danger. Generally, metal-on-metal sounds imply total loss of lining and the dragging of shoes or pad backs against a drum or rotor. These symptoms quickly degenerate into damaged rotors or drums, often beyond the point of repair.

Periodic inspection of your truck's brakes can help prevent this trouble. Check for leaks, worn lining and heat damage. Look closely at hoses and brake pipes, especially in those areas exposed to debris and trail abuse. Periodically, remove brake drums to assess lining wear.

> *WARNING —*
> *Brake friction materials such as brake linings or brake pads may contain asbestos fibers. Do not create dust by grinding, sanding, or cleaning the pads with compressed air. Avoid breathing any asbestos fibers or dust. Breathing asbestos can cause serious diseases such as asbestosis or cancer, and may result in death. Use only approved methods to clean brake components containing asbestos.*

Brake Fluid Precautions

Safety is at stake when you replenish your truck's fluids. Accidental use of mineral-based oils in the hydraulic brake or clutch system can cause swelling of rubber seals and complete failure of the brakes or clutch.

> *WARNING —*
> *• Brake fluid is poisonous. Wear safety glasses when working with brake fluid, and wear rubber gloves to prevent brake fluid from entering the bloodstream through cuts and scratches. Do not siphon brake fluid with your mouth.*
>
> *• Always use DOT 3 or higher rating brake fluid in the master cylinder/braking system or hydraulic clutch system of your truck. Never add motor oil or any substance other than brake fluid to a hydraulic brake system. Do not mix silicone brake fluid with conventional brake fluid.*

Clean, moisture-free brake fluid is fundamental to brake safety. The master cylinder cover must seal tightly. When topping off fluid, use clean brake fluid with the DOT rating specified by Toyota—or better.

Exposed to the atmosphere, brake fluid has a short shelf life. Keep lids sealed snugly and never store fluid in an open container. DOT 3 fluid, fresh out of a new can, boils at 401° F or higher, while the absorption of only 3% moisture reduces the boiling point to 284° F. This is ample justification for the annual flush and replenishment with clean brake fluid. (See maintenance chapter for further details.)

Apply special care when handling brake service parts and brake fluid. Since brake fluid has an affinity for water, store a tightly resealed brake fluid container in a dry location. The need for cleanliness cannot be overstated, as hydraulic brake cylinders will fail when exposed to abrasive debris or mineral/petroleum based oils, solvents and greases.

Brake Fluid Service

Your truck's brakes require regular attention. Routine concerns include checking the hydraulic brake fluid, inspecting hoses and steel pipes for damage, and noting the lining left on disc brake pads and brake shoes. With clean hands and a clean master cylinder cap, check the brake fluid level at each lubrication interval.

Dusty trails, stream crossings, slush and snow expose various brake parts to water, abrasive dirt and road salts. Many Toyota trucks have atmospherically vented filler caps. These models face the risk of contaminants and moisture entering the reservoir.

The air vent in the master cylinder cap often draws dust and moisture into the master cylinder reservoir. It is common for abrasive sludge to accumulate in the base of the master cylinder reservoir. A complete system flush and overhaul of each cylinder is the only remedy for this kind of contamination problem.

Fig. 12-11. *Some Toyota trucks have a translucent plastic master cylinder reservoir. On these models, you can inspect brake fluid level without removing the cap. Before removing your Toyota truck's master cylinder fill cap, vacuum or brush away any dirt. With a clean hand, carefully remove cap to add fluid. Fill to level noted on reservoir.*

Fig. 12-12. *1967 and newer Toyota trucks (such as this FJ40) feature tandem master cylinders, mounted high on the firewall, a sensible distance from debris and water. Still, always clean around the master cylinder assembly before removing the fill caps.*

NOTE —
Take care when checking the fluid. Make certain that debris and grit cannot fall into the open brake fluid reservoir. Before removing the master cylinder fill plug or cap, clean the area thoroughly—with a shop vacuum cleaner if necessary.

A positive design feature of many Toyota master cylinders is the removable brake fluid filter at the top of the master cylinder reservoir. This filter/screen will trap larger particles of abrasive dust and grit that would otherwise pose an immediate threat to rubber seals within the cylinder. Keep the filter/screen intact, clean and sealing properly.

NOTE —
A 4x4 truck's brake system can face more hazards than a 2WD model. Submerging the chassis in running stream water, or driving through a deeply flooded roadway, can increase the risk of contaminating the hydraulic braking system.

Most truck owners and mechanics ignore flushing the hydraulic brake system. Years ago, brake parts manufacturers recommended an annual pressure flushing with a special flushing compound (usually containing denatured alcohol) or pumping clean brake fluid through the brake system. Replacement of all rubber cups, seals and boots would follow.

For the Toyota truck that has an atmospherically vented master cylinder, for a truck that sets for long periods, or for the 4x4 that drives through streams on a regular basis, periodic flushing of the hydraulic brake system is a good idea. At the very least, you should pump fresh brake fluid through the system annually and bleed out all air.

Make certain that enough brake fluid passes through to carry away as much stale fluid as possible. If your truck has a master cylinder with a cap that vents the reservoir to atmosphere, periodic inspection and service of your hydraulic system will contribute to the safety and preservation of expensive brake parts.

Even on a master cylinder that does not have a vent-to-atmosphere type cap (such as a master cylinder with a bellows type seal), moisture still enters the hydraulic brake system at approximately 3% volume per year.

For details on servicing, flushing or bleeding air from your truck's hydraulic brake system, consult the OEM Toyota truck repair manual for your model. Toyota truck brake system designs vary widely, and modern brake designs, especially a newer Anti-lock Braking System (ABS), call for much different service procedures and precautions than earlier models.

Brake Service And Overhaul Tips

Avoid introducing contaminants or abrasive foreign material into the hydraulic reservoir(s). Such debris damages sensitive rubber parts within the master cylinder and hydraulic system. Late model trucks with aluminum master cylinder bores are especially vulnerable to scoring.

During brake system overhauls, check the labels on brake parts cleaners. Many contain petroleum solvents or distillates. These cleaners work fine as metal parts degreasers. However, petroleum-or mineral-based solvents and oils can cause the wheel cylinder, caliper and master cylinder rubber parts to swell up and fail.

WARNING —
Never use mineral or petroleum-based solvents or oils around rubber parts.

Denatured alcohol and automotive brake fluid are among the few substances that will not destroy rubber. The traditional cleaner for critical brake parts is denatured alcohol. (Allow alcohol to evaporate completely before filling the system with brake fluid.) Your Toyota truck repair manual should indicate which cleaning substances to use. Read safety precautions before handling any of these cleaning substances.

Always inspect hydraulic brake cylinders for pits and corrosion. If in doubt, replace the cylinder. If rebuildable, remove the cylinder from the system and hone its bore lightly with a suitable brake cylinder hone.

Hone just enough to break the glaze. Be certain not to leave debris or abrasive material in the cylinder. Check the bore diameter. If within tolerance, bath the cylinder in a dishwashing soap (like Ivory Liquid), scrub with a toothbrush, rinse thoroughly in clear water, and dry with clean compressed air. Assemble new rubber parts with clean brake fluid or special brake rubber parts assembly lube.

When servicing disc brakes, make certain that floating (self-centering) caliper assemblies and pistons slide freely. If signs of friction exist, overhaul or replace the caliper.

Fig. 12-15. Many late model master cylinders have aluminum housings. Most shops regard such assemblies as a throw away item, finding them ill-suited for overhaul. Deep scratches and scoring, common traits when these parts require service, can render such a master cylinder useless.

Fig. 12-13. Disc caliper piston scoring resulted from the severe heat generated as a rotor disintegrated. Piston seizure can cause brake lockup or severe brake pull.

Fig. 12-14. Wheel cylinders cannot tolerate scoring. If honed, this cylinder will lose too much material. Pitting and scoring result from moisture and wear. Periodic flushing could have prevented this problem.

Fig. 12-16. Overhauling disc brake calipers requires cleanliness, care and proper tools. Here, a new seal seats in a reconditioned, safely sized bore.

If four-wheeling or off-pavement bashing has caused damage to your truck's hydraulic brake lines or fittings, replace parts only with DOT-approved brake hardware. Tees, hoses, junction blocks, and valving should meet or exceed your vehicle's original equipment brake standards.

Use pre-formed steel brake pipe. This tubing, cut to length and double-flared at each end, comes complete with flare nuts and ready to install. Once you have shaped the new tubing with a tubing bender, use a flare nut wrench to remove and replace the brake pipes. Torque flare nuts to the manufacturer's specifications listed in the OEM Toyota truck repair manual for your model.

> **WARNING —**
> *Avoid introducing debris or contaminants into the hydraulic system when changing brake hoses or pipes. Always bleed air from the system and check for leaks before driving.*

While servicing your brakes, inspect the wheel bearings and axle seals. A leaky rear axle seal can ruin new brake lining quickly. Preserve your truck's braking system. Apply preventive care wherever possible. This is your best safeguard against losing your brakes.

Brake Linings

Whether your Toyota truck is bone stock or highly modified, brake performance is important. Although we refine our engines, transmissions and axles, brakes often get overlooked.

> **WARNING —**
> *Brake friction materials such as brake linings or brake pads may contain asbestos fibers. Do not create dust by grinding, sanding, or cleaning the pads with compressed air. Avoid breathing any asbestos fibers or dust. Breathing asbestos can cause serious diseases such as asbestosis or cancer, and may result in death. Use only approved methods to clean brake components containing asbestos.*

Improving your truck's brake system begins with brake lining. Organic friction materials use asbestos, usually in a phenolic-resin compound. Asbestos, an environmental hazard, places the brake mechanic at risk. Use of an approved respirator and protective wear has become mandatory for asbestos and brake industry workers.

The brake and clutch industry's attraction to asbestos has been its exceptional heat resistance, low wear and minimal noise. Asbestos health risks outweigh benefits, however, and asbestos-bearing organic friction materials now border on extinction.

Bendix, a respected industry supplier of quality brake parts, advises several precautions when purchasing new brake lining: 1) If your truck has semi-metallic brake pads, always refit with semi-metallic lining; 2) Replace asbestos/organic pads and shoes with comparable lining; and 3) Don't replace OEM organic or organic/asbestos lining with semi-metallic lining—unless sanctioned by the vehicle manufacturer.

Fig. 12-17. *Age, fatigue and overheating cause brake lining failure. Thinner lining loses heat resistance, as witnessed by these heat-cracked disc brake pads.*

Fig. 12-18. *Thinned brake lining shows heat crack formation. Replace parts now to avoid the risk of lining separation.*

As of this book's publication, asbestos is still legal for some applications. All manufacturers, however, will stop using asbestos as suitable non-asbestos replacement products become available. Stay informed on this issue, and avoid using asbestos products whenever possible.

Semi-metallic brake lining, suited for front disc pad material, provides cooler operation. Under severe braking conditions and heavy loading, semi-metallic lining rapidly draws heat away from the rotors. Excessive heat, the cause of fade and pad/rotor damage, is less likely with semi-metallic brake materials.

Manufacturers recommend that replacement brake lining match the OEM material standards. Poor braking, short pad life, and rotor scoring or warping will otherwise result. From a safety standpoint, fade leads to complete brake failure. If you have questions about your truck's original equipment brake lining, consult your local Toyota dealership or a brake parts supplier for guidelines.

Fig. 12-19. New brake lining has code marks. Many states require edge coding, which helps consumers determine lining type and quality.

Fig. 12-21. Non-directional finish of rotors assures semi-metallic lining break-in. Some manufacturers recommend a brake lathe grinder for this task, while others find a hand held drill motor and disc sander acceptable. Wear an approved particle mask, or a federally approved respirator if you suspect presence of asbestos, and safety goggles.

Like engines and other automotive components, brakes require break-in. For semi-metallic brake pads, Bendix recommends light use of the brakes for the first 150–200 miles. When pads are new, avoid panic stops if possible. Instead of hard burn-ins, Bendix suggests 15 to 20 slow stops from about 30 mph. Use light to moderate brake pedal pressure and allow at least 30 seconds of recovery between each stop.

As another consideration, semi-metallic lining requires heavier pedal pressure when cold or wet. Some disc brake trucks with heavier (integral with the wheel hub) front rotors will dissipate heat so effectively that a semi-metallic retrofit lining cannot work at peak efficiency.

Reciprocally, a less expensive organic lining will overheat and wear rapidly when installed on a late model, lightweight rotor system designed for semi-metallic lining. This is one more reason to stick with original equipment recommendations.

Drums And Rotors

The trueness of a rotor or drum is essential. Drums and rotors should be checked for scoring, hard spots, warpage, lateral runout (rotors), and proper inside diameter (drums) or thickness (rotors). Micrometers for this task are common to brake shops and automotive machine shops. If the rotor or drum surface is at all suspect, resurfacing on a brake lathe is necessary.

Rotors, drums and lining are expensive. Take care to tighten each set of wheel nuts gradually and in cross. Whenever possible, use a torque wrench for final tightening.

Always recheck air gun tightened wheel nuts when you have new tires mounted commercially. If too tight, jack up the wheel, loosen the whole set of nuts, and retightened properly. If too loose, bring nuts to specification in cross sequence.

Fig. 12-20. Coat new pad backs before installation. The special silicone grease dries quickly and helps prevent brake squeal on disc brake systems.

Semi-metallic Brake Pad Break-in

If your truck can use semi-metallic disc pads, special preparation of the rotors is necessary. When resurfacing your rotors, Bendix recommends a satin-smooth final cut, followed by a non-directional finish. Correct rotor finish will eliminate squeal and hard pedal action.

Semi-metallic pad replacement always includes rotor resurfacing—even if very minor work is necessary to true the rotor and condition the surfaces. The final non-directional finish assures quieter operation and quick seating of pads.

Fig. 12-22. *Read the thickness and wear of the rotor with an outside micrometer. Determine whether to cut the rotors or buy a new pair. Better ventilated, lightweight rotors are often candidates for semi-metallic pads. Your local Toyota dealership's parts department can verify which type of lining is acceptable.*

Fig. 12-24. *Resurfaced rear brake drum assures a quality brake job. Lining will wear-in better and offer complete contact with the drum surface. For safe braking, opposite wheel's brakes should be serviced at the same time. (On a four-wheel drum brake system, service all four wheels at the same time.)*

Fig. 12-23. *A badly scored rotor cannot be reused. Here, disc brake lining and rivets wore into the rotor, destroying its surface and causing complete failure of the front braking system.*

Fig. 12-25. *Professionals install hardware kits with every brake overhaul. Old springs and retainers fatigue from heat, while new pieces contribute to proper shoe alignment and action. New wheel cylinder boots protect against moisture and debris. Once the cylinder overhaul is complete, new brake shoes and hardware fit into place. Toyota has used several brake shoe types. Make certain that the shoes and other hardware fit in the manner described in your OEM Toyota repair manual. Shoes may have different length lining that must fit in the correct position.*

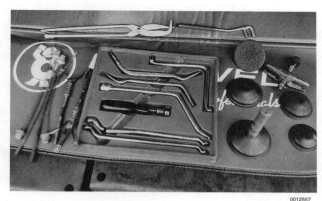

Fig. 12-26. *Specialty tools used for brake work include seal drivers, piston removal tools, adjuster spoons, bleeder wrenches, spring pliers and retainer/removal tool. Seen also is a set of master cylinder bench bleeding hoses.*

Fig. 12-27. *Wheel cylinder cups and dust boots are available in a variety of sizes. Replace these parts at each brake overhaul. Some trucks call for an annual brake system flush and replacement of these cups and boots. The Toyota owner's manual or OEM repair manual for your model describes service intervals and procedures.*

CAUTION —

A common cause of disc brake rotor damage is over-torquing the wheel nuts. Wheel nuts too loose or tight, or tightened out of sequence, can warp a rotor. Use of an impact gun is the easiest way to overtighten nuts. Aside from the risk of breaking lug studs, overtightening enlarges wheel holes and warps disc rotors. Improperly torqued wheel nuts can warp a rotor enough to cause pulsation of the brake pedal and premature pad wear.

Fig. 12-28. *Other damage, like these over-torqued and broken wheel studs, adds to restoration cost. Broken studs usually result from overtorquing during wheel installation.*

Fig. 12-29. *Here is a common cause of premature rear brake lining failure. This semi-floating axle's bearing seal has leaked. Gear oil saturated the brake shoes and rubber dust boots.*

Chapter 13

Body and Detailing

HARSH CLIMATES, brush scratches and off-pavement bashing tear unmercifully at your truck's body. Over the years, a truck also accumulates its share of oxidation. The battle against rust is an endless vigil. You must watch constantly for fresh scratches and exposed metal. In salt air regions, including areas with corrosive salt spread on winter roadways, truck bodies are especially vulnerable. Bright metal, chrome and painted surfaces can oxidize rapidly.

1. BATTLING RUST

Sadly, hundreds of thousands of otherwise restorable Toyota trucks have wound up as rusty hulks at recycling yards. Rust is a chronic problem for any truck, even more so for the 4x4 models. Earlier FJ40 and FJ55 Land Cruisers often succumb to severe rustout of sheet metal.

In addition to environmental hazards, some truck bodies have weak sheet metal areas or a section that provides very poor water drainage. Mid-1980s and newer Toyota models have more extensive use of galvanized (zinc treated) metals, plastic or rubberized trim and special paint processes. These models can resist rust much better than older trucks.

The popularity of early Land Cruisers continues at a feverish pace, however, many restorers discover these early models were built with a scant amount of rust protection. Despite their age, Toyota's oldest trucks remain desirable because of outstanding chassis and drivetrain design. Body sheet metal, surprisingly, has been the weak link in older Land Cruiser and pickup quality.

The most susceptible areas for rust are the front fenders, tail lamp and tailgate areas, the tub/floorboards on FJ25 and FJ40 models, and the huge rear quarter panels of FJ45 and FJ55 Station Wagons. Recycling yards, body shops and sheet metal and fiberglass parts vendors have done a thriving business around replacement body panels for these trucks.

Rust on an older Land Cruiser or Toyota pickup reads like a regional road map of North America. In fairness to Toyota, the model years most affected by rust also repre-

0019620

Fig. 13-1. *Maintaining an FJ40 means preventing body rust, a major concern with vintage Toyota trucks. Painstaking detail* *work has preserved this exceptional 'Cruiser.*

sent those periods when winter road salt was used extensively in the U.S. As a consequence, Midwestern and Northeastern trucks have fared the worst. In drier climates of the West and Southwest, Toyota trucks have done a far better job of resisting rust.

Rust forms at hood hinges and other parts of the body where paint can wear thin. Bare metal on inner fender panels, the cowl, floorboards, grill shell and front fenders will rust quickly in corrosive or moist air.

With the body and chassis thoroughly cleaned, inspect your truck for rust. Pay close attention to areas with add-on accessories, which can expose bare sheet metal. Look for poor sealing and exfoliation (bubbling), an indication of rust formation beneath the paint.

If you suspect rust, remove the accessory and treat the area with thorough sanding, primer/sealing and paint as needed. When damage is excessive, consult a local body shop.

Fix It Yourself

The flatter panels on a truck body make a good place to enhance your metalwork and painting skills. Restoration and maintenance can include sealing, priming and painting your truck.

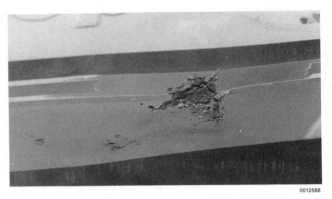

Fig. 13-3. *This is insidious rust. Hidden behind a trim panel, rust now presses through the sheetmetal. Watch for high spots like this.*

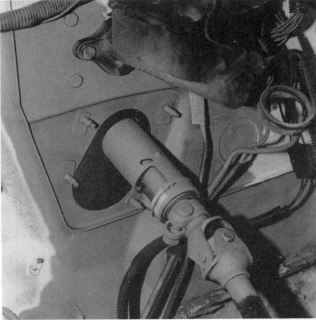

Fig. 13-2. *This area may look ominous because of surface rust. A professional body worker sees this as salvageable. Surface rust on firewall, although unsightly, does not effect the integrity of base sheetmetal. Sandblasting reveals that underlying metal is strong and serviceable.*

Fig. 13-4. *When the carpet rolls back, so can the metal! A small bulge at the outer body surface never suggested this major rust. On older Toyota trucks, especially Land Cruisers, floorboard, door sill and fender bib rust is a major problem. If your truck or a prospective buy needs restoration, look closely for rust. You must always seal around any drilled holes. Carpets may hide an area where water can accumulate and menacing rust forms. Always take rust bubbles or exfoliation seriously.*

Fig. 13-5.   Sandblasting at this metal bulge tells a broader tale. Hidden between an aftermarket trim panel and interior carpet, major rust damage resulted from improper metal seal during installation of the add-on roll bar.

As for your Toyota truck's frame, although made of metals which resist rust perforation, frames also build up surface oxidation. Wear a particle mask and safety goggles, and clean rust with a drill-powered wire brush. Prime and paint surfaces to prevent further problems, using a rust inhibiting primer or paint.

Rust Repairs

Louie Russo, Jr., owner of L. J. Russo's Paint and Body Shop at Lakeside, California, is an auto body and paint master. If your truck restoration includes rust removal, Louie's step-by-step rust repair system provides a good lesson.

Consider these procedures carefully before tackling your truck's rust. Techniques shown here provide a like-new fix and prepare the truck for a quality paint job. This particular repair is common to FJ25 and FJ40 Land Cruiser body tubs and also applies to many other Toyota trucks.

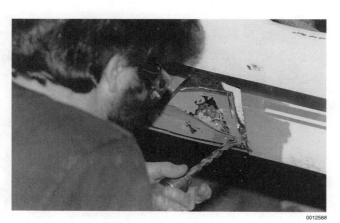

Fig. 13-6.   Factory rivets drilled, Louie Russo separates floorpan from the interior body brace. Extent of rust is still deceptive at this point. This kind of rust can occur on FJ40-type Land Cruiser tubs.

Fig. 13-7.   Louie carefully removes rotted metal. Here, a carbide disc cuts quickly through the sheetmetal brace. Structural integrity of the body is a consideration with this repair. Use an approved particle mask or respirator and goggles around carbide grinding.

Fig. 13-8.   Remove or treat all rust affected metal. At this point, wire brushing and sandblasting will determine strength of metal and pinholes to fill.

Fig. 13-9.   Heavy-gauge metal section from an ancient truck fender has become a replacement piece for the OEM brace. Louie welds the hand-formed repair section into place. Note use of salvageable segment of the original brace. This small portion of metal helps maintain alignment and contours.

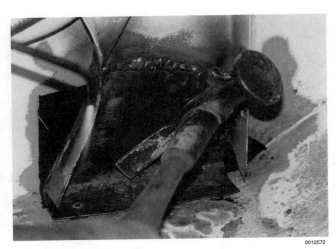

Fig. 13-10. *MIG welded into place, section now fits against the cleaned floorpan. Heat applied to lower bracket flange allows shaping with a body hammer until new brace matches OE fit perfectly. Louie also welded pinholes in floorpan. Surface grinding of welds will restore original appearance.*

Fig. 13-11. *Louie cuts and forms flat piece of sheetmetal to fit cutout. He purposely keeps the original lower roll of body lip to avoid having to reform edge. Drilling and spot-welding outer panel to inner brace duplicates OE engineering. MIG confines heat. Louie strategically lays down welds while carefully quenching hot sheetmetal to maintain shape.*

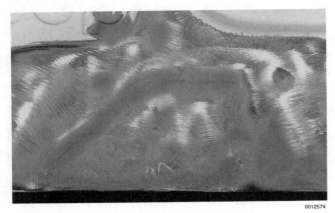

Fig. 13-12. *Surface grinding reveals careful handling of metal. Masterful heat isolation, shrink/stretch control and correct heat diffusion results in near perfect surface straightness.*

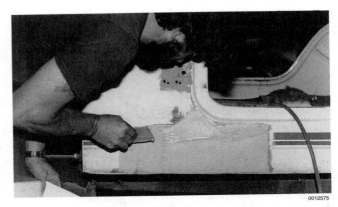

Fig. 13-13. *Louie applies a light coat of plastic body filler to sanding scratches and very slight depressions. Once shaped and sanded, only a tiny amount of plastic will remain. Louie Russo prefers the challenge of metal working to the simpler, plastic fill approach. His work shows good-as-new quality.*

2. BODY DETAILING

As a Toyota truck owner, get to know your local self-service car wash. Here, the combination of soap and high pressure spray can transform a mud-caked truck into respectable suburban driveway material. In minutes, pounds of mud and debris will stream from the body, wheel wells, frame, axles and suspension.

Detailing your truck begins with a thorough wash. Many trucks face as much dirt, sun and abrasive wind as a desert camel, yet there's no protective hair or hide to seal the elements from your truck's paint finish. Magnetic abrasives cling tenaciously to the paint pores, while scorching sun and road salts oxidize the trim and rubber. A cleaner must be gentle enough to leave healthy paint intact, yet still cut and flush the grit from the paint.

There are many commercial car wash solutions on the market. The main objective with any good car soap is to dissolve road oils and gently flush dirt away. Although dishwashing liquids work well, commercial products

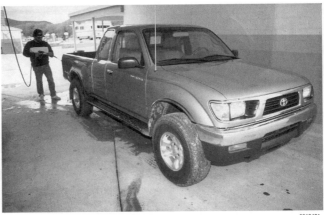

Fig. 13-14. *Local car wash or a home pressure washer will remove major debris after a hard day's work or off-pavement driving.*

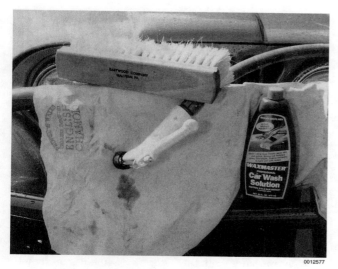

Fig. 13-15. *A spray nozzle, car wash solution, horse hair brush and a genuine English chamois are tools for a safe wash job.*

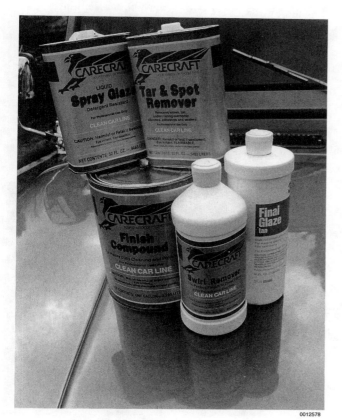

Fig. 13-16. *Eastwood Company's mail order catalog features products for a show-winning appearance. (See text and appendix.)*

might be part of a complete cleaning system, chemically engineered to work with specific waxes or polishes.

Even more important is your washing technique. For a safe wash job around grit and abrasives, avoid scratching the finish. A sponge or wash cloth is hazardous. Special car wash mitts work much better, but hand pressure can still cause grit to press into the paint or drag across the surface.

I always begin with a thorough wash-down using a high pressure washer that attaches to an air compressor source and garden hose. This washer can easily clean dirty engine bays, inner fender wells and the chassis.

CAUTION —
Make sure engine is cool before cleaning. Keep water away from intake and distributor.

For hand washing painted surfaces and trim, the gentle bristles and cushion provided by a horse hair brush reduce the risk of scratches yet still massage foaming soap into paint pores. Your truck's panels will cleanse easily, followed by a gentle rinse of clear water. Use a quality, rubber-nosed faucet nozzle, capable of controlling pressure while protecting the vehicle's finish.

Why Fight Your Paint Finish?

Most truck owners can find better things to do with their weekends than wash and polish a vehicle. Playing in the backwoods and seasonal four-wheeling hold a lot more fun than performing a wax job! In recent years, however, professional detailing equipment has drastically sped up detailing work. Shifting away from disc-sander type buffers, the orbital polishers now appear everywhere—and for good reason.

Traditional buffing methods, especially hand or disc polishing, can leave the paint finish full of swirls. Worse yet, the risk of buffing right through the paint edges scares most non-professional detailers from even attempting to use a disc-type buffer! The gentle orbital buffers, by contrast, offer the first-time user a chance to do a professional polishing job without ruining an expensive paint finish.

As for the risk of paint removal from orbital buffing, I once interviewed Loren E. Doppelt, Senior Product Manager for Waxmaster/Chamberlain. Loren noted, "I've buffed and polished a sample hood at car shows. The hood receives 1,000 buffings before we routinely re-paint it.... Frankly, even then, there's no evidence that the paint is damaged."

Your First Orbital Buffing Job

When your new paint finish turns dull from road film and caked mud, don't panic. Armed with the right detailing chemicals and a quality orbital buffer, you can produce a professional wax job in less than an hour! Park your truck in the shade, and begin by washing it thoroughly. With the metal cool, apply a smooth coating of wax.

The body contours and accessory hardware on many trucks can pose a nightmare for buffing. A steep sloping

Fig. 13-17.   A random orbital waxer/polisher is your best investment and incentive for detail work. Chamberlain's Waxmaster and other quality units are available from retail suppliers.

Fig. 13-18.   This buffer bonnet's grey debris came from a fully cured new paint job after a thorough wash. An orbital buffer, used with a wide range of detailing chemicals, can strip/clean, apply wax or polish and buff the finish to a high luster. Uniform results make hand or disc-type polishing obsolete.

cab, trailer pulling mirrors and abutments sticking out everywhere create a real challenge for an orbital buffer. Still, the promise of uniform buffing action, as opposed to sluggish, ineffective hand waxing, will spur your polishing job forward.

Carnauba based semi-paste wax, mixed with a liquid polish, works best with the orbital buffer. Although the buffer easily works with other chemical products, the combination polish and wax allows a faster, more thorough job. Carnauba based waxes provide better paint breathing and protection from atmospheric hazards.

Apply the wax and polish solution simultaneously to the terry cloth buffing bonnet. Movement of the orbital buffer is easy to master. The technique is much like operating a floor polisher. Application of wax/polish will take

---

Paint Scratch Repairs

Light trucks and four-wheel drive utility vehicles have close scrapes with trees, limbs and brush. Small scratches and rock chips detract from the appearance of your truck, and brush-on touch up paints often leave ugly scars.

Armed with a random orbital buffer, some brush touch-up paint, a sheet of 1200-grit color sanding paper, a 3M Soft Hand Pad and some swirl remover, here's my formula for a super-fast, professional scratch repair:

9:00 a.m.—Slight scratch in hood surface is carefully cleaned and filled with touch-up paint. (5 minutes)

11:00 a.m.—Left in direct sunlight, touch up is completely dry. Move the truck into the shade.

11:30 a.m.—Gently color sand with 1200-grit paper and 3M pad, confining your sanding to the crown of the touch-up paint. Sanding stops when adjacent paint shows signs of ultra-fine, uniform discoloration. (10 minutes)

11:40 a.m.—Swirl remover is applied to orbital buffer pad. Buffing the discolored area, focus directly on the repair. Light use of the buffer edge will concentrate the polishing effort. (2 minutes or less buffing time)

11:48 a.m.—Wipe away remaining swirl remover. Treat the beautifully matched surface to a new coat of wax/polish. (6 minutes)

12:00 p.m.—Load fishing poles into the cab, bed or cargo area of your truck. Grin broadly and drive to the hottest local angling spot. Catch your limit before heading for camp. Note: Releasing fish is optional, if such is your ethic. (Time involved depends on fishing action.)

Fig. 13-19.   An orbital buffer works with any number of specialized products. Shown are Waxmaster and Mothers brands of waxes and polishes.

from thirty to fifty minutes on bodies ranging from a Land Cruiser or 4Runner to the Toyota pickup—including the exterior and interior surfaces of a bed.

The buffer will lay down a uniform blend of wax. Hard to reach and hand applied areas rub easily with the remaining wax/polish on the polishing bonnet. Install a clean cloth and begin buffing. In minutes, the surface will glisten from every angle! Hand buffing with a terry cloth towel brings the inaccessible areas to a high lustre.

Orbital buffing leaves your truck's finish with a protective, penetrating coat of Carnauba wax. Surface oxidized material has transferred to the buffing pads.

Conventional hand waxing, a tedious, unfulfilling task, is now passe. An orbital buffer produces professional results, the first time out. For a sharp appearance that lasts for years, treat your truck to quarterly polish jobs with a random orbital buffer and a quality Carnauba wax/polish.

Weather-beaten Paint

A grossly oxidized finish may still respond to a finishing compound buff out. Seek a quality compound that lifts dead paint by chemical action, not abrasion, and leaves no swirl marks. Follow buffing with a careful polish and wax job.

Badly oxidized finishes may take a full morning and several orbital buffer pads to fix. Bonnets are washable and reusable if you keep them wet after use.

Finishes raked with disc buffer swirls respond impressively to orbital buffing with a quality swirl remover. Applied directly to the buffer pad, this non-scratching substance is more like a polish than a rubbing compound. I've played with ultra-fine sanding scratches left by 1200 grit wet-sanding paper and found that an orbital buffer can remove all traces in minutes—without cutting into the finish.

The Rest of the Details

When your truck's paint finish comes back to life, a sparkling surface with deeply colored lustre, there's a real incentive to complete the detailing chores. Here, too, I recommend fast, high quality chemical products for highlighting the interior and exterior trim.

Flat stainless steel and chrome moldings respond readily to the gentle buffing action of the orbital machine, and the balance of the stainless hardware will polish easily by hand. Rubber and vinyl, the two most vulnerable materials after paint, require a hand-applied combination cleaner/protectant product that will counter oxidation.

The principal cause of oxidation on paint and rubber is sunlight. Use of a protective UV-blocker agent on vinyl, leather and plastic trim extends the life of these materials. I get good results with 303 Protectant.

> **CAUTION —**
> *Avoid silicone oils and other chemistry that leave a "wet" look on vinyl.*

A gentle cleaner, 303 claims to provide a protective barrier against oxidation without damaging the vinyl's top-coat chemistry. Sensitive vinyl surfaces must flex and breathe. Any coating that either draws away the special surface chemistry or seals the top-coat from breathing will eventually cause embrittlement. According to Orvis,

Fig. 13-20. *The boating and outdoor equipment industries highly recommend 303 Protectant for vinyl and fiberglass. 303 can protect tires, dash pads, door rubber seals and bumper inserts.*

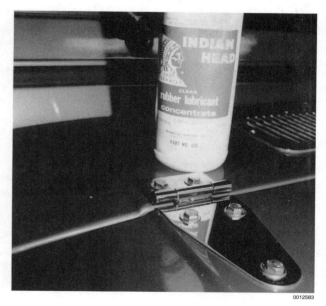

Fig. 13-21. *Permatex's Indian Head Rubber Lubricant has a long history. Claims have it harmless to vinyl, rubber and canvas, with many uses around your truck. This substance also works as an emergency tire mounting lubricant. Used regularly on shock bushings, sway bar bushings and other chassis rubber, this lubricant can enhance service life.*

the noted fishing tackle company, 303 will also lengthen your flyline cast as much as 30 feet!

Wheel cleanup is simple on most truck models. Painted steel rims respond readily to a light coat of Carnauba wax. If wheels are chrome or alloy and dull, hand rubbing with a metal polish such as Simichrome does the trick. If the wheel surface has oxidized, polishing with a die-grinder driven buffer pad will restore its surface.

Quick Tips to a Better Detail Job

1) Wash your truck thoroughly. Use bug and tar remover and other specially formulated chemicals to treat problem areas.

2) When using a buffer, make sure your polish and waxes are compatible. Chemical bases differ, and some chemicals react adversely when mixed.

3) Use several terrycloth towels when hand waxing. Don't apply towels used for buffing the sides and rocker panels to the upper body surfaces. Avoid introducing road oxidants and corrosives to the upper panels.

4) Wax your truck in the shade. Many polishes and waxes have chemistry that will evaporate rapidly in direct sunlight. A hot paint surface is also more vulnerable to damage.

5) Apply polish to the cloth or bonnet. Pouring it onto the painted surface may cause uneven chemical action, including stains.

6) Avoid use of any product that seals paint permanently. Such materials may prevent normal expansion and contraction of paint and seldom offer protection against UV radiation. Auto painters lament the fish-eye effect that results when repainting finishes sealed with permanent protectants.

7) Invest in the miracles of modern science. Special detailing chemicals not only leave more time for recreation, but they often provide superior results.

8) Allow vinyl surfaces to breathe. Most vinyl has a chemically engineered top-coat that needs protection. Choose your vinyl treatment carefully.

9) Use a small detail brush to reach difficult areas. A freshly polished finish draws attention to those small crevices and crannies that you miss. A few extra minutes makes the difference between a show-stopper and a shoddy job.

10) Pay attention to quality. There's a reason for higher priced products, and all waxes are not the same. The longest lasting stuff may not serve your paint finish best. Look for breathable Carnaubas and anti-oxidants. They can extend the life of your truck's finish.

NOTE —
A light coat of Carnauba-based wax will allow porous surfaces to flex and breathe. This prevents UV absorption and permanent dulling, "yellowing" or damage.

The final step in detailing your truck is interior cleanup. Professional shampoos, cleaners and specialized chemicals work quickly on the interior. Carpet stains and other tough challenges respond best to professional cleaners.

Stripping Film and Wax Buildup

Improperly applied waxes and polishes, particularly those which seal the paint surface, will permit oxidation and yellowing. The worst victim is the familiar sun-bleached truck with a dulled color base coat and a yellowed clear-coat finish.

Some aftermarket paint sealant/protectant products also pose a threat to paint. Claiming long term paint protection and ease of maintenance, many of these products actually smother the original paint. Sealed and unable to breathe, the treated paint or clear coat surface succumbs to cracking, weather checking and other damage caused by ultraviolet sunlight.

The most common cause of wax buildup is poor application technique. The paint finish likely had untreated surface oxidation, and uneven hand rubbing has built up successive layers of wax. Although most one-step waxes and polishes employ a cleaner to cut through and loosen the old layer of wax, this chemistry often fails.

Chemistry 101 for Detailers

Effective detailing is knowing which chemicals to use on a given surface. For washing your truck, look for solutions that prevent streaking. Professional car soaps remove very little wax and allow several cleanings between re-wax jobs. Tar and spot removers are actually high-grade cleaning solvents designed for work around interior and exterior finishes.

CAUTION —
Tar and spot remover may affect the top-coat of some vinyl and plastic items. Read labels carefully. These chemicals are also useful for removing wax and silicone before painting stripes or applying touchup.

Rubber dressing and protectants generally have a polymer or silicone base. Renewing tires, moldings, floor mats, pedal pads, dashpads, vinyl materials and other items is as easy as applying the right chemistry to the surface. Some materials require slight hand buffing.

Rubbing and finishing compounds meet several uses. Cleaning or cutting into the painted surface, these materials remove dull paint, "orange peel" and water spots. Often, new paint or even clear coatings require color sanding, which leaves a mildly scratched, dull surface. Power (orbital) buffing with non-abrasive chemical compounds can make the finish smooth and shiny.

Products like Carecraft's Swirl Remover fit a special niche. Carecraft calls its product a buffing cleaner capable of removing fine scratches and oxidation. Swirl Remover contains no wax or silicone, yet it lubricates the buffer pad. As a follow-up to rubbing compound or a poor detail job, Swirl Remover has no harsh abrasives and can be a mild, effective alternative for restoring a slightly oxidized finish.

Additionally, there are treatments and cleaners for upholstery, rugs, chrome, stainless steel and every other material found on a truck. The concern here is chemical compatibility. With questionable materials, always test chemicals first. Discoloration and damage can result from improper use or poor mixing of chemicals.

Let modern tools and chemistry do the work. Save your time and energy for family, friends and outdoor recreational pursuits.

After using a random orbital buffer and professional chemical products, it's obvious why hand polishing leads to wax buildup. A truck waxed regularly by hand will turn a terrycloth buffer bonnet blacker than the tire sidewalls! Successive layers of wax simply seal off the paint. Paint cracking or severe fade then develops. A proper wax job should lightly coat the surface and allow paint to breathe.

Use a chemical finishing compound and an orbital buffer to reverse the damage of wax buildup. (Avoid the use of rubbing compounds. They are abrasive and remove paint.) The goal is to eliminate old wax and gently lift oxidized, dead paint from below the wax. (Yellow simply means that oxidation has occurred.)

Once the finishing or cleaning compound has removed wax and oxidized paint, the surface will regain its luster. The fresh finish can receive a coat of quality polish or wax.

3. PICKUP BED AND TUB LINERS

Did your pickup truck go off to work, only to return all bashed and battle scarred? Does your cargo bed rattle with tools, jacks and other menacing items? Forget the dents and raw paint! An aftermarket slide-in bed liner or sprayed-in polyurethane bed coating can prevent utility bed damage. Both the looks of your truck and its resale value will benefit from bed protection.

The traditional plastic tub liners now compete with a new generation of spray-in materials. Advocates of plastic tub liners assert that the liner is replaceable (or removable on resale of the truck), while spray-in materials are permanent.

By contrast, a spray-in polyurethane coating will rust-proof far better than a slide-in tub. Polyurethane sprays adhere to every square inch of a pickup bed, Land Cruiser FJ40 or FJ25 "tub" or a cab's floor.

This last point is important. A major concern with slide-in bedliner installations is that moisture can creep beneath the liner. Once there, collected water waits patiently for bare metal to appear. Hidden rust forms,

Fig. 13-22. Slide-in tub liners have the advantage of easy removal if you sell the truck. If you use this kind of liner, periodically remove the tub and check for rust. A heavy coat of wax on the bed floor can help prevent the formation of rust on sheet metal beneath the liner/tub.

spreading beneath the bedliner. Often, rust perforation through the bottom of the bed is the first clue that oxidation has occurred.

If a bedliner is installed in a new truck, the odds of rust formation can be drastically reduced. Most rustout develops when owners install bed protection after scratches and seam spreading have already scarred the bed. For a bedliner installation in a used truck, first eliminate all rust, caulk or seal each seam, and prime any repaired or scratched surfaces.

Tub or polyurethane spray-in bedliners offer protection against chemicals, corrosives and denting. For loading and handling materials, however, another factor should also influence your choice of a liner: anti-skid protection.

Fig. 13-23. Spray-in polyurethane bed coatings have gained popularity. This material, applied properly, offers durability and anti-corrosion protection, plus a waterproof barrier against rust. When textured, the coating has anti-skid quality. Color can be added to contrast with your truck's paint scheme.

My choice is a spray-in polyurethane coating that offers a permanent barrier to rust. In many parts of North America, a moist climate or harsh and wet winters make a slide-in bedliner unwise.

By comparison, if the bed is prepared properly and sprayed correctly with a quality polyurethane bedliner material, rust is no longer an issue. An aftermarket spray-in bedliner can preserve your bed and prevent rust formation.

These spray-in bed coatings require special equipment and spray booths for installation. They adhere so well that it would be virtually impossible to remove the cured material without damaging paint—and possibly the bed metal! If damaged, the coating can be retouched.

An alternative to the slide-in liner or permanent spray foam installation is a bed mat. Bed mats, custom fitted to cover the entire floor of your truck, provide substantial protection. Better mats offer skid resistance and a cushioned cargo surface.

Mats insulate the bed or floor from cargo damage. Additionally, you can remove a quality mat periodically to thoroughly clean and wax the bed to reduce the risk of rust formation. Better quality bed mats are resistant to oil, chemicals and marring. They provide years of service.

Chapter 14

Electrical System Basics

TRUCK RESTORATION AND MAINTENANCE include the electrical system and wiring. Repair work and routine service frequently mean the renewal of wiring and changing connectors. Often, the frame-up restoration of an older truck chassis requires wiring the truck from scratch.

A successful wiring job can be gratifying. I well remember my first job as a truck fleet mechanic. My employer bought a two-ton capacity stake truck. The vehicle came really cheap, via a U.S. government surplus source, as someone had cut every wire behind the instrument/dash panel and left the truck paralyzed.

My first task was to re-wire the entire chassis and engine electrical system. Armed with a wiring schematic from the local truck dealership, I chose the proper wire

gauge for each circuit and carefully began routing the scores of new wires.

When I finished and turned the key, the engine started—and the lights, turn signals, wipers, accessories and all instrument gauges worked, too. In fact, everything operated safely, as I had routed all circuits through an OEM fuse panel for reliable service. The truck had a fine six-cylinder engine and rugged geartrain, and we got excellent service from the workhorse chassis.

Your truck works dependably when the lights glow, turn signals flash, heater blows, starter spins, wipers swish, spark plugs fire, alternator charges and electric fuel pump pulses. Understanding the dynamics of a truck's electrical system can enhance your troubleshooting skills, a vital asset when traveling in remote country.

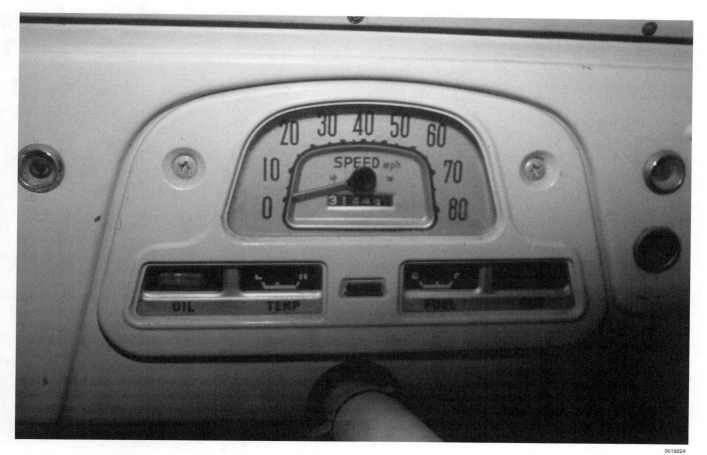

Fig. 14-1. *This FJ25 Land Cruiser featured 12-volt, negative ground electrics, with directional signals and accessible electric wipers. Wiring was simple and easy to troubleshoot. Today's trucks have complex electrical systems.*

CHAPTER 14

1. THE ELECTRICAL SYSTEM

Fortunately, Toyota's entry into the U.S. market was at a time when plastic wire insulation and 12-volt, negative ground electrical systems were already popular. Beginning in the mid-1950s, domestic vehicle manufacturers switched to plastic wrapped wiring and 12-volt electrics, each of which improved the performance and reliability of the accessories, starting circuit and lighting. Toyota FJ25 Land Cruiser electrical systems were of 12-volt, negative ground type.

> **NOTE —**
> Both cloth and plastic wiring insulation deteriorate over time. Trucks used off-pavement, in agriculture, harsh climates or around corrosive industrial settings are ongoing candidates for electrical wire repairs.

System Overview

Toyota trucks all use a 12-volt wet storage battery to supply current. Toyota trucks have used a variety of starter motor designs, however, the two most common have been a layout similar to the popular GM/Delco-Remy starter with piggyback solenoid and the later gear reduction starters.

The piggyback solenoid type starter system assigns the starting operation to the key switch. The solenoid unit, which mounts atop the starter motor, engages the starter drive and also delivers current to the starter motor.

Solenoid activation begins when low amperage current flows from the key switch's start pole to the solenoid. As magnetism moves the solenoid plunger, the drive gear engages and high amperage current flows to the starter motor.

Toyota truck starter motors have been conventional and reliable field coil/pole shoe "series wound" armature types—despite the industry-wide push toward the use of permanent magnet motors. Series wound motors are easily serviceable.

The starter mounted solenoid switch most often doubles as a junction block terminal for the main leads of the electrical system. As the starter draws more amperage than any other item in the electrical system, the battery's hot lead cable attaches directly to the solenoid switch to minimize resistance.

Toyota electrical components have always been reliable and easy to service. 12-volt generators served the battery charging needs of the earliest Land Cruisers, while higher output alternators became standard equipment by the time Toyota introduced the first mini-pickups. Considering the wide array of electrical accessories that all Toyota trucks have offered, an alternator's higher amperage output was welcome. Many generator-equipped Land Cruisers have been upgraded with a retrofit alternator.

What Is An Alternator?

Although alternator designs have evolved since the 1960s, their operation remains much the same. Typically,

Fig. 14-2. Toyota's use of a starter motor mounted solenoid dates back nearly four decades. Type at top is common to 1958–80 trucks. In 1978, Toyota introduced the newer reduction type starters (bottom), a design prevalent in later models.

as the ignition switch turns ON, a wire lead with 12-volt current feeds to the alternator or external regulator. Through transistor and diode switching, current reaches a field coil. While the engine cranks, a high field current is generated to increase available voltage. This is the pre-charging mode.

Once the engine starts, the alternator's rotor spins at speed, with alternating current produced within the stator winding. Typically, the stator sends AC current to an internal rectifier bridge and diodes, which convert the AC current to usable 12-volt DC current. Diodes also prevent battery current from draining at the alternator.

The battery (BAT) pole on the alternator or regulator can perform two roles: 1) act as a route for charging current returning to the battery, and 2) serve as an information source for the battery's state of charge or electrical loads on the system.

During normal operation, all amperage drains on the battery send a voltage reading to the alternator's regulator. (Later trucks feature voltmeters on the instrument panel. The voltmeter signals the correlation between battery drain and volts.)

While the engine cranks, a 12-volt battery momentarily reads approximately 9 or 10 volts. At times, an electric winch can draw this kind of heavy load. Headlights, air conditioning or any other electrical demand will also drop voltage at the battery.

How the Alternator Charges the Battery

When your battery has a low state of charge, the alternator returns high amperage current to the battery. Although this current flowing from the battery is actually a quantity of *amperage*, the battery and regulator interpret the flow in terms of *voltage*.

Charging a 12-volt battery requires meeting a range of voltages at various temperatures. At very low temperatures, for example, the regulator may test at 14.9–15.9 volts. The same regulator at 80° F may operate between 13.9 and 14.6 volts, while 140° F produces 13.3–13.9 volts. Above 140° F, the same regulator may offer 13.6 volts.

Since a fully charged battery reads approximately 12.6 volts, the charging circuit must at least maintain that voltage. This requires enough current flow to recharge the battery plus the amperage necessary to operate the entire range of electrical accessories and lights while the engine is running.

For generator equipped vehicles, and even for early lower output alternators, accessories like air conditioning place an exceptional load on the charging circuit and battery. Often, such charging systems cannot keep up with battery drain at an idle. Today's 100- to 140-plus ampere hour alternators can easily meet engine idling requirements.

Charge Circuit Routine Service Tips

Battery condition and state of charge are very important to your truck's performance. Later models with electronic fuel and spark management systems depend upon very accurate voltage readings and a strong current supply. All trucks, regardless of the environment in which they operate, require a quality battery in premium condition.

NOTE —
The new generation of high cold cranking amperage (CCA) batteries exceeds older OEM requirements by a good margin. (For details on battery service, see the lubrication/service chapters.)

For early Toyota Land Cruiser DC generators, periodic service and drive belt inspection is crucial. A spare belt is a mandatory item for back country trips. All Toyota generator systems have external voltage regulators, which are adjustable. Most mechanics, however, prefer to replace a unit that reads out of range.

Polarity is a concern when servicing or replacing either the generator or generator regulator. You must polarize the generator/regulator to prevent damage and permit charging. As the regulator adjusts current flow back to the battery, correct wiring of the charging system is essential.

Polarizing the generator is important when you replace the generator or voltage regulator. Different types of automotive regulators (with either an internally or externally grounded field) require different polarizing procedures.

CAUTION —
Know which type of regulator your early Land Cruiser uses, and consult the OEM Toyota truck repair manual or a professional-level service guidebook for instructions on how to polarize the generator system when you install a new or rebuilt generator or regulator. Failure to polarize the system will immediately cause severe damage to expensive—and rare—electrical components.

Lights and Other Circuits

Truck lighting is basic, with current simply flowing through switches, fuses/relays, then to the headlights, tail lamps, turn and brake lights, warning lights and interior lamps. To avoid shorts and unreliable service, your truck's lighting system requires safe routing of wire, correct wire size and secure connections.

Aftermarket accessories pose a challenge. Sound systems, add-on lighting, auxiliary fuel pumps and other additions to your truck's electrical system demand careful consideration. Where should components source their current supply? What wire gauges are suitable? How do you route wires safely? (You'll find more information about these issues in the accessory chapter.)

Your truck's electrical system follows a layout common to U.S. built light trucks. Earlier Toyota trucks have very simple electrical systems, built around common components still available at any auto supply house.

Later models boast modern electrical systems with more complex switches and power accessories. By the early 1980s, Toyota trucks entered the automotive electronic era, introducing the first use of modules and computer components that depend on constant voltage levels, perfect wire connections and secure grounds.

The modern Toyota truck electrical system proves very demanding. Air conditioning, closed loop emission controls, electronic fuel and spark management, and automatic transmission shifting systems create a maze of wires. ABS braking has its own demanding circuits, with speed sensors and other components dependent upon the integrity of the chassis wires.

Work on a late model Toyota electrical system involves use of detailed wiring diagrams, an understanding of wire gauge requirements and a clear sense for wire routing.

Electrical wire shorts and poor ground connections can leave your truck stranded or cause expensive damage.

Relays

Toyota truck electrical systems employ relays. The main advantage of relays is that minor amounts of current can control major power flow. For heavy amperage (a measurement of electrical resistance), this is useful. Systems like the starter motor can use lighter wiring to activate a relay that controls the flow of heavy current. Shorter lengths of heavy cable reduce resistance.

Relays have two basic designs, each with a different function. Electro-*magnetic* relays typically control circuits with larger current flows. The relay, activated by a low amperage current, directs high amperage current to systems like the starter motor or horn. Smaller gauge wiring from the horn button activates the relay, then current flows from a higher amperage (heavier wire gauge) battery source lead to the horn. The starter solenoid, which must deliver very high amperage battery current directly to the starter motor, also receives its activating signal by way of a much lighter gauge ignition/starter switch wire. An electro-magnetic starter solenoid also engages the starter's drive teeth with the flywheel ring teeth.

Electro-*thermal* relays receive and deliver current to a bi-metallic contact set. After exposure for a given interval of heat, the switch opens, stopping current flow. As the contacts cool down, the switch closes. The traditional turn signal flasher switch is this type of relay.

Volt/Ohmmeter: The Perfect Troubleshooting Tool

Of all my automotive testing equipment, one of the most valued tools is a combination volt-ohmmeter (VOM). The ohmmeter can read circuit continuity levels and ohms resistance. A volt meter reads the actual voltage available at a given circuit. Adjusted for alternating current (AC) or direct current (DC), a volt meter can measure line voltage between any two points. For automotive electrical troubleshooting, these tools provide a wealth of useful information.

Ohms, a measurement of electrical resistance, follows the engineering formula: 1 ohm = 1/siemens = 1 volt/ampere. Simply, each ohm is a precise increment of resistance to current flow. Conductive liquids or solids (such as electrical wiring) serve as mediums through which we can measure ohms resistance.

Aside from testing alternator diodes or components in a fuel injection or electronic ignition system, most automotive electrical troubleshooting centers around continuity of current flow and availability of voltage. The ohms segment of a VOM will quickly satisfy a wide range of these continuity checks, helping you find shorts and either partially or fully open circuits.

An inexpensive needle meter can handle basic voltage and resistance tests. For less than twenty-five dollars, you can buy a quality pocket-size tester. (My Radio Shack tester, purchased in 1982 for $10, still functions flawlessly.)

Designed for light use, these handy testers can perform a wide range of effective tests and still fit neatly into

Fig. 14-3. Relays and fuses come in a variety of sizes and meet various needs. Circuit or reset breakers work well with vehicles that are temporarily exposed to shorts or grounding, especially a 4x4 model that wades through streams.

Fig. 14-4. This unique fuse/relay holder, available through Wrangler Power Products, features popular ATO-type fuses and circuit breakers that fit ATO sockets.

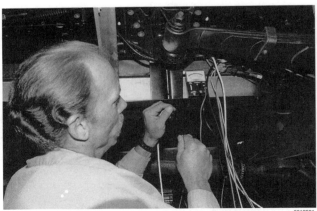

Fig. 14-5. Grounds are as important as hot sources. Ohmmeters take the guesswork out of testing your engine, chassis and body grounds.

Fig. 14-6. *Trailer connectors demand more than a test lamp check. You can detect insufficient current flow or resistance at a ground lead with your volt/ohmmeter.*

your truck's on-board toolbox. For testing fuel injection and other electronic components, however, you must use a more precise digital volt-meter.

> **CAUTION —**
> • *Connect or disconnect multiple connectors and test leads only with the ignition off. Switch the multimeter functions or measurement ranges only with the test leads disconnected.*
>
> • *On later model vehicles with sensitive electronic components, do not use a continuity/test lamp with an incandescent bulb to test circuits containing electronic components. Use only an LED (light emitting diode) test lamp. Do not use an analog (swing-needle) volt-ohmmeter to check circuit resistance or continuity on electronic (solid state) components. Use only a high quality digital multi-meter with a high input impedance rating (at least 10 meg-ohms).*

2. ELECTRICAL TROUBLESHOOTING

Four things are required for current to flow in any electrical circuit: a voltage source, wires or connections to transport the voltage, a consumer or device that uses the electricity, and a connection to ground. For trouble-free operation, the ground connections, including the battery ground cable and the body ground strap, must remain clean and free from corrosion.

> **NOTE —**
> Most problems can be found using only a multi-meter (volt/ohm/amp meter) to check for voltage supply, for breaks in the wiring (infinite resistance/no continuity and such), or for a path to ground that completes the circuit.

Electric current is logical in its flow, always moving from the voltage source toward ground. Keeping this in

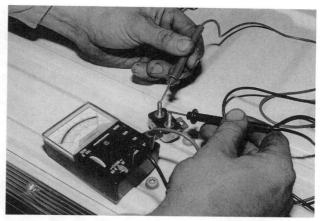

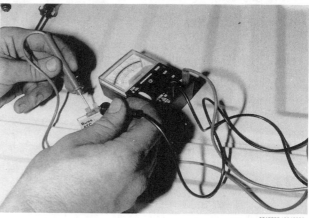

Fig. 14-7. *This 20 amp breaker and a late ATO style Buss fuse each pass the ohmmeter test. Test any suspect circuits and switches for high resistance readings.*

Fig. 14-8. *Test variable voltage devices with the volt meter. Although most trailer brake controllers are now electronic, they still send voltage signals to the trailer brakes, much like earlier rheostat devices.*

mind, electrical faults can be located through a process of elimination. When troubleshooting a complex circuit, separate the circuit into smaller parts. The general tests outlined here may be helpful in finding electrical problems. This information is even more valuable when used in conjunction with OEM wiring diagrams. You will find diagrams in the OEM Toyota repair manual for your truck.

Testing For Voltage And Ground

The most useful and fundamental electrical troubleshooting technique is checking for voltage and ground. A voltmeter or a simple test light should be used for this test. For example, if a parking light does not work, checking for voltage at the bulb socket will determine if the circuit is functioning correctly or if the bulb itself is faulty.

To check for battery voltage using a test light, connect the test light wire to a clean, unpainted metal part of the truck or a known good ground. Use the pointed end of the light to probe the hot lead of the connector or socket.

To check for continuity to ground, connect the test light wire to the positive (+) battery post or a battery source. Now use the pointed end of the light to probe the connector/socket's ground lead. In either case, the test lamp should light up.

> **WARNING** —
>
> *Do not create electrical sparks at or near the battery. A hot or defective battery emits explosive gases. Perform battery and current draw tests away from the battery at terminal blocks or junctions. Do not scratch test probes at battery posts, as this could create a spark and ignite battery gases.*

> **CAUTION** —
>
> *Do not use the pointed end of the test light to pierce through a wire's insulation. This could permanently damage the wire or insulation.*

> **NOTE** —
>
> A test light only determines if voltage or a ground is present. It does not determine how much voltage or the quality of the path to ground. If the voltage reading is important, such as when you test a battery or when you need a precise reading of a circuit's voltage, use a digital voltmeter. To check the condition of a ground connection, check for voltage drop on the suspected connection as described below.

To check for voltage using a voltmeter, set the meter to DCV and the correct scale. On 12-volt Toyota systems, connect the negative (-) test lead to the negative (-) battery terminal or a known good ground. Touch the positive (+) test lead to the positive wire or connector.

On a 12-volt negative ground system check for ground, connect the positive (+) test lead to the positive (+) battery terminal or voltage source. Touch the negative (-) test lead to the wire leading to ground. The meter should read battery voltage. When using an analog (swing needle) voltmeter, be careful not to reverse the test leads. Reversing the polarity may damage the meter.

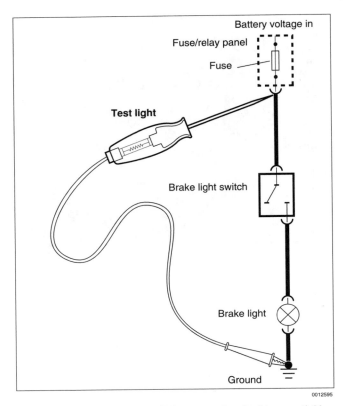

Fig. 14-9. *This is a test light set-up for checking available current. A test light makes a quick check of voltage sources and a complete ground.*

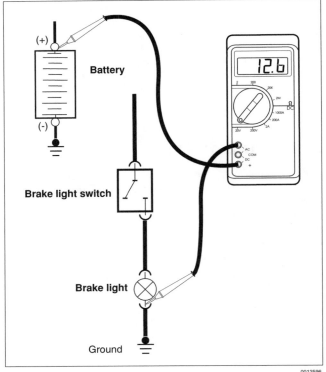

Fig. 14-10. *Here, a voltmeter checks for proper ground.*

Continuity Test

The continuity test can be used to check a circuit or switch. Because most automotive circuits are designed to have little or no resistance, a circuit or part of a circuit can be easily checked for faults using an ohmmeter or a self-powered test light. An open circuit or a circuit with high resistance will not allow current to flow. A circuit with little or no resistance allows current to flow easily.

When checking continuity, keep the ignition off. On circuits that are powered at all times, disconnect the battery. Using the appropriate wiring diagram, a continuity test can easily find faulty connections, defective wires, bad switches, defective relays, and malfunctioning engine sensors.

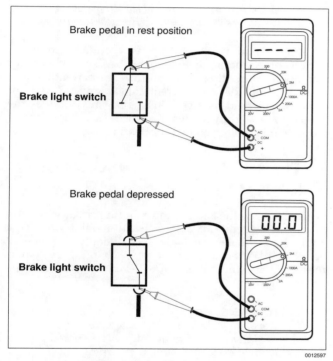

Fig. 14-11. *This is a brake light switch being tested for continuity. With the brake pedal in a resting position (switch open), the test reveals no continuity. With brake pedal depressed (switch closed), there is continuity.*

Short Circuit Test

A short circuit is exactly what the name implies. The circuit simply takes a shorter path than intended. The most common short that causes problems is a short to ground where the insulation on a hot lead wire wears away, and the metal wire becomes exposed. If the exposed wire is live (positive battery voltage on a 12-volt Toyota negative ground system), either a fuse will blow or the circuit may become damaged.

Shorts to ground can be located with a voltmeter, a test light, or an ohmmeter. However, these shorted circuits are often difficult to locate. Therefore, it is important that you use the correct wiring diagram when troubleshooting your electrical system.

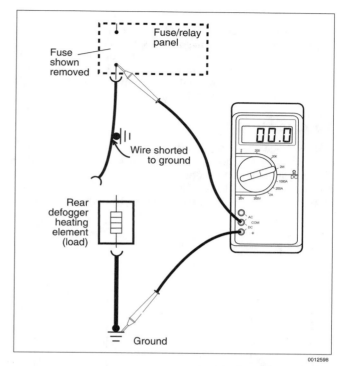

Fig. 14-12. *Ohmmeter being used to check for short circuit to ground.*

CAUTION —
On circuits protected with large fuses (25 amp and greater), the wires or circuit components may be damaged before the fuse blows. Always check for damage before replacing fuses of this rating. Always use replacement fuses of the same rating.

Short circuits can be found using a logical approach based on the path that current follows. To check for a short circuit to ground, remove the blown fuse from the circuit and disconnect the cables from the battery. Disconnect the harness connector from the circuit's load or "consumer." Using a self-powered test light or an ohmmeter, connect one test lead to the load side fuse terminal (terminal leading to the circuit) and the other test lead to ground.

A short circuit can also be located using a test light or a voltmeter. Connect the instrument's test leads across the fuse terminals (fuse removed) and turn the circuit on. If necessary, check the wiring diagram to determine under which circumstances the circuit should be live.

Working from the wire harness nearest to the fuse/relay panel, move or wiggle the wires while observing the test light or your meter. Continue to move down the harness until the test light blinks or the meter displays a reading. This will pinpoint the location of the short.

Visually inspect the wire harness at this point for any defects. If no defects are visible, carefully slice open the harness cover or the wire insulation for further inspection. Make sure that you find the trouble. Repair the defects to OEM standards.

NOTE —

On critical circuits, like the EFI system, you will likely need a new harness to ensure circuit integrity and the quality of connections. Consult the OEM Toyota truck repair manual for recommendations on repairing a particular electrical circuit.

Voltage Drop Test

The wires, connectors, and switches that carry current have very low resistance so that current can flow with a minimum loss of voltage. A voltage drop results from higher than normal resistance in a circuit. This additional resistance actually decreases or stops the flow of current.

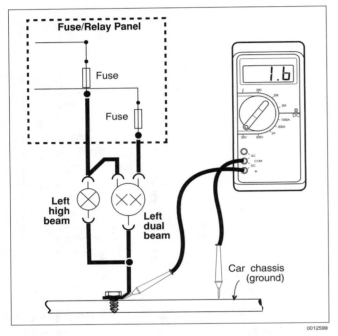

Fig. 14-13. Example of voltage drop test on dim headlights. Voltmeter showed 1.6-volt drop between ground connector and chassis ground. After removing and cleaning headlight ground, voltage drop returned to normal and headlights gained brightness.

A voltage drop produces symptoms and problems ranging from dim headlights to sluggish wipers. Some common sources of voltage drop are faulty wires or switches, dirty or corroded connections or contacts, and loose or corroded ground wires and ground connections.

Voltage drop can only be checked when current is running through the circuit, such as by operating the starter motor or turning on the headlights. Making a voltage drop test requires measuring the voltage in the circuit and comparing that reading to what the voltage should be. Since these measurements are usually small, a digital voltmeter must be used to ensure accurate readings. If you suspect a voltage drop, turn the circuit on and measure the voltage when the circuit is under load.

A voltage drop test is generally more accurate than a simple resistance check because the resistances involved

are often too small to measure with most ohmmeters. For example, a resistance as small as 0.02 ohms results in a 3 volt drop in a typical 150 amp starter circuit. (150 amps x 0.02 ohms = 3 volts).

Keep in mind that voltage with the key on and voltage with the engine running are not the same. With the ignition on and the engine off, full charge battery voltage should be approximately 12.6 volts. With the engine running (charging voltage), voltage should be approximately 14.5 volts. For exact measurements, first measure voltage at the battery with the ignition on, then with the engine running.

WARNING —
Do not create a spark near a hot or possibly defective battery. An explosion could result. If necessary, take your battery voltage reading at the primary battery terminal block (typically at the starter solenoid), well away from the battery.

The maximum voltage drop, as recommended by the Society of Automotive Engineers (SAE), is: 0 volt for small wire connections; 0.1 volt for high-current connections; 0.2 volt for high-current cables; and 0.3 volt for switch or solenoid contacts. On longer wires or cables, the drop may be slightly higher. In any case, a voltage drop of more than 1.0 volt usually indicates a problem.

3. TESTING BATTERY AND CHARGING SYSTEM

When checking the battery and charging circuits, be careful and considerate of battery hazards. High amperage applied to a defective battery is, literally, a potential bombshell. When you know your charging system is functional yet the battery acts dead, proceed with extreme caution.

WARNING —
A minute spark near an overcharged or defective battery is a safety hazard. Avoid the risk of igniting explosive hydrogen gas. Always unplug your battery charger before connecting or disconnecting the clamp leads. If in doubt, make VOM tests well away from the battery, at the alternator, a factory wire junction or the fuse/breaker panel.

Find a good ground, and attach the correct meter probe (based on your system's polarity). Attach the other probe to the hot wire source and read battery voltage. If you get a reading of 12.30 or less volts on a 12-volt system, with all known current drains (including lights, ignition and accessories) shut off, the battery's state of charge is at 50% capacity or lower. This indicates poor electrical connections, weak generator/alternator output, excessive current drain from accessories or a defective battery.

You can check each of these possible problems with the VOM. Start the engine and begin at the alternator. The battery signal to the voltage regulator should say, "I'm low on voltage, flow some current my way!"

In response, the normal charge circuit will call for a heavy amperage flow. Use the voltmeter mode of the

Fig. 14-14. *The solenoid junction block and other points that lie well away from the battery provide alternate battery testing sources. Avoid direct voltage checks at the battery, especially after heavy charging from the alternator or a battery charger. Explosive hydrogen gas can surround the battery and ignite from the slightest spark.*

Fig. 14-15. *Check your ignition cables periodically with an ohmmeter. Late electronic ignitions with higher firing voltages place more stress on high tension carbon cables*

tester, and probe the charge wire at the alternator or generator with the positive lead. On a negative ground system like your Toyota truck, attach the negative lead to ground. (On a positive ground system, you would attach the positive lead to ground and the negative lead to the charge wire.)

Charging properly, the alternator/generator should now read well over 12.6 volts on a 12-volt system. (See your repair manual to determine regulator settings and correct readings.) With current flowing toward the battery, voltage could read 14.8 volts or higher, depending upon the parameters of the voltage regulator and output capacity of the 12-volt generator or alternator.

If you see no increase in voltage over your static battery test reading, the generator/alternator or regulator is not performing properly. However, before condemning these expensive parts, troubleshoot further.

Shut the engine off and leave the meter set for the 12-volt range. Touch the heavy (BATTERY or BAT) lead at the 12-volt system's alternator or generator with the positive (red) meter probe. Using a quality engine ground for the negative probe, again read available voltage at the alternator or generator. This should be approximately the same as the battery's voltage reading.

If you cannot read voltage here, a wiring or fusible link problem exists. Trace the route of the generator/alternator BAT lead. At the first junction between the alternator and the battery, your ohmmeter test can begin.

Zero the meter and set for DC-Ohms and K-Ohms. Check the wire for continuity and conductivity by holding a probe at each end of the wire and reading the scale. If no opens or shorts exist, the meter will rest at the zero line. If there is too much resistance, as with a slight open in the lead or a poor connection, the needle will read upward on the scale. An actual open in the wire prevents the needle from registering at all.

Repeat this procedure along the wire path toward the battery. Eventually, you will locate the short or open. Resistance readings help locate corrosion within wire leads, too. Battery cables or terminal clamp connections often develop such problems. Unseen in a visual inspection, a current blockage cannot fool your ohmmeter. The force necessary to keep current flowing is measurable.

When the generator/alternator unit is defective, your OEM Toyota repair manual will provide test information and overhaul procedures. Most bench tests of alternators, generators, starters, coils and ignition modules involve a VOM. You can also test headlight and dimmer switches, relays, breakers, fuses, and turn signal switches with the meter. Tracing poor ground wires, troubleshooting faulty gauges, finding nuisance shorts, isolating worn spark plug cables and most other electrical tests are well within the VOM's ability.

Getting a Charge Out Of Your Generator/Alternator

Alternator and generator output tests are similar. (For simplicity, I use the term *alternator* for this section.) If your early Land Cruiser has a generator, you will find the majority of these troubleshooting and test suggestions useful and applicable.

Any concern about alternator output should begin with checking the drive belt tension. Next, inspect all wire connections. To test the alternator and regulator output, test the current flow from the alternator with an induction ammeter. Compare the ammeter flow to the OEM specifications for your truck, beginning at an idle, then 1500 rpm, then finally 2000 rpm.

NOTE —
Perform the induction meter test with the battery charge low. You want the alternator near its maximum output.

An induction ammeter, although not as accurate as more expensive test equipment, provides a quick sense for alternator output. Since the meter simply fits over the cable or wire insulation, you can test without removing any electrical component. (Make certain that magnetic interference from adjacent wires does not influence the readings.)

My two alternator (charging) and starter (draw) induction meters have served for over twenty years. If your equipment includes an ohms-resistance meter, you can perform additional field tests. When you suspect an alternator problem but cannot find its source, sublet the alternator and regulator to an automotive electrical repair shop. The shop can help distinguish regulator troubles from alternator defects.

> **NOTE —**
> An OEM Toyota truck repair manual will detail the troubleshooting guidelines for your generator/alternator and regulator. Also, most public libraries maintain a reference section that contains professional level automotive and light truck service manuals that contain details on charging system components.

Shorts and Voltage Leak-off

If starter and alternator circuits check okay and the battery's cells read normal specific gravity at a full charge, then chronic low battery voltage is still possible. Accessories like the clock or the improper hook-up of an aftermarket sound system can cause the battery to go dead. Be sure to wire your sound system through a fused and ignition switched accessories (ACC) source.

A defect in the ignition switch, air conditioning clutch, lighting equipment, the turn signal switch, a radio, tape deck or hazard lamp can each draw excessive current from the battery. The dome, underhood and hazard lamps operate without the ignition switch on, so check these areas first. When an aftermarket accessory taps directly to a battery source, disconnect the accessory and see if the problem resolves.

If a current drain persists, suspect the ignition switch. A shorted ignition switch can deliver current, even when the key is in the off position. Current may be passing to the coil, ignition module or EFI computer (on later truck models). You can confirm current flow at each of these areas by taking voltage readings with your volt-ohmmeter.

Testing Ignition and Fuel System Components

Most automotive tool boxes include test lamp type continuity and hot lead testers. The VOM serves far beyond these tools, however, giving precise readings about the underlying condition of your electrical system.

For example, spark plug misfires or engine balking under load are often the result of excessive resistance in the primary or secondary ignition circuits. Here, the VOM can provide an ideal tool for diagnostic work.

Many ignition and late model fuel system parts rely on electrical switches and electronic components. Given the ohms-resistance values for these pieces, you can easily test them with your meter. The troubleshooting and service guidelines in an OEM Toyota repair manual for your model can provide useful test criteria.

Ballast resistors, spark plug wires and electronic ignition modules each have specified tests. Voltage and ohms-resistance readings at the ends of a ballast resistor can determine whether the unit works properly. Likewise, an ignition coil has a specified resistance in its winding. Ohms resistance tests of a coil can identify most shorts and internal defects.

You can also test spark plug cables with an ohmmeter. Read resistance to identify defective wires or those that demand excessive firing voltage. Continuity/ohms tests can also identify rotor shorts.

> **NOTE —**
> When worn excessively, electronic ignition rotors can short to ground through the distributor shaft. You may experience this problem on a high output ignition.

Used creatively, the tests performed with a VOM often serve the same purpose as diagnostic analyzers that cost a thousand times more. Although fancy oscilloscope patterns and digital electronic readouts are valuable, the VOM's simple, pragmatic answers often serve better than expensive and bulkier diagnostic equipment.

4. THE STARTER MOTOR AND COLD CRANKING CHORES

Engines resist cranking as compression, valve spring tension and spinning belt-driven components fight the starter motor's efforts. Toss in a bit too much ignition spark advance, and it's clear why some starter drive housings break.

A 12-volt starter is a high torque electric motor, with or without an internal gear reduction drive. Heavy "lock test" amperage draw, well in excess of 450 amps on a large domestic V-8 engine application, is considered normal.

Such a starter may demand over 100 amps just to spin freely on a bench test. A defective starter motor may draw over 500 amps while cranking the engine, enough to fry both the battery and its cables. The typical Toyota starter might still draw 150 to 210 amps during cranking.

A 12-volt automotive starter motor can spin as high as 8500 rpm on the bench. However, while cranking the engine at 160 crankshaft rpm, with an 18-to-1 flywheel-to-starter drive tooth ratio, this same starter motor might spin 2900 rpm. Considering the amperage necessary to rotate the flywheel or flexplate, the starter motor has a major job.

Brush-type, series-wound starters consist of typical electrical motor components: an armature, field coils and brushes that ride on the armature's commutator. From a service standpoint, these motors require nothing more than periodic brush changes and replacement of the armature end bushings. There are other wear factors, however, that can also retire the starter motor from service.

Starter Solenoid

For massive current flow to reach the starter, without cooking the wiring circuits, the starter utilizes a solenoid switch. Simply put, the solenoid is an electrical switch that handles heavy current flow. The switch receives its signal from the ignition/starter switch via a small wire.

On non-reduction type Toyota starting systems, the ignition/start mode current causes magnetism to move the plunger inside the solenoid. When the plunger moves (engaging the drive gear), the circuit closes between the solenoid's heavy battery pole and the starter motor's hot lead. Battery cable current now flows to the starter motor.

Sequencing of this action is such that the starter drive gear engages the flywheel or flexplate ring gear teeth before the starter motor spins. To prevent severe clash of teeth or starter motor damage, starter drives have a one-way overrunning clutch mechanism.

Starter Drive

There are two types of starter drives common to Toyota truck models described within this book. One design engages when an electro-magnetic solenoid switch moves a shift lever. The other starter drive, found on late reduction type starter motors, works with a series of gears, a drive/clutch mechanism and an electro-magnetic solenoid switch.

On models with an electro-magnetic solenoid and a lever actuated starter drive, the lever attaches to the solenoid's plunger. When the ignition switch's start mode flows current to the solenoid (mounted astride the starter motor), two events occur: 1) The plunger moves the starter drive toward the flywheel teeth, and 2) just upon tooth engagement, a second phase begins as the solenoid closes

Fig. 14-16.   Release lever relationship is clear here. Solenoid's magnetic core draws lever and also closes a high amp current switch. Forward of lever is drive clutch and drive gear.

the heavy amperage switch and battery current flows to the starter motor.

The common wear points of lever action, non-reduction starters are the solenoid, brushes, armature bushings, engagement lever and clutch/drive gear. Although each of these components can be readily serviced in the field, most of today's owners and mechanics simply exchange a worn or defective starter motor assembly and solenoid switch for a relatively inexpensive rebuilt starter and a new or rebuilt solenoid switch.

NOTE —

Your starter motor may spin but not engage the flywheel or flexplate gear properly. This sounds like a high speed electric motor whir without the engine cranking over. (Or perhaps the drive only partially engages, causing a raucous grating noise as the gear teeth gnash.) Usually, the culprit is a worn starter drive and/or shift lever.

All starters must compensate for drive gear shock. Torque loads at the point of gear tooth mesh is where most starter housing damage occurs.

Starter housing nose end breakage is often the result of a poor starter motor mounting and bracing method. This problem is far less likely on a four-cylinder Toyota truck engine than a high output Chevrolet V-8 conversion engine. The starter mounting bolts/studs that attach to the front face of an iron clutch housing, like the early six-cylinder Land Cruiser design, tend to hold the starter more securely and help keep it on a straight plane.

If your Toyota Land Cruiser has a high output Chevrolet V-8 engine transplant and a starter that mounts directly to the engine block, be aware that the starter motor requires a metal brace between its endplate (commutator end frame) and the side of the engine block. If this brace is either missing or not attached properly, the starter motor can flex. This movement usually breaks the aluminum nose or drive housing of the starter. To completely eliminate this problem, I use a cast iron (earlier) Chevrolet V-8 truck-type bellhousing that doubles as the mounting location for an iron nosed starter motor. (See engine performance chapter for details on this engine swap, bellhousing and starter.)

Starter Motor Troubleshooting

Assuming that your truck's engine won't crank over, you need to answer a few questions. Does the starter solenoid click? Is the starter motor turning too slowly? Can you hear the starter motor spin, but the engine isn't cranking?

Always check the neutral safety or clutch pedal start switch before condemning the starter motor, starter solenoid switch or battery.

If the battery and cables check okay and the solenoid simply clicks, the trouble is either 1) a defective solenoid, or 2) a defective starter motor (bad brushes, armature, or internal windings). Also check the starter drive shift lever or fork, if so equipped.

When the starter motor turns too slowly, you must consider internal engine problems. With the ignition switch turned off and the coil high tension lead discon-

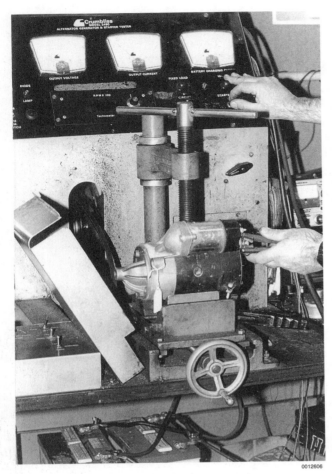

Fig. 14-18. *Induction ammeter can check starter current flow. Without removing the starter or any other parts, place the meter over the battery cable's insulation. Used in conjunction with a volt-ohm meter, the induction ammeter can help pinpoint defects and malfunctions by showing excessive current draw while the engine cranks over.*

Fig. 14-17. *A Crumbliss test bench at North County Rebuilders tests this starter motor. If you suspect trouble with your starter, an auto electric shop can assess its performance.*

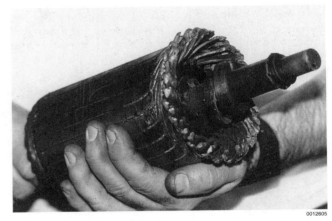

Fig. 14-19. *Here, a worn GM/Delco-Remy solenoid has welded its contacts and kept the drive and starter motor engaged. The motor winding unraveled from the heat—not a healthy prospect for a truck used in back country. Although Toyota has used a similar solenoid and drive design, failure of this kind is very uncommon.*

nected, rotate the engine by hand and observe any friction. (If necessary, remove the spark plugs to reduce load.) If the crankshaft turns okay, the trouble is likely within the starter motor assembly or solenoid switch.

There are two exceptions to this conclusion: 1) a jammed starter drive or 2) water in the engine's cylinders (hydro-lock). Either will prevent the engine from rotating. If you suspect water in the engine, remove the spark plugs and crank again. (If you find that internal engine friction keeps the engine from turning freely, refer to the troubleshooting chapter.)

Attach a starter motor induction meter to the heavy starter cable and observe the current flow necessary to crank the engine. If an abnormally high amp draw is evident (above the level of 150–210 amps), remove the starter motor for a bench test and determine the damage. Should the starter motor spin quickly and loudly, without rotating the engine, suspect a defective starter drive.

On Toyota truck starters with the solenoid mounted at the motor housing, the starter drive or the starter shift lever could be faulty. Noise also suggests teeth missing from either the starter drive, flexplate or flywheel ring gear. The latter prospect is costly and difficult to repair.

Replacing a damaged starter ring gear (flywheel/flexplate) requires removal of the transmission and clutch or the torque converter. In the ranking order of starter motor related repair costs, a solenoid switch is the least expensive item next to brushes and armature bushings.

For popular Toyota truck engines, rebuilt starter motors are available and inexpensive. However, if you have modified your engine with performance parts, a generic rebuilt starter may not handle the cranking load of a modified engine. You may need a starter application that serves a high compression/high output engine or perhaps an aftermarket high-torque starter.

If the field coils and armature are intact, your starter's major overhaul should include new end bushings, properly installed and reamed to fit. New brushes, re-dressing (cleaning and resurfacing) of the commutator, replacement of a worn starter shift lever/fork (if so equipped), a renewed solenoid and general clean-up of components will complete the job.

Starter Motor Overhaul

Your truck's reliability depends on an engine that will crank and start readily. Especially with an automatic transmission model that cannot be "bump" or push started, starter performance is critical.

Depicted in the step-by-step photos are starter motor rebuilding procedures that apply generally to Delco-Remy and Toyota lever shifted (non-reduction type) truck starters. For specific details on your truck's starter motor and electrical system, refer to the repair manual that covers your model.

Fig. 14-20. On this starter design, overhaul begins with solenoid switch removal. This particular starter has a GM/Delco-Remy type solenoid that mounts to the nose section.

Fig. 14-21. Brush inspection is possible once you remove the end plate. You will likely replace brushes and the end plate bushing during a starter repair, as these parts are readily available and inexpensive.

Fig. 14-22. Brushes are accessible with the commutator end frame (end plate) removed. At this point, brushes can be replaced. Lay parts out carefully and in order. Note the way wires attach to brushes.

Fig. 14-23. This commutator and armature show wear. Note the angle of the shaft (arrow), an indication of end bushing wear.

Fig. 14-24. These two armature/commutators are identical—except for the diameters of the commutators. Smaller diameter results from resurfacing on lathe.

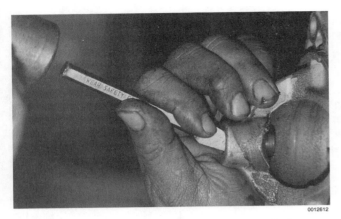

Fig. 14-25. *End bushing replacement is a standard procedure.*

Fig. 14-26. *Loosening brushes precedes field coil removal. An impact driver or special tool is necessary for removing field coil screws (arrows). These screws are really seated firmly and should only be removed if field coils require service.*

Fig. 14-27. *Bench tester charges armature. Time-honored "hacksaw blade" test indicates shorts or opens. I recall performing this test as a fleet truck mechanic during the 1960s. The procedure was already old at that time.*

Fig. 14-28. *Commutator receives resurfacing in a metal lathe. This operation requires professional skill. Sublet the work to a local starter rebuilding shop.*

Fig. 14-29. *A new or rebuilt drive is a must. This item wears over time.*

Fig. 14-30. *On some applications, a selective fit thrust washer(s) controls end play of the armature. Consult the OEM Toyota truck repair manual for end play specifications.*

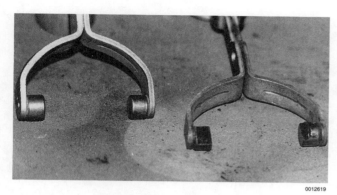

Fig. 14-31. *Release fork wear is evident here. This fork needs replacement to assure starter's reliability.*

Fig. 14-33. *This kit would overhaul a modestly worn starter. Brushes, a new drive and end bushings make up the necessary pieces. A new or rebuilt solenoid unit will round out the rebuild parts unless the coils or armature show damage. Turning the commutator is a sublet task, if required.*

Fig. 14-32. *Rebuilt solenoids are not all the same. On the right is a cheap replacement item of approximately 80 winds. 140-wind wire at left is a high quality rebuild, similar to a new OE unit.*

Chapter 15

Accessories

BY THE TIME TOYOTA'S Land Cruiser hit the U.S. shores, light truck accessorization had become a booming industry. Many of the original Toyota Land Cruiser trucks were themselves the product of "aftermarket" body builders in Japan, especially the Station Wagon models.

Cab-and-chassis Land Cruiser models like the FJ43-Series often acquired custom utility beds. During the mid-1970s, as fuel costs rose and interest in motorhomes prevailed, Toyota built many cab-and-chassis small trucks for Chinook's mini-motorhomes and also for fleet, commercial and utility users.

Toyota Truck Accessorization

Since early on, the Toyota dealership parts department has been a source for aftermarket accessories and enhancements to satisfy a wide range of truck users. The first Toyota import trucks were tough 4WD Land Cruisers, which came with a fine complement of features and provision for some utility upgrades. Turn signals, a rear factory floor heater (found on many FJ40 models) and electric wipers gave U.S. buyers a well-equipped truck. Still, the Land Cruiser was a 4x4 off-pavement vehicle, so spare gas can holders, power take-off (PTO) driven acces-

Fig. 15-1. *The light truck aftermarket has developed along two distinct paths. While commercial fleets create a demand for utility products, a growing number of recreational and multi-purpose users now personalize their trucks with cosmetic and convenience accessories.*

CHAPTER 15

Fig. 15-2. *Even the earliest Land Cruisers were well equipped, with electric wipers, turn signals, a small tool kit, and touch-up paint. A valuable factory item for FJ40 models was the rear floor heater. This was a luxury compared to Willys/Kaiser Jeeps, which offered front heat only as an accessory.*

sories and aftermarket winches soon expanded the versatility of these roguish trucks.

Add-on traction devices have always been popular with 4WD vehicles, however, the Land Cruisers were so tractable that no pressing need existed for limited slip or locking axles. These aftermarket items have become available more recently, primarily for highly specialized terrain like California's Rubicon Trail, Moab, Utah and the Rocky Mountains.

Popular aftermarket items often become original equipment or factory options on later truck models. As a Toyota truck owner, you can select from a huge array of aftermarket upgrades, including safety enhancements, high performance components, specialized wheels and tires, utility products and cosmetic accessories.

Toyota trucks have always allowed room for an owner's personality stamp and accessorization. If your Toyota truck needs more personality, better on-board work tools, styling improvements or a less spartan interior, there's likely an aftermarket solution. Often, an older truck can provide the features and conveniences of a later model by simply adding the right accessories.

1. WINCHES

Nearly as important as four-wheel drive systems, power winches have enhanced truck utility for half a century. Pioneered by Claude C. Ramsey, front mounted power take-off (PTO) winches were the first truck designs. By 1948, Ramsey's winch popularity was widespread. A recognized dealer-installed option, Ramsey winch systems were often "factory-approved" products offered through U.S. truck dealerships.

Early Toyota Land Cruisers had PTO transfer case drives, and power take-off driven winches have been fitted to many of these early 'Cruisers. Some PTO winches are Japanese (OEM-type equipment), while U.S. units from Ramsey and Koenig also found their way onto Land Cruiser chassis.

A power take-off (PTO) drive taps into either the transmission or transfer case PTO access and uses all forward speeds and reverse speed of the transmission. Power flows to a front mounted winch gearbox via an accessory PTO driveshaft. OEM Toyota winches have a worm gear drive.

Fig. 15-3. *Some truck transmissions have PTO drive access. This convenient feature is one power source for PTO winch units. Land Cruisers also used a transfer case access point (arrow).*

Toyota's own PTO winches and the Koenig/King and Ramsey PTO products drowned in the wave of electric winch sales. By the early 1970s, the bulky PTO winches, with scores of moving parts and massive installation and repair tasks, made the PTO winch far less attractive than the growing number of powerful electric winch designs.

Ramsey Winch Company made a successful transition to electric winches. The highly respected Koenig Iron Works, however, disappeared from the recreational accessory market. Today, PTO-driven winches are still available, although their use is largely limited to commercial and utility company service.

Electric Winches

Since the late 1960s, a heated debate has waged between PTO winch advocates and electric winch users. PTO buffs argue that battery power limits the usage of the electric winch. Stranded with the engine stalled in a rushing stream, will the battery last long enough to pull the truck free? Electric winch advocates counter with the argument that a stalled engine can't spin a PTO shaft. In either case, the operator could be in real trouble.

Dual battery installations, isolators and high output alternators have virtually eliminated the shortfalls of electric winches. Today, electric winches furnish the quality—and quantity—of service that users demand. Notable manufacturers in the truck mounted electric winch market include Ramsey, Warn and Superwinch. Contemporary winch marketing emphasizes gear and motor design, integrity of components, amperage draw, load capacity and utility.

Fig. 15-4. *Warn's XD-9000 winch is an electric planetary design. Compact and inconspicuous, the unit ranks a hefty 9000 lbs. single line rating. This winch is rated to pull twice the weight of a Land Cruiser FJ40. Select a winch capable of pulling at least 1.5 times your truck's gross weight.*

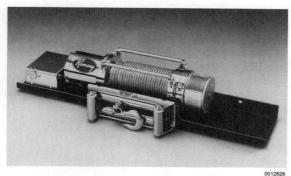

Fig. 15-5. *Ramsey REP 8000 is a popular winch unit. Optional roller fairlead is shown. This is one of Ramsey's heavier duty planetary gear models and weighs 61 pounds. RE 8000 and even stronger RE 10000 or 12000 models feature worm gear drives and choice of Hawse or roller fairleads.*

Determining Your Winch Needs

Electric winches have a variety of ratings. Speed (defined as feet-per-minute or fpm spooling) results from the gear reduction ratio and electric motor speed. Popular electric winch designs feature worm, spur or planetary gear systems.

The vehicle's battery (and/or an auxiliary battery) powers the winch motor, which basically resembles the motor portion of an automotive starter. In turn, the winch motor spins either a drive gear, worm shaft or sun gear.

Worm-and-gear systems rotate the worm gear inside a bull gear. Typically, the bull gear attaches to the cable spool drum. A major advantage of the worm drive is its ability to stop abruptly or "load-reverse" when power flow ceases. Planetary and spur gear arrangements, by contrast, require a brake mechanism to prevent reverse rotation when the motor stops.

Worm gear systems, with their low efficiency factor (the ability to transmit energy from one gear to another),

require no brake. By contrast, if a winch gear system could develop 100-percent efficiency, it would spool in either direction with equal ease, whether loaded or unloaded.

Gear efficiency of less than 45% creates a self-locking capability. Here, the relationship and ratios of the gears create a lesser incentive for free-spooling, even with a load on the cable. Worm gear systems, although extremely strong, offer only 35–40% efficiency.

Spur gear drives like Warn's classic Model M8274 work at 75% efficiency. This requires a braking mechanism to prevent load-reversal. Similarly, the popular planetary gear systems offer 65% efficiency.

One variation, the compound planetary gear, produces 40% efficiency, which provides for self-braking action. The compound planetary gear system requires a high speed motor, generally in the 4000–5000 rpm range.

The planetary systems provide both strength and smooth operation. Compact planetary winches have good resistance to torque loads. Direct power flow through the sun gear permits lighter weight, a low profile and high output.

Winch Motors

At present, the heaviest duty winches feature series wound motors. These motors provide maximum torque with a price: maximum amperage draw. The series wound brutes demand a heavy duty battery or the use of an auxiliary battery.

Permanent magnet motors require far less amps, draw less battery power, and save weight. On light and medium load winches, these motors work fine. After all, many newer autos and trucks feature permanent magnet starter motors. These motors serve well here, as engine cranking takes a short time and seldom generates excess heat.

The arguable disadvantage of permanent magnet motors is overheat. Under sustained and heavy loads, the permanent magnet motor tends to overheat. The operator needs to monitor the winching effort and time involved, allowing the motor to cool at safe intervals. (Most winch motors have circuit breaker protection against extreme overload.)

Winching and R.V. Batteries

Modern batteries offer higher cold cranking amperage or CCA. These types of batteries are far more practical for series wound motors. A dual battery system, once mandatory for high output winch systems, remains an option.

If your battery rates above 650 CCA (preferably 850 CCA or higher), the normal needs of a high output series wound winch motor could be met with a single battery. For extreme duty use or very long winch pulls, consider a second battery and an automatic battery isolator. The isolator prevents draining your main battery below the level necessary to start the engine.

Selecting A Winch

Determine your truck's gross vehicle weight (GVW) before choosing a winch. This is the combined weight of the truck, your cargo, fuel, oil and any other items on board.

Include your spare tools, the mounted winch and any accessories attached to the truck.

Also account for other motorists and four-wheelers. As a rescue or emergency tool, your truck (especially a 4x4 model) has a wide range of uses. Consider not only your GVW but also the weight of other vehicles that you might assist.

Engineers compute the winch safety factor at 1.5 times the working GVW of your truck. Working GVW is the real world, loaded version of your vehicle. If in doubt, take your fully loaded vehicle to a truck scale. Multiply the amount of working GVW by 1.5. Example: If your fully loaded truck weighs 4500 lbs., the minimum winch capacity should be 4500 x 1.5, or 6750 lbs.

Many buyers, even those who own lighter half-ton rated trucks, seek 8000-pound or higher capacity winches. The added margin of safety is obvious with a high output winch. A winch motor rated to pull heavier loads than you have planned will last longer and hold up better when worked hard.

Also be clear of a winch's rating method. "Single-line pull" or "double" makes a major difference. Applying the physics of a snatch-block (making a 180° turn of the cable and coming back to a tow hook near the winch) provides almost twice as much pulling strength and far less strain on your winch unit.

> **CAUTION —**
> *Although physics shows nearly a doubling of pulling power, engineers advise a 15% safety factor. If your winch's single line pull is rated 6000 lbs., a 180° turn of the cable should increase pulling power by 85% or 5100 lbs. This would make your total pull rate 11,100 lbs. Any deviation from the 180° pull angle will reduce load capacity. Also, always consider the cable's load limit when using a snatch block.*

Although doubling and even tripling the cable is possible, the cable length eventually becomes an issue. Also, it is very hard on larger wire cables to bend them 180-degrees around a snatch block pulley. Even with a high output winch, conservative loads make a good strategy.

Mounting a Winch

Mounting position is important. Winches that mount at or above the frame/bumper height seem better for off-pavement use. Often, when you most need a winch, the front of the truck is low to the ground. If above the bumper height, the cable and spool will still be easy to reach.

In the worst instance, a below bumper mount could actually become buried in snow, mud or a creek. As with any front bumper extension, the truck's approach angle may also suffer from a below-the-bumper mount. A winch near the ground increases the likelihood of dragging the cable during pulls.

Many truck owners, however, prefer hiding the winch behind the bumper. An open grill frontal area is important. In very hot climates, under severe loads, a high mount winch may compromise the engine and automatic transmission cooling system. Decreased air flow over the radiator core can reduce radiator efficiency.

Options are another factor when selecting your winch. Winch manufacturers frequently offer extra equipment. A roller fairlead, winch cover, remote controls, a portable/receiver mount, handtools or a wiring harness may be items you'll want—either when you purchase your winch or later.

Mechanical engineers design winch mounts to match a given winch installation. As life, limb and expensive property are at stake, proper installation is a necessity. Your safest strategy is a manufactured winch mount. Installation kits available from the winch manufacturer will fit the frame and vehicle requirements of your truck. Mount kits address load points, the strength of frame attachments and the ease of access to the winch. Engineers take the rated load capacity of the winch and apply that force safely to the truck's frame.

> **WARNING —**
> *Eliminating any part of a winch installation package could compromise safety and the load capacity. Use only the graded and designated hardware included in the kit. If your truck has other modifications that make a kit difficult to install, consult the winch manufacturer for possible solutions.*

Fig. 15-6. *A snatch block and 180° reversal of the cable can reduce load on the winch motor by nearly one-half. Always allow a 15% safety margin. Note that my son Jon has raised the hood as a safety precaution.*

Sadly, operators often underestimate the load forces involved with winching. A cable drawn to maximum load capacity must transfer force safely to the frame. This concern goes beyond the winch mount and hardware.

If the winch attaches to the OEM bumper or brackets, that hardware must also be at factory standards. If the bumper has been removed, make certain that the attaching bolts and nuts meet or exceed OEM standards for your truck. Winch kit engineering assumes that the truck's frame and hardware will meet or exceed OEM guidelines.

Portable Winches

A recent development in winch mounting is the portable winch receiver. Recognizing the versatility of a detachable front or rear mounted winch, manufacturers now build winches and winch frames that fit a Class III (2" square) or better trailer receiver.

Fig. 15-7. *Portable winches allow quick removal. A Class III or stronger frame mounted receiver serves at either end of your truck. The portable winch is highly versatile for recovery work.*

Using a quick disconnect electrical cable and pin-type receiver hitch, these winches install and disconnect in minutes. The main advantage of a quality portable winch is out of the way storage. Protected from theft and foul weather, the winch can stow in a covered pickup bed or bed tool box. Ready for an emergency, the winch assembly is free of ice, mud or rusted cable. Additionally, the portable winch is useful at either end of the vehicle.

Portable winches rely on the integrity of your truck's receiver mount or hitch kit. Commercially made, most frame mounted hitches that have a two-inch receiver rate as Class III or higher. The load capacity of a properly installed Class III hitch is 5000 lbs., with a maximum tongue weight of 500 lbs. Graded bolts and reinforcement plates generally accompany a frame mount hitch kit.

> **WARNING —**
> *Failure to install a safe hitch is hazardous. Under heavy load, a bumper mounted hitch could break away, causing personal injury or damage to your truck. Cosmetic tube bumpers seldom rate even a Class II hitch status.*

> **CAUTION —**
> *Many homemade and poorly installed hitches fall short of Class III standards. If you find that a portable winch suits your needs, have your hitch inspected by a specialist or install an approved frame mounted hitch with the correct class rating recommended by the winch manufacturer.*

Winch Controls and Installation

Winch installation kits offer either direct or remote controls. The remote cable allows control of the winch feed from twenty or more feet away, well away from the cable, spool and gearworks. This gives an optimal view of the pull without your standing in line with the load.

When mounting the control box, follow the suggestions of the manufacturer. Since distance equates to amperage loss and resistance, many control units have a specified location. The switch box should be easily accessible, in an airy space, preferably out of the weather.

Modern electric winch controls include solenoids, breakers or relays. In most instances, the control box is a plastic case, sealed from the weather. Since relays and/or solenoids receive direct battery current, you must isolate them from moisture. If ice, snow or sleet were to freeze inside the switch box, a current drain could sap your bat-

Fig. 15-8. *The remote winch control is a must. Never stand in the line of a winch cable. If the cable breaks and recoils under load, severe bodily injury could result. Note Jon's use of gloves when handling winch cable.*

Carry-on Winch Accessories

Once you've mounted and wired your new winch, a few accessory items, handily stored in your truck, will help your winch perform at maximum capacity.

Accessory kits offer compact storage for important winching gear. Warn's kit includes a snatch block, forged steel shackle, tree protector, leather work gloves and a carrying bag. Ramsey and other winch manufacturers also offer such kits.

An industrial or logging supply provides an excellent assortment of high grade snatch blocks, pulleys, shackles and swivels. Swivels protect cable from twisting under load, a major source of damage. Load rated assortments of hooks are also available. Watch for rough inner edge of hooks. Protect your nylon tree saver and recovery straps by carefully bevelling forging scars with a grinder or file.

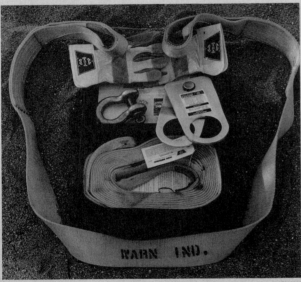

0012630

Recovery Strap. Quality winch accessory kits always include a recovery or tow strap. Often, you can free a stuck vehicle with a tug rather than setting up your winch. Many strap designs provide controlled stretch, which reduces shock loads.

Snatch Block. Known in other circles as a pulley block or block and tackle, the snatch block is an anchor plate with a pulley inside. Attached in front of the truck with a 180-degree return of the line, the snatch block offers 85% (with safety factored) load reduction when the cable hook attaches near the winch.

Choker Chain. A term familiar to woodsmen and loggers, the choker is a high tensile strength link chain with hooks at each end. The chain is very versatile, acting as a vehicle recovery tool or reinforcement between two anchor points. You'll find it handy for wrapping around huge rocks, truck frames or other anchor points. You can easily store a six- to ten-foot choker in your truck.

Tow Hooks. Factory or aftermarket front and rear frame mounted tow hooks require high tensile strength bolts and self-locking aircraft quality nuts. Attaching points and hardware must meet OE frame requirements. Never mount a tow hook directly to the bumper. Hooks are available with spring clips to prevent straps from slipping off. These are especially useful for one-person operation. Mounted upward, downward or sideways, tow hook bolts should align in the direction of pull. Mount the hook(s) at frame height and remember that the safest pull is a straight line. If possible, avoid welding tow hooks into place. These hooks may need replacement at some time.

D-Shackle. Most popular winch accessory kits include a D-shackle and pin. This is a highly versatile device for attaching and joining straps, rings, chain and even cable. When using a D-shackle with straps, make certain that nylon material rubs against the inside of the smooth looped end. Otherwise, fraying and damage to the strap will result. Tighten threaded bolt, then back off 1/2-turn to prevent thread seizure during heavy pulling.

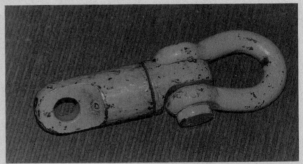

0012631

Gloves. Every accessory kit should include a pair of hefty (preferably leather) work gloves. These gloves must resist weather, cable friction burns, scraps and abrasions. Frayed cable and sharp sheet metal edges can cut fingers to the bone. Wear gloves.

Tree Saver Strap. This is vital. For attaching a winch cable or anchoring your vehicle to a tree, the tree saver strap protects the bark and live sections. The eyes of the saver strap provide an attachment point for your D-shackle, which in turn becomes the snatch block anchor.

Pull Pal. An anchor designed to set firmly in the ground as winch load increases—useful when there are no rocks or trees nearby to function as anchor points.

Shovel and Hand Tools. A simple, often overlooked tool is the folding shovel. Vital hours are wasted when shovels, handyman jacks and proper handtools get left at home. Many winches provide the framework for mounting a shovel, axe and jack. Also, bring along strong wire cutters, as a broken cable can easily wrap up in the winch or the truck's chassis. The MAX multi-purpose tool kit and a High Lift or Handyman jack are must items for serious off-pavement adventures.

tery. Likewise, operating the winch under such conditions could create a short circuit.

A properly grounded electrical system is fundamental, and the issue becomes more critical with a winch. A 400–600 amp resistance load, even for a brief time, will tax your truck's electrical system to its limit. Poor grounding is a fast way to establish a power robbing voltage drop.

Grounds and Winch Wiring

As a rule, the best ground system takes the 12-volt battery negative cable directly to the engine block. Next, the alternator housing, or its ground post, connects to the engine, with a ground strap from the engine block to the frame completing the circuit. (To assure a good body ground, add a strap from the frame or engine to the cab.) The winch system may now ground directly to the block or frame.

Each manufacturer furnishes specific electrical requirements for its various winch models. Consult your kit instructions for details. As an additional item, consider an accessible master disconnect switch. Mount the switch in an easy to reach place, out of line from the winch.

NOTE —
Under extreme load, winch motors and the electrical system can overheat. An accessible master switch allows shutting the system down completely without placing your limbs in jeopardy.

If your winch electrics interface with a complex electrical system (sound system, lights and an extra battery), you may need a complete, high amperage cable and wiring harness.

Using a Winch

Before operating your winch, raise the hood. A broken winch cable is potentially lethal and could easily break your truck's windshield. (For this reason, a brush/grill guard makes a smart addition to a winch mount.) Make sure that the cable can spool evenly onto the drum, and attach the hook to a substantial anchor point.

If possible, stand far to the side when winching, well outside the cable's path. Many operators lay a blanket over the cable, assuming that this will reduce recoil if the cable breaks.

Although a cover or blanket may help contain the cable, no cloth blanket can absorb the immense force of a snapping cable under load. Pull as straight as possible. Always use leather work gloves when handling wire cable.

Always leave a reasonable length of cable on the winch spool. Your winch manufacturer has guidelines for the necessary length. Paint the cable red from the starting wrap to the length specified. This will signal when the maximum length of cable has spooled out.

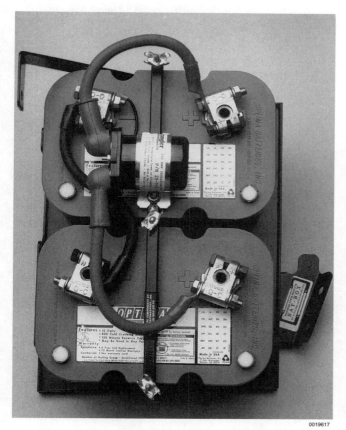

Fig. 15-9. Use of dual batteries is smart when running an electric winch. Two batteries, separated by an isolator system, can provide adequate engine cranking after a thorough draining of the winch battery. If you accidently over-use the winch, this Wrangler Power Products dual battery system with isolator will keep the charged battery off line until you are ready to start the engine.

Fig. 15-10. Loads on cables are fully capable of launching a tow hook, D-shackle, snatch block, bumper section, bumper bracket or frame piece through the windshield. Never stand in the line of a loaded cable. Many truck owners raise their hoods to protect the windshield in the event of a cable failure. Use your remote winch control to keep clear of the cable.

Preventive Maintenance For Your Winch

Your winch is a safety device and lifeline. When a four-wheeling trip requires the use of your winch, you're way out there! A secluded box canyon or a muddy creekbed is no place for winching errors or a poorly maintained winch.

The modern electric winch is easy to maintain. Unlike PTO winches, with their oil-filled transmissions and mechanical driveshafts, the electric winch requires simple service.

Cable Inspection. The major wear item is the cable. Properly used, the wire winch line will last for years. One careless moment, however, can weaken or kink the cable. If a night time or blizzard winching episode leaves your winch cable coiled wrong, free-spool the cable entirely and check for damage. Kinks, broken outer strands and twists that leave the cable distorted are all signs of weakness. Clean the cable thoroughly to allow close inspection.

Lubrication. Your winch may have grease fittings and require periodic lubrication. If you have an oil bath drive (usually on PTO winches), the gear oil must be clean and up to the full level. Check for seal leaks. If your winch operates in a dusty and wet environment, always wipe zirk fittings clean before greasing. Use the manufacturer's recommended grease or a water-resistant chassis/bearing lube. Cable friction leads to fatigue and unnecessary stress. Many users lube the cable with special cable lubricants.

As greases often attract unwanted dirt and dust, special lubricants are available for use on cables. Industrial supplies sell chain and cable lubricants that cure like cosmoline. This reduces messy handling and resists dirt accumulation. Such lubes also work well on clevis pins, hook pivots and the snatch block. They provide a good moisture barrier against rust, too.

Mounts, Hooks, Pulleys and Straps. Inspect your hooks and straps. Make certain clevis pins are free of moisture and lubricate them lightly. Dry out your nylon straps before storing them. Check tow hook and winch mount bolts and nuts for tightness and signs of fatigue. Inspect parts closely for bending or possible fatigue cracks. Clean and lubricate pulleys and the snatch block at regular intervals.

Electrical System. Inspect your remote control cable, control box and all cable leads to the winch. Insulation on these leads must be in good condition and free from nicks. Amperage passing through the winch motor cables is high enough to weld metal. If a hot cable shorts to ground, a fire or severe damage might result. Inspect the cable routing to make certain no cable lays across sharp metal edges. You can reduce the effects of moisture through the use of silicone sprays and dispersing chemicals. Make certain that the control box and remote connectors are free of debris and corrosives.

Freeing a vehicle often will require more than one run of the cable's length. If the vehicle wants to roll faster than the cable spools, apply the vehicle's brakes slightly. Many winches operate at both a minimum and maximum operating load. Proper cable spooling depends upon working within this load range.

When winching, keep in mind that the winch's maximum pulling ability is rated as the first few wraps of cable. As the cable spools in, the larger diameter wraps offer less load capacity than the first wraps. For this reason, you should spool out as far as safely possible when moving a heavy load. If necessary, use a snatch block and 180-degree cable return (back to the vehicle's tow hook) to reduce cable length and add pulling power.

Fig. 15-11. *A sensible anchor point for your tow chain or strap is the receiver of a safe, frame mounted hitch. A Class III hitch/receiver rates a 5000 pound load capacity and will withstand the stress of moving another light vehicle. Avoid use of elastic or bungie cord-type recovery straps. The load of a stretched cord places far too much stress on tow hooks and other attachment points.*

WARNING —
Always assume that a loaded winch cable is dangerous. Imagine the path a snapped cable might take. Stay out of that space.

2. ELECTRICAL SYSTEM UPGRADES

Automotive electrical wire must meet various current loads. Amperage determines the proper wire gauge for each area of your truck. Since resistance increases with distance, longer runs of wire require heavier gauge sizes.

For rewiring and repair work, safety standards must apply. Heavy duty devices demand more amperage draw and larger wire sizing. OEM standards assume a specific distance between the current source and each device.

As a rule, 12-volt ignitions draw between 1.5 and 3.5 amps. A pair of horns draw 18–20 amps, while electric wipers demand 3–6 amps. A pair of back-up lights drain 3.5–4 amps, while an air conditioner drains 13–20 amps.

On a 12-volt and four-lamp system, headlights demand 8–9 amps on low beam and 13–15 additional amps for high beam operation. Assume slightly less draw if your truck has a two-headlight system.

The cigar lighter, often used for plug-in accessories, drains 10–12 amps from the battery. A radio draws up to 4 amps (tape decks more), while power antennas drain 6–10 amperes. Instrument lamps, engine gauges, a clock or dome light each pull from 1–3 amps, a relatively mild load. Wire type ranges accordingly, and gauge size increases with wire length.

Fig. 15-12. *A heavy duty engine, alternator, frame and winch ground system assures full power. Here, Wrangler Power Products' custom 1/0 welding type cables (heavier cable) provide both positive and negative battery current and the complete ground circuit. Lighter conventional battery cables supply current to the winch.*

By contrast, the 12-volt starter motor, requiring an arc welding size lead from the battery, draws 150–450 amps during cranking. (This is a generalized range for modern automotive engines. An OEM level shop manual offers specific data for your truck's engine and starter.) These amperage requirements demand safe wire sizes.

Determining Wire Gauge

Distance also fits into the wiring equation. A device demanding 10 amperes of current requires a minimum 18-gauge wire for a seven foot flow. The same device needs a heavy 10 gauge wire at 75 feet.

> **NOTE —**
> When choosing wire, the higher the wire's AWG number, the smaller the wire size.

Undercapacity wire creates an excess voltage drop (the inherent loss of current due to a wire's resistance), causing lights to burn dimly, motors to turn slowly or accessories to operate below capacity. If the wires are grossly undersize, resistance rises to the point that the insulation melts, usually followed by a short to the closest chassis or body ground.

For auxiliary lighting (lightbars, emergency lights, floods, halogen lamps and such), look closely at the Watt ratings. Manufacturers list the Watt output, and there's a simple formula for converting watts to amperage: Wattage divided by voltage = amperage.

Example: On a 12-volt electrical system, a 100W lamp equals 100W divided by 12, or 8-1/3 amps. Therefore, an exotic string of ten 100 Watt lamps draws 83.3 amps.

For computing your electrical needs, consider the typical amperage draws for various accessory and OEM items on your truck. Add up the on-line components, and build your charging and battery system around these guidelines.

Wire, available at local auto supplies, usually comes in spool lengths of 25–100 feet. Once you determine the

proper amperage draw for each electrical component in your truck's system, select wire by gauge size.

Carry the amperage needs through the fuses and relays, those safety devices that will prevent wires from frying in the event of an overload or short. When matching fuses to electrical components, each fuse should allow just slightly more amperage flow than the device requires. This covers upstart surges and hot operation (when amperage draw increases slightly).

> **WARNING —**
> *Never install a higher amp fuse as a cure for an OE circuit that keeps blowing fuses. Always find the reason for an overload or voltage drop. (See electrical chapter for details on troubleshooting the electrical system.)*

Fuses blow for valid reasons: a defective electrical component, a bare wire short in the circuit, a weak ground, loose connections, or a charging circuit defect. Resolve the problem and install the correct fuse. A small volt-ohmmeter makes the ideal tool for troubleshooting resistance and the continuity of wiring circuits. (See chapter on electrical system.)

The backside of an early Land Cruiser dash is readily accessible. This reflects the utility and ease of service found in older light trucks. By the time RN11 mini-pickups came on line, electrical system access was already becoming complex. For the late Land Cruiser, 4Runner or pickup, a wire repair, switch replacement, stereo radio/cassette removal and other underdash tasks have become as complicated as working on an exotic automobile.

Matching Accessories and Wiring

When selecting the right wire gauge for your add-on accessories, note the relationship between amperage draw, Watt ratings, candle power and length of the wire runs.

Auxiliary lights, a sound system or a winch each have an assigned amperage draw. Cover that rating with a safety margin. You can always go bigger and be safe. Wherever possible, use fuses or circuit breakers. Protect higher amp items and wiring with reset breakers. Protective devices are available from 1.0 amp to 250 amp ratings and higher.

A winch's current draw is similar to a starter motor. Route cables very carefully to avoid high amperage shorts and possible fire. Review the winch manufacturer's guidelines for circuit protection and cable routing.

Remember: more wire means added resistance. Resistance raises amperage draw. Note the length of wire feeding each accessory. Select the recommended amperage ratings from an automotive wire manufacturer's guidebook, and match wire size accordingly. Account for the entire distance that current will flow, from the battery source to the accessory.

If your truck has a camper or aftermarket fiberglass body panels, you must run a ground wire to any accessory mounted on non-conductive material (fiberglass, plastic, wood, etc.). In this case, choose a wire gauge that satisfies the *total length of the power lead and ground wire*. A ground lead must always match the gauge size of the power lead.

High Work Standards

Safe routing of the long wires that run from the front to the rear of your truck requires close watch. A quality wiring job ensures that vibration and road shake will not separate or damage wires.

> CAUTION —
> *Improperly installed plastic wire ties, clamps and straps have a nasty habit of wearing through wire insulation.*

A yardstick I like to apply is the worst case scenario. (Some call this "Murphy's Law," but I don't believe Murphy or anyone else can stake sole claim to the phenomena.) Assume that the wire you're routing will face tension, heat and friction. Are there sharp metal edges just waiting to whittle at your vital wiring loom? Can engine heat melt the plastic off wires? Will chassis movement tear a crucial connection apart?

You must depend on your wiring in blizzards, on remote desert moonscapes, atop craggy and windswept mountains—and even in the fast lane of the freeway during rush hour. Take the time to route, shield, tape and secure all wires.

Wire Looms and Connections

For assuring quality work, use universal plastic wire shields, quality wire connectors, ties and straps. Rewiring and repairs often involve use of insulated, solderless connectors. These connectors match wire gauge sizes. When using solderless connectors, be certain to select the correct size for the wire involved.

Color coded solderless connectors have become popular over the last three decades. They are easy to fit, quick to secure in tight places and offer long service life. A special crimping pliers is necessary for installation. Don't cut corners when buying this tool. Tight, neat connections depend on professional caliber tools.

Expect to waste a few connectors practicing your crimping skills. Too tight or loose won't do. On connectors and crimp terminal ends with seams on the metal sleeves, make certain your crimp is on the solid side, not the seam.

The factory (OE) wire connections are often solder type, with molded insulation. In some cases, aftermarket pigtails are available to restore OE integrity to electrical connections. Some fitups, however, benefit from the use of an entire OE wiring harness, tailored to your truck's needs. Pre-formed harnesses, insulated properly, provide the best connections possible.

> NOTE —
> Late model Toyota trucks with electronic/solid state components depend upon proper circuit resistance and voltage signals. On such a system, it may be necessary to repair damaged wiring with the installation of a complete new harness assembly. Consult the OEM Toyota truck repair manual before attempting wire repairs on a late model truck.

Some forethought and a factory schematic of your truck's electrical system will contribute to a quality wiring job. Electrical work, done properly, is very gratifying. It also provides a better understanding of how your truck operates. Armed with this knowledge, you'll feel more confident about traveling to isolated regions.

Consider the Load

When amperage load rises, so does the need for a high performance electrical system. Light trucks, and especially four-wheel drive models, offer more room for accessorization than any other vehicle. These trucks press their electrical systems to the limit.

Fig. 15-13. *Wrangler Power Products at Prescott, Arizona offers this crimping tool for the do-it-yourselfer. These crimps in heavy duty copper battery terminals offer maximum conductivity and a long-lasting cure for resistance problems. Note size of heat shrink sleeve.*

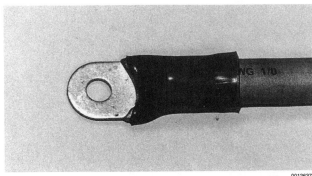

Fig. 15-14. *This is a quality wire connection. After crimping, the copper terminal receives a coating of special adhesive-lined heat shrink tubing.*

Fig. 15-15. *When running a winch, dual batteries are a smart choice. Wrangler's 'Battery Management System' features a dash-mounted switch for three mode protection for using and charging both batteries. System helps prevent risk of becoming stranded with a dead battery.*

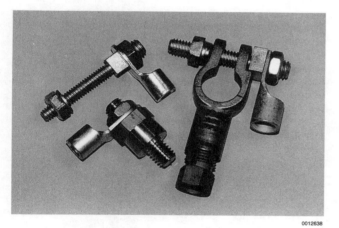

Fig. 15-16. *Various types of battery attachments are available. Shown are two crimp type terminals and a unique compression nut clamp. Each meets high industrial/automotive standards and feature durable, high quality copper.*

Installation of an aftermarket high output alternator can serve your high amperage charging needs. Along with high amps from the alternator, you must consider the wiring and safety devices needed to support such a high output charging and accessory system.

Protecting Your Electrical System

Once you've selected the right alternator to meet your amperage needs, heavy duty wiring can begin. In external regulator systems, wiring starts with the alternator-to-regulator harness. Needs here include proper wire sizing and use of quality terminals. If the alternator unit has an integral regulator, an adequate charge wire, routed directly to the battery, is necessary.

If your alternator delivers 130 or less amps, the appropriate (minimum) requirement for a 10-foot or less length

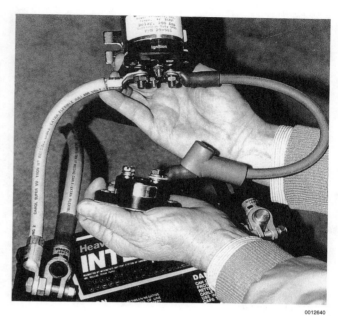

Fig. 15-17. *In-line relays and isolators are available in high amperage ratings. These devices service heavy accessory circuits.*

alternator lead is 4-gauge wire. A positive battery cable with the proper ring size end for the alternator output stud is more than adequate. (Protect this lead with a 150 amp circuit breaker or fusible link.)

For the battery cable or a higher output alternator charge lead, premium 1/0 size copper welding-type cable is more than adequate. The fine strands of the welding cable, with quality crimped or compression clamped ends, will easily handle high resistance loads.

Unlike battery cables, which are relatively rigid and of lower grade, welding wire meets the highest industrial standards for carrying amperage. Fine-strand wire permits oversizing without excessive resistance, voltage drop or false battery/current signals to the voltage regulator.

When building the charging/battery wiring with 1/0 welding cable, make sure you also use 1/0 cable for all grounds, including the engine-to-frame and battery. The 12-volt battery system of a Toyota truck is direct current (D.C.), and this means the ground circuit wire gauge must match both charging and starter draw demands.

Dual Battery Electrical Needs

Many truck owners with heavy duty electric winches add an extra battery to their system. For electrical systems with auxiliary batteries, I recommend use of Wrangler Power Products' Battery Management System.

The system provides an automatic low voltage battery response designed to disconnect the current flow from the auxiliary battery when voltage drops to a critical level. This prevents abuse of your truck's expensive accessories and also protects the auxiliary battery from severe discharge. Upon recharging the battery to a full state of charge, the system reconnects the circuit.

A quality dual or auxiliary battery management system performs two functions: 1) delivers maximum bat-

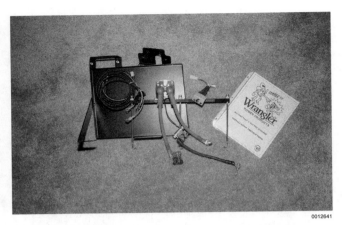

Fig. 15-18. Dual batteries require a quality management system. Wrangler Power Products' Battery Manager System is a driver switched dual battery circuit controller. The reliable battery isolator and switching components make it virtually impossible to get stranded by a discharged battery. This is my choice for a safe and reliable dual battery management system.

tery current for starting and 2) charge system protection. In the event that the chassis main battery(s) become low, a management system can bring the auxiliary battery on line to help start the engine.

The system monitors the two batteries once the engine starts, applying current solely to the main battery until it reaches a full charge state. Then the management system reads the charge state of the auxiliary or winch battery and feeds current to both batteries as required.

Other types of battery isolators are also available. Both electronic and electro-magnetic/mechanical relays, ranging in amperage limits from 100 to 200 amps, can handle major current flow chores. A hefty 250 amp battery switch will also meet heavy current requirements.

Circuit breaking relays, gaining popularity over traditional fuses, work very well on truck electrical systems. In environments where temporary shorting is likely, such as submersion in a running stream of water, a circuit breaker will reset when the hazard passes and the components dry—a helpful prospect.

Circuit breakers range from huge devices to small two-spade ATO fuse size relays. ATO type fuses have become popular in later model trucks.

Assessing Your Electrical System's Reliability

Building a first class wiring system involves use of high grade copper terminals and wire products. Regardless of style, judge switches by two criteria: amperage load capacity and a switch's designated number of service cycles.

> **NOTE —**
> Better quality switches have amperage load and service cycle ratings. You will find these switches listed in automotive and electrical/industrial parts catalogs.

If you want maximum performance from your truck's electrical system, each piece of hardware, including crimped and compression terminals, should bear either a military, commercial or industrial (UL) rating. The switches found at discount auto supply outlets seldom have these ratings.

For heavy duty purposes, be suspect of any electrical component without a recognizable rating. When in doubt, seek out an industrial/commercial supplier or high quality automotive sources like NAPA's Belden line or Wrangler Power Products. (See appendix for parts sources.)

High grade hardware, including both brass and copper battery attachments and wire terminals, eliminates trouble in heavily worked electrical systems. Protection from battery acid and the corrosion of salty winters is a must. Underhood heat becomes your nemesis in desert climates, gnawing away at wire insulation and taxing the voltage regulator and other relays. Quality electrical hardware is the best protective measure.

Some Unusual Electrical Hardware

Among the electrical specialty items is a battery jumper system that mounts permanently to the front or rear of your truck. Quick connect cables can serve easily in emergencies, enabling your truck to park nose-to-nose with a stalled vehicle.

Quick disconnect jumper cables help you avoid the hazard of hanging your truck out in the road or sliding over a cliff while trying to pull alongside a vehicle. The best system I've found yet comes from Wrangler Power Products. These kits feature 1/0 welding cable, copper terminals and industrial grade connectors.

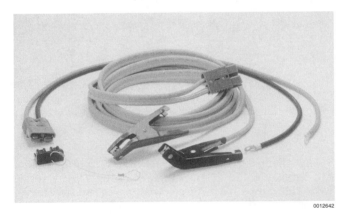

Fig. 15-19. Here is the best way yet to jump batteries, with special quick-connect system that terminates at front bumper. This avoids the spark-and-explosion risk of hooking jumper cables directly to a battery.

Selecting a Battery

Batteries have an ampere hour rating and cold cranking capacity. The engine and electrical system dictate their needs, with air conditioning, power options, the engine size and compression ratio determining the necessary battery group size.

An under-capacity battery will discharge quickly and require excessive, high amperage recharging. Such cycling leads to short battery life. If your truck has a heavy electrical load, or has been hybridized with an engine transplant, battery selection should favor the engine.

Find a listing for a truck equipped with your engine type and approximately the same accessory package. Note its battery size. Select a similarly rated battery that will fit your Toyota truck's battery box, if possible, or change boxes to an adequate size. Secure the battery safely, and use the best battery cable connections available.

A 12-volt battery will operate best above 12.3 volts. A full state of charge is 12.6 volts. When you crank the engine for a long period or the headlights have burned without the engine running, the battery voltage drops below 12.3 volts. Healthy and adequately sized batteries will recover some voltage if left alone for awhile (regain a "surface charge"), however, to completely restore a battery's state of charge, the generator or alternator must flow amperes.

Maintaining and Monitoring Battery Charge

Earlier Toyota truck charge systems (both generator and alternator versions) have ammeters that read the amperes of electrical current that flow either toward or away from the battery. Current flow is regulated by an external voltage regulator. It acts as an electrical current monitor, directing charge flow to the battery. The regulator receives battery voltage signals and adjusts current to achieve a full charge.

Later trucks feature integral voltage regulators and voltmeters instead of ammeters. Voltmeters show the battery's actual state of charge, or the charge state as current flows from the alternator to the battery. Most truck owners prefer a voltmeter and find it more useful. I certainly do.

A worn battery with bad cells loses more voltage while spinning the starter motor, which may bring the battery's volt reading down to 10 volts or less. When this occurs, the alternator floods the battery with heavy amps of current, and a vicious cycle begins. The already tired battery suffers from this fast charge, which heats the battery and reduces its life even further. Soon, the worn battery is nothing more than a source of lead for recycling.

Likewise, an engine rebuild or performance modifications may finish off a lighter duty or worn out battery. Heavy voltage depletion followed by maximum charging after each engine start-up will quickly ruin any battery. Battery drain from heavy lighting or an electric winch can also create a high-rate charging situation. This can quickly destroy the battery.

High Performance Charging System

A high output alternator can restore the battery's state of charge in minutes. OE alternator output usually improves with power options like air conditioning, electric door locks and power window lifts.

Even with a high output factory alternator, however, truck owners find ways to overwhelm their electrical system. Auxiliary lighting, an electric winch, high Watt sound systems, and dual-battery installations leave the alternator with a heavy burden.

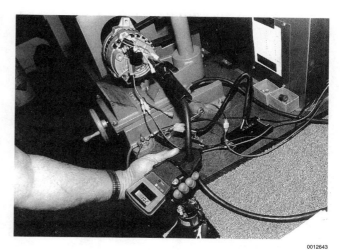

Fig. 15-20. *OEM GM CS-130 style alternator is potent. This Delco-Remy unit, capable of 100 amps at an equivalent of 1500 crankshaft rpm, tests a top end output of 103 amps. Characteristic of many late model alternators, the CS-130's most impressive attribute is 61 amp output at an engine idle.*

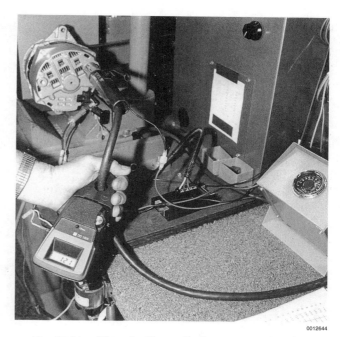

Fig. 15-21. *Wrangler Power Products tests a GM factory CS-144 alternator, which stormed to a 121 ampere output by 5000 rotor rpm. Idle speed amperage read 61. Wrangler builds the GM CS-133 or CS-144 alternators into even higher output 140 and 160 amp systems that can be retrofitted to meet demands of a Chevy V-8 conversion 4WD Land Cruiser or 2WD and 4WD pickups with a domestic V-6 engine swap.*

The alternator's strongest advantage over older generator designs is the ability to produce a higher charge rate at slower speeds. Alternators can meet the demands of a vehicle that idles in traffic with air conditioning and other luxury accessories gnawing at the battery. Worse yet, high amp draw auxiliary lighting or a winch often operates with the engine either idling or stopped in a precarious off-pavement situation.

Late OEM alternators have outstanding charge rates at an idle. By comparison, trucks built before the 1980s, even with high output factory alternators, lag at lower rpm. The typical high output alternator of 1970s vintage produces 55 amps @ 6500 alternator/rotor rpm but only 9 amps at an engine idle. In fairness, this alternator at 1500 engine rpm jumps to a 44 amp output, but the message is clear: At a curb idle, or when you're crawling off-pavement in the desert, the older alternator has limited output.

As a high output alternator retrofit for an early Land Cruiser, consider the features of later factory alternators.

An On-board Welder

We were five tortuous, rock crawling hours into the Rubicon. In our whole group, only one rig had given us mechanical trouble. Compared to the two guys now standing in the trail, the trip was a breeze.

A powerful Saginaw power steering gear, manhandled by two burly arms, had ripped out the section of frame rail that supports the steering gearbox. In three hours time, the CJ model Jeep had moved only a couple of healthy stone's throws.

As much as we wanted to help these guys, our tools fell short. What we really needed was a welder. An alternator-powered frequency welder takes a fabrication welder wherever your truck goes. Mounted either underhood or in the bed, the compact unit is powerful stuff.

Better frequency welders perform serious welding, including the use of 5/32" rod on heavy steel plate. Since the principle is frequency, not amperage, cable length/distance is no barrier. Some designs also provide a 110-volt DC outlet with enough wattage to run brush motor power tools or a string of camp lamps. A battery booster mode assists stranded vehicles in minutes.

A high-output alternator is at the core of a frequency welder system. At 1500 engine rpm, the alternator reaches 135 or more amps, enough to deliver peak welding voltage.

Options include all welding accessories and even TIG (heliarc) or MIG (wire weld) equipment. From my view, this is the ultimate tool for the serious outback traveler. (See Appendix for sources.)

Fig. 15-22. *Here are high quality components for building longevity into a charging system. Your new alternator is just the beginning. Shown is a junction block for high amperage, battery size leads.*

By 1982, a popular 80 amp domestic Delco-Remy alternator produces 55 amps at 2000 engine rpm. The newest Delco high output units produce in excess of 60 amps at a 675 rpm idle. Now that's progress!

Always upgrade your battery size when installing a high output alternator. Running a winch from a single, low ampere hour battery is dangerous. Completely draining a battery then forcing massive current back into it (which is the voltage regulator's normal response to a fully discharged battery) will heat up the battery plates and cause their failure. Weak batteries produce gases that can explode violently under such conditions.

3. ROLL BARS

By design, light trucks need ground clearance, which means that your truck has a higher center of gravity than a passenger car. Concerns about a hazardous rollover are valid, with taller 4x4 models especially vulnerable.

> **WARNING —**
> *A cabover camper or roof rack full of cargo raises the vehicle's roll center and also affects center of gravity. When you carry such a load, your truck should have stabilizer bars and other devices to offset the risk of rollover. Wheel and tire width also play a role here. For ideas on how to reduce risk, see the chapter on chassis/suspension upgrades.*

It's unnerving when a trail or roadway shifts off-camber and your truck's tilt meter runs off the safe zone. When you drive in these kinds of environments, the best protection against bodily injury and major vehicular damage is a roll cage and ample seat belt/harnesses.

Greater concern for product liability has encouraged aftermarket manufacturers to classify cab bars and other steel tubular assemblies into distinct classes: the bonafide roll bar (chassis or cab mounted) and a group of lighter weight, largely cosmetic tube or bed bars.

Fig. 15-23. *Where does the roll cage/frame end and the suspension begin? On desert race trucks and stadium race trucks, the line is thin. Bracing angles reflect nature's strongest design, the triangle. This shape repeats itself throughout the chassis and cage.*

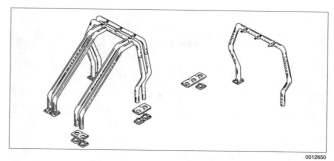

Fig. 15-25. *Hobrecht, Grizzly, Smittybilt and others make attractive truck bars for Toyota pickup beds. These bars provide mounts for lighting and minimal protection. Mounted to the bed sheet metal, they do not qualify as bonafide roll bars. Hobrect and Smittybilt also offer more protective cab cages for pickups.*

Fig. 15-24. *Roll bars require padding. If your bars are shaped oddly or you want protection, padding is available from aftermarket sources.*

Cab cages, built for light trucks and multi-purpose sport/utility 4x4s, resemble race truck protection. The critical differences between a hard-core Baja race truck cage and a manufactured cab cage are the bracing and attachment methods.

A Racing Roll Cage

Off-road racing is the best test for roll cages. The standards set by the High Desert Racing Association (HDRA) and SCORE say a lot about our safety needs. Whether you are building your own truck roll cage or shopping for quality aftermarket rollover protection, racing requirements offer the highest standards.

For racing, the minimum tubing size for a 2000-3000 lb. truck is 1-3/4" diameter for open cockpits and 1-1/2" for closed cabs. Tubing wall thickness is minimum 0.120". A 3000-4000 lb. race vehicle requires 2" x 0.120" for open cockpits and 1-3/4" x 0.120" for a closed cab. In trucks over 4000 lbs., tubing size increases to 2-1/4" x 0.120" for open cockpits and 2" x 0.120" for closed cabs.

Materials and construction follow strict guidelines. HDRA/SCORE recommends CRW, DOM, WHR, or WCR mild carbon steel or 4130 Chromoly steel. Light weight and high strength make 4130 popular.

According to official rules, "All welded intersections should be stress relieved by flame annealing. Welds must be high quality with good penetration and no undercutting of the parent metal. No oxy-acetylene brazing on roll cage tubing is permissible. No square tubing is permitted. Use of other materials is subject to prior HDRA/SCORE approval."

Along with these minimum material standards, HDRA/SCORE has strict construction guidelines. The cage must mount securely to the frame or body. All intersection points must have gussets and bracing.

Officially, "Cab or body mounted cages must not be attached to the body structure by direct welding, but must be bolted through and attached by the use of doubler plates (one on either side) with a minimum thickness of 3/16"...Roll cage terminal ends must be located to a frame or body structure that will support maximum impact and not shear..."

The required tubing sizes apply to front and rear hoops, front and rear hoop interconnecting bars, rear down braces and all lateral bracing. Minimum bolt size for any attachments is 3/8", with Grade 5 or better strength. A minimum requirement for HDRA/SCORE racing is a roll cage with one front hoop, one rear hoop, two interconnecting top bars between the hoops; two rear down braces and one diagonal brace.

NOTE —
Gussets are mandatory at all welded intersections on the main cage and down braces. Fabricators must also use gussets at any single weld where a fracture could affect driver safety.

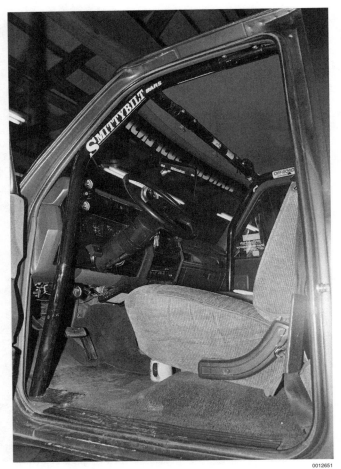

Fig. 15-26. *Cab cages like the one in this 4x4 pickup truck can serve well in a crisis. Quality Smittybilt kit makes installation easier, with minimal amount of assembly time. Carpet and seat removal are part of the installation.*

Triangular gussets at the top corners may be halves of a 3" x 3" x 1/8" flat plate. Another approach is split, formed and welded corner tubing, or tubing gussets the same thickness as the main cage material. When making the rear down braces and diagonal bracing, the angle cannot be less than 30 degrees from a vertical plane.

HDRA/SCORE rules provide another valuable insight. If a race truck has no steel doors to protect the driver and co-driver, side bars are mandatory. A minimum of one bar per side, as near parallel with the ground as possible, must provide protection yet allow the driver and co-driver (i.e., passenger) to get in and out of the vehicle quickly.

The side bars, formed from the same tubing as the roll cage, must attach to the front and rear hoops of the cage. Gussets and other such braces are also necessary. Sure, it might be tougher to crawl in and out of such a truck, but if rocky terrain or high speed in the desert is part of your game plan, the added protection could prevent severe injury in a rollover or T-bone accident.

Racing rules also state that the roll cage bars must be at least 3" in any direction from the driver's or co-driver's helmets while in their normal driving or riding positions.

Poorly constructed cages have many back country four-wheelers knocking themselves silly against their roll bars. For off-pavement driving, bar padding is a must.

In addition to the roll cage requirements, HDRA/-SCORE requires head and neck restraints to minimize whiplash. The restraint is usually 36 square-inches with at least 2" of padding. Rules also call for padding at all areas of the roll bar or bracing that the occupants' helmets might reach. For an off-pavement or race truck, full padding of the whole interior cage is practical.

Practical Alternatives

Few drivers will ever experience a rollover at high speed or the catastrophic impact forces that regularly threaten desert racers. For a reasonable margin of safety, short of a racing-specification cage, manufactured cab cage systems will often suffice. Better manufactured kits have the advantage of pre-fabricated pieces, with all necessary bends in place. Manufacturers like Smittybilt and Hobrecht work hard to assure proper fitup and ease of installation.

While HDRA/SCORE standards assure maximum protection, less elaborate designs can serve most off-high-way situations. At lower speeds, especially while rock crawling, a rollover is generally the less extreme matter of slowly laying a truck on its side. Here, a quality roll cage with side protection, proper seat mounts and secure belts will meet most needs.

WARNING —
Loose objects in your truck can become lethal weapons during a rollover. A latched or locking box to contain pieces like tool boxes, metal jacks and jack handles is a very important off-pavement or 4x4 accessory.

4. SEAT BELTS AND SAFETY HARNESSES

Rough terrain driving means odd angles and plenty of bounce. Vehicles can roll over, even at a snail's pace. With very few exceptions, an occupant is safest when safely seat belted within the truck.

If, however, your truck faces a situation like rolling off the edge of a ledge above a steep cliff or into a deep and swift running body of water, consider getting out. (The same rule applies if you might be crushed or impaled by an object in your path as the truck heads for a very low speed rollover.)

WARNING —
Faced with such a foreboding choice, be sure to exit your truck as safely as possible, at the point furthest away from the hazard. Avoid being crushed or trapped by your vehicle as it rolls over. Use extreme caution if you choose to jump from the vehicle. This is always a tough call to make—and on extremely short notice.

Beyond these kinds of situations, you're usually better off seat belted within the protection of your cab and, optimally, a roll cage. That's why you have one.

Fig. 15-27. *Factory seat belt anchors are quality attachment points for lap belts. OE engineering accounts for high strength and proper angles.*

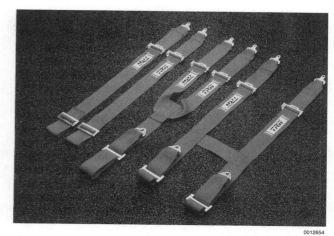

Fig. 15-29. *TRW shoulder harnesses demonstrate two popular styles: H and Y types. TRW is popular in off-road and other forms of sanctioned racing.*

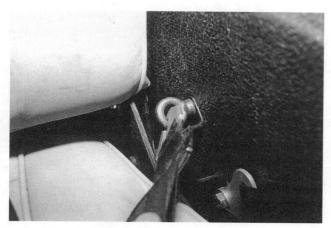

Fig. 15-28. *Grade 8 or better quality hardware, including this eye loop anchor from Filler Safety, assures safe seat belt and harness attachments. A 3" square reinforcement plate backs up sheet metal where harness tail strap attaches.*

Racing Harnesses

HDRA/SCORE racing standards provide a yardstick for measuring seat belt and harness quality. The minimum standard for racing is a five-point fast release seat belt and shoulder harness assembly. Buckles must be metal-to-metal, with the single anti-submarine strap attached "as close to the front edge of the seat as practical so that it will exert maximum restraint to the upward movement of the belt and harness."

Seat lap belts are 3" width, the submarine belt 2", and shoulder straps must be 2–3". Harness materials must be Nylon or Dacron Polyester and in new or perfect condition with no cuts or frayed layers, chemical stains or excessive dirt.

HDRA/SCORE recommends that belts be changed after one year of use. They *must* be changed three years from the date of manufacture. The mounting position of the shoulder harnesses is approximately 4" below the top of the driver's and co-driver's shoulders. This issue is critical, as severe injury can result from poorly positioned belt anchor points.

By HDRA/SCORE guidelines, "Lap belts should be kept at a minimum at least 2-1/2" forward of seat and backrest intersection. All belts must be mounted directly to a main structure member with the strength at least 1-1/2" x 0.090" tubing with gussets." HDRA/SCORE also recommends keeping adjustment buckles a minimum distance of 1-1/2" from the seat to prevent accidental loosening or chafing.

Avoid Submarining

Submarining is your body sliding beneath the lap belt during a frontal impact. In desert racing, submarining also occurs when a truck or buggy flies over a rise and lands nose first in a silt bed or the edge of a streambed.

Spinal and head injuries can result from submarining. By sliding down into the seat, the body's alignment during the recoil-phase (when the body slams rearward after impact) is awkward. Your head may hit the space between the headrest and seat back, causing severe neck injury.

A series of factors cause submarining: poor design of the safety-belt, bad location of the belt's attachment points, and the wrong seat configuration.

Many shoulder belt designs actually pull the lap belt up during a collision. Schroth, a major producer of rally and racing seat belts, discovered that evenly distributed loads on the shoulder belts were more likely to pull the lap belt up and cause submarining.

As a remedy, Schroth's ASM (AntiSubMarining) system is designed to allow one shoulder belt to readjust very slightly on impact, turning the body a few degrees. The slight shift in position causes the lower body to press into the lap belt earlier (approximately 20 milliseconds sooner). This tiny delay before the shoulder belts begin to pull is just enough time to tighten against the lap belt.

Using a precalculated energy change also cushions head and shoulder force as the belts begin to tighten. An additional benefit, Schroth notes, is that the design prevents hard pressure on the sternum and breastbone.

> **WARNING —**
> *Like all other seat belts or harnesses, once the ASM shoulder belts have experienced a heavy frontal impact shift (enough to lengthen the belt), they require replacement.*

Filler Safety Products, very popular with racers, also stresses the importance of proper seat belt mounting. On 5- and 6-point harnesses, Filler recommends that lap belts angle 45-55 degrees to the tangent line of the thigh. Filler shoulder harness tailstraps require a 45-degree angle from the seat top, tying to a roll bar cross brace 4-inches below the shoulder line.

The lap belt anchors 2" forward of the point where the driver's back line and the floor intersect, or 2-1/2" forward of the intersect point of the seat and backrest. Belts should attach to the floor at the same width as the occupant, with brackets aimed in the direction of belt pull. The crotch strap should anchor in line with the driver's chest. Filler's guidelines comply with HDRA/SCORE rules.

Engineers work continuously to improve seat belt and roll bar systems. Light truck and four-wheel drive users have a lot to gain from that effort. If you and your truck have an appetite for the rough stuff, give yourself a fighting chance.

5. TRAILERING

My trailering experience includes two- and four-wheel drive light trucks and 4WD SUVs. I once pulled a tandem axle travel trailer with our 4WD Land Cruiser FJ40's 90-inch wheelbase. Although that worked reasonably well (due largely to elaborate chassis/wheel/tire upgrades and the use of safety trailering equipment), trucks and SUVs with a wheelbase shorter than 110 inches are generally poor candidates for pulling a sizeable trailer. For long-term towing use and overall safety, I prefer a hefty, longer wheelbase truck or SUV chassis.

As a rule, short wheelbase vehicles don't track well in front of long framed trailers. Even without a trailer, a short wheelbase vehicle can be a handful on ice, slick pavement or when turning at excess speed.

The shorter the wheelbase, the tighter the turning radius, though, and that's where some mini/compact 4x4 pickups and sport utility (SUV) models reign. These shorty SUVs and light 4x4 trucks are often ideal for a tight, twisty off-pavement trail. Once such a vehicle crosses up or skids sideways on a firm roadway surface, however, they're in big trouble. Events happen very quickly with a shorter wheelbase and frame. Add to this a higher center of gravity, and a full spinout or rollover is possible.

When towing a trailer, steering control is the main drawback for a shorter wheelbase vehicle. Trucks under 110-inch wheelbase have insufficient frame length for absorbing the side sway and whip of a trailer. Additionally, a lightweight truck chassis is easily overrun by a bigger trailer during braking.

A truck's higher center of gravity compounds the short wheelbase problem, making risk of a rollover even greater with a trailer out of control. A two-ton load pushing at the rear bumper centerline of a light duty, short wheelbase truck will tax both the vehicle's design and intent.

For the truck better suited to towing, a set of beefier springs, heavy duty shock absorbers, sway controls and an increased tread width can help add stability. A wider-than-stock tread width, accomplished with appropriate wheel rims and oversized tires, can improve the vehicle's directional control. My FJ40 Land Cruiser trailering experiment benefitted from each of these upgrades. (See

Fig. 15-30. *Incredibly, your truck can set almost exactly at its unloaded ball height with a twenty-plus-foot travel trailer attached. Here, my FJ40 sets ready to tow a Starcraft travel trailer.*

Although I do not recommend this wheelbase length for towing, the use of a load distributing hitch, sway control and electric trailer brake controller made towing substantially safer.

suspension/chassis upgrade chapter for details about wheels and tires.)

Stable Hitch Assemblies and Equalizers

Equalizers have revolutionized trailer towing. An equalizer is the ultimate torsion bar suspension system, designed to neutralize chassis load on the tow vehicle.

The equalizer looks inconspicuous enough, basically two unassuming bars that trail rearward from the truck hitch's ball mount. They swing in their hitch mounting sockets, attached by link chains to brackets that mount on the trailer frame. The adjusting links of the chain are significant, actually loading tension between the truck's hitch and the trailer frame.

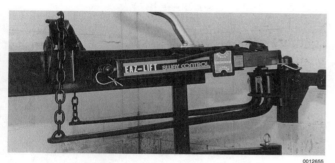

Fig. 15-31. *Drawtite equalizer and EAZ-Lift Sway Control provide ingenious means for stabilizing a trailer in tow. The trailer and truck chassis move in unison, offsetting road forces while distributing the load.*

The theory is ingenious. As you load the bars, the tongue weight that would otherwise push downward at the rear of the truck becomes "equalized" by the torsion bar tension. When properly adjusted, the trailer's weight becomes distributed over the entire length (each of the axles' spring sets) of both the trailer and truck frames.

Visualize pulling a long and hefty trailer without an equalizer. Imagine hard braking with a 3500-lb. trailer rocking forward. Consider the interaction between the two chassis when your truck encounters dips. Picture the truck loaded with additional gear in the back, its front tires too light to steer and the rear springs slamming against the bump stops.

The equalizer attacks each of these problems, allowing the truck and trailer chassis to move together. These torsion bars aren't just responsible for balancing the load, they also exert a counterforce as they flex.

An equalizer assembly works effectively to counter uncontrolled chassis movement. With an equalizer hitch assembly, the truck and trailer frames can move closely together on nearly the same plane.

Sturdy Trailer Hitches

Pre-fabricated trailer hitches are available for many Toyota truck models. Your local Toyota dealership or a trailering/RV center can supply a bolt-on assembly that meets a wide range of needs and load ratings. In some

Fig. 15-32. *A Class III fabricated hitch rates strong enough for a 5000 lb. load. These hitches accommodate Warn and Ramsey portable winches. Similar hitches are available from your local Toyota dealership or most RV outlets.*

Fig. 15-33. *Hefty Drawtite receiver ball mount adjusts horizontally and also for tilt angle. Massive sockets for equalizer torsion bars can be seen here. The welded miniature ball bracket holds a sway control ball head. Sway control and equalizer assemblies make the whole package work. Without these devices, a light truck and trailer could wind up in serious trouble.*

cases, however, a custom hitch will better suit your trailer or the truck's design.

A capable shop can build the right hitch for your truck. When choosing a custom trailer hitch, look carefully. You want a well-equipped shop, with all the necessary tools, welding apparatus, and quality steel for building a good hitch.

The highest grade steel, 1/4" thick, should be used for braces and gussets. Two-inch square, 0.188" wall thickness rectangular tubing provides a safe hitch framework. To prevent stresses inherent to heat-and-bend methods, make tubing bends on a press. Likewise, all construction welds and actual frame attachment welds should follow rigid standards that reduce heat stress to frame members and other vital parts.

Fig. 15-34. *Pulling a travel trailer is no light matter. Rick's R.V. Center and Hitch Shop custom-built this frame mount hitch for my FJ40 'Cruiser, which pulled a 1600 lb. tent trailer with ease. Hitch will now receive additional fore and aft upgrade bracing at the receiver. (The muffler will be relocated, and brace will tie receiver to forward crossmember of truck's frame.) The greater load will also require an equalizing hitch.*

Trucks and 4x4s used off-pavement, like the FJ40 Land Cruiser, occasionally bury their rear bumpers in the dirt. For this reason, a receiver-type hitch, tucked in close to the rear frame member, works well.

You can remove the detachable ball mount assembly when the trailer is not in use. This will reduce rear departure angle hang ups and also discourage theft of expensive pieces. Use of a pin-and-clip disconnect on the ball mount, with a nut welded to the side of the receiver to accept an anti-rattle bolt, provides for quick installation and removal of the ball mount.

Rick Preston is one of the best hitch fabricators around, an experienced and innovative designer of safe, custom built towing hitches. When Rick's crew builds a custom hitch, they often incorporate two rearward facing side gussets, triangular in shape. Safety chain-holed plates brace the receiver. The trailer's safety chains, which can route through the hitch and index with chain slots, help meet mandated safety requirements.

For Rick's R.V. Center and Hitch Shop at El Cajon, California, final fit-up includes strategically placed welds for frame mounts, then installation of cross-bracing and support. (Added braces can raise the class rating of the hitch.) A trailer electrical connector bracket and glossy black engine enamel complete the job.

Before towing any trailer with your truck, get an expert opinion about the vehicle's towing equipment. Shops like Rick's know the requirements and can quickly identify an unsafe hitch.

Big League Trailering

If a 1500 pound or larger trailer fits your vacation or utility needs, consider towing with a truck of 112" or longer wheelbase. (For pickups and SUVs, I prefer wheelbases in excess of 120 inches, which Toyota offers in the T100 and some extended cab compact trucks. The later 4WD Land Cruiser is very stable at 112.2 inches, as are the earlier 'Cruiser FJ Station Wagons.)

For trailer pulling, the strikes against a shorter wheelbase model are not only the wheelbase length. Trucks under 112-inch wheelbase also have lighter duty braking capacity, weaker axle sizing and lower spring rates.

Good trailer brakes, a frame-mounted Class III or better hitch and an equalizer (load distributing) assembly can help bring your truck and trailer to a quick, straight and safe stop. Add a sway control (basically a friction brake mounted between the trailer tongue and hitch) to reduce the effects of cross winds and whip on curvy roads. Most trailer whip can be controlled with a matched equalizer assembly and sway control.

Chapter 16

Toyota Engine Performance

1. ENGINE PERFORMANCE AND SMOG LEGAL MODIFICATIONS

The United States Clean Air Act of 1990 was a watershed measure to curb environmental pollution. "This landmark bill will result in deep and lasting reductions in acid rain, of toxic industrial air pollutants and urban smog," President George Bush noted. "It also will limit U.S. greenhouse gas emissions and sharply reduce our potential contribution to climate change."

The President expressed this nation's commitment to protect the environment and added, "While national governments have an important role to play, progress in protecting our environment is also made community by community, street by street, person by person." Targeting engine modifications that defeat pollution controls, the U.S. Environmental Protection Agency (EPA) has given aftermarket performance manufacturers a higher level of accountability. Product disclaimers that read "off-highway use only" are no longer enough.

The Message Is Clear

The California Air Resources Board and the U.S. EPA mean business. Cars and trucks manufactured and licensed for public road use must comply with clean air standards and emission control guidelines.

0019573

Fig. 16-1. NWOR Specialties and California Mini-Truck each offer the proven Camden supercharger retrofit kit for 20R and 22R four-cylinder engines. Shown here is NWOR/Camden kit installed on a 22R. NWOR claims 135 rear wheel horsepower using "hi-tech forged pistons" and 8–11 psi of boost. For a stock carbureted or EFI engine, however, NWOR and California Mini-Trucks each recommend a milder five psi maximum boost for long engine life.

CHAPTER 16

An EPA letter addressed to automotive parts manufacturers, distributors, retailers and installers clarifies the amended government policy: "The Clean Air Act now prohibits any person from manufacturing, selling, offering for sale, or installing any part or component intended for use with, or as part of, any motor vehicle, where a principal effect of the part or component is to bypass, defeat, or render inoperative any device or element of design, and where the person knows or should know the part or component is being put to such use."

As an example, the letter notes, "...EPA has determined that a catalytic converter replacement pipe, also known as a test pipe, is a part or component intended for use with a motor vehicle for which a principal effect is to bypass, defeat, or render inoperative a vehicle's catalytic converter...EPA believes it is illegal for any person to manufacture, sell, offer for sale or install a catalytic converter replacement pipe...The penalty for violations is up to $2500 for each such device which is manufactured, sold, offered for sale or installed on a motor vehicle."

Ignorance is no excuse. Simply saying that the pipe cannot be used on pollution controlled vehicles won't satisfy the law. The manufacturer of such a device must now take full responsibility for the actual use of the product. The EPA warns, "We intend to focus our enforcement efforts not only on the manufacturers of these defeat devices, but also on auto parts houses and repair facilities who stock, sell or install such devices."

Taboos Under The Law

How does this policy affect your Toyota truck? Using the catalytic converter as an example, you cannot remove the converter for off-road driving. According to the EPA, "The federal tampering prohibition pertains to motor vehicles, which are defined by section 216(2) of the Act as 'any self-propelled vehicle[s] designed for transporting persons or property on a street or highway.'"

The EPA emphasizes that in each model year, vehicle manufacturers certify engine-chassis configurations to meet certain tailpipe emission standards. Under the 1990 mandates, "...it is not legal for anyone to de-certify a motor vehicle for off-road use." This means that Toyota, as a vehicle manufacturer, has certified your model, its engine and the emission control system. You cannot compromise any part of your truck's pollution control system.

This same law says that swapping an earlier non-catalyst engine into a later, catalytic-equipped chassis is illegal. The chassis still requires the use of a catalytic converter, and the engine must be either the same year or newer than your Toyota truck chassis/body. Shops are now held accountable for knowing whether a vehicle originally required a catalytic converter.

Importantly, a muffler shop cannot install a non-certified (termed "non-exempt" in California) dual exhaust system in place of a single exhaust system—even if the shop installs dual catalytic mufflers. If your truck was originally a single exhaust model, certified by Toyota in that mode, the new EPA law restricts any kind of non-certified modification by a muffler shop.

So strong is this ruling that the only current exception is a vehicle converted to dual exhausts with double catalytic converters prior to the Clean Air Act of 1990. Although the EPA encourages a shop to retrofit an OEM style single exhaust system in such cases, the agency currently allows shops to install replacement catalytic converters and pipes on a previously retrofit dual exhaust system. The shop must be able to prove, however, that they did not replace the OEM single system with a dual exhaust setup.

Catalytic converter rulings are just the beginning. EPA has adopted California's standards for exemption or certification of aftermarket engine parts. Components that the California Air Resources Board (CARB) finds acceptable also earn a federal stamp of approval. An Executive Order (EO number) from California indicates that an aftermarket part has undergone the testing necessary to meet or exceed OEM tailpipe emission standards.

Legally Exempted Components

Before you limit the utility of your smog-compliance Toyota truck, consider the legal alternatives. EPA and CARB each approve (exempt) many engine components that meet clean air requirements. There are also legally recognized components that have no impact on tailpipe emissions. A high output water pump, an improved cooling system, a high capacity charging circuit or chrome valve covers will not fail your truck's emissions test.

Equally important, engine rebuilding can legally include many upgrade parts that will increase the reliability of your engine. Components like stronger pushrods or rocker arms, hardened exhaust valve seats, better bearings, improved piston rings, quality (stock compression ratio) pistons and a heavy duty timing chain have no effect on tailpipe emissions.

The point here is tailpipe emissions. Changing the camshaft to a long duration grind for maximum mid-range and top end power is a sure way to raise measurable hydrocarbon and carbon monoxide output at lower engine speeds. (California-type biennial smog inspection tests traditionally have taken place at an idle and 2500 rpm.) Likewise, a non-approved high performance retrofit carburetor could raise your truck's tailpipe emissions.

NOTE —
A non-approved replacement carburetor will immediately fail the visual portion of the California-standard smog inspection test.

Many aftermarket manufacturers have taken their components through the California emission certification process. Some performance items qualify as OEM replacement parts. Most of Edelbrock's Performer dual-plane manifolds, for example, provide a mount for the EGR valve and have earned certification.

Although these Edelbrock manifolds improve flow and engine efficiency, they will not increase tailpipe pollution. Several exhaust header and ignition component manufacturers have also passed the CARB tests and received Executive Order (EO) exemption numbers for their products.

For electronic fuel injected and turbocharged engines, a variety of aftermarket improvements in air flow and induction tuning parts have met certification standards. If a part has an official California exemption number for use on your specific engine, you can install these parts without violating the law.

Fig. 16-2. *Both NWOR Specialties and Downey Off-Road offer precision port polished intake plenums for 22R-E fours and 3VZ-E 3.0L V-6 engines. Claims of 20-25% better air flow lead to better fuel economy and performance. Since polishing an OEM Toyota plenum has no effect on air/fuel ratios or EFI computer functions, this part will not interfere with tailpipe emissions standards.*

Clean Air High Performance

Under the amended Clean Air Act, aftermarket manufacturers must certify any induction system component, ignition system piece, performance camshaft or exhaust device that differs from the OEM design or engineering standards. Additionally, each state has statutes or regulations that prohibit defeating or tampering with the pollution control equipment on a certified motor vehicle. EPA emphasizes, "Vehicle owners who tamper with their own vehicles may be subject to substantial penalties under both federal and State law."

These laws, however, encourage lower tailpipe emissions. For this reason, California has no objection to your replacing the carbureted F or 2F in-line OHV six in your 1987 or earlier Land Cruiser chassis with a later model 3F-E Toyota six, a Chevrolet EFI 350 V-8 or a Ford 5.8L EFI engine. Despite the increase in horsepower and torque, the tailpipe pollution from a late and stock EFI engine is a fraction of that allowed for a carbureted engine, especially those built before 1980.

> **NOTE —**
> A late EFI conversion engine must include its OEM computer and all factory engine sensors. You must swap all parts that make up the OEM engine/emissions package.

Buy Legal Performance

A wide range of aftermarket parts have California EO exemptions (50-State legal status). An exemption means the part will not defeat the design or intent of your engine's emission control system.

When you find EO exempted parts, make sure that pieces have approval for use on your particular year and model engine. Some parts might fit your engine but still do not meet the emission requirements. EO exemptions apply to a specific year/model, chassis type and engine

application. There are a variety of devices that have EO numbers. Currently, the EPA accepts CARB tests and exemption criteria. Parts that have California exemption status also meet Federal/EPA standards.

> **NOTE —**
> A complete list of California exempted components is available from the California Air Resources Board, or write to: Haagen-Smit Laboratory, 9528 Telstar Avenue, El Monte, CA 91731-2990, phone 1-818-575- 6800.

A Bright Future

Improvements in engine technology means more likelihood of swapping late EFI engines into earlier Toyota truck chassis. Electronic fuel injection overcomes sidehill flooding and the negative effects of altitude. Also, without exception, later EFI engines have lower tailpipe emissions and potentially better fuel efficiency than earlier carbureted versions of these same engine designs.

California has provided a referee program for smog certification of vehicles with engine conversions. Referees determine whether you have made a complete conversion, including all necessary emission equipment.

> **NOTE —**
> Tailpipe emissions from your new, upgraded engine must not exceed those of the original Toyota truck engine in good operating condition. For details, contact the California Consumer Affairs Department for referral to your local Bureau of Automotive Repairs referee station.

Imagine the performance of a late 350 Chevrolet TBI V-8 with an aftermarket 50-State legal supercharger—in place of the 1971 Toyota Land Cruiser's original 236.7 cubic inch OHV in-line six. How about a late 4.3L Vortec V-6 TBI/EFI engine in place of the 20R four of a 1979 4x4 Toy-

Fig. 16-3. *NWOR Specialties emphasizes both Ford and Chevrolet V-8 conversion kits for Toyota Land Cruisers and 4WD pickups—including a Ford small-block kit that allows installation of 260 to 302 V-8s into 1984–94 4WD pickups and 4Runners with five-speeds (removable bellhousing type). Use of a late EFI/MPI 302 with all OEM emission controls in place could provide legal high output V-8 performance. Ford V-8s of this design are very compact and lightweight.*

ota pickup? Your earlier Toyota truck would gain torque and likely better fuel efficiency, yet produce far less tailpipe pollution.

Aftermarket manufacturers have responded to the EPA requirements. Crane Cams has tested and received California Air Resources Board EO numbers for several camshaft profiles. Crane camshafts with EO numbers have 50-State legal status when used in specific engines.

Gene Ezzell, President and CEO at Crane Cams, has noted, "We are extremely proud to be the first performance camshaft company to receive exemption from ARB and to show the performance industry that it is possible to have products that meet emissions standards."

Ezzell credits the Specialty Equipment Market Association (SEMA) for encouraging the aftermarket to build California/EPA legal products. SEMA's effort helps assure the stability and future of the automotive performance aftermarket.

As an active supporter of TREAD LIGHTLY! and the Clean Air Act standards, I encourage you to protect the environment. Use those aftermarket performance parts with California EO numbers or EPA/50-States Legal status. At the very least, make sure that your truck is emission legal.

2. TOYOTA TRUCK POWER: AN OVERVIEW

Building a truck engine strictly for horsepower, a valid goal for desert racing, may actually inhibit low speed torque output and diminish trailer pulling, trail running and rock crawling ability. Careful planning and selection of components can give your engine more usable torque, better breathing characteristics and greater stamina for tortuous lugging and off-pavement climbs.

> *CAUTION —*
> *• Many engine modifications are illegal for street or public highway use. If your truck must comply with vehicle registration and public highway requirements, make certain that aftermarket parts have California and federal EPA approval. It is illegal to remove, modify or degrade pollution control devices on vehicles licensed for use on public highways.*
>
> *• When making major engine modifications, the rest of the truck's powertrain must be able to withstand the added torque. A light duty transmission, transfer case and drive axle(s) often fail when subjected to great increases in horsepower. Beware. You may need a host of geartrain modifications or upgrades.*

High Performance Begins With The Valvetrain

The typical valve-in-head (OHV) engine's valvetrain consists of the camshaft, camshaft followers (lifters), pushrods, rocker arms, valve springs and valves. Overhead camshaft (SOHC and DOHC) valvetrains eliminate the use of pushrods and, in the case of some Toyota engine designs, even the rocker shaft(s) and arms.

On all F, 2F and 3F-E OHV Toyota Land Cruiser engines, the valves and springs fit in a removable cylinder head. Camshaft followers or mechanical type lifters ride on lobes of the camshaft, low in the engine. Lengthy pushrods link the lifters to the rocker arms, which pivot on a rocker shaft mounted on pedestals atop the cylinder head. Rocker arms press against the valve stem ends. The intake and exhaust valves open and close the ports, allowing gases to enter and leave each cylinder.

For overhead camshaft Toyota truck engines, the camshaft either operates rocker arms or camshaft followers (with adjuster shims) that fit between the cam lobes and valve stems. As the timing chain(s) or belt rotates the single or double camshaft arrangement atop the cylinder head, the valves open ports in sequence.

The camshaft has an important job. Lobes, carefully shaped to open and close the valves at precise times, rotate at one-half the speed of the crankshaft. Each two turns of the crankshaft, the camshaft will open and close each valve, doing so for the entire service life of the engine.

Tension between a camshaft lobe and the lifter's convex base or follower contact point is the highest pounds-per-square-inch load within your truck's engine. Hardness of the camshaft and lifter or rocker arm/follower, plus the compatibility of these materials, will affect the overall reliability of your engine. The severity of lobe lift contours or profiles also dictates the degree of stress placed upon pushrods, rocker arms and valve springs.

Camshaft Lobe Profiles and Valve Timing

Each Toyota engine type and application requires a camshaft with unique lobe profiles. Careful engineering determines the correct lobe shape from low point (heel) to peak lift. Lifter or follower design limitations also influence the lobe "ramp" design or initial lifting contour.

> *CAUTION —*
> *Radically tall lobe contours increase stress and wear between the lobe and the lifter base. Very tall valve lift requires roller lifters and/or rocker arms, special valve springs and other valvetrain upgrades. (See camshaft manufacturer's recommendations.)*

The three basic elements in camshaft design are 1) the total valve lift (over the full range of lifter movement), 2) valve opening duration (the number of crankshaft degrees that each valve stays open) and 3) valve timing (essentially the opening and closing points for the valves). The correct replacement camshaft will have proper valve lift and opening duration with the right valve timing.

Selecting Your Camshaft

Some general rules apply when meeting off-pavement and heavy duty pulling chores. For general four-wheeling and trailer towing, your engine will operate over a broad rpm range, needing power from just off idle to at least 4000 rpm. (By design, four-cylinder and V-6 Toyota truck engines typically require more rpm than this to reach peak horsepower.) Here, a long valve opening

Fig. 16-4. Whenever you upgrade the camshaft of a Land Cruiser six, be sure to install new lifters. Check the camshaft manufacturer's valve spring recommendations, and install new timing gears if there is any indication of wear. Check valve spring tension, spring free-height and timing gear wear against specifications found in your OEM Toyota repair manual. Replace defective parts—for maximum performance, do not shim valve springs to restore tension or height.

duration like the street performance or light racing camshaft is incorrect, as valve timing will have excessive overlap.

Valve overlap is the exhaust valve still closing while the intake valve has already begun to open. Excess valve overlap creates two fundamental problems for an off-pavement 4x4 or towing engine: 1) rough idle and poor low speed throttle response, and 2) low manifold vacuum at slower engine rpm.

Manifold vacuum is crucial to truck pulling power, proper combustion, and fuel economy. In effect, an automotive-type gasoline engine is a vacuum pump. Your truck engine's operating cycle begins with the vacuum characteristics of the intake stroke.

If you plan serious rock crawling and trailer pulling, or want low speed economy and good throttle response, high manifold vacuum will be on top of your priority list. Especially at higher altitudes, engine breathing depends upon efficient manifold vacuum.

> **NOTE —**
> Before considering a camshaft change, assess your engine's overall condition. Check the carburetor, hunt down vacuum leaks, measure compression and analyze the ignition timing and spark. Confirm manifold vacuum. These are each areas where performance is won or lost.

Off-pavement and Towing Camshaft Profiles

The back country truck engine needs a camshaft that works well at highway cruising speeds—generally 2000-3000 engine rpm for in-line six and V-6 engines and a slightly higher range for Toyota's four-cylinder powerplants. Off-pavement, the truck must be able to crawl through your favorite rockpile or carefully claw its way

up a steep, loose traction hill. Similarly, a truck that tows a trailer or carries heavy loads will require strong low speed performance and notable mid-range strength.

If light duty use, highway cruising, occasional trailer pulling and reasonable fuel economy are your goals, a camshaft close to OEM specs will likely work fine. The formula for hard-core off-pavement or trailering success, however, requires more low-rpm torque response and a relatively low speed horsepower peak. This usually requires more valve lift than most OE truck camshafts can provide.

Earlier Toyota four-cylinder truck OEM camshaft grinds have profiles like Toyota passenger cars. Since the introduction of 22R-series and 3VZ-E V-6 engines, engine and camshaft developments have produced higher torque and more horsepower at lower engine rpm, a substantial improvement for truck-type power.

Controllable power in an off-idle rock crawl situation relies more on torque than horsepower. (Good low speed torque is often the product of increased valve lift and a mild valve opening duration.) As lugging the engine can prevent wheelspin, the engine must have good low-end torque and high manifold vacuum at both "tip-in" and very light throttle. (For driving details, see the chapter on operating your truck.)

Traditionally, smaller displacement gasoline engines have realized their full horsepower potential in the mid- to top-end rpm range, speeds upward of 3600 rpm. However, when your truck's tires need a solid grip and rock shale threatens the sidewalls, running the engine at 3600 or more rpm is not only unsafe but also abusive to the engine, geartrain and environment.

Low rpm control requires immediate off-idle torque, the product of healthy valve lift. I always use manifold vacuum as a guide for selecting a utility truck camshaft, looking for a grind capable of delivering at least 16 (preferably 18 or more) in./hg of manifold vacuum at idle.

Such an RV, trailer towing, or economy camshaft grind will work well with milder carburetion or EFI. Four-wheeling and trailer towing always benefit from the strong torque characteristics of a camshaft that delivers good idle and higher manifold vacuum at low speeds.

In general, I look for a camshaft with slightly more valve lift than the OEM profile. (OE specifications are sometimes available in your OEM Toyota truck repair manual or used as a comparative figure in high performance aftermarket camshaft catalogs.) I stay conservative with both valve opening duration (measured in either total degrees or degrees at a specified lift) and valve timing.

Aftermarket Camshaft Options

For high torque within a reasonable rpm range, several camshaft profiles have worked well in Toyota Land Cruiser sixes. For the F or 2F in-line OHV sixes with their long stroke, it's easy to extract serious stump pulling power. A mechanical lifter camshaft of approximately 0.428" gross lift and 260° total duration will work well. Assuming that your Toyota in-line six has a reasonable compression ratio (no more than 9.2:1), the idle with this kind of camshaft is smooth, and your engine can develop strong low-end torque plus respectable mid-range (2000–3500 rpm) horsepower. Expect this type of camshaft grind to flatten its power curve abruptly around 4200 rpm.

If you want towing or heavy cargo power, consider an RV camshaft designed for maximum performance at low engine speeds. This means more lift than an OEM cam and a mild number of valve opening (duration) degrees.

The correct camshaft will have a lower peak rpm ceiling. I would hold F and 2F engines to a redline/maximum of 4000–4500 rpm for non-racing usage. (Small- or big-block V-8 conversion engines work best to a maximum of 5000 rpm, with authentic rock crawl grinds running out of horsepower around 4200 rpm.)

For an in-line six, domestic V-6 or V-8 conversion tow vehicle or rocky trail camshaft, strive for peak horsepower between 4000 and 4500 rpm. This will provide maximum low end torque and lugging power, plus offer considerable manifold vacuum at lower speeds. Toyota four-cylinder and V-6 engines used on the trail and for light towing require an rpm peak of at least 4500.

For towing, heavy loads and cargo hauling, strive for a compression ratio of 8.5–9.0:1 for Toyota fours and V-6s. 8.0–8.5:1 is plenty for the larger displacement Toyota Land Cruiser in-line F and 2F sixes. At these compression ratios (determined by combustion chamber design and volume, piston crown height and head gasket thickness), your engine will work well with a milder RV camshaft grind. Fuel economy will be good, and you can run low octane fuels without risk of harmful detonation.

For Toyota four-cylinder 20R/22R engines, one of the best camshafts available for stump pulling low-end torque is Northwest Off-Road Specialties' #N21800 grind. The split pattern camshaft offers 250-degrees duration for intake valves and 260-degrees at the exhaust valves. Valve lift is 0.414-inch at both the intake and exhaust valves.

This camshaft has special intake and exhaust valve opening and closing points that deliver a huge increase in usable low end torque and a 12% overall gain in horsepower at 4500 rpm. There are camshafts that offer far more mid-range and top-end power than this grind (available from NWOR, Downey Off-Road, Cal-Mini Trucks and others), however, for stump pulling trails or oversized tires, this is a very practical profile.

Camshafts of this type satisfy rock crawling needs, help pull a light trailer and deliver good gas mileage. On a pre-EFI engine, you can use OEM-type carburetion or an improved carburetor with near stock cubic-feet-per-minute (CFM) flow rate.

For carbureted engines, there are many aftermarket intake manifolds and exhaust headers available. Weber carburetors work best on the four-cylinder engines. (See sources described within this chapter.) For the built up Land Cruiser F or 2F six used off-highway only, common approaches include Clifford's four-barrel intake manifold

Fig. 16-5. *High manifold vacuum produced with NWOR Specialities' #21800 camshaft makes this grind compatible with 22R-E and 22R-TE EFI systems. Billet and lobe faces of NWOR camshafts work fine with Toyota's OEM carbide-faced rocker arms.*

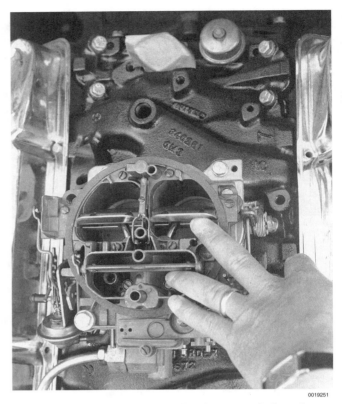

Fig. 16-6. *Flexibility of a GM/Rochester Quadrajet carburetor, especially its ability to cope with altitude changes and twisty off-highway angles, is legend. I used this blueprinted OEM carburetor on my 1976 Land Cruiser's 383 Chevy stroker V-8. Tests of its agility were conclusive.*

with either an adapted Holley two-barrel or four-barrel (square flange) carburetor.

Here I take a conservative approach. By using an ignition distributor with centrifugal plus vacuum advance, you can do well with Specter Off-Road's non-U.S. market OEM Toyota carburetor with its ported vacuum supply. If you need a four-barrel carburetor due to extensive modifications, my choice is a GM Quadrajet designed for a smaller displacement GM V-6 application like the Buick 3.8L or 4.1L V-6 engine. (Avoid use of later closed-loop feedback versions of the Quadrajet.)

Adapted to a Clifford Performance four-barrel intake manifold, the GM Quadrajet requires nothing more than a "blueprint" rebuild and a brass aftermarket float. As for availability, used units abound, and Edelbrock now offers Quadrajet-type replacement carburetors (built by Weber).

Axle Gearing For Your Camshaft

When making a camshaft selection, consider your axle gearing and tire diameter. These two factors determine the cruising rpm and low-speed response demands of your truck's engine.

Unless the tire diameter is oversize, low axle ratios (ranging from 4.11:1 to 5.29:1) will substantially raise the engine's highway cruising rpm. By contrast, mid-1970s and later trucks have taller axle ratios (like the Land Cruiser's switch from 4.11:1 to taller 3.70:1 gearsets in 1979).

Taller axle ratios or oversize tires can drop the truck's highway/cruising rpm range to below 2000 rpm, especially in mini- and compact trucks with an overdrive gear. This will not work with a mid-range or top-end camshaft grind. Here you need either a low-end torque camshaft or lower (numerically higher) axle gear ratios.

Tall gearing (numerically low) and oversize tires require a camshaft that delivers maximum low end torque. Forget about 5000 rpm performance. For the Toyota truck with 33" diameter oversize tires, stock axle gearing and an overdrive transmission, the engine spins way too slow in overdrive at highway cruise speed. If the engine develops peak torque at over 3500 rpm or maximum horsepower around 5,000 rpm, this tire change will surely impede performance and even hamper fuel economy.

By dramatic contrast, a truck with 5.38:1 gears and 30" diameter tires would have the engine spinning 3617 rpm at 60 mph. This speed would not only wear out the engine but also consume an enormous amount of fuel.

When I match gears and tire diameter for strong performance and top fuel economy, my 60 mph goal for a three- or four-speed's high gear (or the overdrive gear of a five-speed transmission) is around 2200 rpm for a torquey V-8 or in-line six, 2300–2500 rpm for a domestic V-6 and 2400–2600 rpm for a four-cylinder or Toyota V-6.

Making an engine's horsepower available and useful is the primary role of axle gearing and OEM tire diameters. With careful planning, your truck can make substantial performance and fuel economy gains both off-pavement and at highway cruise speeds.

Hot and Reliable Ignition Spark

A high performance or working truck engine requires top ignition performance. Spark cannot falter, as a mis-fire at the wrong moment could prove catastrophic. Battling weather, high altitude, extreme climates, precarious road surfaces and marginal fuel grades, your truck's engine needs a quality ignition system.

An excellent starting point for Toyota ignitions is the original equipment high output electronic breakerless system, which served all models by 1978. The only drawback with many of these truck distributors is their lack of adequate vacuum and centrifugal spark advance. Emission era Land Cruisers, in particular, suffer drastically from distributors with a vacuum *retard* mechanism and no provision for vacuum advance.

> **CAUTION —**
> *Do not use GM Delco-Remy distributors for 235/261 Chevrolet engines in the Land Cruiser six. Similarity between the designs has encouraged some owners to install the Delco-Remy unit in the F and 2F engines. The GM drive gear is not of metric proportion nor compatible with the camshaft's drive teeth metallurgy. The result is stripped gears, metal debris in your engine, and the risk of getting stranded in the backcountry without an ignition system.*

Like other centrifugal advance distributors, Toyota's mechanical advance distributors can be enhanced by re-curving the spark timing advance. On emission era 2F

Fig. 16-7. *Aftermarket spark timing re-curve kits are available for the 1979-up (non-EFI) 20R/22Rs. NWOR kit reaches full mechanical spark advance by 4000 rpm and moves more quickly at lower rpm. The result is an engine more responsive under low-speed loads and rock-crawling.*

Fig. 16-8. *MSD is distinguished by a full line of high quality ignition distributors and all-out racing hardware. Many MSD electronic devices interface with OEM, aftermarket or complete MSD ignitions. MSD's Adjustable Timing Control device can provide more complete combustion plus a dashboard mounted fix for altitude changes and poor fuel grades. I have used MSD distributors and ignition enhancements with great success, including this complete distributor in my 1976 Land Cruiser's 383 Chevy V-8. These products are well built and their durability serves 4WD back country needs.*

Land Cruisers, the use of a non-U.S. or earlier F-engine vacuum-and-centrifugal advance distributor can enhance performance substantially.

Accel Performance Products and MSD offer a wide range of high performance ignition components. Racing coils, like the MSD Blaster and Accel Super Coil can work in conjunction with various OEM Toyota pre-EFI ignition systems. Electrical accessories, including ballast resistors and coil brackets, are also available.

Mallory pioneered high performance ignitions and offers high performance distributors, coils, electronic conversion kits, modules, rev limiters and more. The Mallory catalog covers OE replacement upgrades, including the popular Unilite breakerless distributors or a Unilite conversion kit to provide plenty of dependable spark. Racing Unilite units are also popular. I find spark curves on the Mallory Unilite distributors, available for the Land Cruiser F and 2F engines, very easy to adjust.

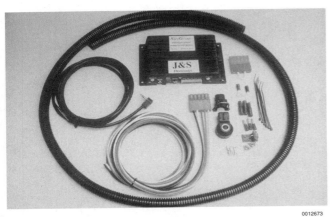

Fig. 16-9. J&S's SafeGuard is 50-State legal. Electronic module provides settings for knock sensitivity plus an adjustable engine rpm limiter. Mode settings can retard either all cylinders simultaneously or just those cylinders that knock. Other cylinders remain just below their detonation threshold, where optimal power and economy occur.

Lubrication and Engine Oil Cooling

Internal combustion engines depend upon heat as hot, expanding gases move the pistons. However, thermal loss from the cylinders is tremendous, as heat dissipates throughout the engine. The cooling system must draw this excess heat away. A radiator, the engine fan and coolant play a key role here, yet there's far more to cooling an engine.

Oil, expected to lubricate and battle friction, is a major outlet for heat. On later truck engine designs, emission control and fuel economy standards lean the fuel mixes while spark timing advances to the detonation threshold. As smaller engines do bigger jobs, upper cylinder temperatures increase.

The buildup of engine heat also increases the oxidation rate and acid content in the oil. Oxygen combines with oil hydrocarbons, producing easily recognizable sludge. This sludge may include varnishes, waxes, corrosive acids and the water of hydration compounds. According to Hayden, a respected manufacturer of engine and transmission oil coolers, each 20° F of excess oil temperature doubles the oil oxidation rate and bearing wear.

Engine Tuning With An Oxygen Sensor

Fig. 16-10. J&S Electronic's combined anti-knock system (shown here), K&N's A/F meter and a similar device from Edelbrock can each indicate approximate air/fuel ratios across the rich to lean scale. This is a tremendous tuning tool for carburetor jetting and troubleshooting fuel and spark system problems. You can perform real world exhaust analyzer simulations at a fraction of the cost of an infrared tester or dynamometer.

A number of aftermarket engine tuning devices use an exhaust system mounted oxygen sensor to indicate the air/fuel ratio or mixture. Sending a signal to LED display lights, such an instrument can provide an instant account of a carburetor or EFI system's air/fuel ratio delivery and jetting.

Deviations from the ideal 14.7:1 (stoichiometric for gasoline) air/fuel ratio are easy to detect. Tuning an aftermarket fuel injection system or jetting a carburetor is simple. I find that road tuning with an exhaust stream (oxygen sensing) air/fuel ratio meter is much like using a wheel dynamometer. Equipped with this technology, you can quickly become a proficient engine tuner.

Few out-of-the-box aftermarket carburetors will produce exactly the right air/fuel ratios for your performance engine buildup. By using an air/fuel ratio meter, you can analyze the carburetor's performance over the entire span of fuel circuits—from idle to the full-on power cycle, from partial throttle response to cruising mixture.

The gains of tuning with an air/fuel ratio meter are better fuel economy, maximum performance and the assurance that the engine will not run too lean or be over fueled. Over-fueling of a newly rebuilt engine can damage the cylinder walls, prevent piston ring seating and radically shorten engine life by fuel diluting the lubricant in the crankcase. Too lean, an engine can burn up valves, a piston or worse.

Threaded plugs are available for simple oxygen sensor installation into an exhaust pipe or header collector. If a muffler shop positions the plug to match the heat requirements of the oxygen sensor, the meter will offer concise and quick data response.

Launching A Second Front Against Heat

Traditionally, water/coolant circulation and dissipation of heat through a fan-assisted radiator have provided reasonable cooling for trucks. Porsche and Volkswagen, however, proved the effectiveness of direct oil-to-air cooling. The Porsche and VW air-cooled engines have survived in desert dune buggies and Baja racers, illustrating that enough air, moving through the right oil cooler, can offer sufficient engine cooling.

Sceptics of air cooled engines need only look at their own water cooled truck engine. Outside the block's water jackets and cylinder head coolant ports, your entire engine is oil cooled. The valves and valvetrain, including the camshaft and timing chain or gear mechanisms, the connecting rods, pistons, rings, all bearings, and even the crankshaft rely on the oil's ability to continuously carry heat away.

For many years, truck and industrial users have recognized the effectiveness of engine oil coolers. Newer trucks offer OEM engine oil coolers, an obvious choice for the aware buyer. Mini-cooler/radiators also appear on other automotive systems, including the power steering and automatic transmission units of many trucks—and even the emission system EGR valve inter-cooler of mid-1970s and later Land Cruisers.

Aftermarket automatic transmission coolers, offered since the 1960s, have drastically extended transmission life. Despite OEM radiator cooling, in-line automatic transmission fluid coolers and engine oil coolers are a must for trailer pulling and other heavy duty uses.

Subjected to loads, hills and towing, oil heat rises rapidly. The best radiator and fan can only address coolant temperature, while oil temperature continues to increase. An add-on, external oil-to-air cooling system could prove vital to your truck's engine. If hot climate driving, off-pavement four-wheeling or travel trailer pulling fit your plans, OEM and aftermarket engine and transmission oil coolers add practical protection.

Oil Cooler Installation Tips

Like any other accessory, an engine oil cooler requires careful fitup. Mounted improperly, the cooler may actually inhibit air flow through the radiator. Most oil cooler kits provide detailed instructions. Necessary hardware should include quality hose and fittings, designed for exposure to high temperature oil under pressure. Usually, an oil filter spacer/adapter provides the attachment point for both pressurized oil and the return flow.

Many aftermarket kits include quality coolers and adapters, but they fall short with attaching hardware. For simple installation, manufacturers have resorted to through-the-radiator plastic ties to secure the cooler. For off-pavement use and situations where vehicles jar, vibrate and twist, plastic ties lead to trouble.

I agree with radiator experts who suggest fabricating a lightweight metal framework for the oil cooler. The cooler may still mount in front of the radiator, isolated from the expensive fins and tubes of the radiator core. Also route hoses carefully, and consider potential road hazard damage or any risk of hose chafing on the body or chassis edges.

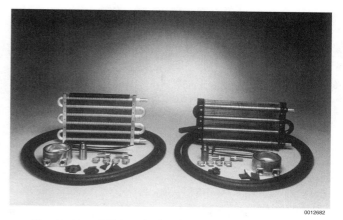

Fig. 16-11. *OEM and aftermarket engine and transmission oil coolers make a good investment. Oil plays a crucial role in cooling your truck's engine and transmission. Cooling the oil can extend engine and transmission life.*

Supercharging

Toyota introduced the use of an exhaust turbocharger on the gasoline 22R-TE engine. Toyota four-cylinder engines have considerable stamina and the capacity to handle supercharging. In step with demands for greater fuel economy and performance, it is likely that more trucks will offer models with OEM supercharging.

Acceleration, mid-range power, and volumetric efficiency improve drastically with supercharging, yet a sensibly staged blower or turbocharger usually has no impact on engine start-up, idle quality or off idle tip-in performance. As rpm rises, the blower boosts both manifold and cylinder pressures. The higher the speed, the greater the performance and efficiency.

Blower Basics

Mechanical superchargers or blowers receive power directly from the engine via a belt- or gear-drive mechanism. Altering the blower shaft speed regulates air displacement. There are five popular mechanical blower designs: Roots-type, sliding-vane, spiral, centrifugal and rotary piston.

GM's Detroit diesels popularized the Roots-type blower. Plentiful and relatively inexpensive, the 6-71 and 4-71 blowers have served the racing community for nearly four decades. Fitted to a gasoline engine, a blower increases torque, mid-range and top-end power.

The Roots-type blower, like other positive-displacement superchargers, provides smooth volumetric flow rates and high pressures—even at relatively low blower speeds. Although some pressure loss occurs through backflow, Roots-type superchargers provide useful boost over a wide speed range.

In the Roots-type blower, two rotors spin in a blower housing/cavity. (These twin rotors never touch each other or the housing.) The close tolerance fitup between the rotors and housing create high boost pressures.

Other mechanical superchargers share a common theme: Timed phases first draw air then squeeze, forcing air into the plenum. (Centrifugal superchargers compress air in the blower rather than the intake plenum.) On OEM diesels, injectors spray pressurized fuel into each combustion or pre-combustion chamber as compression peaks.

When retrofitting Roots-type blowers to gasoline engines with carburetion or Throttle Body Injection (TBI), fuel passes through the compressor chamber. For Tuned Port Injection (TPI) or multi-point injection (MPI), the high speed, close tolerance centrifugal blower has become popular, as fuel does not pass through the compressor. Centrifugal blowers work well for late engines equipped with TPI or MPI, like Toyota EFI engines use.

Exhaust Turbocharging

Turbochargers receive their power from the exhaust gas exiting the engine. The exhaust spins a turbine mounted on a shaft. On the other end of the shaft, in the intake, is a vaned wheel. As the vane turns, it compresses the intake air flow. The result is an energy gain, as boost occurs when engine rpm (i.e., exhaust pressure/turbine speed) reaches a suitable level.

Turbochargers are usually of single-flow turbine design, and deliver a slight excess of boost. Excess boost bypasses through a wastegate system. The wastegate prevents cylinder overcharging and minimizes the energy spent spinning the turbine/compressor.

> **NOTE —**
> High intake manifold vacuum reduces exhaust pressure and also the demand for boost. Reciprocally, low manifold vacuum (heavy loads) increases exhaust pressure and creates turbo boost. The adjustable wastegate sets a ceiling on boost pressure.

Intercoolers provide a major breakthrough for turbocharging. Compressed air generates heat. This heat expands the air/fuel mix and absorbs vital space. Cooling the air between the turbo unit and the intake plenum provides a denser air/fuel mass (and more power) for each cylinder.

Aftermarket Blowers

B&M Products: B&M has put years of product development into a complete line of blowers and an extensive blower accessory line. B&M offers a Powercharger 66 blower kit for all carbureted 20R/22R truck engines. Using a stock Toyota carburetor or an aftermarket Weber or Holley 5200 style carburetor, this kit is available in 4-6 psi or 5-7 psi boost. All factory emission controls can be left in place. Kits permit use of stock factory accessories, which can be a real savings in cost and time.

B&M also offers the *Supercharger Technical Manual*, drafted by Jim Davis, former B&M executive, with insight into designing a blower system. See your local B&M dealer for details.

Camden Superchargers: John Camden began supercharging the very first 265 and 283 Chevrolet small-block V-8s. Camden's Road Warrior blowers pioneered several design features, including a highly efficient pressurized lubrication system with insert-type rotor shaft bearings.

Fig. 16-12. *Supercharger retrofit kits come with drive pulleys, accessory adapters, installation hardware and instructions. When shopping for a blower or exhaust turbocharger kit, consider the whole package.*

Low profile for underhood clearance, the Camden street unit for small-block V-8s claims a 30% horsepower increase for engine compression ratios up to 8.5:1. Six-pound maximum boost helps assure engine longevity for stock, low compression engine applications. Camden offers kits for Chevrolet V-8s, some sixes and the Toyota four-cylinder engines.

Supercharging Compression Ratios, Camshafts and Air Filtration

Supercharging a gasoline engine requires compression ratios of 7:1 to 9:1 on engines with good cylinder sealing (10% maximum leakdown). Blower drive ratios determine the boost levels. Forged aluminum pistons, quality stainless steel exhaust valves, and hard steel exhaust valve seats are minimal requirements for higher boost pressures.

Weiand, a highly reputable manufacturer of automotive, marine, racing and pro-street type blowers, has found that all-out performance camshaft grinds for blower use feature 112 to 114 degree lobe centers, 0.450" to 0.500" lift and 220-234 degree valve opening duration at 0.050" lift (272 to 288 degrees gross duration). Logically, the exhaust valve must remain closed while the intake valve is open to prevent pressurized air/fuel charges from racing out the exhaust port.

True performance blower grinds also have slightly longer duration on the exhaust to totally clean out cylinders during the exhaust cycle. For mild or street-legal supercharging, a stock or RV camshaft grind works fine.

Air/fuel ratios are critical with blowers, so carburetor jetting and adequate air flow are essential. K & N Filtration and similar filtration systems provide the protection needed for expensive, close-tolerance blower systems. Although carburetor flow or CFM requirements may rise above stock demands, many OEM air cleaner assemblies still provide ample flow capacity when used with a K & N-type element.

Engine Modifications for Supercharging

Before considering a blower installation, assess the condition of your engine. Weiand, with extensive experience in this area, offers some general recommendations. To begin, the optimal engine compression ratio for a street blower installation is 8.5:1. This works nicely for 1971–up smog engines, but inhibits blower usage on 1960s muscle engines and others that sport 9.5:1 and higher compression ratios.

If pistons are cast, the boost limit should range from four to seven 7 psi, with an engine rpm ceiling in the 4500–5000 range. Regardless of piston type, detonation should be avoided. Lower boost levels, a milder spark timing curve and/or a boost in fuel octane will help offset detonation.

CAUTION —
Detonation is the number one cause of damage in a supercharged engine.

Fuel leanout or starvation, an additional cause of detonation, can be avoided through use of larger fuel supply lines and a higher volume fuel pump. Attention to detonation cannot be overstated, as broken pistons, burned valves and crankshaft damage result from sustained periods of detonation.

An engine overhaul should be performed if excess wear exists on an engine intended for supercharging. Forged pistons, moly rings, close attention to tolerances and a general blueprinting philosophy should prevail. The blown engine produces far more cylinder pressure, and valve and gasket sealing become critical.

Although the Weiand and other blower kits will work with a street engine in good condition, any effort to improve engine stamina and longevity will also enhance performance. Select block and valvetrain parts with a known ability to last longer than OEM pieces.

Weiand has emphatic suggestions about carburetion and jetting, recommending that primaries be opened five to ten percent, and that secondaries provide 10 to 20% extra flow. For those contemplating a carburetor switch, a stock size carburetor works adequately with Weiand's Pro-Street Supercharger kits or a similar mild boost (street) system.

For the V-8 street blower or 4WD Land Cruiser Chevota small-block V-8 sand drag racing installation, a 600-750 cfm flow rate with vacuum secondaries has proven appropriate. A Holley double pumper may be needed for a more modified engine. Weiand's massive 6-71 Supercharger works best with a pair of 600 cfm vacuum secondary carburetors on a small-block V-8 engine, while a big-block may require a pair of 750 cfm carburetors.

Aside from a healthy cooling system, increased fuel supply network and tight sealing air cleaner to prevent debris from ruining the rotors and blower housing, the ignition spark timing is critical. Initial, static spark timing should fall within six to ten crankshaft degrees advance, with the curve swinging to a combined static and mechanical maximum spark advance of 32 crankshaft degrees by 3400 rpm. Weiand notes that no more than 38 total crankshaft degrees of spark timing advance should be attempted with a blower under any circumstance.

The late model electronic spark control and closed loop carburetor/EFI engines create an obstacle. OEM computer systems cannot accurately control spark and air/fuel ratios with a blower installed. Weiand recommends replacing the electronic fuel and spark management with a conventional electronic ignition and carburetor for strictly off-highway use.

NOTE —
Removal of any emission control components or the electronic fuel and spark management system is for off-highway/racing use only and violates Federal/EPA, state and local laws for pollution controlled vehicles driven on public roads. On a vehicle intended for highway or public road use make sure the kit has 50-State legal status.

When installing a blower, large tubing headers provide the best exhaust flow. Turbo-type or other low restriction mufflers also enhance performance. Proper tuning, including use of the correct spark plugs, will assure desired results.

3. BUILDING A HIGH PERFORMANCE LAND CRUISER SIX

Beginning with the earliest F and 2F OHV in-line sixes, Toyota engine quality has always been tops. From a high performance buildup standpoint, however, I shy away from the pre-1974 236.7 cubic inch Land Cruiser F engines. The by-pass type lubrication/oil filtration design of these engines will always hinder reliability and efforts to build an all-out performance engine.

If you have an interest in the F engine, the last year (1974) of U.S. market use is the best design. Like the later and improved 2F and 3F-E OHV sixes, the 1974 engine has a full-flow oil filtration system.

For racing and sustained high speed operation, a major design limitation of the F, 2F and 3F-E Land Cruiser engines is their four main bearings. Despite exceptional size and quality, the four bearings and a massive crankshaft in Toyota's OHV sixes share the inherent weakness of earlier domestic in-line sixes.

Domestic truck manufacturers overcame this inhibiting design with the introduction of seven main-bearing in-line sixes. In 1963, Chevrolet pioneered the use of seven main bearings with the 230 OHV in-line six-cylinder engine. (This design first came on line in 1962 Chevy II cars as the 194 cubic inch engine.)

Kaiser's Jeep Corporation soon adopted the AMC seven main bearing 232 sixes and Ford trucks introduced the seven main bearing 240 and 300 in-line sixes. Toyota Land Cruisers stubbornly adhered to their four-main bearing crankshaft through the 1992 3F-E engine.

The F and 2F block and head designs are strikingly similar to a mid-1950s 235 Chevrolet or 248 GMC OHV six. If you have a restoration/performance need around these kinds of early engines, Jack Clifford of Clifford Performance (see appendix) shares your interest.

Jack once led me on a tour of his facility, a veritable shopping center for in-line six performance parts. From

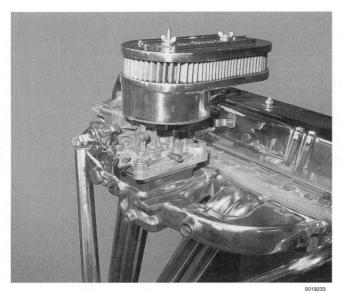

Fig. 16-13. *Despite four main bearing design, F, 2F and 3F-E Land Cruiser sixes have tremendous durability. Downey Off-Road, Specter Off-Road, NWOR Specialties and Clifford Performance devote many catalog pages to performance upgrades for Land Cruiser in-line OHV sixes. Here, Downey Off-Road Mfg. offers a 6-into-2-into-1 tuned header and Holley carburetor retrofit kit.*

Fig. 16-14. *Specter Off-Road and Downey Off-Road focus on vacuum-and-centrifugal advance Toyota OEM distributors for improving Land Cruiser performance. These units are essentially non-U.S. market breaker point types with better spark advance curves. A ported vacuum (non-U.S. market) carburetor is also available from Specter Off-Road. These components are for "off-highway use only" and not legal for public road use on pollution controlled vehicles.*

Fig. 16-15. *GM Quadrajet four-barrel has proven worthy for emission legal OEM V-6 and V-8 off-pavement conversion engine applications. I like this carburetor's flexibility and ability to compensate for altitude, and the design functions reasonably well at odd angles. Versions for smaller displacement GM engines can also serve a Land Cruiser F or 2F engine built for "off-highway use only." Use with a Clifford four-barrel manifold and base plate adapter.*

camshafts, exhaust headers, valvetrain components, pistons and manifolds to exotic carburetion or retrofit EFI systems, lightweight flywheels and ignition upgrades, Clifford Performance can supply the goods for extracting more performance from in-line sixes, including your 'Cruiser F or 2F engine. The blueprint for F or 2F performance is virtually identical to an early Chevrolet 235/261 or GMC 228/248/302 in-line OHV six.

Likewise, other aftermarket suppliers can provide specialized pieces to upgrade and improve the performance of F and 2F engines. Headers, camshafts, intake manifolds, distributors and carburetion systems are the more common aftermarket components available.

I am most familiar with rock-crawling six cylinder engine build-ups, and here are some of my conclusions: 1) use a high lift, short duration camshaft; 2) balance the reciprocating engine parts, along with the large OEM steel flywheel and a Centerforce clutch assembly; and 3) use a compression ratio between 8.5:1 and 9.0:1.

Add cylinder head porting, a three-angle valve grind, Clifford's four-barrel intake manifold and headers. Blueprint an appropriate GM/Rochester Quadrajet four-barrel carburetor and re-curve an old OEM type Toyota centrifugal-and-vacuum advance distributor. Specter Off-Road and Downey Off-Road offer "non-U.S." OEM Toyota distributors for "off-highway use." Specter Off-Road also offers non-U.S. ported vacuum Land Cruiser OEM-type carburetors.

For wilder performance buildups of an F or 2F engine, Clifford Performance provides more exotic carburetion and EFI systems. Be aware, however, that for trail use, a more complex buildup leads to less flexibility. High rpm horsepower at the expense of legendary Land Cruiser bottom end crawling torque is disappointing when the

going gets tough. Fuel economy will suffer severely, and the horsepower barely approaches that of a stock 350 Chevy V-8. If performance is the goal, you would be better off, and dollars ahead, building a 350 cubic inch or larger domestic V-8.

The cost of building up a Land Cruiser six is very high. OEM replacement pieces cost considerably more than counterpart domestic engine parts, especially when comparing Chevrolet small-block V-8 and 230/250/292 in-line six components to Land Cruiser pieces.

If I were committed to in-line six-cylinder performance in a Land Cruiser, which has certainly proven its worth along backcountry trails, I would consider adapting an in-line OHV six cylinder engine like the 292 Chevrolet or 300 cubic inch Ford six to the Land Cruiser chassis, using either an OEM Toyota Land Cruiser or domestic truck transmission. (See geartrain upgrade chapter.)

Although hard numbers are not available, it has been estimated that there are more Chevrolet V-8 engine conversions in U.S. market FJ40 and FJ55 model Land Cruisers than models still operating with F and 2F type engines. This is likely, as higher mileage trucks tend to fall into the hands of owners with multiple use or performance interests—and also because of the cost of F or 2F engine rebuilding and performance upgrades.

Additionally, the Land Cruiser's large engine bay, strong chassis and rugged gear assemblies more than lend themselves to a powerful V-8 conversion. The hefty F, 2F and 3F-E sixes weigh more than a Chevrolet small-block V-8—or even a big-block V-8 with some aluminum accessories and tubular steel exhaust headers. The choice is yours.

4. FOUR-CYLINDER AND V-6 POWER

Like the Land Cruiser in-line sixes, Toyota four-cylinder and V-6 engines have a rugged record for dependability and heroic performance for their cylinder displacement. Quality engineering plus exceptional component integrity make some applications suitable for performance upgrades.

Generally, modifications focus on camshaft profiles (altered valve opening duration and lift), induction system, and spark timing. Four-cylinder engines receive the largest attention.

Although the pre-1975 18RC engine has a good track record, its use in fuel efficient two-wheel drive mini-trucks and Toyota passenger cars created little interest in performance modifications. Developments like induction system upgrades, exhaust headers and fine tuning did occur, but mostly in response to the sub-compact car racing programs of that era.

Serious buildups of four-cylinder Toyota engines turn to the 20R and 22R. These similar designs have reliable castings, durable internal parts and a single chain valvetrain mechanism—a distinct advantage over the more complicated 8RC/18RC double chain mechanism with its failure-prone hydraulic tensioner.

The performance aftermarket was quick to recognize the 1975-80 20R engine, especially its propensity to run for 200,000 trouble free miles if serviced regularly. This engine was Toyota's showcase for superior engineering and components. Iron cylinder blocks, with comparatively high nickel content, rivaled the high ticket European luxury car engines.

My appreciation for Toyota truck engines began with in-chassis overhauls and valve jobs on four-cylinder engines that had accrued more than 150,000 miles. At this mileage, even without the use of synthetic oil, the piston ring edges were razor blade sharp, but the block still showed OEM machining with cylinder cross-hatch patterns rising from the base of bores to the block deck.

Fig. 16-16. *One swap option is the 22R-TE, Toyota's potent EFI with turbocharger engine. Short of a Toyota V-6 or larger domestic (Buick or Chevy Vortec) V-6 transplant, this is a good choice for a mini-pickup buildup. In stock, emission legal form, the 22R-TE raises the performance ante considerably. (See section on 22R-E swap within this chapter. Conversion steps would be similar.)*

Fig. 16-17. *Toyota's development of the 3RZ-FE 2.7L DOHC four and 5VZ-FE 3.4L DOHC V-6 (shown here) truck engines will spur interest in some Toyota engine-to-earlier Toyota pickup truck and 4Runner swaps. Drawbacks with such a conversion would be no available adapters plus the exotic nature and cost of such a DOHC/EFI engine—new or used. Domestic pushrod V-6s make easier, cost effective swap material for earlier 2WD and 4WD Toyota pickups.*

A domestic engine at this mileage typically shows wear in the form of cylinder taper, with at least several thousandths of an inch of bore material worn away at the top of each compression ring's run.

What this says is that Toyota (and some other Japanese engine builders) can produce a four-cylinder engine that takes the kind of punishment we apply to a V-8 engine, without showing any block wear. Often, a simple glaze-breaking hone job, careful washing of the cylinder bores, cleaning up the original pistons, installing new standard size piston rings and fitting new standard size crankshaft bearings will restore a Toyota block assembly at 200,000 miles. Original pistons, wrist pins and the crankshaft might show no wear whatsoever.

For the owner of a 1975-up 20R or 22R powered truck, there is a large assortment of aftermarket engine parts for enhancing performance. Throughout this chapter, you will find products offered by sources that have worked closely with these engines for two decades.

Since 1988, the popularity of the 3.0L Toyota V-6 has soared. From a high performance buildup standpoint, the 3.0L engine has potential, however, severe emission control limitations coupled to a very crowded engine and accessory package leave little room for improvements. As a result, most view the 3.0L engine as better off left alone. Exhaust, intake air-stream and plenum tuning rank among the available upgrades.

Some consider swapping the later 22R-E, 22R-TE, 2.4L DOHC (2RZ-FE) and 2.7L (3RZ-FE) DOHC fours, and even the 3.0L SOHC and 3.4L DOHC V-6s, into the earlier mini- or compact-truck chassis. A few Land Cruiser loyalists have even swapped the 3F-E EFI six and other Toyota industrial strength engines, including non-U.S. market

diesels, into their earlier 'Cruisers. (The newer 1FZ-FE DOHC in-line six with seven main bearings could be another possibility.)

Such changeovers, however, typically involve expensive OEM pieces plus custom machine work. Some chassis and sheet metal fabricating is often necessary, along with detailed electrical system and wiring changes.

3F-E Land Cruiser Six Retrofit

Loyal Land Cruiser owners have a hard time giving up their in-line six cylinder engines. While I would look to the seven-main bearing 292 Chevrolet in-line six or Ford 300 six as viable swap material, many stick staunchly with OEM Toyota iron monsters.

One impressive Toyota-to-Toyota swap is Jim Leininger's 1976 FJ55 Land Cruiser with a later FJ62/FJ80 3F-E EFI conversion engine. The 3F-E choice preserves the rugged block and head design of the original 2F engine while providing a modern electronic fuel and spark management system. By retaining all emission and EFI components in their original form, this vehicle qualifies as a California emission legal conversion. Tailpipe emissions read much lower than a 1976 2F engine in top shape. Still, because this is an engine change, a referee station must inspect and certify the vehicle with its new engine/emission package.

Fig. 16-18. *3F-E is essentially a 2F engine with a shortened stroke. For earlier Land Cruiser swaps, this eliminates the need for an aftermarket or custom built bellhousing. Jim Leininger mated the 3F-E engine to a later FJ60 four-speed transmission using OEM parts. 2F flywheel was used by carefully resizing the bolt holes.*

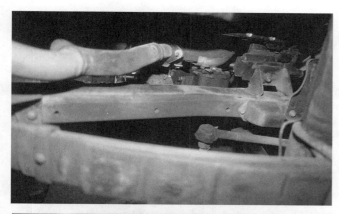

Fig. 16-19. For manifold and emission control devices to clear the original steering gear, Jim chose to move the engine to the right and forward. Use of a Saginaw power steering conversion (see chassis/suspension upgrade chapter) could eliminate this need, as the steering gear relocates far forward.

Fig. 16-20. 3F-E's clutch-type fan protrudes at front of engine. Here Jim remedied the problem by relocating radiator further forward. This required some fabrication work to secure the radiator at its new location. (As an alternative, you might experiment with a Flex-A-Lite stainless steel fan and spacers. See cooling system chapter for details.) Proper hoses completed the installation. Leininger's FJ55 has factory air conditioning, a rare item for a 1976 Land Cruiser.

Fig. 16-21. Wiring work, including installation of a harness and computer for the fuel and spark management system, was necessary during this 3F-E swap into a 1970s carbureted model Land Cruiser.

Fig. 16-22. To avoid fuel supply problems, Jim developed a unique fuel system. Pump delivers fuel from main tank to an auxiliary fuel tank. Auxiliary tank remains full at all times, and here the high pressure pump picks up flow to the OEM Toyota EFI system, preventing chance of fuel aeration within the high pressure lines.

Toyota 4WD Pickup-to-Domestic V-6 Swaps

Since the late 1970s, especially with the introduction of the 1979 4x4 pickup, interest in domestic V-6 and V-8 swaps has increased. (Land Cruiser/Chevy V-8 swaps have been popular since the mid-1960s.) Although the exceptional stamina of Toyota mini- and compact-truck geartrains and chassis is legendary, I do not recommend the use of a small-block domestic V-8 in pickup models.

The popularity of swapping Buick 231/3.8L and 252/4.1L engines into a Toyota 4WD pickup or 4Runner owes much to Downey Off-Road, Advance Adapters and Northwest Off-Road Specialties. Transmission adapters, mounts, accessory brackets and upgrade cooling systems have become available for swapping Buick V-6s and, more recently, Chevrolet's 4.3L Vortec V-6.

Although these V-6s will fit 2WD engine bays (with considerable fabrication work), I do not recommend their use here. 4x4 pickups and 4Runners offer a more substantial front chassis and axle that can support the heavier weight and torque twist of a domestic V-6 engine—especially when horsepower exceeds the 150–160 range. With higher horsepower, the use of a heavy duty domestic manual truck transmission (with a large clutch assembly) or a durable automatic transmission is advisable.

Perhaps the most practical reason for considering a domestic V-6 swap for a Toyota pickup is availability of performance parts and adapters. The Buick and Chevrolet 90-degree V-6s have a wide range of OEM variations plus the support of the entire high performance aftermarket. For these domestic V-6s, high output ignition, induction, exhaust, camshaft and internal hard engine parts fill the pages of popular high performance catalogs.

If you find the Chevrolet 4.3L Vortec V-6 of interest, I highly recommend the *Chevrolet Power* book, a genuine General Motors/Chevrolet Division publication available through your local Chevrolet dealer. This GM book is the best information source available for a Chevrolet 60 or 90° V-6, small-block V-8 or big-block V-8 "off-highway" engine buildup. The book makes "must" reading.

For Buick V-6 buildups, another GM book, *Buick Power*, is available through Buick and other GM Division

Fig. 16-24. *Typical domestic V-6 engine swap involves a 1979–85 solid front axle 4x4 pickup or 4Runner. Along with GM engines, the Turbo 350 automatic is commonly adapted to the Toyota 4WD transfer case. Downey Off-Road's precision adapter package shown here.*

dealerships. This book offers comprehensive, engineering level suggestions on how to build the ultimate off-highway Buick powerplant.

I am partial to the later 4.3L L35 and R8Y V-6 engineering with CPI (Central Point Injection). These GM S/T-truck versions employ a balance shaft to overcome the inherent imbalance of any 90° V-6. The balance shaft delivers smoother and more efficient performance than 1985 and newer 4.3L engines that do not offer a balance shaft. CPI's innovative electronically activated (variable flow) plenum vane contributes to better fuel economy, improved torque and added horsepower.

5. V-8 SWAP FOR THE LAND CRUISER

When I removed the 2F engine from my 1976 Land Cruiser chassis, the original six-cylinder engine showed all its shortcomings. A crankshaft "hand crank" nut that dated to antiquity faced forward, while the engine sideview showed yards of emission control plumbing and vacuum hoses that had turned an otherwise simple engine removal into a marathon.

I was sure to keep the valuable emission hardware intact. Any auto recycler in a mandatory smog test region will acknowledge that F and 2F emission control components are as much in demand as the heavy iron cylinder head that can roast an exhaust valve or two on occasion. (Like the early Chevrolet and GMC in-line sixes, F and 2F cylinder head cracking is not that uncommon, either.)

Fitting a Chevrolet V-8 with lightweight intake and exhaust manifolds into the chassis would ultimately lower the truck's curb weight by nearly 300 pounds. Horsepower would more than double, torque would increase enormously, and the Chevy V-8 performance buildup and conversion parts would cost less than simply rebuilding the stock 2F six-cylinder engine.

In addition to rock crawling at high elevations, my Land Cruiser FJ40 would also pull a travel trailer. Econo-

continued on 3rd page following

Fig. 16-23. *Downey Off-Road Manufacturing, Advance Adapters and Northwest Off-Road (NWOR) Specialties have developed lines of conversion adapters, bracketry and accessories for installing domestic V-6 and V-8 engines into Toyota pickups and 4Runners. Here is Downey Off-Road's Buick 3.8L V-6 conversion package for a 4x4 pickup. Adapter brackets accept power driven accessories. Heavy duty Downey Off-Road radiator handles cooling.*

22R-E Swap Into Earlier Toyota 4wd Pickups

1986 22R-E engine looks at home in 1984 4x4 pickup.

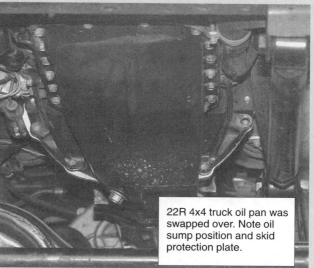

22R 4x4 truck oil pan was swapped over. Note oil sump position and skid protection plate.

Newer Toyota trucks boast electronic fuel injection and computer-driven spark timing. Although the legendary stamina of the 22R engine remains virtually the same, the later induction system brings a host of driveability advantages, both on- and off-road. Generally, EFI enhances fuel economy, too, and later pickups deliver exceptional gas mileage.

With earlier 20R/ 22R carbureted engines so similar to the newer EFI engines, a later EFI (22R-E) swap is practical for some owners. My friend Jerry Steele of Tucson, Arizona and his fellow four-wheeler, Ken Francisco, successfully performed such a transplant using a 1986 22R-E pickup (2WD) engine and Ken's 1984 4x4 chassis.

To Arizona and Moab crowds, Ken's truck is familiar. Its red shiny finish has embraced the blue skies of several Western states. With well over 100,000 miles on the odometer, and five years of continuously toting a 4200 lbs. truck and payload combination, the original engine lost its piston rings.

(Actually, it's atypical for a 22R to make less than 140,000 miles before the rings fail, but Ken had played with a fuel-rich, mis-jetted Weber carburetor at one point, and this had gas washed the engine's cylinder walls.)

Ken and Jerry, both electronics whizzes, decided to pursue an upgrade swap. "After all," they guessed, "some 1984 Toyota 2WD trucks had EFI. Surely, the swap would work with existing parts and electrics....."

Not necessarily so. Ken secured a very low mileage 22R-E engine from a Phoenix salvage yard, complete with all accessories, air intake pieces and the entire *intact* wire harnesses for the engine and EFI systems. This last fact would ultimately assure success.

The Mechanical Swap

Once the old engine set on the ground, Ken realized that since the 1984 Toyota chassis accommodated both 22R and 22R-E engines, most components would interchange. The 2WD truck had an automatic, and that added a small task. Ken swapped his flywheel to the new engine, along with a

new pilot bearing. Other pieces remained the same, though, even the motor mounts.

Fitup of the engine presented no major obstacles. Several details, like mounting the intake air box and EFI ballast, readily fell into place. Body panels on the 1984 were engineered for these pieces. (Earlier trucks may require more thought and effort.) The alternator and all engine accessories came with the newer engine, and Ken kept all wiring harnesses intact.

Also included in the mechanical swap was the fuel tank from the 1986 truck. The high pressure pump in the tank is necessary. All neoprene fuel hoses must be changed to high pressure lines, as EFI pressures run way in excess of the conventional (carburetor system) fuel hose capacity.

Other components, like the fan, alternator and such, fit okay. The EFI coil/igniter and wiring are also a requirement with this swap.

Wiring: An Electronics Degree Helps

When I asked where the greatest challenge lies in this swap, Jerry and Ken replied in harmony, "The wiring..." In explaining the effort required, Jerry insisted that the wiring job is impossible without *two* OEM Toyota repair manuals: one for the swap engine year and model, the other to complement your earlier truck chassis.

After wiring the 2WD-type EFI system's engine harnesses into the 4WD (formerly carbureted) truck, Jerry and Ken took an hour to review their work. Overall, they had followed their electronics training and encountered few problems with the installation. Jerry noted that a non-electronics person might have more difficulty here. He noted that the wiring system provides more challenge than any other aspect of the swap.

From their swap, Jerry and Ken have highlighted these tips: 1) Keep all wiring intact and gather every wire that connects to an engine accessory or the EFI computer; 2) all EFI connec-

continued on next page

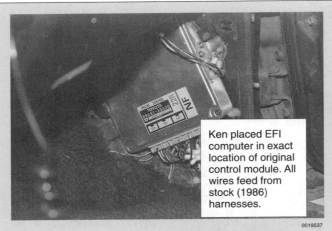

Ken placed EFI computer in exact location of original control module. All wires feed from stock (1986) harnesses.

Here Ken sets base ignition timing. distributor base timing normally requires no attention beyond one-time adjustment.

Coil and igniter from EFI truck were a requirement. Computer-based ignition of EFI engine was retained, including distributor, wiring, and computer.

With the computer mounted at the original control module location, the completed job looked stock. Jerry and Ken elected to route wires on the engine side of the firewall, encased in plastic wire shielding. Only a few power source leads require mating to the truck's original wiring harness. Jerry emphasizes that the underdash wires remain virtually undisturbed, and this is surely desirable.

Driving Impressions

To test the EFI swap firsthand, my wife Donna and I joined Jerry and Melody Steele and Ken for a fun romp near Sedona, Arizona. Ken's Toyota climbed steep and rocky trail faces and step rock, close on the tail of the Steele's surefooted Jeep CJ-7. Odd slopes and angles had no effect on the EFI engine. Performance was quick and ample.

Ken's truck, with a sleeping rack, large stowage box, and a full complement of camp equipment, weighs 4200 pounds. This is a lot of weight for a 2.4L four. Never tiring, the truck travels at freeway speeds and doubles as a virtual off-highway mule---a real tribute to the prowess of Toyota trucks and their engines.

After a day of rough four-wheeling, including several stout rock climbs, the truck started easily, shook off its coat of dust and effortlessly headed down the pavement—just like a Toyota 4x4.

tors are of high quality and waterproof—preserve these connectors and their wiring; and 3) as a general rule, any wire splicing should include both twisting and soldering—popular crimp connectors won't work with EFI caliber wiring.

This cannot be overstated. Computer signals require concise voltage readings and resistance levels. Loose connections, too much resistance, shorts or weak current flow can cause EFI and spark malfunctions.

As various truck schematics differ, we discussed some general fitup rules. Ken and Jerry spent several hours on a kitchen floor, sorting out the wires within the EFI harness. All connectors received electrician's stick-on numbers, a means for quickly identifying the wire junctions. Non-EFI wires were identified and separated from the EFI leads.

Does all this sound intimidating? No factory manual will spell out hybridizing jobs like this, yet Jerry and Ken found the factory data essential. A clear set of goals emerged, as the overall swap focuses on tie-ins of ground and power leads. Power must come from three distinct sources: 1) hot at all times, 2) hot while ignition is ON, or 3) hot while cranking the engine.

The EFI fuel pump receives its power source from the EFI/computer circuitry. This is a must. Likewise, harnesses include necessary grounds. The computer integrates the ignition system, fuel supply and EFI fuel distribution. An exhaust stream oxygen sensor and several other devices must also relay their signals to the computer.

Sturdy rack above truck bed is Ken's creation. MIG welded precisely, the rack holds compressed air—enough to air down and top off tires for the trail four times.

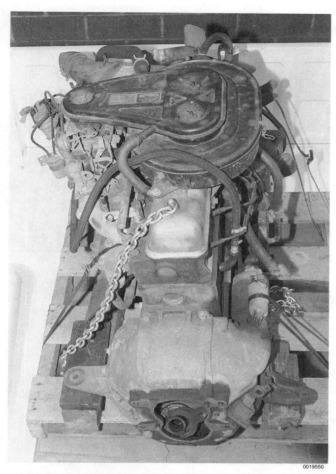

Fig. 16-25. *Later six-cylinder 2F engine, loved by many Land Cruiser owners, has one of the rarest anomalies around: a crankshaft hand cranking provision on an engine overwhelmed with modern emission control plumbing. These Toyota engines are heavy, limited by four main bearing design, and vulnerable to exhaust valve burnout. Despite all this, many of us have thoroughly enjoyed the 2F's impressive torque characteristics.*

my remained a concern, too, and the hardtop truck would still weigh a hefty 3900 pounds—even with small-block Chevy V-8 power.

My engine buildup of choice was a 383 stroker engine, designed around the basic 350 cubic inch, four-bolt main bearing Chevrolet V-8. For emission legality, the engine block assembly was a late 1970s version.

To achieve 383 cubic inches, a 350 block and replacement pistons combine with either small-block 350 or 400 connecting rods. (See 383 Chevy V-8 buildup for details.) The 400 crankshaft is re-ground 0.200-inch undersize to match the 350 main bearing saddle and bearing sizes. A cleanup re-bore of 0.030-inch over standard completes the 383 configuration.

The long 3.750" crankshaft stroke with a 4.030" slightly over-bored 350 block, noted for its superior cooling over the 400's siamesed cylinder block design, develops massive low-end torque and great mid-range horsepower with the right camshaft grind.

Off-pavement four wheeling is not like drag racing or cruising with a street truck. When the rocks get thick and speed slows to near standstill, you want an ultra smooth idle and throttle tip-in response—an engine that wouldn't stall when stumbling through a rocky stream bed. Crawl-ability is a primary need.

On the highway, where we spend a lot of time commuting and driving to our favorite trails, mid-range power is vital. For this kind of service from a Chevrolet or similar OHV V-8 engine (or from a domestic V-6 engine intended for a Toyota 4WD pickup conversion), you need a very mild camshaft that builds quick low-end torque and tops its horsepower between 4000 and 4500 rpm.

One of the secrets of the F and 2F powered Land Cruiser successes is the very heavy iron flywheel. This large rotating mass keeps the engine turning over when the rocky trail would have other engines stalled. Here, the Land Cruiser simply ticks its way along the trail at an idle, the huge iron flywheel smoothing out the bumps and boulders.

You can duplicate this behavior with a properly built Chevy V-8 by attaching a heavy iron, 168-tooth factory 14-inch flywheel. Popular small-block or big-block Chevrolet engines will accept this type of flywheel, and similar big diameter iron flywheels are available for other GM V-8 and V-6 engines that have the common Buick, Cadillac, Oldsmobile and Pontiac bellhousing pattern.

Although I repeatedly refer to the 383 small-block stroker hybrid, many other domestic V-8s have served well in FJ Land Cruisers. One worthy installation is the 472 or 500 cubic inch Cadillac engine, with either a Turbo 400 or a flywheel and manual GM truck transmission (adapters and oil pan available from Cadillac Motorsports Development. See Appendix for address.).

These surprisingly light weight Cadillac V-8s, or the rugged and light weight Buick 455 V-8 alternative, provide massive torque. The low compression smog era versions also deliver good fuel economy and tolerate low octane fuels.

Multi-National Engine and Transmission Marriage

For adapting the Chevrolet V-8 to a Land Cruiser chassis and gearbox, Advance Adapters, Northwest Off-Road Specialties (NWOR) and Downey Off-Road Manufacturing have the products. There are a number of approaches that I find well suited to the multi-purpose four-wheeler.

OEM Land Cruiser manual three- and four-speed transmissions are rugged but offer no overdrive. Some builders have no need for an overdrive unit. (In such a case, the truck is driven primarily off-highway or runs oversized tires that provide a facsimile of overdrive.) Here, the aftermarket suppliers can provide time-honored adapters to mate a Chevrolet, Ford or other GM engines to an original Land Cruiser transmission.

For those who do not need overdrive but desire a more rugged transmission with an exceptionally low (numerically high) first gear ratio, the aftermarket suppliers can provide a kit to mate the popular GM SM420 (7.05:1 first gear) and SM465 (6.54:1 first gear) to the Land Cruiser transfer case.

Using this method, the engine and transmission become entirely Chevrolet, with the transfer case and axles

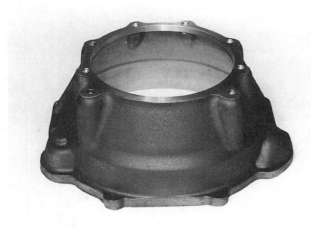

Fig. 16-26. *Northwest Off-Road Specialties (NWOR) is a Toyota 4x4 performance supermarket. One of the many unique NWOR items is this bellhousing to adapt a popular Chevrolet V-8 to the Land Cruiser FJ80's automatic transmission. Engineering enables a swap without the need to move or modify the OEM transmission, transfer case or drivelines.*

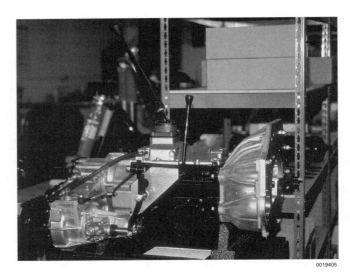

Fig. 16-27. *Advance Adapters has developed a practical NV4500 heavy duty five-speed overdrive to Land Cruiser transfer case conversion. I really support this approach for its overall simplicity and use of mostly OEM parts from the engine through the transmission. Here, BTB Products' linkage and other enhancements help complete the conversion.*

remaining Toyota components. These truck four-speeds can provide the proven rock crawling gearsets, with low range, low gear final crawl ratios approaching 70:1.

More recently, the success of GM's New Venture 4500-series heavy duty iron case five-speed overdrive has provided a superb alternative. Available in GM full-size light truck chassis above 8,500 pounds GVWR, first generation versions of the NV4500 (D-Spec) boast a synchromesh first gear ratio of 6.34:1 and a 27% overdrive fifth gear.

This transmission, although currently expensive, is the one-stop approach. Using a prototype Chevrolet truck engine and transmission assembly, the adapters needed fit between the transmission and Land Cruiser transfer case plus a custom bellhousing.

Another alternative is the use of Advance Adapters' Ranger Torque Splitter two-speed transmission (available with a 1:1 ratio direct drive gear and an over- or underdrive gear). This unit is a bonafide two-speed gearbox that fits between the engine bellhousing and the transmission of trucks up to 20,000 pounds GVW capacity.

Advance Adapters offers a Ranger Torque Splitter unit that fits in front of Chevrolet truck four-speed transmissions and also units that fit Landcruiser four-speeds. One unit can even mate the stock Chevrolet truck bellhousing to a Land Cruiser four-speed transmission.

The lengthy Land Cruiser six requires a long engine compartment. Unless you use the Ranger Torque Splitter transmission, a V-8 needs to be moved forward during fit-up to provide driveline, oil pan, header and distributor clearance. This means shifting the transmission and transfer case forward, which also requires lengthening of the rear driveshaft and shortening of the front shaft. You must relocate cables, possibly hoses, the transmission/transfer case shift mechanisms and other accessories.

Use of the Ranger overdrive gearbox, which is approximately seven to eight inches long (depending upon application), may require moving the transfer case and transmission *rearward* slightly to provide enough room

Fig. 16-28. *NV4500-to-Land Cruiser aftermarket adapter pieces consist of bellhousing with proper location for clutch slave cylinder, a transmission and transfer case adapter, and conversion engine/transmission mounts. Advance Adapters and BTB Products can even fit this transmission to an F, 2F or 3F-E six-cylinder engine.*

for a mechanical (engine-driven) fan. Driveshaft lengthening, re-fitting sheetmetal for shift levers and sizing of cables may be necessary when you relocate the transmission and transfer case.

Relatively Easy Engine Swap

No engine conversion is without glitches. When I swapped engines on Project Rubicon I, all of my work was performed in space provided by Rick's R.V. Center and Hitch Shop at El Cajon, California, a shop fully equipped for fabricating steel products. Although the conversion work can be done with a buzz box welder and more modest equipment, I had the distinct advantage of access to a shop with hoists, a fork lift, die punches, MIG welders, gas cutting equipment, cold cutting and bending equipment, graded hardware—and four highly skill and accomplished metal worker/welders: Barry Lowrey, Henri Koers, Stu Ehrich, and shop owner Rick Preston.

The conversion begins with a simple yet crucial step. To ensure proper alignment of parts, install the aftermarket Advance Adapters' or Downey Off-Road type rear support plate to the rear of the transfer case. With the six cylinder engine still in place and the truck *driveable*, estimate the motor mount cushion thickness and crush, then lightly tack weld or tightly clamp the rear frame side mounts into place.

In cases where the elevation of the engine-transmission-transfer case assembly may need adjustment, wait until you have exact dimensions before locating the rear mounting plate and side mounts. I like the idea of getting the engine far enough forward to give room for servicing the ignition distributor. Also, it is best to provide proper spacing for the mechanical fan and fan shroud. This may require raising the engine, and possibly the gearbox assemblies, to center the fan—Otherwise, the V-8 fan will mount considerably lower than the fan on a stock Land Cruiser six, in most cases too low for effective cooling.

Once my rear frame mounts and transfer case rear mounting plate were in position, I supported the transmission from the ground level, with cushions installed *loosely* at the rear adapter mount plate. Following customary steps, I removed the grill, unbolted the radiator and core support and began the engine removal. After a few hours of wrestling with hoses, old exhaust flange hardware and a massive and bulky engine and bellhousing, the old 2F powerplant rested solidly on the ground.

To use the Ranger overdrive required removal of the transmission's front bearing retainer and cleaning the front of the case carefully. I then carefully fitted the Advance Adapters' Ranger overdrive and supported the transmission and overdrive gearboxes.

Once the gearboxes were in place, the job became routine. I found a Chevy V-8 cast-iron bellhousing at a local recycling yard. The unit came from a late Sixties/early Seventies four speed truck model. This provided the mandatory 5.125" bearing retainer bore diameter for the Advance Adapters overdrive or an SM465 Muncie four-speed truck box. The bellhousing was hot tanked and checked for cracks, then I carefully measured the deck alignment and concentricity of the index bore.

NOTE —

For the earlier and smaller SM420 index bore size, simply use a 1955-67 Chevy V-8 iron truck bellhousing.

Stock Chevrolet truck parts finalized the fit-up. The front face and input gear of the Ranger unit was identical to a Chevrolet truck transmission, so all parts forward of the overdrive were bone-stock Chevrolet truck pieces—very simple and reliable.

Fig. 16-29. *1960-62 and 1963 K-model GM light trucks use a right-side clutch release lever with a hydraulic clutch linkage system. This bellhousing has been popular in some Toyota truck swap applications where there is limited clearance at the left side of the engine and transmission. The transmission index bore is 4.686-inches (common SM420 four-speed size) on these 1960-63 bellhousings and can be custom machined to 5.125-inch for use with the later Muncie 465 or NP435 four-speed truck transmission.*

Fig. 16-30. *An iron bellhousing incorporates a starter motor mount for a common and durable iron nosed starter. Attaching bolts lay on a horizontal plane, unlike passenger car and later truck starters that have long bolts running vertically into the block casting.*

The aftermarket can furnish the necessary pieces to simplify this kind of swap or similar swaps involving Toyota pickup truck models. Available pieces include a bracket for mounting the stock Toyota clutch slave cylinder near the left hand Chevrolet throwout arm. An aftermarket alternator pulley, adapter bracket and special fittings allow easy use of the original alternator, temp sender and other hardware.

With the 168-tooth flywheel and a Centerforce II clutch mounted to the engine, I installed the iron bellhousing, a new clutch fork boot, and an iron Chevrolet clutch release fork (early V-8 truck style). Now the engine was ready for the chassis.

NOTE —
Iron starter noses and iron bellhousings are more durable than the later aluminum types. Since most cast iron truck bellhousings accept the larger 168-tooth flywheel, you also have the choice of a larger clutch assembly.

Fig. 16-31. Your engine conversion will require the installation of adapters and machined accessory brackets. Like other engine builders, I have developed a healthy respect for Loctite 242 and other liquid fasteners on critical bolts. Here is Downey Off-Road's pulley assembly for a Buick V-6 swap into 4WD Toyota pickups.

NOTE —
You cannot be too safe with fasteners and liquid thread locker, however, avoid use of permanent type stud-and-bearing mount liquids unless they have been recommended by the component manufacturer or your OEM Toyota repair manual. Some thread lockers require special procedures—or even heat—for disassembly.

If located properly, the engine should set in easier than the 'Cruiser six cylinder. In my installation, the bellhousing bolts could be installed without laying under the vehicle. Properly located, the engine's distributor will clear the firewall, the fan will clear the radiator, and the oil pan will clear the front axle and driveline. I reached the bellhousing bolts by laying over the front of the engine. Tubular aftermarket exhaust headers fit easily.

The engine can be leveled once the bellhousing has been coupled and secured properly. Driveshaft angles and U-joint relationships are critical to performance and reliability, so spend time with a protractor level and make sure of correct driveshaft and yoke angles before installing front/side engine mounts. (See discussion of driveshaft angularity in geartrain upgrade chapter.)

Fig. 16-32. On domestic V-8 engine conversions, use molded radiator hoses available through OEM and aftermarket sources. If parts counterperson draws a blank stare, ask to see some 350 or 400 Chevy V-8 truck applications. If this does not work, make a mockup of hose shapes with a piece of welding rod, and become friends with the parts manager. Wade through OEM replacement hoses in the back of the parts store until you find appropriate shapes and inlet/outlet sizes—When you find the right hoses, record part numbers for future reference.

A correctly positioned engine will be on nearly the same planes and lines (side view and top-view) as the stock six cylinder engine, using crankshaft centerlines as your reference points. (The entire assembly may need to be raised on this side-view plane to center the fan.)

Measure U-joint angles closely, then fit the front engine mounts. Once you have correct U-joint angles and a properly angled engine, the adapter motor mounts and transmission/transfer case mounts can now be permanently welded into place.

Check suspension (spring, frame, axle, etc.) clearance carefully. One area that deserves close attention is the engine's oil pan clearance with the axle and driveline. (With aftermarket "lift" springs, there is more clearance than a stock set of springs will provide.) Watch for clearance between the crankshaft pulley and axle housing. Height of the engine, transmission and transfer case determines the crankshaft pulley clearance above the front axle.

Tightening all engine and transfer case mounting bolts and nuts (provided in the aftermarket motor mount kit) completes the engine installation. At this point, the engine accessories, fuel and exhaust systems and some cooling system work lie ahead. Relocation of the battery, electrical system hookups, carburetor linkage and miscellaneous fabrication work also remain.

Fig. 16-33. *If you have a spring lift, make sure that the spring rebound snubbers will prevent axle movement into the area of the crankshaft pulley or oil pan. Also, axle limiter straps can help prevent the front axle from hyper-extending downward, which could cause the driveshaft to separate at its spline coupler. This truck is owned by Ross Stuart of Land Cruiser Advanced Handling. Note chassis modifications and flexibility. FJ40 features a 396 Chevy big block V-8.*

Fig. 16-34. *You need the right oil pan and pickup screen for your engine conversion. You may need an aftermarket or custom fabricated pan. Solid axle Toyota 4WD chassis require a rear oil sump and pickup, common to Chevrolet V-engines (as shown) and available in Ford 4WD truck V-8 engine applications like the Bronco or F-series trucks.*

Keeping A "Chevota" Cool

Your high mileage Land Cruiser radiator is likely shot. Tubes become plugged and corrosion eats enough fin material to disqualify the old radiator for reliable service. A "desert cooler," using a quality brass and copper core from a source like Well Built of Los Angeles, can assure quality cooling in the rough backcountry.

Fig. 16-35. *Hot tanked clutch fork and bellhousing look new. Fitted with a new dust boot, fork works with Centerforce's throwout bearing. All parts forward of overdrive are stock Chevrolet, except for 11" Centerforce diaphragm clutch. Resurfaced heavy duty (14-inch/168-tooth) Chevrolet truck flywheel will aid off-pavement torque demands. Skid plate protects light duty Chevrolet oil pan from road debris. Note adapter for a 600-Series Oberg "Tattle Tale" oil filtration system. Oberg units offer remote means for protecting an engine and have a serviceable screen filter.*

Fig. 16-36. *Final installation places 383 Chevrolet engine slightly to driver's side of chassis. This is normal and follows stock layout. Chassis and steering modifications were performed at same time to simplify installation. Note front spring Advance Handling kit and power steering assembly with narrow steering shaft. (See chassis/suspension upgrade chapter for details.)*

A quality Land Cruiser based radiator core upgrade will have seamless tubes and provide four-row coolant flow. Stock 'Cruiser side straps, tanks, and custom inlet/outlet necks can work well with most Chevrolet V-8 installations. Careful and secure fitup in the chassis is essential, taking clearance with the water pump and fan into account. Always use a functional shroud. (See cooling system chapter for tips on installing a high performance radiator, fan and shroud.) A custom crossflow radiator may be necessary for high horsepower V-8 swaps.

V-8 Land Cruiser Performance Record

When I finished my project buildup, the 1976 'Cruiser's chassis sported an emission legal 383 cubic inch Chevrolet V-8 engine, a 27% Ranger Torque Splitter overdrive unit and the original Toyota four-speed transmission with its two-speed transfer case. Advance Adapters' Ranger overdrive gave two options for final drive gearing: In direct gear, the unit provided 4.11:1 axle ratios, while the 27% overdrive yielded an equivalent of 3:1 axle gearing. With 33" tires, such gearing in overdrive was way too "tall" (numerically low) for the original six cylinder 2F engine, but fine for the 383 V-8.

Toyota's Land Cruiser FJ40 is a formidable machine with a reputation for exceptional stamina and off-pavement crawling ability—attributes worth preserving. I soon discovered that the truck not only maintained its old Land Cruiser lugging performance and off-road versatility but also made "muscle car" strides on asphalt. With less than five-hundred miles on the new engine and an assurance that the cooling system and accessories were

Fig. 16-37. Advance Adapters' Ranger two-speed Torque Splitter overdrive, offering direct drive plus a 27% overdrive gear, doubles as the transmission adapter. Rear of unit mates to front end of Toyota four-speed box, while front of overdrive is virtual match for a stock Chevrolet truck four-speed. Unit is tough enough for 20,000 pound GVW rated trucks and provides this 'Cruiser with 16 speeds forward and 4 in reverse.

functioning properly, I qualified the truck's new performance parameters.

FJ40 Chevota Tractor?

I wanted proof that the FJ40 could still tackle a good hill, without a lot of ruckus and wheelspin. A more fickle small-block, fitted with a "bigger" camshaft than I chose, would likely labor under the bulky weight of a Land Cruiser chassis. Such an engine will either stall or dig a pair of deep tire ravines in its wake. Would my choice of a mild and short duration/high lift camshaft do the same?

The velvet smoothness of a Centerforce diaphragm type clutch gave no hint of the engine's torque capacity— nor did the smooth rotational force of a hefty 168-tooth iron flywheel. This was my very first encounter with a low range, first gear hill climb, and the engine produced *over two times* the horsepower of the original 2F six. I worked the throttle lightly....

Approaching the steep incline, the truck idled at a smooth 500 rpm with the clutch engaged and no throttle applied. The gearing and power met perfectly, effortlessly raising the nose end of the truck at nearly the limit of its approach angle. Without a bit of engine hesitation, lope, stumble, or lunge, the 383 V-8 simply walked its payload up the steeply angled slope.

When the going got really rough, ruts and rocks dictating the speed, the engine willingly accepted an application of the brakes while in gear. The tachometer read less than 400 rpm, but the heavy flywheel and 0.270-inches of extra piston stroke length triumphed. The 383 stroker small-block could easily out-lug a stock 'Cruiser, with twice as much horsepower available on demand.

The awesome throttle response required some driver adjustment. With a 90-inch wheelbase and instant acceleration, dirt road driving required a new approach. My FJ40, with a chassis lift of several inches, oversized tires, a Saginaw integral power steering conversion (see suspension/chassis upgrade chapter) and a weighty OEM hardtop, now had faster steering, more agility and gearing that responded readily to a high torque V-8 engine.

> NOTE —
> See the following section for more information on building a 383 stroker engine.

For Land Cruisers Only: Stump-pullin' Chevrolet V-8 Power

For the real world of everyday driving, in terms of fuel economy and in the interest of occasional trailer pulling, I find that the best overall small-block Chevrolet engine buildup is the 383 V-8 stroker motor.

After researching OEM performance formulas, comparing my engine building and field testing experience with that of others, and consulting top aftermarket R&D facilities like Racing Head Service (RHS), I can suggest a 383 Chevrolet V-8 buildup that really works.

A 383 engine consists of parts from both the 350 Chevrolet V-8 and the 400 (small-block) engines. The Chevrolet 350 V-8 has a good record and was first offered in 1968 passenger cars and 1969 light trucks. 350 V-8s share the same 4.00" bore as the legendary 327 small-block. A longer stroke of 3.48" and a durable big (main bearing) journal crankshaft contribute to this engine's stamina and reliability.

High output Chevrolet small-block V-8 engines, which by design benefit from over-square features (bigger cylinder bore/shorter stroke lengths like the legendary 4.00" x 3.00" 302 Camaro Z-28 V-8), generally require high compression ratios to develop peak performance. With emission controls and low octane unleaded fuel, it is difficult for engines to operate at high compression ratios.

The 283, 302, 327 and 350 put out their best performance with large valves, a 10:1 or higher compression ratio, a healthy fuel supply and 100-plus octane fuel. The potent 327, last used in 1969 trucks, loses its performance effectiveness when compression drops below a 9:1 ratio. A 350/5.7L V-8, due to its longer stroke design, can still pull reasonably well at 8.5:1 compression ratio.

Fig. 16-38. Although 400 small-block design offers a substantial stroke increase at 3.75", cooling suffers from "siamesed" middle cylinders. Chevrolet's 400 small-block bore, a large 4.125-inches, relies on same bore centers as other small block engines.

From a production standpoint, the 400 small-block was a useful concept. Having the same bore centers as other small-block engines, the 400 allowed for ready parts interchangeability, using similar cylinder head castings, manifolds and ignition system. Missing, however, is space for coolant circulation between the middle cylinders.

Role Model: The 305 V-8

Chevrolet's 305 small-block V-8 was a 1976 response to heavy emission constraints. A strong running, small displacement engine, the 305 uses the 350's 3.48" stroke and a small 3.75" bore that more closely approaches the "square" point (equal bore diameter and stroke length). The 3.75" bore also has significance as the same bore dimension found in the original 265 cubic inch small-block Chevrolet V-8.

Like an industrial or medium duty gasoline truck engine, the 305 develops substantial low-speed torque. This

Fig. 16-39. 305 V-8 has worked adequately in many Land Cruisers and even some 4WD Toyota pickups. In stock form, truck version of 305 and the rarer 262 emission era Chevy V-8s are two exceptions to my sanction against using a V-8 in Toyota 4WD pickups or 4Runners. Shown here is Steve Frank's Land Cruiser FJ40 sporting an EFI/Tuned-Port Injected 305 IROC Camaro V-8 with plenty of muscle.

helps meet emission and fuel economy demands, which require higher (lower numerical) axle gear ratios.

The formula has proven a success. 305 engines generate nearly as much torque and pulling power as their larger 350 brethren, albeit with less total horsepower at higher rpm. Flexibility also makes the long stroke 305 okay for low GVWR light trucks and later High Output passenger cars like the Camaro/Firebird Cross-Fire EFI engines (circa 1982–83) and the 1985-up IROC 305 Tuned Port EFI engine.

The 305 achieved the goal that the 400 narrowly missed. Both engines proved that a closer to square bore/stroke ratio better serves in a low compression, low octane, leaner burning world. With better block and head cooling, the 400 may well have survived.

Basis for the 383

Although the 400 itself has faded like the 307 and 262 designs, its unique torque, produced by its long 3.75-inch stroke crankshaft stroke, has given the 400 a key role in the world of high performance auto and truck racing.

Horsepower and torque losses result from stringent emission standards and the demands of low octane fuels that require lower compression ratios, especially in pre-EFI carbureted engines. This can be offset by increasing the stroke length. High performance engine builders capitalized on this phenomena by mating a 3.75" stroke 400 crankshaft to the 4.00" bore 350 V-8 block.

A stock 400 crankshaft has 0.200" larger diameter main bearing journals than the 350. The 400 cast crankshaft can easily part with this excess metal, and the machining takes only a bit more effort than a standard crankshaft grinding and polishing job. Severe duty testing and the rigors of racing environments have proven that a properly undersized cast 400 crankshaft is both strong and reliable.

NOTE —

The popularity of Chevy 383 hybrid engines has opened a market for *new* crankshafts, specially built by the aftermarket. As cores of the original cast-type 400 crankshaft run short, an even greater market will exist for new "stroker" crankshafts, including heavy duty forged types.

A remachined 400 crankshaft with 400 connecting rods and short skirt forged aluminum pistons easily fits the 350 V-8 block. An alternative is use of stock 350 rods with special pistons that compensate for the longer stroke by relocating the piston pin hole. Either way, substantial low-rpm torque and a major horsepower increase at the mid- and upper-rpm ranges will result.

The term "383" addresses two factors. Use of a 400 crankshaft provides a 0.270" longer stroke, while the standard cleanup rebore of a recyclable 350 engine block is 0.030" oversize. Since most hybrid 383 engines begin with a used four-bolt main 350 Chevrolet block, 0.030" oversize has become a standard for the 383 buildup.

383 Torque Goals

Torque is a measurement of the twisting force available at the crankshaft. In automotive uses, torque overcomes inertial loads and allows an engine to perform work. There is a distinct relationship between torque and horsepower, and in basic terms, automotive engines cannot develop peak horsepower before exceeding their maximum torque output.

An engine's torque rating, often overlooked when building a Rubicon Trail rock crawler or trailer pulling truck, is the single most important measurement of strength and efficiency. Torque and gearsets provide the means for moving weight. The ideal utility truck engine provides high torque at the lowest possible rpm.

454 Chevy TBI big-blocks built through 1995, with their 4.251" bore and long 4.00" stroke, run a 7.9:1 compression ratio and develop maximum torque of 385 lb/ft at an impressively low 1600 rpm. This TBI 454, equipped with roller lifters, reaches 230 peak horsepower at only 3600 rpm. For off-highway use and trailer pulling, this is optimal power on a somewhat hefty gasoline bill.

Properly built, the "stroked" 350/383 engine makes an ideal truck alternative. Coupled to either a manual transmission or a TH350 or TH400 GM automatic, a 383 buildup can maintain all OEM emission devices for compliance. Power accessories, like power steering and air conditioning, can make an easy adjunct to this conversion package.

For a truck like my 1976 Land Cruiser, a carbureted 1976 350 Federal emissions package V-8 truck engine could provide the foundation for an emission legal swap. In its original form, the 1976 GM 350 3/4-ton 4WD truck V-8 was a four-barrel carbureted 8.5:1 compression (Federal 49-State form) emission engine that produced 265 lb/ft torque @ 2400 rpm and 160 horsepower @ 4000 rpm.

Proving the 383 Point

Based upon my experience combined with the expertise of Racing Head Service (RHS) at Memphis, Tennes-

383 Superflow Dynamometer Tests

As a special service, RHS took a blueprint engine like I recommend for Land Cruiser conversions and ran it for three hours on a Superflow dynamometer during break-in. Off the assembly line, preliminary checks included the compression (which ranged from 215 to 220 psi at test stand speeds), bearing oil flow and oil pressure (68 psi with a new high volume pump). The engine then went on the dynamometer for eleven full test sequences.

Equipment used for running the engine on the dynamometer included an Edelbrock Performer (dual plane) manifold, 600 cfm Edelbrock carburetor and a set of 1-5/8" Hedman headers. (On Land Cruiser installations, you will find that the factory iron intake and exhaust manifolds and the original, unmodified Quadrajet carburetor work fine.) An aftermarket manifold and headers could be legal for some older FJ Land Cruiser applications; otherwise, you will find it necessary to use factory iron intake and exhaust manifolds plus the original and unmodified Quadrajet carburetor, which actually serves as an excellent fuel source.

Figures for the test sequence reflect Unocal regular grade gas, standard correction factor to 29.92 in./hg atmosphere, 60° F air temperature and, notably, a dry air environment:

RPM	Lb./Ft. Torque	Horsepower	Volumetric Efficiency
2000	384.7*	146.5	92.6%
2500	416.6	198.3	94.2%
3000	411.4	235.0	96.1%
3500	414.6**	276.3	96.9%**
4000	402.7	306.7	95.3%
4500	361.7	309.9**	90.1%
5000	306.5	291.8	83.7%

* 2000 rpm is lowest point for accurate readings on dyno. Here, 383 engine has already matched the *maximum* torque of a 454 TBI engine.

** Peak performance for 383 tow engine.

see, I begin the 383 truck engine buildup with a proven 350 four-bolt main bearing truck block. This design is ideal for snail paced trail running, hill climbing, high altitude lugging, overall economy and even trailer pulling.

For emission compliance, I maintain the use of all OEM 350 smog devices, plus the OEM manifolds (or 50-State legal aftermarket designs), a stock or mildly recurved Delco-Remy HEI ignition and a blueprinted Quadrajet four-barrel carburetor. Complete with all emission controls and engine accessories, this package can be street legal. (See this chapter's section on emission requirements.)

NOTE —

The late EFI/TBI engine is an alternative, although the block must be fitted with a Chevrolet Race Shop rear main seal adapter kit to accept the re-machined 400 type crankshaft with its earlier two-piece rear main seal.

Fig. 16-40. *RHS Tow Torque Special 383 engine accepts all OEM 350 hardware. Here, manifolding has been installed. (Impressive chrome valve covers were soon replaced by OEM items to comply with emission control needs.) Installed properly, 383 engine is indistinguishable from original 350.*

Fig. 16-41. *World Product SR cylinder heads accept 1976 Chevy engine brackets for air conditioning, power steering and alternator. Stock intake manifold and Quadrajet carburetor provided bonafide comparison of 350 versus 383 engine designs. Likewise, end dump factory exhaust manifolds, although notably restrictive in flow, were also re-used.*

A mild compression ratio ceiling of 8.7:1 will permit use of regular grade fuel yet still develop high manifold vacuum. *Usable* torque and horsepower, along with improved fuel economy, should be your goals. According to RHS's dynamometer tests of the kind of 383 engine I am suggesting, we have found that a properly built 383 can exceed the output of a 454 TBI engine while delivering lower tailpipe emissions than the original 350 V-8. Fuel economy is much better than the stock 350 truck engine.

Although any competent machine shop can construct a 383 stroker engine from a 350 block and 400 crankshaft, RHS has developed a specialized engine for severe duty trailer pulling, the kind of power that also serves 4WD off-pavement users. The goal for a trailer puller or a rock crawlin' 4x4 Land Cruiser is the same: strong low speed torque with maximum horsepower by 4,000–4,500 rpm. This is the *maximum practical operating rpm for tow vehicles subjected to severe loads.*

RHS's 383 Tow Torque Special buildup reuses a thoroughly cleaned and remachined 350 four-bolt main bearing block, custom machined 400 crankshaft and 5.7" (350 type) connecting rods. All other parts, including the cylinder head assemblies and engine bolts, are new.

For cylinder heads, RHS chooses the 76cc combustion chamber World Products design, which feature thick walled bronze valve guides, special hardened exhaust valve seats, stainless steel 1.5" diameter exhaust and 1.94" diameter intake valves, new valve springs and chrome moly spring retainers.

One version of RHS's 383 buildups uses Silv-O-Lite/Keith Black hypereutectic D-cup pistons, Speed Pro plasma moly piston rings, Vandervell engine bearings, heavy duty ARP rod bolts and main studs, a complete Competition Cams heavy duty valve train with 1.5:1 (stock) ratio roller tip rocker arms, and a new GM harmonic balancer and transmission flexplate for proper external balance of the 400 crankshaft.

Fig. 16-42. *400 crankshaft is externally balanced. RHS includes a new factory harmonic balancer and flexplate with these engines. (A pre-1986 350 flywheel or flexplate will fit the 400 engine but will not provide proper balance.) RHS also match-weights and balances other reciprocating pieces.*

For high altitude operation, RHS and I recommend the CompCams CS 252H-10 grind camshaft designed for RV use. Valve opening duration of this torque camshaft is a mild 252-degrees (intake and exhaust) measured from 0.006" tappet lift. Single pattern lobe centerlines of 106 degrees with a healthy 0.431" intake/exhaust lift provide for very stable manifold vacuum at all engine speeds plus a rapid torque rise to get a heavy load rolling.

383 Real-World Driving Performance

We translated the impressive dynamometer figures to real world driving conditions, subjecting both the original 350 V-8 and new RHS 383 engine assemblies to the same tests, using regular pump gas and stock base timing advance of 8° BTDC. The altitude at our test site is 1400 feet above sea level. Air temperatures during both tests ranged from 86 to 92° F. We conducted tests using a truck equipped with an automatic transmission. Shifter remained in Drive mode and allowed automatic upshifts of the stock Turbo 350 transmission*:

Test Criteria	Original 350	New 383
0–60 mph without trailer (weight of truck was 6,450 pounds.)	17.85 seconds	10.27 seconds
40–60 mph Run without trailer	9.10 seconds	4.97 seconds
O–60 mph with 4,100 pound trailer	37.82 seconds	24.16 seconds
40–60 mph with trailer	21.83 seconds	9.53 seconds(!)
Combined fuel economy w/o trailer	10 mpg	11.2 mpg
Fuel economy with trailer	8 mpg	11 mpg

*1976 Chevrolet K-20 pickup has original full-time 4x4 system. We reinstalled original torque converter. Axle gearing was 4.10:1 with a 31.25-inch dia. 235R85/16 tire size. Shift and passing gear linkage adjustments were identical with both tests. Tests conducted when engine had three dyno hours and less than 800 miles clocked on the odometer. (Expect slight gains after full break-in.) Typical FJ40 weighs one ton less than this truck, so expect performance and economy gains.

Fig. 16-43. *Using all of a 1976 350 engine's accessories, emission equipment and peripheral pieces, new RHS 383 long block produced tailpipe emission levels much lower than California's current allowable guideline for a 1976 Chevrolet 350 V-8 truck engine in top condition. GM decal on air cleaner notes September 1975 build date of original 350 engine and Federal (EPA) compliance guidelines.*

Variations on the 383 Theme

Some design alternatives for a 383 engine include use of shorter 400 connecting rods, higher compression ratios and camshafts ranging from original equipment grinds to all out racing profiles. The RHS tow formula, however, makes a practical model for the severe duty Land Cruiser under load.

Faced with today's low octane fuels and the heat buildup of rock crawling or trailer pulling, avoid higher compression ratios when building your Land Cruiser V-8. Also, although a stock profile 350 or 400 camshaft could easily work with a mild compression ratio 383 stroker en-

Manifold Vacuum: Test of Fuel and Energy Efficiency

A simple manifold vacuum test says a lot. After adjusting the spark timing and idle mixture on the original 350 V-8, I conducted several vacuum tests. I repeated the same tests with the new engine.

Stationary and not under load, the 700, 1000, 1500 and 2000 rpm readings for the original 350 engine were 20, 20.5, 22 and 23 in/hg manifold vacuum, respectively. The same rpm tests on the new 383 produced 20, 21, 23 and 24 in/hg vacuum, respectively. This indicates a practical matchup of the camshaft, compression ratio and overall design.

Despite these very healthy readings for the new 383, the most impressive figure was a stall/load test that I conducted. With each engine, we placed the transmission in drive, holding one foot firmly on the brake. Bringing the engine to precisely 1250 rpm, I took manifold vacuum readings.

The original 350 engine yielded 10 in/hg of vacuum under this loaded condition. 383 tests produced a whopping 14.5 in/hg vacuum at the same load and speed. Manifold vacuum equates directly to energy efficiency and power, and this test illustrates a major low rpm gain from both the 400 crankshaft and CompCams CS252-H10 camshaft grind.

Manifold vacuum is an excellent test of both engine condition and energy efficiency. Readings of both original 350 and new 383 reveal similar low speed (unloaded) vacuum patterns, with 383 running slightly higher. Under stall load at 1250 rpm, however, 383 pulls 14.5 in/hg vacuum versus weaker 10 in/hg of stock 350 carbureted truck engine.

gine, RHS's RV/torque grind will provide a quicker torque rise, which serves better in rough terrain.

As for shorter 400 rods versus the 5.7" length 350 type rods, I have compared these two rod lengths on Alan Lockheed's *Engine Expert* computer software, a sophisticated engine design program. The 5.7" center-to-center rod length used by RHS requires a specially located piston pin (nearer the piston crown), while 400 rods of 5.56" length will work with short-skirted forged aluminum 350 replacement pistons.

My primary concern is durability, and *Engine Expert* revealed that a 383's critical tension (failure point) is at 7839 rpm with 5.7" 350 rods and 7814 rpm with the 5.56" 400 rods. As maximum horsepower for a Chevy 383/Land Cruiser engine should be reached by 4500 rpm, either rod length will work fine, with pistons currently available to accommodate each approach.

Fig. 16-44. *This RHS 383 has 8.7:1 compression, uses a mild RV/torque camshaft and relies on original HEI spark timing curve. Engine tested well below pollutant limits set for either a 350 V-8 engine in a 1976 3/4-ton Chevy truck or a stock 1976 Land Cruiser 2F non-catalyst engine.*

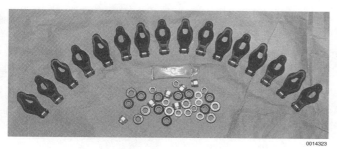

Fig. 16-45. *Tow Torque Special 383 engine uses RHS/CompCams replacement roller tip rocker arms. Precise rocker arm ratio is same as stock (1.5:1), however, smoother operation and improved performance result from less friction plus more accurate valve lift and duration figures.*

6. ENGINE REBUILDING

As your truck engine reaches the upper end of its service life, you have two options: an in-the-chassis "ring and valve job/overhaul" or a complete, out-of-chassis engine "rebuild."

An in-chassis overhaul is relatively easy with earlier in-line six- and four-cylinder Toyota truck engines. Following your OEM Toyota repair manual, you would begin by removing the cylinder head, oil pan and timing cover.

The next steps would be reaming the cylinder ridges before removing the rods and pistons, then protecting the crankshaft from debris as you hone the cylinders to break glaze. After carefully washing and oiling the cylinder walls with clean oil, re-assembly would include fitting new rod and main bearings, along with new piston rings.

Other new pieces would be a timing chain/sprocket set (or timing gears on a Land Cruiser F, 2F or 3F-E engine), plus a new or reconditioned oil pump. The cylinder head would take a trip to the machine shop for thorough reconditioning. New gaskets, changing the accessible freeze plugs and a major tune-up would complete the job.

Overhauls work on mildly worn engines and those having hard, durable cylinder walls. An overhaul buys extra miles of driving yet falls short of a complete rebuild. Restricted by the chassis and body, many rebuilding steps are neglected during an in-the-frame overhaul. By contrast, a complete, professional engine rebuild involves replacement or precision machining of every moving part in the engine.

The "Real" Engine Rebuild

Emission control hardware and a maze of carburetor plumbing overwhelm most 1972-up Toyota truck en-

Fig. 16-46. *During in-chassis overhaul, you will sublet the cylinder head assembly to a machine shop for reconditioning, then carefully hone the cylinder bores while protecting the crankshaft bearing journals from any debris or abrasive materials. A new or reground camshaft and lifters (if so equipped), re-machined rocker arms, a new oil pump, new timing chain(s) or gears, plus a new tensioner if so equipped, will round out the job. Here, camshaft journal/bores and saddles receive machining to restore centerline and salvage a slightly heat-warped Toyota four-cylinder head.*

gines. Basic long-block engine designs, however, remain relatively unchanged. Once out of the chassis (see your OEM Toyota repair manual for removal procedures), your four- or six-cylinder engine can undergo a thorough rebuild.

A quality rebuild will virtually remanufacture your engine. Caustic block and head cleaning, replacing hard-to-reach freeze plugs and installing camshaft bearings are just a few of the procedures.

Unless run on a high grade synthetic oil from day one, the high mileage Toyota truck engine will have some degree of cylinder taper. (A simple ring-and-valve job overhaul would serve little purpose if much taper exists, as rings cannot seal properly against a tapered cylinder wall.) Here, restoration to OEM bore tolerances can take place during a machine shop remanufacture of your engine.

Some Engine Assembly Survival Tips

Sometimes it is easier to have the machine shop completely assemble your "long block" (cylinder head or heads plus all block assembly parts). If, however, you plan to assemble your newly machined engine parts, you will need to follow some important guidelines. Although your OEM Toyota repair manual can help with step-by-step procedures, there are some additional concerns that I will share.

For example, never fill hydraulic lifters with oil by compressing their plungers in an oil bath. New lifters take many crankshaft revolutions to bleed down, and if the camshaft profile has a high degree of valve overlap, the normal pre-load setting may cause valves to interfere with the piston crowns upon cranking. Before installing lifters in a domestic conversion V-8, V-6 or in-line six engine with hydraulic lifters, apply lifter lube to the block's lifter bores and the base of each lifter.

Fortunately, Toyota truck engines have reasonable compression ratios and can tolerate today's lower fuel octane ratings. For the purpose of rebuilding your engine, a compression ratio of 8.5:1 to 9:1 works very well on a carbureted engine. I've found that longer stroke engines, like the carbureted 258 cubic inch 2F engine, can survive nicely at 8.7:1 compression.

Usually, spark timing adjustments (like mild base/initial timing, a modest spark advance curve and a conservative spark timing advance limit) will permit use of a slightly higher compression ratio. Most Toyota engines can tolerate 9:1 or even higher compression, and surviving with such a ratio may be possible by simply retarding the spark timing slightly to prevent detonation. The yardstick that I use for truck purposes is to be able to run 87–88 octane fuel without detonating. This will prevent damage to pistons and pitting of valve faces.

On an engine with an undesirably high compression ratio, one means of lowering the compression is to replace the OEM head gasket with a thicker (Detroit or similar type) composition gasket. Apply sealant, if required, and install the gasket according to the manufacturer's guidelines. Use Permatex's Teflon Thread Compound on any head bolt threads that enter water jackets.

During an engine overhaul or rebuild, you can upgrade performance with high-quality aftermarket parts. Wiseco and others recognize the potential of Toyota engines and offer race-quality pistons and piston ring sets.

For the less stressed engine, OEM Toyota components work fine.

After refinishing and measuring each cylinder wall, wash your bores thoroughly and coat them with clean oil. Many shops recommend quality aftermarket rings, fitted to the stock/OEM type alloy pistons. For greater durability, use forged type pistons and recommended rings. Likewise, a full set of high performance valves (typically stainless steel type) and a three angle valve seat grind on hardened valve seats will assure consistent cylinder sealing and longevity. Make sure valve guide material is compatible with your chosen valve types.

Knowing When To Rebuild Your Engine

An engine rebuild is necessary when oil loss increases and fixing the leaks doesn't help. A noticeable decrease in oil pressure is also a bad sign, or when a subtle, deep in the engine knock develops. Another portent of serious trouble is a power decrease to the point that your torquey Land Cruiser six feels more like an 18RC mini-truck four cylinder engine, even after a thorough tune-up—or when a steady miss is neither fuel system nor spark related.

The story can only worsen, and if ignored, a connecting rod might well say, "Good-bye"—just as an off-highway hill places a load on the engine. Assuming the rest of the truck still stands tall, the engine wear can easily be remedied by a proper rebuild of the long block. By catching damage in time, your old engine can serve as a thoroughly useful and rebuildable core.

> **NOTE** —
> Due to scarcity of numbers, Land Cruiser and early mini-truck engines should be protected from irreparable damage. If you suspect mounting troubles, stop pushing the engine and plan a rebuild. If a rod should let go and ruin the crankshaft, other rods, the block and head, you could be out considerable expense and time trying to find another engine core for rebuilding.

As for the merits of a seasoned cylinder block, many racers insist that these blocks are far better than new ones. Heat and stress have likely distorted and twisted the castings to their final form, and assuming that magnafluxing or sonic testing of cylinders has shown no casting flaws or cracks, the remachined older block may actually hold closer tolerances under severe service.

Since all engines wear and tire with age, tune related troubles are easily separated from major engine wear, which can be confirmed through basic diagnostic tests. Categorically, tune problems relate to two areas of concern: the fuel supply system and ignition spark. Once adequate fuel supply has been confirmed, with proper air/fuel ratios for all engine speeds and driving conditions, adequate spark and correct ignition timing can be verified. After addressing these factors, you can confirm long block (block assembly and cylinder head) condition.

I have found that engine parts often wear at uneven rates. Timing chain and valve/carbon problems usually have a head start on other parts. Sometimes, in fact, a valve job and timing chain replacement can buy tens of thousands of miles before a major rebuild is necessary.

Piston ring wear, however, will follow. (In off-pavement use, air filtration is critical, or rings will fail even sooner than normal.) Cylinder walls generally taper toward the top (compression end) of their bores, and ring replacement usually calls for re-boring and refitting with new, oversized pistons. Sometimes, especially in the case of high nickel/chrome content in an engine block, the cylinders can simply be power honed, with new rings fitted to the original pistons (if they remain in good condition).

Any need to replace rings will warrant a valve grind and new engine bearings. Since carbon and sludge find their way into most engine assemblies, a complete teardown will afford hot tanking the engine parts to remove all traces of grime and deposits. Once piston ring, crankshaft, or block work becomes necessary, the best cure is removal of the engine from the chassis and either a complete teardown and rebuild or an exchange of the core for another long block.

Engine Diagnosis Leading To A Rebuild

Before jerking your engine from the chassis and floating a short-term loan at the credit union, be certain the engine needs a rebuild. Start with a standard compression test, isolating the lowest cylinder readings. Follow up with a leakdown test to distinguish valve from piston ring wear. I am so sold on the superior accuracy of a leakdown test that I only use a conventional compression gauge to pinpoint lowest cylinder readings. At that point, I use my portable Snap-On or vintage Sun scope's leakdown tester to isolate wear and specific defects.

I hold to a maximum compression variance of 10% between the highest and lowest cylinder readings on any engine that calls for a normal compression reading under 160 psi. Although OEM guidelines may allow more latitude than this, especially on high cylinder pressure engines, an engine with 15-25% or more compression variance definitely has ring or valve wear.

Using my 10% standard, a cylinder with a normal reading of 150 psi on a compression gauge test will tolerate *no less than* 135 psi pressure on the engine's lowest cylinder. Ideally, even this imbalance should be eliminated if possible. If valve or carbon troubles are not suspected, follow up with a leakdown test to confirm whether there is piston ring trouble.

A properly performed leakdown test should yield 8-12% cylinder leakage in an engine at top efficiency. (10% leak is the maximum allowed for retrofitting a supercharger.) By 20% leakage, the engine definitely requires attention. Should ring wear be noted, I would remove and tear down the engine for rebuilding.

Although traditional ring-and-valve jobs, in the chassis, meet with success in some instances, they do not constitute rebuilding. Such approaches simply buy time, and seldom do these in-chassis overhauls last as long as a completely remachined/rebuilt engine. Toyota truck engine parts are expensive—don't pay for them twice.

In all cases where crankshaft bearings have failed or a loss of oil pressure results from bearing wear, the engine must be torn down for complete rebuilding. The failure of bearings will contaminate the lubrication system, leaving metal particles to tear up new bearings. Complete disassembly and hot tank cleaning of parts is necessary to assure that the engine is clean.

When camshaft lobes grind away, I would also advise a major engine teardown. Hard metal has circulated through the engine, and the oil filter is not always able to catch all of the metal that has worn away. This is especially true of earlier Toyota Land Cruiser F-type engines with by-pass oil filtration systems.

Long Block Versus Short Block Replacement

When faced with the choice to rebuild an engine, two alternatives exist: 1) rebuilding the short block (fitted engine block without the cylinder head or heads) or 2) rebuilding the entire long block.

If your choice is to have an automotive machine shop assemble the engine, a long block will come with the head gaskets, head(s), and all valve train parts installed. The valve lifters, pushrods, rocker arms, and related parts will be assembled, and valve clearances will likely be set. Your job would simply be the installation of the manifolds, fuel supply and ignition systems, the water pump and all engine accessories.

The second alternative, the short block, consists of an engine block assembled with the crankshaft, rods, pistons/rings, bearings, camshaft (on OHV 'Cruiser engines), timing gears or chain/sprockets, and possibly the oil pump and pan. Your cylinder head(s) could be rebuilt separately, and you would install the head(s) plus all related parts and valvetrain components.

The final alternative would be subletting the machine shop work only. If your skills include complete disassembly and reassembly of an engine, money can be saved by assembling the engine yourself.

Rebuilding Your Toyota Engine

Once you've decided to rebuild and re-machine your engine, the machine shop is the next stop. Find a machine shop with a good reputation. (AERA or PERA membership is a good sign.)

Make sure the shop's customary work load runs the full range of automotive machine shop services and that they have all the machine tools and equipment on site to remanufacture or rebuild a gasoline or diesel engine.

> *CAUTION —*
> *Start-up of a newly rebuilt engine is the most critical moment in its life. Cleanliness during assembly is a must. Use engine assembly lube on all bearings, the lifter bases and bores, rocker arm shafts and rocker tips, and the valve stems. Oil the timing chain or gears, and prime the oil pump and oiling system to prevent a dry start.*

The job begins with a complete teardown for cleaning. To enable proper cleanup of the block, all oil artery plugs, freeze plugs, engine bearings, and seals must be removed. The crankshaft, rods/pistons, valve timing mechanism (chain or gear type), camshaft and camshaft bearings, plus any loose gasket material, are also separated from the block.

Then, stripped to its basic casting, the block is placed in a highly caustic hot tank solution and, literally, boiled until there is nothing left but bare casting metal and badly etched camshaft bearings (on Land Cruiser pushrod type engines). As for other ferrous metal parts, including the oil pan, cylinder head(s), crankshaft, and connecting rods, these may also be dipped in the caustic.

After thoroughly scouring all debris, carbon, and sludge from the block, a thorough wash, rinse and brush cleaning of oil galleries and other passages takes place. Once clean, the block will later be carefully refurbished with new Teflon tape wrapped artery plugs and sealant coated brass type freeze plugs. Now, however, cylinder boring and piston fitting will take place.

Boring cylinders is precise work. Tolerances run to the *ten-thousandths* of an inch, and machining tools must be deadly accurate. Depending upon engine use and the machinist's preference, torque plates may be mounted to the block deck before boring. These plates, thick steel and attached to the cylinder head bolt holes, simulate the mounted cylinder head with its attendant torque stress on the block deck. (Iron cylinder head engines are more apt to be torque plate bored.)

Regardless of whether torque plates are used, the boring is critical. Pistons come in standard oversizes ranging 0.010", 0.020", 0.030", 0.040", and 0.060" (U.S.) or, in the case of OEM Toyota standards, metric oversizes of 0.25mm, 0.50mm, 0.75mm, 1.00mm, 1.25mm, and 1.50mm.

Piston to cylinder wall clearances must be on tolerance for the piston and ring design and/or OEM engine standards. Too close, and piston seizure could occur. Excessive, and oil consumption or piston damage will be likely.

For a quiet and long running engine, I recommend a Sunnen CK-10 or equivalent cross-hatch hone job to assure very true cylinder walls. (The CK-10 can counter out-of-round and distortion caused by hard spots in the cylinder walls.) Under these conditions, I will run 0.0015" (fifteen ten-thousandths of an inch) piston to wall clearance with cast, OEM type replacement pistons and cast/moly rings. For forged type replacement pistons, 0.0025" to 0.003" is optimal for a somewhat quiet and trouble-free engine.

Some forged alloy racing piston designs demand 0.005" to 0.0075" piston to wall clearance, far more than suitable for a highway driven engine. For anything less than an all-out racing effort, avoid these piston types, as their cold start-up noise level and increased oil consumption can be troublesome. High clearance pistons typically serve racing applications and use zero-gap piston rings.

When fitting new pistons and rings, always follow the piston and ring manufacturers' recommendations and compare them with your OEM Toyota repair manual guidelines.

Once cylinder wear has determined the correct oversize required, boring begins with setup of the engine block. Clamped securely in position, with the crankshaft centerline absolutely perpendicular to the boring bar, each cylinder is centered carefully and bored. Constant measurements are taken by the machinist to assure that results conform to the planned buildup for this engine.

For a Toyota truck engine subjected to heavy loads, I prefer a maximum rebore of 0.030" (0.75mm) over standard. 0.040" (0.100mm) oversize is tolerated by many engines, but 0.060" or more presses the limits of engine cooling and into the realm of block core shift concerns.

Fig. 16-47. *Gary Sweetwood begins his post-boring finish work. The block benefits from Sunnen's CK-10 machine, which precisely trues the bore while leaving a perfect "cross hatch" pattern Here, Gary works within ten-thousandths of an inch standard to assure proper fitup of the pistons to cylinder walls. Clearances established here will increase engine*

Fig. 16-48. *Coarseness of cutting versus finishing stones can be seen on these two cylinder walls. Proper cylinder wall finish helps control oil consumption and regulates piston ring wear and break-in.*

Once bored to near finished size, enough material is left in each bore to allow finish honing. The goal is a true, perfectly finished cylinder wall with the correct, predetermined angle in the cross-hatch pattern. This is determined by piston ring and piston design, with each ring type demanding a specific finish. An incorrect cross-hatch pattern angle or improper wall coarseness can ruin piston rings and/or cause oil consumption problems.

By now, you can see the difference between precision machining versus in-the-chassis ring jobs with a glaze buster. Remanufacturers or machine shop rebuilders actually restore seasoned engine blocks, rods, crankshafts, and cylinder heads to OE standards of performance.

The Rebuild Continues

While the block is being prepared, including thorough rewashing and brush cleaning after finish honing, the machinist refurbishes the crankshaft and connecting rods. Crankshafts can be reground to 0.010", 0.020", and 0.030" U.S. or 0.25mm, 0.50mm, and 0.75mm metric undersizes.

When the rod journal with the worst wear or out-of-round condition has been determined, all rod journals will be turned to that size. Likewise, main bearing journals will be undersized uniformly—This follows the same logic as boring and honing all cylinders to the same oversize for even performance.

If a rod or main journal has been severely damaged, it can often be safely repaired by a special welding process. Once welded, a lighter undersize or even standard size bearings can be utilized after machining. Ideally, the least amount of undersizing (.010" by U.S. standard or 0.25mm on a metric engine) is desirable. This leaves ample material and adheres closer to the original engine balance.

Like cylinder boring, crankshaft grinding is an art. The crankshaft must be on dead center, as the main bearings and rod journals, or throws, are machined on an offset. For proper bearing clearance, the crankshaft machinist must decide whether "high" or "low" sided tolerances will work best on a given engine.

Bearing clearances also control the oil pressure. The type of oil pump volume employed will also affect the

Fig. 16-50. *Franco puts the finishing touch on crankshaft journals that have been ground. His polishing technique and chamfering of oil holes will give better than new service to this crankshaft.*

grinder's decision. Excessive clearance with a lower volume pump may not provide the necessary bearing protection, and failure of bearings could result.

In addition to a proper radius, the grinder may chamfer the oil feed holes and, finally, polish the surface of each journal to enhance service life and increase the refinement of the tolerances.

> **NOTE —**
> The crankshaft and rod/piston assemblies hold a critical role within the engine, and this is a good place to invest in precision finishing work and balancing.

After the crankshaft is ground and finished, a thorough cleanout of all passages takes place. Brush, solvent, and air pressure cleaning is not overkill, since *any* debris within a newly machined crankshaft can cause immediate and irreparable damage to rod or main bearings. Remember, debris in crankshaft passages will immediately hit the bearings.

Fig. 16-49. *Super tough, heavy duty steel Chevrolet 1182 crankshaft is being machined here. Cast crankshafts, like the 400 uses, can also give substantial service at more moderate rpm, especially when machined to tolerance and balanced.*

Fig. 16-51. *Rod shanks are decked before big end of the rod is honed. The roundness of the rod bores helps determine bearing clearance and correct fitup of parts.*

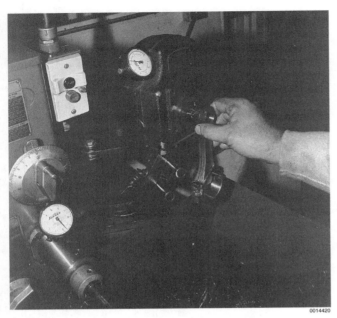

Fig. 16-52. *Honing and sizing of the connecting rods can increase engine life considerably. In conjunction with rod alignment, true piston travel can be assured.*

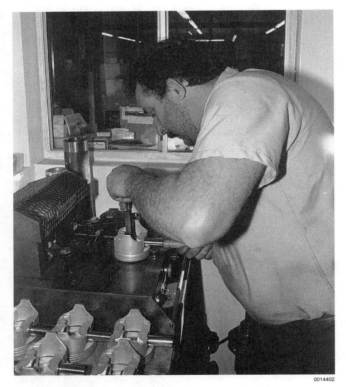

Fig. 16-53. *Using heat, Nick Bongiorno precisely fits new pistons to remachined connecting rods. Last step is check for rod alignment and piston squareness. With the block bores now perfectly perpendicular to the crankshaft centerline, these straight parts will run friction free.*

With a clean block and crankshaft, cam bearings can be carefully fitted to a Land Cruiser OHV six. (On OHC and DOHC engines, camshafts run in the cylinder head.) Installed with special driving tools and a heavy hammer by most shops, the cam bearings must be true and centered perfectly to align oil passages. Oil pressure control can often be affected by misaligned cam bearings, and even slight misfitting can cause serious engine damage.

With cam bearings installed, a new rear cam plug and new Teflon or sealant coated artery plugs, the block is ready for parts reassembly. The new pistons have by now been fitted to the refurbished connecting rods. The small and big end bores of the rods are machined and honed to assure concentricity, and rod alignment is checked after the pistons have been pin-fitted. (Modern shops use a special piston warmer to allow easy installation of the wrist pins.)

Once the ring end gaps have been verified in their cylinder bores, piston rings are carefully installed on the pistons. The pistons/rods are ready for installation.

Assembling The Short Block

If you have the right tools and can keep a work area super clean, assembly is not very difficult. With freshly machined and cleaned parts ready for installation, a careful job can be performed in a few hours.

Most builders like to install the crankshaft first. "Laying" the crank involves carefully placing the main bearings in their saddles and coating them with assembly lube or oil. Keep the rear main seal area dry. For engines with two-piece seals, apply sealant to the outer surface of seal halves and their joining junctions (unless otherwise recommended) before installation.

Toyota engines use excellent one-piece (full circumference) rear main seals. I apply a thin film of Permatex's Ultra-Blue silicone sealant to the outer edge of the seal during installation. I prefer this sealant to any other product currently available. Avoid rear main seal leaks.

With the main seal half installed (on engines with a two-piece seal), the clean crankshaft is carefully centered over the upside down block. Having the block in this position, the crankshaft can be lowered directly onto the bearing half-shells. Once in position, the main bearing caps will center easily.

> **CAUTION —**
> *Main caps cannot be mixed, switched, turned around or borrowed from another engine. Every block has matched and fitted main caps. If you find a damaged main cap on teardown, a new or used cap can only be used after line boring. (Line boring aligns the main bearing bores.)*

Bearing halves centered and seated, with all clearances correct, the main cap bolts can be installed finger tight. As dry threads create friction and poor torque readings, engine oil or a graphite thread dressing is often recommended to help assure torque uniformity.

With bolts installed and main caps setting flush, the torque sequence begins. Follow OEM repair manual guidelines for proper tightening sequence and torque, starting with a lower measurement, then increasing tension on the entire set uniformly. Three or four steps, over the entire bolt set, will provide good results.

> **CAUTION —**
> *When tightening critical engine bolts and nuts, note the torque specifications in your repair manual and whether these figures are with oiled or dry threads.*

Once the final tightening tension has been reached at every bolt, I let them set for a few minutes, then check each one again. Thread friction can cause one or two bolts to be *slightly* loose. After the threads cool and bolts stabilize, slight torque gains can sometimes be made.

There's no such thing as a "tight" engine. In fact, a properly machined engine, with correct clearances at critical points, should turn as easily during assembly as

Fig. 16-54. Once main bearings and crankshaft have been "laid," piston ring installation, with care and proper alignment of rings, readies the rod/piston assemblies for placement in the block. Read piston ring installation instructions carefully—pay close attention to which side of each ring faces up.

Fig. 16-55. Conventional ring compressors work well. Lightly oiled and square, the tool allows for an easy hammer handle tap to insert pistons into their cylinders. Note the plastic caps over rod bolts to protect the fresh and precisely polished crankshaft from accidental nicks.

when the rings have seated after break-in. No part should create friction severe enough to prevent rotation. Ring drag on the cylinder walls, valve spring tension, and the general mass of moving parts will provide whatever rotating resistance a new engine has. Of course, rotation gets tougher after the spark plugs have been installed.

> **CAUTION —**
> *The crankshaft should rotate smoothly as you torque the bolts in sequence. Floating in oil or assembly lube, no part should resist rotation in a fresh engine.*

With the crankshaft installed, the rod/piston/ring assemblies can be fitted. If OEM rods from the original engine are being re-used, the rods are each numbered for their respective cylinders. Pistons generally have arrows or similar marks on their crowns designating the front of the engine. In many Toyota light truck engines, the goal is to install each rod and piston with the rod's oil squirt hole facing correctly in the block. This consideration is critical to engine survival. Check with the machinist or your OEM Toyota repair manual if you are unsure of the location of the rod oil holes or piston direction.

Plastic boots are placed on the rod bolts to protect the crankshaft during assembly. The rod's crankpin is rotated as far away from the top of the block as possible, and the rings are "staged" or staggered according to the manufacturer's recommendation. With the rings in their proper alignment, the ring compressor is oiled and installed.

Holding the piston squarely in the cylinder bore, I use a soft hammer handle to *gently* tap the rings through the compressor and into the bore. Watch the rod to be certain that it drops easily and free of any parts. Guide the centered rod, carefully, toward the crankpin.

Some mechanics have already installed the rod bearing shells before installing the piston/rod assembly, while others insert the bearings just before attaching the rod. Either way, the bearing shells must be in place, oiled or coated with assembly lube before the rod reaches the crankpin.

Fig. 16-56. With crankshaft rotated to place rod journals at the bottom of their arc, pistons are carefully installed. Cleanliness and careful handling of these parts will pay big dividends in extra miles of service.

With the rod gently drawn squarely to the crankpin journal, the rod cap can be installed. The cap should only be installed *one way*, generally marked or numbered to match the rod. Care must be used here, as the rod bearing saddles have been trued, and only the correct installation direction will provide a perfectly round bearing bore.

As each rod is fitted to the crankshaft, the fasteners can be firmly and evenly secured. Stay below the actual torque setting until the rod is squarely attached. Final torque can then be met before installing the next rod.

Be certain that rod cap fasteners are tightened sequentially and in stages, and always rotate the crankshaft after setting torque to be certain the parts are free of friction. Re-check torque at each rod after turning the crankshaft to be certain torque settings have held.

Read your OEM-level repair manual before installing the oil pump and its drive shaft. When all of the rods have been secured, install the oil pump and torque the oil pump mounting bolt(s) carefully. Install and adjust the new or thoroughly cleaned oil pickup screen. The oil pan

Major Gains From Balancing Your Engine

Precision balancing engine parts provides a major benefit. For instance, a quarter ounce of imbalance just 4" from the center of the crankshaft becomes a seven pound force at 2000 rpm and 120 pound force at 8000 rpm. Claims of *doubling* the life of production engines are not far fetched, since balancing can come within *tenths of a gram* accuracy.

Any engine, including the Toyota truck types, can benefit from balancing the crankshaft and reciprocating parts. (An in-line six or four is inherently smooth, however, the V-6 requires careful balancing.) For Land Cruiser conversion V-8s, the Chevy 400 small-block and 454 big-block crankshafts have external balancing, while 350 and other small-blocks are internally balanced.

For long and smooth engine life, I always balance the damper, crankshaft, flywheel/flexplate and manual clutch assembly. Match weighting the rods, pistons, rings and other reciprocating parts also contributes to top engine performance and longevity. Here is a look at my 383 Chevrolet V-8 hybrid Land Cruiser conversion engine as it underwent balancing by Cliff Priest at Santee, California.

Cliff uses Stewart-Warner Model 2000D balancing equipment for crankshafts, flywheels, and clutch covers. He begins an engine balancing job with boxed pistons and separate connecting rods. Cliff cuts each piston to the exact gram weight of the lightest in the set, and follows by matching the rods. Then, with exact measurements of reciprocating versus rotating weights, balancing can begin.

Cliff determines reciprocating weight on a V-8 and other engines by adding one piston, piston pin, piston pin lock set (when utilized), the ring set weight for the one piston and the estimated weight of oil. Rotating weight for a V-8, with two rods sharing each crankpin, would be the weight of two rod big ends, their insert bearings, nuts and locking hardware, plus oil weight.

Once these calculations are made, bobweights can be attached to the crankshaft. The bobweights strive for a simulated 100% of rotating weight and 50% of reciprocal weight on a V-8 engine balancing job like this one.

As the crankshaft spins on the balancer, Cliff adjusts for its front and rear weightiness and imbalance. On my 383 Chevy stroker crankshaft balancing job, the flywheel was easily drilled to correct imbalance, and the clutch pressure plate got a similar treatment.

When I assembled this engine, the results were dramatic. Compared to a small-block Chevrolet assembly line pro-

duction V-8, this precisely weight matched engine, even with less than 100 miles wear-in time, sung happily from a s-m-o-o-t-h 650 rpm idle to an impressive and heavy throttled 5000 rpm.

A precisely balanced engine just loves to spin. Very regular, even power strokes distinguish these engines, and the results of balancing can be heard in the exhaust note and felt in the extra miles between gas stops.

Connecting rod weight is precisely determined.

Bobweights simulate the reciprocating and rotating mass of the rods, pistons/pins, rings, bearings, and even motor oil.

can now be carefully installed with the engine still upside down on the stand.

CAUTION —

Oil pump pickup screen height is critical to proper engine oiling. You must follow the guidelines in your OEM repair manual when setting the screen height.

On some engines, it is wise to install the oil pan last, as the timing cover should be securely in place to allow easy fitup of the front pan seal. On OHV engines, I install the camshaft and its timing chain/sprockets or gears either after or just before installing the oil pump.

Once the timing cover is securely in place, the oil pan can be fitted. Follow oil pan installation instructions, carefully using Ultra-Blue or its equivalent at the junction corners where the seals meet the side rail gaskets. Tighten pan bolts lightly and evenly from one end toward the other in cross, or adhere to the OEM installation tightening sequence. Check all bolts several times, taking care not to overtighten.

Whether the timing cover needs installation before the oil pan or not, the camshaft on an OHV six (or, for that matter, the Toyota OHC engines) must be carefully installed. The camshaft is a critical valve train component and requires careful installation to assure proper break-in.

OHV Land Cruiser Camshaft Installation Footnotes

Camshaft, lifter or rocker arm installation should follow instructions found in your OEM Toyota repair manual. Use of lifter lube is vital, applying a liberal coating to the lifter bases and lifter bores to assure a safe initial start up for the new engine. With its bearing journals well lubed, the camshaft can be carefully installed.

Installing a camshaft on Toyota OHV Land Cruiser engines can be tricky. With the timing gear installed properly (see OEM Toyota repair manual) on the camshaft, you can hand access the cam through the lifter bores. To make a safe installation, without galling the new cam bearings, the camshaft must be supported from its front end and *carefully* fed through each cam bearing.

Crossing areas where the cam does not have bearing support is most critical, as the sharp edged lobes could nick or otherwise damage the cam bearings. Here, you must grasp the long camshaft from within the block and use the timing gear for leverage at the front end of the camshaft. Once the camshaft and crankshaft gear timing marks align properly, the camshaft thrust plate can be bolted to the block. If this is an engine rebuild, coat the block's new camshaft plug (at the rear of block) with sealant and install it carefully.

Valve timing is critical. There's no room for "maybe" as you align two timing gears or sprockets. On an OHC engine, follow Toyota's marks and the alignment method described in the OEM Toyota repair manual. The camshaft sprockets can be aligned using a straight-edge before bolting a sprocket into place. Loctite 242 or its equivalent should be applied to any camshaft sprocket bolts, whether or not they use OEM locking hardware.

The ideal method of setting and checking valve timing is with a degree wheel and dial indicator. Attached to the crankshaft or camshaft, the wheel can detect minute chain or sprocket deviations from straight-up (zero-indexed) valve timing. The use of a dial indicator on a magnetic stand can help locate the exact TDC (top-dead-center) point for #1 cylinder's piston.

Fig. 16-57. *Final touch in verifying piston heights and accuracy of machining and fitup is the use of a dial indicator. I find TDC by this method before installing the camshaft and indexing the valve timing. This tool can assure proper valve timing and help set the timing cover tab for accurate ignition timing.*

Fig. 16-58. *After setting valve timing, rotate crankshaft slowly in direction of normal rotation. Stop just short of two full turns. Then, without passing timing marks, continue rotating the crankshaft as you watch carefully for valve timing marks to align. Confirm that valve timing is still correct.*

With #1 piston at exact TDC, the degree wheel can be aligned precisely or indexed to zero. The crankshaft can then be rotated carefully, while the dial indicator checks the movement of #1 piston. Valve timing can be calibrated within 0.001" of piston location, resulting in substantial performance gains. Error is nearly impossible when you use a dial indicator and degree wheel for your camshaft installation.

On many engines, the timing mark must indicate exact TDC or precise degrees of advance for #1 piston. On some engines, however, timing cover alignment or the index tab may be inaccurate.

To avoid ignition timing error, the timing cover and crankshaft pulley/damper should be trial fitted before the cylinder head(s) installation. Using the dial indicator at #1 piston, find TDC for that piston. Observe the location of the pulley's timing mark and the mark(s) or pointer on the timing cover tab. (You can do the same with a Land Cruiser's F, 2F or 3F-E flywheel marks and the bell-housing pointer.) Look from approximately the same angle as you would shine a timing light. Depending on the timing pointer design, if marks don't align, try carefully bending the pointer slightly—or carefully scribe a new mark on the crankshaft pulley or flywheel.

Crankshaft pulley degree tape is available through aftermarket sources for specific diameter pulleys. This can enable a look at spark timing at higher engine speeds. Index pulley (or Land Cruiser flywheel) to #1 piston's exact TDC before aligning degree tape.

Upper Engine Rebuilding

Machining now done, the block fitted with the crankshaft, pistons, rings, rods, bearings and camshaft (on an OHV engine), you can address the rest of the valve train and cylinder head work. The overall goals here should be long service both off- and on-highway.

Cylinder head machine work and the type of camshaft and valve train parts will determine the performance character of an engine. Once the compression level has been decided, and the correct pistons fitted to achieve that ratio, the rest of the performance story will be told through the camshaft grind, valve and cylinder head work, and finally, tune related components like the rocker arms, manifolds, fuel system and ignition.

Cylinder head choices should follow an engine's intended use. The intake and exhaust valve sizes, port shapes, and combustion chamber design might be entirely different for two engines of identical size and type. For off-pavement crawling, low- to mid-range horsepower may dictate smaller intake valves than a mud bog, tractor pull, or sand drag engine would require—These racing engines will run for maximum horsepower and be geared to operate well over 4000 rpm at all times.

Combustion chamber area and shape will determine both compression ratio (by the volume of space into which air/fuel is compressed) and spark or flame characteristics. Again, the rpm operating range of the engine and loads placed on the engine at various speeds will dictate flow and the combustion flame-front angles. Compression ratios vary according to fuel octane availability, horsepower expectations, camshaft demands and the nature of the load the engine will sustain.

When building a workhorse or reliable utility engine, I shy away from high horsepower expectations. My goal is an engine with lots of torque, good mid-range performance, and a reasonable redline between 4200 and 5500 rpm, determined by engine size and number of cylinders. Variations on this engine design can suit your individual requirements, but for highway and back country use, *utility* should be your principal goal.

0014416 / 0014424

Fig. 16-59. With camshaft and sprockets indexed, the timing cover is installed. I match the ignition timing indicator tab precisely to the crank pulley mark, using my dial indicator above #1 piston crown to find absolute TDC. This assures a precise reference for ignition timing.

Fig. 16-60. *Depending upon space and tools available, many home mechanics prefer working with a "short engine," placing the block assembly in the chassis at this point. The heads, remaining valvetrain components, and intake/exhaust systems must then be installed over the fenders. To assure cleanliness, you may prefer building the "long" engine on your engine stand, then install the engine in complete form.*

Fig. 16-61. *Head surfacing is common on Toyota alloy heads and even iron Land Cruiser cylinder heads. Any kind of over-heat will warp a head, and some heads simply lose their deck flatness during normal service. Machine shops can re-surface deck if warpage is within Toyota's OEM tolerance.*

Whichever engine you choose to build for your Toyota truck, understand that selecting the right cylinder head(s) is as important as choosing the right carburetor or ignition spark advance curve. Once the proper heads have been chosen, a thorough hot tanking at the local machine shop, followed by magnafluxing (on ferrous iron castings) or pressure checking (on non-ferrous alloy heads) for cracks, will start your cylinder head work.

Remachining Your Cylinder Heads

Head service has become a specialty. Years ago, when engines were lower in compression, the proverbial ring-and-valve job or carbon-and-valve job was performed by a general service garage. Although many contemporary garages can perform quality head service, AERA- or PERA-member full-service machine shops have become the central source for consistently high quality work.

Machine shops can either rework your heads or furnish heads on an exchange basis. Regardless, cylinder head rebuilding begins with an initial cleanup. Carbon, burnt oil, and deposits disappear as caustic tanking or heat oven cleaning scours castings to a like-new appearance. Once clean, the machinist examines the head(s) closely. The focus is casting integrity, valve guide wear, the condition and depth of the valve seats and the overall condition of the valves, springs and related hardware.

Valves often can be reused, as long as their stems and faces are straight and not excessively worn. Valve faces must be free of cracks, with enough material still available for safe regrinding. If any question of excess wear or distortion exists, or if heat has damaged the valve stems or head, the valve(s) should be discarded.

Valve springs can also be inspected for heat damage, and their free standing height and tension checked. If height or tension is slightly erratic, many shops install shims beneath the springs upon reassembly. Any questionable spring should be tossed out, as a broken valve

spring can cause a valve to interfere with the piston or cause other serious damage. Likewise, crystallized valve stems often break, dropping the valve's head into the cylinder. The resulting damage can be catastrophic if the valve head wedges between the piston crown and the cylinder head's combustion chamber.

Loose valve guides are trouble. Excess valve stem clearance in the guide allows oil to be sucked past the guide on the intake stroke. Worn guides also impair proper valve seating and reduce the compression seal. Manifold vacuum suffers, as does compression, and the engine's performance falters.

A good deal of controversy exists over the various alternatives for valve guide service, but the traditional method of knurling worn guides has generally fallen from practice. Most machinists and I would agree that knurling of old guides simply buys a little time. I would place their lifespan at anywhere from one-tenth to one-half that of the OEM valve guide—even when service is performed properly.

Various methods for both service and replacement of guides exist, including installation of bronze valve guide sleeves or the complete replacement of the guides with either new cast iron or bronze types. Current service technology favors complete replacement. Bronze works well with racing or high performance stainless steel or stellite valve stems, while cast iron replacement guides better suit the softer OEM type steel valve stems.

Bronze, copper, and silicone bronze guide liner sleeves have also become popular with the engine remanufacturing industry, due largely to a sleeve's quick and inexpensive ability to salvage even badly worn guide bores. Service life of sleeves exceeds that of knurling but does not match the replacement of the entire guide. Cost often dictates the use of liners or sleeves, however.

With guide service performed, valve seat grinding can start. Inspection reveals whether the existing valve seats are free of cracks and of ample thickness. Cracked valve seats, especially those that do not involve a water jacket, can be repaired or replaced with ultra hard steel inserts. These replacement seats far exceed the quality of the original casting material.

Today, engines are more apt to generate valve seat cracks, especially at exhaust valves. Heat kills valve seats. Properly installed nickel/stellite seats are often recommended as an aid for improving engine reliability, even when the original seats show no evidence of cracking. Once valve seats have been restored, grinding can begin.

NOTE ——
Beginning with unleaded fuel engines of the mid- to late-1970s, Toyota and other manufacturers' cylinder heads switched to hardened exhaust valve seats. If your engine has non-hardened valve seats (your machinist can determine the type of casting and seats involved), especially a Land Cruiser F or earlier 2F engine, I strongly advise the installation of hard steel exhaust valve seats and stainless exhaust valves to prevent valve seat recession and abnormal valve wear from the use of unleaded fuel.

Valve seat grinding follows some general rules: Seats should be concentric, not too narrow or wide, and centered on the face of the refinished valve. Normal wear will widen the original seat considerably. Grinding will widen it further yet, so reshaping of the seat becomes necessary. The usual procedure calls for precise, *three-angle* seat cuts. This requires three sharpened stones or hard steel cutters.

If the normal seat angle is 45°, one cutter will be 45°. To lower the top portion of the widened seat, a 30° cutter might be utilized, while the port or inside edge of the seat can be *raised* with the use of a 60° cutting stone. This process requires critically sharp and properly angled stones or cutting tools, enabling the seat width to finish on specification, with the seat centered.

Once all intake and exhaust seats have been cut and finished, the cylinder heads should be cleaned again. This final cleaning will remove ground particles and machining debris that could otherwise damage the piston rings and cylinder walls. As with every process of engine assembly, cleanliness translates to longevity.

Re-usable valves can be ground on the valve refacing machine. I bathe the valve in oil during grinding, and generally set my valve face angle to 44-1/2° (for a specified 45° valve and seat). My machine shop mentor taught that this slight variance, 1/2° flatter, assures a slight crush force to prevent carbon buildup and allow correct valve seating during engine break-in.

NOTE ——
If the head-to-block mating surface requires machining to correct warp or assure head gasket seal, such work should take place before the valve grind to assure thorough cleanup of any casting debris before the valve work begins.

After grinding the valves, traditional lapping may be useful. (Smoothly dressed grinding stones usually eliminate the need for such work.) The use of lapping compound and blue dye, however, does enable a machinist to see whether the valve face and seat have mated properly. As an alternative, some shops employ a vacuum check to

Fig. 16-62. Valve seat grinding at three angles will be necessary to restore these heads. Stones need continual sharpening to produce quality results. Careful grinding is repeated at each seat.

test a valve's sealing ability, and this can detect unwanted seepage at the seats or valve guides.

In assembling the valves, new guide seals will be installed. A variety of OEM seal types exist. Additionally, several aftermarket seals, like the original Perfect Circle (PC) nylon wiper type, can improve sealing quality by providing a better fit at the stems and tighter sealing around the valve guide boss.

Fig. 16-63. *Finished seats show three angles: 30, 45 and 60°. On most general use truck engines, the goal is a seat width of 3/64" to 1/16" on intake valves and 1/16" to 3/32" on exhaust valves. (See your repair manual for metric and U.S. specifics on your engine.) Seat angles are 45°, and the fresh seat must be concentric and center on the valve face.*

Fig. 16-64. *Valve stems and valve guides are carefully fitted. Guides often require sizing to fit. Here, valve stem heights are compared and machined to match.*

NOTE —

When cutting the mating deck (surfacing) an overhead camshaft cylinder head, or when lowering the camshaft centerline by line boring the camshaft bearing bores, be aware that valve timing changes slightly. As the camshaft moves closer to the crankshaft, the timing chain and valve timing shift. Consider this factor when calculating your engine's camshaft timing.

Valve springs must be installed correctly, noting whether the spring is progressively wound (more tightly wound on one end than the other). Tight winds fit against the head boss, and improper installation can cause poor spring action or worse: valve and/or piston damage.

Valve stem keepers or locks must also receive close attention. Many mechanics and machinists rap the end of the valve stem lightly with a plastic hammer head after assembly to be certain that the lock and spring retainer have seated.

Fig. 16-65. *Popular Toyota OHC engines do not use insert camshaft bearings. Instead, the camshaft rotates in machined bearings that are an actual part of the head casting. When the head has warpage or the camshaft bearings show abnormal wear, you can sometimes salvage the head.*

Fig. 16-66. *My friend and machinist, Nick Bongiorno, operates his Italian engineered line-boring machine that salvages OHC cylinder head bearings. After Nick surfaces head deck and bearing caps, he torques shortened bearing caps into place. Bore bar "line bores" bearings to OEM journal diameter and parallel with deck surface.*

At this stage the heads are ready for new freeze plugs. With new brass freeze plugs installed, the head is ready for installation on the block assembly.

Valvetrain and Cylinder Head Installation

Cylinder head installation begins with careful placement of the head gasket(s). Often, the gasket should fit only one way, requiring proper assembly to assure good sealing. Look for notations like "This Side Up," "Top" or "Front."

Place the head *evenly* and *gently* on the head gasket. In most cases, the head gasket will not require sealant. (Felpro, Victor and others offer "one torque" materials with impregnated sealant, usually including silicones or Teflon.) Clean, straight head installation will prevent problems later. Be careful not to dent or nick the new gasket(s).

Unless otherwise specified in your OEM Toyota repair manual, head bolts should be coated with sealant. I use Snap-On's Never-Seez compound or Permatex/Loctite's Teflon Sealant on those bolts that enter water jackets. A good size can with brush applicator will last for years.

Snap-On's compound is a graphite-based paste, non-electrolytic, that resists heat to 2000-degrees Fahrenheit. On some engines, head bolts reach the coolant, with rusted threads, corrosion, and bolt seizure developing over time. After long operation, bolt threads coated and protected with Never-Seez will readily unfasten, leaving the block threads clear and undamaged.

I like to lightly install all bolts and follow the torque tightening sequence, beginning with a 30 ft/lbs setting. This will seat the parts evenly and compress the head gasket flatly. Start the tightening sequence again, this time splitting the difference between 30 ft/lbs and the final torque required. Finally, follow through with the actu-al torque required, and then allow the engine to set for several minutes before repeating the sequence at the final torque specification once more.

On engines using "one torque" gaskets, the head bolts will require no more attention. Older gasket styles may dictate re-torquing after initial engine warm-up, but with the use of modern sealant impregnated gaskets, that method is now rare.

Once you install the head on a Land Cruiser OHV in-line six, lube the lifter bases and their bores, then fit the lifters and pushrods. On OHC fours or V-6s, you can now install the camshaft(s) and either the shims and followers or the rocker shaft(s) and rocker arm assemblies, depending upon the engine design.

> **NOTE** —
> Follow the OEM Toyota repair manual guidelines for your engine when installing these parts and setting up the valve timing or chain tensioner on a Toyota OHC type engine. On Toyota engines with rocker shaft assemblies, like the F, 2F and 3F-E Land Cruiser in-line OHV sixes, the rocker shaft and arms (with adjuster screws backed way off) can be installed once the lifters and pushrods are in position.

Once valve timing is set, run #1 piston to TDC on its compression stroke and make sure that camshaft lobes are at the lowest point (heel) of their profiles. With the camshaft in this position and both valves closed completely, you can gently tighten each rocker arm adjusting screw. Tighten the adjuster until the proper clearance exists between the rocker arm tip and valve stem. (See your OEM Toyota repair manual for guidelines and settings.)

Once you have set #1 cylinder's intake and exhaust valves, you can proceed with valve adjustment by following steps described in the OEM Toyota repair manual for a static engine. Refer to the tune-up section of this book for additional information on static valve adjustment for several of the four-cylinder Toyota engines.

On Land Cruiser F, 2F and 3F-E OHV engines, one safe means for static valve settings is to make sure all valve adjuster screws are loose, then turn the crankshaft and observe the valve openings at each cylinder. With a given cylinder's intake valve fully open, adjust its exhaust valve (a few thousandths of an inch looser than specification to allow for the cold engine temperature). Then rotate the crankshaft until that adjusted exhaust valve is fully open and adjust the intake valve—again, a few thousandths of an inch looser than specification to allow for the cold engine temperature.

Repeat these steps at each cylinder until you have adjusted all twelve valves. When you start the engine with the valve cover removed, quickly verify valve clearance and make adjustments as necessary. Then warm the engine completely and recheck valves.

An adjustable rocker arm or shim/follower must be set with the camshaft lobe at its lowest point. Be sure of camshaft lobe location before setting any valves. Keep adjuster screws safely loose until each valve is in position for adjustment. This will prevent risk of severe engine damage from pressing a tightly adjusted valve into a piston crown while rotating the crankshaft.

Fig. 16-67. Head bolts coated with an anti-seize compound will seal well, provide accurate torque settings, and permit ease of removal years after installation. Set the head carefully atop its gasket to assure a good seal.

Fig. 16-68. When installing rocker arms and adjusting valves for the first time, note that rocker arm adjusting nuts and screws have been loosened several turns. If adjusters are too tight, the valves will interfere with the piston crowns when you rotate the engine. This could ruin your entire rebuilding effort.

Prepping the Long Block for a Successful Start-up

Valves adjusted, at least for preliminary run-in, the intake manifold can be installed. The manifold gaskets should be coated with sealant in accord with Toyota's repair manual specifications, giving special consideration to corners and gasket junctions. Torquing and tightening a manifold should follow the recommended sequence of three torque steps to the final setting.

With the intake manifold installed, you can prime the engine's lubrication system on F, 2F or 3F-E in-line OHV sixes using an old, "dummy" distributor and hand drill. Remove the dummy distributor's drive gear and modify the top of the shaft to accept a drill chuck.

Fill the crankcase to FULL (as indicated on the dipstick). Install the dummy distributor, making sure to fully engage the oil pump drive, and chuck on the drill. Maintain steady downward pressure to prevent damage to the oil pump drive, and make sure that the drill is turning in the distributor's normal rotation. The drill will turn the oil pump as though the engine were running. Use a high torque, low speed drill motor, and allow the pump to spin for a couple of minutes. This will charge all oil galleries with fresh oil.

NOTE —
Toyota OHC fours and V-6s have their oil pumps at the front of the crankshaft, and they cannot be primed. Here, use of engine assembly lube on critical bearing surfaces is essential to engine health during initial start-up after a rebuild.

By charging the lubrication system thoroughly, your engine will crank over in a pre-primed state, and bearing scoring from dry cranking will not occur. The engine should have been assembled with fresh oil, lifter lube, or engine assembly compounds on critical wear surfaces. Despite this, priming helps prevent oil starvation, aeration and cavitation.

Once the oil system has been primed, the engine can be installed in the chassis. With mounts secured and exhaust manifold(s) attached, the ignition distributor and plug wire installation can proceed. Many engine builders successfully complete all phases of the long block assembly, only to mess up the ignition timing.

In Chapter 8, you will find my methods for static timing the engine. Follow these procedures closely, and your new engine will be correctly timed before you touch the starter. Make sure number one piston is at the top of its *compression stroke* before static timing the engine. (Intake and exhaust valves will have clearance in this position.) Confirm the distributor cap location for #1 plug wire, then follow the firing order and direction of rotor rotation as you install the rest of the plug wires.

Later, upon start up, you can verify the timing with a timing light. Although this method may require some practice, static timing will place your engine within two crankshaft degrees of exact timing, a very safe range for starting even the most exotic engine.

Now the engine is ready to run. Install all accessories, cooling system components and the fuel system pieces. Make preliminary adjustments on the carburetor, if necessary, and get ready...Your fresh engine will soon burst into life. Assuming that spark and fuel needs are properly met, the engine should start immediately. Try it, and appreciate your effort.

NOTE —
See the engine run-in recommendations in the Appendix of the book. A new or freshly rebuilt engine must be cycled during its initial start-up and first hours of running.

Fig. 16-69. *With care and a methodical approach, the end result is an engine that runs. These steps or exchanging your worn old engine for a completely assembled, ready to run long block could be just what your truck needs.*

Adjuncts To An Engine Rebuild

Your newly rebuilt engine will produce more horsepower and greater torque. The engine now needs proper break-in and care. This requires adequate cooling, good water pump circulation and a working fan. A marginal OEM radiator, erratic fan clutch or worn water pump becomes a glaring problem when new found horsepower places higher demands on the cooling system.

Protect your rebuilt engine's scale-free block and cylinder head. Have the radiator hot tanked, rodded and pressure checked to assure adequate coolant flow.

Plugged, soldered and damaged radiator cores, or a radiator filled with rust and scale, will prevent your new engine from cooling adequately. Engine break-in heavily taxes the cooling system. If in good shape, your truck's cooling system helps the engine meet the variety of challenges that the vehicle will face.

In addition to installing a new water pump and reconditioning the radiator, pay attention to all hoses, clamps, the thermostat and drive belts. New parts here are cheap insurance. Test the fan clutch and replace if necessary.

Any transmission or clutch parts that were sub-standard before the overhaul now need attention. The new engine will place a higher load on worn geartrain parts, especially when you drive in the off-pavement environment. Replace the clutch assembly (if necessary, re-surface the flywheel), service the transmission, and be certain that the gear assemblies work well before installing the fresh engine.

Chapter 17

Geartrain Modifications

LAND CRUISER FOUR-SPEED synchromesh transmissions came on line in 1975 models, and I would characterize this OEM transmission as highly rugged and far more versatile than the earlier three-speed units. Unfortunately, Toyota also changed the transfer case with these four-speeds, and although very durable, the 1975–up transfer unit has a taller (numerically lower) low range ratio than the earlier three-speed equipped models.

For the Toyota performance enthusiast, transmission stamina is an important issue. When building up a 4WD truck for off-highway use, reliability is paramount. Here, owners planning a high horsepower engine swap or high performance modifications to a stock engine need to consider the heavy duty replacement transmission options.

1958–74 Land Cruiser models offered two types of three-speed transmissions. Neither version has synchro-

Fig. 17-2. *Transmission countergears show relationship between a "real" truck four-speed and lighter duty OEM offerings. Left to right, the T-18, T-90, T-14, and T-5 gears stand next to GM's impressive 465 Muncie countergear. I would rank Toyota Land Cruiser four-speed gearboxes with Ford T-18 four-speed.*

Fig. 17-1. *Toyota manual transmissions have helped build a legendary record of reliability around these trucks. Beginning in 1975, Land Cruisers offered a fully synchromesh closer ratio four-speed transmission that offers enough stamina to handle a high output V-8 conversion—I tested such a unit thoroughly in my 1976 FJ40 with a hybrid 383 cubic inch Chevrolet V-8. Engine torque peak was near 400 ft./lbs, and the transmission, with over 90,000 miles of use when I installed the engine, held up fine.*

mesh on first gear. Unless your budget is very restricted, replacement of this transmission with a later model fully-synchromesh Land Cruiser four-speed or domestic truck transmission makes good sense. Whether you plan a V-8 conversion or want to keep the original F engine, your pre-1975 Land Cruiser will benefit from a transmission upgrade.

Owners building a hard-core rock crawling 'Cruiser will often retrofit a domestic V-8 engine and domestic truck four-speed transmission. On 1975–up conversions, builders sometimes add the earlier three-speed type transfer case for a lower crawl ratio. With a compound low gear type domestic truck four-speed, 4.11 or lower (numerically higher) axle ratios and an early Toyota Land Cruiser two-speed transfer case, crawl ratios approaching 70:1 can be attained.

For General Motors V-8 swaps into the Land Cruiser chassis, I am partial to GM's SM420 and SM465 four-speed gearboxes. The non-synchromesh first gear is such a low ratio (7.05:1 in the SM420; 6.54:1 in the SM465) that the 1975–up transfer case can work very well here.

Unquestionably, the best transmission swap option is the NV4500 D-Spec five-speed. The NV4500 heavy duty five-speed was designed specifically for 3/4-ton and larger (over 8500 pound GVWR) trucks. This transmission offers every feature an off-highway or severe duty four-wheel drive truck could require: synchromesh on each of the five forward speeds, a durable iron case, two PTO

Fig. 17-3. *In considering a domestic transmission transplant, this crop of units says a lot: Massive gearbox at left is GM's 465 Muncie box, which dwarfs a compact truck T-5 overdrive. Three-speed Borg-Warner T-14 and T-90 (early Jeep application with V-8 adapter attached) set in middle, while T-18 Ford truck four-speed box rests to right. In foreground is an early (pre-1968) GM Muncie SM420 truck four-speed. GM's 420 and 465 Muncie iron units clearly offer superior stamina and accompany many domestic V-8 engine transplants into the Toyota Land Cruiser chassis.*

Fig. 17-4. *For supreme off-/on-highway performance with either a domestic V-8 or a Land Cruiser six, a retrofit NV4500 transmission makes a great swap. Advance Adapters and BTB Products offer kits to install the NV4500 behind stock or transplant engines. NV4500 could also work with a 4.3L Vortec V-6 engine swap into a heavy duty Toyota 4WD pickup or 4Runner.*

drive outlets, a fifth gear overdrive for fuel economy and outstanding ratio spacing between gears.

The first generation GM version of the NV4500 offers ideal ratios for multi-purpose use. The earlier design offers a 6.34:1 first gear and 3.44:1 second, while the 1995 and newer edition has a 5.61:1 first gear and 3.04:1 second. Third gear is 1.67:1, fourth rates 1.00:1, and fifth offers a 27% (0.73:1) percent overdrive on the earlier design and 25% (0.75:1) overdrive on 1995–up applications. Reverse is 6.34:1 on the first design and 5.61:1 on 1995–up versions.

1. HEAVY DUTY MANUAL TRANSMISSION CHANGEOVER

Compound low gear gives a 4x4 truck both crawling and pulling advantages. Such low gearing can save your chassis and powertrain. In hard-core rock-crawling, your truck can inch its way through the roughest terrain, with light use of the brakes, less tire spin and less skidding.

Stalled on a precarious slope, you can engage the clutch with the transmission in compound first gear and the transfer case in low range four-wheel drive. The 12-volt starter motor can pull the truck up a steep incline while firing the engine.

Fig. 17-5. Use of oversized tires provides an overdriving effect, so a three-speed automatic or four-speed manual transmission will often work fine in 4WD pickup/4Runner or Land Cruiser buildups that use larger tires. If your truck originally came with overdrive and you plan to keep the stock axle gearing and tire size, an overdrive retrofit transmission would be practical—Without such an overdrive, your engine would run at a higher rpm on the highway, burn excessive fuel and wear out prematurely.

Unless your truck has a load, little starter drag will occur. The low-low gearing will afford a smooth chug forward as the engine catches (providing you have your foot very lightly on the throttle).

> **WARNING —**
> *Know how your truck will respond to a start-up in gear. Practice this technique before traveling dangerous terrain. Be aware that you cannot start your truck with the clutch engaged if the truck's starter wiring includes a neutral or clutch pedal safety switch.*

Installing a four-speed or NV4500 five-speed truck transmission eliminates chassis abuse in rough terrain. Tall geared trucks bend springs and twist their frames as they bash and skid their way through rockpiles. Your Toyota 4x4 truck with a two-speed transfer case and a very low first gear (compound low) ratio will perform far better, as ultra-low gearing yields great dividends in extending chassis parts life, vehicle safety, and driver/passenger comfort.

High output engines have great difficulty breaking an iron domestic truck four-speed or NV4500 five-speed gearbox in good condition. For most domestic truck four-speeds, the second gear ratio is lower than first gear in a three-speed Toyota Land Cruiser transmission. Such a four-speed has synchromesh down to second gear, and most starts are in second gear—until you need heavy crawling power. A truck equipped with correct axle gearing only uses compound low gear under heavy loading.

A GM SM420 or Muncie 465, or the New Process 435 truck four-speed, can easily handle high horsepower in a Toyota Land Cruiser or 4WD truck—so can the newer NV4500 five-speed.

Consider the cost of either recycled or new components that will complete such a conversion. If the changeover is cost effective, consider the labor involved and look closely at the catalog/information manuals available from Advance Adapters, Downey Off-Road, BTB Products and NWOR Specialties. These manuals offer tried methods for installing the transplant engine and transmission of your choice. Evaluate these steps and techniques before undertaking such a project.

As for sourcing a heavy duty domestic truck four-speed transmission, the GM SM420 was available from 1947–67. In 1968, the heavy duty Muncie 465 truck four-speed replaced this unit. (During the closed or torque-tube driveline era, only the SM420 was available.)

A basic fitup difference between the SM420 and 465 Muncie is the index bore of the bellhousing. The 465 has a larger 5.125-inch bore. Previous GM truck three- and four-speed transmissions share a common 4.686-inch diameter.

When replacing your Toyota transmission, first review the aftermarket adapter catalogs, then select the domestic replacement transmission that will work with available adapters. A light truck recycling yard is a good source for your heavy duty replacement transmission.

> **NOTE —**
> A recycling yard has interchange manuals that can determine year, make and model sources for transmissions, axles and related parts.

A transmission changeover sometimes will require use of a larger diameter flywheel, different bellhousing and starter change. Domestic truck four-speeds and the NV4500 five-speed have high torque ratings and come with a larger diameter clutch assembly. You will want this added stamina when you make a truck type four-speed or NV4500 transmission changeover.

> **CAUTION —**
> • *Use the correct flywheel for your engine. GM crankshafts, for example, have either internal or external balancing. An externally balanced crankshaft and flywheel differs from internally balanced pieces. Be sure your conversion engine's flywheel selection matches the engine's balancing method.*
>
> • *When selecting a bellhousing, always be certain the index hole that centers the transmission is of the correct diameter to accept the four- or five-speed's front bearing retainer collar. This bore helps keep the transmission in alignment and also centers the input shaft with the crankshaft pilot bearing. The fit should be nearly snug, and the housing bore must index on center for proper transmission and clutch alignment.*

> **NOTE —**
> Aftermarket formed steel racing bellhousings are available, often with universal bolt patterns and detailed instructions for custom fit machining.

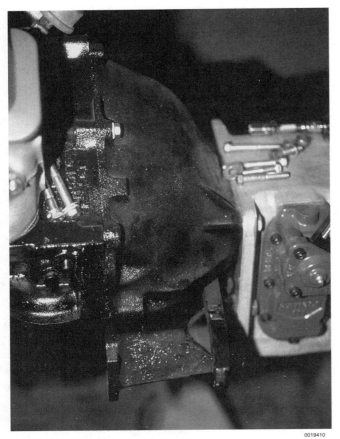

Fig. 17-6. For Land Cruiser engine/transmission swaps using available commercial adapters, I encourage the use of a cast iron bellhousing. Four-speed iron truck transmissions and an attached transfer case make a very heavy mass to hang off the rear of the bellhousing.

Fig. 17-7. With the long span between Land Cruiser front engine mounts and a rear transfer case adapter/mounting plate, an OEM aluminum alloy bellhousing is under tremendous stress. For some engine applications, there is a cast iron clutch housing available from an earlier truck model, like this pre-1973 Chevrolet V-8 truck bellhousing design. This rugged FJ40 is under construction at BTB Products.

Extra Considerations

When planning a transmission swap, determine the driveline length required. You may need to change driveshaft length or U-joint type. An alternative is to have a driveline constructed. (See earlier chapters for details.)

A new four- or five-speed domestic transmission may come with a speedometer gear assembly that served different axle gearing or tire diameters. You may also have a metric versus U.S. thread issue. Check your speedometer error, and secure the correct speedometer drive gear from your local truck dealership or recycler. If you have difficulty resolving this detail, consult a speedometer shop. They can install a speedometer speed correction kit if necessary.

> NOTE —
> For a conversion transmission upgrade, you must also account for the transmission input shaft length. This is the distance from the crankshaft pilot bearing to the front face of the transmission.

Clutch linkage will likely differ between transmission types. Release fork or throwout bearing designs for heavy duty transmissions have heavy iron release arms and use a large throwout bearing. When securing parts, make sure to include all changeover pieces, and note their assembly order. Use the correct clutch release arm, linkage, hydraulic slave cylinder mount and return spring(s)—be sure to attach them properly. Pay close attention to the adapter kit's instructions.

Fig. 17-8. Advance Adapters offers the two-speed underdrive or overdrive Ranger Torque Splitter gearbox. Mounted between the clutch/bellhousing and transmission, this auxiliary transmission provides a durable synchromesh shift mechanism and an extra range of forward and reverse gears. Although NV4500 five-speed swap will become increasingly more popular, Torque Splitter appeals to those who need 16 split shifts forward and four reverse gear speeds.

2. AUTOMATIC TRANSMISSION OPTION

For those who prefer an automatic transmission, Advance Adapters, Downey Off-Road and NWOR Specialties each offer a wide range of options. Adapters are available to use some of the late Toyota OEM automatics, including the later FJ80 Land Cruiser's unit and 1984–up 4WD pickup/4Runner OEM Aisin/Warner designs. These automatic transmissions have electronic shift controls, so their use is mostly limited to an engine swap into a later Toyota truck chassis that already features this type of transmission.

Most builders who plan domestic V-6 or V-8 swaps find it simpler to use a domestic automatic transmission. Popular adapters mate the GM THM350 or THM400 three-speed, the GM 700R-4 overdrive four-speed, and even the Ford C-4, to various Toyota transfer cases.

For a GM muscle V-8 swap into a Land Cruiser, I would use the THM400 unit. Two basic styles of OEM transmission cases permit use of any GM OHV V-8. GM V-6 engines into the Toyota 4WD pickup do well with either a THM350 or TH700R-4.

I am not convinced that the later and improved TH700R-4 is suitable for Land Cruisers, as the weight of such a vehicle, combined with high horsepower and hard-core off-highway use, could break such a design. Early TH700R-4 units have serious design flaws that received upgrade improvements through 1984. You need to either upgrade an earlier unit with 1985–up replacement parts or use an 1985–up transmission unit. An upgraded TH700R-4 should hold up in a domestic V-6 powered 4WD pickup or 4Runner....Late 4L60E electronic shift versions would require the ECM computer and a vehicle speed sensor to affect shifts. Unless used in combination with a late TBI/EFI engine unit, complete with all OEM wiring, the computer and speed sensors, the 4L60E is not good swap material.

If I were swapping a Buick or Chevy/Vortec V-6 into a 4WD Toyota pickup, my first transmission choice would be a 1984–up manual five-speed Toyota OEM unit. This would be a durable transmission with overdrive, using stock Toyota pieces from the transmission rearward. For an automatic transmission, either the GM THM350 or a non-electronic shift THM700R-4 overdrive would work.

3. CLUTCH UPGRADES

Eventually, your truck's clutch will fatigue and fail. When it does, the aftermarket clutch industry offers a variety of rebuilt and new clutch units to restore or improve performance. You can select a clutch that will handle your engine's torque and horsepower demands.

Traditionally, a high performance clutch was a non-diaphragm design. Two varieties include a centrifugal arm/fulcrum arrangement (Long) and a high spring-rate type.

Centrifugally weighted clutch fingers allow two distinct clutch behaviors. To ease take-off and reduce shock loads to the transmission, transfer case or axle, the initial squeeze or clamp pressure is lower. As engine rpm increases in each gear, the centrifugal weights move out-

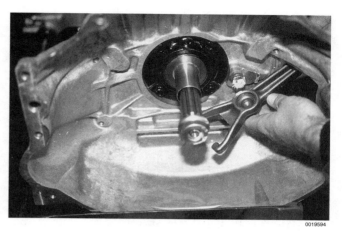

Fig. 17-9. *OEM service guidelines prevent trouble. See your OEM Toyota repair manual for critical measurements and proper tightening techniques to prevent warpage of a new clutch cover. Apply high temp grease sparingly to clutch lever release stud (shown here) and crankshaft pilot bearing bore (if a bronze bushing type).*

ward. At speed, the fingers' fulcrum leverage applies increasingly more pressure to the clutch disc.

The complaint with older centrifugal clutch designs is high pedal pressure at higher rpm. In racing and high performance activities, applying the clutch pedal at high revs with hydraulic clutch linkage can actually blow out the slave and clutch master cylinder seals. Under these same circumstances, mechanical linkage will place an overwhelming load on the driver's clutch foot. Reciprocally, lowering the apply pressure often allows damaging clutch slippage.

Borg&Beck Type Clutch

An alternative design, the non-centrifugal, three-finger clutch popularized by Borg & Beck, eliminates guesswork about apply pressure at any given rpm. Spring pressure clutches apply the entire force of the pressure plate at one time. This means that the spring rate built into the clutch cover unit is exactly the rate sandwiching the clutch disc against the flywheel face.

Accurate clutch pressures can be set for vehicle weight, engine power output and the vehicle's usage. In heavy duty towing and 4x4 applications intended for brute work, the clutch apply pressure (static) is 2200 pounds or better. Users generally choose a non-centrifugal clutch of 2200–2400 pounds clamping force for heavy hauling or a large increase in horsepower.

In a lighter duty vehicle, say a Toyota 4WD pickup or 4Runner with a stock 3.8L Buick or Chevy 4.3L Vortec V-6 engine, the maximum pressure demands would seldom require more than 2000 static pounds. While adding static pressure will decrease the chance of slippage, it also increases the shock to vital geartrain parts during initial clutch engagement.

Diaphragm Clutch

The third common clutch design is the multi-fingered diaphragm type. General Motors popularized the use of diaphragm clutches many years ago, and early high performance enthusiasts discarded these types of clutches regularly in favor of Borg & Beck and Long type clutches. Most Toyota trucks have used diaphragm type clutches.

Traditionally, diaphragm clutches were unable to handle high performance demands, as they offered few means for increasing apply pressures. Worse yet, clutch overheat quickly damaged the flat diaphragm clutch springs.

A diaphragm clutch has two advantages, however. The pedal pressure to disengage the diaphragm clutch is minimal, as sixteen fingers apply leverage instead of three. The long spring fingers allow relatively high apply pressures with minimal effect on the driver's left foot. Pedal take-up distance is relatively short with a diaphragm design, and clutch engagement occurs very smoothly.

Fig. 17-11. *Midway's Centerforce clutch is a firm clamping diaphragm design with the advantage of centrifugal weights for high clamp pressures as rpm increases. Centrifugal weights apply tremendous pressure at higher rpm. Pedal pressure is light and easy on Toyota's hydraulic linkage.*

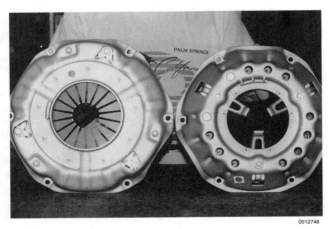

Fig. 17-10. *OEM-type diaphragm clutch (left) shows multiple spring/lever design. Spring tension alone squeezes the disc between the pressure plate and flywheel. At right is a common Borg & Beck style OEM replacement clutch.*

Aftermarket Clutches

Thanks largely to aftermarket innovation, several performance clutch designs are available for your truck. One of the more exciting options is Midway's Centerforce clutch. A diaphragm clutch with unique centrifugal weights, the Centerforce unit uses the best features of each popular clutch design.

Borrowing from the diaphragm unit, the Centerforce clutches have low release pressure, short pedal effort and smooth take-up. Drawing on centrifugal principles, the Centerforce clutch cover design incorporates an ingenious weighting of the diaphragm fingers to allow higher apply pressure as clutch rpm rises. Centerforce claims increased disc and pressure plate life, and weights can be designed to accommodate a variety of user needs.

Although many clutch manufacturers build healthy aftermarket replacement clutches, Midway's Centerforce II and Dual Friction designs have a wide reputation for

their rugged performance, reliability and light pedal apply pressure. For multi-purpose truck usage, I prefer the Centerforce centrifugal weight clutch assembly over all other designs.

Clutch Linkage

Toyota trucks have relatively trouble-free hydraulic clutch linkage. This linkage design lends itself to engine and transmission conversions. If you have plans to replace your engine or transmission with domestic parts, see the many slave cylinder mounts and linkage adapters available from BTB Products, Downey Off-Road, Advance Adapters and NWOR Specialties.

> *CAUTION —*
> *Toyota truck hydraulic clutch cylinders have aluminum housings. The bores of such cylinders can easily become damaged if abrasive contaminants enter the system. Use care and cleanliness when inspecting clutch fluid or servicing the system. Keep parts together during service work.*

As interior bellhousing parts are difficult to reach, I highly recommend the use of a new, high quality throwout bearing. Install the best pilot bearing type available, and make sure it fits the crankshaft and transmission input gear properly. Look closely for any release arm/fork and pivot stud wear.

Aftermarket hydraulic throwout/release bearings are available, and some OEMs have even turned to this design. I avoid such systems, especially on 4x4 models. This is a poor concept, as the simplest leak repair or seal replacement could require removal of two driveshafts, the transfer case, the transmission and other parts.

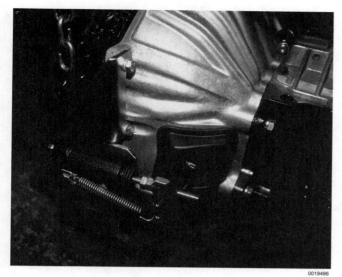

Fig. 17-12. *OEM Toyota hydraulic clutch linkage makes engine and transmission conversions much easier. Reliable linkage can be readily adapted to fit your conversion engine and work with a domestic clutch release arm. With attention to details, this can be one of the easier aspects of a conversion. Hydraulic clutch linkage offers less pedal pressure and smooth clutch engagement. Shown here is BTB Products' slave cylinder mount for Chevy V-8 into FJ40 Land Cruiser.*

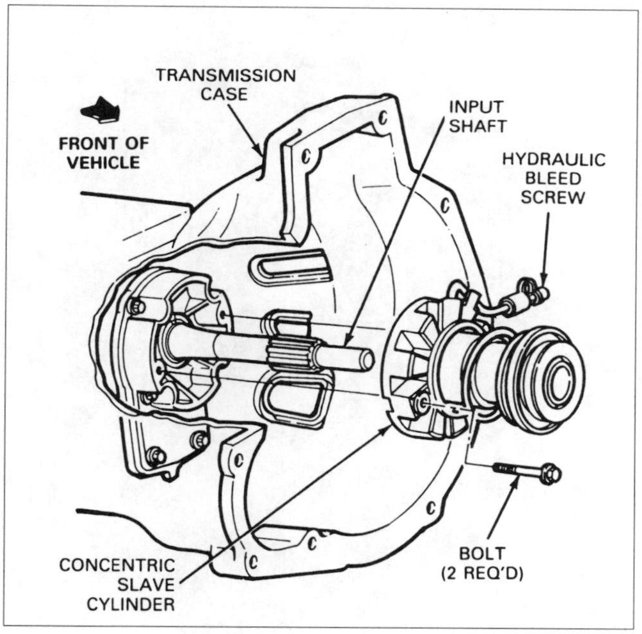

Fig. 17-13. *When fabricating a clutch linkage system, I avoid use of hydraulically actuated clutch release bearings. Although this design eliminates mechanical clutch linkage, a hydraulic leak could ruin the clutch disc and require a major amount of labor to repair—especially on a 4x4 model.*

4. AXLES AND TRACTION

4x4 Toyota trucks prove their worth battling climate extremes, stretching over rocks, clawing at mud in fast flowing streams and pulling through deep snow on barren winter paths. Four-wheelers, seasoned by unruly trails, argue that there's no such thing as too much traction.

For Toyota trucks, engine power flows through the clutch or torque converter, transmission, transfer case (4WD models) and driveline(s). The driveshaft rotates the axle's pinion gear. At the differential, power changes direction. The differential also determines the amount of power (torque) that flows to each wheel.

Conventional differential action has a severe limitation: When the truck encounters a loose traction surface, the differential mechanism directs power to the wheel with the least resistance.

This inherent weakness in open differentials has a major impact on a truck's traction. In loose terrain, it's easy to spot the truck with a conventional or open differential because one wheel spins furiously while the opposite wheel, on a better traction surface, stands still.

Traction Differentials: Controlling Wheelspin

A factory/OEM positive-traction or limited-slip differential helps deliver traction yet still provides vital differential speed between the axle shafts. Traction axles have used a variety of trade names, including Posi-Traction, Power-Lok and NoSPIN (Detroit). A number of aftermarket performance systems, well suited for severe on- and off-pavement traction demands, are also available.

The typical Toyota truck posi-traction or limited slip differential (LSD) unit features a clutching mechanism within the differential. Loss of traction at one wheel reads as no resistance in the differential unit. Most clutching devices apply torque to the axle shaft with more resistance, which is the same as delivering power to the wheel with better traction.

One variation of this design is the later GM governor type locking differential. These systems rely on a fly-weighted governor to telegraph wheel spin and initiate the process of applying torque to the opposite wheel. Such a system strives to match or balance the rotational speed at each wheel of the axle.

Most OEM limited slip units incorporate a multi-plate spring loaded clutch assembly with a standard spider and side gear arrangement. Under normal driving conditions, these differentials flow power through the spider and side gears in the conventional manner. They can also direct power from the differential case directly to the side gears when the clutches apply.

When one tire loses traction and spins, the clutches within the differential provide power to the other wheel by directly driving its side gear. The spider gears, driving through beveled teeth, want to separate or spread the side gears. As the side gears move apart, they exert force on the clutch plates. When the load increases, so does the side gear pressure against the clutch plates. This directs more power to the wheel with traction.

Fig. 17-14. *This spool, shown for a 9-inch Ford axle application, is the ultimate traction device. Axle shafts fit directly into spool splines, eliminating the differential completely. Spools serve strictly for sand drags, pulls and other forms of all-out racing. Retrofit 9-inch Ford axle is a common desert racing device for Toyota pickups.*

While part of the load on the clutches comes from springs in the differential assembly, the majority of the force is from spreading the side gears. Torque load acting as the decisive factor, this explains why slight application of the brakes will cause a limited slip differential to direct more power to the wheel with good footing.

The clutch type limited slip unit, which retains the standard spider gears and side gears, still allows wheel speed to vary on corners. Varied wheel speed under normal load causes the clutches to slip, which allows the spider gears to perform their function. Applying heavy power in a turn, however, can load the clutches enough to lock the side gears against the differential case. This will cause both wheels to turn at the same speed.

Although various clutch styles exist, the principle remains the same: provide a direct flow of power from the differential case to each of the side gears and wheels rather than only to the wheel with the least traction. Although their method of delivery is entirely different, aftermarket lockers also accommodate this need.

Which Differential?

Your highway driving environment or off-pavement tastes dictate which traction differential to buy. Yes, there is such thing as too much traction, and driver caution is a must with any traction differential. A truck with a limited slip or locking differential can go sideways when both wheels lose traction at the same time.

As an expert on differentials, Tom Reider, president of Reider Racing Enterprises notes, "While differential choices vary enough to satisfy most everyone's needs, the differential that satisfies everyone's wants still hasn't been invented. For most highway situations, an open differential is all that most people need and is, therefore,

found in 90% of all vehicles. Its ability to move the vehicle, however, is limited by the minimum traction available to any of the driving wheels. When operated in slippery conditions or with minimum weight on any of the drive wheels, it often causes the vehicle to become a land-locked barge.

"The alternatives available to us are to install limited slip or locking type differentials which will then provide the type of power flow to the ground that we expect out of our vehicle. Benefits and drawbacks exist for both types of differentials."

WARNING —
On ice or slick off-camber pavement, torque application at both ends of an axle assembly can create unwanted trouble. If your truck has a traction differential(s) and you're traveling on ice, be very careful. The truck could easily slip sideways if both wheels spin at the same time and the road camber is steep.

While manual and automatic lockers have the advantage of providing 100% traction to the opposite wheel when an axle shaft breaks, if you break a semi-floating axle shaft, or if you snap a 4x4's front axle shaft anywhere near the steering knuckle, you cannot drive safely.

Fig. 17-15. *Safety tire chains are a primary "traction device." Meeting needs of truckers for nearly half a century, Burns Bros., Inc., also owns Security Chain Company, the largest safety chain plant in the United States. Innovative Z-Chain cable design works well with latest ABS braking systems and is officially rated as a high speed safety chain. Easy to install in a blizzard, Z-Chain devices complement a limited slip differential.*

Fig. 17-16. *OEM-quality limited slip differentials are available through TRD U.S.A., Downey Off-Road, NWOR Specialties, California Mini-Trucks and Reider Racing/Precision Gear. Engineered for various Toyota truck applications, unit features replaceable multiple plates and serves Toyota pickup and 4Runner rear axles plus front axles of pre-IFS 4x4s. Users find that OEM style limited slip units deliver high traction without risk of severe shock loads.*

Fig. 17-17. *Multiplate OEM style differential provides power to the wheel and axle shaft with traction. Spider gears press side gears against the clutches to deliver more torque to wheel with traction.*

Traction Buyer's Guide

A variety of aftermarket and OE-type traction differentials are available for your truck. The need for these devices depends upon your driving environment and the importance of delivering maximum torque or traction at each wheel. (On some 4x4 applications, this could mean a traction device at both the front and rear differentials.) Several manufacturers offer traction differential kits for improving your truck's axle(s).

Detroit Locker/NoSPIN: A highly respected differential unit that has stood the test of time is the Detroit Lock-

Fig. 17-18. *The Detroit Locker/NoSPIN has a loyal following. The Detroit Locker features positive engagement of wheel with greater traction. Cutaway display model shows high quality and simplicity of mechanism. Display model has survived years of customer abuse on this parts counter.*

er or NoSPIN unit, built by Tractech, Inc., a subsidiary of Dyneer Corporation. Years ago, the NoSPIN was an OEM and dealer installed option for domestic trucks.

Speed sensitive, the NoSPIN allows your truck to maneuver corners and operate over irregular terrain. The unique design offers the equivalent of a completely locked differential (similar to a spool) during straight ahead driving conditions.

For differential action, the NoSPIN has a central spider assembly with dog teeth on both sides, two driven clutches (one for each axle shaft) with dog teeth to engage the spiders, and a pair of side gears. This spider assembly fits in the middle of the differential case. The case drives the spider assembly, while the driven clutch assemblies ride on splines machined on the outside of the side gears. Coil springs keep the clutches engaged with the spider assembly. This directs power from the spider to the side gears.

As the truck corners and the outside wheel speeds up, cam ramps on the inside edges of the spider unit cause the clutch assembly for that wheel to disengage from the spider. The wheel now coasts freely. As with conventional or factory limited slip differentials, NoSPIN also prevents axle binding on turns. The method differs, however, as NoSPIN completely disconnects the power flow to the outer wheel as the vehicle makes a turn.

When wheel speeds are again equal, the free-wheeling clutch engages with the spider. Power now flows evenly to both wheels. The unique factor with this differential is that power flow is either equal at both wheels or going to the wheel with the greater amount of traction.

If one wheel hangs in the air, the NoSPIN unit stays locked, providing as much power to the wheel on the ground as traction will allow. If you spin the inside wheel on a turn, once the inner wheel's speed reaches that of the outside wheel, the unit will return to a locked mode.

ARB Air Locker: After seven years of severe use in Australia, the ARB Air Locker hit the U.S. market by storm several years ago. This differential locking system now has a loyal following among those who prefer manual control of the differential(s). Winner of the coveted

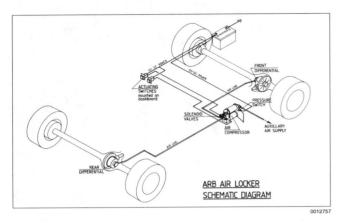

Fig. 17-19. *ARB's Air Locker leaves traction to the driver. With the push of a switch, the differential locks up and both axle shafts rotate in unison, much like a spool. When disengaged, Air Locker provides the smooth highway operation of a conventional axle.*

1989 SEMA Best Product Award, the ARB Air Locker is a popular item with hard-core off-pavement users.

By design, the Air Locker provides conventional open differential operation for normal driving conditions. When your truck needs power to both wheels, Air Locker has a pneumatically operated shift mechanism for completely locking the spider gears and side gears within the differential assembly.

Inside the differential case, the Air Locker has a slider shift mechanism, much like sliders found in manual transmissions or a transfer case. The outside of the slider has splines. They engage and slide inside the differential case.

The slider also attaches to a hollow piston which surrounds the spider and side gears. Actuated by pressurized air, the piston moves the slider. Teeth on the inside of the slider match a set of teeth on the outside of one side gear. When the piston moves the slider over the outer teeth of the side gear, the side gear, slider and differential case lock up as a single unit. The locked side gears and spiders rotate both axle shafts at the same speed as the differential case.

An ARB Air Locker can engage solid power flow to each wheel, much like a racing spool. This is unsurpassed tractability, however, the driver now bears full responsibility for locking and unlocking the unit.

For durability, most ARB Air Locker applications have four spider gears, compared to the two spiders found in most OEM conventional axle designs. An Air Locker fitup requires electrical wiring and the installation of an air compressor and air lines to the differential(s). Although installation is more involved than other traction devices, each kit includes instructions and all necessary parts.

I have installed and tested the ARB system. The differential installation was much like changing a ring-and-pinion gear set and requires use of a dial indicator for setting up the ring and pinion gears plus blue dye to perform tooth contact tests. It takes time to fit and route air hoses carefully and mount the compressor. Wiring, which features nicely made harnesses, also requires effort to assure a neat and reliable installation. From my experience with a common Toyota-type truck axle, the task should take the reasonably equipped home mechanic from 10–16 hours to perform. Despite the time involved, I was very pleased with the results and unique advantages of this system.

Auburn Gear: For truck owners looking for a high-quality limited-slip differential, Auburn Gear provides a smart alternative. Although Auburn focuses mainly on the high-performance automobile market, its heavy duty limited-slip design has applications for popular light truck axles.

Like OEM limited-slip designs, Auburn Gear delivers power to both wheels through a clutching mechanism. However, instead of using clutch plates with high frictional loads, Auburn Gear uses a cone type clutch system. (A cone attaches to the back side of a side gear and nests inside a matching machined surface in the differential case.) When loaded by either the differential springs or the spider gears, the side gear wedges itself within the differential case.

Fig. 17-20. *Auburn Gear's SureGrip is a rugged, heavy duty limited slip unit.*

By design, much less force is necessary to lock the side gear to the differential case. Since there is direct steel-to-steel contact without clutch plates to wear out, peak performance can last much longer than with other units. Auburn traction differentials also boast large spider and side gears that deliver exceptional strength and durability for a limited slip type differential.

Torque delivery to the wheel with traction is superior with this design. If I were to consider a limited slip traction device, the latest Auburn design would be my choice.

LA Locker/LOCK-RIGHT: LA Locker's differential functions much like the NoSPIN/Detroit Locker. Originally designed for military Dodge trucks and larger W300 civilian Power Wagons, this design has gone widely civilian since 1986. In addition to larger domestic truck axles, LA Lockers fit Toyota truck differentials and many other OEM axle applications.

The dramatic difference between LA Locker and other traction devices, including the NoSPIN, is its quiet operation during clutch lockup. Like the popular NoSPIN, LA Locker delivers 100% of the available power to the trac-

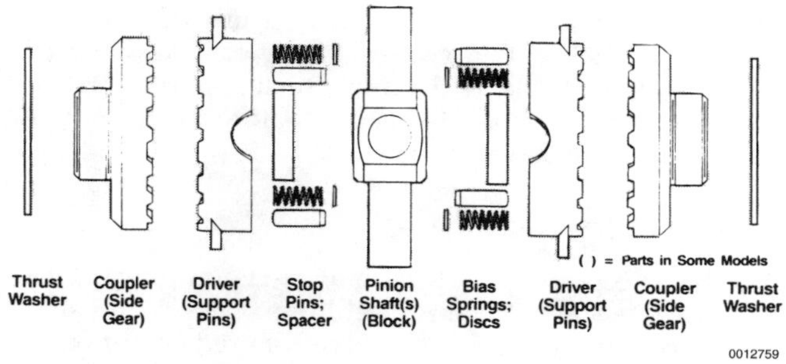

Thrust Washer | Coupler (Side Gear) | Driver (Support Pins) | Stop Pins; Spacer | Pinion Shaft(s) (Block) | Bias Springs; Discs | Driver (Support Pins) | Coupler (Side Gear) | Thrust Washer

( ) = Parts in Some Models

0012759

Fig. 17-21. LA Locker diagram shows components of the differential. Cam teeth on each coupler allow overrun and disengagement when the axles rotate at uneven speeds.

tion wheel(s) at all times. This design offers a very simple cam action and lockup, shifting smoothly enough for use at rear or front (4x4 model) axles.

WARNING —

Although many four-wheelers use an LA Locker at both the rear and front axles, this design exaggerates the usual understeer associated with running a four-wheel drive truck on a hard surface with the front hubs engaged. You should use manual locking hubs and unlock your front hubs as you normally would for driving in 2WD mode on hard pavement. An LA Locker up front will not affect steering in 2WD with the hubs unlocked. Always follow the traction device manufacturer's operating guidelines for using two- or four-wheel drive.

The Lock-Right unit installs in the existing differential case, which saves considerable cost. During installation, there's no demand to remove differential bearings, so resetting ring gear backlash is often unnecessary. The LA Locker/LOCK-RIGHT is a tough, military-proven design. If you're attracted to the no-nonsense traction of a Detroit Locker/NoSPIN or ARB Air Locker, this rugged automatic locker deserves a look.

OEM-Type Limited Slips: Many trucks have factory-installed limited slip differentials. For Toyota trucks, Downey Off-Road, NWOR Specialties, Reider Racing/Precision Gear, California Mini-Truck and others supply quality Japanese built OEM-style traction differentials. (See these vendors' catalogs for a variety of axle traction devices.)

NOTE —

Users who prefer a milder application of power and subtler traction at the front axle often choose a factory-type limited slip or positive traction differential. An OEM type limited slip in front and Detroit, Lock-Right or Air Locker at the rear is a popular combination for four-wheelers seeking maximum off-pavement traction. See suppliers' cautions, however, as some Toyota front axles, especially 4WD IFS types, cannot tolerate a limited slip differential.

Traction Differential Footnotes

Installing a differential carrier assembly involves close tolerances. Ring gear backlash settings require a dial indicator and patience. Before buying a traction differential, read the installation instructions carefully. Decide whether to send the job to a capable shop or do the work yourself.

Give the broader traction issue some thought, too. Consider tires, traction bars and shock absorbers. Added traction to the wheels means a greater challenge keeping traction on the ground. Expect more wheel hop and spring wrap up, especially with large tires.

There is such thing as *too much traction*, especially when driving on icy, off-camber pavement. I like an open differential (non-locking/non-limited slip unit) in this kind of environment, as it allows for better vehicle control and straighter, more stable steering.

ARB's Air Locker allows the driver to use an open differential under these kinds of driving circumstances, yet provides a locking provision for off-pavement rock crawling or loose dirt hill climbs. In my experience, a device like ARB's Air Locker will better serve the multiple uses expected of the typical four-wheel drive truck.

Rating Differential Traction Devices*

Differential style	Smoothness of operation	Tractability	Adverse effect on tires/driveline	Cost	Used for
Conventional (open)	Excellent	Poor	None	Lowest	Highway
OEM Limited slip	Very good	Good	Very little	Modest	Modest off-road
Aftermarket limited-slip	Good	Very good	Modest	Moderate	Modest off-road
Automatic lockers (Lock-Right and Detroit)	Good to poor	Extremely good	Modest	Higher	Heavy off-road
Manual locker (ARB)	Good to excellent	Excellent (locked) Poor (unlocked)	Poor (locked) None (unlocked)	Highest	Heavy off-road
Spool/welded diff.	Poor	Excellent	Poor	Modest	Racing

*Source: Tom Reider, Reider Racing Enterprises

Conversion Axles

When considering an upgrade or retrofit rear axle for a Toyota truck, one choice would be a GM 12-bolt (twelve differential cover screws) Saginaw type. If you can find the correct width, which will pose a real challenge, the 1/2-ton 4x4 truck versions of this GM axle can provide a six wheel-stud pattern similar to Toyota's Land Cruisers and 4WD pickups or 4Runners. This could simplify the conversion in terms of wheel requirements.

The more likely retrofit candidate is a Ford 9-inch axle. Wheel-studs pose no real problem, as a quality local machine shop or M.I.T. at El Cajon, California (see Appendix) can machine Ford-type axle flanges to accept Toyota type wheel-studs. Select the axle type that will work best. Custom machine work can complete the job.

> **CAUTION —**
> *Compatibility with a later model's ABS braking system is a concern. Do not interfere with safe braking. With any axle swap, you will likely need to perform fabrication work (such as spring perch relocation, a perch design change, brake line fitup and an emergency brake cable/control adaptation). Matched brake sizing is also of concern.*

Although a domestic 3/4-ton full-floating rear axle (like the Dana 60 or GM Corporate 14-bolt) is superior to any semi-floating design, such an axle would be overkill for a Toyota pickup or 4Runner. The unsprung weight and eight-stud wheel pattern requirements would raise havoc with your springs and overall chassis dynamics.

There is a lighter semi-floating version of the Dana 60 axle that GMC and International-Harvester used in heavy duty 1/2-ton trucks. This unit, although somewhat scarce, offers exceptional stamina. (GMC applications even offered a six-stud wheel pattern axle flange.) This could conceivably work for a Land Cruiser or Toyota

0019263

Fig. 17-22.   For a pre-runner or all-out Toyota racing pickup truck, many builders turn to the Ford 9-inch semi-floating axle assembly. Curry Enterprises and others specialize in custom applications of these well engineered Ford truck and full-size passenger car axles. This 2WD Toyota pre-runner, equipped with Downey Off-Road suspension components, has a beefy 9-inch Ford semi-floating axle retrofit.

4WD pickup. (I-H versions would require machining axle flanges to accept the correct size and number of wheel studs.) Whichever axle you select, be certain that track width is compatible with your truck's chassis. Earlier (1960s) applications of this semi-floating Dana 60 offer the narrower track widths.

Heavy Duty Axle Upgrades

With the exception of motorhome, special cargo van chassis, and late Land Cruisers, all Toyota 2WD and 4WD trucks sold in the U.S. market have offered semi-floating rear axles. Motorhomes and cargo vans require superior stamina and safety, and here Toyota has opted for a full-floating rear axle with dual wheels at each side.

Until 1980, GM, Dodge, Ford, I-H and several other domestic truck manufacturers offered the added stamina and safety of a full-floater type rear axle in 3/4-ton models. In 1980, Ford initiated the switch to semi-floating rear axles on F250 models, a move soon followed by GM 3/4-ton trucks and the Suburbans.

Loss of full-floating wheel hub support is not the only drawback with 1980–up 3/4-ton and other semi-floating axles. While GM's traditional Corporate 14-bolt full-floaters featured a huge 10-1/2" diameter ring gear, the semi-floating 14-bolt axles have a smaller 9-1/2" diameter ring gear. A 9-1/2" ring gear is still very tough, larger than a 9-inch Ford or Dana 44 ring gear, and just a quarter-inch smaller than the massive Dana 60.

Toyota trucks, by comparison, have smaller ring gear diameters. Most 2WD pickups and the front axles of IFS 4WDs offer 7.5-inch diameter ring gears. 4WD pickups/4Runners and some 2WD pickups have 8-inch diameter rear axle ring gears (in a semi-floating type axle). Pre-IFS model 4x4s (solid axle type) use an 8-inch diameter ring gear—tough stuff.

> **NOTE —**
> All 4x4 Toyota trucks to date have full-floating front wheel hubs. Solid axle 4WD Land Cruisers and solid axle pickup/4Runner models have bonafide full-floating front axle assemblies.

The Land Cruisers offer a larger ring gear and axle design, but U.S. market Land Cruisers have semi-floating rear axles until very recent models. There is a full-floating axle available for non-U.S. application Land Cruisers, and some owners retrofit this unit to U.S. models. Specter Off-Road can supply the OEM Land Cruiser full-floating rear axle.

Characterizing a Full-floating Rear Axle

A full-floating axle is easy to spot, as its hub flange protrudes through the rear wheel centers. The outside flange of a floating axle shaft bolts to the outer face of the wheel hub. You can safely remove a full-floating axle shaft with the truck's wheels attached and on the ground.

For large trucks that carry a heavy load, the full floating axle has a distinct advantage. An inner and outer bearing set support the load, much like the wheel bearings of a 4x4's full-floating front axle. These bearings ride on spindles that extend outward past the brake shoe set.

Fig. 17-23. When Toyota has offered 3/4-ton trucks, the rear axle has been a heavy duty semi-floating type, much like later model domestic trucks. Semi-floating axle shaft supports weight of vehicle. Vehicle load and weight bear directly on outer section of axle shaft. If shaft breaks, the flange, brake drum, wheel and tire could separate from truck. Prior to 1980, nearly all domestic 3/4-ton and larger capacity trucks used full-floating rear axles.

Fig. 17-24. OEM Toyota full-floating rear axles for the Land Cruiser are available through Specter Off-Road. These axles originate on non-U.S. market Land Cruisers and late 'Cruiser wagons. Some builders upgrade the 'Cruiser with a 9-inch (ring gear diameter) custom fitted Ford semi-floating axle assembly.

Fig. 17-25. Typically, a semi-floating axle shaft (right) is much heavier than a full-floater. Semi-floating axle shaft must bear load and weight of vehicle. Full-floater shaft simply acts as a power link between the differential side gear and outer flange of the full-floating hub.

Fig. 17-26. Here is spindle section of full-floating axle housing. Wheel hub rides on inner and outer bearing sets, with an adjusting nut/lock nut holding the hub in place. If axle shaft breaks, hub still rides safely on bearing sets.

The hefty spindles of domestic truck full-floating axles are an integral part of the axle housing.

By design, the full floating axle shaft simply connects the differential's side gear with the wheel hub. If the axle shaft breaks, the wheel remains in place, safely supported by the hub's inner and outer bearings.

In a semi-floating axle, commonly used at the rear of Toyota trucks, the inner end of the axle shaft engages the side gear at the differential. In this design, the side gear engagement keeps the axle aligned and the wheel flange straight. Compared to a full-floater, however, the vehicle load presses directly against the outboard section of the axle shaft, where a bearing supports the shaft just inside the wheel flange. Loss of inner end C-lock or a broken axle shaft could prove catastrophic with a semi-floating axle.

On a semi-floating axle, when the axle shaft or bearing wear, the shaft can become scrap and must be replaced at great expense. Also, although Toyota offers substantial size and strength in these semi-floating axle shafts, under severe stress, shaft breakage could allow the hub, brake drum and wheel/tire assembly to separate from the vehicle.

A full-floating axle is typically stronger, safer and better equipped to handle heavy working loads. If your truck demands ultimate stamina, consider a retrofit heavy duty semi-floating or full-floating rear axle assembly.

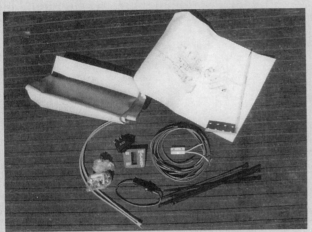

0012763

Hub-A-Lert: Watchdog for 4x4 Front Hubs

Knowing whether your truck's hubs have engaged or disengaged depends on more than the 4-Wheel Drive light on the console or dashboard. In many applications, the OEM 4x4 indicator lamp signal originates at the transfer case and simply indicates that the shifter/fork has moved to 4-High or 4-Low.

This means that power is flowing to the front axle, but if the hubs are not completely engaged, torque cannot rotate the front wheels. Similarly, with automatic locking hubs, simply backing the truck up is no guarantee that the automatic hubs have disengaged. Dash lights cannot see inside the front hub mechanisms.

There's a better way to monitor front axle activity. Hub-A-Lert, an easy-to-install device built by 4x4 Specialty Products, can read front driveshaft rotation. The device sends a signal to an LED dash lamp and takes the guesswork out of hub disengagement.

During normal two-wheel drive operation, no shaft rotation (other than the minor lubricant spin common to some geardrive transfer cases) will display on the LED lamp. If a defective hub begins to drag, however, the front driveshaft will spin and flash a signal on the dashboard.

Simple and designed by a savvy victim of several automatic hub malfunctions that resulted in transfer case failures, Hub-A-Lert is automatic hub insurance—at a fraction of the cost for a damaged front axle, transfer case or wheel hub assembly.

5. DRIVESHAFT UPGRADES

Use the largest practical U-joint sizes when dealing with a high output engine. You do not want driveline trouble while pre-running a race or along a backcountry trail.

0019267

Fig. 17-27. *Toyota typically uses a flat, bolt-on yoke flange to support drivelines and U-joints, and joints are of metric sizing. You will likely need to mate Toyota and domestic pieces when retrofitting a domestic axle. A qualified local driveline shop can perform this kind of work.*

As a yardstick, many half-ton domestic trucks use the common 1310 Spicer or similar size U-joints. These U-joint styles work with appropriate axle, transfer case and transmission flange yokes. Replacement OEM and aftermarket U-joint flanges can help when making upgrades.

When driveshaft parts must handle more than 300 horsepower under heavy throttle, you need heavy duty 3/4-ton or one-ton truck size U-joints (Spicer 1350 type minimum), if such a fitup is possible. This is also necessary for a high output powertrain in a 4x4 desert pre-runner/race truck.

> **NOTE —**
> For a radical 4x4 chassis lift, double Cardan type CV-joints will help reduce vibration caused by steep driveshaft angles.

A complete U-joint conversion can include heavier driveshaft tubing and larger U-joint flanges. For most truck owners, the 1350-series Spicer joint (or its equivalent size in another design) can handle severe loads. Domestic Dana/Spicer 44 and 60 axle units can easily be fitted with 1350 size replacement flanges, and so can many GM and Ford axles, domestic transfer case inputs and outputs, and domestic transmissions.

> **NOTE —**
> In four-wheel drive, the torque splits between front and rear axles, reducing overall load on each U-joint. Two-wheel drive mode is actually much harder on driveline U-joints than running a truck in four-wheel drive. A 2WD Toyota pre-runner with a high horsepower domestic V-6 will require a heavy duty rear axle and hefty driveline.

Chapter 18

Chassis, Suspension, and Tire Upgrades

MOST STATES NOW HAVE MANDATES setting limits on vehicle chassis height and body modifications. Motor vehicle safety administrators, law enforcement agencies and a wary citizenry have targeted unsafely customized street trucks and poorly modified off-pavement prototype "pre-runner" and 4x4 trucks registered for public road use.

Evidence of sensational accidents and senseless traffic deaths supports this sentiment. The more reputable aftermarket suspension manufacturers share many views with the state legislators. Increasing a truck's height, for example, raises issues like correct safety engineering versus a homespun botch job to achieve a particular look.

Teams of factory engineers work endlessly at improving the ride, handling, safe steering and brakes of Toyota pickups, 4Runners and the Land Cruiser. These mechanical engineers, versed in chassis dynamics and equipped with elaborate computer CAD programs and laboratory equipment, build trucks to comply with the highest standards for safe handling and braking.

> **WARNING —**
> *Any suspension modification will affect the handling of your truck. Poor braking, risk of a rollover, loss of vehicle control, chronic failure of driveline parts and marginal braking each can result from improper modifications. When in doubt, always follow OEM standards or the information furnished by a reputable aftermarket equipment manufacturer.*

1. CHASSIS MODIFICATIONS

Chassis and suspension engineering provide a challenge with any multi-purpose truck. Highway driving,

Fig. 18-1. *Custom fabrication work on Ivan "Ironman" Stewart's Toyota race truck reveals complex engineering and ultra-heavy duty components. A homespun look-alike cannot duplicate the stamina and materials displayed here. For high performance chassis tuning, issues of safety, predictable han-dling and reliability become top priorities. Toyota's unparalleled SCORE/HDRA off-road racing success reflects the Ironman's world renowned talent and exceptional commitment as a driver plus the professional engineering of his Toyota race trucks.*

trailer pulling, trail running and hard-core desert racing each call for different chassis dynamics.

Visualize your truck sweeping through corners, fighting a crosswind with a trailer in tow, braking hard, bracing against a loose traction surface or negotiating a precarious, off-camber sidehill. The interaction of the springs, shocks, stabilizers, brakes and tire/wheel mass is a blur. An automotive engineer or race truck fabricator must address each of these conditions.

On the test course or skidpad, a safe truck meets many criteria. Along with center of gravity, terms like Ackerman steering angles, lateral acceleration, roll axis, roll center, roll couple distribution, roll steer and toe change; roll stiffness, shock damping, spring/wheel rate, and vertical load transfer each apply to handling. The frame, suspension and axle design (Hotchkiss, solid hypoid, twin A-arm, rear coil-and-link, coil spring or torsion bar IFS, live IFS or mono-beam) also enter the equation.

At speed, aerodynamics and road load add to the burden. Braking is critically dependent upon load distribution and the anti-dive/anti-lift characteristics of the overall chassis design. Tire slip angle also becomes a factor, and the safest truck chassis balances each of these demands into a reasonably compliant package.

Modifying Your Toyota Truck's Chassis

Changes in front end geometry, roll center, center of gravity, unsprung weight and tire design each have an effect on your truck's handling. Toyota truck engineers

Fig. 18-2. Wider wheel track offsets higher center of gravity created by aftermarket suspension lift. Here, oversized tires and wider wheels help restore original chassis design and handling.

generally set up a chassis for good ride, safe steering control and manageable braking. Aftermarket components often meet the additional needs of special terrain, extra loads and exceptionally harsh driving conditions.

The better engineered aftermarket spring and shock absorber kits offer substantial improvements for your truck. Additional clearance for specialty tires, improved spring rates, massive shock absorbers and a stouter steering damper shock can make our vehicles far better suited for off-highway perils. Many of these parts enhance the truck's handling and control under a variety of driving conditions.

For some Toyota truck owners, trends and fads also motivate chassis modifications. Achieving a certain status may even override safety concerns. Poor braking, risk of a rollover, loss of vehicle control, chronic failure of driveline parts and marginal braking characterize the worst modifications.

The Culprits

Unfortunately, some truck owners go far beyond the OEM and aftermarket parts sources, seeking to establish their own records for the highest, biggest, fastest and fattest truck. Without the benefit of engineering credentials or a sense for chassis dynamics, builders of homespun, radically lifted trucks have encouraged the wrath of motor vehicle and public safety administrators.

A large number of improperly modified trucks sport crude and unsafe spacer block lifts, disfigured springs, bound up steering linkage, stretched brake hoses, overheight bumpers and ridiculous headlamp angles that glare menacingly into the eyes of oncoming drivers.

These same trucks, with massively oversize tires creating an unsprung weight imbalance, have overtaxed brake systems that prevent safe stops. Radically sloped steering linkage and drag link angles, common to poorly constructed chassis lifts, create bump steer—the slightest blip in the road can cause the truck to veer uncontrollably.

Many law enforcement officers are also truck owners and recreationalists, yet most have a profound bias against radically lifted trucks. Each state's motor vehicle safety offices has files on highway mayhem caused by

Fig. 18-3. The ride height may look "hot," but this front end geometry is unsafe. Note the radical slope angle on the draglink. As springs compress and the solid axle rises, bump steer shifts the wheels to the right.

Fig. 18-4. *Here's an illegal setup by many state standards. Two sets of stacked spacer blocks make up this rear lift. Shifting of blocks and failure under load are possible. Never stack rear spacer blocks. Never install spacer blocks at the front leaf springs.*

poorly crafted, radically lifted 4x4 trucks. Horror stories of homespun junk run the gamut, including cases of monstrous 4x4 trucks rear ending other vehicles—with the lower edge of the front bumper overrunning the entire trunk of the car.

Equally appalling, some of the homemade "street truck" chassis systems include hastily "slammed" or lowered suspension and marginal steering hardware. All would agree that personal expression is a fundamental human right. Highway safety, however, is a collective responsibility.

State Lift Laws And Accountability

Although a few states have no current laws directly regulating chassis lift or excessively oversize tires, a trend is clear. Federal safety laws, interstate highway funding, and the issues of public liability make each state accountable to the same issues.

The aftermarket suspension and body lift manufacturers have similar accountability. For a reputable company to survive, product liability insurance is essential. The cost of this insurance can become prohibitive, which provides a large incentive for building safely engineered kits. A good safety record can effectively reduce product liability and operating overhead.

Massachusetts' Suspension Modification Formula

Here's an example of a practical lift law as it applies to 4x4 (and other) vehicles. Massachusetts devised a formula for allowable mechanical (body and suspension) lift that accounts for both vehicle stability and safe handling: Wheel base multiplied by Wheel Track (the tire tread center-to-center measurement at the wider axle) divided by a factor of 2200. Wheel track width may be increased up to four inches—by way of rim offset only; no wheel spacers allowed.

The test is relatively easy. Suppose your solid front axle Toyota 4WD pickup has a 102.2" wheelbase and wide rims that provide a 59.9" front axle tread centerline width (four inch increase over the OEM tread width of 55.9-inches). 102.2" x 59.9" = 6121.78 divided by 2200 = 2.78" lift. Under Massachusetts' Sections 6.04 and 6.05, the tire diameter (based on the largest size available as an OEM option) may also be increased the same amount as the mechanical lift.

Simply put, this Toyota truck could have tires up to 2.78" larger in diameter than the stock/OEM tire size plus a 2.78" mechanical lift by way of chassis and/or a body lift kit. Accordingly, the body/door sill height could set a total of 4.17" (2.78" plus the 1.39" tire radius increase) over stock with installation of these wide rims, oversized tires and the mechanical (chassis or body) lift.

Example: If the OEM maximum tire diameter was 31 inches, you could install 33" diameter tires on a wide offset rim size (equal to a two-inch wider track/wheel centerline measurement per wheel) and add a 2-1/2" chassis lift kit for tire clearance. Within the Massachusetts formula, the added track width restores the center-of-gravity when you increase suspension height and tire diameter.

All parts must be equal to or better than OEM standards, and the vehicle safety cannot be compromised. Massachusetts has addressed OEM vehicle design, roll center, center-of-gravity and all other handling concerns with this statute. Other equipment on the truck must comply with general safety standards. This is a sound approach, allowing reasonable lifts for both off-pavement and highway use.

OEM standards remain the best baseline for safety. Toyota and other new vehicle manufacturers must comply with U.S. Department of Transportation (D.O.T.), Society of Automotive Engineers (SAE) and other professional engineering guidelines when constructing their vehicles.

"Lifting" your truck means an increase in tire size, suspension modifications or installation of body mount spacers. Before investing time and money either raising your truck's chassis/body or mounting a set of expensive oversize tires, review the laws for your state.

> **NOTE—**
> If you've heard rumors of a height limit change, consult your nearest state police or highway patrol for the new rulings. These agencies will prove very helpful. Their primary concerns are public safety and compliance with motor vehicle regulations.

CHAPTER 18

IFS Pickup/4Runner Lift Kits

1979-up 2WD and 1986-up Toyota 4WD pickups have independent front suspension with torsion bars. A variety of lift kits serve these popular models and the IFS 4Runners as well.

For an overview of the typical IFS 4WD truck lift kit installation, I have highlighted the Black Diamond kit (formerly Rugged Trail, now built by Warn Industries), plus other quality kits and components available from SuperLift, Rancho Suspension, Trailmaster, NWOR Specialties and Downey Off-Road (Mfg).

Fig. 18-5. Black Diamond's Toyota IFS 4WD suspension lift begins with lowering brake lines, then disassembling the front sway bar and crossmember. Once committed to a lift package, there's no going back—crossmember tabs must be cut off. This and other modifications make restoration back to OEM difficult. Be determined before starting this job.

Fig. 18-6. Differential is "dropped" to maintain axle half-shaft alignment and fitup. Kits vary, along with engineering approaches. Rancho, SuperLift and others use new custom fabricated upper control arms that eliminate need for a steering knuckle/upper control arm spacer. Review various kits available before committing to this project.

Fig. 18-7. OEM lower control arms fit new drop brackets. This is where Black Diamond achieves IFS lift. Upper control arm removal is much like a front end rebuild, and kit comes with instructions. At upper control arm, a cast spacer fits between upper ball joint and steering knuckle/spindle.

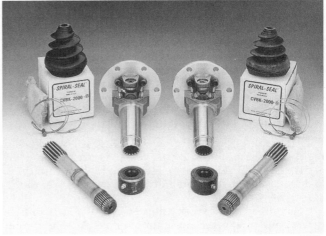

Fig. 18-8. Downey Off-Road offers this innovative kit to eliminate OEM CV-joints, replacing them with short slip-yoke type driveshafts. These half-shafts serve Downey Off-Road and other chassis lifts. Downey has concentrated on fast desert Toyota trucks for many years.

0019577

Fig. 18-9. NWOR Specialties offers an assortment of lift kits for Toyota trucks. While offering manufactured kits from SuperLift, Trailmaster and Rancho Suspension, NWOR also offers many supplementary upgrades. NWOR's IFS idler arm truss (shown) helps overcome a weakness created by over-tensioned torsion bars and severe off-pavement pounding.

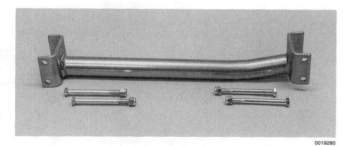

0019280

Fig. 18-10. Downey Off-Road's IFS 4WD control arm truss brace is a must item for any off-pavement four-wheel drive user—especially trucks with oversized tires. Frame shops often see stock suspension systems with their lower control arms and vertical frame supports spread apart. This truss aims at protecting your truck's frame, suspension and steering linkage.

0019279 / 0019287 / 0019281

Fig. 18-11. Downey Off-Road's 1990-up 4Runner coil spring lift kits complement a set of two-stage torsion bars. Extra travel plus useful chassis/suspension lift make this a practical approach—with an OEM spring rate and ride quality. Longer brake hose and hardware included in this kit.

Fig. 18-12.   SuperLift's lift kit for IFS Toyota 4WD trucks boasts a 3-1/2" to 5-1/2" lift range and departure from other designs. After dropping lower control arm and axle, kit establishes new upper control arm locations with ball-joint points at OEM steering knuckles. Adjustable rocker assembly takes torsion bar twist down to new upper control arms. This provides normal wheel travel and permits use of other stock components.

Fig. 18-13.   T100 has not been overlooked. Downey lift kit for Extra Cab T100 provides a desired ride height and room for oversized tires.

Lift Kit Footnotes for FJ40 and Other Models

I installed suspension lift kits in two of my Land Cruisers and have written many magazine articles and tech column responses on such installations. My experience and research have turned up several concerns, especially around the issue of premature urethane bushing failure.

Underlying causes of premature urethane spring bushing failure center around the two distinct spring designs: 1) 1981-up FJ-40 spring eyes are ten millimeters larger than earlier models, and 2) spring *shackles* are wider on these later 'Cruisers. Some aftermarket spring manufacturers have attempted to use the later spring eye diameter for *all* Land Cruiser applications, and for pre-1981 models, this means use of a narrow shouldered, oversize diameter spring bushing that will fail in service.

Choosing A Quality Lift Kit

When selecting an aftermarket lift kit, consider these features:

1) On a solid axle model, make sure the kit uses new replacement leaf spring sets at the front. Avoid shackle extensions and front add-a-leafs.

2) If lift is substantial, make sure that longer brake hoses, dropped sway bar brackets, bump stop drop kits, longer shock absorbers, a raised steering arm or dropped pitman arm (whichever is applicable) and other parts compensate for the longer distance between the frame and axles.

3) On later IFS 4WD or 2WD, make sure the lift kit includes either new steering knuckle/arm assemblies or properly engineered control arms that allow for adequate wheel travel. Avoid IFS kits that simply jack up the torsion bars (or add taller front coil springs in the case of 1978 and older 2WD mini-trucks).

4) Quality kits attempt to restore OEM wheel travel, steering arcs and sway control. Consult a high performance/4WD frame and alignment shop that does this kind of installation before selecting a kit for your chassis.

5) Make sure that the kit addresses driveline slope, driveshaft length and axle pinion angles. A stretched driveshaft or bad U-joint angle means trouble.

6) Consider CV-joint and boot/seal angles on later IFS models, and make sure the chassis lift kit does not compromise these angles or cause stress to these parts.

7) Have a frame and alignment shop check out your kit's installation and fine-tune the caster, camber and toe-in.

8) Go with a known product, as its research and development budget is more apt to produce quality results.

9) Make sure that the lift is necessary. Lifts and the attendant work to fine-tune a chassis can get expensive and prove very time consuming. Do you really need big tires? *That big?* Is this where your money is best spent? Consider the degree of change that your truck will undergo. Will this enhance its value? Can you restore the truck to stock if necessary? Will legal rulings ban your truck from public roads soon? Think this through before spending hard earned money on a lift, big wheels and oversized tires.

With these late style (big eye diameter) springs, the military wraps rub the frame supports of earlier models, and the urethane bushings have too thin a side flange for use with the earlier width shackles. The best solution to this problem is use of stock-width springs with your truck's stock diameter spring eye design. This will allow for normal bushing fitup, use of stock or aftermarket type shackles and longer parts service life.

Brake hoses and lift kits pose a safety concern. As the axle and chassis gap spreads, brake hoses can become too short. While a custom aftermarket brake hose can solve this problem (expensively!), there's another alternative that may be simpler and less costly: an OEM replacement hose that fits.

Fig. 18-14. *For any suspension lift, brake hoses usually wind up short. When safe, pipes and support brackets can sometimes be relocated to restore normal movement and clearance for the hoses. In other cases, like with my 1976 Land Cruiser and a 3-1/2" lift, longer brake hoses will be necessary.*

When I lifted my 1976 FJ40, the frame-to-axle flexible hoses stretched like bow strings as the chassis and axle moved. I sought out a *Bendix Illustrated Identification Guide* and *Bendix Brake Application Catalog* for brake parts and looked for suitable brake hose replacements.

I found that a hose designated as "rear" for a 1979 4x4 Toyota pickup (part #77264) actually matched the fittings and layout of the 1976 Land Cruiser's front hose. Although the length of the 77264 hose was much longer than needed, this furnished a prototype configuration.

Turning to the *Identification Guide*, I found the 77264 hose listed with several others. These hoses varied in length, with the 77264 listed as 18 inches. My particular chassis lift called for somewhere around a 13" hose, which was available through Bendix under another part number. (The #77264 Bendix hose is also available from Toyota—as a rear axle brake hose for a 1979 4x4 mini-pickup.)

I found that replacing the Land Cruiser's rear hose was unnecessary, as the factory had drilled another hose bracket hole further rearward on the frame rail. The brake pipe had excess length bent into the tube, just in front of the hose attachment point. By very carefully straightening the frame pipe (while not disturbing its routing or protection from road debris), I attached the hose further back, bolting the support bracket to the rearward frame

Axle Trusses

Pounding off-pavement can bend or break axle housings. Often, 4x4 owners add stiff spring rates and hefty shock absorbers without concern for the axles. If serious trail running or high performance driving is your truck's lot, consider axle trusses as part of your suspension buildup.

Fig. 18-15. *1979–85 Toyota pickup/4Runner solid 4x4 front axle is strong, however, later axle version has a "doubler" on long side of the housing to increase housing support. For 4WD pickups and 4Runners, aftermarket retrofit trusses, like this stout item from Downey Off-Road (Mfg), serve well if your truck receives much off-pavement pounding.*

Fig. 18-16. *Here is Downey Off-Road's combination skid plate/truss for a Toyota truck's rear axle. For low running clearance and rock-crawling, skid plates provide the best protection. Downey, Specter Off-Road, NWOR Specialties, Con-Ferr, and others offer an array of skid plate protection for Toyota truck engine/transmission assemblies. This can add stiffness to the frame while protecting your vital engine and geartrain pieces.*

hole as if it were designed to fit there. The result was exactly enough slack in the flex hose to meet the truck's suspension lift and wheel travel needs. Had the OEM rear hose not worked, I may have found a suitable match in the Bendix catalog.

CAUTION —

When matching hoses, fittings must have the same thread pitch, thread depth, and seats for the pipe flare type (inverted, 45-degree, SAE, etc.). A hose must attach to the bracket in a manner similar to the original hose, assuring solid support at the junction. The hose must provide adequate length without rubbing on the chassis, tires, steering linkage or body parts. When mounting the hose, keep seams running straight. Do not twist the hose (barber pole effect). The hose should move through its entire arc, flexing without kinking or undo stress.

Fig. 18-17. *Brake hoses cannot be neglected on lifted trucks. Here, FJ40's original front hose had little room to move. BTB Products turned to Earl's custom brake hose and fittings (shown) for a solution.*

Fig. 18-18. *With spring/suspension lift, rear hose has become dangerous on this Toyota pickup. Note tension on the hose when springs extend with wheel travel. Cure in this case will involve carefully repositioning the support bracket to place hose in better alignment with axle housing to gain correct slack.*

2. OFF-PAVEMENT SUSPENSION TUNING

Suspension tuning can enhance off-pavement performance. An upgraded spring and shock absorber package transforms a multi-purpose 4x4 into a highly versatile trail machine. The right handling, suspension travel and shock damping provide better vehicle control, stability and greater utility.

Several factors determine the need for spring rate and chassis changes. Conversion to a heavier engine, the addition of a hefty front mounted winch or installing a protective front bumper/brush guard each place a load on the front springs. An oversize fuel tank, heavy duty truck-type manual or automatic transmission, a trailer towing package, a camper shell/cap, a utility or tool box, and heavy fuel and water containers can weight the rear springs.

When your fatigued OEM shocks and sagging springs need replacement, an upgrade spring and shock absorber package can improve your truck's performance. Sagging coil or leaf springs allow the axle housing(s) to rest close to the rubber bump stops. Weak front springs create bounce, sagging and loss of steering precision.

Loss of suspension travel means that your truck will have difficulty negotiating twisty terrain. Traction off-pavement becomes poor, with body roll and steering control problems. If the springs and shock absorbers now show these symptoms on your Toyota truck, or if modestly oversize tires create tire-to-body interference, consider an aftermarket suspension package.

Aftermarket Suspension Improvements

Your goal should be a reasonably firm spring rate and solid traction—without unduly harsh rebound and overly stiff leaf stacks. Spring rebound damping and deflection control remain vital to maximum traction, yet timid shocks lose effectiveness in just a few miles of trail pounding. The best all around kits have "easy ride" springs and quality shock absorbers.

From my experience, a mild lift/soft-ride suspension package provides several benefits. Once installed, these kits maintain a legal frame/front bumper height when used in conjunction with 31- to 33-inch diameter tires. The truck now has greater tire-to-body clearance, a much improved spring rate and improved handling, both on- and off-pavement.

WARNING —

• Use extreme caution when installing a lift kit or otherwise working under your truck. Always support the truck's frame on jackstands rated for the load. Do not rest the vehicle only on a floor jack, on cinder blocks or on pieces of wood.

• Limit your truck's lift to just that amount necessary for safe tire installation and a full range of suspension travel. Select your tire size with care. Follow practical and safe tire and chassis guidelines, and make certain the wheel rim size is correct for your tires.

NOTE —
Before considering a suspension lift kit, consult your state's lift laws on height and track width limits. Select your chassis lift and tire size accordingly.

Shock Absorbers

Single shocks, dual shocks, gas shocks and more...The market is ripe with shock absorbers. What does your Toyota truck need? Which shock works best? Is there a formula for choosing the right shock absorbers? You bet!

Shock absorbers wear out. For some trucks, the shock absorbers fail fast. Why? Shocks deteriorate from high heat, excess friction and overload—symptoms caused by washboard roads and off-pavement poundings.

Most truck shock absorbers look similar, and despite different designs, they each meet the same goals: damping the springs' oscillating motion, limiting the effects of uneven loads transferring to each wheel, and keeping the wheels safely on the ground when the suspension moves violently. This translates as better steering control and an easier seat-of-the-pants ride.

Off-pavement, your truck's suspension travels constantly, with full extension and pounding compression. Damping such forces, the shock absorbers pay severely, often succumbing to leakage or ineffective performance. Driver discomfort and unnecessary chassis or body rattles will usually follow.

The Right Features

When buying replacement shock absorbers for your Toyota truck, consider a twin-tube type, preferably a gas pressurized or cellular gas shock design. Piston head size, rod diameter, seal types and valving design determine the strength, reliability and performance of a shock absorber.

Most OEM telescoping shocks offer meager 1" to 1-1/8" piston diameters. Replacement shocks should have pistons of 1-5/16" or larger size. Popular for many years, the 1-3/8" piston head has satisfied all but the most brutal off-pavement maulers and heavyweight haulers.

Severe Duty Shocks

For heavy duty use, look to a nitrogen gas pressurized shock with a 1-5/8" piston diameter. These brute shocks hover around 200 psi, demanding tremendous piston/rod strength.

Pistons should be O-ring sealed, cylinders double walled and tough. Larger fluid reservoirs provide better cooling and greater resistance to fading. Lastly, precise valving gives the shock absorber its real advantage. The valve's ability to sense terrain and load demands will determine the shock absorber's worth. When working properly, the shock absorbers are a basic element in your truck's suspension system.

Shock mounting grommets and eyes must hold up. A loose shock absorber is useless, and a weak set of grom-

---

Rancho Suspension's RS9000 Shock Absorbers

The term *adjustable shock absorber* has a variety of meanings. Non-air adjustable shocks mean crawling under your truck, removing the units from the chassis and rotating their housings a number of clicks. Adjusting these kinds of shocks is such a hassle that most users wind up using only one setting.

Rancho Suspension has eliminated these obstacles with its RS9000 shock absorber system. The five-position adjustable shocks offer an easily accessible manual valve for setting the compression and rebound damping. An air-compressor actuated option is also available for cab control of the settings while you drive.

Position 1 provides a good highway ride; 2 makes for slightly firmer control; 3, programmed much like the classic RS5000 shock, offers versatile on- and off-road performance; position 4 addresses light to moderate off-roading; and position 5 provides a heavy off-pavement pounding or trailer lugging mode.

A pin-and-slider design, the adjustable valve enhances a proven cellular gas shock design that features 15-stage valving and an advanced tri-tube, mono-flow design.

I have tested the RS9000 shock absorbers and optional air-actuated Remote Control adjusting system. Tests exceeded the point where a standard shock absorber would fade completely—challenges like running a truck repeatedly through desert dry washes, whoops and a modest simulation of an off-road course. This is my top choice for multi-purpose use.

Fig. 18-19. *Rancho RS9000 adjustable shocks offer an optional air-actuated cab control system. Standard valving allows quick five-position adjustment at each shock absorber. Air-actuated adjustment kit allows even faster driver adjustment from the dashboard, even while on the highway or off-pavement.*

mets permits wasted movement and undamped travel. Proper shock absorber angles (a crucial engineering decision) also contribute to handling.

Single Versus Multi-shock Installations

Show trucks, street trucks, lifted trucks and even some OEM suspensions feature multiple shock absorbers. On factory dual-shock installations, the mounting angle and position of the additional shock is vital to the truck's handling. The shocks must counter jarring, chassis/spring oscillation and friction forces along critical paths of frame motion and suspension travel.

Many homespun, multi-shock assemblies defy logic. Few hobbyists have the engineering expertise to properly reposition shock absorbers. Unless looks override every other consideration, do your homework. If your Toyota 4x4 truck or 2WD pre-runner pickup operates off-pavement, begin your suspension buildup around a healthy set of aftermarket replacement shocks.

Urethane Bushings

Polyurethane, a product of mid-1930s German pharmaceutical technology, meets a wide range of automotive chores. Urethane is used in dashboards, arm rests, paints, door panels, foam seats and suspension components.

Urethane suspension and roll cage bushings provide the chassis tuning and durability that many desert racers demand. Recreational four-wheelers and street truck builders also benefit from urethane suspension pieces.

Fig. 18-20. This Toyota 2WD pre-runner pickup boasts a full complement of Downey Off-Road (Manufacturing) suspension modifications. Note shock absorber mounting and generous use of urethane bushings. Urethane comes in a variety of colors. The correct hardness of finished bushings, however, is far more important than color considerations.

Why is urethane desirable? First, unlike rubber products, urethane resists road salt, ozone, gasoline and automotive oils. Precise hardness control provides a variety of stiffnesses for suspension uses. More importantly, urethane offers high resistance to abrasion, yet engineers can factor elasticity into the product during the molding process. Manufacturers of urethane suspension bushings have a large measure of control over the finished product.

The Right Mix For Your Truck's Chassis

Don Bunker, founder of Energy Suspensions in San Clemente, California, comments on the differences in urethane materials. "Obviously," Don notes, "bump stops have to be somewhat soft to perform their duties, where high performance control arm bushings are generally of a firmer durometer hardness for maximum control. Urethane can be as soft as the Slime toys that kids buy or as hard as a bowling ball."

Poor ratio mixes create low quality finished products. Noting the disparity between good and poor product, Don Bunker states flatly, "All urethane is not created equal." He cites the bitter experience of early urethane users who broke eyelets loose from their shock absorbers. Although owners often condemned the shocks, the real problem was the bushings. When excessively hard, the urethane acts as rigid as metal. Shock eyes, which actually travel in an arc, can bind up if the bushings are too hard. Eyelets break from the force.

If you upgrade your truck's chassis with urethane suspension bushings, squeak is not uncommon, especially in twisting situations. Several manufacturers have addressed this problem. Some have graphite-impregnated bushings to counter noise and friction.

Urethane Parts Under Construction

There are two methods of urethane bushing production: injection molding and liquid cold pour casting. Injection molding provides the more precise results. Liquid cold pour castings serve in parts that require less critical tolerances.

Aftermarket urethane producers invest substantially in each bushing mold. Molds determine the fitup and ultimate reliability of the parts. Intricate machining is necessary to produce a quality mold. Correct mixture ratios complete the process, while colorful finishes are merely an aesthetic consideration.

NOTE —
When looking for quality in a urethane sleeved bushing, seek out a product with seamless sleeves.

Where Does Urethane Work Best?

Use in suspension arm, radius rod and stabilizer bushings is popular. Polyurethane bushings allow greater application of force at front and rear stabilizers (unlike the loose action of factory rubber bushings).

Polyurethane mounts offer a major gain over factory rubber cab and body mounts. Unlike aftermarket aluminum spacers, which deliver a rigid and harsh ride, urethane can provide firm yet functional suspension while maintaining the alignment of body panels.

Most lift kits offer urethane bushings for leaf springs and mounting pins, A-arms, and linkage. The trick is to select the right bushings for your particular driving style. Before grabbing the most colorful set off the shelf, consider options like graphite-impregnated products.

If your truck demands more stamina and a finely tuned suspension system, consider the urethane bushing option. The right bushings can drastically improve your truck's steering control and responsiveness.

3. TOYOTA-TO-GM STEERING GEAR CONVERSIONS

The early Toyota Land Cruisers offer less efficient worm-and-roller steering gears. These models, and even the later FJ40 and FJ55 models with recirculating ball manual steering gears, make prime candidates for a GM Saginaw power steering conversion.

GM pioneered the much improved and innovative Saginaw recirculating ball-and-nut manual steering gear in 1940. Twenty-five years later, GM introduced the Saginaw integral power steering gear, relying on the same recirculating ball principle proven in the Saginaw manual type gears.

These Saginaw manual and integral power steering gear assemblies have become the most respected designs in automotive history, the basic design emulated by scores of manufacturers around the globe—including Toyota.

Primitive worm-and-roller type manual steering gears are high in friction and offer much shorter service lives than recirculating ball-and-nut or ball-and-power rack/piston gears. Fortunately, with the exception of only the pre-1973 4WD Land Cruisers, all Toyota trucks covered within this book have benefitted from the use of smooth and durable OEM recirculating ball type steering gears. (T100 4WD models use a recirculating ball integral power gear, while the 2WD chassis uses an innovative power rack-and-pinion assembly that also serves Tacoma 2WD and 4WD pickups.)

RN11 and newer Toyota mini-trucks and all pre-Tacoma compact trucks feature advanced recirculating ball steering gears (power-type available by the late 1970s as an option). 1973-up 4WD Land Cruiser models also benefit from this design. For the Land Cruisers, however, models through the FJ40-series and FJ55 still retain the cumbersome fore-and-aft draglink and center arm (bellcrank) type steering linkage.

GM/Saginaw recirculating ball-and-power piston rack steering offers many benefits. Land Cruiser owners commonly convert to Saginaw power steering using a mounting and steering linkage kit available from Advance Adapters and other suppliers. One of the added advantages of such a kit is the elimination of the bulky center arm steering linkage.

> **WARNING —**
> *When converting to modern power steering, do not weld, cut, bend or modify steering linkage or other steering components. Find the mix of OEM and aftermarket pieces that will enable a simple and safe installation.*

For Land Cruisers, Advance Adapters and BTB Products (see Appendix) offer a pitman arm, steering linkage and plate for mating a Saginaw integral power or manual steering gear to the truck's frame. BTB can provide mounting hardware for installing a GM pump and steering gear in an FJ40 or FJ55 with F or 2F engine.

Instructions found in Advance Adapters' catalog explain the wide range of Saginaw steering gears that will work with your Land Cruiser upgrade. This even includes manual gears for those owners who do not want power steering. These gears are readily available through recycling sources, and in addition to the steering gear assembly, you will need the correct power steering hoses and a matching pump unit, plus engine brackets and drive pulleys.

Retrofitting an integral power steering gear unit may involve welding, fabricating and engineering. If you have limited expertise in this area, do not attempt such a changeover. Seek out a professional shop with experience

Fig. 18-21. *Due to scarcity of 1979–83 Land Cruiser integral OEM power steering gears, most owners opt for the less expensive and practical GM Saginaw retrofit. Advance Adapters' approach eliminates the center arm linkage and provides a direct pitman arm-to-steering arm "short tie-rod" (draglink) for more positive steering. For 1979-up solid axle 4WD pickups with a manual steering gear, Toyota's OEM power steering works best, providing a bolt-on factory retrofit.*

at this type of conversion, and be sure that they have a working knowledge of the task at hand. Some of the credentials needed for a safe installation would include a history of building similar systems on Toyota trucks and also certification as a professional welder. Do not take shortcuts on this kind of work. Controlled and predictable steering is a fundamental requirement for your truck.

Fig. 18-22. *Advance Adapters makes universal brackets for adapting popular Saginaw integral power steering gear units to a Toyota 4x4 Land Cruiser chassis. If your FJ40, FJ45 or FJ55 Land Cruiser needs a power steering conversion, you may find this weld-on frame adapter useful. Wide use of Saginaw integral power steering can provide a range of OEM components to safely complete your installation.*

Choosing the Right Steering Gear

If you make a power or manual steering gear conversion with a Saginaw steering gear assembly, consider the steering gear's ratio and related engineering. The quicker (approximately three turns lock-to-lock) gears are entirely too fast for a Toyota Land Cruiser, and they make a shorter wheelbase model steer like a sprint race car. Avoid these ultra-quick steering ratios. Saginaw four-turn or slower (lock-to-lock) gear assemblies make much

better sense and provide safer steering for your Land Cruiser.

Length of the Pitman arm or steering arms also contributes to the final steering ratio. If you have a choice, select a Pitman arm or steering arms that provide good road feel and still offer correct travel of the steering linkage.

> **CAUTION —**
> *Make sure steering linkage moves freely and on OEM proscribed arcs. Assess how the linkage will react as the wheels turn and as the suspension moves to its extremes.*

When setting up a retrofit steering gear and linkage on a solid front axle 4x4 truck like the Land Cruiser, keep the steering draglink/short tie-rod as close to a level plane as possible. This will help prevent bump steer. Check steering linkage alignment and draglink slope with the truck setting on flat ground and loaded normally.

Make certain that the steering gear does not reach its full range of movement before the knuckles reach their stops. Hyper-extending the steering gear can severely damage the ball races, nut or power rack. Always make sure that the steering gear is on its center with the front wheels and tires in the straight-ahead position.

> **CAUTION —**
> *Power steering retrofit systems require careful engineering. The force of an integral power unit is sufficient to rip a gear loose from the frame. When setting up a power gear and pitman arm, care must be taken to prevent excess pressure build-up when the knuckles turn against their stops.*

Fig. 18-23. *Many 4x4 lift kits contain a raised or dropped pitman arm. NWOR Specialties offers a full line of chassis/suspension lift kits for Toyota 4x4 trucks. Kits use specially engineered and rated new springs, and NWOR can provide the custom pitman or steering arm, or a dropped draglink (bottom) to help prevent bump steer.*

CAUTION —
Consult OEM repair/service manuals for pump and gear pressure specifications. Test your system for correct travel and pressure in all positions.

Handling Kit and Saginaw Steering Conversion

Typically, a V-8 conversion goes along with a suspension lift kit and larger than stock tires. If this is your plan, consider BTB Products' Steering Correction Kit or Ross Stuart's Land Cruiser Advanced Handling/Suspension Correction Kit. These kits reverse the front leaf spring anchor and shackle ends, placing the anchor end at the leading (front) end of the springs—where they belong. This design is similar to the more modern 1979–85 4WD Toyota pickup front end, and the improvement is considerable.

When the springs *trail* from the anchor instead of *pushing forward* as they do with the OEM anchor points, the 4WD Land Cruiser tracks far better and handles much more predictably. When a Land Cruiser FJ40 with stock spring anchors meets an obstacle, the axle wants to drive the front leaf springs into the frame rails. With reversal of the front spring anchor ends, the Land Cruiser's front springs and axle rise gently over obstacles, as the front springs pivot easily from the front end of the springs.

Both kits add approximately one inch to the front end height of the FJ40 chassis. Before mounting a Saginaw conversion steering gear, install the anchor end reversal kit and any suspension/spring lift kit you have planned.

Fig. 18-25. *We installed Ross Stuart's Advanced Handling/Suspension Correction Kit on 1976 "Project Rubicon I" Land Cruiser, along with Saginaw power steering. MIG welder was utilized, although the kit came with premium grades of bolt-on mounting hardware.*

You will want a fixed chassis height before positioning a steering gear and aligning the draglink/short tie-rod with the long tie-rod.

When retrofitting a Saginaw integral power steering gear to the Toyota 4WD Land Cruiser, it's the small items that can hold up the job. For example, General Motors builds many of these power steering gears with common 3/8" tubing, but one flare nut fitting is the popular 5/8" size while the other is an obscure 11/16" (generally found with larger 7/16" tubing).

On my 1976 FJ40 project, this fitting nemesis turned an "I'll be back in twenty minutes." parts run into a three hour tail chase. Finally, the hydraulic hose builder at a tractor and heavy equipment outlet fabricated a high pressure hose and matching couplers to accommodate the odd thread and tubing sizes.

Ironically, the least involved part of the conversion was the steering gear installation. After careful alignment and angling of the gear, coupler shaft, pitman arm and short tie-rod/draglink, the Advance Adapters frame mounting plate was wire-feed MIG welded into place.

NOTE —
Downey Off-Road also offers a steering box mounting plate for 3- and 4-bolt mount Saginaw steering gears. Downey's mount is cast of low carbon mild steel and can be readily welded to the frame.

Fig. 18-24. *I find that reversing the anchor ends of the front springs is a must for an FJ40 Land Cruiser used on hard-core trails. BTB kit (shown) puts your 'Cruiser's front spring anchors where they belong—at the front end of each front spring.*

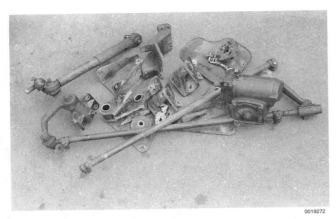

Fig. 18-26. *Each of these steering linkage pieces was discarded with the installation of a GM/Saginaw integral power steering system. Areas where frame rivets were removed, such as the original steering gear pedestal and the original front motor mount supports, were filled by MIG weld to regain strength.*

Fig. 18-27. *Left fender exit tube was modified slightly at #7 cylinder to clear the upper universal joint of the new steering shaft. Shaft was painstakingly routed to allow proper steering gear/pitman arm angle with the least possible angularity at shaft's U-joint. When hybridizing a steering system, even with an aftermarket kit, you must align parts according to your particular chassis and engine requirements.*

Fig. 18-28. *With the original steering linkage removed, a Rancho Suspension damper/stabilizer kit with RS5000 shock absorber makes a functional substitute. Damper helps absorb impact that could otherwise damage power steering gear. This FJ40 was set up by Brian Schreiber of BTB Products.*

I adjusted the draglink with the front wheels pointed dead straight ahead, making sure that the steering gear was at its lock-to-lock dead center point when the tires were in this position. Clamps were secured, and the steering wheel was placed on center, spokes aligned, before the new column coupler was safety MIG-welded to the Toyota steering shaft. The remaining job consisted of hooking power steering hoses to the stock Chevrolet V-8 power steering pump.

NOTE —
If you plan to install a Saginaw power gear and pump on a six-cylinder F or 2F engine, BTB Products offers a pump bracket and pulley and belt system to drive the pump. A power steering pump should have its own drive belt if at all possible.

For tight V-8 conversions (rare with long Land Cruiser engine bays), use the correct water pump and fan spacing to allow for power steering pump clearance. In my case, a Flex-a-Lite stainless steel fan and spacers, used with the correct mid-1970s Chevy V-8 water pump and pulley set, eased the power steering pump installation.

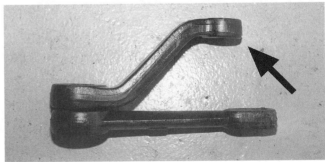

Fig. 18-29. *Steering installation (top) shows Advance Adapters' pitman arm, mounting plate and "spud shaft," which passes through a pair of drilled holes that angle slightly upward at crossmember. Short tie-rod/draglink has metric tie-rod joint at steering arm end and domestic joint for pitman arm end. Overall lift of 3-1/2" created more draglink/short tie-rod slope than planned. Dropped pitman arm (arrow) provided bump steer cure and a shorter center-to-center length that slightly slowed steering ratio. Land Cruiser steered well with this configuration.*

Fig. 18-30. *Driveshaft angles reflect use of a Rancho Suspension lift kit and Land Cruiser Advanced Handling's Suspension Correction kit. Higher chassis height has caused steeper driveshaft departure angles. U-joint/shaft angles match, however, since chassis lift is level, axle caster and pinion shaft angles remain correct, and transfer case output shaft angles still fall within OEM guidelines.*

The addition of power steering to my Land Cruiser, especially with its 33"x12.50"x15" tires on 10-inch wide rims, was the most significant addition I made to the truck's chassis. Use of custom built aftermarket lift springs, Rancho's RS5000 shock absorbers and a new RS5000 steering stabilizer/damper kit added further to the truck's handling.

The Advanced Handling/Suspension Correction Kit lent a new dimension to the steering smoothness and stability of my 1976 Land Cruiser. When tracking over bumps and irregularities, the FJ40 showed no loss of steering control—with stock Land Cruiser steering and suspension, even in "good" condition, the steering wheel must be clutched firmly while the driver remains constantly on the lookout for trail obstacles.

> *CAUTION —*
>
> *Be cautious of driveline length when lifting your truck's chassis with a spring/suspension kit. If necessary, lengthen driveshaft tubes to prevent shafts from separating at splined couplers. Make sure splined couplers operate within their original range of movement. (See chapter covering driveshaft construction.)*

4. TIRES

Preparing your truck for a special environment always includes tires. For maintaining stability on wet or icy roads, rock crawling in rough terrain or scaling a wagon road to an abandoned silver mine, you need the right rubber. Ground clearance, superior traction and resistance to rock abrasions each depend on your tire choices.

Wider wheels and oversize tires will affect the handling characteristics of your truck. Take extreme care when selecting your truck's wheels. When in doubt, always follow the recommendations of the manufacturer.

Fig. 18-31. *Wider wheels are necessary with most oversize tires. This 33"x12.50x15 Bridgestone Desert Dueler tire mounts on Golden Wheel Corporation's Enkei 89-series one piece alloy rim. Rim bead width is ten inches. These tires could safely fit a chassis/suspension lifted Toyota Land Cruiser or properly modified 1979–85 Toyota solid front axle 4WD pickup.*

> *CAUTION —*
>
> *Wider wheels and oversize tires usually require other changes to your truck. Larger tires and wheels may place excessive stress on suspension components, including bearings, hubs, spindles, knuckles, and brakes.*

There are mildly and wildly oversize wheels and tires. Oversize tires run anywhere from one or two sizes larger than your stock Toyota truck's rubber to monstrous tires. Concerned with safety and liability issues, the majority of light truck tire manufacturers limit their maximum tire sizes to 35" diameter.

For highly specialized uses, 36" to 44" tires are available from a small number of producers. An even smaller number of wheel manufacturers cater to the safety standards necessary for handling specialty rubber.

Why is 35" the usual limit? When it comes to mounting massive rubber on a light truck, tire manufacturers don't have time to conduct safety schools. Product abuse and consumer negligence occur regularly in this realm.

Where Do Monster Tires Serve Best?

Lifted show trucks and boulevard cruisers have monster tires. Are these tires simply an artistic expression?

Not always. The 35" to 44" tire is also a workhorse. At highly specialized jobsites, such as logging and mining operations, heavy loads and deep mud packs make a rubber-tire loader cringe. Here, a heavy duty 3/4- or one-ton rated truck, given the unceremonious task of lugging supplies and equipment over miles of primitive road, can benefit from jumbo tires.

Warren Guidry of Interco Tire Corporation comments on the merits of monster tires. "For 4WD vehicles to obtain their full potential, bigger tires need to be used. Nothing will raise the axles except the tires, which in turn gives greater ground clearance, and this is very important to off-road use."

Obviously, there's a limit to monster tire use. These tires, which mount on specially built rims, fit a radically lifted truck. Huge tires require an elaborate spring and body lift for clearance, plus many other modifications to the engine, chassis, geartrain, steering and brakes.

Way Up Has Its Downside.

While a certain look and self-expression has its place, mounting huge 100 pound tires on a half-ton rated Toyota 4WD pickup or 4WD Land Cruiser equipped with four-wheel drum brakes overrides all safety considerations. For some Toyota trucks, even a 32" diameter tire could threaten chassis and axle safety and create a precariously high center of gravity.

Making any mini-, compact or intermediate class truck safe with the mass and unsprung weight of 36–44" tires involves radically altering the track width, brakes, power-

Fig. 18-32. *Handling big rubber means serious chassis, engine and geartrain modifications. Full-floating 3/4-ton truck rear axles are common on show trucks, and a very large tire size demands the safety advantages of a full-floater. Sadly, some Toyota 4WD pickup owners attempt to run this size tire with a stock powertrain and geartrain, which results in dangerously overtaxing the steering, brakes, engine, clutch, transmission and axles.*

train, steering and suspension. Neither Toyota nor any other truck builder in these classes offers an OEM brake

---

Tire Glossary

Bias (Diagonal) Ply: Before radial tires, all trucks rode on bias ply tires. Bias plies run in a diagonal direction to the tire centerline. Plies cross in an X pattern, making a very strong but stiff tire. Today's truck owners demand the better ride and handling of radial ply designs.

Load Carrying Capacity: All highway-legal tires have load capacity ratings (A, B, C, etc.). Inflation pressure, however, affects a tire's load capacity. Ratings apply to each tire size and design. Lower pressures decrease load carrying capacity.

Maximum Inflation: This is a tire's air pressure limit, which influences load carrying capacity. A tire with a load range C and a maximum inflation pressure of 36 PSI may have a 3,000 pound rating. This means that the tire can support 3,000 pounds at 36 PSI inflation. As pressure drops, so does the tire's carrying capacity. Beware.

Ply Rating: Plies are supporting layers of synthetic cord and/or steel built into a tire casing. These layers or belts mold within the tire's rubber. Ply ratings for big radial tires can get confusing. Load range C tires qualify for a traditional 6-ply rating. A closer look, however, may reveal a 4-ply tread and 2-ply sidewall. Plies also vary in thickness and strength, so evaluate a tire by its load rating, the ply materials and overall construction.

PSI: Pounds per Square Inch refers to the air pressure in your tires. Adding air increases PSI, while airing down reduces pressure. Always maintain your tires at recom-

mended inflation levels. If you drop pressure too low, your tubeless tire may unseat from the rim. Excess air pressure can damage the plies or destroy a bead.

Radial Ply: Belts, whether steel or synthetic cord, circle the tire at a perpendicular angle to its tread centerline. Radial belts flex, allowing the sidewalls to cushion the ride. Tread conforms to the road, providing a better grip. Most new tires, including 36" to 44" monster tires, are radials.

Rim Offset: Wheel rim offset determines track width and frame/tire clearance. Rarely is a wheel's mounting flange aligned with the centerline of the tire. OEM rims offset toward the brake assembly. Aftermarket wheels must take OEM engineering into account, including back-spacing and negative (outboard) or positive (inboard) rim offset from the wheel mounting flange. Otherwise, stress to wheel bearings, spindles, axle shafts and steering components can occur. Steering geometry, tire wear, and handling are all affected by rim offset.

Rim Width: Rim width is the space between the outer faces of the tire beads. This measurement is crucial, and every tire has a rim width requirement. Sidewall and tread shape, the bead angle and even the vehicle's handling depend on rims that correctly match the tires.

Speed Rating: Although most trucks with big tires stay within posted speed limits, speed ratings also indicate a tire's margin of safety. Symbols represent maximum speed: S to 112 mph; T to 118 mph; H to 130 mph; V to 149 mph; and Z over 149 mph. Take heed.

system capable of safely handling the rolling mass of four 44" diameter, 130-pound tire and wheel assemblies.

In my experience, a 33"x12.50x15 tire on a 10-inch wide rim is the largest practical tire for a safe suspension lift (2-1/2" to 3" maximum chassis lift) on a 4WD Land Cruiser or 4WD Toyota solid front axle pickup. 1986-up IFS 4WD models have rim offset and front end geometry limitations that restrict safe tire diameter to a maximum of 32-inches on an 8- or 9-inch rim width. Some users go well beyond these rim and tire sizes—at their own risk.

Furthermore, manufacturers match gearing to their trucks' OE tire diameter. If your Toyota truck has 30" diameter OE tires and a 4.11:1 axle gear ratio, a switch to 44" tires (if you could ever find a way to fit such a size) would require an axle ratio(s) slightly over 6:1 to restore the engine's original operating rpm.

For Toyota 4WD trucks, the switch to 4.88:1 and 5.29:1 gearsets is a somewhat common antidote for oversized tires. Be aware that 4.88:1 or 5.29:1 ring and pinion gear strength is less than that of 3.70:1 or even 4.11:1 gears. Lower (numerically higher) axle gearsets require a smaller pinion gear tooth count, while ring gear diameter remains nearly the same.

This weakens tooth strength, and it is not uncommon to lose the pinion gear teeth on an ultra low gearset under severe load. The only solution is a larger axle assembly with a bigger ring gear diameter and larger pinion gearhead. I do not support the practice of fitting Toyota 4WD axles with gearsets lower (numerically higher) than 4.56:1 or 4.88:1 ratio.

The radically lifted 4x4 show trucks have extensive frame, suspension, geartrain and engine upgrades to handle their taller vehicle profile and huge rubber. If you're serious about duplicating this look, don't stop with wheels, tires and a spring and body lift. Pay attention to the rest of your truck's needs, those engineering measures that will maintain tractability plus safe handling, steering and braking. Protect your engine, clutch and geartrain as well.

Safety First

"The truth is," Warren Guidry notes, "if a vehicle is professionally modified to accommodate larger tires, and if the larger tires are not just taller but also wider, the vehicle can be more stable than when it was stock..."

Guidry concludes, "The wider tire and wheel combination increases the track of the vehicle and adds a tremendous amount of stability. The bigger, wider tires can carry more load with the same air pressure, and because of the greater volume of air are not under the load stresses that the smaller tires have to bear, and are thereby safer."

There's a clear relationship between track width and center of gravity. The savvy state laws, those that aim at restoring a stable center of gravity, suggest the use of a wider track width whenever height changes have been made to a vehicle.

As Warren Guidry suggests, the professional modification of a vehicle takes safety factors into account. If you're unsure of the safety requirements for your truck, consult a race or show truck fabricator who has built his or her credential around truck safety.

In general, larger tires represent more unsprung weight, which immediately suggests stouter springs,

Fig. 18-33. *The B.F. Goodrich Baja T/A tire (right), developed through actual desert racing tests, is an excellent off-pavement performer. Hard compound makes a harsher ride, but sidewall stamina is outstanding in rocky terrain.*

hefty gangs of shock absorbers, added steering stabilization, traction bars or torsion arms and a whole arsenal of heavy duty wheel and brake parts. Oversize brake rotors, pads, rear brake shoes and drums—even heavier drive axles—may be necessary.

NOTE—
Most custom 4x4 trucks that run 39" and larger diameter tires have full-floating rear axles. The full-floater adds stamina plus better wheel and axle bearing support.

Shock loads transfer back through the entire geartrain to the engine. U-joint upgrades, increased driveshaft wall thickness and/or diameter and other precautions help assure parts survival. Also, by changing axle gearing to restore the original engine speed at a given road speed, you'll give the manual clutch or automatic transmission a chance to survive. Even so, consider upgrading the clutch or torque converter to handle the extra inertial loads of big tires.

A Tried Trail Running Formula

I've never installed tires larger than 33" diameter on any of my 4x4 trucks, including domestic 3/4-ton 4x4 models with full-floating axles. I firmly believe that driving skill and a decent tire will handle even the most challenging off-pavement environments. Beyond a mud-bog racer, logging rig or swampland runner, successful traction for your truck is as close as a good tread pattern on a set of moderately oversized tires.

Specifically, I believe that a 31"x10.50x15 tire is adequate for a relatively stock Toyota 4x4 truck. This size tire should not require modifying the body or chassis height. These tires are very popular for this chassis type.

Wider and bigger tires, like a 33"x12.50x15 will also work on Land Cruisers and solid front axle (1979–85) 4WD pickups with a suspension lift kit. Match the tire load range to your truck's fully loaded weight.

The only drawback to a very wide tire on a light-weight truck is the high flotation effect of the wide tire print. Such tires work great on sand, but a narrower tire would provide safer traction on ice and snow.

The 7.60x15 and 7.00x16 size tires and narrow wheel rims on early FJ43 and FJ45 4WD Land Cruiser pickup models teach a good lesson. These trucks, at curb weights of around 3,500-3,800 pounds and GVWRs of 5,000 to 6400 pounds, get exceptional traction in rock and packed snow. The narrower tread places more weight on each tire print.

Tread design advantages provide a more realistic indicator of tractability, which often has little to do with tire size. The newer 15- and 16-inch diameter (narrower) OE wheels will work fine if you select an appropriate tread pattern for your driving environment.

You can choose from a host of tire tread patterns. Fifty years of off-pavement testing, complemented by three decades of desert racing, have produced specialized and multipurpose tread patterns for a wide range of light truck uses.

Tire Inflation and Other Safety Concerns

Despite nail holes, rock punctures and other natural hazards of four-wheeling or back country driving, the number one cause of tire blowout is under-inflation. Low tire pressure places tremendous stress on sidewalls and generates unsafe heat levels.

Interco tire, manufacturer of Super Swamper tires, notes, "Do not allow the air pressure to get below 20 PSI regardless of how light the vehicle may be. Pressures below 20 PSI may let the bead of the tire become unseated, especially from lateral forces. An exception would be while running in soft sand, where you may wish to reduce air pressure below 20 PSI. This should be an emergency procedure only. As soon as possible, pressure must be brought back up. Remember, overloading and/or under-inflation causes excessive heat build up which can cause separation of the tire body."

Like all other tire manufacturers, Interco recommends that you maintain correct air pressure, checking each tire cold at least once a month. (Cold means the truck has parked out of direct sunlight at least 3 hours.)

Match pressure to the weight of your truck and its current load. Remember, maximum load capacity is at the maximum pressure rating for the tire. If you lower the pressure to improve the ride, or for any other reason, load capacity also decreases. Deceptively, big tires stand up easily, so give them more than a glance.

CAUTION —
Invest in a quality tire pressure gauge—cheap gauges seldom read the same pressure twice.

Tire wear depends on proper wheel alignment, inflation pressures, balancing and rotation. Interco recommends tire rotation at 2,500 to 4,000 miles. The traditional pattern of rotation for radial tires has been front-to-rear and rear-to-front. Some manufacturers now recommend a modified cross-rotation method. Consult your tire manufacturer for proper tire rotation procedures.

Many oversize tires benefit from balancing on the truck. When you have your tires balanced with a floor balancer (wheels mounted on the truck), tire rotation in-

Fig. 18-34. *An extra set of tires, mounted and balanced on less exotic steel rims, make a good investment for your truck. Consider a specialized tread pattern designed for your recreational driving terrain. Install the mounted and balanced tires when you're ready to tackle the rough stuff.*

volves one more step: Your tires will require re-balancing. Once rotated, or even re-positioned on the wheel hub, the tire balance changes. Beware!

Installing Wheels On The Truck

Your new tires, safely mounted to the correct rim, may be ready to install—but are the OE wheel studs and nuts ready? Grossly oversize wheel and tire packages have a lot of mass. Even if your new wheels fit the axle hub flange properly, there's still the matter of stamina. The inertial load may place excess stress on your truck's OE wheel studs.

WARNING —
Some aftermarket wheel flanges are much thicker than a stock-length OEM wheel stud can safely handle. If wheel nuts do not fit securely onto the studs, you should install longer wheel studs or select another wheel type.

Toyota trucks use metric size wheel studs. Toyota 2WD trucks have five wheel studs, while 4WD trucks use six wheel studs. Typically, wheel stud diameter increases with GVWR, and some Toyota cargo van and motorhome chassis use metric wheel studs and nuts designed like those found on one-ton and larger load capacity domestic trucks with full-floating rear axles and dual wheels.

NOTE ——

Before mounting a set of monster alloy wheels and big tires, consider the OEM wheel stud size. Consult your wheel and tire manufacturers for their recommendations. Your tires and wheels may demand an upgrade in either stud diameter or length.

Be sure to tighten the wheel nuts securely. Use a torque wrench to prevent under- or over-tightening. Overtorquing is a common cause of wheel damage and stud breakage, especially on models that use smaller diameter studs. Toyota and aftermarket wheel manufacturers recommend specific torque settings. (Consult your Toyota truck repair manual or owner's glovebox handbook for tightening specifications.)

Factory torque settings take load, braking, vehicle weight and stud diameter into account. For safety sake, use a torque wrench whenever possible to establish and verify the final torque setting. Always tighten wheel nuts gradually and in cross. This prevents distortion of the rim and damage to nut seats.

Choosing Wheels

Big tires increase unsprung mass, raise load capacities and present special mounting concerns. Many OE and aftermarket wheels cannot match the big tire loads. Mickey Thompson/Alcoa and Clement Composite wheels address big tire requirements.

Other wheel suppliers, including Golden Wheel Corporation, Ultra Wheel and American Racing Equipment, satisfy a broad cross-section of user needs. Before selecting wheels, make sure that the load rating and warranty will satisfy your big tire demands.

Sources For Big Specialty Tires

CAUTION ——

Many of the tires and wheels described in this section exceed reasonable size standards for stock or commonly modified Toyota 4x4 trucks, and much of this information will be applicable only to the show or "monster" truck builder. The entire chassis, geartrain and engine must undergo upgrading to accommodate the more radical tire and wheel sizes. Check your state's lift and chassis height laws before considering any of the radical tire and wheel sizes described here.

For most four-wheel drive uses, tires built by major tire companies like B.F. Goodrich, Goodyear, General Tire, Michelin, Yokohama or Bridgestone provide excellent selection and tread patterns for back country and multi-purpose use. When your plans lean toward the ex-

traordinary, however, several specialty manufacturers produce 36" and larger diameter monster tires.

When shopping for your truck's tires, look closely at construction, ply ratings and the load capacity, not just diameter and price.

Interco's Swamper Tires: The original 78-series Swamper tire has been around for over a quarter century. Originally a 6- or 8-ply bias ply tire, Swamper offers a popular tread pattern. Interco also builds grossly oversize tires, including the Super Swamper TSL 36"x12.50-15LT through 18.5/44-15 sizes and a 18.5/44-16.5 tire. These heavy duty bias ply tires with massive lugs and self-cleaning ability meet on- and off-pavement demands for the 4x4 truck with an ultra stout, highly modified chassis and appetite for massive rubber.

Super Swamper Radial/TSL tires come in LT315/85R15, 38x15.50R15 and 38x15.50R16.5LT sizes. These are smooth riding, low noise level biggies with a six-ply rating. If noise, handling and ride are top priorities, consider these tires. For severely rugged and rocky terrain, Super Swamper's TSL/SX comes in 36x12.50-15 and 16.5 sizes and rates six plies with a nylon bias body and steel belt reinforcement under the tread. Sidewall lugs protect and add extra traction in ruts and rocks.

Gateway Buckshot and Gumbo Mudders: Campfire talk has the Buckshot Radial Mudder pegged as the hot setup for tall, narrow traction. The QR78-15LT and QR78-16 varieties fit the 36" big tire category, yet they still fit a 7JJx15 or 6.5Hx16 rim. These are tubeless, 6-ply rated tires with a polyester and steel belt cord. Stiff bead areas and

Fig. 18-35. Buckshot Radial Mudder provides a high traction option for users who want a narrower wheel width.

provision for ice and snow studs make the Buckshot a versatile choice, without the need for exotic wheels.

Also available are the Buckshot Wide Mudder, Buckshot Metric Radial Mudder and the famed Gumbo Monster Mudders. Gumbo Monster series tires fit the big tire category with ease. These tires begin at 36-inch diameter and grow to 43.6" giants for 15" or 16.5" rims. Tread widths for the 6-ply rated tires range from 10.4" to 14.1", which requires wide rims. For the radial user, the Gumbo Monster Radial Mudder is available in 36–38" sizes with a width of 10.4" to 10.7" (cross-sections 14.2" to 15.2"). These radials require 10x15 and 9.75x16.5 rims.

Mickey Thompson Tires/Alcoa Wheels: Mickey Thompson and off-road desert racing go back to the beginning. Mickey Thompson's Baja-Belted polyester and fiberglass belt tires offer an aggressive tread pattern with a soft ride, long wear and Sidebiters for extra traction. The Tall Baja-Belted tire line offers several big tire sizes, including 15/39 and 18/39 for 15" and 16.5" rims.

Mickey Thompson has joined with Alcoa Aluminum to produce the M/T Alcoa Aluminum Wheel. Most wheel manufacturers void their warranties when you mount really big tires. Alcoa has engineered these wheels of one-piece forged aircraft aluminum, with a non-porous and leak proof surface. Polished and machined for a 0.020" maximum runout, these wheels have a 2600 or 3000 pound load rating, depending upon application. Available in 15" x 10", 12" or 14" width (3000 pound rated) and 8" width (2600 pound rated), these wheels are available in popular 5- and 6-lug truck patterns.

Dick Cepek Tires: Dick Cepek is a household name among four-wheeling recreationalists. A full line of vehicle parts and accessories, plus outdoor equipment, makes Cepek a one-stop shopping center for four-wheelers. When buyers want tires, Dick Cepek has a full line to match every need.

Radial F-C/Fun Country tires aim at mileage. As a steel belted flotation tire, these tires run quietly, yet the tread design offers self-cleaning. These are legitimate

Fig. 18-37. Dick Cepek Radial F-C offers the ride and handling benefits of a radial tire. Radial tires satisfy users who do most of their driving on the highway but still need superior traction off-pavement.

mud and snow tires, much like the popular Fun Country nylon bias-ply design. Dick Cepek's Mud Country I tires can be used for snow plowing or logging trails, while Mud Country II boasts better flotation characteristics.

Cepek has also introduced a Super Wide Radial F-C tire available to 38" diameter. These tires concentrate on width, providing all around performance in mud, snow, sand, rock and on the highway. Quietness, an aggressive tread design, steel belts (for a 50,000 mile limited warranty) and tread at least 4" wider than competitors' tires distinguish the Super Wide Radial F-C.

Goodyear—One Big Wrangler RT: Goodyear Tire and Rubber Company is the only major tire producer to offer a tire in the really big category. The Wrangler RT-GC0530 provides a rugged, multipurpose tread design and is available in 36-12.50-16.5 size only. Hummer drivers would recognize this design, as Goodyear developed the tire for military use on this vehicle.

Although Goodyear offers a complete line of Wrangler light truck radial tires, the RT is its only entry in the 36" or larger market. If you're looking for big tires, these load range C biggies may meet your needs. (Order under Goodyear's product code No. 309-552-321.)

Denman Tires' Ground Hawg: Denman's line of big tires has a huge following with the 4x4 show truck crowd. The Ground Hawg is a beefy tire, hell-bent for maximum traction. For a flexible tread and superior traction, Denman delivers radial benefits with a deep, self-cleaning tread design. The biggest Ground Hawg tire is 18.5/44x16.5 inches.

Fig. 18-36. M/T Alcoa aluminum wheels carry a rating for big tires. Load capacity to 3000 pounds with 8", 10", 12" or 14" widths.

Fig. 18-38. Goodyear builds highway and light off-pavement tires like the all-weather Wrangler GS-A and Aqua-Tred light truck types. These tires suit winter commuters, skiers and those who spend long hours on pavement with occasional gravel road jaunts. I particularly like the ride quality and longevity of the Wrangler GS-A. Goodyear's Workhorse Extra Grip is an industrial-commercial design that also deserves attention.

5. BRAKE SYSTEM UPGRADES

Years ago, one cure for undersize brakes on domestic trucks and early (pre-1971) Toyota Land Cruisers was to retrofit an in-line Bendix Hydrovac booster (common to older medium duty trucks with hydraulic brakes). This fix applies more pressure to the hydraulic cylinders and brake shoes, which also raises the likelihood of either hazardous brake fade or rupture of a fluid seal. *This is not the fix for a weak brake system.*

Fortunately, even the earliest Land Cruisers have adequate brake shoe and drum sizing for models of their era. In good condition, with the hydraulic system functioning properly and the brake shoe and drum surfaces in top shape, an early four-wheel drum brake Toyota Land Cruiser or mini-pickup truck can stop reasonably well.

Before the introduction of disc front brakes, a Toyota truck with four-wheel drum brakes could match the braking performance of any other truck in its weight class. When I restored the braking system of my stock 1971 Land Cruiser FJ40 (four-wheel drum brakes with an OEM

vacuum-assist power booster), I found the brakes matched or exceeded the brake capacity and performance of any 4x4 domestic light truck with four-wheel drum brakes.

By comparison, however, my 1976 FJ40's four-piston caliper, power assisted disc front brakes were vastly superior to the earlier 'Cruiser four-wheel drum braking. In fact, for its curb weight, the 1976-up FJ40 has exceptionally good brake performance. Similarly, when Toyota mini-pickups switched to power-assisted disc front brakes in 1975, they also gained considerable brake performance— including greater resistance to fade when under load.

Hydraulic Brake System Improvements

Before 1967, most brake system manufacturers recommended annual flushing and rebuilding of all hydraulic brake cylinders. Although some vehicles tolerate years of neglect without a brake system flush or rubber cup/seal replacement, 4x4s and other off-pavement use trucks are far more susceptible to fluid contamination and subsequent parts failure.

Many 1967-up domestic truck tandem master cylinders have air bellows in the master cylinder cap gasket. A bellows gasket completely seals the system and eliminates the need for a master cylinder vent to atmosphere. Problems like moisture damage and contamination from debris, dust or corrosives occur far less often with a bellows type master cylinder seal.

NOTE —

Although 1967 and newer Toyota trucks have safer tandem master cylinders, Toyota remained committed to master cylinder filler caps that do not offer the full-seal capability of a tightly secured bellows gasket. Serving as a vent to atmosphere, a filler cap can draw moisture and dust particles over time. (See brake chapter for more details.)

A tandem master cylinder is a safety item for the Land Cruiser or 4WD pickup/4Runner that travels the backcountry. If you accidently tear a brake pipe or hose at the front or rear axle, the hydraulic brakes still work at the opposite axle. For the pre-1967 single line master cylinder, a leak anywhere in the system can quickly lead to complete failure of the hydraulic braking system—with no warning to the driver.

One cure for the pre-1967 Land Cruiser single line master cylinder is to custom fit a 1967 or newer Toyota or domestic tandem master cylinder system, including necessary pedal linkage and hydraulic hardware. If you use a domestic master cylinder, you will need metric adapter fittings that meet DOT standards for use on a hydraulic braking system. You may also need a brake proportioning or "combination" valve to properly meter front-and-rear brake fluid flow.

Toyota's hydraulic clutch master cylinder is a separate unit, so you can retain the Toyota hydraulic clutch master cylinder. Along with the tandem brake master cylinder, you might also consider a vacuum brake booster with proper pedal linkage—make certain that your hydraulic wheel cylinders are in top condition. Always use brake hardware approved and rated by the SAE and D.O.T., including fittings and double-flared brake tubing.

> **WARNING —**
> *On any hydraulic system modification, make certain that the master cylinder bore and brake pipe sizing can move enough fluid to safely operate the brakes.*

Upgrading or modernizing the wheel brake system of any truck may require special hydraulic system components to meet the demands of a disc brake rotor/caliper conversion or the retrofitting of bigger brake shoes, drums, wheel hubs and wheel cylinders. For baseline engineering, begin with a prototype OEM braking system that will meet your braking demands. Select wheel brake parts and hydraulic components that make up this prototype system. Try to duplicate the complete OEM package to assure a proper match of wheel brake components and hydraulic system parts.

> **WARNING —**
> *Find a safe place to perform braking tests. Determine whether front-to-rear brake system balance (proportioning) is correct. If required, a variety of OEM or adjustable aftermarket proportioning valves are available.*

MANUALS AND BOOKS

Your first source of information for the repair and maintenance of a Toyota truck is the genuine OEM Toyota repair manual and owner's handbook for your model. Become familiar with the wording and flow of these factory manuals. They are the best beginning for learning how to repair any sub-system of your Toyota chassis, engine or geartrain. The only limitation is tools, work space, parts availability, and your own repair skills.

OEM Toyota repair manuals are often available through your local Toyota dealership. For rarer or older model Land Cruisers, you will find Specter Off-Road is a valuable resource; Downey Off-Road also carries some of the genuine Toyota workshop manuals. If demand for information on these models continues, I am optimistic that reprints of early OEM Toyota truck repair manuals will become available.

An OEM Toyota repair manual covers a specific range of body types, powertrains, geartrains and chassis for a given model year or series of years. Some factory manuals require sets, such as *Engine* and *Chassis*, the latter consisting of gear, body, chassis (steering and suspension) and electrical coverage. Models covered in an OEM Toyota repair manual typically address the Land Cruiser, Pickup, Tacoma, 4Runner, or T100.

See your local Toyota truck dealership's parts department for availability of official Toyota repair manuals. For an older model, you may need to consult a used book source that specializes in automotive literature. (Several advertise in *Hemmings Motor News*.) Insist on original OEM Toyota manuals if you want the most up-to-date and model-specific data.

Catalogs from Advance Adapters (engine and transmission conversions for trucks, including Toyota models) serve as useful reference guides for geartrain interchangeability and component applications. Similarly, catalogs from Specter Off-Road, Downey Off-Road, BTB Products and NWOR Specialties offer valuable reference information.

MAPS AND TRAVEL GUIDES

A variety of map sources and atlas guides serve back country travelers. My favorite references are U.S. Forest Service and B.L.M. topographical maps and the popular state-by-state atlas guides built around these types of maps.

Specialty map sources include the series by Sidekick, which produces a range of maps on California and Baja California four-wheel drive trails. A Sidekick Map details each region, including highlights of local sites, the area's history, minesites, ghost towns, directions from major highways, access costs, camping facilities and public agency offices in the area. Sidekick map/pamphlets are printed on high quality paper stock and include color pictures.

Sidekick
12475 Central Avenue, Suite 352
Chino, CA 91710
714-628-7227

PARTS

Your Toyota truck is a popular vehicle, and parts availability seldom presents a problem. The local Toyota dealer can provide pieces for most 1970 and newer models, and experience has taught me to buy Genuine Toyota filters whenever available.

In addition to Toyota dealerships, you will find a wide variety of Toyota parts sources throughout the United States and Canada. Outfits like Specter Off-Road and local retail auto parts houses can supply tune-up, powertrain and even chassis/steering parts. (Not many aftermarket/OEM-replacement chassis or steering parts are available for older Land Cruisers. Here, Specter Off-Road's can help.)

For geartrain parts, try your local Toyota dealership, Specter Off-Road (especially for older Land Cruisers), 4-Wheel Parts, BTB Products, Dick Cepek, Inc., and Reider Racing Enterprises/Precision Gear. These outlets can provide OEM or aftermarket performance components.

APPENDIX 1: SOURCES

Axle, Transfer Case and Transmission Service

ARB Air Locker
564 Valley Street
Seattle, WA 98109
206-284-5906
Traction differentials

Dyneer/Tractech
11445 Stephens Drive
P.O. Box 882
Warren, MI 48089-3860
313-759-3850
Traction differentials

Lock-Right/Powertrax
245 Fischer Ave., #B-4
Costa Mesa, CA 92626
714-545-7400
Locking differentials

M.I.T.
1112 Pioneer Way
El Cajon, California 92020
619-579-7727

TSM
4321 Willow Creek Road #7
Castle Rock, CO 80104
303-688-6882
Disc brake conversions

Electrical

Wrangler Power Products
P.O. Box 12109
Prescott, AZ 86304
602-717-1771
Upgrades, portable welders

Premier Welder/Pull-Pal
P.O. Box 639
Carbondale, CO 81623
800-541-1817
Portable welders

Ron Francis's Wire Works
167 Keystone Road
Chester, PA 19013
800-292-1940
Custom wiring/harnesses

Engine/Transmission Conversion Kits

Advance Adapters
P.O. Box 247
Paso Robles, CA 93447
805-238-7000

Novak Enterprises
P.O. Box 1185
Whittier, CA 90609-1185
213-921-3202

Engine/High Performance

ACCEL
175 N. Branford Road
Branford, CT 06405-2810
203-481-5771
Performance Ignition

Bonded Motors
7522 S. Maie Avenue
Los Angeles, CA 90001
213-583-8631
Engine rebuilding

Cadillac Motorsports Development
3705-3 Century Blvd.
Lakeland, FL 33811
Cadillac V-8 conversions

Camden Superchargers
401M E. Braker Lane
Austin, TX 78753
512-339-4772

Clifford Performance Products
2330 Pomona-Rincon Road
Corona, CA 91720
714-734-3310
In-line six-cylinder specialists

Crower
3333 Main Street
Chula Vista, CA 91911-5899
619-422-1191
Specialty camshafts

Edelbrock
2700 California St.
Torrance, CA 90509
213-781-2222
Manifolds, camshafts, carburetors

Flex-A-Lite Fans
P.O. Box 9037
Tacoma, WA 98409
206-475-5772
Engine and transmission cooling

J&S Engineering (Electronics)
Box 2199
Garden Grove, CA 92642-2199
714-534-6975
Electronic spark retard system

Jacobs Electronics
500 N. Baird St.
Midland, TX 79701
800-626-8800
Ignition specialty items

K&N Engineering
P.O. Box 1329
Riverside, CA 92502
714-684-9762
Filtration products

MSD/Autotronic Controls Corp.
1490 Henry Brennan Drive
El Paso, TX 79936
915-857-5200
Ignitions

Paxton Superchargers
1260 Calle Suarte
Camarillo, CA 93012
310-450-4800

Racing Head Service/RHS
3410 Democrat Road
Memphis, TN 38118
901-794-2830
Custom engines and buildup kits

Speed-Pro Performance/Sealed Power
100 Terrace Plaza
Muskegon, MI 49443
616-724-5688
OEM/high performance components

T.C.K. Enterprises
9540 Pathway Street #102
Santee, CA 92071
619-448-0899
4WD engine/transmission conversions

Toyota Racing Development: TRD, U.S.A.
335 E. Baker St.
Costa Mesa, CA 92626
714-444-1188

Exterior Trim, Tops, Light Bars, Roll Cages, Seat Harnesses, Misc.

Azara International
4701 S.W. 45th Street
Ft. Lauderdale, FL 33314
305-791-3451
Grilles and brush guards

Beachwood Canvas Works
39 Lake Ave.
Island Heights, NJ 08732
908-929-3168
Restoration canvas and upholstery

Bell Auto Racing
Route 136 East
Rantoul, IL 61866
217-893-9300
Harnesses/safety equipment

BMC/Hi-Lift Jack Company
46 West Spring Street
Bloomfield, IN 47424
1-800-233-2051
Jacking and tie-down systems

BTB Products
825 Civic Center Drive #8
Santa Clara, CA 95050
408-984-5444
Land Cruiser suspension, conversion kits, roll cages

Bushwhacker
9200 N. Decatur
Portland, OR 97203
503-283-4335
Fender flares, protective trim items

California Mini Trucks, Inc.
6600-B McDivitt Drive
Bakersfield, CA 93313
1-800-255-MINI
Performance and bolt-on accessories

Colorado Consoles
1024 E. Costilla
Colorado Springs, CO 80903
1-800-859-0668
Cab consoles

Con-Ferr Mfg.
123 South Front St.
Burbank, CA 91502
818-848-2230
Suspension, skid plates, fuel tanks, seats, etc.

Country Craft
P.O. Box 62
Norco, CA 91760
714-279-4360
Sidebar covers

Dee-Zee Manufacturing, Inc.
P.O. Box 3090
Des Moines, IA 50316
1-800-779-2102
Body accessories, running boards, etc.

Explorer/Pro-Comp
14111 So. Kingsley Drive
Gardena, CA 90249
310-323-7767
Suspension kits, lighting, bumpers

Filler Products
9017 San Fernando Rd.
Sun Valley, CA 91352
818-768-7770
Racing safety equipment

Garvin Industries
316 Millar Avenue
El Cajon, CA 92020
Grilles, bumpers

Grant Products
700 Allen Avenue
Glendale, CA 91201
213-849-3171
Steering wheels

Grizzly/Mercury Tube
1802 Santo Domingo Ave.
Duarte, CA 91010
818-301-0226
Steel tubing bumpers; utility products

Hobrecht
15632 Commerce Lane
Huntington beach, CA 92649
714-893-8561
Roll cages/steel tubing products/ running boards

I Love Trucks
18327 Napa Street
Northridge, CA 91325
818-993-3111
Body accessories, A/C parts

J. Craig
P.O. Box 723852
Atlanta, GA 30339
1-800-551-3524
4Runner, Pickup accessories

Malotte Manufacturing Company
P.O. Box 305
Lincoln, CA 95648
1979–83 fiberglass replacement beds

Man-A-Fre Catalog
5076 Chesebro Road
Agoura, CA 91301
Land Cruiser parts

Mark's Off Road Enterprises
437 N. Moss
Burbank, CA 91502
1-818-953-9230
FJ40 Land Cruiser parts

Mountain Enterprises
P.O. Box 537
El Toro, CA 92630
1-800-869-LIPS
Fender well liners

Northwest Off-Road Specialties, Inc.
P.O. Box 1617
Bellingham, WA 98227-1617
206-676-1200
Parts, accessories, engine, suspension

Ozone Off-Road Center
86 Freeman's Bridge Road
Glenville, NY 12302
518-346-8849
Land Cruiser parts and conversions

PIAA Corporation, USA
15370 SW Millikan Way
Beaverton, OR 97006
1-800-525-7422
Racks and lighting

Schroth
(See your local performance parts outlet)
Safety harnesses/rally belts

Smittybilt
2090 California Ave.
Corona, CA 91719
714-272-3176
(Roll cages/steel tubing products)

SNUGTOP
1711 Harbor Avenue
Long Beach, CA 90801
310-432-5454
Pickup tops

TRW
(See your local performance parts outlet)
Safety harnesses/equipment

Tuffy Security Products
12540 W. Cedar Drive
Lakewood, CO 80228
303-988-8833

Front Hubs, Winches

HUB-A-LERT
4x4 Specialty Products
P.O. Box 813
Highland, CA 92346

Ramsey Winch Company
1600 N. Garnett
Tulsa, OK 74116
918-438-2760

Superwinch
Winch Drive
Putnam, CT 06260
203-928-1143

Warn Industries
13270 S.E. Pheasant Court
Milwaukie, OR 97222
503-786-4462.

Rare, OEM and Restoration Parts

Note: Specter Off-Road is one of the best sources for new OEM-type early Land Cruiser restoration parts. For Hi-Lux and early mini-Pickups, find a well stocked Toyota recycling yard. You can find sources for specialty restoration services in *Hemmings Motor News*. If you plan to authentically restore an older Toyota truck model, Hemmings lists many services and parts sources.

Specter Off-Road
21600 Nordhoff Street
Chatsworth, CA 91311
818-882-1238

Restoration and Specialty Tools

Bob Cash/B & B Happy Ranch
1318 Rolling Meadow Lane
Buellton, CA 93427
805-686-3088
Land Cruiser restoration and parts

Eastwood Company Tools
Box 296
Malvern, PA 19355
1-800-345-1178

Easco/K.D. Tools
(Contact Eastwood Company or your local tool supplier)

Suspension/Chassis

Air Lift Company
P.O. Box 80167
Lansing, MI 48908-0167
517-322-2144
Air suspension kits

Doetsch Tech
10728 Prospect Avenue #A
Santee, CA 92071
619-562-8773
Shock absorbers

Downey Off Road Manufacturing
10001 So. Pioneer Blvd.
Santa Fe Springs, CA 90670
310-949-9494
Suspension, conversions, engine performance

APPENDIX 1: SOURCES

Energy Suspension Systems
960 Calle Amanecer
San Clemente, CA 92672
714-361-3935
Urethane bushings

FABTECH Motorsports Engineering
4010 S. Palm Street
Unit 103
Fullerton, CA 92635
714-870-9422
Suspension mods for 1984-up 2WD
pickups

Heckethorn Off Road
P.O. Box 526
Dyersburg, TN 38024
901-285-9000
Shocks/steering stabilizers

JT Industries
8157 Wing Avenue
El Cajon, CA 92020
619-562-3390
Urethane bushings

Land Cruiser Advanced Handling, Inc.
1029 24th SE
Albany, Oregon 97321
503-926-8122
Suspension, handling kits

National Spring Company
1402 N. Magnolia Avenue
El Cajon, CA 92020
619-441-1901
Leaf spring lift kits

Rancho Suspension (USA)
6925 Atlantic Ave.
Long Beach, CA 90805
213-630-0700
Complete suspension packages

Rugged Trail/Black Diamond
A Division of Warn Industries
(See your local Warn products dealer)
Suspension kits

Skyjacker
P.O. Box 1878
West Monroe, LA 71291-1878
318-388-0816
Suspension kits

Superlift
211 Horn Lane
West Monroe, LA 71292
318-322-3458
Suspension kits, traction bars

Suspension Techniques
13546 Vintage Place
Chino, CA 91710
714-465-1020
Suspension upgrades

Trail Master
649 E. Chicago Road
Coldwater, MN 49036
517-278-4011
Suspension kits

Tires

Bridgestone Tire
See your local dealer

Dunlap & Kyle Co.
P.O. Box 720
Batesville, MS 38606
601-563-7601

Dick Cepek, Inc.
17000 Kingsview Avenue
Carson, CA 90746

Denman Tire Corporation
216-898-5256

The Goodyear Tire & Rubber
Company
See your local dealer

B.F. Goodrich T/A
See your local dealer

Interco Tire Corporation
P.O. Box 486
Rayne, LA 70578
318-334-3814

Mickey Thompson Performance Tires
P.O. Box 227
Cuyahoga Falls, OH 44222
216-928-9092

Manual Clutch and Automatic Transmission

Centerforce Clutches/Midway
2266 Crosswind Drive
Prescott, AZ 86301
520-771-8422
Manual clutch and flywheel

Mean Green
P.O. Drawer 336
Laughlintown, PA 15655
412-238-7319
Clutch parts

REGIONAL 4WD ASSOCIATIONS

Arizona State Association Of 4-Wheel
Drive Clubs
P.O. Box 23904
Tempe, AZ 58282
602-258-4BY4

California Association Of 4-Wheel
Drive Clubs
2856 Arden Way, #231
Sacramento, CA 95825
916-974-3984

Colorado Association Of 4-Wheel
Drive Clubs
P.O. Box 1413
Wheat Ridge, CO 80034
303-321-1266

East Coast 4-Wheel Drive
Association, Inc.
101 South Miami Avenue
Cleves, OH 45002
513-941-1450

4-Wheel Drive Association Of British
Columbia
Box 284 Surrey, B.C. V3T 4W8
604-590-1502

Great Lakes 4-Wheel Drive Association
13911 Townline Road
St. Charles, MI 48655
517-865-6983

Indiana 4-Wheel Drive Association
2203 Osman Lane
Greenfield, IN 46140
317-326-2329

Midwest 4-Wheel Drive Association
RR2, Box 70
Crystal, MN 56055
507-726-2598

Montana 4x4 Association, Inc.
516 N. 4th
Bozeman, MT 59715
406-587-8307

Pacific Northwest 4-Wheel Drive
Association
948 18th
Longview, WA 98632
800-537-7845

Southern 4-Wheel Drive Association
Box 3473 Oak Ridge, TN 37831
815-482-6912

Toyota Land Cruiser Association, Inc.
(TLCA)
P.O. Box 607
Placerville, CA 95667-0607
916-642-2330

Utah 4-Wheel Drive Association, Inc.
P. O. Box 20310
Salt Lake City, UT 84120
801-250-1302

Virginia 4-Wheel Drive Association
P.O. Box 722
Mechanicsville, VA 23111
804-883-6115

Wisconsin 4-Wheel Drive Association
203 Greunwald Ave.
Neenah, WI 54956
414-722-3777

United Four-Wheel Drive Associations
For information about UFWDA or regional associations, phone:
1-800-44-UFWDA

TRAILSIDE TOOLBOX AND SPARE PARTS KIT

Your properly maintained Toyota truck might never break down in the back country. Yet for long trips, like the Alaska Highway, Baja California or the Far North, bringing along a full set of tools and spare parts can safeguard your adventure and provide a reasonable level of self-reliance.

CAUTION —
Store your tools and spare parts safely and securely. Take into account the worst case scenario, the possibility that your truck could break in desolate country. Under such conditions, you would need quick access to your winching accessories or tools.

On-board Tools for Remote Trailside Fixes

1. A complete socket set
2. A full set of common hand tools
3. Oil filter wrench
4. Compact volt-ohmmeter
5. Induction ammeter and starter current meter
6. Flare nut wrench set
7. Plumber's small chain wrench
8. Snap ring pliers set
9. Front wheel bearing spindle nut wrench
10. Pry bar
11. Vacuum gauge
12. Compact timing light
13. Wire repair kit and crimping pliers
14. Tubing flare tool and repair kit
15. Grease gun with chassis lube
16. Enough tools to break down and repair a tubeless tire
17. Air compressor
18. On-board welder
19. Jacks for tire repairs and transmission/axle work
20. A Hi-Lift jack and Pull-Pal anchor
21. A quality winch and winch accessory kit

Spare Parts for the Long Trail

1. Fuses, light bulbs and at least one headlamp
2. 25-foot rolls of 12-, 14- and 16-gauge automotive wire
3. Two rolls of electrical tape
4. Solderless crimp connectors and terminals
5. Roll of duct tape
6. Package of radiator and gas tank repair putty
7. Fuel hose and spare clamps
8. Spare drive belt(s)
9. Upper and lower radiator hoses
10. Thermostat and housing gasket
11. Tubes of silicon gasket sealant
12. Tube of metal mender (Permatex's LocWeld or equivalent)
13. Exhaust system patch kit
14. Thread locker
15. Teflon tape
16. Clean brake fluid
17. A fuel pump and pump gasket
18. Roll of mechanic's wire
19. Spare tire valve stems
20. Patch kit for repairing tubeless (radial or bias ply) tires
21. Spare universal joints
22. Front wheel grease seals (full-floating axles and wheel hubs)
23. At least one oil filter and enough oil for a crankcase refill
24. An oversized and self-tapping oil pan drain plug
25. Two squeeze bottle quarts of gear lubricant
26. Wheel bearing grease
27. Clean rags or shop towels
28. Fuel filter(s)
29. Air cleaner element
30. Spare fuel and potable water (minimum 5 gallons of each), ignition distributor cap, rotor, points or module
31. Ignition spark plug wire set
32. Carburetor float and air horn gasket
33. Water pump and gasket
34. Suitable fire extinguisher(s)
35. Axe, bucket, shovel (preferably a Max toolkit)
36. Backup C.B. radio and cellular phone (if within transmission range)

CAUTION —
Always carry a quality first aid kit and safety flares. Stow a ground cloth, shelter materials and rope for setting up an emergency habitat. Freeze dried or canned rations will provide a means for survival in the event that your truck becomes stranded.

APPENDIX 3: ENGINE BREAK-IN

NEW OR REBUILT ENGINE BREAK-IN PROCEDURE

There is little information available on the proper break-in of a new or freshly rebuilt engine. Your truck engine's performance and longevity depend upon correct break-in. The following procedures are those recommended by Sealed Power Corporation, a major supplier of parts to the engine remanufacturing industry.

> CAUTION —
>
> *These run-in schedules are good basic procedures to follow for engine break-in. They are recommended as a practical guide for engine rebuilders who are not advised of specific factory run-in schedules. If available, follow OEM guidelines for engine break-in.*

Engine Run-in Procedure (engine in vehicle)

Before starting the engine: Make preliminary adjustments to the carburetor or diesel injection system where applicable, adjust tappets and set ignition timing. Always install new oil and air filters. Prime the engine lubrication system before attempting to start the engine. Clean crankcase ventilation components—breathers, road draft tubes or positive crankcase ventilation system. Carefully check coolant and crankcase oil levels.

> CAUTION —
>
> *When an engine is started for the first time, the most common cause of bearing scuff and seizure is a dry start. This can happen in the short length of time before the oil, under pressure, is delivered to bearings and other vital parts. Pre-priming the oil system can be accomplished with a pressure tank or pre-lubricator attached to the system or by mechanically driving the oil pump to supply the necessary oil throughout all oil passages.*

Initial Starting Steps (before run-in schedule)

1) Start engine and establish throttle setting at a fast idle (1000 to 1500 RPM) and watch oil pressure gauge. If oil pressure is not observed immediately, shut engine down and check back on assembly of oil pump and lubricating system. When engine running is resumed, continue at the fast idle until coolant reaches normal operating temperature.

2) Stop engine and recheck oil and water levels.

3) Make necessary adjustments to carburetor (or injectors), ignition timing, tappets, fan belt tightness, etc.

4) Retorque cylinder heads following engine manufacturer's recommendations.

5) Check for oil and coolant leaks, making corrections where necessary.

Run-in Schedule for Light and Medium Duty Trucks

Set engine at a fast idle. Put vehicle under a moderate load and accelerate to 50 miles per hour with alternate deceleration. Continue this intermittent cycling under this load for at least 50 miles. Additional time is desirable.

Note: Harmful Practices

(A) Avoid lugging under any load condition. Lugging exists when the vehicle does not readily respond as the accelerator is depressed. The engine speed being too low, does not allow the engine to develop sufficient horsepower to pull the load. (Keep rpm up.)

(B) Avoid long periods of idling. Excessive idling will drop engine temperature and can result in incomplete burning of fuel. Unburned fuel washes lubricating oil off cylinder walls and results in diluted crankcase oil and restricted (poor) lubrication to all moving parts. The relatively dry cylinder walls depend upon oil throw-off to lubricate them and a speed above a slow idle is necessary for this. Long idling periods produce glazing of cylinder walls, detrimental to ring and cylinder wall seating.

(C) Avoid stopping engine too quickly. When an engine has completed the test run-in schedule or at any time it becomes heavily worked, it is a good policy to disengage the load from the engine and decelerate gradually. Allow it to idle a few minutes before turning the ignition to the off position.

The few minutes of idling will allow the engine to cool gradually and promote a desirable dissipation of heat from any localized area of concentrated temperature. Such good practice avoids the rapid cooling that can cause valve and seat warpage, block distortion, etc.

Engine Run-in procedure (engine on dynamometer)

> NOTE —
>
> *Follow necessary preliminary procedures outlined for engine in vehicle.*

Engine Run-in, Gasoline Engines: Light Truck and Passenger Car

Stage of test	Complete test cycle of dynamometer break-in						
	1st	2nd	3rd	4th	5th	6th	7th
RPM	800—1200	1500	2000	2500	3000	3000	800
Manifold vacuum in inches of mercury	No load	15 in.	10 in.	10 in.	6 in.	Full load	No load
Time limit	Warm-up 10 min.	10 min.	15 min.	15 min.	15 min.	5 min.	3 min.

RULES AND REGULATIONS FOR 4X4 VEHICLE TRIALS

Revisiting the Rubicon in the summer of 1988, I saw many four-wheelers place unnecessary stress on both their machines and the environment. It was clear that these drivers believed a heavy throttle and plenty of power were the only ways to overcome this brutal trail. Believing very strongly that the opposite is true, I sought a useful way to illustrate my point.

In the ensuing months, I carefully drafted a guideline for 4x4 Trials, a competitive event that discredits a driver for displaying wheelspin, misusing power or failing to maintain smooth progress in rough terrain. As the concept unfolded, California Association of 4WD Clubs' Central District (CA4WDC) endorsed the idea of a pilot competition at the 1989 Molina Ghost Run.

I worked with Bruce Swanson and other Central District members at constructing a special course, and we officially established our first 4x4 trials event. The participant drivers and crowd showed real enthusiasm for the project, and we realized that the program could work.

At the 1990 Molina Ghost Run, Bruce Swanson set up an outstanding course. (The low environmental impact of trials competition permits quick course construction, a factor that makes 4x4 trials well suited to clubs with limited space and resources. A large lot and some imagination can produce an event!) Bruce's course was tight and twisty, laced with rocks, and steeper than our first effort.

As Sunday morning's sunlight pierced the deep ravine, each competitor got a first glimpse of the 1990 trials course. The 1989 winners, brothers Harry Hetzer and Alvin Hetzer, Sr., looked over the steep starting bank and shook their heads. "Boy," Harry exclaimed, "my truck's wheelbase is plenty long for this course!"

Minutes before the start, Bruce walked the attentive drivers through the course. For the next hour and a half, seven hard-core four-wheelers battled against the stopwatches as they squeezed through a ravine, inched over two rockpiles, straddled a nasty trench and crept up and down two steep slopes.

These veteran four-wheelers caught on quickly. Few points were lost to tire spin, and high torque again joined forces with driving skill to produce a winning score.

The "Brothers Hetzer," as we now called them, pulled an upset. Alvin, who placed a solid second in the 1989 event, had shown up with a 101" wheelbase 1959 Jeep CJ-6. A transplant Chevrolet V-8 with a high carburetor float level (which caused flooding and rough idle) quickly troubled his score.

Harry Hetzer, the 1989 first-place winner with a 103" wheelbase Jeep Scrambler (CJ-8), triumphed once again over nimbler CJ-5s and others. Despite wide skepticism about the longer CJ-8 wheelbase, Harry proved once more that 4x4 trials is a driver's sport.

Creeping and crawling his retrofit T-18 truck four speed and AMC in-line 258 six (bone stock with OE carburetion and a maze of California smog hardware!), Harry Hetzer ran to a tight tie with highly skilled Mark Booker from Fresno. Mark and his CJ-5 outperformed everyone except Harry, who racked up another *zero tirespin* score with his CJ-8. In a hair splitting run-off, Harry edged out Mark for first place.

CA4WDC/Central District trophies went to Mark Booker for 2nd Place, and Harry Hetzer took another 1st Place home to Daly City, California. 4x4 trials became a reality at Molina, and these crawl masters now know what it takes to win.

When the course got tougher, the driver skills just came on stronger. Bruce Swanson even hinted about trying a log tee-ter-totter at a future 4x4 Trials event. Winching skills may also enter into the competition.

I encourage all 4x4 clubs and individuals with a competitive spirit to pick up the trials challenge. A trials course is very easy to construct, and you can spend a fun afternoon competing for trophies or other prizes. 4x4 Trials promotes better driving skills, heightens awareness of the environment and provides a chance to work your four-wheel drive truck through its low-range paces with minimal engine and geartrain stress.

Use these rules and regulations to foster friendly competition—and always remember to TREAD LIGHTLY!

Official Rules and Regulations For 4x4 Trials

In the interest of safe and environmentally sound off-pavement recreation, the following rules and regulations have been established. The sole intent of 4x4 Vehicle Trials is to promote, within a friendly, competitive atmosphere, those driving techniques and skills that minimize vehicle impact upon terrain and natural habitat.

4x4 trials will enhance the off-pavement driving skills of both new and experienced four-wheel drive vehicle operators. The goals set forth for 4x4 trials competition provide a far-reaching model for all off-pavement driving. Safety and preservation of the natural environment underlie these standards, rules, regulations and amendments for conducting trials events.

I. Vehicle Requirements—Any street-legal, four-wheel drive truck or sport/utility model may compete. Engine size, wheelbase and wheel/tire size are optional, providing that 1) the vehicle complies with local, state, and federal regulations for safe use on public highways, 2) tires are of conventional, highway legal "mud and snow" or "highway" tread design, recognized as commercially available, and 3) no aspect of the vehicle has been modified in a manner that would increase impact on the trials road course, terrain or local habitat.

APPENDIX 4: 4X4 TRIALS

Safety equipment should include, but not be limited to, a Red Cross approved First Aid Kit, a charged and "tagged" fire extinguisher, a four-point (or better) padded roll cage, a properly mounted and operational winch*, minimally of 6000 lbs. (single line) capacity, and an approved "tree saver" strap. Vehicle inspection for operationally safe hydraulic and emergency brakes, lights and brake lamps, and assurances of reasonable operating condition will take place before each event.

(*Events may test operator skills at safely utilizing a winch, with due consideration for trees, fauna and local habitat.)

II. Driver Requirements—Drivers must possess a valid state vehicle operator's license or legally recognized international driver's license. Learner's permits will not be acceptable, and proof of license is a requirement. A valid driver's license with notable restrictions shall not disqualify any driver, unless such restrictions either 1) prevent driving the vehicle during hours in which the trials event has been scheduled or 2) place the driver, passenger/occupants, other drivers/vehicles or spectators at unusual risk.

The driver must be in good physical condition. Use of illegal drugs, alcohol* or medical prescriptions and over-the-counter drugs that impair driving skills shall be cause for disqualification. Reckless, erratic or aberrant driving displays shall be cause for immediate disqualification and removal from the event. In all instances, the officials and judges of the event shall make the final decision regarding qualification and disqualification of drivers.

(*Alcohol at legally acceptable levels for safe vehicle operation on public highways shall be the maximum allowable under any circumstances. Additionally, any driver believed to be adversely influenced or impaired by the use of alcohol must prove his or her ability to compete safely. In each instance, use of alcohol by competitors shall be discouraged. No competitor is to carry alcoholic beverages in or about the vehicle.)

III. The Course—For each 4x4 trials event, the selection of a designated course shall meet with appropriate local, state and federal regulations. Public use permits and use of the 4x4 trials course shall comply with applicable land use regulations. Every reasonable effort shall be made to meet land use regulations. Officials of the 4x4 trials event shall provide participants and spectators with a list of rules, regulations and land use standards for the area assigned for the event. Whenever possible, land use agencies shall be encouraged to assist or participate in the establishment and layout of the trials course. Impact to the local environment will be minimized, and trials event damage to terrain, fauna or local waterways shall be reasonably alleviated by the 4x4 trials organizers or their assignees.

III. Scoring—An ideal score shall be zero ("0"). During the event, each participant will be penalized points according to the methods set forth in Section IV. OBJECTIVES. Penalty points shall be added to the starting score of zero, winners to be the driver(s) with the lowest number of penalty points. Each event's obstacles shall be clearly indicated, and officials will monitor times between course markers in 1/100ths of a second. Penalty points accrue as both the drivers' time errors and technique infractions.

IV. Objectives—There is only one 4x4 Trials winning criterion: TRAVEL THE COURSE IN THE DESIGNATED TIME OR SLOWER, WITHOUT STOPPING AND WITHOUT TIRE SPIN. Trials is not a speed contest, and any exhibition of speed shall be cause for points deduction or disqualification. Points shall also be deducted for running off course or excess abuse of terrain, as determined by the offical(s). Damage to the vehicle or "high centering" on chassis, body or powertrain components shall also be cause for points deductions. The overall winner is a highly competent driver, in full control of his or her vehicle at all times. Such a competitor leaves the least impact upon the course, the environment, his or her vehicle and passengers.

A. Designated Time: Well marked Start and Stop points shall be noted throughout the course. Upon starting from a given marker, the competitor/driver has a specific, minimum time to reach the next stop point. The driver must keep the vehicle moving without leaving the course or spinning tires. (As an option, a co- driver or passenger may assist by keeping time with a conventional stopwatch.)

B. Tire Spin: Each tire of competitors' vehicles shall be marked with one (1) swath of white, washable paint. Paint shall be applied with a 3-inch wide brush, from the wheel center outward to the tread area of each tire. Officials will watch the rotation of tires over the varied course terrain. Points shall be deducted for any occurrence of tire/wheel spin. Spin shall be defined as 1) the rotation of any tire without forward movement of the vehicle or 2) any moment in which one tire/wheel rotates faster than the other three tires/wheels, the one exception being a required, safe maneuver in which a wheel temporarily becomes suspended above the ground. One (1) point shall be deducted for each instance of tire/wheel spin observed.

C. High Center: For the purpose of 4x4 Trials competition, "high centering" shall be defined as interference or contact of vehicle undercarriage components with the course terrain. Such interference refers to, but is not limited to, chassis, suspension, powertrain and body components. Specific course requirements may involve the application of washable paint to undercarriage components. In such instances, officials will judge and penalize drivers for each indication of paint removed by undercarriage interference/contact with terrain. Such a course shall afford sufficient opportunity to avoid high centering.

Water crossings, log climbs, and other obstacles may be designed into any 4x4 trials course. In events with such special obstacles, additional rules and scoring methods shall be thoroughly discussed with all drivers at the "DRIVER'S PRELIMINARY MEETING." To qualify for competition, each driver must attend any and all such meetings. Special obstacles will be clearly marked on course maps and en route.

V. Entry Fees—Organizers of 4x4 Trials events may assign vehicle/driver entry fees for each eligible competitor. These fees shall be clearly designated and posted for the benefit of interested participants. Entry fees must be paid as stated, before each scheduled event. Any eligible competitor who becomes disabled or is unable to participate in an event must notify a designated official one (1) hour before the scheduled start of his or her event. A refund of entry fees or a portion thereof, according to posted and established guidelines, may then be afforded. Any competitor disqualified from competition for any rule or regulation infraction shall forfeit his or her paid entry fees.

VI. Rules Philosophy—4x4 Trials competition is a thorough test of driving skill. Skillful off-pavement driving requires total vehicle control and an awareness of road hazards and obstacles. When driving on off-pavement trails, respect for the natural environment is equally important. 4x4 Trials, conducted over a specified course, simulates the trying situations encountered in serious four-wheeling. Under the watchful eyes of officials and spectators, 4x4 operators can develop and display greater off-pavement/trail driving ability. "RULES AND REGULATIONS FOR 4X4 VEHICLE TRIALS" is for the sole purpose of achieving these goals. Such rules may be changed, amended, or modified to improve this competitive sport. Any changes must promote safety and driving habits that protect our public lands.

ART CREDITS

Index

INDEX

Automotive Books From Robert Bentley

ENTHUSIAST BOOKS

Jeep Owner's Bible™ *Moses Ludel*
ISBN 0-8376-0154-1

Ford F-Series Pickup Owner's Bible™
Moses Ludel ISBN 0-8376-0152-5

Chevrolet & GMC Light Truck Owner's Bible™ *Moses Ludel*
ISBN 0-8376-0157-6

Chevrolet by the Numbers™: **1955-1959**
Alan Colvin ISBN 0-8376-0875-9

Chevrolet by the Numbers™: **1960-1964**
Alan Colvin ISBN 0-8376-0936-4

Chevrolet by the Numbers™: **1965-1969**
Alan Colvin ISBN 0-8376-0956-9

Chevrolet by the Numbers™: **1970-1975**
Alan Colvin ISBN 0-8376-0927-5

Alfa Romeo Owner's Bible™ *Pat Braden,
foreword by Don Black* ISBN 0-8376-0707-9

Think To Win *Don Alexander with foreword
by Mark Martin* ISBN 0-8376-0070-7

Sports Car and Competition Driving
Paul Frère, with foreword by Phil Hill
ISBN 0-8376-0202-5

The Technique of Motor Racing *Piero
Taruffi with foreword by Juan Manuel Fangio*
ISBN 0-8376-0228-9

**The Design and Tuning of Competition
Engines** *Philip H. Smith, 6th edition revised
by David N. Wenner* ISBN 0-8376-0140-1

**New Directions in Suspension Design:
Making the Fast Car Faster** *Colin
Campbell* ISBN 0-8376-0150-9

**The Scientific Design of Exhaust and
Intake Systems** *Philip H. Smith and John C.
Morrison* ISBN 0-8376-0309-9

Vintage Racing British Sports Cars *Terry
Jackson with foreword by Stirling Moss*
ISBN 0-8376-0153-3

FUEL INJECTION

**Ford Fuel Injection and Electronic
Engine Control: 1980-1987** *Charles O.
Probst, SAE* ISBN 0-8376-0302-1

**Ford Fuel Injection and Electronic
Engine Control: 1988-1993** *Charles O.
Probst, SAE* ISBN 0-8376-0301-3

**Bosch Fuel Injection and Engine
Management** *Charles O. Probst, SAE*
ISBN 0-8376-0300-5

BMW SERVICE MANUALS

**BMW 3-Series Service Manual: 1984-
1990 318i, 325, 325e(es), 325i(is), and 325i
Convertible** *Robert Bentley*
ISBN 0-8376-0325-0

**BMW 5-Series Service Manual: 1982-
1988 528e, 533i, 535i, 535is** *Robert Bentley*
ISBN 0-8376-0318-8

AUDI OFFICIAL SERVICE MANUALS

**Audi 100, 200 Official Factory Repair
Manual: 1988-1991** *Audi of America*
ISBN 0-8376-0372-2

**Audi 5000S, 5000CS Official Factory
Repair Manual: 1984-1988 Gasoline,
Turbo, and Turbo Diesel, including
Wagon and Quattro** *Audi of America*
ISBN 0-8376-0370-6

**Audi 80, 90, Coupe Quattro Official
Factory Repair Manual: 1988-1991
including 80 Quattro, 90 Quattro and 20-
valve models** *Audi of America*
ISBN 0-8376-0367-6

**Audi 5000, 5000S Official Factory Repair
Manual: 1977-1983 Gasoline and Turbo
Gasoline, Diesel and Turbo Diesel** *Audi
of America* ISBN 0-8376-0352-8

**Audi 80, 90, Coupe Quattro Electrical
Troubleshooting Manual: 1988-1992**
Robert Bentley ISBN 0-8376-0375-7

**Audi 4000S, 4000CS, and Coupe GT
Official Factory Repair Manual: 1984-
1987 including Quattro and Quattro
Turbo** *Audi of America*
ISBN 0-8376-0373-0

**Audi 4000, Coupe Official Factory
Repair Manual: 1980-1983 Gasoline,
Diesel, and Turbo Diesel** *Audi of America*
ISBN 0-8376-0349-8

VOLKSWAGEN OFFICIAL SERVICE MANUALS

**GTI, Golf, and Jetta Service Manual:
1985-1992 Gasoline, Diesel, and Turbo
Diesel, including 16V** *Robert Bentley*
ISBN 0-8376-0342-0

**Corrado Official Factory Repair Manual:
1990-1994** *Volkswagen United States*
ISBN 0-8376-0387-0

**Passat Official Factory Repair Manual:
1990-1992, including Wagon** *Volkswagen
United States* ISBN 0-8376-0377-3

**Cabriolet and Scirocco Service Manual:
1985-1993, including 16V** *Robert Bentley*
ISBN 0-8376-0362-5

**Volkswagen Fox Service Manual: 1987-
1993, including GL, GL Sport and
Wagon** *Robert Bentley* ISBN 0-8376-0340-4

**Vanagon Official Factory Repair
Manual: 1980-1991 including Diesel
Engine, Syncro, and Camper** *Volkswagen
United States* ISBN 0-8376-0336-6

**Rabbit, Scirocco, Jetta Service Manual:
1980-1984 Gasoline Models, including
Pickup Truck, Convertible, and GTI**
Robert Bentley ISBN 0-8376-0183-5

**Rabbit, Jetta Service Manual: 1977-1984
Diesel Models, including Pickup Truck
and Turbo Diesel** *Robert Bentley*
ISBN 0-8376-0184-3

**Rabbit, Scirocco Service Manual: 1975-
1979 Gasoline Models** *Robert Bentley*
ISBN 0-8376-0107-X

**Dasher Service Manual: 1974-1981
including Diesel** *Robert Bentley*
ISBN 0-8376-0083-9

**Super Beetle, Beetle and Karmann Ghia
Official Service Manual Type 1: 1970-
1979** *Volkswagen United States*
ISBN 0-8376-0096-0

**Beetle and Karmann Ghia Official
Service Manual Type 1: 1966-1969**
Volkswagen United States
ISBN 0-8376-0416-8

**Station Wagon/Bus Official Service
Manual Type 2: 1968-1979** *Volkswagen
United States* ISBN 0-8376-0094-4

**Fastback and Squareback Official
Service Manual Type 3: 1968-1973**
Volkswagen United States
ISBN 0-8376-0057-X

SAAB OFFICIAL SERVICE MANUALS

**Saab 900 16 Valve Official Service
Manual: 1985-1993** *Robert Bentley*
ISBN 0-8376-0312-9

**Saab 900 8 Valve Official Service
Manual: 1981-1988** *Robert Bentley*
ISBN 0-8376-0310-2

VOLVO SERVICE MANUALS

**Volvo 240 Service Manual: 1983-1993 DL,
GL, Turbo, 240 DL, 240 GL, 240 SE** *Robert
Bentley* ISBN 0-8376-0285-8

Robert Bentley has published service manuals and automobile books since 1950. Please write Robert Bentley, Inc., Publishers, at 1033 Massachusetts Avenue, Cambridge, MA 02138 or call 1-800-423-4595 for a complete listing of current automotive literature, including titles and service manuals for **Jaguar**, **Triumph**, **Austin-Healey**, **MG**, and other cars.

Acknowledgments

My interest in trucks began before kindergarten. As the family tale goes, I could recite the names Peterbilt, Autocar and Jimmy while heavy duty trucks with these badges rolled past on the highway. That innate curiosity, later fueled by the enthusiasm of peers, co-workers and eventually magazine and newspaper readers, has never waned.

Commitment to detail stems from work with "old-school" professional truck mechanics, desert racers, topnotch parts personnel, engineers, fabricators, machinists, and truck experts, individuals like Tom Reider, Jeff Sugg, Tom Telford, Scott Salmon, Kevin Healey, Greg Williams, Lloyd Novak, Keith Buckley, John Partridge, Richard Corgiat, Marv Specter, Ross Stuart, Jim Sickles, John Hendricks, Brian Schreiber and Steve and Randy Kramer.

Some of my best insights, however, I owe to my students at the San Diego Job Corps mechanics program. They taught me how to convey information in a useful manner.

In assembling archival graphics for this book, I have relied upon Warn Industries, Toyota Motor Sales, U.S.A., Downey Off-Road, NWOR Specialties and California Mini Trucks. Personnel within these organizations, especially Scott Salmon at Warn Industries, provided useful materials and information. For my own photography, Jim Sickles, Marv Specter, and Brian Schreiber provided generous access to their businesses, and my good friend, Steve Shaw, made his immaculate 1982 Land Cruiser FJ40 available as a photo subject.

I thank Michael Bentley and Fred Newcomb for their encouragement and promotion of my work, which has established our enduring and creative author/publisher relationship. Likewise, John Kittredge deserves my profound thanks for his exceptional professionalism and willingness to handle the monumental amount of material, photographs and text that I found essential for the project.

Last mentioned but of foremost consideration, I thank my wife, Donna, and son Jacob for their patience and understanding. My commitment to this book was intensive and time consuming, yet our home remains whole and happy. Thanks, family, for your support, presence and interest in my passions!

About the Author

An avid fly fisherman, hunter, canoeist and four-wheeler, Moses Ludel took his first driver's test in the family 4x4 truck. Two years later, at age eighteen, he drove the Rubicon Trail by the back route (traveling east to west), starting at Miller Lake and tracking the unmarked trail across the Sierra Nevada Mountains to Placerville, California.

Moses worked as a journeyman truck mechanic and heavy equipment operator before receiving a Bachelor of Science degree with honors from the University of Oregon. He has taught Adult Education level courses in Automotive/Diesel Mechanics and established himself as an automotive journalist, columnist and photographer, with a specialty in four-wheel drive trucks and sport utility vehicles (SUVs).

Since 1982, Moses has published over 1,500 technical features and columns. His magazine credits include *OFF-ROAD, Four-Wheeler, 4WD Action/SUV, 4x4 Magazine (Japan), Trailer Life, Motorhome, Popular Hot Rodding, Street Truck, Truckin', Sport Truck, Super Chevy, Corvette Fever, Chevy Truck, JP* and many others. He currently fields several magazine technical columns and also writes the Portland *Oregonian*'s weekly "DriveTime" technical column.

In response to his *Owner's Bible* series of light truck and SUV books (Robert Bentley, Publishers), Moses has been a guest on radio talk shows and has appeared on TNN cable television's "Truckin' U.S.A." He is active with the TREAD LIGHTLY! organization, having served as Media Representative, a National 4WD Clinic Instructor, and a member of the Environmental Relations Committee.

Front cover: John Thawley

Back cover: Top: courtesy of Warn Industries (photo by Bryan F. Peterson); Vintage FJ40 Land Cruiser (upper right), 1995 T100 Pickup (lower right), and 22R-TE engine (lower left): Moses Ludel; Ivan "Ironman" Stewart's Toyota race truck (middle right): Toyota Motorsports; 1995 Land Cruiser (upper left): Toyota Motor Sales

Unless otherwise indicated, all other photographs on the inside of this book are by the author.